POET'S MARKET

2016

includes a one-year online subscription to **Poet's Market** on

Where & How to Sell What You Write

THE ULTIMATE MARKET RESEARCH TOOL FOR WRITERS

To register your *Poet's Market 2016* book and **start your one-year online genre-only subscription**, scratch off the block below to reveal your activation code, then go to www.WritersMarket.com. Find the box that says "Purchased a Deluxe Edition?" then click on "Activate Your Account" and enter the activation code. It's that easy!

PM-Y26EC524

UPDATED MARKET LISTINGS FOR YOUR INTEREST AREA
EASY-TO-USE SEARCHABLE DATABASE • RECORD-KEEPING TOOLS
PROFESSIONAL TIPS & ADVICE • INDUSTRY NEWS

Your purchase of *Poet's Market* gives you access to updated listings related to this genre of writing (valid through 12/31/16). For just $9.99, you can upgrade your subscription and get access to listings from all of our best-selling Market Books. Visit **www.WritersMarket.com** for more information.

WritersMarket.com
Where & How to Sell What You Write

Activate your WritersMarket.com subscription to get instant access to:

- **UPDATED LISTINGS IN YOUR WRITING GENRE:** Find additional listings that didn't make it into the book, updated contact information, and more. WritersMarket.com provides the most comprehensive database of verified markets available anywhere.

- **EASY-TO-USE SEARCHABLE DATABASE:** Looking for a specific magazine or book publisher? Just type in its name. Or widen your prospects with the Advanced Search. You can also search for listings that have been recently updated!

- **PERSONALIZED TOOLS:** Store your best-bet markets, and use our popular recording-keeping tools to track your submissions. Plus, get new and updated market listings, query reminders, and more—every time you log in!

- **PROFESSIONAL TIPS & ADVICE:** From pay-rate charts to sample query letters, and from how-to articles to Q&As with literary agents, we have the resources writers need.

YOU'LL GET ALL OF THIS WITH YOUR INCLUDED SUBSCRIPTION TO

WritersMarket.com
Where & How to Sell What You Write

29th ANNUAL EDITION

POET'S MARKET

2016

Robert Lee Brewer, Editor

WRITER'S DIGEST
BOOKS

WritersDigest.com
Cincinnati, Ohio

Publisher: Phil Sexton

Writer's Market website: www.writersmarket.com
Writer's Digest website: www.writersdigest.com
Writer's Digest Bookstore: www.writersdigestshop.com

Distributed in Canada by Fraser Direct
100 Armstrong Avenue
Georgetown, Ontario, Canada L7G 5S4
Tel: (905) 877-4411

Distributed in the U.K and Europe by F&W Media International
Brunel House, Newton Abbot, Devon, TQ12 4PU, England
Tel: (+44) 1626-323200, Fax: (+44) 1626-323319
E-mail: postmaster@davidandcharles.co.uk

Distributed in Australia by Capricorn Link
P.O. Box 704, Windsor, NSW 2756 Australia
Tel: (02) 4577-3555

ISSN: 0883-5470
ISBN-13: 978-1-59963-941-3
ISBN-10: 1-59963-941-6

Attention Booksellers: This is an annual directory of F+W Media, Inc. Return deadline for this edition is December 31, 2016.

Edited by: Robert Lee Brewer
Cover designed by: Alexis Brown
Page layout by: Claudean Wheeler
Production coordinated by: Greg Nock

CONTENTS

RESOURCES

INDEXES

FROM THE EDITOR

Every year, I come to this book with the same goal: Let's make this book more useful for poets than ever! For this year's edition, I attempted to pack in more listings than ever for poets in every section: Magazines/Journals; Book/Chapbook Publishers; Contests & Awards; Conferences, Workshops & Festivals; and even Organizations.

This edition of *Poet's Market* still includes articles covering the business, promotion, and craft of poetry, because I believe there's always a need for that extra advice that helps poets find more success than they did before picking up this book. Some of the new articles this year include "6 Ways to Promote Your New Book," "How to Take Poetry to New Audiences," and some craft pieces. I may be biased, but I think the *Poet's Market 2016* is the best edition yet.

That said, I'm probably already trying to figure out how to make the next edition even better. If you have any ideas, be sure to send a tweet to my Twitter handle below and leave me a comment at the Poetic Asides blog (URL below). Because as a poet myself, I want this book to help other poets as much as possible.

By the way, don't forget to take advantage of your free poetry-related webinar by heading to http://www.writersmarket.com/pm16-webinar.

Until next time, keep poeming!

Robert Lee Brewer

Senior Content Editor, *Poet's Market*
http://www.writersdigest.com/editor-blogs/poetic-asides
http://twitter.com/robertleebrewer

HOW TO USE POET'S MARKET

Delving into the pages of *Poet's Market* implies a commitment—you've decided to take that big step and begin submitting your poems for publication. How do you *really* begin, though? Here are eight quick tips to help make sense of the marketing/submission process:

1. BE AN AVID READER. The best way to hone your writing skills (besides writing) is to immerse yourself in poetry of all kinds. It's essential to study the masters; however, from a marketing standpoint, it's equally vital to read what your contemporaries are writing and publishing. Read journals and magazines, chapbooks and collections, anthologies for a variety of voices; scope out the many poetry sites on the Internet. Develop an eye for quality, and then use that eye to assess your own work. Don't try to publish until you know you're writing the best poetry you're capable of producing.

2. KNOW WHAT YOU LIKE TO WRITE—AND WHAT YOU WRITE BEST. Ideally, you should be experimenting with all kinds of poetic forms, from free verse to villanelles. However, there's sure to be a certain style with which you feel most comfortable, that conveys your true "voice." Whether you favor more formal, traditional verse or avant-garde poetry that breaks all the rules, you should identify which markets publish work similar to yours. Those are the magazines and presses you should target to give your submissions the best chance of being read favorably—and accepted.

3. LEARN THE "BUSINESS" OF POETRY PUBLISHING. Poetry may not be a high-paying writing market, but there's still a right way to go about the "business" of submitting and publishing poems. Learn all you can by reading writing-related books and magazines. Read the articles in this book for plenty of helpful advice. Surf the Internet for a wealth of sites filled with writing advice, market news and informative links.

4. RESEARCH THE MARKETS. Study the listings in *Poet's Market* thoroughly; these present submission guidelines, editorial preferences and editors' comments as well as contact information (names, postal and e-mail addresses, and website URLs). In addition, the indexes in the back of this book provide insights into what an editor or publisher may be looking for.

However, studying market listings alone won't cut it. The best way to gauge the kinds of poetry a market publishes is to read several issues of a magazine/journal or several of a press's books to get a feel for the style and content of each. Websites may include poetry samples, reviews, archives of past issues, exclusive content, and especially submission guidelines. (If the market is an online publication, the current issue will be available in its entirety.) Submission guidelines are pure gold for the specific information they provide. However you acquire them—by SASE or e-mail, online, or in a magazine itself—make them an integral part of your market research.

5. START SLOWLY. It may be tempting to send your work directly to *The New Yorker* or *Poetry*, but try sending your work to less competitive markets as well. As you gain confidence and experience (and increased skill in your writing), you can move on to more recognized markets. Although it may tax your patience, slow and steady progress is a proven route to success.

6. BE PROFESSIONAL. Professionalism is not something you should "work up to." Make it show in your first submission, from the way you prepare your manuscript to the attitude you project in your communications with editors.

⊘ market does not accept unsolicited submissions

♺ Canadian market

⤵ market located outside of the U.S. and Canada

$ market pays

⮞ tips to break into a specific market

○ market welcomes submissions from beginning poets

◐ market prefers submissions from skilled, experienced poets; will consider work from beginning poets

◖ market prefers submissions from poets with a high degree of skill and experience

◎ market has a specialized focus

Follow those guidelines. Submit a polished manuscript. Choose poems carefully with the editor's needs in mind. Such practices show respect for the editor, the publication and the process; and they reflect *your* self-respect and the fact that you take your work seriously. Editors love that; and even if your work is rejected, you've made a good first impression that could help your chances with your next submission.

7. KEEP TRACK OF YOUR SUBMISSIONS. First, do *not* send out the only copies of your work. There are no guarantees your submission won't get lost in the mail, misplaced in a busy editorial office, or vanish into a black hole if the publication or press closes down. Create a special file folder for poems you're submitting. Even if you use a word processing program and store your manuscripts digitally, keep a hard copy file as well (and be sure to back up your electronic files).

Second, establish a tracking system so you always know which poems are where. This can be extremely simple: index cards, a chart created with word processing or database software, or even a simple notebook used as a log. (You can enlarge and photocopy the Submission Tracker in this book or use it as a model to design your own version.) Note the titles of the poems submitted (or the title of the collection if you're submitting a book/chapbook manuscript); the name of the publication, press, or contest; date sent; estimated response time; and date returned *or* date accepted. Additional information you may want to log: the name of the editor/contact, date the accepted piece is published and/or issue number of the magazine, type/amount of pay received, rights acquired by the publication or press, and any pertinent comments.

Without a tracking system, you risk forgetting where and when manuscripts were submitted. This is even more problematic if you simultaneously send the same manuscripts to different magazines, presses or contests. And if you learn of an acceptance by one magazine or publisher, you *must* notify the others that the poem or collection you sent them is no longer available. You run a bigger chance of overlooking someone without an organized approach. This causes hard feelings among editors you may have inconvenienced, hurting your chances with these markets in the future.

8. DON'T FEAR REJECTION. LEARN FROM IT. No one enjoys rejection, but every writer faces it. The best way to turn a negative into a positive is to learn as much as you can from your rejections. Don't let them get you down. A rejection slip isn't a permission slip to doubt yourself, condemn your poetry or give up.

Look over the rejection. Did the editor provide any comments about your work or reasons why your poems were rejected? Probably he or she didn't. Editors are extremely busy and don't necessarily have time to comment on rejections. If that's the case, move on to the next magazine or publisher you've targeted and send your work out again.

If, however, the editor *has* commented on your work, pay attention. It counts for something that the editor took the time and trouble to say anything, however brief, good or bad. And consider any remark or suggestion with an open mind. You don't have to agree, but you shouldn't automatically disregard the feedback, either. Tell your ego to sit down and be quiet, then use the editor's comments to review your work from a new perspective. You might be surprised by how much you'll learn from a single scribbled word in the margin—or how encouraged you'll feel from a simple "Try again!" written on the rejection slip.

SUBMISSION TRACKER

Poem Title	Publication/ Contest	Editor/Contact	Date Sent	Date Returned	Date Accepted	Date Published	Pay Recieved	Comments

FREQUENTLY ASKED QUESTIONS

The following FAQ (Frequently Asked Questions) section provides the expert knowledge you need to submit your poetry in a professional manner. Answers to most basic questions, such as "How many poems should I send?," "How long should I wait for a reply?" and "Are simultaneous submissions okay?" can be found by simply reading the listings in the Magazines/Journals and Book/Chapbook Publishers sections. Also, see the Glossary of Listing terms.

Can I submit handwritten poems?

Usually, no. Now and then a publisher or editor makes an exception and accepts handwritten manuscripts. However, check the preferences stated in each listing. If no mention is made, assume your poetry should be typed or computer-printed.

How should I format my poems for online and print publications?

If you're submitting poems by regular mail (also referred to as *postal mail* or *snail mail*), follow this format:

Poems should be printed on white 8½×11 paper of at least 20 lb. weight. Left, right and bottom margins should be at least one inch. Starting ½ inch from the top of the page, type your name, address, telephone number, e-mail address and number of lines in the poem in the *upper right* corner, in individual lines, single-spaced. Space down about six lines and type the poem title, either centered or flush left. The title may appear in all caps or in upper and lower case. Space down another two lines (at least) and begin to type your poem. Poems are usually single-spaced, although some magazines may request double-spaced submissions. (Be alert to each market's preferences.) Double-space between stanzas. Type one poem to a page. For poems longer than one page, type your name in the *upper left* corner; on the next line, type a key word from the title of your poem, the page number, and indicate whether the stanza begins or is continued on the new page (i.e., MOTHMAN, Page 2, continue stanza *or* begin new stanza).

If you're submitting poems by e-mail:

In most cases, editors will request that poems be pasted within the body of your e-mail, *not* sent as attachments. Many editors prefer this format because of the danger of viruses, the possibility of software incompatibility, and other concerns associated with e-mail attachments. Editors who consider e-mail attachments taboo may even delete the message without opening the attachment.

Of course, other editors do accept, and even prefer e-mail submissions as attachments. This information should be clearly stated in the market listing. If it's not, you're probably safer submitting your poems in the body of the e-mail.

Note, too, the number of poems the editor recommends including in the e-mail submission. If no quantity is given specifically for e-mails, go with the number of poems an editor recommends submitting in general. Identify your submission with a notation in the subject line. While some editors simply want the words "Poetry Submission," others want poem titles. Check the market listing for preferences. **Note:** Because of spam, filters and other concerns, some editors are strict about what must be printed in the subject line and how. If you're uncertain about any aspect of e-mail submission formats, double-check the website (if available) for information or contact the publication for directions.

Some publications may also accept submissions only via online submission forms, such as Submittable or Submishmash. These typically require setting up a log in and then either pasting the poems into a text box or attaching a digital file.

What is a chapbook? How is it different from a regular poetry book?

A chapbook is a booklet, averaging 24-50 pages in length (some are shorter), usually digest-sized (5½×8½, although chapbooks can come in all sizes, even published within the pages of a magazine). Typically, a chapbook is saddle-stapled with a soft cover (card or special paper); chapbooks can also be produced with a plain paper cover the same weight as the pages, especially if the booklet is photocopied.

A chapbook is a much smaller collection of poetry than a full-length book (which runs anywhere from 50 pages to well over 100 pages, longer for "best of" collections and retrospectives). There are probably more poetry chapbooks being published than full-length books, and that's an important point to consider. Don't think of the chapbook as a poor relation to the full-length collection. While it's true a chapbook won't attract big reviews, qualify for major prizes or find national distribution through chain bookstores, it's a terrific way for a poet to build an audience (and reputation) in increments, while developing the kind of publishing history that may attract the attention of a book publisher one day.

Although some presses consider chapbooks through a regular submission process, many choose manuscripts through competitions. Check each publisher's listing for requirements, send for guidelines or visit the website (absolutely vital if a competition is involved), and check out some sample chapbooks the press has already produced (usually available from the press itself). Most chapbook publishers are as choosy as book publishers about the quality of work they accept. Submit your best poems in a professional manner.

How do I format a collection of poems to submit to a book/chapbook publisher?

Before you send a manuscript to a book/chapbook publisher, request guidelines (or consult the publisher's website, if available). Requirements vary regarding formatting, query letters and samples, length, and other considerations. Usually you will use 8½×11, 20 lb. white paper; set left, right and bottom margins of at least one inch; put your name and title of your collection in the top left corner of every page; limit poems to one per page (although poems certainly may run longer than one page); and number pages consecutively. Individual publisher requirements might include a title page, table of contents, credits page (indicating where previously published poems originally appeared) and biographical note.

If you're submitting your poetry book or chapbook manuscript to a competition, you *must* read and follow the guidelines. Failure to do so could disqualify your manuscript. Guidelines for a competition might call for an official entry form to accompany the submission, a special title page, a minimum and maximum number of pages, and specific formatting instructions (such as paginating the manuscript and not putting the poet's name on any of the manuscript pages).

What is a cover letter?

A cover letter is your introduction to the editor, telling him or her a little about yourself and your work. Most editors indicate their cover letter preferences in their listings. If an editor states a cover letter is "required," absolutely send one! It's also better to send one if a cover letter is "preferred." Experts disagree on the necessity and appropriateness of cover letters, so use your own judgment when preferences aren't clear in the listing.

A cover letter should be professional but also allow you to present your work in a personal manner. Keep your letter brief, no more than one page. Address your letter to the correct contact person. (Use "Poetry Editor" if no contact name appears in the listing.) Include your name, address, phone number and e-mail address (if available). If a biographical note is requested, include 2-3 lines about your background, interests, why you write poetry, etc. Avoid praising yourself or your poems in your letter (your submission should speak for itself). Include titles (or first lines) of the poems you're submitting. You may list a few of your most recent publishing credits, but no more than five; and keep in mind that some editors find publishing credits tiresome—they're more interested in the quality of the work you're submitting to *them*.

Show your familiarity with the magazine to which you're submitting: comment on a poem the magazine published, tell the editor why you chose to submit to her magazine, mention poets the magazine has published. Use a business-style format for a professional appearance and proofread carefully; typos, misspellings and other errors make a poor first impression. Remember that editors are people, too. Respect, professionalism and kindness go a long way in poet/editor relationships.

What is an SASE?

An SASE is a self-addressed, stamped envelope—and you should never send a submission by regular mail without one. Also include a SASE if you send an inquiry to an editor. If your submission is too large for an envelope (for instance, a bulky book-length collection of poems), use a box and include a self-addressed mailing label with adequate return postage paper-clipped to it.

What does it mean when an editor says "no previously published" poems?

If your poem appears *anywhere* in print for a public audience, it's considered "previously published." That includes magazines, anthologies, websites and online journals, and even printed programs (say for a church service, wedding, etc.). See the explanation for rights below, especially *second serial (reprint) rights* and *all rights* for additional concerns about previously published material.

One exception to the above guidelines is if your poem appears online in a *private* poetry forum, critique group, etc. As long as the site is private (i.e., a password is required to view and participate), your poem isn't considered "published." However, if your poem is printed on an online forum or bulletin board that's available for public viewing, even if you must use a password

to post the poem or to comment, then your poem is considered "published" as far as rights are concerned.

What rights should I offer for my poems?

Editors usually indicate in their listings what rights they acquire. Most journals and magazines license *first rights* (a.k.a. *first serial rights*), which means the poet offers the right to publish the poem for the first time in any periodical. All other rights to the material remain with the poet. (Note that some editors state that rights to poems "revert to poets upon publication" when first rights are acquired.) When poems are excerpted from a book prior to publication and printed in a magazine/journal, this is also called *first serial rights*. The addition of *North American* indicates the editor is the first to publish a poem in a U.S. or Canadian periodical. The poem may still be submitted to editors outside of North America or to those who acquire reprint rights.

When a magazine/journal licenses *one-time rights* to a poem (also known as *simultaneous rights*), the editor has *nonexclusive* rights to publish the poem once. The poet may submit that same poem to other publications at the same time (usually markets that don't have overlapping audiences).

Editors/publishers open to submission of work already published elsewhere seek *second serial (reprint) rights*. The poet is obliged to inform them where and when the poem previously appeared so they can give proper credit to the original publication. In essence, chapbook or book collections license reprint rights, listing the magazines in which poems previously appeared somewhere in the book (usually on the copyright page or separate credits page).

If a publisher or editor requires you to relinquish *all rights*, be aware that you're giving up ownership of that poem or group of poems. You cannot resubmit the work elsewhere, nor can you include it in a poetry collection without permission or by negotiating for reprint rights to be returned to you. It's highly recommended that poets refuse such an arrangement.

What is a copyright? Should I have my poems copyrighted before I submit them for publication?

Copyright is a proprietary right that gives you the power to control your work's reproduction, distribution and public display or performance, as well as its adaptation to other forms. In other words, you have the legal right to the exclusive publication, sale or distribution of your poetry. What's more, your "original works of authorship" are protected as soon as they are "fixed in a tangible form of expression," i.e., written down or recorded. Since March 1989, copyright notices are no longer required to secure protection, so it's not necessary to include them on your poetry manuscript. Also, in many editors' minds, copyright notices signal the work of amateurs who are distrustful and paranoid about having work stolen.

If you still want to indicate copyright, use the © symbol or the word *copyright*, your name and the year. If you wish, you can register your copyright with the Copyright Office (directions and form available for download from www.copyright.gov). Since paying per poem is costly and impractical, you may prefer to copyright a group of unpublished poems for that single fee.

HOW TO INCREASE YOUR ODDS OF PUBLICATION

....

by Sage Cohen

//

Writing poetry is an art, and so is the process of submitting your poems for publication. If you'd like to increase your odds of getting noticed and getting published, this article can help you align your best work with the right opportunities—so you can give your poems the chance they deserve.

IDENTIFY THE RIGHT PUBLICATIONS FOR YOUR POETRY

You'll have the greatest odds of publication when you submit your poems to journals or contests that are most suited to your work—and therefore most likely to appreciate it. If you're not sure how to identify such possibilities, consider the following:

Read the work of poets you love

A good way to get a feel for publishing possibilities is by reviewing the acknowledgments pages of the poetry collections you admire. If you connect to a particular poet's work, chances are good that your poet-

ry could also be well suited to the journals where s/he has been published.

Do your due diligence

Let's say you've collected a list of possible journals and contests based on the tip above. And let's say you've never sent out work for publication before. You can research here in *Poet's Market* to learn more about how your poetry and these opportunities might line up. For example, you'll want to submit only to journals that say they publish work by emerging as well as established poets. You'll want to confirm that contest submission fees and guidelines are in alignment with what you're willing to send and spend. And you may want to make sure your themes, poetic forms, and approach to language are compatible with the publication's description of what it is seeking. I also suggest learning what you can about the editors or contest judge(s)—and reading their poetry, if possible, so you get a feeling for their personal aesthetic.

Always experience a journal before submitting

Before submitting your work to a publication, purchase its latest issue or view content online to get a sense of the poets and poems it features. Also consider how the publication's front cover, inside art, website design, production, paper quality and font choice create a particular kind of experience. If you can imagine seeing your poetry in these pages, that's a good indication that the journal or site may be the right fit for you.

Track what you learn to grow your knowledge base

I suggest creating a simple system—a document, binder or folder—where you track what you've learned about each publication and record your thinking about how your poems align or do not align. This way, you'll have a growing knowledge base about the poetry market—and how various opportunities may be suited to your goals—as you investigate, submit and publish over time.

CHOOSE THE RIGHT POEM/S

When you've chosen a publication or contest to which you'd like to submit, it's time to gather the poems for this opportunity. Consider running the poems you are considering through these filters of inquiry:

Does something significant or resonant happen?

Poems get editors' attention when they introduce a new possibility, provide a palpable experience or revelation, and say something in a way it has never been spoken (or written) before. Ask yourself:

- What happens in this poem? (Or, if the poem is non-narrative, do the language, sound and/or imagery create the kind of experience or journey I intended?)
- If this poem is about or addressed to someone I know, does it also reveal something meaningful or relevant to people outside of the dynamic?
- What is discovered or transformed or revealed?

Because it can be tricky to experience your own, highly subjective material objectively, you may want to share your poems with a reader or two you trust and ask these questions of them. If you're not sure you are creating an experience that has impact or resonance, your poem may not yet be ready for publication.

Have I found something fresh to say about a familiar theme?

If you're writing about a historical person or event or one that's been covered in the news in recent years, chances are good that most readers will have a good handle on the facts. To ensure that your poem makes an impact, ask yourself:

- What happens in this poem that is fresh, surprising, and different than the information already available on this topic?
- How is this poem departing from the work of "reporting" and moving into the territory of "illuminating"?

- How is this event or person serving as a leaping-off point for my own inquiry or discovery about myself, history, the natural world, or the human condition?

IS MY WORK AS POLISHED AS POSSIBLE?

These 10 revision tips may help you identify opportunities to nip, tuck, and shine. Ask yourself:

1. Could I trim exposition at the beginning or summary information at the end that is not serving the poem?
2. Could I use a different voice to influence the experience of this poem? (For example, consider changing a third-person voice into the first person and see if this shift in intimacy is of benefit.)
3. Could my similes and metaphors be more distilled or powerful? If I've used an extended metaphor, does it hold up throughout the poem?
4. Where can I bring more energy to the language I've used? Can I use more active language to communicate similar ideas? Can modifiers be cut?
5. What if I changed past-tense verbs to the present tense (or vice versa)?
6. How might I shape the poem (line length, stanza breaks, white space) to more fully enact the emotion and rhythm of its content?
7. Are punctuation and capitalization and verb tense consistent? Would different choices (such as removing punctuation or capitalization) improve the experience?
8. Is there a music of repeating sounds throughout the poem? What words could I replace to create a more cohesive sound experience?
9. Are there opportunities to break lines in ways that give attention to important words or pace the momentum of the narrative more powerfully?
10. How might the title better encapsulate and add dimension to the experience of the poem? Could some of the exposition cut in step one be used to set the context of the poem in its title?

ARRANGE YOUR POEMS INTENTIONALLY

The order of the poems you've submitted can make a difference in an editor's experience and opinion of your work—even if you're just submitting three to five poems. Think about the arrangement as a single composition that provides a coherent reading journey. Where do you want the reader to start—and finish? How do you want them to enter the realm of your poetry, and how are you intending to send them off?

MAKE SUBMISSION GUIDELINES YOUR BIBLE

Every literary publication and contest will offer detailed guidelines about how and when they want to receive poems. Your job is to follow every single detail of those guidelines fanatically to ensure you don't rule yourself out with a simple oversight. Because it's easy to miss a detail when scanning instructions online, I recommend printing out the submission guidelines for any opportunity and then checking off each requirement as you meet it. Specifically:

- Follow simultaneous submission instructions. Some publications accept simultaneous submissions (meaning that you've sent the same poems to more than one publication for consideration at the same time), and others don't. Be careful to understand and honor each journal's parameters.
- Get your timing right. Publications have contest deadlines and specific reading windows. Send your work in advance of the specified deadline.
- Choose poems that fit. Ensure that you have chosen poems that match any specific requirements, such as: theme, form, length (number of lines or pages), number of poems allowed or required.
- Be deliberate about where you include your name. Some publications read and choose poems "blind," others don't. Be sure to understand whether the publication wants identifying information on the poems or not—and follow these guidelines carefully.
- Double-check the mailing address and editor names. No editor wants to see his or her name misspelled or receive mail addressed to his or her predecessor. It's also a good idea to confirm the gender of the person you are addressing if you have any doubt.

- Follow binding requirements. Publications often specify whether they want paper clips, staples or loose pages.
- Provide SASE (self-addressed, stamped envelope) if this is required or requested by the publication. Follow whatever process is requested.
- Include a check if you are submitting to a contest with a required reading fee. Make sure you make it out to the organization as requested in the amount required and specify the name of the contest to which you are submitting.

FORMAT, PROOF, AND POLISH

First impressions are often the last impression. Think of your submission package as a gift that an editor or selection committee will enjoy opening and experiencing—whether you're submitting online or by mail:

- Use a standard font that is easy to read—such as Times New Roman or Garamond or Calibri—using 12-point font, unless instructed otherwise. Your priority should be legibility and ease for the person(s) who will be considering your poem.
- Unless you are doing so for a very specific reason, think twice about bolding or italicizing fonts. Let your images, word choice and line breaks do the work of creating emphasis.
- Print your poems on white, unrumpled and unscented paper.
- Ensure your toner is working or that your photocopies are clear and crisp.

WRITE A COVER LETTER THAT CONNECTS

Your cover letter should first and foremost provide whatever information is requested in the submission guidelines, if any. In the absence of specific instruction, write a concise note that covers the following:

- Explain you are submitting poems for [name of contest, issue, or general consideration].
- Describe in a sentence or two what you admire about the publication and why you chose to submit your work—if you have something authentic to say. Or, if you've had a previous communication with an editor (such as, they sent an encouraging rejection with a note inviting you to submit again in the future) you can mention that here.
- Lists the names of the poems being submitted. If this is a simultaneous submission, it is good form to mention this and confirm you intend to follow whatever process this publication has requested in its submission guidelines.
- Provide a brief biographical paragraph that describes key publishing or education highlights to reflect your literary experience and expertise. If you haven't

published yet or don't have anything else relevant to report, no need to say anything here.
- Be polite and gracious.

Remember, this is a business communication. Some mistakes to avoid:

- Do not provide explanations about why you chose these poems for submission, why you wrote them, what they mean to you or your family, or how you have revised them.
- Do not advise editors about when you expect to hear back from them.
- Do not send a follow-up letter with a batch of poems that are edited versions of a previous submission.
- Do send a follow-up letter to withdraw any poems you have submitted as soon as they have been accepted elsewhere.

Over time, you'll get more efficient and adept with this process. Preparing your poems for submission will get faster, easier and more automatic as you know what steps to take and mistakes to avoid. Your commitment to consistently putting your best work forward—and willingness to learn from the feedback you get along the way—will give you the very best odds of publication.

SAGE COHEN is the author of *Writing the Life Poetic* and *The Productive Writer*, both from Writer's Digest Books, and the poetry collection *Like the Heart, the World*. She holds an MFA in creative writing from New York University and a BA from Brown University. Sage has won first place in the Ghost Road Press poetry contest, been nominated for a Pushcart Prize and published a number of articles in *Writer's Digest* magazine. In 2011, she judged the Writer's Digest contest for non-rhyming poetry. To learn more about Sage, visit pathofpossibility.com.

READY YOUR WORK FOR PUBLICATION

9 Techniques for Perfecting Poems

....

by Lauren Camp

Poetry is a sublime art form, but making it takes time. Breathtaking poems generally emerge from a slow, considered approach and a long gestation period.

Writing technical and magazine articles taught me structure, concision, and reporting strategies. Poetry teaches me to analyze the colors of each thought, and to look for ways to sculpt the statement. If every poem came out perfect right away, the experience would feel too clipped. I want the project to take a while, to "marinate" and evolve into language both exquisite and weirdly unexpected.

To ensure your poems get picked out from the editors' slush pile, take some time to prime your work for publication. Here are nine hands-on, critical techniques to help you assess your poems from different perspectives, and improve your writing.

#1—LISTEN TO MILES DAVIS.

On his 1959 album *Kind of Blue,* trumpeter and composer Miles Davis named a composition "So What." Ask that question of your poem. *So what* if you have a distinctive voice? *So what* if there's melody? Why should others care about your poem?

To create a poem with staying power, you have to be able to answer one tough question: is this worth saying? If you are writing the poem just to share an experience, the poem isn't done yet. Consider what the experience taught you. Would an audience be interested in that? Most experiences are universal in some way. Give readers an insight that they can connect to their lives.

#2—EAT THE BANANA.

Think hard about "the."

"The" means "the one and only." The ultimate. The whole enchilada. The all and everything of a subject.

Look at every single place you've used it. Is this what you're trying to infer? Did you really sit on "the" park bench? (I can think of a lot of benches—and a lot of parks). Did you really eat "the" banana? The one and only?

You see what I mean. It's easy to say it and write it, but when you start picking apart what you mean…well, maybe you shouldn't use "the." Try substituting "a"—a park bench, a banana, a trip to Peru—or see if the poem works without any articles at all.

#3—STOP GOING & DOING.

Another easy fix is to shorten and tighten verbs. Why are you "going" when you could just "go"—or better yet, "fly" or "trudge"?

Gerunds ("ing" words) are so kind. They whisper over readers with a tinge of apology. They are almost always less effective than a lean verb—one without fat. Be insistent in your writing for a change. Make those verbs muscular. Ask them to really do something, to lift the line. Be more authoritative than you think you can; stop "ing-ing" around.

After you've made these changes, re-read your lines in a big, vigorous, and certain voice. How does the poem sound now?

Clearly, you can't cut all "ing" words all the time. Look for a balance of tensile strength with breathing space.

#4—PULL YOURSELF OUT.

We all write about ourselves in some way, but sometimes poems are just loaded with… well, us.

How many times do you have to say "I" for your readers to know the poem is happening to you? I bet you could safely eliminate some references to self, and readers would still be clued in. Try it. Take one "I" out, and see if it matters. Take out another. Don't forget to read out loud to make sure you haven't lost the flow—or the human quality of the poem.

Remove yourself just enough that you aren't ever-present, but be careful. If you take yourself completely out, the poem will seem choppy and abstract.

#5—LOOK FOR SOFT SPOTS.

My students step into soft spots all the time. So do I, and you will, too, because you must write first for you, and then, revise for someone else.

Where readers sink is the quicksand of the poem. The weight of messy language pulls them down. Sometimes our writing is thick and circular—especially if we are trying to say too much. Because we often write to figure something out for ourselves, rather than writing what we already know, we may be uncertain how to draw the map of what we're exploring. What a writer thinks is solid might not always be so to a reader.

How can you avoid these spots? Let the poem sit for a while. The irony of this technique is that the quick answer to finding your soft spots is time. Let the poem exist on your hard drive, unopened, until it becomes a little unfamiliar to you.

When sufficient time has passed, read it. Anything confusing or abstract will now be evident. You'll see where you've taken readers on a side journey, and forgotten to bring them back. Because the poem is again new to you, you'll know if you've complicated its map, and if there is a more direct route.

You want readers to get somewhere specific: your revelation. Take out references that send them to the wrong places.

#6—WEAR THE STRONG SUIT OF SPECIFICITY.

Be particular in your writing. Give details without drowning your readers in adjectives. Tell us which street, the hour it happened, the type of insect you heard in the air, the color of buttons on his shirt.

Israeli poet Yehuda Amichai once wrote that you must "put real things in your poems." Ask the poem every possible question you can. Is everything defined precisely? One of my students wrote about how, as a young child, she was instructed to put her small, cold hand inside the pocket of her mother's wool coat as a way for her mother to keep her close on dangerous urban streets. Holding fast to the pocket, the girl felt the nubbly texture. Because she described it, I could also feel the pocket lining, and the sense of security that came with it.

#7—SMASH IT.

Auguste Rodin advised young sculptors to stop gently picking at the clay and plaster of their sculpture when something wasn't going well. Instead, he encouraged them to "drop it on the floor and see what it looks like then."

It's easy to draw an analogy between this and poetry revising. Both creative acts sometimes require drastic changes to find the form your piece needs. Revision is all about seeing new options, but you might not be able to do this when you're trying to stay true to your initial intent.

If you are convinced that a poem isn't working and will never work, you are free to do anything at all to it. Construction workers often relish demolition work. Why not use their approach? Destruction frees the poem of the ghost of its earlier structure. Rather than remedying little parts, rebuild the whole.

Pick a line or phrase that seems strong. Let that chosen line become a new jumping off place, and jump in an unexpected direction.

Of course, if you're an archivist, and the idea of tossing big parts of the poem gives you hives, by all means, save the gems. (I collect the lines that I still like in a separate document.) But eviscerate them if they don't serve the poem you're revising.

#8—INTERLACE.

Have you ever tried splicing two poems together? In a way, it's like braiding hair. You pull a line from here and a line from there, again and again, until you have created a more complex structure, woven with new thoughts.

Take those good lines, and plait them into another poem. If they are on the same subject, aha! an easy fit. If not, well… your job as poet becomes more challenging. How to match them together…?

In the mid-1960s, John Lennon wrote lyrics inspired by a news headline about a car accident and other events current at the time. His musical partner Paul McCartney had written a simple ditty about a man heading out late on a bus, and moving into a hazy dream. These were totally separate stories, neither quite complete in itself. Twined together, the lyrics became "A Day in the Life," on the *Sgt. Pepper's Lonely Hearts Club Band* album. Lennon said, "I had the bulk of the song and the words, but [Paul] contributed this little lick floating around in his head that he couldn't use for anything."

Isn't that how it is sometimes with a poem; a perfect phrase that needs a new home? Move it to another poem. Encourage it to be a strand in something larger, something with a separate music—maybe even one you didn't realize could exist. Take it from two lyrical masters; poetry interspersed with poetry can double the emotional impact.

#9—CHANGE PACING.

Revision is about taking innumerable steps to write the best possible poem. One technique worth trying is to change the speed of the poem.

If you're writing about something urgent or disturbing, and you want readers to keep moving through the poem—if, in fact, you believe readers should be nearly breathless when reading, try enjambment. In other words, don't let your lines end comfortably with commas or periods. Don't let anyone stop reading. Keep the thought in motion.

Think like a movie director for a thriller. When one of the characters is in danger, you want to design the scene to keep viewers on the edge of their seats, blood racing. How

will you do this? Lighting, sound...whatever it takes to keep the suspense constant.

That's what you're after as a poet, too. Make your readers keep hurrying ahead to the next line, and the next. This doesn't mean you can't use punctuation. Instead, place those punctuation marks in the middle of lines, where periods are significantly less weighty and powerful.

For a different way to speed up, incorporate a full line of monosyllables. You'll get a ticker-tape effect from the rapid short words, hurtling readers through the line.

What if you want to move more slowly, and let readers revel in your images? Lines that are end-stopped (with periods) allow them to pause deeply. Stanza breaks take this even further—a maximum full stop. A complete resting place.

Switch the stride of your poem. As the writer, you know whether it should meander along or hurtle forth; now make your line decisions fit the mood of the piece, so readers know how to "hear" the poem.

It takes work to get a poem right, but this work can also be a joy. My students call this work "revisioning." Whatever techniques you employ, don't be too controlling. Allow spontaneity to guide the work.

LAUREN CAMP is the author of the collection This *Business of Wisdom* (West End Press), an interdisciplinary artist, and an educator. Her poems have appeared in *J Journal, Linebreak, Beloit Poetry Journal*, and you are here, among other journals. Her work gets accepted almost as frequently as it gets turned down, which she considers good odds. She has also guest edited special sections for *World Literature Today* (on international jazz poetry) and for *Malpaís Review* (on the poetry of Iraq). Lauren blogs about poetry at *Which Silk Shirt*. On Sundays, she hosts "Audio Saucepan," a weekly global music and poetry program on Santa Fe Public Radio. www.laurencamp.com

THE ORGANIZED POET

....

by Patricia Kennelly

If you're like many poets I've talked with, it's not uncommon to have your poems everywhere. My desktop held overflowing notebooks, file folders and piles of random pieces of paper, scribbled with favorite words, lines, and poem starts. My computer's desktop wasn't any better. Although I knew most of my work was saved, my lack of organization made finding a particular poem time-consuming.

This wasn't too much of a problem until I started submitting my body of work. I struggled with getting my work to the right market. I missed good opportunities and important deadlines and created unnecessary stress by entering my poems at the last minute. Finding contests, markets and journals was the easy part; tracking down a poem or trying to read my illegible note about a "must enter" contest became challenging.

Most organizational experts agree that organizing any part of your life will save you time, money and help to eliminate stress. So why do so many poets have resistance to organizing their work? Some poets think that organization is the opposite of creativity and that being too businesslike will stifle their voices. I found the opposite to be true. Working on organization fueled my desire to write poetry and get my poems published.

When I decided to take ownership of my body of work and organize, I naturally approached the submission process in a professional manner. Doing the hard work ahead of time meant I had more time to find and research markets. The result? More published pieces and a clearer picture of where I wanted to go with my poetry.

Whatever system you choose (pen and paper, computer based, online or a combination of all) make sure it's one that will work for you. And if it doesn't work, consider trying another. The best organizational systems only function if you're ready to get organized and if they fit your personality. If any of these tips seem too daunting, consider asking a fellow poet to work with you in exchange for doing the same for them.

10 WAYS TO GET ORGANIZED

If you don't already have an uncluttered writing space, create one. It's difficult to work on organization if your space causes additional stress or distraction. These tips might help you become a more organized poet:

1. Find all of your publishable poems as well as your incomplete poems. This may take some time. Don't rush this process; finding, reading and organizing your forgotten words may inspire new work. Consider typing up your poem starts into one document so you know where to begin when you're stuck for inspiration.

2. Print hard copies of all work and separate publishable poems and poems that need revision into separate accordion files or three-ring binders. You can choose to file by title, subject/theme or type/form. Other poets include length of poem and tone.

3. Generate a virtual folder on your desktop. I titled mine "All Poetry" and created subfolders entitled "Publishable Poems," "Needs Work," and "Published Poems." Choose subfolder titles that make sense to you—you can use poem title, subject matter, form, or theme. Your goal is to be able to find your poems easily.

4. Create or find a submission tracker. If your goal is publication, having a system that tracks your submissions and that is easy to use and update will help create a sense of order.

5. Write or type up a list of goal markets for the year. I do this by going through *Poet's Market* and my favorite poetry newsletters and websites to find markets that seem to be a good fit. This document will grow every month as you discover more markets, contests and literary journals. Some poets find including the hyperlinks to be helpful.

6. Make an appointment with yourself. At least once every week I set aside some time to follow up with upcoming deadlines and to write a to-do list. More productive writers than myself do a to-do list every day, but with a full-time job I find that this weekly check-in is enough to keep me on task.

7. Subscribe to poetry newsletters and set Google alerts for specific contests you'd like to enter. Here is the challenging part–as soon as you receive the newsletter or alert, fill in your paper or virtual poetry calendar. And then delete the newsletter.

8. Keep office supplies including: envelopes, paper, file folders, printer ink and stamps stocked. While many magazines and journals are set up for e-mail submissions, there are still some journals that require a hard copy submission.

9. Organize your books by genre. I keep chapbooks, craft books, journals, and poetry magazines on one shelf for reference and inspiration. While the Internet makes it easy to access informa-

tion, having all of your reference materials within easy reach could prevent you from getting distracted online.

10. Do set a date for completion of your new organizational system by choosing a realistic goal date and sticking to it. As Barbara Sher writes in *Wishcraft: How to Get What You Really Want*, "… your true goal, or target, has to be a concrete action or event, not only so you'll know for sure when you get there, but so that you can make that date with success in advance!"

SET UP A POETRY CALENDAR

At the beginning of every year or starting today, consider purchasing a large spaced desk calendar specifically for poetry. Because I'm sitting at the desk every day it's easy to jot down poetry contests and submission deadlines I don't want to miss, especially the "no-entry fee" contests. If it's on my goal market list, I use different colored highlighters to show when the journal is open to submissions.

Writer Phyllis Kaelin also uses a similar paper-based calendar system but uses colorful sticky notes to chart her progress on a particular project. Her paper calendar system works hand in hand with her computer files. She says, "Within the project folder, I keep a running "notes document" where I put comments, plans, progress, word count etc. When I decide to submit I make a note there too."

If you don't already use an online calendar specifically for poetry set one up. If you're serious about poetry this can be used to track submissions, deadlines and markets but also helps keep you on track with readings, writing groups and poetry events. Popular online calendars include: Google Calendar (www.google.com/calendar), Convenient Calendar (www.convenient-calendar.com), and 30 Boxes (www.30boxes.com). I like using an online calendar that integrates with my smartphone so that I can send reminders to my phone, e-mail and/or virtual desktop.

WHY USE A SUBMISSION TRACKER?

Even if you have a good memory, once you get in the habit of sending out your poems it's very easy to lose track of when and where your poems were sent. And there's nothing more frustrating than finding a good market for a particular poem and not remembering where or if it was sent out.

Poet's Market includes a basic submission tracker that you can enlarge and copy. Or if you're feeling creative, you can design your own paper submission tracker using headlines that make sense to you. Another option many poets use is index cards or a simple journal log. Alternatively you can convert *Poet's Market*'s submission tracker to a computer spreadsheet program such as Excel. If you're not comfortable setting up your own tracking spreadsheet on your computer, there are several free submission trackers available online.

The most popular submission trackers include: Duotrope (www.duotrope.com), Luminary Writer's Database (www.writersdb.com), and *Writer's Market* (www.writers-market.com).

Rooze, an award-winning poet who is currently pursuing her MFA, says about Duotrope, "I like that they have a theme calendar and a deadline calendar. For each journal, they also list the average response time, percentage of submissions accepted, and the last time a response was received. This gives me a better context to know what to expect. Duotrope also specifies additional criteria, such as requirements around simultaneous submissions and previously printed poems."

The benefits of using a submission tracker far outweigh the time it will take to set one up. If you choose to include comments you can easily recognize when a poem needs a second look. If you use an online submission tracker your timely follow-up can also help other poets who use the database. Knowing that we're all in this submission process together, helping fellow poets just feels right.

If spreadsheets and submission trackers seem too left-brain, you might consider poet Jessy Randall's process. She says, "I write, with my hand and a pen, a poem. I mess around with, cross things out, rewrite lines, for a day or two. Then I set it aside for, if possible, at least a month, or even better, three months. Then I take a look at it again. If I think it's any good, I type it into a giant Word document that contains typed versions of all my poems, with the newest ones at the top. I fiddle around with it some more as I type it. I set it aside again for a while, maybe another month. If I still like it after

all that, I submit it to a journal, bundling it together with other poems that somehow go with it. I keep track of where I've sent it, and when, in a Word document (to tell the truth, it's the same giant document). I also try to keep track of the general response time so I know when I should send a query. So I'll have something like:

"Name of Journal: Poem Title 1, Poem Title 2, Poem Title 3, sent January 2012, should respond in 6 months."

For the submission process Randall adds that the "submission information is in the top of my Word document, along with a list of the poems that aren't sent out anywhere at the moment. Then come all the typed poems. At the bottom of this giant document is where I keep track of rejections, in alphabetical order by journal name. If I need to, I can do a word search in the document to see if a particular journal has already seen a particular poem."

YOU'RE PUBLISHED!

Unfortunately just being organized doesn't guarantee publication. But if you're committed to poetry and part of that commitment includes being organized and businesslike, with time and persistence, there's a very good chance that your work will be accepted.

When you do receive the letter or e-mail that your work is being accepted make sure to follow through. Update your submission tracker as well as your computer and/or paper files. It's very rewarding to move the poem (physically or virtually) from the publishable folder to the published folder and/or to write where and when your poem will be published. If the poem was a simultaneous submission be professional and notify the other publications that you are withdrawing your work.

Blogger and poet Sonya Fehér of Mama True (www.mamatrue.com) includes a Published Worksheet as part of her organizational system.

"The Published Worksheet includes the following fields:

- **MARKET**—Name of market in which the poem was published
- **DETAILS**—Volume # and other details from publication
- **LINK**—If the poem was published on-line, this gives me the location."

For poet Jessy Randall, being organized makes poetry more gratifying: "This may sound weird, but I particularly enjoy the housekeeping side of poetry, the keeping-track-of-submissions part. When I open up the file that shows me what's where, what's been rejected, what's forthcoming, I feel a real sense of accomplishment even if I didn't write anything that day. Because look at all the stuff that's percolating along without me doing anything!"

That's the favorite part for me too; once I set my organizational system in place I had more fun with the submission process. I missed fewer deadlines and felt more in control of my poetic career. Whether your body of work consists of five or 50 poems there's no time like today to start organizing. Taking the time to organize your work goes beyond the practical; it's a way to honor your time, work, and commitment to craft. It could very well be the inspiration you need to get published.

PATRICIA KENNELLY is a published poet, business owner and editor in Colorado Springs, Colorado. Her poems have most recently appeared in *Haibun Today*, *Messages from the Hidden Lake* and *The Denver Post*. She gently nags about writing daily and creativity at www.writingnag.com.

THE HABITS OF HIGHLY PRODUCTIVE POETS

by Scott Owens

If they held a convention for all the people who have made a fortune off poetry, I'm not sure anyone would show up. The external rewards of writing poetry are relatively minimal. Writing poetry doesn't produce googobs of money. Any fame generated by the act is rather limited and usually accompanied by equal amounts of misunderstanding, suspicion, and other forms of notoriety. Even moral support is often lacking as family and friends may resent the time that poetry takes away from them, and readers and other poets may not support your particular aesthetic or the subjects you choose to write about.

Still, there are thousands of people who write poetry, some obsessively, some successfully, if productivity and a small following can be construed as success. The questions, then, are *Why do they do it?* and *How do they do it?* Ultimately, of course, the answers to both questions are as diverse as the people who write poetry, but some reasons and ways are common enough to merit general discussion.

W.S. Merwin claims that *poetry reconnects us to the world.* Gerald Stern gets a bit more specific when he writes that *poetry is a kind of religion, a way of seeking redemption, a way of understanding things so that they can be reconciled, explained, justified, redeemed.* Certainly these are wonderful reasons for why people write poetry, and they ring true to my own experience as both a writer and reader of poetry. They also relate to the first answer to the second question.

HABIT #1: BELIEF

The first habit of productive poets is that they **believe** in poetry. They believe that it is more than a game with words, more even than just writing about the world (an admirable enough ambition in itself). They believe that it is, in fact, both an ontological and an epistemological act—both a way of being in the world, and a way of making meaning out of the world. They understand that the act of writing poetry helps them pay attention to, appreciate, and make meaning out of their existence, and they enjoy the way in which poetry deepens their experience of people, moments, and things. They believe poetry, and their poetry more specifically, matters, and they will not be dissuaded from engaging with poetry and engaging with the world through poetry.

HABIT #2: CONFIDENCE

This is, of course, intimately related to the second habit of productive poets in that it necessitates that poets are **confident and courageous**. In other words, they believe in the significance of what they are doing no matter how many times and ways they are told by society, family, friends, even other poets that poetry, especially their poetry, doesn't matter or isn't right. Perhaps the best answer to why people write poetry is simply because they have to or because they like doing it. If, as Merwin suggests, writing poetry makes you feel closer to the world, then you'll probably keep doing it no matter what anyone else says. And if, as Stern suggests, writing poetry helps you make meaning, significance, and value out of your perceptions and experiences, then it's likely you'll seek every opportunity to do it.

HABIT #3: RECEPTIVE

Often, it is less a matter of seeking the opportunity than it is of being ready for it. The third habit of highly productive poets is that they are **ready to receive**. Ideas, images, lines for poetry are everywhere, every minute of every day, but our ability to remember the fine details of any particular

event or perception is constantly eroded by the sheer mass of events and perceptions we encounter on a daily basis. Thus, highly productive poets are never without pen and paper so that they can jot down these observations when they occur. My writer's notebook goes with me everywhere. It's on the seat next to me when I drive; it's on my nightstand when I sleep; it's in my bookbag or binder when I go out; and on those rare occasions when I can't have it with me, I'm sure to have a folded up piece of paper in one pocket or another. And I don't use just any notebook either. I use a notebook that I like to spend time with, that I like the feel and heft of, that I want to open even when I don't think I have anything to write, and that I won't get confused with any other notebook. For me it's a Moleskine journal with about 200 unlined pages. Similarly, I keep one of my favorite pens with me at all times. For me that means a heavy, metallic-bodied, gel-type pen. Whatever your favorite is like, having it available enhances the likelihood that you will write with relish rather than discomfort, and thus will do so longer and more frequently.

HABIT #4: ATTENTION

Suitably armed for recording the significant details we encounter throughout every day, the fourth, and perhaps most important, habit of highly productive poets is referenced in Mary Oliver's unforgettable poem, "Summer Day," where she says, "I don't know exactly what a prayer is. / I do know how to **pay attention**." Paying attention consists of learning to notice the finer details, the significance of those details, and the connections between them that most people, caught up in the necessaries of daily existence, miss, or fail to remember for more than a moment. As simple as that sounds, this habit requires more development than any of the others. Perhaps the best method for developing it is to begin by doing it consciously. Set aside 30 minutes every day and pay close attention to something, somewhere. You might sit at a coffee shop and pay attention to people, or take a walk and pay attention to something in nature; you might practice yoga or meditation and learn to pay attention to more internal landscapes. After a while of doing this intentionally, you'll discover that you begin to pay closer attention to such details without having to make yourself do it. You'll notice more; you'll be conscious of the significance of things that most people take for granted; and you'll appreciate the connections between things that too often go unnoticed.

HABIT #5: ATTUNED

Highly productive poets also **stay tuned in** to poetry. I am convinced, in fact, that most successful poets read a great deal more poetry than they ever undertake to write. They read poetry in books and magazines; they attend workshops, classes, and readings; they participate in critique and peer groups; they volunteer to edit journals and anthologies and judge contests; they read and write reviews; and they create opportunities for others to experience poetry, all of which keeps them thinking

about poetry and honing their poetic skills and aesthetic. They do this because they love poetry; they do it because they believe that given the opportunity everyone will love and benefit from poetry; and in the process they make themselves better poets. My own hometown lacked a poetry reading series for local poets, so I partnered with a locally-owned coffee shop and created one that has been going on monthly for 7 years and has an average attendance of about 40 people. I also took on writing a semi-weekly poetry column, editing a quarterly online poetry journal, coordinating a quarterly ekphrastic reading series at the local art museum, and serving as an officer of the state poetry society. I think every state has such a society, and joining it is a great way to get tapped into the network of poets and poetry lovers, and to stay on top of opportunities to experience and participate in the world of poetry wherever you might be.

HABIT #6: INIATIVE

Just as highly productive poets dive in to the world of poetry, they also **dive in** to the subjects they choose to write about. As the first habit suggests, whether they write about politics, personal experience, memory, perception, etc., they approach their subjects without letting fear occlude their vision or censor their words. They also dive in in the sense that they immerse themselves in the subject, not rushing to complete the poem, but luxuriating in it, granting it the time it deserves, writing way too much before beginning to whittle down the language and perceptions to the essentials that will form an effective final poem. Examining any act of creation will reveal that creation always involves waste, or "leftovers." Effectiveness comes through a process of sharpening, whittling away what is ineffective. Thus, most poets begin by overwriting, and then eliminate unneeded elements through the process of editing and shaping the poem. This is another one that takes a bit of practice in a world that encourages focusing on the end result and instant gratification rather than relaxing into and fully experiencing the process. Poets will use any number of techniques to help them expand upon the possibilities they venture into: clustering, free association, automatic writing, meditation, focused freewriting, etc. My suggestion is to use them all, sometimes on the same poem, and then make up your own as you discover what works. Driving long distances helps me; another poet friend of mine does his best work while mowing.

HABIT #7: ENJOYMENT

Of course, the correlative habit is just as essential. A highly productive poet will also **enjoy the process**. I've encountered many people who claim to hate revising, but I can't think of a successful poet who has ever said so. Good poets tend to understand that the real craft of writing comes in the rewriting, and as difficult and sometimes painful as that process can be, it is the part of writing that they enjoy the most. It is, in fact, often a form of play for them. They work on a poem for weeks, months,

sometimes years, trying out different perspectives, metaphors, arrangements of lines. They seek out criticism from others; they revise after poems are published, or after giving public readings. They see the poem as "finished" perhaps only after their own death has made it so. If Whitman could have at least 8 versions (some say as many as 19) of *Leaves of Grass*, then surely no lesser poet should doubt or fear the process of continual revision.

HABIT #8: THICK-SKINNED

The eighth habit of productive poets, and for some the most difficult, is that they **grow thick skin**. They learn to distinguish between themselves and their work such that they can accept criticism of their work without internalizing it as criticism of themselves. Often poetry is about personal experience, and some writers struggle to separate criticism of the poem from criticism of who they are, what they've been through, or how they view things. Productive poets, however, come to understand that once written and shared, any poem is an artifact, an object, something to be handled and shaped, and not a part of who they are. Thus they are able to consider the poem coldly and critically and ask of it what will make it more effective without taking such questions, regardless of the source, as a personal affront. From that perspective, productive poets strive to listen to criticism objectively. Even if they cannot manage that level of objectivity, however, knowing that ultimately all decisions regarding the poem rest with them, productive poets learn to accept commentary about the poem and move on with the writing they have undertaken.

Good habits are essential to prolonged success in virtually any endeavor. Inspiration is a nice idea, and a wonderful thing when it happens, but I think it unwise to count upon its striking very often without developing certain practices that increase the likelihood of its coming to be. This list of practices for those who wish to be productive poets is far from exhaustive, but it has been useful for me, and I hope that it will prove to be so for other poets as well.

SCOTT OWENS holds degrees from Ohio University, UNC Charlotte, and UNC Greensboro. He currently lives in Hickory, North Carolina, where he teaches at Catawba Valley Community College, edits *Wild Goose Poetry Review* and *234*, writes for the *Outlook Newspaper*, and serves as vice-president of the NC Poetry Society. His 11th book of poetry, *Eye of the Beholder*, was recently released by Main Street Rag. His work has received awards from the Academy of American Poets, the Pushcart Prize Anthology, the Next Generation/Indie Lit Awards, the NC Writers Network, the NC Poetry Society, and the Poetry Society of SC.

10 CHAPBOOK DESIGN TIPS EVERY POET SHOULD KNOW

by Amy Miller

There's never been a better time to publish a chapbook. These days, desktop-publishing software is so easy to use that practically any poet who can turn on a computer can put together a chapbook—a small booklet of poems to sell at readings and book fairs. That's the good news. But the bad news is that it's easy to go mad with all that power and crank out a quick chapbook that doesn't do your poems justice. From cramped typography to scary author photos, there are lots of ways—some obvious, some subtle—to go wrong with a chapbook. But with a handful of tips and techniques, you can design a book that lures readers into its pages and presents your work in the best light.

And you don't have to be printing your own chapbook to take advantage of these tips. If you're just sending your work out to literary journals, some basic typography tweaks can help your poems look more polished on the page. And if you've been lucky enough to have your manuscript—chapbook-size or full-length—accepted by a publishing house, knowing a few tricks of the trade will help you communicate your wishes to your publisher in a language you both understand, perhaps making the difference between a book that just gets the job done and one that really pops.

FIGURE OUT THE BEST TYPE SIZE AND LEADING

This bit of typography-speak is one of the most important factors—some would say the most important—in making your poems look good on the page. Put simply, this is the relationship between the size of the letters (type size) and the vertical distance between the lines (leading). A common mistake is to make the leading too tight, resulting in lines that are too close together. It's a subtle business—this cramping won't make the type illegible, but even leading that's just a bit too tight will make it hard for the reader to discern one line from the next, making for an uncomfortable reading experience.

A good rule of thumb for poetry is to make your type size three points smaller than the leading: for instance, 11-point type on 14-point leading, or 12 on 15. But not all fonts are created equal; one font may look best at 11.5 on 15, while another may shine at 12 on 14.75. If you're trying to fit more lines onto the page (say, a poem is a line or two over), think twice before just decreasing the leading; you may be better off shrinking both the type size and the leading by a quarter or half point, resulting in smaller type but easy reading because the leading is still comfortable on the eye. And if you have to shrink the type on one page, do it for the whole book to keep your design consistent throughout.

CHOOSE A GOOD FONT

This may seem very basic, but picking out a font for poetry can be surprisingly difficult. There are many schools of thought on what makes a good poetry font—browse through a dozen chapbooks, and you'll probably see a dozen different text fonts. But if you look closely, you'll find that many fonts are too blocky, too narrow, or too rounded to make for smooth reading.

When in doubt, go with the old favorites—Garamond's a classic font for poetry, or something in the Times family may be a good choice. For a more modern look, try sans-serif fonts like Franklin Gothic or Helvetica. The most important thing is that the font should not be distracting—as your reader settles into her easy chair to enjoy your chapbook, you don't want her first thought to be, "What the heck font is that?"

BONUS TIP: When trying out a font, print out a poem or two in that font before deciding on it, and really scrutinize the printout—what looks good on your screen may look very different on the printed page, and your printer may render some fonts more crisply than others. Plan to use up some scrap paper while you experiment with printing out fonts.

PUT A GOOD POEM IN THE CENTER OF THE BOOK

Most chapbooks are simply a stack of papers, folded in the middle and stapled along that fold. So when someone picks up your book to browse through it, it's likely to fall open to the center spot where the staples are. Because of this little chapbook phenomenon, that center spread is usually the third thing a reader will see, after the front cover and back cover, and the first poem he or she will read. So think of that center spot as prime real estate, and put a strong poem or two there that can be read without turning the page.

USE WHITE SPACE TO HELP YOUR READER

By its nature, poetry is a rich, dense reading experience. And as with a rich meal, it's wise to give your guest a little time to breathe between courses. Leaving some white space on the last page of a poem, or putting a blank left page before a new section (if you have sections) gives the reader a brief break to contemplate what he's just read and gear up for the next poem. One place where you should always have a blank page is on the left page before your first poem in the book.

That first poem should start on a right-hand page, and the blank page to its left serves as a little drumroll that lets the reader know the show's about to begin. And in the body of the book, it's fine to have the occasional poem spill over onto an extra page by five or six lines; again, the white space at the end of the poem gives the reader a mental resting spot.

PERFECT PUNCTUATION

Chapbooks, even ones from well-known publishers, seem to suffer more than their share of careless punctuation: double spaces, straight quote marks, two hyphens standing in for an em-dash, and other small glitches that a spell-check might not catch. Most typographers hate straight quotes and prefer curly ones, but there's nothing really wrong with straight quotes; just make sure you choose one or the other and don't mix them. As for em-dashes (—), you can get a true one on a PC by typing ctrl-alt-<minus sign on the number pad>; on a Mac, it's shift-option-hyphen. Set aside some time at the end of your design process to do some search-and-replaces and root out these inconsistences. This seemingly simple step will make a big difference to your reader.

EMBRACE ODD SIZES

Most chapbooks are 5½ x 8½ inches—not surprisingly, that's what you get when you take a stack of standard 8½ x 11 sheets and fold them in half. That's all very convenient, but with a $30 guillotine-style paper trimmer (or the fancy one at the office), you can experiment with all sorts of other sizes—tall, small, square—and come up with something unusual that will really pique your reader's interest. One popular size is a book that fits nicely in one hand—about 4 × 5 inches. And square books have an alluring power at the book table.

The challenge is getting your poems to fit into the format; poems with long lines will have a hard time squeezing into a narrow book, for instance. Sometimes fitting the trim size to the poems is part of the fun.

BEWARE THE HASTY BACK COVER

Back covers are where a lot of otherwise good chapbooks go bad. It's not unusual to see strong poems and a good interior design marred by a back cover that was obviously thrown together in a hurry. Some poets opt out and just leave the back cover blank.

That's OK, but a missed opportunity; the back cover is a big chunk of free advertising space, a chance to give your prospective reader a taste of what's inside—a snippet of a poem, a short bio, and maybe an author photo. But don't try to jam too much on there; crowded typography is a common malady in back covers, often because of our old nemesis, type size vs. leading (see tip #1).

And if you do include an author photo, make it a good one. Whether it's serious or friendly, just make sure your photo isn't off-putting—a stiff grammar-school-type picture, or a badly lit mug shot that looks like it was ripped out of somebody's passport. If you can't find a good photo of yourself, leave it out; it is better to have no author photo than a bad one.

BONUS TIP: Steal your back-cover design. A chapbook's back cover can look exactly like one on a full-length poetry collection, so grab a stack of poetry books from big publishers, study their back covers, and steal design elements that you like.

ENDPAPERS ADD ELEGANCE

Endpapers are the easiest way to add a hint of artistry to a chapbook. An endpaper is a single, blank sheet of paper inside the cover of your book—a page that's there purely for decoration. These are fun to pick out, and the possibilities are almost limitless: a translucent vellum, textured stationery paper, a delicate sheet embedded with flower petals, or something bold and contrasting.

But there's some room for error—nothing says "cheap" like wrinkle-prone colored paper that you bought at the dollar store, and overly ornate endpapers may make your book look more like a tchotchke than a serious book of poetry.

BONUS TIP: When shopping for endpapers, take a sheet of your interior paper and cover stock (or, better yet, a printed cover) to the store with you to make sure the colors don't clash.

TRIM OFF THE OUTER EDGE

Any time you take a stack of papers and fold it in the middle, the outer edge—the right edge of your book, if you're looking at your front cover—will have a "peak" to it where the edges of the inner pages get pushed out beyond those of the outer pages. This isn't the worst thing in the world, but trimming off that outer edge so that it's flat, smooth, and flush with the edge of the cover will give the book a more finished, professional feel. A $40 rotary trimmer with a wheel-shaped blade, like the kind scrapbookers use, can do the trick with a little practice.

If you have patience and a steady hand, you can trim off the edge with an X-Acto knife and a ruler. Another option is to take the books to a print shop and have them trim off the edges (for a few dollars) using one of their professional cutting machines.

BIND THE BOOK WITH STITCHING

This one's an especially good trick because it looks hard to do, but it's actually very easy. All it takes to add this classic touch of elegance is a needle, an awl to make a few holes, some heavy thread in a color that complements or contrasts with your cover design, and a simple stitching diagram that you can find online (google "chapbook stitching").

This little upgrade will get an "ooh" out of almost everyone who picks up your book, making it that much more memorable—which is the whole point of having a chapbook in the first place.

AMY MILLER is the author of eight chapbooks of poetry and prose, and her writing has appeared in *Northwest Review, ZYZZYVA, Many Mountains Moving, Fine Gardening, The Writer's Journal,* and many other publications. During her 35-year career in publishing, she has worked as a layout artist, editor, and project manager for several magazines and book publishers. She blogs about writing, disaster movies, and life at writers-island.blogspot.com.

MISTAKES POETS MAKE

//

In putting together listings for *Poet's Market*, we ask editors for any words of advice they want to share with our readers. Often the editors' responses include comments about what poets should and shouldn't do when submitting work—the same comments, over and over. That means a lot of poets are repeating similar mistakes when they send out their poems for consideration.

The following list includes the most common of those mistakes—the ones poets should work hardest to avoid.

NOT READING A PUBLICATION BEFORE SUBMITTING WORK

Researching a publication is essential before submitting your poetry. Try to buy a sample copy of a magazine (by mail, if necessary) or at least see if an issue is available at the library. It may not be economically feasible for poets to purchase a copy of every magazine they target, especially if they send out a lot of poems. However, there are additional ways to familiarize yourself with a publication.

Read the market listing thoroughly. If guidelines are available, send for them by e-mail or regular mail, or check for them online. A publication's website often presents valuable information, including sample poems, magazine covers—and guidelines.

SUBMITTING INAPPROPRIATE WORK

Make good use of your research so you're sure you understand what a magazine publishes. Don't rationalize that a journal favoring free verse might jump at the chance to consider your long epic poem in heroic couplets. Don't convince yourself your experimental style will be a good fit for the traditional journal filled with rhyming poetry. Don't go into denial about whether a certain journal and your poetry are made for each other. It's counterproductive and ultimately wastes postage (not to mention time—yours and the editor's).

SUBMITTING AN UNREASONABLE NUMBER OF POEMS

If an editor recommends sending three to five poems (a typical range), don't send six. Don't send a dozen poems and tell the editor to pick the five she wants to consider. If the editor doesn't specify a number (or the listing says "no limit"), don't take that as an invitation to mail off 20 poems. The editors and staff of literary magazines are busy enough as it is, and they may decide they don't have time to cope with you. (When submitting book or chapbook manuscripts to publishers, make sure your page count falls within the range they state.)

Don't go to the other extreme and send only one poem, unless an editor says it's okay (which is rare). One poem doesn't give an editor much of a perspective on your work, and it doesn't give you very good odds on getting the piece accepted.

IGNORING THE EDITOR'S PREFERENCES REGARDING FORMATS

If an editor makes a point of describing a preferred manuscript format, follow it, even if that format seems to contradict the standard. (Standard format includes using 8½ × 11 white paper and conventional typeface and point size; avoid special graphics, colors or type flourishes; put your name and address on every page.) Don't devise your own format to make your submission stand out. Keep everything clean, crisp and easy to read (and professional).

Be alert to e-mail submission formats. Follow directions regarding what the editor wants printed in the subject line, how many poems to include in a single e-mail, whether to use attachments or paste work in the body of the message, and other elements. Editors have good reasons for outlining their preferences; ignoring them could mean having your e-mail deleted before your poems are even read.

OMITTING A SELF-ADDRESSED STAMPED ENVELOPE (SASE)

Why do editors continuously say "include an SASE with your submission?" Because so many poets don't do it. Here's a simple rule: Unless the editor gives alternate instructions, include a #10 SASE, whether submitting poems or sending an inquiry.

WRITING BAD COVER LETTERS (OR OMITTING THEM COMPLETELY)

Cover letters have become an established part of the submission process. There are editors who remain indifferent about the necessity of a cover letter, but many consider it rude to be sent a submission without any other communication from the poet.

Unless the editor says otherwise, send a cover letter. Keep it short and direct, a polite introduction of you and your work. (See "Frequently Asked Questions" for more tips on cover letters, and an example.)

Here are a few important don'ts:

- **DON'T** list all the magazines where your work has appeared; limit yourself to five magazine titles. The work you're submitting has to stand on its own.
- **DON'T** tell the editor what a good poet you are—or how good someone else thinks you are.
- **DON'T** tell the editor how to edit, lay out or print your poem. Some of those decisions are up to the editor, assuming she decides to accept your poem in the first place.
- **DON'T** point out the poem is copyrighted in your name or include the copyright symbol. All poems are automatically copyrighted in the poet's name as soon as they're "fixed" (i.e., written down), and editors know this.

NOT MAINTAINING GOOD EDITOR/POET RELATIONS

Most editors are hard-working poetry lovers dedicated to finding and promoting good work. They aspire to turn submissions around as quickly as possible and to treat all poets with respect. They don't want to steal your work. Often they aren't paid for their labor and may even have to dip into their own pockets just to keep their magazines going.

Poets should finesse their communications with editors regarding problems, especially in initial letters and e-mail. Editors (and their magazines and presses) aren't service-oriented businesses, like the phone company. Getting huffy with an editor as if arguing with your cable provider about an overcharge is inappropriate. Attitude isn't going to get you anywhere; in fact, it could create additional obstacles.

That's not to say poets shouldn't feel exasperated when they're inconvenienced or ill-treated. None of us likes to see our creations vanish, or to pay good money for something we're never going to receive (like a subscription or sample copy). However, exasperated is one thing; outraged is another. Too often poets go on the offensive with editors and make matters worse. Experts on how to complain effectively recommend you keep your cool and stay professional, no matter what kind of problem you're trying to work out.

For additional advice on editor/poet relations, see "Dealing With Problem Editors."

DEALING WITH PROBLEM EDITORS

There *are* problem editors out there. Some rip people off, prey on poets' desires to be published, or treat poets and their work with flagrant disregard. Fortunately, such editors are in the minority.

Now and then you may discover the disorganized editor or the overwhelmed editor; these two cause heartache (and heartburn) by closing up shop without returning manuscripts or failing to honor paid requests for subscriptions and sample copies. More often than not, their transgressions are rooted in chaos and irresponsibility, not malicious intent. Frustrating as such editors are, they're not out to get you.

There are many instances, too, where larger circumstances are beyond an editor's control. For example, a college-oriented journal may be student-staffed, with editors changing each academic year. Funds for the journal may be cut unexpectedly by administration belt-tightening, or a grant could be cancelled. The editorial office may be moved to another part of the university. An exam schedule could impact a publishing schedule. All of these things cause problems and delays.

Then again, a literary journal may be a one-person, home-based operation. The editor may get sick or have an illness in the family. Her regular job may suddenly demand lots of overtime. There may be divorce or death with which the editor has to cope. A computer could crash. Or the editor may need to scramble for money before the magazine can go to the printer. Emergencies happen, and they take their toll on deadlines. The last thing the editor wants is to inconvenience poets and readers, but sometimes life gets in the way.

Usually, difficulties with these kinds of "problem" editors can be resolved satisfactorily through communication and patience. There are always exceptions, though. Here are a few typical situations with problem editors and how to handle them.

AN EDITOR IS RUDE.

If it's a matter of bad attitude, take it with a grain of salt. Maybe he's having a rotten

COMPLAINT PROCEDURE

If you feel you have not been treated fairly by a market listed in *Poet's Market*, we advise you to take the following steps:

- First, try to contact the market. Sometimes one phone call, letter, or e-mail can quickly clear up the matter. Document all your communications with the market.
- When you contact us with a complaint, provide the details of your submission, the date of your first contact with the market and the nature of your subsequent communication.
- We will file a record of your complaint and further investigate the market.
- The number and severity of complaints will be considered when deciding whether or not to delete a market from the next edition of *Poet's Market*.

day. If there's abusive language and excessive profanity involved, let us know about it. (See the complaint procedure .)

AN EDITOR HARSHLY CRITICIZES YOUR POEM.

If an editor takes time to comment on your poetry, even if the feedback seems overly critical, consider the suggestions with an open mind and try to find something valid and useful in them. If, after you've given the matter fair consideration, you think the editor was out of line, don't rush to defend your poetry or wave your bruised ego in the editor's face. Allow that the editor has a right to her opinion (which you're not obligated to take as the final word on the quality of your work), forget about it and move on.

AN EDITOR IS SLOW TO RESPOND TO A SUBMISSION.

As explained above, there may be many reasons why an editor's response takes longer than the time stated in the market listing or guidelines. Allow a few more weeks to pass

beyond the deadline, then write a polite inquiry to the editor about the status of your manuscript. (Include an SASE if sending by regular mail.) Understand an editor may not be able to read your letter right away if deadlines are pressing or if he's embroiled in a personal crisis. Try to be patient. If you haven't received a reply to your inquiry after a month or so, however, it's time for further action.

AN EDITOR WON'T RETURN YOUR MANUSCRIPT.

Decide whether you want to invest any more time in this journal or publisher. If you conclude you've been patient long enough, write a firm but professional letter to the editor withdrawing your manuscript from consideration. Request that the manuscript be returned; but know, too, a truly indifferent editor probably won't bother to send it back or reply in any way. Keep a copy of your withdrawal letter for your files, make a new copy of your manuscript and look for a better market.

Also, contact *Poet's Market* by letter or e-mail with details of your experience. We always look into problems with editors, although we don't withdraw a listing on the basis of a single complaint unless we discover evidence of consistent misbehavior. We do, however, keep complaints on file and watch for patterns of unacceptable behavior from any specific market.

AN EDITOR TAKES YOUR MONEY.

If you sent a check for a subscription or sample copy and you haven't received anything, review your bank statement to see if the check has been cashed. If it has, send the editor a query. Politely point out the editor has cashed your check, but you haven't yet received the material you were expecting. Give the editor the benefit of the doubt: An upcoming issue of a magazine could be running late, your subscription could have been overlooked by mistake, or your copy could have been lost in transit or sent in error to the wrong address.

If your check has *not* been cashed, query the editor to see if your order was ever received. It may have been lost (in the mail or on the editor's desk), the editor may be holding several checks to cash at one time, or the editor may be waiting to cash checks until a tardy issue is finally published.

If you get an unsatisfactory response from the editor (or no response at all), wait a few weeks and try again. If the matter still isn't resolved, let us know about it. We're especially interested in publishers who take money from poets but don't deliver the goods. Be sure to send us all the details of the transaction, plus copies of any correspondence (yours and the editor's). We can't pursue your situation in any legal way or act as mediator, but we can ban an unscrupulous publisher from *Poet's Market* and keep the information as a resource in case we get later complaints.

Should you continue trying to get your money back from such editors? That's your decision. If your loss is under $10 (say, for a subscription or sample copy), it might cost you less in the long run to let the matter go. And the fee for a "stop payment" order on a check can be hefty—possibly more than the amount you sent the editor in the first place. Yes, it's infuriating to be cheated, but sometimes fighting on principle costs more than it's worth.

If your monetary loss is significant (for instance, you shelled out a couple hundred dollars in a subsidy publishing agreement), consider contacting your state attorney general's office for advice about small claims court, filing a complaint and other actions you can take.

IS IT A 'CON'?

Think Before You Trust

What is a "con?" Con is short for "confidence," an adjective defined by *Webster's* as "of, relating to, or adept at swindling by false promise," as in "confidence man" or "confidence game." While the publishing world is full of legitimate opportunities for poets to gain honor and exposure for their work, there are also plenty of "cons." How can you tell the difference? The following are some of the most common situations that cost poets disappointment, frustration—and cash. Learn to spot them before submitting your work, and don't let your vanity be your guide.

ANTHOLOGIES

Has this happened to you? You see an ad in a perfectly respectable publication announcing a poetry contest with big cash prizes. You enter, and later you receive a glowing letter congratulating you on your exceptional poem, which the contest sponsor wants to include in his deluxe hardbound anthology of the best poetry submitted to the contest. The anthology costs only, say, $65. You don't have to buy it—they'll still publish your poem—but wouldn't you be proud to own one? And wouldn't it be nice to buy additional copies to give to family and friends? And for an extra charge you can include a biographical note. And so on.

Of course, when the anthology arrives, the quality of the poetry may not be what you were expecting, with several poems crammed unattractively onto a page. Apparently everyone who entered the contest was invited to be published; you basically paid cash to see your poem appear in a phone-book-like volume with no literary merit whatsoever.

Were you conned? Depends on how you look at it. If you bought into the flattery and believed you were being published in an exclusive, high-quality publication, no doubt you feel duped. On the other hand, if all you were after was seeing your poem in print, even knowing you'd have to pay for the privilege, then you got what you wanted. (Unless you've deceived yourself into believing you've truly won an honor and now have a worthy publishing credit; you don't.)

If you don't want to add insult to injury, resist additional spiels, like having your poem printed on coffee mugs and T-shirts (you can do this yourself through print shops or online services like www.cafepress.com) or spending large sums on awards banquets and conferences. And, before you submit a single line of poetry, find out what rights the contest sponsor acquires. You may be relinquishing all rights to your poem simply by mailing it in or submitting it through a website. If the poem no longer belongs to you, the publisher can do whatever he wishes with it. Don't let your vanity propel you into a situation you'll always regret.

READING AND CONTEST FEES

Suppose you notice a promising market for your poetry, but the editor requires a set fee just to consider your work. Or you see a contest that interests you, but you have to pay the sponsor a fee just to enter. Are you being conned?

In the case of reading fees, keep these points in mind: Is the market so exceptional that you feel it's worth risking the cost of the reading fee to have your work considered? What makes it so much better than markets that do not charge fees? Has the market been around awhile, with an established publishing schedule? What are you paid if your work is accepted? Are reasonably priced samples available so you can judge the production values and quality of the writing?

Reading fees don't necessarily signal a suspicious market. In fact, they're increasingly popular as editors struggle with the costs of publishing books and magazines, including the man-hours required to read loads of (often bad) submissions. However, fees represent an additional financial burden on poets, who often don't receive any monetary reward for their poems to begin with. It's really up to individual poets to decide whether paying a fee is beneficial to their publishing efforts. Think long and hard about fee-charging markets that are new and untried, don't pay poets for their work (at the very least a print publication should offer a contributor's copy), charge high prices for sample copies or set fees that seem unreasonable.

Entry fees for contests often fund prizes, judges' fees, honorariums and expenses of running and promoting the contest (including publishing a "prize" collection or issue of a magazine). Other kinds of contests charge entry fees, from Irish dancing competitions to bake-offs at a county fair. Why not poetry contests?

That's not to say you shouldn't be cautious. Watch out for contests that charge higher-than-average fees, especially if the fees are out of proportion to the amount of prize money being given. (Look through the Contests & Awards section to get a sense of what most competitions charge.) Find out how long the contest has been around, and verify whether prizes have been awarded each year and to whom. In the case of book and chapbook contests, send for one of the winning publications to confirm that the publisher puts out a quality product. Regard with skepticism any contest that tells you you've won something, then demands payment for an anthology, trophy or other item. (It's okay if a group offers an anthology for a modest price without providing winners with free copies. Most state poetry societies have to do this; but they also present cash awards

in each category of the contest, and their entry fees are low.)

SUBSIDY PUBLISHERS, PRINT-ON-DEMAND

Poetry books are a hard sell to the book-buying public. Few of the big publishers handle these books, and those that do feature the "name" poets (i.e., the major prize winners and contemporary masters with breathtaking reputations). Even the small presses publish only so many books per year—far less than the number of poets writing.

No wonder so many poets decide to pay to have their poetry collections published. While some may self-publish (i.e., take full control of their book, working directly with a printer), others turn to subsidy publishers (also called "vanity publishers") and print-on-demand (POD) publishers.

There are many differences between subsidy publishing and POD publishing, as well as similarities (having to pay to get published is a big one). Whether or not you get conned is entirely up to you. You have to take responsibility for asking questions, doing research on presses, and reading the fine print on the contract to make sure you know exactly what you're paying for. There are landmines in dealing with subsidy and POD publishers, and you have to investigate thoroughly and intelligently to avoid damage.

Some questions to keep in mind: Are fees inflated compared to the product and services you'll be receiving? Will you still own the rights to your book? Does the publisher put out a quality product that's attractive and cleanly printed? (Get a sample copy and find out.) How many copies of the book will you receive? How much will you have to pay for additional copies? How will your book be sold and distributed? (Don't count on seeing your volume in bookstores.)

Will you receive royalties? How much? Does the publisher offer any kind of promotional assistance or is it all up to you? Will those promotion efforts be realistic and results-oriented? (Sometimes "promotion" means sending out review copies, which is a waste—such volumes are rarely reviewed.) Don't wait until *after* you've signed a contract (and a check) to raise these issues. Do your homework first.

Obviously, poets who don't stay on their toes may find themselves preyed upon. And a questionable publishing opportunity doesn't have to be an out-and-out rip-off for you to feel cheated. In every situation, you have a choice *not* to participate. Exercise that choice, or at least develop a healthy sense of skepticism before you fling yourself and your poetry at the first smooth talker who compliments your work. Poets get burned because they're much too impatient to see their work in print. Calm your ego, slow down and devote that time, energy and money toward reading other poets and improving your own writing. You'll find that getting published will eventually take care of itself.

BLOGGING BASICS

Get the Most Out of Your Blog

....

by Robert Lee Brewer

In these days of publishing and media change, writers have to build platforms and learn how to connect to audiences if they want to improve their chances of publication and overall success. There are many methods of audience connection available to writers, but one of the most important is through blogging.

Since I've spent several years successfully blogging—both personally and professionally—I figure I've got a few nuggets of wisdom to pass on to writers who are curious about blogging or who already are.

Here's my quick list of tips:

1. **START BLOGGING TODAY.** If you don't have a blog, use Blogger, WordPress, or some other blogging software to start your blog today. It's free, and you can start off with your very personal "Here I am, world" post.

2. **START SMALL.** Blogs are essentially simple, but they can get complicated (for people who like complications). However, I advise bloggers start small and evolve over time.

3. **USE YOUR NAME IN YOUR URL.** This will make it easier for search engines to find you when your audience eventually starts seeking you out by name. For instance, my url is http://robertlee-brewer.blogspot.com. If you try Googling "Robert Lee Brewer," you'll notice that My Name Is Not Bob is one of the top five search results (behind my other blog: Poetic Asides).

4. **UNLESS YOU HAVE A REASON, USE YOUR NAME AS THE TITLE OF YOUR BLOG.** Again, this helps with search engine results. My Poetic Asides blog includes my name in the title, and it ranks higher than My Name Is Not Bob. However, I felt the play on my name was worth the trade off.

5. **FIGURE OUT YOUR BLOGGING GOALS.** You should return to this step every couple months, because it's natural for your blogging goals to evolve over time. Initially, your blogging goals may be to make a post a week about what you have written, submitted, etc. Over

time, you may incorporate guests posts, contests, tips, etc.

6. **BE YOURSELF.** I'm a big supporter of the idea that your image should match your identity. It gets too confusing trying to maintain a million personas. Know who you are and be that on your blog, whether that means you're sincere, funny, sarcastic, etc.

7. **POST AT LEAST ONCE A WEEK.** This is for starters. Eventually, you may find it better to post once a day or multiple times per day. But remember: Start small and evolve over time.

8. **POST RELEVANT CONTENT.** This means that you post things that your readers might actually care to know.

9. **USEFUL AND HELPFUL POSTS WILL AT-TRACT MORE VISITORS.** Talking about yourself is all fine and great. I do it myself. But if you share truly helpful advice, your readers will share it with others, and visitors will find you on search engines.

10. **TITLE YOUR POSTS IN A WAY THAT GETS YOU FOUND IN SEARCH ENGINES.** The more specific you can get the better. For instance, the title "Blogging Tips" will most likely get lost in search results. However, the title "Blogging Tips for Writers" specifies which audience I'm targeting and increases the chances of being found on the first page of search results.

11. **LINK TO POSTS IN OTHER MEDIA.** If you have an e-mail newsletter, link to your blog posts in your newsletter. If you have social media accounts, link to your blog posts there. If you have a

helpful post, link to it in relevant forums and on message boards.

12. **WRITE WELL, BUT BE CONCISE.** At the end of the day, you're writing blog posts, not literary manifestos. Don't spend a week writing each post. Try to keep it to an hour or two tops and then post. Make sure your spelling and grammar are good, but don't stress yourself out too much.

13. **FIND LIKE-MINDED BLOGGERS.** Comment on their blogs regularly and link to them from yours. Eventually, they may do the same. Keep in mind that blogging is a form of social media, so the more you communicate with your peers the more you'll get out of the process.

14. **RESPOND TO COMMENTS ON YOUR BLOG.** Even if it's just a simple "Thanks," respond to your readers if they comment on your blog. After all, you want your readers to be engaged with your blog, and you want them to know that you care they took time to comment.

15. **EXPERIMENT.** Start small, but don't get complacent. Every so often, try something new. For instance, the biggest draw to my Poetic Asides blog are the poetry prompts and challenges I issue to poets. Initially, that was an experiment—one that worked very well. I've tried other experiments that haven't panned out, and that's fine. It's all part of a process.

SEO TIPS FOR WRITERS

Most writers may already know what SEO is. If not, SEO stands for *search engine opti-*

mization. Basically, a site or blog that practices good SEO habits should improve its rankings in search engines, such as Google and Bing. Most huge corporations have realized the importance of SEO and spend enormous sums of time, energy and money on perfecting their SEO practices. However, writers can improve their SEO without going to those same extremes.

In this section, I will use the terms of *site pages* and *blog posts* interchangeably. In both cases, you should be practicing the same SEO strategies (when it makes sense).

Here are my top tips on ways to improve your SEO starting today:

1. **USE APPROPRIATE KEYWORDS.** Make sure that your page displays your main keyword(s) in the page title, content, URL, title tags, page header, image names and tags (if you're including images). All of this is easy to do, but if you feel overwhelmed, just remember to use your keyword(s) in your page title and content (especially in the first and last 50 words of your page).

2. **USE KEYWORDS NATURALLY.** Don't kill your content and make yourself look like a spammer to search engines by overloading your page with your keyword(s). You don't get SEO points for quantity but for quality. Plus, one of the main ways to improve your page rankings is when you...

3. **DELIVER QUALITY CONTENT.** The best way to improve your SEO is by providing content that readers want to share with others by linking to your pages. Some of the top results in search en-

gines can be years old, because the content is so good that people keep coming back. So, incorporate your keywords in a smart way, but make sure it works organically with your content.

4. **UPDATE CONTENT REGULARLY.** If your site looks dead to visitors, then it'll appear that way to search engines too. So update your content regularly. This should be very easy for writers who have blogs. For writers who have sites, incorporate your blog into your site. This will make it easier for visitors to find your blog to discover more about you on your site (through your site navigation tools).

5. **LINK BACK TO YOUR OWN CONTENT.** If I have a post on Blogging Tips for Writers, for instance, I'll link back to it if I have a Platform Building post, because the two complement each other. This also helps clicks on my blog, which helps SEO. The one caveat is that you don't go crazy with your linking and that you make sure your links are relevant. Otherwise, you'll kill your traffic, which is not good for your page rankings.

6. **LINK TO OTHERS YOU CONSIDER HELPFUL.** Back in 2000, I remember being ordered by my boss at the time (who didn't last too much longer afterward) to ignore any competitive or complementary websites—no matter how helpful their content—because they were our competitors. You can try basing your online strategy on these principles, but I'm nearly 100 percent confident you'll fail. It's helpful for oth-

er sites and your own to link to other great resources. I shine a light on others to help them out (if I find their content truly helpful) in the hopes that they'll do the same if ever they find my content truly helpful for their audience.

7. **GET SPECIFIC WITH YOUR HEADLINES.** If you interview someone on your blog, don't title your post with an interesting quotation. While that strategy may help get readers in the print world, it doesn't help with SEO at all. Instead, title your post as "Interview With (insert name here)." If you have a way to identify the person further, include that in the title too. For instance, when I interview poets on my Poetic Asides blog, I'll title those posts like this: Interview With Poet Erika Meitner. Erika's name is a keyword, but so are the terms *poet* and *interview*.

8. **USE IMAGES.** Many expert sources state that the use of images can improve SEO, because it shows search engines that the person creating the page is spending a little extra time and effort on the page than a common spammer. However, I'd caution anyone using images to make sure those images are somehow complementary to the content. Don't just throw up a lot of images that have no relevance to anything. At the same time...

9. **OPTIMIZE IMAGES THROUGH STRATEGIC LABELING.** Writers can do this by making sure the image file is labeled using your keyword(s) for the post. Using the Erika Meitner example above (which does include images), I would

label the file "Erika Meitner headshot.jpg"—or whatever the image file type happens to be. Writers can also improve image SEO through the use of captions and ALT tagging. Of course, at the same time, writers should always ask themselves if it's worth going through all that trouble for each image or not. Each writer has to answer that question for him (or her) self.

10. **USE YOUR SOCIAL MEDIA PLATFORM TO SPREAD THE WORD.** Whenever you do something new on your site or blog, you should share that information on your other social media sites, such as Twitter, Facebook, LinkedIn, online forums, etc. This lets your social media connections know that something new is on your site/blog. If it's relevant and/or valuable, they'll let others know. And that's a great way to build your SEO.

Programmers and marketers could get even more involved in the dynamics of SEO optimization, but I think these tips will help most writers out immediately and effectively while still allowing plenty of time and energy for the actual work of writing.

BLOG DESIGN TIPS FOR WRITERS

Design is an important element to any blog's success. But how can you improve your blog's design if you're not a designer? I'm just an editor with an English Lit degree and no formal training in design. However, I've worked in media for more than a decade now and can share some very fundamental and easy tricks to improve the design of your blog.

Here are my seven blog design tips for writers:

1. **USE LISTS.** Whether they're numbered or bullet points, use lists when possible. Lists break up the text and make it easy for readers to follow what you're blogging.

2. **BOLD MAIN POINTS IN LISTS.** Again, this helps break up the text while also highlighting the important points of your post.

3. **USE HEADINGS.** If your posts are longer than 300 words and you don't use lists, then please break up the text by using basic headings.

4. **USE A READABLE FONT.** Avoid using fonts that are too large or too small. Avoid using cursive or weird fonts. Times New Roman or Arial works, but if you want to get "creative," use something similar to those.

5. **LEFT ALIGN.** English-speaking readers are trained to read left to right. If you want to make your blog easier to read, avoid centering or right aligning your text (unless you're purposefully calling out the text).

6. **USE SMALL PARAGRAPHS.** A good rule of thumb is to try and avoid paragraphs that drone on longer than five sentences. I usually try to keep paragraphs to around three sentences myself.

7. **ADD RELEVANT IMAGES.** Personally, I shy away from using too many images. My reason is that I only like to use them if they're relevant. However, images are very powerful on blogs, so please use them—just make sure they're relevant to your blog post.

If you're already doing everything on my list, keep it up! If you're not, then you might want to re-think your design strategy on your blog. Simply adding a header here and a list there can easily improve the design of a blog post.

GUEST POSTING TIPS FOR WRITERS

Recently, I've broken into guest posting as both a guest poster and as a host of guest posts (over at my Poetic Asides blog). So far, I'm pretty pleased with both sides of the guest posting process. As a writer, it gives me access to an engaged audience I may not usually reach. As a blogger, it provides me with fresh and valuable content I don't have to create. Guest blogging is a rare win-win scenario.

That said, writers could benefit from a few tips on the process of guest posting:

1. **PITCH GUEST POSTS LIKE ONE WOULD PITCH ARTICLES TO A MAGAZINE.** Include what your hook is for the post, what you plan to cover, and a little about who you are. Remember: Your post should somehow benefit the audience of the blog you'd like to guest post.

2. **OFFER PROMOTIONAL COPY OF YOUR BOOK (OR OTHER GIVEAWAYS) AS PART OF YOUR GUEST POST.** Having a random giveaway for people who comment on a blog post can help spur conversation and interest in your guest post,

which is a great way to get the most mileage out of your guest appearance.

3. **CATER POSTS TO AUDIENCE.** As the editor of *Writer's Market* and *Poet's Market*, I have great range in the topics I can cover. However, if I'm writing a guest post for a fiction blog, I'll write about things of interest to a novelist—not a poet.

4. **MAKE IT PERSONAL, BUT PROVIDE NUGGET.** Guest posts are a great opportunity for you to really show your stuff to a new audience. You could write a very helpful and impersonal post, but that won't connect with readers the same way as if you write a very helpful and personal post that makes them want to learn more about you (and your blog, your book, your Twitter account, etc.). Speaking of which...

5. **SHARE LINKS TO YOUR WEBSITE, BLOG, SOCIAL NETWORKS, ETC.** After all, you need to make it easy for readers who enjoyed your guest post to learn more about you and your projects. Start the conversation in your guest post and keep it going on your own sites, profiles, etc. And related to that...

6. **PROMOTE YOUR GUEST POST THROUGH YOUR NORMAL CHANNELS ONCE THE POST GOES LIVE.** Your normal audience will want to know where you've been and what you've been doing. Plus, guest posts lend a little extra "street cred" to your projects. But don't stop there...

7. **CHECK FOR COMMENTS ON YOUR GUEST POST AND RESPOND IN A TIMELY MANNER.** Sometimes the comments are the most interesting part of a guest post (no offense). This is where readers can ask more in-depth or related questions, and it's also where you can show your expertise on the subject by being as helpful as possible. And guiding all seven of these tips is this one:

8. **PUT SOME EFFORT INTO YOUR GUEST POST.** Part of the benefit to guest posting is the opportunity to connect with a new audience. Make sure you bring your A-game, because you need to make a good impression if you want this exposure to actually help grow your audience. Don't stress yourself out, but put a little thought into what you submit.

ONE ADDITIONAL TIP: Have fun with it. Passion is what really drives the popularity of blogs. Share your passion and enthusiasm, and readers are sure to be impressed.

....

ROBERT LEE BREWER is an editor with the Writer's Digest Writing Community and author of *Solving the World's Problems* (Press 53). Follow him on Twitter @robertleebrewer.

....

6 WAYS TO PROMOTE YOUR NEW BOOK

(Without Alienating Your Friends)

by Jeannine Hall Gailey

When your new book arrives, you naturally want to shout the news from the rooftops, run and put a copy in everyone's hand, proudly take a selfie with your box of books and put it on Facebook. But what else can you do to promote your book that won't leave your online reputation in shambles?

In an ideal world, all you'd have to do is write the book, and everyone else—your publisher, your readers, your friends and family—would get word out about your book for you. Sadly, no matter who your publisher is you will be your book's best publicist. You can keep a social media presence with Tumblr, Twitter, Facebook, a blog, etc. But you know those annoying spammy tweets from authors clogging up your feeds with yet another glowing blurb or Amazon rank? You don't want to be that person.

My personal two "golden rules" of promotion—one of which looks a lot like the actual golden rule—are:

1. Do unto others as you would have them do unto you. Whether it's reviews, retweets, or just kind mentions on blogs, remember that you don't live in a vacuum, and you can hardly expect others to enthusiastically support your book if you haven't done much for your peer's books. Show up to your friends' book parties and debut readings, and you'll have a higher likelihood of a full house at your own.

2. Don't do anything online you wouldn't do in real life. If you wouldn't knock on your best friend's doorstep and tell them three days in a row to buy your book, don't do it in e-mail or Facebook messages, either.

Now, here are six ways to create positive buzz about your new title in a seemingly endless sea of new titles, and do it without alienating people. These tips will make the whole process as simple and painless for everyone as possible.

START CLOSE TO HOME

Because you have been working as a positive force for poetry in your immediate community the last few years (right??) you should have some friends and well-wishers who will be happy to help "boost your signal." The greater your involvement in building up your local poetry community and the more people you positively impact, the better.

For instance, I frequently write poetry book reviews for different outlets and write blurbs for writers I like, because I see it as "giving back" to the literary community. I also do it because someone once said to me when I was a young poet: "How can you hope for others to read and review your book if you don't read and review other people's books?" But reviewing isn't the only way to give back. You can run a reading series, edit a literary magazine, or even start your own press. Now that you have a book out, you'll realize that seemingly small gestures such as "liking" a post on Facebook, retweeting a book announcement, or reviewing a great book on Amazon or Goodreads, count more than you thought.

Also remember that it's much easier to sell your book of poetry in your hometown, at a reading full of friends and family, than it will be to sell it to strangers and students you've never met before. Remember, they're already cheering you on.

Similarly, you can reach out to people who have been kind to you in the past—reviewers who liked your previous work, mentors who have offered you help, your writing group—although this can only work if you're keeping either a list of people (with contact information, be it an e-mail address or a physical address) who might be interested in more of your work in the future.

So keep up a list that I call it my "literary Christmas card list," and I actually use it to send Christmas cards, not just literary announcements. Again, being genuine friends with a lot of people will only help you in your efforts, so it pays to be generous. Karma, etc.

HELP PROMOTE OTHERS

This ties in with the previous tip. It makes sense that if you are kind and generous to others, helping spread the word about their good news, they are more likely to be kind and generous when you need help. When you think about sharing news about your book, think about the ways that news can help others—your publishers, editors, and others who have supported you along the way.

Award-winning poet Aimee Nezhukumatathil, a Professor of English at SUNY-Fredonia says: "I'm a big fan of using social media to post someone's poem that catches my breath, with a link to his/her recent book, or even better, to share my 'discovery' of an up-and-coming writer. On Twitter, even reading a line or two is enough to prick my curiosity. I've looked up poets and bought books from other people's postings. As for my own work, I share the occasional notice about where a recent poem or essay was published to help spread the word about the editors and magazines who believed in my work in the first place."

Being involved in helping other people succeed is a great way to build your literary community, so give others a boost when you can.

BOOK ANNOUNCEMENTS

A well-written, non-spammy (and spell-checked!) e-mail announcement to send to your friends, family, and colleagues is an easy thing a new author can do to let people know their book is available. Be friendly, respectful, and direct, and be sure to include, perhaps at the end, a direct link to buy your new book. If you want to include a few people who might have sent you kind notes in the past, or indicated interest in hearing about your new work, don't feel bad—do it. Remember that this can be a great way to get back in touch with old friends; I often have childhood friends, teachers, or students who write back after years of being out of contact. But please don't buy one of those prefabricated mailing list or send your news to every business acquaintance.

Marie Gauthier, Director of Sales & Marketing for Tupelo Press, reminds us to "remember to treat friends as allies, not customers. They want to help you spread the word; it's your job to make it as easy for them to help as you can, sending them the cover image of your book or a jpeg of a beautiful publicity release, items with visual appeal that are simple to share." She also advises writers to "include something personal or quirky or extra in your email that can help elevate it in the receiver's mind from 'spam.'"

Jericho Brown, award-winning poet, professor, and editor, has a few pieces of practical advice, warning writers to think hard about when and how they announce their book. "It makes sense to pay attention to the world in which we live and to be a real part of it. Don't post that you've won a big award or send an email about your book the same day Zimmerman is declared not guilty. If you do send an email to a group, make sure it's just once a year and that you include a link to the message or site you're promoting. Finally, if you want 4,000 people to know your good news at once, know also that you want to thank 4,000 people individually for congratulating you."

Be unique, be yourself, and be socially aware of timing when you send out your announcement.

SOCIAL MEDIA

Yes, it's probably a good idea to have a presence on social media—an author page on Facebook that allows people the option of learning news about your work, for instance, or a good basic website, and maybe a Twitter, Instagram, Pinterest, or Tumblr account. The good news about this kind of promotion is that you can do it in your pajamas! The bad news is that it's easy to overdo it and become unintentionally obnoxious. The other downside? Most people aren't constantly reading their Twitter or Facebook feeds, or checking your blog, so it's hard to know when those messages are being missed by a particular audience.

So, be smart about the way you promote your new book on social media.

Catherine Trestini, Digital Marketing and Social Media Strategist, suggests: "One author kept sending me messages on LinkedIn about his book IN ALL CAPS for weeks. It became so irritating that I eventually removed him from my network. So my first rule of thumb is to leave your spam at the front door. Readers need a reason to want your book. Make a good impression. But let him set the example of what not to do on social media. Similarly, remember to post different and new things about your book. Every day, we're zombie-scrolling through our Facebook feeds, subconsciously looking for great things to 'like' or comment on. Use your wit, empathy, and brainy attitude to engage me. My second piece of advice is: do something awesome that speaks about who 'you' are on your Facebook page, and do it often (at least once a day). It will collect "likes" and comments and woo your readers. Only write what you would want to read, including talking about your book online."

Make your posts authentic, and only talk about your own book part of the time—again, be sure to post other people's news, interesting relevant articles (whether that's on Buffy the Vampire Slayer's impact on pop culture or the latest news on Fukushima) and try to give your followers more than just advertising.

POSTCARDS, BOOKMARKS, AND OTHER "SWAG"

I know it's a new media world, but don't discount the power and pleasure of real mail and the physical object. In my own experience, sending out postcards is one of the best ways to give people a tactile reminder that your book is out—as well as show off a brilliant cover design. You should include a direct link to purchase the book on the postcard somewhere, as well as a way to contact you to get a signed copy, so it will be as easy as possible for them to purchase it. And a personal note on the postcard never hurts.

I've seen fascinating "swag" at readings, from intricate mini-books the size of a business card to elaborate bookmarks, magnets and stickers. The idea is to leave an audience member at a reading or conference-goer a physical memento that will perhaps lead them later to think about your book and purchase it.

READINGS

With a new book coming out, of course you're planning a few readings, maybe around your own town, maybe a more ambitious tour across several states. This one you cannot do in your pajamas, but there are a lot of ways you can make readings more fun for your audience and give your friends a real reason to come out and cheer you on.

Don't just plan a reading—plan a book release party, where you can celebrate and spend time with your friends and family afterward. If your friends are so inclined, they could even host a poetry salon, an informal gathering with cocktails or snacks where you might read a few poems, offer to sell and sign books, but mostly, give writers an excuse to socialize with you and with each other.

For example, when you go to a reading out of town, make sure you're paired up with a popular local writer as well, and try to do something fun to connect—set up a workshop beforehand, or an informal reception afterwards.

Kelly Davio, former editor of *LA Review* and author of *Burn This House*, gives this advice from her recent first book tour: "Anytime I give a reading, I make sure to stay and listen attentively to every other poet, whether that's another featured reader or someone who has just come for the open mic. Listening to others is an important way that we poets can show respect for our readership; if we're asking others to listen to our poems or buy our books, we need to give our attention to their work as well."

In the end, you really want to be able to share your excitement about your book without being pushy or disrespectful, and a lot of that comes down to being genuine and self-aware.

JEANNINE HALL GAILEY recently served as the second Poet Laureate of Redmond, Washington and is the author of three books of poetry, *Becoming the Villainess, She Returns to the Floating World,* and *Unexplained Fevers.* Her website is www.webbish6.com and you can follow her on Twitter @webbish6.

POETRY ON STAGE

Practical Advice for Live Performance

....

by Daniel Ari

Butterflies. Cottonmouth. Sweaty palms and the sound of your own heart beating. Knowing that these are natural reactions to entering the spotlight—even for seasoned speakers—might make them only slightly easier to endure. But preparation and practice can boost your confidence, so you can enjoy the rewards that come with performing your poetry for an audience.

FACING THE FEAR

If you're not someone who intrinsically loves being on stage, you may decide never to go there. But there are benefits of public reading that can make it worthwhile to work through stage fright.

YOUR POETRY IMPROVES. Going through the process of presenting can help clarify your poetic voice and give you the perspective to catch words or phrases that make you stumble or that cloud your meaning. You might also receive constructive input from friends and supportive audience members.

YOUR AUDIENCE GROWS. Getting on stage can help you build your following. People who like what you do will want to read what you've written and become advocates of your work. Having a venue gives you the opportunity to sell books, plug your blog, add to your mailing list, and so on.

YOUR SPEAKING ABILITY IMPROVES. Becoming a more confident speaker can benefit other areas of your life. If you regularly address groups or run meetings, then café poetry readings are a good place to practice in a situation with lower stakes.

IT CAN BE EXCITING. Connecting with an audience can be truly exhilarating, and the chance to feel proud of your work can be the biggest reward.

AUDIENCES WANT TO HEAR YOU. Audiences at readings have made the decision to be there, and they are ready to receive you. Rise to the occasion with good material that's well prepared, and enjoy their appreciation.

PREPARE TO PERFORM

Attend enough readings, and you're likely to encounter a few brilliant writers—who have no sense of delivery. As you listen, you might notice their richness of language and deft handling of thematic subtleties. But their monotone voice and apparent lack of sensitivity to the audience will have you involuntarily glancing toward the exit.

Though any poet can simply walk up to a microphone and start reading, it's better to think of your reading as a theatrical performance and to devote time and attention to the project. A reading that satisfies both you and your audience takes preparation.

CHOOSE POEMS THAT WORK WELL IN YOUR VOICE. Gather more than enough poetry, too much for the stage time you will be given. Read each piece you are considering out loud a few times, and narrow down your selection to those poems that you can recite most fluidly and sincerely.

PREPARE FOR PRACTICE. Double-check the pronunciation of any difficult or unusual words. Listen carefully to what you are saying in the poem and think how you might emphasize and intone the words appropriately. Would the poem benefit from a brief introduction? If so, consider scripting and practicing that part as well so you can keep it to the point.

THINK LIKE A DIRECTOR. As you start to practice, consider how you want the poem to sound. Formal or conversational? Energetically quick or suspensefully slow? How loud do you want to speak? Will your tone, tempo or volume change? Consider your options, and look for what most naturally supports the poem in your voice.

TAKE NOTES. Many performers mark up practice copies of their poems to remind themselves how they want the reading to sound. You can highlight words you want to emphasize and make notes about when to speed up or slow down. Some poets I know who have studied music use musical notations to indicate crescendos, accents, pauses and so on.

MEMORIZE. The subject of an entire article in its own right, memorization doesn't come naturally to everyone; however, getting off paper can make a huge difference in performance. When you speak from memory, your hands are free to gesture more naturally. Your eyes can engage the audience, and the audience will clearly sense your commitment to the poem when you have committed it to memory.

Here are two techniques I use to memorize poems: 1) Recite the first two lines of your poem until you can speak them from memory; then add lines three and four. Keep adding lines as you reciting the whole poem from the beginning, until you've assimilate the whole piece. 2) Record the poem and play it for yourself. Speak along with the recording of your voice. Repeat until you can recite along with yourself without pausing or mistakes.

These techniques can take hours or extend over days. Both are possible to do while you're doing something else like washing dishes, commuting to work, gardening, etc.

Once you have your poems in your memory, be sure to keep them there. Practice at least once a day until your reading date and a couple times a month afterward so the poems stay ready for the next time.

SLOW DOWN AND RELAX. When you're on stage, your tendency will be to speak more quickly than when you rehearse. This will be less of an issue if, when you rehearse, you consciously slow yourself down. Doing so will help offset your natural acceleration in the spotlight.

PRACTICE MORE. It's nearly impossible to over-rehearse. Instead, you're likely to discover new meanings and interpretations in your poems the more your practice them.

VIDEOTAPE YOURSELF. As you critique your performance, seeing yourself as an audience will see you can give you useful insights. Some readers pace as they read; others repeat a gesture or stand unnaturally still. With video, you'll see any unconscious habits you have—and then you can let go of them or consciously change them. Remember to be gentle with yourself. As you watch, focus on what you can improve, but also focus on how cool you are for preparing a performance. Make a point of feeling proud of yourself.

DO A PRE-SHOW. Gather a couple of close friends, a spouse, a supportive sibling or neighbor and recite for them. This is like easing into a hot tub. Reciting for a couple of friendly faces is your warm up to getting on stage in front of strangers. If you'd like feedback from your pre-show audience, ask them direct and specific questions such as:

- Was my voice loud enough?
- Did you understand each word?
- Did you understand and enjoy the poem?

FIND YOUR VENUE

An Internet search for "Poetry Readings" in your area will turn up cafes, bookstores, clubs, bars, theaters, galleries, speakeasies, or other venues. Contact them online or by phone to find out what's going on and how you can participate.

It's a good idea to visit the venue to watch and check out the scene before you go to read, especially if you're new to public reading. By watching other performers and talking to event hosts, you can find out how much time performers get and any other parameters you need to know. You'll also get a sense of what the audience appreciates.

Poetry Slams, for example, usually keep readers to a strict limit of three minutes of high-energy recitation—from memory—before penalties apply in the form of docked points from the volunteer judges. Yes, judges. Delivering a poem significantly different from the usual style at a poetry slam increases the chance of audience heckling, which is not meant to be hurtful, but is a traditional part of some poetry slams. Café open mics, on the other hand, are typically laid back with looser time limits in a wider range of styles. The main thing is to know in advance what you can expect from the venue and its audience.

Many organizers of ongoing events select featured readers whom they've come to know. If you want to be a featured reader at a regular event, a good way to get there is to keep showing up. Introduce yourself to the organizers, and when it seems right, let your interest be known. They'll let you know how you can earn a featured slot.

If performing for strangers worries you, consider arranging your own reading at a private residence. You can decide who to invite, how to decorate, when to start and end, what to charge, what food or beverages to serve, who else will perform, and so on. Though it takes more effort and leadership on your part, setting up your own reading lets you create exactly the event you want.

When you know where and when you're performing, spread the word. If it's your first time and you could use some moral support, invite close friends to be there or to go with you. If you're a seasoned performer doing a featured reading or a one-person show, be sure to advertise. Use Facebook and Evite to get on your desired audiences' calendars. You can also send a quick press release to your local arts weekly, radio station and online calendar sites.

Note that people respond more consistently to personal phone calls, e-mails or texts. If there are people you really want to be there, take the extra time to contact them directly.

BEFORE YOU PERFORM

The poems you choose to recite should be ones that move you and that you're enthusiastic to share. As you practice, you claim the words; they enter your mind and soul. So when it comes time to read, trust the words. Draw confidence from the excellence of the poetry and the time you've put into your performance. On the day or evening of your performance, these steps can support your sense of confidence and help your reading go just right:

DRESS FOR THE VENUE. Attractive, clean and hip are always appropriate. You can do something flashy, but don't let your clothes distract from your words. Dress like Lady Gaga, and your clothing will overshadow your poetry.

EAT LIGHT. If you're feeling nervous, don't eat for a couple of hours before your performance, but stay hydrated.

SET UP YOUR CAMERA. If you're recording or having someone record you, be sure to get connected early and test your equipment before the show starts.

WARM UP. Try to find some time backstage or outside to warm up your voice. It will help you relax and improve your projection, pacing, breathing and enunciation. Here are some easy warm ups:

1. Yawn or sigh deeply a couple of times. Make the natural yawning sounds to relax your throat and vocal chords.
2. Recite a few tongue twisters. Red leather, yellow leather. She sells sea shells by the sea shore. You know New York; you need New York; you know you need unique New York.
3. Recite one or two lines of your poem while grotesquely over-enunciat-

ing each word. This will loosen your tongue, lips, jaw and nasal passages.

4. Blow air through your lips with and without engaging your vocal chords.

5. With your fingertips, massage your jaw, lips, cheeks and chin.

6. Make exaggerated chewing motions as though you are chomping twenty pieces of gum at once. Make the sounds that would go with the motions.

7. Finish by taking three slow, deep breaths. This is especially good to do before you go on stage. If an emcee introduces you, take that time to breathe consciously, deeply and slowly. And then...

You're on!

DO IT.

Once you're on, you're on. Go with the words of the poem and the performance you prepared. When you practice, it will help to develop these good habits so they come naturally when you're on stage:

- Stand up straight so your lungs and throat are fully open.
- Put your breath behind your voice and project your words to the far end of the room.
- Speak slowly and let the words take their resonance in sound and meaning.
- Let yourself pause between stanzas or thoughts.

Your voice when performing shouldn't sound exactly like your everyday conversational voice, even if you're reciting in a conversational tone. Your words will be somewhat slower, more distinct, more fully enunciated. It may sound funny to you until you're used to it, but an audience depends on the enhanced clarity and resonance to get the full effect of what you're saying.

When you're on stage, strive to make eye contact with the audience. I find it helps to imagine that everyone there is an old friend of mine, even the person dourly glaring up at me from the fourth row.

If there's a microphone, simply project into it with your mouth positioned about a foot away. Many novice performers get distracted trying to adjust the mic stand or cord. The less of that you can do the better—you don't even have to touch the microphone. And if there are any issues with the microphone or sound system, politely ask if you can get some help before you start your recitation.

If you lose your place in the poem or stumble over a word, simply take a breath and start the line or stanza again. It's okay for you to take a moment in quiet to find your place and to look at the audience. You'll see that they are ready for you to continue, and they want you to succeed. Remember: you own the poem. Trust the words and let them come through you.

At the end of your reading, I suggest doing what feels right to you in terms of acknowledging your applause and thanking your emcee or host; but usually a bow of the head is polite and sufficient.

When I get off stage, I try to take a few deep, calming breaths before I talk to anyone. It's good to let your endorphins settle before you start meeting and greeting. But do let yourself receive kudos from your audience.

If you want feedback on your performance, watch the video if you have one and look for ways to inflect words differently or improve your delivery. Don't be overly critical. Focus only on your words and your delivery. Consider asking friends and other performers you trust for honest and constructive input. It's also good to watch other poets perform so you can see what styles and behaviors you want to model and make your own.

For the long term, keep doing it. Keep building your confidence, your repertoire, and your audience. Be sure to practice a few times a month to keep poems ready for opportunities to share. You might find your recitations welcome in your place of worship, among wedding toasts, or at informal social gatherings. When the moment's right, you'll be ready to make the gentle offer, "Would you like to hear a poem?"

DANIEL ARI's forthcoming book, *One Way to Ask*, pairs poems in an original form called queron with imagery by more than 60 artists. Besides being a professional copywriter, he writes and publishes poetry and organizes poetry performances and events throughout the Pacific Northwest. He blogs at fightswithpoems.blogspot.com. This is his third appearance in *Poet's Market*.

HOW TO TAKE POETRY TO NEW AUDIENCES

by Susan Hoskins Miller

When we write poetry, we reach deep inside ourselves so our work is as authentic as we can make it. At some point, we finally feel comfortable sharing it with others, so we go to poetry readings at coffee houses and read our work. Eventually, we submit it to literary journals and get published in as many as we can. The audiences we reach are safe. They are people who will always read and listen to poetry no matter what.

But, wouldn't it be great if our poetry could be heard or read by people who might not have the opportunity to experience poetry? And what about people who might like poetry if they were exposed to it, but probably don't even know they would like it? Wouldn't it be fun to open their minds by surprising them with an unexpected gift of poetry?

PROMISE OF PARTNERSHIPS

The key to reaching these normally out-of-reach audiences is through partnerships. Brick Street Poetry in Indianapolis forges some unlikely liaisons to bring poetry to groups of people who might otherwise not be motivated to take the time to hear or read poetry.

Poetry and quilting

One such group of people attends quilt shows. These shows for colorful works of textile art are attended by not only quilters, but others who enjoy sewing, by those who appreciate the history and tradition behind the art of quilting, and by those who simply enjoy the visual experience of seeing the quilts. Every year, a group of Indiana quilters partners with Brick Street poets to create something bigger and better than either group could host on its own.

Months prior to the event, poets are paired with individual quilters to inspire each other's work. At the exhibition, called Poetry in Free Motion, each quilt is showcased one-by-one while a poet reads the literary art it inspired. The addition of literary art to the quilt show gives it a depth that other quilt exhibits don't have and can't compete with. The event gets bigger every year.

Poetry and farming

Brick Street's Word Hunger project took poetry to Indiana's farmers with help from the Indiana Humanities Council. This long-term project, which is still ongoing, begins with a town hall-type meeting in each of the participating rural counties. The county's residents talk about how agriculture impacts their lives. A poet assigned to interpret the conversation writes a poem that is then painted on a farmer's barn in that county by a local artist.

Eventually, the project will create a statewide poetry trail through Indiana's countryside, giving all the state's residents and visitors a visual literary record of what farming means to the people who live there. Indianapolis' PBS station taped a documentary about the project, featuring a poetry reading at each of the barns. The program has aired several times.

Poetry and preserving

Indiana's Landmarks preservation organization worked with Brick Street Poetry to raise awareness about some of the state's most endangered historic sites and buildings. This partnership, called Landmark Lyrics, got the word out about endangered sites to more people while the state's historic preservationists saw the landmarks with new eyes through the poetic interpretations they inspired.

This partnership culminated in an evening event that drew history, preservation and literary enthusiasts to a beautifully-restored historic landmark in downtown Indianapolis. Poets who had been paired with a historic landmark read their poems while slides of the landmark that inspired them were displayed on a large screen.

Poetry and the arts

Brick Street has partnered several times with visual arts groups because the two art forms naturally complement each other. If funding is needed for such projects, it can sometimes be found through local arts or humanities councils, state arts commissions and community foundations.

Art in the Park was a partnership between Brick Street and local sculptors, who were found through the arts council in the Indianapolis suburb of Zionsville. Each of the outdoor sculptures they created, ranging from the traditional to the funky, inspired two works of poetry. The park served as the gallery for the outdoor exhibition and public poetry reading that showcased the work of both the artists and poets in a new way.

People who came to see visual art along with people strolling through the park got an unexpected dose of poetry that evening. They heard the interpretations of two different poets inspired by the same piece of art.

In another partnership with local artists, Brick Street poets worked with art galleries on a Friday night gallery walk. The galleries opened their doors for open house visits from the public while a Brick Street poet read a work of ekphrastic poetry inspired by a pre-selected work of art. Visitors looked at visual art while experiencing literary art, too.

Christmas at the Creek was a partnership with an art gallery north of Indianapolis on a country creek that hosts a large exhibition every Christmas season. A few weeks before the show, Brick Street posted photos of paintings on its Facebook page that would be in the gallery's Christmas exhibition. Poets selected the piece of art to write about and submitted their work to Brick Street judges ahead on the show. On the night of the Christmas show's opening, the artists, art lovers and supporters of the gallery were also treated to poetry about the art they were seeing.

Every year during National Poetry Month in April, Brick Street Poetry partners with the Arts Council of Indianapolis to bring poetry to the public. The Arts Council owns and operates a gorgeous, glass-enclosed structure—the Indianapolis Artsgarden—in the heart of downtown Indianapolis. The Artsgarden is attached to the city's Circle Centre Mall, which makes it the favorite spot of shoppers and employees of the mall and downtown businesses to take a break with a cup of coffee or lunch. Brick Street poets conduct public poetry readings throughout the month so those who wander into the Artsgarden receive an unexpected gift of literary art during their break.

Brick Street Poetry has gone beyond arts groups to take its poetry even further into its community.

Poetry and cuisine
Brick Street conducted a poetry contest in a partnership with local restaurants called Poetic Palate. Poets were assigned to eat at restaurants that agreed to participate. Poets paid for their own meals and wrote about their experience.

Poets are at their best writing about sensual experiences like eating. A poet-

ry professor from Indiana University was brought in to judge the contest. All the poems were read at an evening dinner, sponsored by one of the restaurants. Each participating restaurant received its poem in a frame that is still hanging in a prominent spot on the restaurant's wall.

Poetry and history
To commemorate the speech President Abraham Lincoln made while on his way to his presidential inauguration in 1861, Brick Street Poetry partnered with the Zionsville Parks Department to host an event at the spot where he stopped. Today that former train depot is Lincoln Park, which is surrounded by a split rail fence and has a plaque marking the spot where President-elect Lincoln spoke.

Poems were solicited months in advance to honor Lincoln, and were judged prior to the event, which was held on the 150th anniversary of his visit. A costumed Lincoln re-enactor was hired to speak to the attending crowd while a high school band played Hail to the Chief. The top five poems were read by the poets who wrote them. To inject a little humor, the winning poet received $150 (in honor of 150 years) all in $5 bills because they have Lincoln's picture on them. This event drew people from the whole community who were interested in the historic commemoration.

Brick Street partnered with Indianapolis's most famous cemetery—Crown Hill Cemetery—for a Dead Poets celebration. U.S. President Benjamin Harrison is buried at Crown Hill and so is Chicago gangster, John Dillinger. There are also some accomplished

Indiana poets buried there, including James Whitcomb Riley, Etheridge Knight, Ruth Lilly, Meredith Nicholson and Sarah T. Bolton. Brick Street volunteers dressed themselves in period costume to portray how each of the dead poets would have dressed during their lifetimes. They entertained those who gathered in the cemetery's chapel by reading the dead poets' works.

Poetry and the community

Brick Street is currently working with two Indianapolis children's hospitals to perform kids' poetry to their young hospitalized patients. This project includes partnerships with local university and high school theater departments so that costumed theater students accompany the poets to interact with the sick children.

This brings poetry to kids who might otherwise not experience it and, it is hoped, opens their minds to poetry's gifts, but also helps uplift their spirits during their hospital stay. It also exposes hospital staff and some parents to the art, as well.

The Eiteljorg Museum of American Indians and Western Art is partnering with Brick Street to bring a black Native American poet from Los Angeles to Indianapolis for a special program called "Who's Afraid of Black Indians?"

Poetry and recreation

Sports enthusiasts have also been exposed to poetry through Brick Street's partnership with a sports museum that hosted a poetry night with poems that focused on sports.

One of Brick Street's board members worked with the Indianapolis Zoo when it opened its new orangutan exhibition. Poet Joyce Brinkman spent several days with the orangutans to get to know their personalities and then wrote poems inspired by each one. The project, called Poetry and Primates, culminated in a public poetry reading and slide show of the orangutans.

THINK OUTSIDE THE BOOKSTORE

Look around your region with an open mind to gather ideas and inspiration for partnerships that would enrich your community by adding poetry to what is already there. Figure out ways that a partnership could benefit both your organization and your partner's so both of you gain by raising awareness of the work you do.

While it's always a good idea to continue to work to bring more people to your poetry readings, you can reach even more people by taking your poetry on the road to new audiences.

SUSAN HOSKINS MILLER has a 20-year background as a journalist for newspapers, magazines and, more recently, websites. Her work has been published in the *Huffington Post*, *USA Today*, the *Chicago Sun Times*, the *South Bend Tribune*, *Rotarian* magazine, *Indianapolis Star* and other publications. She is a co-founder and board member of Brick Street Poetry Inc., a 501 (c) 3 not-for-profit that sponsors the monthly series, Poetry on Brick Street, and publishes the *Tipton Poetry Journal*.

SOCIAL MEDIA PRIMER FOR POETS

How to Use Social Media the Right Way

by Robert Lee Brewer

Beyond the actual writing, the most important thing writers can do for their writing careers is to build a writer platform. This writer platform can consist of any number of quantifiable information about your reach to your target audience, and one hot spot is social media.

HERE'S THE THING: It's more important to chase quality connections than quantity connections on social media.

Social media is one way to quantify your reach to your target audience. If you write poetry, your target audience is people who read poetry (often other folks who write poetry). If you write cookbooks, your target audience is people who like to cook.

In both cases, you can drill down into more specifics. Maybe the target audience for the poetry book is actually people who read sonnets. For the cookbook, maybe it's directed at people who like to cook desserts.

4 SOCIAL MEDIA TIPS

Anyway, social media is one way to connect with your target audience and influencers (like agents, editors, book reviewers, other writers) who connect to your target audience. Sites like Facebook, Twitter, LinkedIn, YouTube, Pinterest, Goodreads, Red Room, and so many more–they're all sites dedicated to helping people (and in some cases specifically writers) make connections.

Here are my four social media tips for writers:

1. **START SMALL.** The worst thing writers can do with social media is jump on every social media site ever created immediately, post a bunch of stuff, and then quit because they're overwhelmed on the time commitment and underwhelmed by the lack of response. Instead, pick one site, complete all the information about yourself, and start browsing around in that one neighborhood for a while.

2. **LOOK FOR CONNECTIONS.** Notice that I did not advise looking for leads or followers or whatever. Don't approach strangers online like a used car

POPULAR SOCIAL NETWORKING SITES

The social media landscape is constantly shifting, but here are some that are currently popular:

- Bebo (http://bebo.com)
- Digg (http://digg.com)
- Facebook (http://facebook.com)
- Flickr (http://flickr.com)
- Google+ (http://plus.google.com)
- Habbo (http://habbo.com)
- Hi5 (http://hi5.com)
- Instagram (http://instagram.com)
- LinkedIn (http://linkedin.com)
- MeetUp (http://meetup.com)
- Ning (http://ning.com)
- Orkut (http://orkut.com)
- Pinterest (http://pinterest.com)
- Reddit (http://reddit.com)
- StumbleUpon (http://stumble upon.com)
- Twitter (http://twitter.com)
- Yelp (http://yelp.com)
- YouTube (http://youtube.com)
- Zorpia (htttp://zorpia.com)

salesman. Be a potential friend and/or source of information. One meaningful connection is worth more than 5,000 disengaged "followers." Seriously.

3. **COMMUNICATE.** There are two ways to make a mistake here. One, never post or share anything on your social media account. Potential new connections will skip over your ghost town profile assuming your account is no longer active. Plus, you're missing an opportunity to really connect with others. The other mistake is to post a million (hopefully an exaggeration) things a day and never communicate with your connections. It's social media, after all; be social.

4. **GIVE MORE THAN YOU TAKE.** So don't post a million things a day, but be sure to share calls for submissions, helpful information (for your target audi-

ence), fun quotes, great updates from your connections (which will endear you to them further). Share updates from your end of the world, but don't treat your social media accounts as a place to sell things nonstop. Remember: Don't be a used car salesman.

ONE FINAL TIP: Focus. Part of effective platform building is knowing your target audience and reaching them. So with every post, every status update, every tweet, every connection, etc., keep focused on how you are bringing value to your target audience.

9 THINGS TO DO ON ANY SOCIAL MEDIA SITE

Not all social media sites are created the same. However, there are some things poets can do on any site to improve the quantity and quality of the connections they make online.

1. **USE YOUR REAL NAME.** If the point of social media is to increase your visibility, then don't make the mistake of cloaking your identity behind some weird handle or nickname. Use your real name—or that is, use your real byline as it appears (or would appear) when published.

2. **USE YOUR HEADSHOT FOR AN AVATAR.** Again, avoid concealing your identity as a cartoon image or picture of a celebrity or pet. The rules of online networking are the same as face-to-face networking. Imagine how silly it would be to see someone holding up a picture of a pet cat while talking to you in person.

3. **COMPLETE YOUR PROFILE.** Each site has different ways to complete this information. You don't have to include religious or political views, but you do want to make your site personal while still communicating your interest and experience in poetry. One tip: Give people a way to contact you that doesn't involve using the social networking site. For instance, an e-mail address.

4. **LINK TO WEBSITES.** If you have a blog and/or author website, link to these in your profile on all social media sites. After all, you want to make it as easy as possible for people to learn more about you. If applicable, link to your previously published books at points of purchase too.

5. Make everything public. As a poet, you are a public figure. Embrace that state of mind and make everything you do public on social media. This means you may have to sacrifice some privacy, but there are pre-Facebook ways of communicating private matters with friends and family.

6. Update regularly. Whether it's a status update or a tweet, regular updates accomplish two things: One, they keep you in the conversation; and two, they let people you know (and people you don't know) see that you're actively using your account. Activity promotes more connections and conversations, which is what poets want on social media sites.

7. **JOIN AND PARTICIPATE IN RELEVANT GROUPS.** One key to this tip is relevancy. There are lots of random groups out there, but the ones that will benefit you the most are ones relevant to your interests and goals. Another key is participation. Participate in your group when possible.

8. **BE SELECTIVE.** Piggybacking on the previous tip, be selective about who you friend, who you follow, which groups you join, etc. Don't let people bully you into following them either. Only connect with and follow people or groups you think might bring you value—if not immediately, then eventually.

9. **EVOLVE.** When I started social media, MySpace was the top hangout. Eventu-

ally, I moved on to Facebook and Twitter (at the urging of other connections). Who knows which sites I'll prefer in 5 months, let alone 5 years, from now. Evolve as the landscape evolves. In fact, even my usage of specific sites has had to evolve as user behavior changes and the sites themselves change.

FINAL THOUGHT

If you have a blog, be sure to use it to feed your social media site profiles. Each new post should be a status update or tweet. This will serve the dual purpose of bringing traffic to your blog and providing value to your social media connections.

30-DAY PLATFORM CHALLENGE

Build Your Poet Platform in a Month

....

by Robert Lee Brewer

Whether writers are looking to find success through traditional publication or the self-publishing route, they'll find a strong writer platform will help them in their efforts. A platform is not marketing; it's the actual and quantifiable reach writers have to their target audience.

Here is a 30-day platform challenge I've developed to help writers get started in their own platform-building activities without getting overwhelmed. By accomplishing one task for one day, writers can feel a sense of accomplishment and still handle their normal daily activities. By the end of the month, writers should have a handle on what they need to do to keep growing their platform into the future.

DAY 1: DEFINE YOURSELF

For Day 1, define yourself. Don't worry about where you'd like to be in the future. Instead, take a look at who you are today, what you've already accomplished, what you're currently doing, etc.

EXAMPLE DEFINE YOURSELF WORKSHEET

Here is a chart I'm using (with my own answers). Your worksheet can ask even more questions. The more specific you can be the better for this exercise.

NAME (AS USED IN BYLINE): Robert Lee Brewer

POSITION(S): Senior Content Editor - Writer's Digest Writing Community; Author; Freelance Writer; Blogger; Event Speaker; Den Leader - Cub Scouts; Curator of Insta-poetry Series

SKILL(S): Editing, creative writing (poetry and fiction), technical writing, copywriting, database management, SEO, blogging, newsletter writing, problem solving, idea generation, public speaking, willingness to try new things, community building.

SOCIAL MEDIA PLATFORMS: Facebook, LinkedIn, Google+, Twitter, Tumblr, Blogger.

URLs: www.writersmarket.com; www.writersdigest.com/editor-blogs/poetic-asides;

http://robertleebrewer.blogspot.com/; www. robertleebrewer.com

ACCOMPLISHMENTS: Named 2010 Poet Laureate of Blogosphere; spoken at several events, including Writer's Digest Conference, AWP, Austin International Poetry Festival, Houston Poetry Fest, and more; author of Solving the World's Problems (Press 53); published and sold out of two limited edition poetry chapbooks, **ENTER** and **ESCAPE**; edited several editions of **Writer's Market** and **Poet's Market**; former GMVC conference champion in the 800-meter run and MVP of WCHS cross country and track teams; undergraduate award-winner in several writing disciplines at University of Cincinnati, including Journalism, Fiction, and Technical Writing; BA in English Literature from University of Cincinnati with certificates in writing for Creative Writing-Fiction and Professional and Technical Writing.

INTERESTS: Writing (all genres), family (being a good husband and father), faith, fitness (especially running and disc golf), fantasy football, reading.

IN ONE SENTENCE, WHO AM I? Robert Lee Brewer is a married Methodist father of five children (four sons and one daughter) who works as an editor but plays as a writer, specializing in poetry and blogging.

As long as you're being specific and honest, there are no wrong answers when it comes to defining yourself. However, you may realize that you have more to offer than you think. Or you may see an opportunity that you didn't realize even existed.

DAY 2:
SET YOUR GOALS

For today's platform-building task, set your goals. Include short-term goals and long-term goals. In fact, make a list of goals you can accomplish by the end of this year; then, make a list of goals you'd like to accomplish before you die.

EXAMPLE GOALS

Here are some of examples from my short-term and long-term goal lists:

SHORT-TERM GOALS:

- Promote new book, Solving the World's Problems.
- In April, complete April PAD Challenge on Poetic Asides blog.
- Get Writer's Market 2016 to printer ahead of schedule.
- Get Poet's Market 2016 to printer ahead of schedule.
- Lead workshop at Poetry Hickory event in April.
- Etc.

LONG-TERM GOALS:

- Publish book on platform development for small businesses.
- Raise 5 happy and healthy children into 5 happy, healthy, caring, and self-sufficient adults.
- Continue to learn how to be a better husband and human being.
- Become a bestselling novelist.
- Win Poet Laureate of the Universe honors.
- Etc.

Some writers may ask what defining your-self and creating goals has to do with plat-form development. I maintain that these are two of the most basic and important steps in the platform-building process, be-cause they define who you are and where you want to be.

A successful platform strategy should communicate who you are and help you get where you'd like to be (or provide you with a completely new opportunity). If you can't communicate who you are to strang-ers, then they won't realize how you might be able to help them or why you're impor-tant to them. If you don't have any goals, then you don't have any direction or pur-pose for your platform.

By defining who you are and what you want to accomplish, you're taking a huge step in establishing a successful writing and publishing career.

DAY 3:
JOIN FACEBOOK

For today's task, create a profile on Face-book. Simple as that. If you don't have one, it's as easy as going to www.facebook.com and signing up. It takes maybe 5 or 10 min-utes. If that.

10 FACEBOOK TIPS FOR WRITERS

Many readers probably already have a Face-book profile, and that's fine. If you have al-ready created a profile (or are doing so today), here are some tips for handling your profile:

- Complete your profile. The most checked page on most profiles is the About page. The more you share the better.
- Make everything public. Like it or not, writers are public figures. If you try to hide, it will limit the potential platform.
- Think about your audience in everything you do. When your social media profiles are public, anyone can view what you post. Keep this in mind at all times.
- Include a profile pic of yourself. Avoid setting your avatar as anything but a headshot of yourself. Many people don't like befriending a family pet or cartoon image.
- Update your status regularly. If you can update your status once per day, that's perfect. At the very least, update your status weekly. If your profile is a ghost town, people will treat it like one.
- Communicate with friends on Facebook. Facebook is a social networking site, but networking happens when you commu-nicate. So communicate.
- Be selective about friends. Find people who share your interests. Accept friends who share your interests. Other folks may be fake or inappropriate connections try-ing to build their "friend" totals.
- Be selective about adding apps. If you're not sure, it's probably best to avoid. Many users have wasted days, weeks, and even months playing silly games on Facebook.
- Join relevant groups. The emphasis should be placed on relevancy. For in-stance, I'm a poet, so I join poetry groups.

- Follow relevant fan pages. As with groups, the emphasis is placed on relevancy. In my case, I'm a fan of several poetry publications.

In addition to the tips above, be sure to always use your name as it appears in your byline. If you're not consistent in how you list your name in your byline, it's time to pick a name and stick with it. For instance, my byline name is Robert Lee Brewer—not Robbie Brewer, Bob Brewer, or even just Robert Brewer.

There are times when I absolutely can't throw the "Lee" in there, but the rest of the time it is Robert Lee Brewer. And the reasoning behind this is that it makes it easier for people who know me elsewhere to find and follow me on Facebook (or whichever social media site). Name recognition is super important when you're building your writer platform.

DAY 4:
JOIN TWITTER

For today's task, create a Twitter account. That's right. Go to www.twitter.com and sign up—if you're not already. This task will definitely take less than 5 minutes.

As with Facebook, I would not be surprised to learn that most readers already have a Twitter account. Here are three important things to keep in mind:

- **MAKE YOUR PROFILE BIO RELEVANT.** You might want to use a version of the sentence you wrote for Day 1's task. Look at my profile (twitter.com/robertleebrewer) if you need an example.

- **USE AN IMAGE OF YOURSELF.** One thing about social media (and online networking) is that people love to connect with other people. So use an image of yourself—not of your pet, a cute comic strip, a new age image, flowers, robots, etc.
- **MAKE YOUR TWITTER HANDLE YOUR BYLINE—IF POSSIBLE.** For instance, I am known as @RobertLeeBrewer on Twitter, because I use Robert Lee Brewer as my byline on articles, in interviews, at speaking events, on books, etc. Be as consistent with your byline as humanly possible.

Once you're in Twitter, try finding some worthwhile tweeps to follow. Also, be sure to make a tweet or two. As with Facebook, people will only interact with your profile if it looks like you're actually there and using your account.

SOME BASIC TWITTER TERMINOLOGY

Twitter has a language all its own. Here are some of the basics:

- **TWEET.** This is what folks call the 140-character messages that can be sent on the site. Anyone who follows you can access your tweets.
- **RT.** RT stands for re-tweet. This is what happens when someone shares your tweet, usually character for character. It's usually good form to show attribution for the author of the original tweet.
- **DM.** DM stands for direct message. This is a good way to communicate with someone on Twitter privately. I've ac-

tually had a few opportunities come my way through DMs on Twitter.

- **#.** The #-sign stands for hashtag. Hashtags are used to organize group conversations. For instance, Writer's Digest uses the #wdc to coordinate messages for their Writer's Digest Conferences. Anyone can start a hashtag, and they're sometimes used to add humor or emphasis to a tweet.
- **FF.** FF stands for follow Friday—a day typically set asides to highlight follow-worthy tweeps (or folks who use Twitter). There's also a WW that stands for writer Wednesday.

DAY 5: START A BLOG

For today's task, create a blog. You can use Blogger (www.blogger.com), WordPress (www.wordpress.com), or Tumblr (www.tumblr.com). In fact, you can use another blogging platform if you wish. To complete today's challenge, do the following:

- **CREATE A BLOG.** That is, sign up (if you don't already have a blog), pick a design (these can usually be altered later if needed), and complete your profile.
- **WRITE A POST FOR TODAY.** If you're not sure what to cover, you can just introduce yourself and share a brief explanation of how your blog got started. Don't make it too complicated.

If you already have a blog, excellent! You don't need to create a new one, but you might want to check out some ways to optimize what you have.

OPTIMIZE YOUR BLOG

Here are some tips for making your blog rock:

- **USE IMAGES IN YOUR POSTS.** Images are eye candy for readers, help with search engine optimization, and can even improve clicks when shared on social media sites, such as Facebook and Google+.
- **USE HEADERS IN POSTS.** Creating and bolding little headlines in your posts will go a long way toward making your posts easier to read and scan. Plus, they'll just look more professional.
- **WRITE SHORT.** Short sentences (fewer than 10 words). Short paragraphs (fewer than five sentences). Concision is precision in online composition.
- **ALLOW COMMENTS.** Most bloggers receive very few (or absolutely zero) comments in the beginning, but it pays to allow comments, because this gives your audience a way to interact with you. For my personal blog, I allow anyone to comment on new posts, but those that are more than a week old require my approval.

DAY 6: READ AND COMMENT ON A POST

For today's task, read at least one blog post and comment on it (linking back to your blog). And the comment should not be something along the lines of, "Hey, cool post. Come check out my blog." Instead, you need to find a blog post that really speaks to you and then make a thoughtful comment.

Here are a few possible ways to respond:

- **SHARE YOUR OWN EXPERIENCE.** If you've experienced something similar to what's covered in the post, share your own story. You don't have to write a book or anything, but maybe a paragraph or two.
- **ADD ANOTHER PERSPECTIVE.** Maybe the post was great, but there's another angle that should be considered. Don't be afraid to point that angle out.
- **ASK A QUESTION.** A great post usually will prompt new thoughts and ideas—and questions. Ask them.

As far as linking back to your blog, you could include your blog's URL in the comment, but also, most blogs have a field in their comments that allow you to share your URL. Usually, your name will link to that URL, which should either be your blog or your author website (if it offers regularly updated content).

It might seem like a lot of work to check out other blogs and comment on them, but this is an incredible way to make real connections with super users. These connections can lead to guest post and interview opportunities. In fact, they could even lead to speaking opportunities too.

DAY 7:
ADD SHARE BUTTONS
TO YOUR BLOG

For today's challenge, add share buttons to your blog and/or website.

The easiest way to do this is to go to www.addthis.com and click on the Get AddThis button. It's big, bright, and orange. You can't miss it.

Basically, the site will give you button options, and you select the one you like best. The AddThis site will then provide you with HTML code that you can place into your site and/or blog posts. Plus, it provides analytics for bloggers who like to see how much the buttons are boosting traffic.

If you want customized buttons, you could enlist the help of a programmer friend or try playing with the code yourself. I recently learned that some really cool buttons on one friend's blog were created by her husband (yes, she married a programmer, though I don't think she had her blog in mind when she did so).

Plus, most blogging platforms are constantly adding new tools. By the time you read this article, there are sure to be plenty of fun new buttons, apps, and widgets available.

Here's the thing about social sharing buttons: They make it very easy for people visiting your site to share your content with their social networks via Facebook, Twitter, LinkedIn, Google+, Pinterest, and other sites. The more your content is shared the wider your writer platform.

DAY 8:
JOIN LINKEDIN

For today's challenge, create a LinkedIn profile. Go to www.linkedin.com and set it up in a matter of minutes. After creating profiles for Facebook and Twitter, this task should be easy.

LINKEDIN TIPS FOR WRITERS

In many ways, LinkedIn looks the same as the other social networks, but it does have its own quirks. Here are a few tips for writers:

- **USE YOUR OWN HEAD SHOT.** You've heard this advice before. People want to connect with people, not family pets and/or inanimate objects.
- **COMPLETE YOUR PROFILE.** The more complete your profile the better. It makes you look more human.
- **GIVE THOUGHTFUL RECOMMENDATIONS TO RECEIVE THEM.** Find people likely to give you recommendations and recommend them first. This will prompt them to return the favor.
- **SEARCH FOR CONNECTIONS YOU ALREADY HAVE.** This is applicable to all social networks. Find people you know to help you connect with those you don't.
- **MAKE MEANINGFUL CONNECTIONS WITH OTHERS.** Remember: It's not about how many connections you make; it's about how many meaningful connections you make.
- **MAKE YOUR PROFILE EASY TO FIND.** You can do this by using your byline name. (For instance, I use linkedin.com/in/robertleebrewer.)
- **TAILOR YOUR PROFILE TO YOUR VISITOR.** Don't fill out your profile thinking only about yourself; instead, think about what your target audience might want to learn about you.

LinkedIn is often considered a more "professional" site than the other social networks like Facebook, Google+, and Twitter. For one thing, users are prompted to share their work experience and request recommendations from past employers and current co-workers.

However, this site still offers plenty of social networking opportunities for people who can hook up with the right people and groups.

DAY 9: RESPOND TO AT LEAST THREE TWEETS

For today's task, respond to at least three tweets from other tweeps on Twitter.

Since Day 4's assignment was to sign up for Twitter, you should have a Twitter account—and you're hopefully following some other Twitter users. Just respond to at least three tweets today.

As far as your responses, it's not rocket science. You can respond with a "great article" or "cool quote." A great way to spread the wealth on Twitter is to RT (retweet) the original tweet with a little note. This accomplishes two things:

- One, it lets the tweep know that you appreciated their tweet (and helps build a bond with that person); and
- Two, it brings attention to that person for their cool tweet.

Plus, it helps show that you know how to pick great resources on Twitter, which automatically improves your credibility as a resource on Twitter.

DAY 10:
DO A GOOGLE SEARCH ON YOURSELF

For today's task, do a search on your name.

First, see what results appear when you search your name on Google (google.com). Then, try searching on Bing (bing.com). Finally, give Yahoo (yahoo.com) a try.

By searching your name, you'll receive insights into what others will find (and are already finding) when they do a search specifically for you. Of course, you'll want to make sure your blog and/or website is number one in the search results. If it isn't, we'll be covering SEO (or search engine optimization) topics later in this challenge.

OTHER SEARCH ENGINES

For those who want extra credit, here are some other search engines to try searching (for yourself):

- DuckDuckGo.com
- Ask.com
- Dogpile.com
- Yippy.com
- YouTube.com

(Note: It's worth checking out which images are related to your name as well. You may be surprised to find which images are connected to you.)

DAY 11:
FIND A HELPFUL ARTICLE AND LINK TO IT

For today's task, find a helpful article (or blog post) and share it with your social net-work—and by social network, I mean that you should share it on Facebook, Twitter, and LinkedIn at a minimum. If you participate on message boards or on other social networks, share in those places as well.

Before linking to an article on fantasy baseball or celebrity news, however, make sure your article (or blog post) aligns with your author platform goals. You should have an idea of who you are and who you want to be as a writer, and your helpful article (or blog post) should line up with those values.

Of course, you may not want to share articles for writers if your platform is based on parenting tips or vampires or whatever. In such cases, you'll want to check out other resources online. Don't be afraid to use a search engine.

For Twitter, you may wish to use a URL shortener to help you keep under the 140-character limit. Here are five popular URL shorteners:

- bit.ly. This is my favorite.
- goo.gl. Google's URL shortener.
- owl.ly. Hootsuite's URL shortener.
- deck.ly. TweetDeck's URL shortener.
- su.pr. StumbleUpon's URL shortener.

By the way, here's an extra Twitter tip. Leave enough room in your tweets to allow space for people to attribute your Twitter handle if they decide to RT you. For instance, I always leave at least 20 characters to allow people space to tweet "RT @robertleebrewer" when retweeting me.

DAY 12:
WRITE A BLOG POST AND IN-CLUDE CALL TO ACTION

For today's task, write a new blog post for your blog. In the blog post, include a call to action at the end of the post.

What's a call to action?
I include calls to action at the end of all my posts. Sometimes, they are links to products and services offered by my employer (F+W Media) or some other entity. Often, I include links to other posts and ways to follow me on other sites. Even the share buttons are a call to action of sorts.

Why include a call to action?
A call to action is good for giving readers direction and a way to engage more with you. Links to previous posts provide readers with more helpful or interesting information. Links to your social media profiles give readers a way to connect with you on those sites. These calls to action are beneficial to you and your readers when they are relevant.

What if I'm just getting started?
Even if you are completely new to everything, you should have an earlier blog post from last week, a Twitter account, a Facebook account, and a LinkedIn account. Link to these at the end of your blog post today. It's a proper starting place.

And that's all you need to do today. Write a new blog post with a call to action at the end. (By the way, if you're at a loss and need something to blog about, you can always comment on that article you shared yesterday.)

DAY 13:
LINK TO POST ON SOCIAL MEDIA PROFILES

For today's challenge, link your blog post from yesterday to your social networks.

At a minimum, these social networks should include Facebook, Twitter, and LinkedIn. However, if you frequent message boards related to your blog post or other social networks (like Google+, Pinterest, etc.), then link your blog post there as well.

I understand many of you may have already completed today's challenge. If so, hooray! It's important to link your blog to your social media accounts and vice versa. When they work together, they grow together.

Is it appropriate to link to my blog post multiple times?
All writers develop their own strategies for linking to their articles and blog posts, but here's my rule. I will usually link to each blog post on every one of my social networks at least once. Since I have a regular profile and a fan page on Facebook, I link to each of those profiles once—and I only link to posts once each on Google+ and LinkedIn. But Twitter is a special case.

The way Twitter works, tweets usually only have a few minutes of visibility for tweeps with an active stream. Even tweeps with at least 100 follows may only have a 30-minute to hour window of opportunity to see your tweet. So for really popular and timely blog posts, I will tweet them more often than once on Twitter.

That said, I'm always aware of how I'm linking and don't want to become that an-

noying spammer that I typically avoid following in my own social networking efforts.

LINKING TIPS

Some tips on linking to your post:

- Use a URL shortener. These are discussed above.
- Apply title + link formula. For instance, I might Tweet this post as: Platform Challenge: Day 13: (link). It's simple and to the point. Plus, it's really effective if you have a great blog post title.
- Frame the link with context. Using this post as an example, I might Tweet: Take advantage of social media by linking to your blog posts: (link). Pretty simple, and it's an easy way to link to the same post without making your Twitter feed look loaded with the same content.
- Quote from post + link formula. Another tactic is to take a funny or thought-provoking quote from the post and combine that with a link. Example Tweet: "I will usually link to each blog post on every one of my social networks at least once." (link). Again, easy stuff.

DAY 14:
JOIN GOOGLE+

For today's task, create a Google+ (plus.google.com) profile.

Many of you may already have G+ profiles, but this social networking site is still rather new compared to Facebook and Twitter. Plus, Google+ status updates often show up in search results on Google's search engine.

I've heard people describe Google+ as a mix between Facebook and Twitter, and I don't think that's too far off the mark. Personally, I think it's still growing, which can be a good and bad thing.

The good news is that you could still be one of the first G+-users on the block; bad news is that you have to wait (and hope) for other people to migrate over to the block. Of course, Google has a huge reach online, so there's no reason to doubt that people will migrate...eventually.

One tool I've really learned to appreciate on Google+ is the Hangouts feature, which makes it easy to record video chats with other people, including experts in your field on Google+ and then share permanently on YouTube. Since I feel video is the future of online, I think this is really cool.

As with Facebook and LinkedIn, keep these tips in mind:

- Complete your profile completely. Use your name. Provide easy to find contact information. Describe who you are.
- Use an image of yourself. Not a cartoon. Not an animal. Not a piece of art. Remember that people like to connect with other people.
- Post new content regularly. Let people know you are using your account. That means connecting with other G+'ers as well.

DAY 15:
MAKE THREE NEW CONNEC-
TIONS

For today's task, make an attempt to connect with at least three new people on one of your social networks.

Doesn't matter if it's Facebook, Twitter, LinkedIn, or Google+. The important thing is that you find three new people who appear to share your interests and that you try to friend, follow, or connect to them.

As a person who has limited wiggle room for approving new friends on Facebook, I'd like to share what approach tends to work the best with me for approving new friend requests. Basically, send your request and include a brief message introducing yourself and why you want to connect with me.

That's right. The best way to win me over is to basically introduce yourself. Something along the lines of, "Hello. My name is Robert Lee Brewer, and I write poetry. I read a poem of yours in *XYZ Literary Journal* that I totally loved and have sent you a friend request. I hope you'll accept it." Easy as that.

Notice that I did not mention anything about checking out my blog or reading my poems. How would you like it if someone introduced themselves and then told you to buy their stuff? It sounds a bit telemarketer-ish to me.

While it's important to cultivate the relationships you already have, avoid getting stuck in a rut when it comes to making connections. Always be on the lookout for new connections who can offer new oppor-

tunities and spark new ideas. Your writing and your career will benefit.

DAY 16:
ADD E-MAIL FEED TO BLOG

For today's challenge, add an e-mail feed to your blog.

There are many ways to increase traffic to your blog, but one that has paid huge dividends for me is adding Feedblitz to my blog. As the subscribers to my e-mail feed have increased, my blog traffic has increased as well. In fact, after great content, I'd say that adding share buttons (mentioned above) and an e-mail feed are the top two ways to build traffic.

Though I have an account on Tumblr, I'm just not sure if it offers some kind of e-mail/RSS feed service.

The reason I think e-mail feeds are so useful is that they pop into my inbox whenever a new post is up, which means I can check it very easily on my phone when I'm waiting somewhere. In fact, this is how I keep up with several of my favorite blogs. It's just one more way to make your blog content accessible to readers in a variety of formats.

If I remember, this task didn't take me long to add, but I've been grateful for finally getting around to adding it ever since.

DAY 17:
TAKE PART IN A TWITTER
CONVERSATION

For today's task, take part in a Twitter conversation.

Depending upon the time of month or day of week, there are bound to be any number of conversations happening around a hashtag (mentioned above). For instance, various conferences and expos have hashtag conversations that build around their panels and presentations.

Poets will often meet using the #poetparty hashtag. Other writers use #amwriting to communicate about their writing goals. Click on the hashtag to see what others are saying, and then, jump in to join the conversation and make new connection on Twitter.

DAY 18:
THINK ABOUT SEO

For today's task, I want you to slow down and think a little about SEO (which is tech-speak for search engine optimization, which is itself an intelligent way of saying "what gets your website to display at or near the top of a search on Google, Bing, Yahoo, etc.").

So this task is actually multi-pronged:

- Make a list of keywords that you want your website or blog to be known for. For instance, I want my blog to be known for terms like "Robert Lee Brewer," "Writing Tips," "Parenting Tips," "Platform Tips," "Living Tips," etc. Think big here and don't limit yourself to what you think you can actually achieve in the short term.
- Compare your website or blog's current content to your keywords. Are you lining up your actual content with how you want your audience to view you and your online presence? If not, it's time to think about how you

can start offering content that lines up with your goals. If so, then move on to the next step, which is...

- Evaluate your current approach to making your content super SEO-friendly. If you need some guidance, check out my SEO Tips for Writers below. There are very simple things you can do with your titles, subheads, and images to really improve SEO. Heck, I get a certain bit of traffic every single day just from my own SEO approach to content—sometimes on surprising posts.
- Research keywords for your next post. When deciding on a title for your post and subheads within the content, try researching keywords. You can do this using Google's free keyword tool (googlekeywordtool.com). When possible, you want to use keywords that are searched a lot but that have low competition. These are the low-hanging fruit that can help you build strong SEO for your website or blog.

A note on SEO: It's easy to fall in love with finding keywords and changing your content to be keyword-loaded and blah-blah-blah. But resist making your website or blog a place that is keyword-loaded and blah-blah-blah. Because readers don't stick around for too much keyword-loaded blah-blah-blah. It's kind of blah. And bleck. Instead, use SEO and keyword research as a way to optimize great content and to take advantage of opportunities as they arise.

SEO TIPS FOR WRITERS

Here are a few SEO tips for writers:

- Use keywords naturally. That is, make sure your keywords match the content of the post. If they don't match up, people will abandon your page fast, which will hurt your search rankings.
- Use keywords appropriately. Include your keywords in the blog post title, opening paragraph, file name for images, headers, etc. Anywhere early and relevant should include your keyword to help place emphasis on that search term, especially if it's relevant to the content.
- Deliver quality content. Of course, search rankings are helped when people click on your content and spend time reading your content. So provide quality content, and people will visit your site frequently and help search engines list you higher in their rankings.
- Update content regularly. Sites that are updated more with relevant content rank higher in search engines. Simple as that.
- Link often to relevant content. Link to your own posts; link to content on other sites. Just make sure the links are relevant and of high interest to your audience.
- Use images. Images help from a design perspective, but they also help with SEO, especially when you use your main keywords in the image file name.
- Link to your content on social media sites. These outside links will help increase your ranking on search engines.
- Guest post on other sites/blogs. Guest posts on other blogs are a great way to provide traffic from other relevant sites

that increase the search engine rankings on your site.

DAY 19: WRITE A BLOG POST

For today's task, write a new blog post.

Include a call to action (for instance, encourage readers to sign up for your e-mail feed and to share the post with others using your share buttons) and link to it on your social networks. Also, don't forget to incorporate SEO.

One of the top rules of finding success with online tools is applying consistency. While it's definitely a great thing if you share a blog post more than once a week, I think it's imperative that you post at least once a week.

The main reason? It builds trust with your readers that you'll have something to share regularly and gives them a reason to visit regularly.

So today's task is not about making things complicated; it's just about keeping it real.

DAY 20: CREATE EDITORIAL CALENDAR

For today's task, I want you to create an editorial calendar for your blog (or website). Before you start to panic, read on.

First, here's how I define an editorial calendar: A list of content with dates attached to when the content goes live. For instance, I created an editorial calendar specifically for my Platform Challenge and

"Platform Challenge: Day 20" was scheduled to go live on day 20.

It's really simple. In fact, I keep track of my editorial calendar with a paper notebook, which gives me plenty of space for crossing things out, jotting down ideas, and attaching Post-It notes.

EDITORIAL CALENDAR IDEAS

Here are tips for different blogging frequencies:

- Post once per week. If you post once a week, pick a day of the week for that post to happen each week. Then, write down the date for each post. Beside each date, write down ideas for that post ahead of time. There will be times when the ideas are humming and you get ahead on your schedule, but there may also be times when the ideas are slow. So don't wait, write down ideas as they come.
- Post more than once per week. Try identifying which days you'll usually post (for some, that may be daily). Then, for each of those days, think of a theme for that day. For instance, my 2012 schedule offered Life Changing Moments on Wednesdays and Poetic Saturdays on Saturdays.

You can always change plans and move posts to different days, but the editorial calendar is an effective way to set very clear goals with deadlines for accomplishing them. Having that kind of structure will improve your content—even if your blog is personal, fictional, poetic, etc. Believe me, I used to be a skeptic before diving in, and the results on my personal blog speak for themselves.

One more benefit of editorial calendars

There are times when I feel less than inspired. There are times when life throws me several elbows as if trying to prevent me from blogging. That's when I am the most thankful for maintaining an editorial calendar, because I don't have to think of a new idea on the spot; it's already there in my editorial calendar.

Plus, as I said earlier, you can always change plans. I can alter the plan to accommodate changes in my schedule. So I don't want to hear that an editorial calendar limits spontaneity or inspiration; if anything, having an editorial calendar enhances it.

One last thing on today's assignment

Don't stress yourself out that you have to create a complete editorial calendar for the year or even the month. I just want you to take some time out today to think about it, sketch some ideas, and get the ball rolling. I'm 100% confident that you'll be glad you did.

DAY 21:
SIGN UP FOR SOCIAL MEDIA TOOL

For today's task, try joining one of the social media management tools, such as Tweetdeck, Hootsuite, or Seesmic.

Social media management tools are popular among social media users for one reason: They help save time and effort in managing multiple social media platforms. For instance, they make following specific threads in Twitter a snap.

I know many social media super users who swear by these tools, but I actually have tried them and decided to put in the extra effort to log in to my separate social media accounts manually each day.

Here's my reasoning: I like to feel connected to my profile and understand how it looks and feels on a day-to-day basis. Often, the design and feel of social media sites will change without notice, and I like to know what it feels like at ground zero.

DAY 22:
PITCH GUEST BLOG POST

For today's task, pitch a guest blog post to another blogger.

Writing guest posts is an incredible way to improve your exposure and expertise on a subject, while also making a deeper connection with the blogger who is hosting your guest post. It's a win for everyone involved.

In a recent interview with super blogger Jeff Goins, he revealed that most of his blog traffic came as a result of his guest posting on other blogs. Some of these blogs were directly related to his content, but he said many were in completely different fields.

GUEST POST PITCHING TIPS

After you know where you want to guest blog, here are some tips for pitching your guest blog post:

• Let the blogger know you're familiar with the blog. You should do this in one sentence (two sentences max) and be specific. For instance, a MNINB reader could say, "I've been reading your Not Bob blog for months, but I really love this Platform Challenge." Simple as that. It lets me know you're not a spammer, but it doesn't take me a long time to figure out what you're trying to say.

• Propose an idea or two. Each idea should have its own paragraph. This makes it easy for the blogger to know where one idea ends and the next one begins. In a pitch, you don't have to lay out all the details, but you do want to be specific. Try to limit the pitch to 2-4 sentences.

• Share a little about yourself. Emphasis on "a little." If you have previous publications or accomplishments that line up with the blog, share those. If you have expertise that lines up with the post you're pitching, share those. Plus, include any details about your online platform that might show you can help bring traffic to the post. But include all this information in 1-4 sentences.

• Include your information. When you close the pitch, include your name, e-mail, blog (or website) URL, and other contact information you feel comfortable sharing. There's nothing more awkward for me than to have a great pitch that doesn't include the person's name. Or a way to learn more about the person.

What do I do after the pitch is accepted?

First off, congratulations! This is a great opportunity to show off your writing skills. Here's how to take advantage of your guest post assignment:

- **WRITE AN EXCEPTIONAL POST.** Don't hold back your best stuff for your blog. Write a post that will make people want to find more of your writing.
- **TURN IN YOUR POST ON DEADLINE.** If there's a deadline, hit it. If there's not a deadline, try to turn around the well-written post in a timely manner.
- **PROMOTE THE GUEST POST.** Once your guest post has gone live, promote it like crazy by linking to your post on your blog, social networks, message boards, and wherever else makes sense for you. By sending your own connections to this guest post, you're establishing your own expertise—not only through your post but also your connections.

DAY 23:
CREATE A TIME MANAGEMENT PLAN

For today's task, create a time management plan.

You may be wondering why I didn't start out the challenge with a time management plan, and here's the reason: I don't think some people would've had any idea how long it takes them to write a blog post, share a link on Twitter and Facebook, respond to social media messages, etc. Now, many of you probably have a basic idea—even if you're still getting the hang of your new-fangled social media tools.

Soooo... the next step is to create a time management plan that enables you to be "active" socially and connect with other writers and potential readers while also spending a majority of your time writing and publishing.

As with any plan, you can make this as simple or complicated as you wish. For instance, my plan is to do 15 minutes or less of social media after completing each decent-sized task on my daily task list. I use social media time as a break, which I consider more productive than watching TV or playing Angry Birds.

I put my writing first and carve out time in the mornings and evenings to work on poetry and fiction. Plus, I consider my blogging efforts part of my writing too. So there you go.

My plan is simple and flexible, but if you want to get hardcore, break down your time into 15-minute increments. Then, test out your time management plan to see if it works for you. If not, then make minor changes to the plan until it has you feeling somewhat comfortable with the ratio of time you spend writing and time you spend building your platform.

Remember: A platform is a life-long investment in your career. It's not a sprint, so you have to pace yourself. Also, it's not something that happens overnight, so you can't wait until you need a platform to start building one. Begin today and build over time—so that it's there when you need it.

DAY 24:
TAKE PART IN A FACEBOOK CONVERSATION

For today's task, take part in a conversation on Facebook.

You should've already participated in a Twitter conversation, so this should be somewhat similar—except you don't have to play with hashtags and 140-character restrictions. In fact, you just need to find a group conversation or status update that speaks to you and chime in with your thoughts.

Don't try to sell or push anything when you join a conversation. If you say interesting things, people will check out your profile, which if filled out will lead them to more information about you (including your website, blog, any books, etc.).

Goal one of social media is making connections. If you have everything else optimized, sales and opportunities will take care of themselves.

DAY 25:
CONTACT AN EXPERT FOR AN INTERVIEW POST

For today's task, find an expert in your field and ask if that expert would like to be interviewed.

If you can secure the interview, this will make for a great blog post. Or it may help you secure a freelance assignment with a publication in your field. Or both, and possibly more.

How to Ask for an Interview

Believe it or not, asking for an interview with an expert is easy. I do it all the time, and these are the steps I take.

- **FIND AN EXPERT ON A TOPIC.** This is sometimes the hardest part: figuring out who I want to interview. But I never kill myself trying to think of the perfect person, and here's why: I can always ask for more interviews. Sometimes, it's just more productive to get the ball rolling than come up with excuses to not get started.
- **LOCATE AN E-MAIL FOR THE EXPERT.** This can often be difficult, but a lot of experts have websites that share either e-mail addresses or have online contact forms. Many experts can also be reached via social media sites, such as Facebook, Twitter, LinkedIn, Google+, etc. Or they can be contacted through company websites. And so on.
- **SEND AN E-MAIL ASKING FOR AN E-MAIL INTERVIEW.** Of course, you can do this via an online contact form too. If the expert says no, that's fine. Respond with a "Thank you for considering and maybe we can make it work sometime in the future." If the expert says yes, then it's time to send along the questions.

How to Handle an E-mail Interview

Once you've secured your expert, it's time to compose and send the questions. Here are some of my tips.

- **ALWAYS START OFF BY ASKING QUESTIONS ABOUT THE EXPERT.** This might seem obvious to some, but you'd be surprised how many people start off asking "big questions" right out of the gate. Always start off by giving the expert a chance to talk about what he or she is doing, has recently done, etc.

- **LIMIT QUESTIONS TO 10 OR FEWER.** The reason for this is that you don't want to overwhelm your expert. In fact, I usually ask around eight questions in my e-mail interviews. If I need to, I'll send along some follow-up questions, though I try to limit those as well. I want the expert to have an enjoyable experience, not a horrible experience. After all, I want the expert to be a connection going forward.

- **TRY NOT TO GET TOO PERSONAL.** If experts want to get personal in their answers, that's great. But try to avoid getting too personal in the questions you ask, because you may offend your expert or make them feel uncomfortable. Remember: You're interviewing the expert, not leading an interrogation.

- **REQUEST ADDITIONAL INFORMATION.** By additional information, I mean that you should request a headshot and a preferred bio—along with any links. To make the interview worth the expert›s time, you should afford them an opportunity to promote themselves and their projects in their bios.

Once the Interview Goes Live...

Link to it on your social networks and let your expert know it is up (and include the specific link to the interview). If you're not already searching for your next expert to interview, be sure to get on it.

DAY 26: WRITE A BLOG POST AND LINK TO SOCIAL PROFILES

For today's task, write a new blog post.

In your blog post, include a call to action and link it on your social networks. Also, don't forget SEO.

Remember: One of the top rules of finding success with online tools is applying consistency. While it's definitely a great thing if you share a blog post more than once a week, I think it's imperative that you post at least once a week.

The main reason? It builds trust with your readers that you'll have something to share regularly and gives them a reason to visit regularly.

If this sounds repetitive, good; it means my message on consistency is starting to take root.

DAY 27: JOIN ANOTHER SOCIAL MEDIA SITE

For today's task, join one new social media site. I will leave it up to you to decide which new social media site it will be.

Maybe you'll join Pinterest. Maybe you'll choose Goodreads. Heck, you might go with RedRoom or some social media site that's not even on my radar at the time of this article. Everything is constantly evolving, which is why it's good to always try new things.

To everyone who doesn't want another site to join...

I understand your frustration and exhaustion. During a normal month, I'd never suggest someone sign up for so many social media sites in such a short period of time, but this isn't a normal month. We're in the midst of a challenge!

And no, I don't expect you to spend a lot of time on every social media site you join. That's not always the point when you first sign up. No, you sign up to poke around and see if the site interests you at all. See if you have any natural connections. Try mingling a little bit.

If the site doesn't appeal to you, feel free to let it be for a while. Let me share a story with you.

How I Came to Rock Facebook and Twitter

My Facebook and Twitter accounts both boast more than 5,000 followers (or friends/subscribers) today. But both accounts were originally created and abandoned, because they just weren't right for me at the time that I signed up.

For Facebook, I just didn't understand why I would abandon a perfectly good MySpace account to play around on a site that didn't feature the same level of music and personal blogging that MySpace did. But then, MySpace turned into Spam-op-olis, and the rest is history.

For Twitter, I just didn't get the whole tweet concept, because Facebook already had status updates. Why tweet when I could update my status on Facebook?

But I've gained a lot professionally and personally from Facebook and Twitter—even though they weren't the right sites for me initially. In fact, Google+ is sort of in

that area for me right now. I don't use it near enough, but I started an account, because it just feels like a place that will explode sooner or later. It's not like Facebook is going to be around forever.

The Importance of Experimentation

Or as I prefer to think of it: The importance of play. You should constantly try new things, whether in your writing, your social media networks, or the places you eat food. Not only does it make life more exciting and provide you with new experiences and perspective, but it also helps make you a more well-rounded human being.

So don't complain about joining a new social media site. Instead, embrace the excuse to try something new, especially when there are only three more tasks left this month (and I promise no more new sites after today).

DAY 28: READ POST AND COMMENT ON IT

For today's task, read and comment on a blog post, making sure that your comment links back to your blog or website.

If you remember, this was the same task required way back on Day 6. How far we've come, though it's still a good idea to stay connected and engaged with other bloggers. I know I find that sometimes I start to insulate myself in my own little blogging communities and worlds—when it's good to get out and read what others are doing. In fact, that's what helped inspire my Monday Advice for Writers posts—it gives me motivation to read what others are writing (on writing, of course).

DAY 29:
MAKE A TASK LIST

For today's task, make a task list of things you are going to do on each day next month. That's right, I want you to break down 31 days with 31 tasks for each day—similar to what we've done this month.

You see, I don't want you to quit challenging yourself once this challenge is over. Of course, you get to decide what the tasks will be. So if you aren't into new social media sites, don't put them on your list. Instead, focus on blog posts, commenting on other sites, linking to articles, contacting experts, or whatever it is that you are going to do next month to keep momentum building toward an incredible author platform.

Somewhere near the end of the month, you should have a day set aside with one task: Make a task list of things to do on each day of the next month. And so on and

so forth. Keep it going, keep it rolling, and your efforts will continue to gain momentum and speed. I promise.

DAY 30:
ENGAGE THE WORLD

For today's task, engage the world.

By this, I mean that you should comment on status updates, ask questions, share answers, start debates, continue debates, and listen—that's right, don't be that person who dominates a conversation and makes it completely one-sided.

Engage the world by entering the conversation. Engage the world by having the courage to take risks and share things of consequence. Engage the world by having the courage to make mistakes and fail and learn from those mistakes and failures.

The only people who never fail are those who never try, and those people never succeed at anything except avoiding failure and success. Don't be that person. Engage the world and let the world engage you.

KRISTINA MARIE DARLING

....

by Robert Lee Brewer

///

Kristina Marie Darling is the author of more than 20 books, which include *Vow, Petrarchan,* and *Scorched Altar*, all available from BlazeVOX Books. Her writing has been recognized with fellowships from Yaddo, the Ucross Foundation, and the Helene Wurlitzer Foundation, as well as grants from the Kittredge Fund and the Elizabeth George Foundation.

When I conducted this interview, Darling had been recently selected as a Visiting Artist at the American Academy in Rome. She also had just released her collection *Scorched Altar: Selected Poems & Stories 2007-2014.*

What are you currently up to?

I'm getting ready to leave for a residency at the Kimmel Harding Nelson Center for the Arts and couldn't be more excited. I'll spend my time there working on a new collection of erasure poems, which examines the egregious amount of gender violence in Shakespeare's tragedies. The fragmented, elliptical poems ask reader to consider whether the literature we've inherited has normalized gender violence, since plays like *Hamlet, King Lear,* and *Othello* are so present within the public imagination.

Part critique, part excavation, the poems are intended to redirect the focus of scholarly and readerly attention. It is when we become conscious of underlying beliefs and assumptions in culture, and their roots, that change emerges as a real possibility.

Scorched Altar *is a collection of selected poems and stories published by BlazeVOX [books]. How did this collection come about?*

That's a great question. I initially contacted Geoffrey Gatza, the fabulous editor in charge of the press, to inquire about the possibility of a *Selected Poems.*

It turns out that Geoffrey had the same idea himself, and I simply e-mailed first. Since I had worked with BlazeVOX on numerous previous collections, I knew that my *Selected Poems* was in very good hands.

Was the process of selecting pieces from previous collections different than putting together a new collection?

When I compiled the poems from my previous collections for *Scorched Altar*, it was a much different process than working on a brand new collection. For me, writing a new poem or poetry book is an intuitive process, and I don't reflect much on what I'm doing, at least in the drafting stage. If I allow myself to become too self-aware, that allows me to become self-critical, and then no writing gets done at all.

What I really enjoyed about the process of compiling *Scorched Altar* was that it prompted me to reflect on my body of work as a whole, to see patterns emerge from my writing over the past seven years, and to see progress and growth. The act of examining my poetry over the course of several years also helped me see what ideas, obsessions, and literary forms I returned to most frequently. And as a result, I came away from the process with many ideas for new projects, experiments, and poems that were completely different from anything I'd ever written before.

In many ways, the act of examining my body of work showed me what is possible within it.

Many of your pieces have a very visual element to how they're arranged on the page. Do you ever perform these in readings?

I think every poetry reading has some element of performance. Whether the poet shouts their poems, or sings them, or invites audience participation, I'm positive that all writers have a constructed persona, which is an extension of the work itself. With that in mind, I love performing my footnote poems at readings.

I typically read them in a completely flat, monotone voice, almost like the bad math professor that just about everyone had in college. I love seeing the audience lulled into a sense of comfort by the unexciting presentation of the work, only to be surprised by the wildly imaginative content.

You're an active literary critic. Does this inform your writing? Help? Hinder?

I'm glad you asked about my reviewing and involvement with literary criticism. I love reviewing books, because it exposes me to poetry that is completely outside my comfort zone. This is great because it helps me question and interrogate what I normally do in my own writing. It pushes me to try new things and experiment more within my own practice. And it helps me see more clearly where my poems fit within the larger literary community.

The best thing about reviewing, though, is that it helps build relationships within publishing and writing. I've met friends, collaborators, and even mentors when working on reviews.

And there's nothing better than free books!

You've published 17 collections now. How do you keep the writing flame lit?

By reading and reviewing other poets. As long as you're constantly being exposed to new ideas, literary forms, and aesthetics, you'll always have something to write about.

I also run a small press, Noctuary Press, which has been great for my own creative practice. The press primarily publishes women's writing that takes places across and beyond genre categories. Although I pride myself on my ability to question genre distinctions, reading submissions for the press has shown me the tremendous variety inherent in contemporary cross-genre writing by women.

My work as editor has helped me see what's possible within the hybrid forms I typically inhabit, and it's a great deal more than I had initially envisioned.

One poet who no one knows but should—who is it?

Erin Bertram. She has several magnificent chapbooks out, including one from Kristy Bowen's fabulous Dancing Girl Press. I'm just waiting for someone to realize that her first full-length book needs to be published (so I can buy it and read it!).

Who (or what) are you currently reading?

I'm very excited to check out Donna Stonecipher's *Model City* and Dawn Lonsinger's *Whelm*. I also just picked up Olena Kalytiak Davis's newest collection, which I've been eagerly awaiting for quite some time.

And if you haven't checked out Carl Adamshick's *Saint Friend*, just published by McSweeney's Books, then you sure are missing out. It's a terrific collection, even better than his first book, *Curses & Wishes*.

Could you share how you stay organized and on task for writing, submitting, following up, etc.?

I'm probably going to out myself as a total nerd with this answer, but here goes: Excel Spreadsheets. I keep track of everything (applications I've submitted, review copies sent, deadlines for applications) in a couple of gigantic spreadsheets.

If I could offer one piece of advice to poets, I'd say keep records of where you send your work, whether it's review copies, applications, or poems. If you don't remember where you sent something, then there's no way you'll ever be able to follow up with the decision maker.

And believe me, persistence pays off, especially in small press publishing.

MEGAN VOLPERT

by Robert Lee Brewer

Megan Volpert is the author of five books on communication and popular culture. She is also the editor of *This assignment is so gay: LGBTIQ Poets on the Art of Teaching*. For the better part of a decade, Volpert has been doing three things: teaching high school English in Atlanta, living with ulcerative colitis, and driving a motorcycle.

When I conducted this interview, Volpert was in the process of promoting *Only Ride*, a wonderful collection of prose poems that can be read in order, out of order, but especially out loud.

What are you currently up to?

Well, I finally watched all of *Breaking Bad* this summer. But work wise, there are a few things brewing. Most immediately, Gina Myers of Lame House Press is kindly publishing a chapbook of about a dozen weird little language experiments I built based on something Michel Foucault once said. So we are having a blast contemplating design elements for that.

But I'm also knee deep in research for a book of essays I'm writing about punk rhet-orics of independence during the American Bicentennial year, which is like holding a seance for Hunter S. Thompson. That will be breaking some new nonfiction ground for Sibling Rivalry Press, though I don't think there's anyone left who doubts that SRP is blowing up all kinds of new avenues. Bryan Borland-Pennington is deeply visionary, and moreover, remarkably nice for somebody so successful.

A little further out, I've recently begun to collaborate with the amazing and tender performance artist Craig Gingrich-Philbrook. We are investigating the nature of failure, of shows we imagined but then tossed away before they could become realities. That will be CGP's first book, to which a million people have been looking forward for a very long time, and I'm just proud he wants to make the leap on that with me.

Do you have a process for assembling poems for a collection of poetry?

Yes, I've basically stopped thinking about each piece in isolation. They each have to stand alone, of course, but more and more often I am beginning with the big idea then drilling down to determine its component parts. I know what sort of machines I'm after, so I really proceed more from what the total function of the book will be and then write bits and pieces as I stumble across applications of the project's main functions in my daily life.

Only Ride, in particular, is based on a series of constraints. It's all prose poems between 95 and 110 words, with titles that are complete sentences. My previous collection was the Warhol thing, which was so sprawling and research heavy that I really wanted to work on something more compact and minimal next. I typed most of them on my phone, on the train during my morning commute. I'd let a batch sit in my notepad for a month or so, then revise the whole pile over a couple hours on a weekend. I knew my subjects, so when I reached my target of 66 pieces, I laid them all out on the floor and organized first based on chronological order of the events in the poems then for the right emotional arch within each subject or time period.

Other stuff can present itself for more obvious arrangement, for example, the 1976 book will report historical events in a straightforward chronological order, one month per chapter. I do prefer organic methods like that. My first two collections still feel well organized, but I agonized over those little piecemeal frankensteins, which in hindsight seems unnecessary.

I've seen you read from your collection Only Ride *by getting the audience to select random poems*

to read—kind of like a poetry juke-box. Was that the intention for this collection?

Intention is a strong word, but sure. In the design discussions, I was adamant about no table of contents and no page numbers. Life doesn't have those, and I like it if the physical product of my books can surprise readers in useful ways like that. It contributes something beyond just the quality of the writing. Fonts choices are also of critical import to me, selecting the weight of the paper, and so on. I'm lucky SRP trusts me to participate in those choices.

But as much as I thought about how each poem would be performed aloud and live, it honestly never once occurred to me that I would have no system for putting together a set list. I think it looks silly to put sticky notes on so many pages, especially with these poems that are all just a minute long. I'd have like 20 tabs hanging out, and still the problem of whether to go through the book in order or not. I considered numbering the pages in my own reading copy for reference, but it really felt like cheating.

So I gave up control to the audience, and the first few times they loved it so profoundly that I just kept doing it. It allows me to be much more in the moment, enjoying the connections we make together. And it sure is nice not to have to sit down ahead of time for a half hour and fool myself into believing I know what those future moments of the reading should hold.

Each spread in the collection has a title on one page and a prose poem on the other. What appeals to you about the prose poem?

Ten years ago, I'd have said nothing appeals to me about the prose poem. In grad school, I was notoriously militant about the value of line breaks and could pontificate about the evil vagaries of the prose poem for an hour stretch without breaking a sweat.

But at some point, I gave up on the label of poetry. Truly, I know a lot of people categorize *Only Ride* as a collection of prose poems, but you could just as easily call them flash or micro-essays. I work in a hybrid kind of area and don't see a lot of merit in genre classifications beyond their value as marketing tools.

The Warhol book was hardly clear cut as poetry either. I don't feel I've lost my capacity for line breaks, but I'm genuinely disinterested in them right now. I expect this trend to continue for awhile on into the future as I expand into making texts that are more easily identifiable as nonfiction, like the 1976 book and the collaboration with CGP.

I realize that doesn't answer your question, but it does answer for some of the assumptions sliding around under the question.

You teach high school English. Do you find teaching helps or hinders your writing? Or the other way around?

Oh, teaching helps. No question about that. Because I am essentially a manic person, I am terrible at vacationing. After two or three weeks away from my students, I'm quite refreshed and ready to go back. I did just a sick amount of research and writing for the 1976 book during my eight weeks of summer break. It was so gross. I was inside all day, alone, staring at my computer. My back hurt, my vision got weird, and I went into that freaky liminal writing space for just too long too often. I couldn't be a full time writer, and not because it doesn't pay well enough. I get great inspiration from my students, plus I need the hamster wheel of the school to keep myself from being so focused on writing that I simply go nuts.

Do you have a writing routine?

It varies from project to project because it emerges out of the needs of each project, but I can at least say that I am more productive in the morning or afternoon and that I type almost everything now. I've always enjoyed writing in transit, on airplanes or trains especially, but have no explanation to offer as to why that might be. See also: above discussion of unhealthy manic behaviors.

One poet no one knows but should—who is it?

Brock Guthrie, no relation to Woody. We went to grad school together at LSU. His debut collection, *Contemplative Man*, is out now from Sibling Rivalry Press. When we would workshop together, I thought most of his comments were kind of dopey but all of his poems made me totally jealous. Envy is actually not an emotion I feel very often toward other writers, but wow, I just wanted to steal everything Brock ever wrote. Brock is still not good at promoting himself, or finding a publisher.

I've been helping him out on those ugly business fronts, but as a writer, he nails it every time and I'm not going to attempt to encapsulate it for you. Just buy the book. Brock is the type of guy who will go unnoticed for 40 more years, then up and win a Pulitzer on the merit of the work alone. Get in on it while he's still nobody famous, and later on you can join me in the I-told-you-so fest.

Who (or what) are you currently reading?

I used to be a one book at a time kid of girl, but now I usually have two of three things going. I read tons of monthly pop culture magazines, from *Rolling Stone* to *Esquire*. I've been checking out a lot of Erma Bombeck, which is a 1976 thing. I just finished Bob Colacello's excellent old book about the Reagans' path to the presidency.

And I'm steeped in Lester Bangs just for the sound of him. I've always kept mainly to nonfiction and don't read much new poetry, though I did love Bruce Covey's new book. When I want poetry, I listen to new music. As I type this, I am listening to Tom Petty's new album, *Hypnotic Eye*, on loop.

When I want fiction, I watch television dramas like *Rescue Me* or *Six Feet Under*. Whatever the medium, I pretty much prefer a pile of snark with a dash of morbidity. Surprise.

If you could only share one piece of advice with fellow poets, what would it be?

Fuhgeddaboudit. Stop asking fellow poets for advice and do whatever you damn well know in your heart feels best.

TODD DAVIS

by Robert Lee Brewer

Todd Davis teaches creative writing, American literature, and environmental studies at Penn State University's Altoona College. When this interview was conducted, his most recent collection of poems was *In the Kingdom of the Ditch.*

His other three full-length poetry collections are *The Least of These, Some Heaven,* and *Ripe.* His poetry has been featured on the radio by Garrison Keillor on *The Writer's Almanac* and by Ted Kooser in his syndicated newspaper column *American Life in Poetry.*

What are you currently up to?

The last month or so I've been working on revising my fifth full-length poetry collection. At the moment it's called *Winterkill.* The poems have been written over the past three years, finding homes in journals and magazines along the way, and in May I began to put the poems together to see how they talk to one another.

After two revisions of the manuscript— rearranging the placement of individual po- ems, tinkering with lines in individual poems, and even dropping or adding certain poems to the collection—I've sent it to four of my poetry friends who are reading it and offering commentary.

Once they've finished, I'll do some more revision based upon their observations and critiques and hopefully send it to my publisher, Michigan State University Press, in the spring. After that, I'll keep my fingers crossed that my editor likes what she sees and the press will move the book into production.

Do you have a process for assembling poems for a collection of poetry?

I'm very much a daily writer and thinker. My mind tends to gravitate toward certain subjects based upon my experiences—in the woods, on the rivers, with the books I'm reading.

For example, yesterday I was deep in on a small stream in the 41,000 acres of game lands above the village where I live. My son and I were taking a long hike and fishing for native brook trout. I came across an amazing caterpillar on the walk—it was lime green with what looked like small spines or quills covering its body. At the end of these spines where bright, vivid colors—red and yellow and blue. I hadn't seen this caterpillar before, and when I returned home, with the help of the photos I took, I was able to spend time looking through my field guides, discovering that this was the caterpillar that would later turn into a cecropia moth (*Hyalophora cecropia*), the largest native moth in North America.

Several years ago at the top of the mountain above our village, I was hiking on an extremely foggy morning. Mornings like this many flying creatures settle to earth because nature's "ground traffic control" has cancelled their flights. I've come across a kettle of kestrel and other beautiful raptors on mornings like this. That particular morning, however, it wasn't raptors that I found but a cecropia moth clinging to a long blade of grass in a meadow. I spent more than 30 minutes photographing it, studying it, trying to express how enamored I was by its beauty. (Yes, I tend to talk to the natural world!)

I tell you this story because, like William Stafford whose example means a great deal to me, I go daily into the world simply to be with the miraculous range of human and nonhuman creatures, to observe what is unfolding, to attend to what is too often ignored. Out of this act of paying attention, I write my poems, trying to spend a few hours at my desk each day.

After a few years I begin to see the patterns of what the act of paying attention has afforded me. Once I feel the body of a book beginning to take shape, I place poems on the floor of my office and start to see what happens when a poem makes neighbors with another poem. It's a bit like chemical reactions. Just as individual images or sounds in a poem, when juxtaposed with other images or sounds in the same poem, cause a reaction between them, so do individual poems in a collection. It's fun to see how a poem will be transformed when it finds a particular place in a collection.

Many of the individual poems in the collection were previously published in a variety of literary publications. How do you handle submitting your poems?

I try to keep the act of writing and all such a process entails separate from the idea of publication. I write my poems for myself—a form of meditation or prayer, a way of thinking—and I also write them with my closest friends and family in mind. After that, I'm thrilled if a poem makes its way into the world to be published and read by strangers. But I don't want the idea of publication to control or change the way a poem is created.

Having said that, I use the other half of my brain to be fairly orderly and efficient in sending the work out. I try to send to magazines and journals whose work I've read. A good way to find magazines or journals that might be amenable to your work is to read the acknowledgments page in books of poetry you've connected with. After you have a list of places to send, get the poems in the mail and get back to writing.

This same half of my brain also deals with the rejection. I remind myself when I receive the endless rejections that come every writer's way that the statistical probability of getting a poem accepted is incredibly low. Thus, when I get a rejection, I read the poems again and if I think they are still working, I get them quickly back into the mail to another journal. A poem can't be published unless it's in the hands of editors for it to be considered.

You teach creative writing, in addition to American literature and environmental studies. Could you share one or two common areas in which most students need improvement?

I truly enjoy teaching. I've been very fortunate to work with some amazing students. In fact, just this past two years, four of my former students have published first books of poems with very fine presses.

What I've noticed in my 27 years of teaching—I taught junior high and high school English before receiving my Ph.D. 19 years ago—is a decline in reading. No mystery there, given the radical technological shifts. But if someone wishes to be a writer, there's no substitute for reading the best from the past and the best from the present.

I've also noticed a shift away from delayed gratification. In a consumeristic culture, we're used to desiring something and then purchasing it. No delay to our gratification at all. However, writing demands patience. Writing rewards self-discipline, delayed gratification, the ability to toil for days, for months, even years, to finally make that poem or story "work."

I suppose this is similar to training for an athletic event. If someone was hoping to run a 10k race, for example, they would need to put in time running on a daily basis. Many days the runs will not be great, but they're still necessary. You never know the day you will show up and things will click and your body feels unbelievably good and suddenly you are running effortlessly, turning in your best time.

Like an athlete, I think you have to show up to your desk, knowing that many days will be a slog, nothing seeming to work. But one of those days you'll show up and the fantastical will happen at the desk. It's kept me coming back to my desk for many years now.

I like to share poetic forms on the Poetic Asides blog. Do you have a favorite form?

I don't think I can pick one favorite form, but I can name two that I enjoy reading. (I don't claim to be a good practitioner of either!) The ghazal as practiced or recreated by such contemporary poets as Robert Bly, Galway Kinnell and Jim Harrison, and the sonnet, especially as Gerard Manley Hopkins practiced it.

Could you describe your writing process?

I think I've described quite a bit of this above, but I might add that reading other people's poetry is instrumental to my writing process, as is looking at visual art. I see art as a way of not only expressing something interior in oneself, but also as a way of having a conversation with other artists (living or dead) and their art work. Many poems I've written have begun because of a line or image in a poem, some music I'm hearing in a line, that reminds me of, or calls forth, a narrative or a phrase or an image from my own experience.

I'm a free verse poet, but I love all kinds of sound play. Sound is one structuring device in my poems that shapes what the poem will become. I also enjoy experimenting with different forms that grow organically out of the content and sound play. Thus, my work does take on different shapes on the page, addressing the issue of white space and order/disorder.

One poet no one knows but should—who is it?

I'm going to cheat again. I can't name just one. Sadly, there are so many poets we don't know about because it's difficult to find a bookstore where you can go browse 100 books of poetry that were published in a given year.

So here's a list of poets whose work I truly respect and that many people may not have heard of: David Shumate, Natalie Diaz, Ross Gay, Chris Dombrowski, K.A. Hays, Austin Smith, Nathaniel Perry, Rose McLarney, Jack Ridl, Mary Rose O'Reilley, Dan Gerber, Amy Fleury, and Harry Humes.

And that list only scratches the surface of writers I wish I could tell everyone about.

Who (or what) are you currently reading?

Here's a list of the books that I've either read or am currently reading this summer: In poetry, *The Whole Field Still Moving Inside It,* by Molly Bahsaw; *The Glad Hand of God Still Points Backward,* by Rachel Mennies; *Revising the Storm,* by Geffrey Davis; *It's Day Being Gone,* by Rose McLarney; *Hum,* by Jamaal May; in fiction, *Brown Dog* and *The Road Home,* by Jim Harrison; *Blasphemy,* by Sherman Alexie; *Swamplandiaia!,* by Karen Russell; *Eight Mile High,* by Jim Daniels; *Light Action in the Caribbean,* by Barry Lopez; *The Plover,* by Brian Doyle; in nonfiction, *Distant Neighbors: The Selected Letters of Wendell Berry and Gary Snyder; A North Country Life* by Sydney Lea; *A Fly Fisherman's Blue Ridge,* by Christopher Camuto; *Life Everlasting: The Animal Way of Death,* by Bernd Heinrich.

And, of course, I'm always taking off the shelf books of poems to read a poem or two in the morning by writers I return to again and again. They're my sustenance.

If you could only share one piece of advice with fellow poets, what would it be?

I see many people get caught up in trends, writing work they think will be considered hip, publishable. I have no trouble with experimentation, with the creation of new schools of poetry, poems that push our understanding of what poetry might be. But, again, I'm referring to our hyper-consumeristic culture and the ways that mindset bleeds into the world of poetry in negative ways.

We all become dust and our books will become dust, too. (Or digital files to be lost in the grand cosmos of the digital multi-verse!) I don't say this to depress my fellow poets. I say it to remind myself (and others) that no one can predict who will be read 50 years from now, 100 years from now. So the question then becomes: what art truly moves me, and what art do I wish to spend my time creating, sending into the world, hoping it reaches some other person and impacts them in a way that changes them, moves them?

I've had many poems change the way I live. I suppose that's the kind of poem I'm interested in writing. Whether that poem ultimately becomes dust and is forgotten doesn't matter. It's life in the here-and-now that matters. I suppose such comments are born out of my conviction that poetry is an integral part of the pattern of human community. So what kind of poem do you wish to send to that human community?

POETIC FORMS

by Robert Lee Brewer

Not every poet likes the idea of writing in poetic forms, but for many poets—including myself—poetic forms are a sort of fun challenge. Whether playing with a sestina or working haiku, I find that attempting poetic forms often forces me into corners that make me think differently than if I'm just writing in free verse.

If you don't have any—or much—experience with poetic forms, I encourage you to peruse the following list and try them. If you are very familiar with poetic forms, I hope the following list can act as a reference for when you're unsure of the rhyme scheme for a triolet versus a kyrielle—or shadorma.

Have fun poeming!

ABSTRACT POETRY

Apparently, *abstract* was a term used by Dame Edith Sitwell to describe poems in her book *Facade*. Abstract (or sound) poetry is more about how sounds, rhythms, and textures evoke emotions than about the actual meanings of words.

Acrostic poetry

Acrostic poetry is very easy and fun. The most basic form spells words out on the left-hand side of the page using the first letter of each line. For instance,

> *I like to write*
> *Acrostic poems*
> *Mostly because*
> *Reading them*
> *Out loud is*
> *Bound to be fun.*

If you notice, the first letter of every line makes the simple sentence, "I am Rob." It's very simple, and you can make it as difficult as you want—where the fun part begins.

The brave at heart can even try double acrostics—that is, spelling things out using the first and last letter of each line.

ALPHABET POETRY

There are many different ways to write an alphabet poem. You can write a poem in which the first letter of each word is a different letter of the alphabet. A tactic for writing this poem is to write out the alphabet ahead of time so that you can pay attention to which letters have been used and which letters are still up for grabs. Of course, you can also do this consecutively through the alphabet.

Another method for alphabet poems is to go through the alphabet using the first letter of the first word for each line.

Poets can always flip the alphabet, too. That is, instead of going A to Z, write alphabet poems from Z to A. It's all about having fun and stretching your mind. Kind of like school.

ANAGRAMMATIC POETRY

In Christian Bok's comments about his poem "Vowels" in *The Best American Poetry 2007*, he writes, "'Vowels' is an anagrammatic text, permuting the fixed array of letters found only in the title. 'Vowels' appears in my book *Eunoia*, a lipogrammatic suite of stories, in which each vowel appears by itself in its own chapter." So an anagrammatic poem uses only the letters used in the title.

For instance, if I titled a poem "Spread," it could use only words like red, dresses, drape, spare, pear, pressed, etc.

The real challenge with this kind of poem is first picking a word that has at least a couple vowels and a good mix of consonants. Then, brainstorm all the words you can think of using only those letters (as many times as you wish, of course).

The Blitz Poem

The blitz poem was created by Robert Keim and is a 50-line poem of short phrases and images. Here are the rules:

- Line 1 should be one short phrase or image (like "build a boat")
- Line 2 should be another short phrase or image using the same first word as the first word in Line 1 (something like "build a house")
- Lines 3 and 4 should be short phrases or images using the last word of Line 2 as their first words (so Line 3 might be "house for sale" and Line 4 might be "house for rent")
- Lines 5 and 6 should be short phrases or images using the last word of Line 4 as their first words, and so on until you've made it through 48 lines
- Line 49 should be the last word of Line 48
- Line 50 should be the last word of Line 47
- The title of the poem should be three words long and follow this format: (first word of Line 3) (preposition or conjunction) (first word of line 47)
- There should be no punctuation

There are a lot of rules, but it's a pretty simple and fun poem to write once you get the hang of it.

THE BOP

The Bop is a poetic form that was developed by poet Afaa Michael Weaver at a Cave Canem summer retreat. Here are the basic rules:

- 3 stanzas
- Each stanza is followed by a refrain
- First stanza is 6 lines long and presents a problem

- Second stanza is 8 lines long and explores or expands the problem
- Third stanza is 6 lines long and either presents a solution or documents the failed attempt to resolve the problem

CASCADE POEM

The cascade poem was a form invented by Udit Bhatia. For the cascade poem, a poet takes each line from the first stanza of a poem and makes those the final lines of each stanza afterward. Beyond that, there are no additional rules for rhyming, meter, etc.

So to help this make sense, here's what a cascade poem with a tercet would look like:

A
B
C

a
b
A

c
d
B

e
f
C

A quatrain cascade would look so:

A
B
C
D

a
b
c
A

d
e
f
B

g
h
i
C

j
k
l
D

And, of course, you can make this even more involved if you want.

CONCRETE POETRY

Concrete poetry is one of the more experimental poetic forms available to poets. Concrete poems use space and sound to communicate the meanings of the words. Words can cover other words; and the poem has trouble standing without the structure. Concrete poetry is more visual than other poetic forms.

Of course, concrete poetry has plenty of detractors because of the weight structure has on the words, but as much thought goes into concrete poetry as any other form.

ELEGY

An elegy is a song of sorrow or mourning—often for someone who has died. However, poets being an especially creative and contrary group have also written elegies for the ends of things, whether a life, a love affair, a great era, a football season, etc.

While there are such things as elegiac couplets and elegiac stanzas, form does not rule an elegy; content *is* king (or queen) when writing elegies.

EPITAPHS

The epitaph is a note meant to appear on a tombstone. From the Greek, epitaph means "upon a tomb." Since it has to fit on a tombstone, this note is usually brief and often rhymes. Some epitaphs are funny; most are serious. Most try to get the reader thinking about the subject of the tombstone.

THE FIB

Fibonacci poetry was founded by Gregory K. Pincus as a 6-line poem that follows the Fibonacci sequence for syllable count per line.

For the 6-line poem that means:
- 1 syllable for first line
- 1 syllable for second line
- 2 syllables for third
- 3 syllables for fourth
- 5 syllables for fifth
- 8 syllables for sixth

There are variations where the Fibonacci expands even further with each line, but to understand how to accomplish this, you need to understand the Fibonacci math sequence of starting with 0 and 1 and then adding the last two numbers together to add to infinity.

$$0+1=1$$
$$1+1=2$$
$$1+2=3$$
$$2+3=5$$
$$3+5=8$$
$$5+8=13$$
$$8+13=21$$
$$13+21=34$$

and so on and so forth...

Anyway, those lines can easily get more and more unwieldy the more you let them expand. So, there's another variation that has taken flight in making Fibonacci poems that ascend and descend in syllables. For poets who also like mathematics, this is definitely an interesting form to get your mind working.

FOUND POEMS

Found poetry is all about taking words not originally meant to be a poem (as they originally appeared) and turning those words into a poem anyway. You can use newspaper articles, bits of conversation, instructions, recipes, letters, e-mails, direct mail and even spam e-mail.

With found poetry, you do not alter the original words, but you can make line breaks and cut out excess before and/or after the poem you've "found." The power of found poetry is how words not intended as poetry can take on new and profound meanings as found poems.

Ghazal

The ghazal (pronounced "guzzle") is a Persian poetic form. The original form was very simple: five to 15 couplets using the same rhyme with the poet's name in the final couplet. The main themes were usually love or drinking wine.

Contemporary ghazals have abandoned the rhymes and insertion of the poet's name in the final couplet. In fact, even the themes of love and drinking wine are no longer mandatory—as the poem now just needs the couplets which are complete thoughts on their own but also all work together to explore a common theme (whatever that might be).

If you wish to stay traditional though, here's the rhyme scheme you would follow:

a

a

b

a

c

a

and so on to the final stanza (depending upon how many you include).

Many traditional ghazals will also incorporate a refrain at the end of each couplet that could be one word or a phrase.

HAIKU

Haiku is descended from the Japanese *renga* form, which was often a collaborative poem comprised of many short stanzas. The opening stanza of the renga was called *hokku*. Eventually, haiku evolved from the leftover and most interesting hokku that were not used in renga.

Most haiku deal with natural topics. They avoid metaphor and simile. While most poets agree that haiku have three short lines, there is some disagreement on how long those lines are. For instance, some traditional haiku poets insist on 17 syllables in lines of 5/7/5. Other contemporary haiku poets feel that the first and third lines can be any length as long as they're shorter than the middle line.

Haiku do not have to include complete sentences or thoughts. They do not have titles. The best haiku contain some shift in the final line.

HAY(NA)KU

Hay(na)ku is a very simple poetic form created in 2003 by poet Eileen Tabios. Hay(na)ku is a 3-line poem with one word in the first line, two words in the second, and three in the third. There are no restrictions beyond this.

There are already some variations of this new poetic form. For instance, a reverse hay(na)ku has lines of three, two, and one word(s) for lines one, two, and three respectively. Also, multiple hay(na)ku can be chained together to form longer poems.

INSULT POETRY

There are no hard and fast rules to the insult poem, but it's usually done in a joking (all in good fun) fashion as opposed to seriously trying to annoy anyone. Many insult poems also have a repetitive form or recurring method of delivering the insults. The insult poem is a good way to show just how clever you are (or think you are). But beware writing them! Once you attack someone (even in jest), you are suddenly fair game to receive an insult poem in retaliation.

KYRIELLE

The kyrielle is a French four-line stanza form—with 8 syllables per line—that has a refrain in the fourth line. Often, there is a rhyme scheme in the poem consisting of the following possibilities:

- aabb
- abab
- aaab
- abcb

The poem can be as long as you wish and as short as two stanzas (otherwise, the refrain is not really a refrain, is it?), and, as with many French forms, it is very nice for stretching your poetic muscles.

LIMERICKS

The origin of the limerick is shrouded in some mystery, but most sources seem to point to the early 18th century—one theory being that soldiers returning from France to the Irish town of Limerick started the form, the other theory pointing to the 1719 publication of *Mother Goose Melodies for Children*. Either way, Edward Lear popularized the form in the mid-19th century.

Basically, the limerick is a five-line poem consisting of a tercet split by a couplet. That is, lines 1, 2, and 5 are a bit longer and rhyme, while the shorter lines of 3 and 4 rhyme. After studying many effective limericks, there is not a precise syllable count per line, but the norm is about 8-10 syllables in the longer lines and around 6 syllables in the shorter lines.

LIST POEMS

A list poem (also known as a catalog poem) is a poem that lists things, whether names, places, actions, thoughts, images, etc. Even a grocery list could turn into a poem with this form.

LUNE

The lune is also known as the American Haiku. It was first created by the poet Robert Kelly and was a result of Kelly's frustration with English haiku. After much experimentation, he settled on a 13-syllable, self-contained poem that has 5 syllables in the first line, 3 syllables in the second line and 5 syllables in the final line.

Unlike haiku, there are no other rules. No need for a cutting word. Rhymes are fine; subject matter is open. While there are fewer syllables to use, this form has a little more freedom.

There is also a variant lune created by the poet Jack Collom. His form is also a self-contained tercet, but it's word-based (not syllable-based) and has the structure of 3 words in the first line, 5 words in the second line and 3 words in the final line.

MONOTETRA

The monotetra is a poetic form developed by Michael Walker. Here are the basic rules:

- Comprised of quatrains (four-line stanzas) in tetrameter (four metrical feet) for a total of 8 syllables per line
- Each quatrain consists of mono-rhymed lines (so each line in the first stanza has the same type of rhyme, as does each line in the second stanza, etc.)
- The final line of each stanza repeats the same four syllables
- This poem can be as short as one quatrain and as long as a poet wishes

Personally, I like the rhyme scheme and the repetitive final line of each stanza.

OCCASIONAL POEMS

There are no specific guidelines for occasional poems except that they mark a specific occasion. The poems can be long or short, serious or humorous, good or bad—just as long as they mark the occasion. Good occasions for poems include birthdays, weddings and holidays.

ODES

The ode is a poetic form formed for flattery. There are three types of odes: the Horation; the Pindaric; and the Irregular.

The Horation ode (named for the Latin poet, Horace) contains one stanza pattern that repeats throughout the poem—usually 2 or 4 lines in length.

The Pindaric ode (named for the Greek poet, Pindar) is made up of a pattern of three stanzas called triads. This type of ode can be composed of several triads, but the first (the strophe) and the second (antistrophe) should be identical metrically with the third (epode) wandering off on its own metrical path.

The irregular ode (named for no one in particular) does away with formalities and focuses on the praising aspect of the ode.

PALINDROME POETRY

The palindrome seems like a simple enough form—until you actually try to write a good one. The rules are simple enough:

1. You must use the same words in the first half of the poem as the second half, but
2. Reverse the order for the second half, and
3. Use a word in the middle as a bridge from the first half to the second half of the poem.

At first, the simplicity of the rules made me feel like this would be easy enough to do, but I ran into problems almost immediately. For instance, you can't start the poem with the word "the" unless you plan to end the poem on the word "the." And just because something makes sense in the first half doesn't guarantee it'll pass the same test on the way back.

PANTOUM

The pantoum is a poetic form originating in Malay where poets write quatrains (4-line stanzas) with an *abab* rhyme scheme and repeat lines 2 and 4 in the previous stanza as lines 1 and 3 in the next stanza.

Poets differ on how to treat the final quatrain: Some poets repeat lines 1 and 3 of the original quatrain as lines 2 and 4 in the final quatrain; other poets invert lines 1 and 3 so that the beginning line of the poem is also the final line of the poem.

Also, the pantoum can be as long or as short as you wish it to be, though mathematically it does require at least 4 lines.

PARADELLE

The paradelle is a poetic form that Billy Collins originally introduced as "one of the more demanding French forms," though eventually Collins fessed up that he created it as a joke.

However, Collins was not kidding about the demanding rules of the paradelle. Here they are:

- The paradelle is a 4-stanza poem.
- Each stanza consists of 6 lines.
- For the first 3 stanzas, the 1st and 2nd lines should be the same; the 3rd and 4th lines should also be the same; and the 5th and 6th lines should be composed of all the words from the 1st and 3rd lines and only the words from the 1st and 3rd lines.
- The final stanza should be composed of all the words in the 5th and 6th lines of the first three stanzas and only the words from the 5th and 6th lines of the first three stanzas.

PARODY POEMS

A parody poem is one that pokes fun at another poem or poet. The best parodies are those that are easily recognizable—and funny, of course.

RONDEAU

The rondeau is a form that has a refrain and rhymes. The traditional rondeau is a poem consisting of 3 stanzas, 13 original lines, and 2 refrains (of the first line of the poem) with 8 to 10 syllables per line and an A/B rhyme scheme. The skeleton of the traditional rondeau looks like this:

A(R)
A

B
B
A

A
A
B
A(R)

A
A
B
B
A
A(R)

There are variations of the rondeau, including the rondeau redouble, rondel, rondel double, rondelet, roundel, and roundelay. Of course, poets tend to break the rules on each of these as well, which is what poets like to do.

SESTINA

The sestina is one of my favorite forms. You pick 6 words, rotate them as the end words in 6 stanzas and then include 2 of the end words per line in your final stanza.

Let's pick 6 random words: bears, carving, dynamite, hunters, mothers, blessing.

Here's how the end words would go:

Stanza 1

Line 1-bears (A)
Line 2-carving (B)
Line 3-dynamite (C)
Line 4-hunters (D)
Line 5-mothers (E)
Line 6-blessing (F)

Stanza 2

Line 7-blessing (F)
Line 8-bears (A)
Line 9-mothers (E)
Line 10-carving (B)
Line 11-hunters (D)
Line 12-dynamite (C)

Stanza 3

Line 13-dynamite (C)
Line 14-blessing (F)
Line 15-hunters (D)
Line 16-bears (A)
Line 17-carving (B)
Line 18-mothers (E)

Stanza 4

Line 19-mothers (E)
Line 20-dynamite (C)
Line 21-carving (B)
Line 22-blessing (F)
Line 23-bears (A)
Line 24-hunters (D)

Stanza 5

Line 25-hunters (D)
Line 26-mothers (E)
Line 27-bears (A)
Line 28-dynamite (C)
Line 29-blessing (F)
Line 30-carving (B)

Stanza 6

Line 31-carving (B)
Line 32-hunters (D)
Line 33-blessing (F)
Line 34-mothers (E)
Line 35-dynamite (C)
Line 36-bears (A)

Stanza 7

Line 37-bears (A), carving (B)

Line 38-dynamite (C), hunters (D)
Line 39-mothers (E), blessing (F)

While many poets try to write sestinas in iambic pentameter, that is not a requirement. Also, when choosing your six end words, it does help to choose words that can be altered if needed to help keep the flow of the poem going.

SEVENLING

The sevenling was created by Roddy Lumsden. Here are the rules:

- The sevenling is a 7-line poem (clever, huh?) split into three stanzas.
- The first three lines should contain an element of three. It could be three connected or contrasting statements, a list of three details or names, or something else along these lines. The three things can take up all three lines or be contained anywhere within the stanza.
- The second three lines should also contain an element of three. Same deal as the first stanza, but the two stanzas do not need to relate to each other directly.
- The final line/stanza should act as either narrative summary, punchline, or unusual juxtaposition.
- Titles are not required. But when titles are present, they should be titled Sevenling followed by the first few words in parentheses.
- Tone should be mysterious, offbeat or disturbing.
- Poem should have ambience which invites guesswork from the reader.

SHADORMA

Shadorma is a Spanish 6-line syllabic poem of 3/5/3/3/7/5 syllable lines respectively.

SKELTONIC POETRY

Skeltonic verse is named after the poet John Skelton (1460-1529), who wrote short rhyming lines that just sort of go on from one rhyme to the next for however long a poet wishes to take it. Most skeltonic poems average less than six words a line, but keeping the short rhymes moving down the page is the real key to this form.

SONNET

The sonnet is a 14-line poem that usually rhymes and is often written in iambic pentameter, though not always. Over time, this Italian poem has been pushed to its limits and some contemporary sonnets abandon many of the general guidelines.

The two most famous forms of the sonnet are the *Shakespearean Sonnet* (named after William Shakespeare) and the *Petrarcan Sonnet* (named after Francesco Petrarca). The rhyme scheme for a Shakespearean Sonnet is:

a
b
a
b

c
d
c
d

e
f
e
f

g
g

The rhyme scheme for the Petrarcan Sonnet is a little more complicated. The first eight lines (or octave) are always rhymed abbaabba. But the final six lines (or sestet) can be rhymed any number of ways: cdcdcd, cdedce, ccdccd, cdecde, or cddcee. Of course, this offers a little more flexibility near the end of the poem.

But sonnets don't necessarily need to be Shakespearean or Petrarcan to be considered sonnets. In fact, there are any number of other sonnet varieties.

A few extra notes about the sonnet:

- A crown of sonnets is made by seven sonnets. The last line of each sonnet must be used as the first line of the next until the seventh sonnet. The last line of that seventh sonnet must be the first line of the first sonnet.
- A sonnet redouble is a sequence of 15 sonnets. Each line from the first sonnet is used (in order) as the the last line of the following 14 sonnets.

TANKA

If a haiku is usually (mistakenly) thought of as a 3-line, 5-7-5 syllable poem, then the tanka would be a 5-line, 5-7-5-7-7 syllable poem. However, as with haiku, it's better to think of a tanka as a 5-line poem with 3 short lines (lines 2, 4, 5) and 2 very short lines (lines 1 and 3).

While imagery is still important in tanka, the form is a little more conversational than haiku at times. It also allows for the use of poetic devices such as metaphor and personification (2 big haiku no-no's).

TRIOLET

The triolet (TREE-o-LAY) has 13th-century French roots linked to the rondeau or "round" poem. Like other French forms, the triolet is great for repetition, because the first line of the poem is used three times and the second line is used twice. If you do the math on this 8-line poem, you'll realize there are only three other lines to write: two of those lines rhyme with the first line, the other rhymes with the second line.

A diagram of the triolet would look like this:

A (first line)
B (second line)
a (rhymes with first line)
A (repeat first line)
a (rhymes with first line)
b (rhymes with second line)
A (repeat first line)
B (repeat second line)

VILLANELLE

The villanelle, like the other French forms, incorporates rhyme and repetition. This French form was actually adapted from Italian folk songs (villanella) about rural life. One of the more famous contemporary villanelles is "Do Not Go Gentle Into That Good Night," by Dylan Thomas.

The villanelle consists of five tercets and a quatrain with line lengths of 8-10 syllables. The first and third lines of the first stanza become refrains that repeat throughout the poem. It looks like this:

A(1)
b
A(2)

a
b
A(1)

a
b
A(2)

a
b
A(1)

a
b
A(2)

a
b
A(1)
A(2)

101 POETRY PROMPTS

by Robert Lee Brewer

WRITE A POEM ABOUT A FIRST OR SERIES OF FIRSTS. This first could be a first love, first job, first funeral, first marriage, or first poem.

PUT YOURSELF IN SOMEONE (OR SOME-THING) ELSE'S SKIN AND WRITE A POEM ABOUT THE EXPERIENCE. WHO (OR WHAT) EVER YOU BECOME, MAKE THAT THE TITLE OF THE POEM. If you're Buddy Holly, your poem should be titled "Buddy Holly."

WRITE A WORRY POEM. Anything that causes you worry can be used to help you write this poem. Are you worried about paying the bills? Asking a friend on a date? Circus clowns?

RECORD ALL THE DETAILS OF YOUR DAY AND GENERATE A POEM FROM THAT MA-TERIAL. To make the poem interesting, you probably do NOT want to just list out every-thing from the beginning of the day to the end. But then again, maybe you could prove me wrong on that assumption.

WRITE A RAMBLE POEM. That is, write a poem in which you just start rambling with-out worrying about where you're headed. Very interesting things can happen in these poems. Then, go back through and revise.

Pick a word (any word) and write a poem about it. If you wish, you can make that word the title of your poem. Look up the definition. Think about how the word is used by people and in what situations. Then, write.

WRITE A LOCATION POEM. This poem could be about a room, a city, a country or some other specific place. The location you choose could be a place you've actually vis-ited, or just one you'd like to see someday—or that you've created in your imagination.

WRITE AN APOLOGY POEM. If you're not the type of poet who apologizes for anything, then pretend that someone is apologizing to you in the poem.

LISTEN TO A SONG (OR TWO) AND WRITE A POEM IN RESPONSE. Your poem can take the song to another level, or it can level an argument against the lyrics. Or your poem can spring into a completely new direction.

TAKE THE PHRASE "HOW (BLANK) BEHAVES," REPLACE THE BLANK WITH A WORD OR PHRASE, MAKE THE NEW PHRASE THE TITLE OF YOUR POEM, AND THEN, WRITE YOUR POEM. Sample titles might include: "How My Poem Behaves," "How Robert Lee Brewer Behaves," or "How Children Behave." Don't be afraid to misbehave with this prompt.

....

Take the phrase "I'm so over (blank)," replace the blank with a word or phrase, make the new phrase the title of your poem, and then, write the poem. Example titles: "I'm so over time sheets" or "I'm so over rainy days."

....

WRITE AN INSULT POEM. If you get along with everyone you meet, this might be a tough one to write. However, if you can find something to criticize in everyone you know, then this prompt alone could give an entire collection worth of material.

GIVE YOUR POEM A TWIST ENDING. The easiest way to accomplish a twist ending

might be to write a narrative poem that takes a left when the reader was expecting a right. But it might also be a twist in rhyme scheme, form, or something else completely unexpected.

WRITE A POEM ABOUT A MEMORY OF YOU THAT YOU DON'T PERSONALLY REMEMBER. Maybe a friend or family member remembers something when you were small or a little too intoxicated or asleep. Write about this memory that you've had to hear through another.

FIND A LINE THAT YOU REALLY ENJOY AND USE IT AS THE FIRST LINE OF YOUR POEM. Be sure to give credit to the source that provided you with the first line.

WRITE A LOVE POEM. That's simple enough, isn't it?

PICK AN IMAGE AND WRITE A POEM ABOUT IT. The image could be a painting, a photograph, graffiti, or something else. If you pick a famous image, you may want to identify it in the title of your poem.

WRITE A SNOOPING (OR EAVESDROPPING) POEM. Pay attention to conversations from the next table or room. Watch people from a balcony or behind a bush. Just don't do anything to get yourself arrested or hit with a restraining order.

WRITE A POEM ABOUT GETTING OLDER. It doesn't matter how old you are, you're aging by the minute. The longer you wait to write this poem the older you'll be when you finally get around to it. So poem.

WRITE A NATURE POEM. This poem can celebrate trees, creeks, birds, and clouds. Or it can dive into the psychological natures of people. Or it can attack the nature of writing poetry.

TAKE THE PHRASE "I'M SO OVER (BLANK)," REPLACE THE BLANK WITH A WORD OR PHRASE, MAKE THE NEW PHRASE THE TITLE OF YOUR POEM, AND THEN, WRITE THE POEM. Example titles include: "I'm so over time sheets," "I'm so over bad poetry," or "I'm so over rainy days."

WRITE AN OCCUPATIONAL POEM. Are you a lawyer or paralegal? Write about working in the law field. Do you bus tables or wait on hungry customers? Write about working in a restaurant. Or imagine what it's like to have a job that you don't have.

WRITE A POEM THAT IS ONLY ONE SIDE OF A TWO-SIDED CONVERSATION. Leave the other half of the conversation to the imagination. To help you achieve this poem, you could write both sides of the conversation and then edit out one of the voices.

PICK AN ANIMAL AND WRITE A POEM ABOUT IT. In fact, make the animal the title of your poem so that readers know your subject.

WRITE AN EXERCISE POEM. Either you love it or you hate it, but anyone can write a poem about the act of working out. Plus, there are so many ways to exercise from hitting the gym to stretching or from running around a lake to swimming in a pool.

VISIT A LANDMARK AND WRITE A POEM ABOUT IT. If you're not able to get out of the house, then visit the landmark through a book or the Internet. There are many ways to experience landmarks these days.

WRITE AN ORIGIN POEM. This poem could be about the origin of a superhero or just a regular person. It could be about the origin of a problem or a solution.

THINK ABOUT SOMETHING THAT'S MISSING AND WRITE A POEM ABOUT IT. The missing something might be a physical object (like your keys or a sock) or something more abstract (like an emotion or an idea).

Think about a routine you have and write a poem about it. Or write about the routines of other people (or animals). The tricky part is to make the poem anything but routine.

WRITE AN OUTSIDER POEM. The outsider in the poem could be yourself or someone else. You could even write a poem about an animal or plant that is considered an outsider.

WRITE A CLEAN POEM. This poem could be about cleaning something or something that's clean. Or it could just be a poem that uses clean language. For extra credit, write a dirty poem.

TAKE THE PHRASE "THE PROBLEM WITH (BLANK)," REPLACE THE BLANK WITH A WORD OR PHRASE, MAKE THE NEW PHRASE THE TITLE OF YOUR POEM, AND THEN, WRITE YOUR POEM. Example titles include: "The Problem With Poets," "The Problem With Money," or "The Problem With Love."

WRITE A POEM WITH AN INTERACTION. The interaction could be verbal, physical or emotional. For instance, an interaction could be as simple as two people making eye contact and then looking away from each other.

THINK ABOUT A ROUTINE YOU HAVE AND WRITE A POEM ABOUT IT. Or write about the routines of other people (or animals). The tricky part is to make the poem anything but routine.

....

Write an angry poem. Even the most mild-mannered poets surely get upset from time to time. Unleash the fury with a poem.

....

PICK A DAY OF THE WEEK AND WRITE A POEM ABOUT IT. Or write a short seven-poem collection titled Days of the Week. Explore how a Friday poem might be different from a Tuesday or Sunday poem.

WRITE A REBIRTH POEM. This poem could tackle the rebirth of a person's identity or the changing of a season. There are many ways in which animals, people, plants and ideas are reborn.

SELECT AN OBJECT AND WRITE A POEM ABOUT IT. Think of William Carlos Williams' "The Red Wheelbarrow." Of course, pick your own object and do it in your own style.

WRITE A POEM OF REGRET. Think of something you wish you'd done differently. Write about someone else's regrets. This might be a perfect opportunity to write a blues poem, but a hopeful poem with regret may make it even more interesting.

INCORPORATE A HOBBY INTO A POEM. There aren't enough poems about collecting stamps and bird spotting. Write an ode to collecting baseball cards or dolls.

WRITE A POSTCARD POEM. In about the same confined space you would have to scribble a message on a postcard, write a poem. To make it even more realistic, address your poem directly to a reader.

TAKE THE PHRASE "NEVER (BLANK)," REPLACE THE BLANK WITH A WORD OR PHRASE, MAKE THE NEW PHRASE THE TITLE OF YOUR POEM, AND THEN, WRITE THE POEM. Example titles include: "Never Say Never," "Never Leave Home Without a Pen," or "Never Again."

WRITE A MISCOMMUNICATION POEM. Poems are a form of communication between the poet and the reader. However, good poetry can come from the miscommunication between one character and another.

LOOK AT SOMETHING FAMILIAR IN A NEW WAY OR FROM A DIFFERENT ANGLE AND WRITE A POEM ABOUT YOUR NEW PERSPECTIVE. The something familiar could be a physical object (like a statue or building) or it could be something more abstract (like a relationship or daily routine). Just look for something new in the familiar.

WRITE A POEM OF LONGING. IN THIS POEM, HAVE THE NARRATOR OR A CHARACTER PINING AWAY FOR SOMEONE (OR SOMETHING) ELSE. Some might mistake this for a love poem, but people could be longing for a vacation on a tropical island or a bowl of chocolate ice cream.

PICK A COLOR, MAKE THAT THE TITLE OF YOUR POEM, AND WRITE THE POEM. Your color-titled poem can directly investigate the color itself, or the color could suggest a mood that sets the scene for whatever happens in your poem.

WRITE A POSITIVE POEM. Pulling off an effective happy poem may seem difficult for some, but positive poems are often very refreshing for readers. However, if you want an extra challenge, write a negative poem too.

WRITE A SLOW POEM. This is the perfect opportunity to write about turtles and snails or the slow drip of syrup. Or rush hour traffic.

WRITE A GROWTH POEM. This poem could be about physical growth (like growing a few inches or growing hair) or emotional growth. It could even be about a normal-sized person who comes into contact with radiation and turns into the 50-foot Poet. Or something along those lines.

PICK AN INVENTION AND WRITE A POEM ABOUT IT. The invention could be something real, such as an airplane or food processor. The invention could also be something not so real, such as a time travel machine or teleportation device.

WRITE A SLIPPERY POEM. Maybe the subject matter of this poem is on a slippery slope. Or maybe the poem is about slipping on banana peels or black ice.

TAKE THE PHRASE "IF ONLY (BLANK)," REPLACE THE BLANK WITH A WORD OR PHRASE, MAKE THE NEW PHRASE THE TITLE OF YOUR POEM, AND THEN, WRITE THE POEM. Possible titles include: "If Only It Didn't Snow," "If Only We Remembered to Change the Oil," or "If Only This Poem Were Easier to Revise."

WRITE A POEM ABOUT A MEMORY. Sound familiar? Earlier, I had you write about a memory that you did not remember. However, I want you to write about something you do remember for this memory poem.

CHOOSE A SHAPE AND WRITE A POEM ABOUT IT. For instance, you could write a poem about a crescent moon or box kite. There are a lot of simple and complex shapes out there, and some of them can even be used to describe other people or objects.

Write a construction poem. It's your choice whether you want to write about building construction, highway construction or working with construction paper.

PICK A PLANT AND WRITE ABOUT IT. There are so many plant species on this planet that you're bound to find one that's never been tackled before or on which you can put a new spin.

WRITE A POEM INVOLVING LINES. I know, I know, all poems have lines. Well, you could write about poetic lines, sure, but I also encourage you to write about lines drawn in the sand, lines used in architecture, lines used in sports, or lines used in a sports bar.

CONSIDER SOMETHING THAT WILL AL-WAYS STICK WITH YOU AND WRITE A POEM ABOUT IT. Maybe it's something that happened to you when you were young. Maybe it's a good thing or a bad thing. Maybe it's just a random thing that someone said that has always stuck with you and even played an important role in decisions you've made afterward.

....

Write a poem filled with noise. The noise could be loud, but also soft. Noise could be something mechanical or sounds that build in nature. (Note: I do not advise writing a poem about whether trees falling alone in the forest make a sound, but that doesn't mean you can't go that route anyway.)

....

WRITE A HANGING POEM. There are a lot of things that can hang. Pick one (or more) and write about it.

WRITE AN EMERGENCY POEM. Emergencies can sometimes be a subjective thing, so the possibility for creating tension between two people in a poem is ripe in an emergency poem. Of course, there are other

emergencies that put everyone on edge, and those can be engaging too.

WRITE AN ATTACHMENT POEM. People make all manner of attachments—physical, mental and emotional. Pick one (or two) and write about them.

TAKE THE PHRASE "EVERYBODY SAYS (BLANK)," REPLACE THE BLANK WITH A WORD OR PHRASE, MAKE THE NEW PHRASE THE TITLE OF YOUR POEM, AND THEN, WRITE THE POEM. Example titles include: "Everybody Says the Same Thing," "Everybody Says I Should Quit," or "Everybody Says Things in a Foreign Language." For an alternate option, do the same thing with the phrase "Nobody Says (blank)."

WRITE AN EXPLOSION POEM. Write a poem about fireworks or having an explosion of emotion. For extra credit, write an implosion poem.

WRITE A LONELY POEM. The narrator can be lonely or another character, but there should definitely be some loneliness in the poem.

WRITE A POEM FILLED WITH NOISE. The noise could be loud, but also soft. Noise could be something mechanical or sounds that build in nature. (Note: I do not advise writing a poem about whether trees falling along in the forest make a sound, but that doesn't mean you can't go that route anyway.)

THINK ABOUT HISTORY AND WRITE A POEM ABOUT IT. The history could be ancient history, national history or personal history.

The poem could be about big concepts or a very particular snapshot in time.

WRITE A TOO MUCH INFORMATION POEM. This poem could be one in which the narrator shares a little too much personal information, or it could tackle the information overload of the Internet, social media, and smart phones.

WRITE A DEADLINE POEM. Poems and deadlines don't usually go together, which is why this prompt may deliver some good poems. If you want to put some pressure on your poeming, give this poem a deadline to be written, revised and published.

PICK AN EVENT, MAKE THAT THE TITLE OF YOUR POEM, AND THEN, WRITE THE POEM. The event could be a national celebration or a parade. It could be a local festival, an annual gathering, or even something as mundane as a weekly department meeting.

WRITE A FAREWELL POEM. This poem could be about a person leaving a group or situation, or it could be directed to a specific reader or audience.

THINK SCARY AND WRITE A HORROR POEM. Relate an urban legend. Give a new slant on timeless terror.

TAKE THE PHRASE "PARTLY (BLANK)," RE-PLACE THE BLANK WITH A WORD OR PHRASE, MAKE THE NEW PHRASE THE TITLE OF YOUR POEM, AND THEN, WRITE THE POEM. Example titles include: "Partly Cloudy," "Partly Insane," or "Partly Poetic."

WRITE A WATER POEM. Water can be a main feature of the poem, or it can just factor into the poem in an indirect way, such as a character standing next to a water fountain or a poem that takes place on a yacht.

Write a self-portrait poem. Of course, it's up to every poet whether to airbrush out blemishes or be excessively harsh (or somewhere in between), but I'd really be missing a poetic goldmine if I didn't mention that you can write about yourself.

WRITE A DEATH POEM. You could write about a specific death or consider death in general.

PICK A CITY, MAKE THAT THE TITLE OF YOUR POEM, AND THEN, WRITE THE POEM. Choose your own city, one that you've visited, or one you'd like to visit.

WRITE A SCIENCE POEM. Science encompasses a lot. In fact, science either touches or rubs up against about everything that poetry does.

SELECT A PERSON AND WRITE A POEM ABOUT HIM OR HER. The person could be a famous historical figure, such as Emily Dickinson or Abraham Lincoln, or someone from your own sphere of influence. The person could even be someone you don't personally know, but who you've mythologized over time.

WRITE A LOOKING BACK POEM. There are a couple ways to attack this poem. The narrator could be looking over past events or literally looking over his or her shoulder.

WRITE AN EVENING POEM. Pretty simple—just write a poem that takes place at night.

PICK A TOOL, MAKE THAT THE TITLE OF YOUR POEM, AND THEN, WRITE THE POEM. Tools are everywhere—from writing implements to computers and from hammers to sporks. So while there is plenty of inspiration in the workshop, tools can be found elsewhere too.

....

Write an agreement poem. In this poem, there could be an agreement made between two parties, or the narrator could agree with a statement. Or the poet could lay out a contractual agreement between him or her self and the reader.

....

WRITE A SELF-PORTRAIT POEM. Of course, it's up to every poet whether to airbrush out the blemishes or be excessively harsh (or somewhere in between), but I'd really be missing a poetic goldmine if I didn't mention that you can write about yourself.

TAKE THE PHRASE "LOOKING FOR (BLANK)," REPLACE THE BLANK WITH A WORD OR PHRASE, MAKE THE NEW PHRASE THE TI- **TLE OF YOUR POEM, AND THEN, WRITE THE POEM.** Example titles include: "Looking for Reasons to Write a Poem," "Looking for the North Pole," or "Looking for the Answer to This Question."

WRITE A HOPEFUL POEM. The poem can present a hopeful vision, or the poem can follow someone who is filled with hope. As an alternative, write a hopeless poem.

LET GO OF SOMETHING AND WRITE A POEM ABOUT IT. Let go of junk. Let go of resentments. Let go of self-loathing. Write a poem (or two) that releases something.

WRITE A CONTAINMENT POEM. The poem could cover containers like plastic baggies and cardboard boxes or containers like jails and prisons. There are also more abstract containers, such as our minds and computers.

WRITE A METAMORPHOSIS POEM. This poem is one in which the original subject changes into something else—maybe even multiple times during the poem.

TAKE A STAND ON AN ISSUE AND WRITE A POEM ABOUT IT. Maybe you can take a stand on form poems or pick a side on the political spectrum. Maybe you support public transportation—write a poem that expresses your position.

WRITE AN AGREEMENT POEM. In this poem, there could be an agreement made between two parties, or the narrator could be agreeing with a statement. Or the poet could lay out a contractual agreement between himself and the reader.

WRITE A CROSSROADS POEM. This could be a poem about a physical, mental or emotional crossroads.

THINK OF A QUESTION, MAKE THAT THE TITLE OF YOUR POEM, AND THEN, WRITE THE POEM. The poem could continue asking more questions, or it could attempt to answer the question that was posed in the title. Or it could describe a scene that is heightened by the question in the title.

WRITE A LOST AND FOUND POEM. You could focus on the actual losing and finding. Or your poem might examine how things change after something is lost—or how things change after something is found.

....

Pick a type of person and write about him or her. Your person could be a firefighter, police officer, pedestrian, mountain biker, or any number of other people.

....

TAKE THE PHRASE "BLAME THE (BLANK),"" REPLACE THE BLANK WITH A WORD OR PHRASE, MAKE THE NEW WORD PHRASE THE TITLE OF YOUR POEM, AND THEN, WRITE THE POEM. Example titles include: "Blame the Prompt," "Blame the Barry White Music," or "Blame the Scientists."

WRITE A SPACES POEM. The spaces could be physical spaces, such as an open field or a confined closet. Or the spaces could be spaces in time or logic.

PICK A NUMBER, MAKE THAT NUMBER THE TITLE OF YOUR POEM, AND THEN, WRITE YOUR POEM. Personally, I like the numbers eight and 23, but there are any number of numbers from which to choose. Sorry, I couldn't resist.

WRITE A LESSONS LEARNED POEM. Usually, you can only learn your lesson after you've made a mistake, so keep that in mind. For an alternate prompt, write a poem in which a character never learns.

IMAGINE THE WORLD WITHOUT YOU AND WRITE A POEM ABOUT IT. If this seems too self-centered to you, then you can always imagine the world without someone else and write a poem about that.

WRITE A GOOFY POEM. Who says poetry always has to be serious? It doesn't. However, if you have trouble getting silly with your verse, write a serious poem. Make it deadly serious even.

WRITE A POEM THAT REMEMBERS AN OLD RELATIONSHIP. The poem could be about a romantic relationship, but also about a long lost friend or an estranged or distant family member.

PICK A TYPE OF PERSON AND WRITE ABOUT HIM OR HER. Your person could be a firefighter, police officer, pedestrian, mountain biker, or any number of other people.

THINK ABOUT THE BIG PICTURE AND WRITE A POEM ABOUT IT. This is your chance to write a poem about what's really important in life—or what's unimportant in the big scheme of things.

WRITE A NEXT STEPS POEM. Think about what you're going to do after you write this poem, after you leave this room, after you wake up tomorrow morning.

**TAKE THE PHRASE "THE LAST (BLANK),"
REPLACE THE BLANK WITH A WORD OR
PHRASE, MAKE THE NEW PHRASE THE TI-
TLE OF YOUR POEM, AND THEN, WRITE
YOUR POEM.** Example titles include: "The Last Poem," "The Last Reader," or "The Last Cupcake."

**WRITE A POEM ABOUT ENDINGS OR FIN-
ISHES.** This poem could be about ending a relationship or finishing a poem. If you've finished this list of prompts, I challenge you to start creating your own

SCHEMATIC FOR SCULPTING LANGUAGE

by Lancelot Schaubert

As a young man, I complained I didn't get poetry. The poetry world seemed broken in two: those who rhymed and those who didn't. Rhymers chose their path either out of too much ignorance ("all I know is roses are red; violets are blue") or intelligence ("poema means 'to form' in Greek, therefore abide by forms"). Non-rhymers reacted against them, but did so without a compass, writing anything and everything as long as it didn't look, sound, or taste like a poem.

This begged the question: *Were some free verse poems even poems?*

I've come to enjoy all kinds of poems but this canyon separating poets scares many would-be-poets. Some novices stumble upon rhyming poems, something they can *see* or *hear*, and wonder, "is poetry about good sounds?" Other novices hear free-form poems that focus on metaphor and they wonder, "is poetry only about metaphor?" I suppose the answer to both is "yes."

We'll start with free verse poets who make fun of the "roses are red" crowd. They do have a point. John Milton made the same

critique as those poets, but Milton made it against his contemporary English poets in 1667… and he did it at the start of *Paradise Lost*. Milton said most poets use rhyme "to set-off wretched matter and lame metre" and that some of the best English poems exclude "the jingling sound of like endings."

If we must rhyme, we must consider our rhymes *last*. C.S. Lewis in his forward to *Paradise Lost* said, "Every poem can be considered in two ways—as what the poet has to say, and as a thing which he makes. From the one point of view it is an expression of opinions and emotions; from the other, it is an organization of words which exists to produce a particular kind of patterned experience in the readers."

Your opinions and emotions form your poem's soul—what critics parse apart—but its patterns incarnate your opinions and emotions by giving your reader an *experience*. Smash that up with Milton's thoughts and you'll discover a schematic for any poem you ever want to write or understand:

- your opinion is **matter**
- your emotion is **metaphor**
- pattern… is **meter**
- …experience is **phono-aesthetics**

Some will disagree with my list. Before you do, consider this: (1) without good subject **matter**, your poem means nothing; (2) without good **metaphor** to emulate matter, your poem isn't poetry; (3) without some sort of **meter**—even purposeful arrhythmia—the poetic experience holds no rapture, no *art*; (4) **phono-aesthetics** (the art of sounds) follows the rest like a bright red caboose.

MATTER. It's the most restrictive element of any poem, the size of your canvas. With solid matter, the reader knows we're talking about *this* and not *that*. Genre is part of this, but so is opinion. For instance, some comedy writing schools teach students to pick a subject and pair it with a personal angle:

angle	on	a subject
hopeful	::	divorce
despairing	::	cheese
devious	::	waterfall

Basically, they teach this launchpad so comedians can quickly express opinions. Without a subject, you're a potter without clay. Even if you write about non-entity, nihilism, or antimatter, those still count as poetic *subject* matter. The Psalms of Scripture transcend more languages than any other book of poems by being the poetry of ideas—they don't require sounds to work. Start somewhere other than subject matter and your poem's more than meaningless, it's uninspired, the breath kicked clean out of it. Without it, what you write literally doesn't matter.

METAPHOR. Poetry, as a vessel for birthing and begetting language, draws virility from metaphor. Good matter illuminated by new metaphor is poetry. Nothing else is essential. From Hebrew parallelism to modern free verse, dozens of forms rely on little more than matter and metaphor. Free verse poems that fail, fail because they're either about nothing or about nothing *interesting*. Metaphor's the second bit.

Mixed metaphor *is* metaphor. Granted, some whip up bad mixes, which gave rise to the rule for prose about mixing metaphors. The best illustration I have for good mixed metaphor is in a poem I wrote titled "Silt":

—they (Germanic tribes)
had this word
broka
means "marsh"
sounds like a "mocha"

I've wondered whether
brauchen – "to
use"
like "digest"
—is related to *bruch*…

Our world's stomach
acid eats
soil
away from
stones, anxiety

beats us, erodes or
uses us
well,
how The Brook
deltas Marshland's clothes.

Old English men came
to use *broc*:

stream
in a marsh.
So new words arose:

The Poet tramps through
the marsh then
home
to help his
Misses cook a meal,

drops a plate down
on a stone
where,
shattered, it
reminds him of *broc*.

He points. Says, "*Broc*." Writes.
His village cites.
Then
citation
stops. Revises its source:

Broke. (A word is born).
Two words: one
head,
then mouth. One
spank, then follows sound.

One life-giving muse,
one ruin:
brook
(marsh's veins)
broke (penniless; pain)

We come to now, to
towns how named,
races
split…
or regenerated.

We ask our burrow:
what is this?
What's this?

Oh which will you be, today,
dear Brooklyn?

A modern metaphor like "broken barn" depends on two Old English metaphors. One called a shattered plate "*broc*" as in "brook-like." One meant "barley house." Language is metaphor, in the end. This is a basic tenet in semiotics, the symbolism of language, what Noam Chomsky calls our massive "evolutionary leap." In Narnia, Aslan makes a distinction between animals by giving one set language—a normal horse knows grass is grass and a Narnian horse says to a badger that grass reminds her of fur. Language compares one thing to another so the speaker can build a relationship with the hearer. Every sentence mixes metaphors (words), but poetry invents new mixtures. The better the mix, the better the poem. In the case of the broken barn, this particular mix of metaphors has become cliché or common language, so we could reverse the river of etymology to create something new:

brook through the barley house
its whiskeyrafts of grain

…in place of "broken barn." If I have deferred this new metaphor to subject matter about losing my family's farm, I might be on the right track…

METER. Submit the rhythm or arrhythmia of your poem to metaphor. Find a pace that fits the opinion and emotion behind your budding work. Taste the difference between iambic and troaichic. Analyze the meter in seemingly meterless pieces like Ashbery's *Litany* or Lee's *Porcine Cantacles*. Then pick an appropriate (or glaringly inappropriate) one for your W.I.P. and stick to it.

If you start to use sounds, rhyme or otherwise, that limit your chosen pace, don't let them. Pace limits sound, but sounds don't necessarily limit pace. Break those sounds, enslave them to your patterns and meter. This solidifies the poetry into patterned experiences, historical moments we call "art."

PHONO-AESTHETICS. Half of all bad poems tried to jam square rhymes into round meters. Sounds follow meter. Rhyme and rhythm share the same root word, so we often mix them up. Rhythm (meter) can include rhyme, but encompasses phono-aesthetics. Phono-aesthetics (the art of sounds) sometimes includes rhyme, sometimes dissonance, sometimes phantom rhyme, but all sounds defer to meter —the beat of your song, the pace of your phrasing. Experiment with sounds, like and unlike alike. Draw broadly from rap and Old Norse, from the aisling and roundel. Pay attention to origins because words derived from French land differently on the ear than those derived from Arabic—an eagle is not an albatross, after all. Ask Coleridge's Mariner.

Taken together and in that order, these four categories compose your poem. With this, we put words in the right order and create new language. So what?

So here's why all of us need to *get* and *make* poetry:

Language is an organism—a symbiont, but still an organism. If language ever dies, humanity dies. On the smaller scale, the day poets stop begetting and birthing new English metaphors will be the very day English dies. Language and culture are inseparable like the widow who follows her husband into the grave one week after he passes.

American English in particular is suffering death-by-palliative care. We, unlike Iceland, did not create new English words for new break-throughs whether medical or militant. We stole words from other languages and butchered them for ours. We've let aberrations like "blog" slip in unnoticed because among our people, everyone's a poet.

If the phrase "everyone's a poet" actually inspired Americans, we'd be set. The problem? Few read poetry and almost no one considers himself a poet—*even among poets*. I met a girl last Friday who *read* her poetry at a *poetry* reading that featured three very competent writers in this uber-hip library in Brooklyn and she said, "I'm not good enough to call myself a poet. I just write poems." Offering the power of language creation to three hundred million Americans who consider themselves non-poets is like taking a daycare full of children who haven't learned the word "death" and arming them with assault rifles.

If you think I'm being superlative, just check out how many word origins have N.S. beside them: National Socialist, Nazi. The moment the language shifts, the culture shifts. Hitler's power was his poetry.

At the forefront of our sea of ignorant language creators stand the copywriters. I know. I was one of them. It paid well, but we slaughtered the great phrases of the world on an altar of barcodes. Mother Theresa's *Be the change you want to see in the world* has become *Be the person buying printer cartridges you want to see in the world*. You can't say, "I'm loving it" without thinking about shitty cheeseburgers. These small attacks have added up to a full-scale coup against our language. Left alone and unaided, hers is a death of ten thousand advertisements and elisions and transliterations.

As C.D. Wright says, "It's harder for me to feel that dreamy about poetry nowadays. The art is thoroughly divorced from the multi-million-dollar spectacles that play to the numbers, and entropically inclined from within. It does hang in there. Poetry will not go quietly. You would have to starve it out, and it can live on very little."

Let's put some meat on the bones of our language again. Speak of a new world, poets. Frame the world aright. Birth a new society pregnant with a thousand possibilities with your every poem. Plato feared this and expelled every poet from Athens. One of the most important Ukrainians leading the revolution *right now* is a 26-year-old poet who said, "This is not a garden party. This is a revolution." He has changed their language.

You too. Set your mind on creating a better language for our great-grandchildren. This is poetry.

If no one has yet, I commission you. I hereby arm you to the teeth with a tiny, but effective, schematic for writing and understanding poems. Go speak of a tomorrow stripped clean of the pieces of today you hate. In Perelandra, Lewis tells us of a world that has no word for "murder" or "vanity." What if we woke up tomorrow and discovered that in the middle of the night, American poets had rendered just two words—"rape" and "genocide"—meaningless, as meaning *less* than words like "respect" and "reconcile?"

In the end, write poetry not to publish. Obviously by publishing this article in a book about publishing, I pray you can and do publish. But don't write for that. No, write poetry to ensnare your reader in one historic moment so deep that if they ever escape, they'll remember forever the good we offer the world. This isn't just a schematic for poetry, it's a schematic for tomorrow. As Rilke said, "Because you must." This is humanity, this is art: to find our Self standing at our unique intersection of relationships and offer up to the world all of the good we find in the midst of that intersection using a language we create and teach others to speak.

This isn't a schematic for poetry. It's a schematic for tomorrow:

1. Things that **matter**
2. expressed in moving **metaphor**
3. through memorable **meter**
4. made beautiful by **phono-aesthetics.**

That's a poem.

And for better or worse, poetry is tomorrow.

LANCELOT SCHAUBERT works with guilds of artists in New York City and has sold work to *McSweeney's, Poker Pro, CC&D,* and others.

POETS AND COLLABORATION

The Benefits (and Trials) of Collaborating

by Jeannine Hall Gailey

What is collaboration? For a poet, it is the act of working with another artist (or several artists) to create and produce a new piece of art. It could be a collage that incorporates lines of your poems, a piece of music interpreting your work, an interactive art exhibit, even a play!

Many people think of poets as being solitary types, but there are advantages to stepping away from the laptop and into conversation with other types of artists. Interaction and conversation with artists in a variety of media and genres can spark new ideas and build unexpected connections. The rewards of working in multiple art forms include reaching larger (and new) audiences as well as challenging yourself to think about your work in a new way and in a new medium.

While poetry often lacks a visual or auditory component, I think including all the senses in an experience helps people connect with a piece more fully. For instance, listening to the Star Wars score by itself is pretty stirring, but the John Williams piece is even more moving when accompanied by the sound effects, imagery, and dialogue of the movie.

Collaboration can be a one-way response, or a conversation where artists respond to each other. You may be familiar with book cover art or ekphrastic poems, which are composed in response to a work of art, such as Auden's "Musée des Beaux Arts" that describes the painting "Landscape with the Fall of Icarus." Those are examples of one-way responses. But collaboration can also be two-way, like a conversation between friends, in which there is an exchange of ideas and art over time. Collaborations can happen between poets and sculptors, neon or glass artists, painters, musicians, and filmmakers.

ADVANTAGES TO COLLABORATIONS

What are the advantages of working with other types of artists? It can be hard for poets to get outside of our little "boxes of words" and be vulnerable enough to share our work with others. The rewards include things like: seeing our work brought to life in a way we never imagined, making friends in our community, building support between different artistic communities, increasing opportunities to be inspired by other works of art and the fascinating conversations to be had with other types of artists (my personal favorite), and also increasing the audiences for your work. One of my best-selling readings was when an artist friend invited me along to one of her gallery openings to read poems to accompany the visuals of her work. Almost everyone there, mostly art patrons, bought a book!

I brought collaboration into much of my work as Redmond, Washington's second Poet Laureate, because I thought it was important to incorporate and introduce multiple points-of-view and media types, and because, in a town known for its techie, rather than literary, population, it would be a way to introduce the unknownwn poetry with the more familiar say, art and music. I wanted to enrich our community's experiences with a wider variety of art forms and show how poetry could be relevant to them. It was also a chance to show the often startling beauty of works emerging from cooperation between artists and art forms.

Similar opportunities can come to you through arts organizations, festivals, and art galleries at any time, so it's good to consider with what type of artist you think you would most like to work.

COLLABORATIONS WITH VISUAL ARTISTS

When you think about poets working with visual artists, you might automatically think about cover art. I had a great time working with the cover artist of my first and third books, Michaela Eaves. She took the time to read early versions of my books and create concepts and hire artist's models to pose for the scenes that eventually became the covers of *Becoming the Villainess* and *Unexplained Fevers*. We went on to collaborate on a series of images and poems interpreting Japanese folk tales for one of my Redmond Poet Laureate projects that were later used inside the second edition of my second book, *She Returns to the Floating World*.

Michaela Eaves talks about her experience with poet-artist collaboration: "The expected rules and boundaries are much looser when it comes collaborating with a poet. If you illustrate a straight-up prose story, the publisher, reader, and author expect certain level of illustrative representation. Here's a story about a girl that likes to wear glass slippers, so you create a piece about a girl making the best of her bad footwear choices. Poetry allows you to loosen the reins and explore symbolism and intent, not just act out what's on the page. The poet may mention slippers, but you are illustrating the feel of it rather than the facts. Working directly with the poet is great because you can get to the heart of what she's trying to say by asking questions rather than just relying on guesswork."

Visual artist collaborations can include more than just book covers or illustrations; it can include poetry used to accompany a visual art exhibition. Mary Coss of METHOD Gallery in Seattle paired poets with visual artists of different media for the 2015 show, TEXTure. Carol Milne, a talented glass artist recently featured in the *Boston Globe*, worked with my poems for the show, which also featured Northwest poets Sherman Alexie (paired with neon artists Lia Yaranon Hall and Cedar Mannan) and Daemond Arrindell (paired with fabric artist Maura Donegan.) Carol picked out two poems from my book *The Robot Scientist's Daughter* and created a uranium-glass snowman with words like "Cesium" and "Uranium" woven into the pattern of the glass representing radioactive snow, and then I wrote a poem in response to her work.

Carol Milne, when asked to describe how the project came together: "Well, frankly, I've never been too fond of poetry. Most of it is too brooding and esoteric, where I lean towards the ironic, amusing and down-to-earth. However, I think it's good to challenge one's preconceptions, and I thought it sounded like a fun project. I browsed the meager Northwest poetry section of the library, and then, while surfing the internet for Northwest poets, I ended up on the Jack Straw website where I found Jeannine's poem, 'Cesium Burns Blue.' It struck me with its visual beauty and dark message. I found a kindred spirit working in another medium. It was refreshing to come back to ironic work, making a political/environmental statement, through discovering similar work in written form. Jeannine's work explores innocence and daily life with horrific undertones of environmental hazards. The contrast personalizes and drives home the horror of nucle-

ar contamination. The power of the arts: to get you personally engaged without spewing statistics."

Kelly Davio, the editor of *The Tahoma Literary Review* who collaborated with Redmond, Washington-area visual artists (and me) for the "Voices in the Corridor" project for VALA arts center offers another perspective on collaboration: "Collaborating with the visual artists in the "Voices in the Corridor" project was a wonderful chance to shake up my own artistic process. While I tend to be measured and exact when I write, the visual artists seemed to work intuitively, feeling the ways in which their pieces fit in and adapted to the gallery space. Riffing off their works and making my own process more flexible allowed me to write work I never would have produced otherwise." And Jessica F. Kravitz Lambert, the founder of VALA and one of the two artists who came up with the idea for our collaborative project, said "Working with writers allows visual artists another opportunity to share the themes in their work with another set of artists that can interpret and dialogue with the artwork created, allowing the audience to have yet another way of "seeing" the artwork."

COLLABORATIONS WITH PERFORMANCE ARTISTS–THEATER GROUPS, FILMMAKERS, AND CHOREOGRAPHERS

One of the first collaborations I was even involved with was when I was contacted by a theater group called "The Alley Cat Players." They had a copy of my first book, *Be-*

coming the Villainess, and wanted to use it as the basis for a series of one-act plays they would perform in Florida. I wish I had lived closer to Florida so I could have seen one of the performances!

Other types of collaborations include "videopoems," in which filmmakers might collaborate with a poet to create a video that choreographs with a poem while it is being read, creating an effect similar to a music video.

Dance teams and choreographers can work to interpret poems as well.

COLLABORATIONS WITH MUSICIANS

Of course, you may have thought of poets working with lyrics (such as Wyn Cooper's poem, "Fun," that became Sheryl Crow's pop hit "All I Wanna Do"), but have you ever thought of writing with a musician and songwriter? Bushwick Book Club is a group of collaborative musicians in Seattle. They interpret writings from Shakespeare, the Bible, and contemporary poetry and turn them into songs that they perform in a spirited venue with much joy and riotous musician-like behavior. (I've been to a few of these performances, and let me say, hanging out with a musician crowd, you can definitely tell which are the poets and which are the musicians—rowdier, more attractive, and better dressed.) Geoff Larson, the executive director of Bushwick Seattle, describes the process of collaboration: "The Bushwick Book Club Seattle process of writing original music inspired by others' writings is a unique exercise that allows songwriters to

chase any idea or thread the author's work may spark. Like any writing process, it can be a pretty solitary endeavor, and emerging at the end of it to share the result with audience is a gratifying and interactive moment. When that audience includes the creator of the 'source material,' that interaction is all the more magical when two creative forces feed off of one another in a moment of mutual appreciation, each having generated something and then let it go into the world for others to receive."

Joy Mills, who collaborated with me on one poem/song ("Sleeping Beauty Loves the Needle") for a Bushwick Book Club project, describes her experience working with poets: "Working with Jeannine and other poets in the past has been such a gratifying experience as a musician because I consider poetry to be a foundation for so many creative forms. Poetry is music. The meter, rhythm, word play, rhyme and structure all lend themselves openly to being placed into song. With Jeannine, I much preferred to put her poem to music, rather than interpret it with my own lyrics. To use an already-existing piece and try to wrap the music around it allowed me to broaden my craft through collaborative approach. Poetry and music come from the same motherland in so many ways, allowing us to distill the vast world around us, if only for a fleeting spell." It was truly surreal and a real treat to get up on stage and read my poem, and then hear Joy perform with her guitar the song she interpreted and created from my poem.

Several famous poets, including Yusef Komunyakaa, Margaret Atwood and Dana

Goia, have collaborated with classically-trained composers to create operas from their work, in a practice of collaboration that dates back to the seventeenth century.

COLLABORATIONS WITH OTHER WRITERS

This could be the subject of its own article! Collaborating with other poets can result in wonderful work that yields often work that highlights the strong points of both writers. Denise Duhamel, a frequent and generous collaborator with other poets, highlights this: "I love throwing in with another poet and see where the imagination is ignited by the other. The poem becomes less a force of the will of one writer and a magic revelation full of surprises for the collaborators."

For the previously mentioned "Voices in the Corridor" project for the city of Redmond, not only did Kelly Davio and I respond to the projects for four visual artists, but we also wrote haikus responding to both the Redmond landscape and did a kind of "call and response" to each other's work.

REAP THE REWARDS OF REACHING OUT

In any collaboration, the conversation between poet and artist can enlarge and enlighten.

The risks are worth it, because the chance to include, improvise and bring a larger scope to your work is worth the occasional hiccup and increases your chances of reaching a greater and more diverse audience with your work. Branch out and take advantage of opportunities to exchange ideas and to collaborate. Watch a theater group transform your work with their acting abilities, or a musician take your work to a new level with the addition of a score. With inspiration and a little hard work, the results may take you far beyond what you might have achieved alone.

JEANNINE HALL GAILEY recently served as the second Poet Laureate of Redmond, Washington. She is the author of four books of poetry, *Becoming the Villainess, She Returns to the Floating World, Unexplained Fevers*, and *The Robot Scientist's Daughter*. Her website is www.webbish6.com.

WRITING POEMS FROM PROMPTS

....

by Amorak Huey

The prompt is a thoroughly entrenched part of the pedagogy in creative writing courses from kindergarten to college. "Here's a topic," the teacher will say, "here's a challenge, an idea, a form to try." In return, students dutifully respond with a piece of writing that conforms to the instructions as best as they can manage. Perhaps because these kinds of exercises are so associated with "school writing," prompts may for some writers carry a stigma as something "real writers" don't use, as a trick or gimmick, as a crutch for beginners.

It need not be so.

For many poets, the prompt can be an essential component of an active writing life. The first step to using a prompt successfully is not to think of it as a school assignment that must be followed to the letter. A prompt should be a launching pad for your poems, not a leash that ties them down. The best prompt gives you a quick shove off the edge of a cliff you might not have even known was there—and then disappears as you negotiate the fall yourself.

DEFEATING WRITER'S BLOCK

One of the best things a prompt can do for a poet is to eliminate that most difficult of questions: What do I write about? Much of the world has this notion that poems are mystical gifts from the muses, words bestowed from on high to the poet who waits patiently for inspiration. That sounds nice, and while there's certainly something mysterious and intangible in the creative process, sitting around and hoping for some external inspiration is not a recipe for getting much writing done. Perhaps it worked for Wordsworth or Byron, but my guess is that even the poets we study in literature classes got more accomplished by sitting down with quill in hand than by waiting to be granted some divine gift.

Writer's block is usually some blend of anxiety and self-doubt combined with the many things that demand time in our daily lives. An excuse, in other words. A writing prompt can be just the trick to get past that excuse. It frees you up to write without waiting for inspiration; it also removes some of the pressure we all place on ourselves. If the piece of writing doesn't live up to your hopes, you can always blame the prompt.

T.S. Eliot famously said: "When forced to work within a strict framework, the imagination is taxed to its utmost, and will produce its richest ideas. Given total freedom, the work is likely to sprawl." Think of the blank page (or these days, the blank Word document). It's intimidating, that scary expanse of whiteness, all the emptiness, infinite possibilities. Where to start? How does anyone ever write anything? The answer is in the Eliot quote: You need constraint. A framework. Some limitation: steel against which you can strike the flint of your imagination. That's what the prompt is for. Poet and professor Dean Rader says, "Novice poets tend to rely on abstractions and bigness, so I try to give exercises and prompts that force them to be concrete and specific." The prompt, in other words, shrinks the world, narrows the infinite down to the possible.

SETTING CHALLENGES FOR YOURSELF

For student writers, the prompts given by their instructors might feel restrictive, frustrating, a burden weighing down their creativity. Yet once you're writing outside of the classroom context, all that freedom can be a little dizzying: you can write what you want, when you want, *if* you want. One of the most common things former students say to me is that they miss having writing prompts. I've had students email me

years after graduation asking for some new prompt to kickstart their writing again. Here's a secret, one of the tricks of the poetry trade: Poets have to invent prompts for themselves. As Diane Thiel says, "All writers learn by reading and by setting themselves exercises."

We all, we writers and poets, set ourselves language challenges every time we sit down with our (metaphorical) quill in hand. Write a five-line poem about X. Use this newspaper headline or that Facebook status in a poem. Write a poem in which the letter *I* does not appear. Write a sonnet. Write a sestina. Write a villanelle. The entire concept of formal poetry is itself a kind of prompt, an artificial constraint in the sense Eliot referred to: Write down your feelings about love, only do it in 14 lines of iambic pentameter following a particular rhyme scheme. Even the very choice to write a poem is a prompt. Why not write a short story, a novel, a journal entry, a blog post? A poem makes a particular kind of demand on your creativity, suggests certain things about form and focus in the same way a prompt suggests things about subject matter or approach. Poet and professor W. Todd Kaneko says, "Often the prompt has less to do with topic and more to do with restraint—do something specific with time or rhyming action or sound—anything to help me get something moving on the page. … I think writing prompts are most useful when they are based around an element of craft."

Even if you don't have a teacher to spark your writing with a ready-made syllabus full of assignments, you can always come up with them on your own. Invent whatever restrictions you like. Think of it as a game. (And if you want outside assistance, check out the many prompts provided in the sources at the end of this article.)

BEGINNING AND BEGINNING AGAIN

Here's another secret about poetry: every poet is, in some sense, a beginning poet. Every poem is a fresh start. Sure, some aspects of the craft might grow easier over time, with years of experience in reading and writing, but each new poem offers a new opportunity for discovery, for experimentation—and for failure. Yes, some (much? most?) writing fails. But of course failure is an essential part of writing; as Samuel Beckett said, "Fail again. Fail better." It's easy for a writer to focus too much on product and not enough on process, to see failure as an endpoint instead of a necessary detour on the writing journey.

The best way to think about prompts, then, is to see them as more about process than about product. They are intended to provoke you, to put you into situations that you have to find your way out of, like one of those reality shows where you're dropped on a desert island and have to figure out how to build a hut before it rains. A prompt offers both a challenge and a learning opportunity. Cindy Hunter Morgan says prompts offer a writer "framework and focus." Chris Haven says, "I think poets should think of our writing as responding to an implied assignment. We report on news from worlds

that resemble ours or don't, real ones or imagined ones. A prompt allows us to get outside of our own requirements and widen our scope of what readers might require."

MOVING FROM PROMPT TO POEM

But of course, process is not the only thing that matters. In the end, we do want to create meaningful poems—work that appears to have been hand-delivered by the muses even if it wasn't. It might seem that prompts are an artificial way to achieve this kind of writing; that is, writing from a prompt might feel more contrived than natural. And it's probably true that most published poems probably don't come directly from prompts in the sense of the prompts you were given in your writing classes: What did *you* do on your summer vacation?

The key to getting beyond any sort of artificiality goes back to the idea that a prompt should not limit but inspire your work. The prompt is a starting place, not the destination. Robin Behn and Chase Twichell, in the introduction to *The Practice of Poetry*, an excellent book full of exercises and prompts, write:

> A good exercise serves as a scaffold— it eventually falls away, leaving behind something new in the language, language that now belongs to the writer. … Exercises can result in a new understanding of the relation of image to meaning, or a way into the unconscious, perhaps a way of marrying au-

tobiography with invention, or a sense of the possibility of different kinds of structures, ways to bring a dead poem to life, a new sense of rhythm, or a slight sharpening of the ear. Exercises can help you think about, articulate, and solve specific creative problems. Or they can undermine certain assumptions you might have, forcing you to think—and write—beyond the old limitations.

A scaffold that eventually falls away—it's the perfect metaphor. Here's another: A writing prompt is not a box that your poem must fit into, but a pot that the poem grows out of. Start in the direction your prompt suggests, but if the poem seems to lead somewhere else, follow. If writing about your most recent summer vacation leads to a memory of some youthful July week spent at your grandmother's lake cabin which in turn leads to a memory of your first crush and you wind up writing more about the crush, so be it. Even if those early lines about last summer disappear entirely from the final piece, they have served a purpose.

Not every prompt will lead you to your favorite poem. Some prompts will be easy. Some will seem hard. Often it's the hard ones you should look at more carefully. Ask yourself: What makes this hard? What in particular am I struggling with here? If you really, really hate a particular prompt, try to figure out why. Try to learn something from the difficulty. One of my goals in every creative writing class I teach and with every prompt I assign is to push students outside their comfort zones and away from

their assumptions about themselves and their limitations. Writing should be challenging, every time.

Here are five tips for using prompts effectively:

1. Take the prompt seriously. Work at figuring out what it's asking you do to.
2. Imagine all the different poems that might emerge from a single prompt. Then ask yourself which of those poems you'd like to write.
3. If one prompt is falling flat, combine it with another. The creative process benefits immensely from the friction of two disparate forces.
4. Use the prompt as an excuse to play. Writing poetry should be a playful act most of the time anyway. (That does not mean it's not also serious work. It's both.)
5. Abandon the prompt as soon as it's no longer serving the poem that has emerged on the page.

In the end, to paraphrase Richard Hugo, you owe a prompt nothing and the poem you're writing everything. A poem will never be measured by how well the poet grappled with the prompt that started it. A poem must be measured by its own internal standards, by its music and language and the way it both creates and reflects the world we live in. You won't get to walk around with your poem explaining how the prompt influenced this line or that image. The scaffolding, necessary though it may have been in the composing process, must fall away. Your poem must stand alone.

SIX STELLAR SOURCES OF POETRY PROMPTS

There is no shortage of prompts in the world. A Google search for "poetry writing prompts" yields more than 180,000 hits. If you'd prefer a more curated list, here are six sources of thoughtful, helpful prompts:

- The previously mentioned book *The Practice of Poetry: Writing Exercises from Poets Who Teach* by Robin Behn and Chase Twichell offers a wide range of carefully designed and classroom-tested prompts.
- Natalie Goldberg's classic book *Writing Down the Bones: Freeing the Writer Within* has a Zen approach to writing, with many exercises and activities intended to free you from the self-censor that lurks inside you.
- *Wingbeats: Exercises and Practice in Poetry*, edited by Scott Wiggerman and David Meischen, offers an impressive array of prompts from some of America's preeminent contemporary poets.
- Robert Lee Brewer's "Poetic Asides" blog offers a steady stream of weekly prompts throughout the year and daily prompts for Poem-A-Day challenges in November and April, in addition to poetic form challenges, poet interviews, and more.
- *The Daily Poet: Day-By-Day Prompts for Your Writing Practice* is a fairly new book by Kelli Russell Agodon and Martha Silano designed to lead through a very productive year of writing poems.
- *The Crafty Poet: A Portable Workshop* by Diane Lockward offers model poems and interviews with poets in addition to detailed writing exercises.

AMORAK HUEY, a former newspaper editor and reporter, teaches professional and creative writing at Grand Valley State University, where he assigns all kinds of writing prompts to his students. He is author of the chapbook *The Insomniac Circus* (Hyacinth Girl), and his poems appear in *The Best American Poetry 2012, Poet's Market 2014, The Southern Review, Hayden's Ferry Review, Rattle,* and many other journals.

FRESHEN YOUR POETRYBY REVISING STALE LANGUAGE

by Nancy Susanna Breen

During a recent stint of poetry judging, I decided to keep a running list of the words and phrases that turned up again and again in entries. What I discovered is that too many poets, especially new or developing poets, depend on clichés in their writing. Others simply don't stretch enough for originality when crafting their lines. Instead, they invoke wording and images that have become exhausted with use.

You can freshen your poetry and increase your individuality by targeting stale language during the revising process. Like mold on bread, instances of exhausted images and overused words act as alerts once you know what you're looking for.

CLICHÉS

A cliché is any trite phrase or expression; that is, a phrase or expression that has been run into the ground. Avoid clichés like the plague. (See how easy it is to work clichés into your writing? There are two in those two sentences.) Because of their familiarity, clichés are comfortable and seemingly add a conversational touch to a line of poetry. They seem to guarantee clarity as well, because readers know what the clichés mean.

However, when poets turn to the same tired phrases and overused words, their poems all sound alike. Cliché-ridden lines have a cookie cutter effect. They result in poems that seem prefabricated, assembled of standard parts.

Here's a brief list of clichés that turned up more than three times in the batch of poems I was judging:

lips are/were sealed
blood, sweat, and tears
into thin air
heart and soul
thick and thin
bitter end
on a silver platter
life is precious
time stands still
as far as the eye can see
tore like a knife
sands in an hourglass
sun, moon, and stars

If you need help recognizing clichés, the Internet offers some valuable sites. For example, ClicheList.net provides an alphabetized list of clichés, each example linked to an explanation of its meaning. Cliché Finder (www.westegg.com/cliche) allows you to search its 3,000-plus cliché bank by keyword; "cat" turned up over 50 examples, such as "cat has your tongue," "cat's meow," and "raining cats and dogs." There's also a cliché generator that provides 10 random clichés at a time. Make a practice of reading through those 10 random clichés daily for a month and you'll find it much easier to spot clichés in your poems.

OH, NO! NOT ANOTHER [BLANK] POEM

Clichés include dull, stereotypical ideas and situations. Consequently, entire poems can be clichés. Gather a large enough sample of poems, such as entries in a poetry contest or submissions to a magazine, and you'll see several examples of the same clichéd poem, sometimes with surprisingly little variation. Below are types of poems poets can't seem to resist writing. Exercise heightened originality if attempting these poems.

Butterflies

I have nothing against butterflies, and I appreciate how symbolic they are. However, they turn up constantly as poem subjects, accompanied by all the typical verbs: flit, flutter, and so on. Describing or referring to butterflies emerging from cocoons is also popular. Understand how commonplace butterflies are before writing an entire

poem about them if you really want to set your work apart. For that matter, restrain yourself from using them as images or symbols without plenty of careful thought.

Sea and sand

Poets simply must write about the ocean. (I certainly have.) They stroll through the tide, meditate on the coming and going of the tide, study what the tide leaves behind, and compare life to the movements of the tide.

There's nothing wrong with writing about strolling on the beach, watching the waves, or examining the shells and driftwood at low tide. However, because they're so popular with poets, the ocean and beach are hard to write about in an original way, especially if the physical descriptions basically make up the poem.

Poets consistently choose the same words to describe the sea and shore, and the ring of familiarity isn't a virtue. Even a touching account of a dying person visiting the seaside for the last time or a brokenhearted lover examining a ruined relationship fades into sameness when the speakers' actions are similar and they seem to be viewing the scene through the same pair of eyes.

Seasonal

The most uninspired, and uninspiring, poetry I see usually focuses on one of the seasons or on all four at once. This is primarily because poets pull out all the standard images, as if putting up those colored cardboard cutouts in a classroom: colored leaves and pumpkins for fall, snowflakes for winter, buds and robins for spring, a big, smiling sun for summer. Such images are beloved and iconic; and because of this, you need to move past them when writing about a season. Read enough poems that cite "the golden leaves drift lazily to ground" and you'll wince at the mere thought of autumn.

I'm going to go a step farther and suggest that freshening the seasonal imagery you use isn't enough—you should avoid the seasons as the sole subjects of poems. Instead, use the season as a background. That way your poem develops into sometime more than a laundry list of the same old spring showers, hot July noons, and shimmering blankets of snow on a rolling landscape.

Love

It's a shame so many love poems come across as time-creased valentines. I've rarely read a clichéd love poem that made me doubt the sincerity of the writer's feelings. When such verse seems cribbed from the most mundane greeting card, though, especially when expressed in *oo-aa* rhymes, the poem appears mass-produced rather than the true expression of an individual. Poems about unrequited love or rejection are especially painful, not because of the sadness involved but because a kind of injured, righteous indignation overrides the poet's artistic common sense. And, of course, the same images are evoked and the same flowery language applied as though squeezed out of a tube of frosting.

When writing a poem that addresses a romantic partner or someone who has cast you aside, consider sending it only to the intended recipient or keeping it strictly to yourself. Otherwise, be sure you can treat the work as a piece of literary art, not a love letter. Even then, make it your own. Don't resort to gooey valentine verses or resentful poison notes.

A subset of the love poem is the "love is" poem. If you insist on defining love, have something new to say. "Love is" poems range from a list of clichéd comparisons, both positive and negative (a delicate rose, a knife to the heart, a blanket against the cold) to a series of unsurprising adjectives (kind, understanding, forgiving, harsh, demoralizing, etc.). Throw out the cookie cutter images and the threadbare language or don't bother at all, at least not if you're writing for a general readership. The same goes for "my love is like" poems.

OTHER CLICHÉ PITFALLS

Hearts

In poetry, hearts aren't mere organs that pump blood. Poets have them doing more tricks than a trained poodle in a one-ring circus: pounding, shrieking, weeping, dancing, swelling, bleeding, exploding, freezing, or stopping dead (without killing the poet). Poets assist their hearts in hyperactivity by opening them, shutting them, writing on them, exploring them, hiding things in them, and nursing them. Other people do things to poets' hearts as well: stomp on them, warm them, break them, steal them, stab them, fill them with joy or sadness, play with them, heal them, and reawaken them when they're dead (figuratively speaking).

"Heart" is one of those words you have to handle carefully, if at all. Despite its versatility, in most cases you can leave "heart" out of your poem. It's a cliché that can do more harm than good; and the more animated the heart is in your poem, the more danger of giving the reader a mental image that resembles a Wile E. Coyote cartoon.

Obviously, if you're writing about someone's cardiac event, *heart* is a necessary clinical term, not a cliché. Where emotions are concerned, though, don't go breaking, teasing, or exposing anyone's heart in your poems.

Despair

It's astonishing how many poets "plunge into the abyss" or "descend into oblivion" at some point in their poetry. Sometimes they hurtle their entire beings into the black pit of nothingness; in other instances, their minds or hearts take the dive of despair.

Sadly, it's hard for readers to take you seriously when you're melodramatic. Write with even more finesse when addressing such intense emotional conditions as grief and depression. Imagine an over-the-top actor in 19th-century theater wailing to the balcony, writhing on the stage, or whirling his cape around him like a shroud. This shouldn't be the effect you want your lines to convey.

Read the confessional poetry of Sylvia Plath, Robert Lowell, Anne Sexton, John Berryman, and others to learn how to calibrate your language so you express the most emotion with the least hyperbole.

Tears

Too many poets turn the human face into a Niagara Falls of tears. These tears run, cascade, course, drip, trickle, and flow. Or poets turn to clichés to describe weeping, such as "cried like a baby," "cried a river," or "cried her eyes out."

When you write skillfully, showing rather than telling, you can convey sorrow without using tears at all. Uncontrolled waterworks are just overkill; they don't make the scene more convincing. Think of a movie where an actor cries. It's usually an extreme situation when a character dissolves into heaving sobs; otherwise, the viewers don't buy it. Often a character struggling *not* to cry is more affecting than drenched cheeks. Remember that the next time you're inclined to flood someone's face with tears in your poem.

Colors

Although simply putting "green," "blue," or "red" into your descriptions is pretty mundane, it's almost worse to employ clichéd colors. If you notice "ruby red," "golden yellow," "baby pink," "sky blue," and similar color clichés in your poems, revise them to more specific colors or create original similes—in other words, don't just substitute "red as a ruby" or "blue as a summer sky." Come up with something vivid and new. If your color phrase turns up in the lyrics of pop songs or standards, it's too worn-out to use in your poetry. For inspiration, review some paint company websites for the creative ways they name various colors, then work on original examples of your own.

While I'm discussing colors, I want to mention red, white, and blue. This combination is a favorite of poets writing about the military, patriotism, or the United States in general. Unfortunately, those colors used together have become cliché, detracting from verse that may otherwise make valid statements. There's plenty to say about a soldier's sacrifice, love of one's country, or the esteem for U.S. liberty and democracy without tying everything up in red, white, and blue bunting. Make your poem stirring enough and readers will see the stars and stripes without a specific reference.

ABOUT DEAD METAPHORS

When people repeat a metaphor so often its original imagery gives way to a new, literal meaning, the result is a *dead metaphor*. I once heard the poet Donald Hall cite the use of dead metaphors as one of the most common reasons he rejects poems. One of his examples was *sea of wheat*, which now means an expanse of wheat rather than an ocean-like view of the grain field.

Determining what constitutes a dead metaphor and when to delete it can be confusing. For instance, *eye of the needle* is considered a dead metaphor, yet it's also what we call that opening in the top of a needle. On the other hand, in the phrase *he plowed through the stacks of paper*, "plowed" at first glance seems a vigorous verb choice rather than a dead metaphor. However, consider how many times you hear this metaphor in televised news reports. "The robbery suspect plowed through the festival crowd." "The car plowed into the front porch of the home." *Plow* doesn't conjure up its original imagery of a blade digging through dirt; it's taken on a meaning of its own through heavy repetition as a popular term.

If you're unsure about dead metaphors, apply the yardstick of frequency: If the term in question gets repeated a lot, especially in the media, revise the term whether it's a dead metaphor or not.

BE ALERT, NOT OBSESSIVE

Don't inhibit your writing by being overly conscious about stale language as you're putting the words down. First or even second and third drafts aren't a time for self-editing. When you revise, watch carefully for overused words and tired imagery. They're tricky little devils to catch because we're so used to them. Reread this article and I'm sure you'll target some clichés or dead metaphors that slipped right by me. The point is to be aware of them as you hone your skills. Over time you'll become more astute about when you need to cast them aside to freshen up the lines of your poems.

NANCY SUSANNA BREEN is a poet, freelance writer, and editor. Her poetry is available in e-chapbook form at www.Smashwords.com as is an e-book of writing prompts, *Nudged by Quotes—20 Writing Prompts Inspired by The World's Great Poetry, Volume 10: Poetical Quotations.* She's the former editor of *Poet's Market* and judges poetry contests at the state and national levels.

7 SOMERSAULTS FOR POLISHING YOUR POETRY

by Daniel Ari

When Point Molate became a public beach park, we found sea glass in abundance. My family collected ocean-polished shards in blue, green, red, brown and white. We took home a bag of the smooth, sensual shapes to put in our garden. We filled a second bag with trash, including glass that was still rough and sharp, and threw it away.

I'm not drawing a parallel to poetry to suggest that all polished poems belong in your garden of verse and all rough ones should be thrown away; but in many cases, polishing poems, like glass or shoes or bowling balls, makes them more alluring to human senses. Patient revision often increases poetry's luster and longevity, making it more shareable and more publishable.

That's why revision has to be an enjoyable part of your process. I hope the ideas here help so that you're never inclined to rush revision or skip it altogether. I don't recommend treating revision as a checklist. Remove clichés: check. Cut extra words: check. Replace abstract with concrete: check. After all, your poem may want

clichés, extra words and abstractions. Instead, these somersaults are ways to bring conscious, supple attention to all of your choices.

These techniques work for me because they're fun. They trick me into feeling like I'm seeing my poems for the first time. That gives me the perspective I need to polish and revise with greater freedom and less attachment to my first choices. Each somersault works best at a specific level of revision: the word, the line, the whole poem, etc. I encourage you to use what works for you and to consider the rest as directional signs pointing toward new somersaults that are yours to discover.

THE ALPHABET TRICK— POLISHING LEVEL: WORD

I learned this from *How to Draw a Bunny*, the 2002 documentary about artist Ray Johnson. The method is to run your mind through an alphabet of words until the right one pops out.

I spot the noun stuff, for example, in a poem I'm revising. In the draft, I chose stuff for its aggressive ambiguity, but rereading the poem, I wonder if most readers will feel the punch I intended. Maybe not. It feels now like the line wants greater specificity.

So I go through the alphabet thinking of words that relate, even tangentially, to stuff: Accumulation. Batting. Crust. Debris. Etcetera. Freight. Gravity. Heaviness. Then the word weight comes to me. While it's still general, I like its connotative flavor; plus it fits the rhythm of the poem. I plug in the word and smile. Rereading the stanza, weight works better.

Doing the alphabet trick, I go quickly. I don't get hung up looking for exact synonyms. I'll skip Q, X and Z before I let myself get stuck. Usually, the word I want comes to mind before I get all the way through the alphabet. When you try this, don't use a thesaurus—that would defeat the purpose. The trick is that the part of the brain that loves linear thinking gets occupied in making an alphabet, so the intuitive subconscious can freely slide, leap and land on the best word for your poem.

TISSUE SAMPLES—
POLISHING LEVEL: LINE

Poet and critic Robert Peters taught me this. Take a random line from a poem or manuscript you're editing. You can let your eyes land willy-nilly, or you can roll dice or use some other random-number generator to select a line from a poem. Read the line by itself, out loud if possible. See if the line is interesting to you. Does it suggest a complete idea, moment or image? Evaluate its sound, its sense and its relationship to the poem as a whole.

I'll try this with my own manuscript now. I see an isolated 8 in my field of vision, so I'll extract the eighth line from two different poems. Here they are:

"the alleged subterranean"

"but it's far, away up in the night sky."

For me, the first line sparkles. It could be the name of a jazz band or a mystery novel. It strikes me as a complete and interesting thought. I also like the sound of it; and in the context of the poem, it's clear to me how it fits.

I'm not as excited about the second line. Read aloud, that string of prepositions sounds awkward to my ear. The idea is more or less complete, but it's not very original. (It refers to the moon.) I think this line should add more to the subject of the poem, which is estrangement. I rewrite the line: "It stirs tides and winds into two hoarse cries."

The trick, as you can see, is to focus on your poem in pieces, which helps you confirm your specific choices or see where they need adjustment. If you'd like inspiration from a master, try taking Tissue Samples from Kay Ryan's poetry. Her lines are typically two to five words long, and every one's a wallop.

THE FONT REFRESH—
POLISHING LEVEL: POEM

I don't know about you, but I've never been on a tight deadline to finish poems. Poetry affords me one of a writer's greatest luxuries: the ability to wait before editing. A fortnight, a week, or a weekend away gives me a fresh perspective for revision.

But sometimes I don't want to wait. Even without a deadline, I may feel excited to put a poem draft into the proverbial forge. That's when I bust out the Font Refresh.

I simply change up my font. From Helvetica, I go to Bauhaus or Copperplate, in green or maroon, right- or center-aligned. Or I type up a handwritten poem or write out a typed one. The visual novelty shakes my familiarity with the poem enough to be able to read what I've actually written—rather than what I think wrote. Because the poem no longer looks like the one I wrote, I find I can evaluate it with greater clarity and synthesize revisions with greater freedom. In fact, sometimes I'll put away a poem for a couple of weeks and still change the font before reviewing it.

FEATURED READING— POLISHING LEVEL: SEQUENCE

You're the Featured Reader; present your poetry sequence to an imaginary audience. Read your poems to them at your voice's natural volume and cadence.

I like having my printed poems on hand so I can stop and jot on the drafts. My make-believe audience doesn't mind waiting for me. If I stumble over a word or phrase, or if something sounds wrong, I attempt a revision in the moment, or I circle the spot so I can come back to it later.

Featured Reading helps me isolate and correct places where my diction obscures my meaning, where I've rhymed unintentionally, or where the words jangle when I want them to hum. I look out at my imaginary audience and see their faces as I read. They're a receptive group, but I can tell when I've lost them: their eyes glaze.

A variation is to imagine saying your poems as part of a conversation. Though my language is more heightened than normal speech, when I speak my poems conversationally, I can sense if my meaning is clear and affecting to the person I imagine speaking to. And I can sense when what I'm saying needs more clarity—and more crafting.

52 PICK UP—POLISHING LEVEL: MANUSCRIPT

The last time I compiled a poetry book, I felt daunted at finding the right order. I began by making swaps within the approximately chronological order the book had arbitrarily taken. I moved the sixth poem first and the first poem second and the second poem somewhere near the end. Then the tenth poem seemed like a better first poem, so I moved the prior first poem second, and the second poem fourth, which wasn't right.

In frustration, I threw all the pages at the ceiling. It was fantastic! My frustration instantly vanished. I felt a new sense of wonder, standing among my poetry as it snowed down around me.

Now I had no order, and I could begin fresh by grouping poems and looking for arcs and relationships. 52 Pick Up let me instantly delete all the preconceptions I had about which poems were supposed to be adjacent to others. I figured if the relationship between poems were strong enough, they'd find one another again.

As I sorted my scatter, four distinct piles emerged based on the perspective of the poems. Each pile had about the same number of poems in it, so I knew I was on the right track. Section three was still giving me problems, so I tossed those fifteen poems into the air again, then reshuffled them into three piles based on an intuitive sense of whether they were "early," "middle" or "late." Sure enough, the early stack included an obvious choice for opening the section, the late stack contained an excellent ending, and the other poems jumped into place like stops on the metro.

GET UP—POLISHING LEVEL: POET

Revising poetry takes concentration. Concentration can cause your body to stagnate with inertia. The spine stiffens, the brain stifles, and thinking loses its suppleness. So get up! Go to another room, get some water, go outside, or run an errand.

In my work as a copywriter, I can't tell you how many times the perfect headline comes to me when I'm away from my desk, when I have finally gotten up for a snack or some air, or just to wander around. That's when the words suddenly click—and I have no way of writing them down! I have to repeat them to myself like a mantra while running for a pen and paper or fumbling to launch my notepad app.

Moving the body moves the mind. If you're stuck on a word or a line or an ending—or if you get stuck trying to decide how you feel about something you've written—then Get Up. (But keep writing essentials in your purse or pocket if you're going far.)

Chances are good that getting up will get you unstuck; and if your poem or line or word doesn't click, at least you'll have had a stretch, which is a benefit in itself.

BAD IDEAS—POLISHING LEVEL: ALL

Years ago, I had a quirky rock band. When someone in the band had an inkling to try something new with one of our songs, my friend, multi-instrumentalist Paul "Mockingbirds" McNees, would say, "That's a terrible idea—let's try it!"

If you don't have any terrible ideas for your poems, come up with some. Be mischievous with yourself. To get you started, here are a few bad ideas off the top of my head:

- Recast your poem as prose. Edit as though you were writing a movie review. Then make it back into a poem.
- Slice your poem into 10-syllable lines and edit as necessary.
- If your poem doesn't rhyme, add rhyme; if it does rhyme, remove the rhyme.
- See if you use any specific noun or verb three or more times in your poem. If so, rewrite to eliminate that word entirely. Or replace it with the word cornflakes.

- Rewrite your poem as a different person—as Emily Dickinson, or comedian Louis C.K., or Pocahontas.
- Rewrite your poem in gibberish, then translate it back into your native tongue.
- Stand on your head until a line revision comes to you.

You may end up discarding what your terrible ideas produce, but you might also salvage gems. Failed attempts enrich what writer/painter/teacher Natalie Goldberg refers to as "the compost pile," a creative morass that can volunteer beautiful, nourishing sprouts. So be brash and reckless with your experiments and welcome even the ugliest offspring as a positive result.

You go to a creative, ephemeral, exciting place to find your poem. Go back there to craft it. You'll use your critical faculties, of course, but remember that hammering and honing, testing and tweaking, all have to be part of the same gutsy, sparkling exploration that inspired the poem to begin with. I hope these somersaults—and others you may discover—help make revision your favorite part of the process. Make these your own, and you'll create things far more wonderful than even the choicest piece of sea glass.

DANIEL ARI's book, *One Way To Ask*, pairs poems in an original form called queron with art by 60 different artists. Besides being a professional copywriter, he writes and publishes poetry and organizes poetry performances and events throughout the Pacific Northwest. He blogs at fightswithpoems.blogspot.com and IMUNURI.blogspot.com. He has recently published poetry in *2014 Poet's Market*, *Writer's Digest*, *carte blanche*, *42 Magazine*, *Cardinal Sins*, *Gold Dust* and *McSweeney's*.

MAGAZINES/ JOURNALS

//

Literary magazines and journals usually provide a poet's first publishing success. In fact, you shouldn't be thinking about book/chapbook publication until your poems have appeared in a variety of magazines, journals and zines (both print and online). This is the preferred way to develop an audience, build publishing credits and learn the ins and outs of the publishing process.

In this section you'll find hundreds of magazines and journals that publish poetry. They range from small black-and-white booklets produced on home computers to major periodicals with high production values and important reputations. To help you sort through these markets and direct your submissions most effectively, we've organized information in each listing according to a basic format that includes contact information, magazine needs, how to submit, and more.

GETTING STARTED, FINDING MARKETS

If you don't have a certain magazine or journal in mind, read randomly through the listings, making notes as you go. (Don't hesitate to write in the margins, underline, use highlighters; it also helps to flag markets that interest you with Post-It Notes). Browsing the listings is an effective way to familiarize yourself with the kind of information presented and the publishing opportunities that are available at various skill levels.

If you have a specific market in mind, however, begin with the General Index. Here all the book's listings are alphabetized along with additional references that may be buried within a listing (such as a press name or competition title).

2 RIVER VIEW

7474 Drexel Dr., University City MO 63130. **E-mail:** 1ong@2River.org. **E-mail:** su3m1t@2river.org. **Website:** www.2River.org. **Contact:** Richard Long. *2River View*, published quarterly online, is a site of poetry, art, and theory. Considers unpublished poetry only. Claims first electronic rights and first North American rights, "meaning that publications here at *2River* must be the first publication to feature the work online and/or in print." Publishes ms 3 months after acceptance. Guidelines available online.

MAGAZINES NEEDS Submit up to 5 poems once per reading period (see website for dates). Paste in body of an e-mail. Prefers poems with these qualities: image, subtlety, and point of view; a surface of worldly exactitude, as well as a depth of semantic ambiguity; and a voice that negotiates with its body of predecessors. Publishes 10 poets/issue.

ABLE MUSE

467 Saratoga Ave., #602, San Jose CA 95129-1326. **Website:** www.ablemuse.com. **Contact:** Alex Pepple, editor. "*Able Muse: A Review of Poetry, Prose & Art* published twice/year, predominantly publishes metrical poetry complemented by art and photography, fiction, and nonfiction including essays, book reviews, and interviews with a focus on metrical and formal poetry. We are looking for well-crafted poems of any length or subject that employ skillful and imaginative use of meter and rhyme, executed in a contemporary idiom, that reads as naturally as your free-verse poems." Acquires first rights. Time between acceptance and publication is 3 months. Sometimes comments on rejected poems. Responds in 4 months. Sometimes sends prepublication galleys. Subscription: $24 for 1 year.

○ Considers poetry by teens. "High levels of craft still required even for teen writers." Also sponsors 2 annual contests: The Able Muse Write Prize for Poetry & Fiction, and The Able Muse Book Award for Poetry (in collaboration with Able Muse Press at www.ablemusepress.com). See website for details.

MAGAZINES NEEDS Has published poetry by Mark Jarman, A.E. Stallings, Annie Finch, Rhina P. Espaillat, Rachel Hadas, and R.S. Gwynn. Receives about 1,500 poems/year, accepts about 5%. Submit 1-5 poems and short bio. Electronic submissions only welcome through the online form at www.ablemuse.

com/submit, or by e-mail to editor@ablemuse.com. "The e-mail submission method is being phased out. We strongly encourage using the online submission method." Will not accept postal submissions. Reviews books of poetry. Send materials for review consideration.

ABRAXAS

P.O. Box 260113, Madison WI 53726-0113. **E-mail:** abraxaspress@hotmail.com. **Website:** www.abraxaspressinc.com/Welcome.html. **Contact:** Ingrid Swanberg, editor in chief. *ABRAXAS*, published irregularly (9- to 12-month intervals or much longer) is interested in contemporary lyric poetry, experimental poetry, and poetry in translation. When submitting translations, please include poems in the original language. *ABRAXAS'* new format features longer selections of fewer contributors. Does not want political posing or academic regurgitations. Has published poetry by Ivan Argüelles, Denise Levertov, Ceésar Vallejo, d.a. levy, T.L. Kryss, and Andrea Moorhead. Sample copy: $4 USD plus $1.90 s&h (or $9 international s&h). Subscription: $32 for 4 issues; $52 international for 4 issues. Guidelines online. Unsolicited submissions are considered only during specified reading periods (announced online).

○ *ABRAXAS* is up to 80 pages, digest-sized, litho-offset-printed, flat-spined, with matte or glossy card cover with original art and photography. Press run is 700.

MAGAZINES NEEDS Submit 7-10 poems with SASE. No electronic submissions. Pays 1 contributer's copy and offers 40% discount on additional copies.

ABZ

P.O. Box 2746, Huntington WV 25727. **E-mail:** editor@abzpress.onmicrosoft.com. **E-mail:** abzpress@gmail.com. **Website:** abzpress.sharepoint.com/Pages/default.aspx. *ABZ*, published every other year, wants poetry using interesting and exciting language. Reads submissions May 1-July 1. Sample copy for $8. Guidelines online.

MAGAZINES NEEDS Submit poems by mail with SASE. Does not consider e-mail submissions. Pays 2 contributor's copies and small stipend.

TIPS "We want to read your best poems."

ACM (ANOTHER CHICAGO MAGAZINE)

E-mail: editors@anotherchicagomagazine.net. **Website:** www.anotherchicagomagazine.net. **Contact:** Jacob S. Knabb, editor-in-chief; Caroline Eick, managing editor. "*Another Chicago Magazine* is a biannual literary magazine that publishes work by both new and established writers. We look for work that goes beyond the artistic and academic to include and address the larger world. The editors read submissions in fiction, poetry, and creative nonfiction year round. The best way to know what we publish is to read what we publish. If you haven't read *ACM* before, order a sample copy to know if your work is appropriate." Sends prepublication galleys. Acquires first serial rights. Responds in 3 months to queries; 6 months to mss. Submit online through website.

○ Work published in *ACM* has been included frequently in *The Best American Poetry* and *The Pushcart Prize*.

MAGAZINES NEEDS Length: No more than 4 pages.

TIPS "Support literary publishing by subscribing to at least one literary journal—if not ours, another. Get used to rejection slips, and don't get discouraged. Keep introductory letters short. Make sure ms has name and address on every page, and that it is clean, neat, and proofread. We are looking for stories with freshness and originality in subject angle and style and work that encounters the world."

ACORN

Spare Poems Press, 115 Conifer Lane, Walnut Creek CA 94598. **E-mail:** acornhaiku@gmail.com. **Website:** www.acornhaiku.com. **Contact:** Susan Antolin, editor. "Biannual magazine dedicated to publishing the best of contemporary English-language haiku and in particular to showcasing individual poems that reveal the extraordinary moments found in everyday life." Buys first rights, one-time rights. Publishes ms an average of 1-3 months after acceptance. Responds in 3 weeks to mss. Guidelines and sample poems available online at www.acornhaiku.com.

○ Reads submissions in January-February and July-August only.

MAGAZINES NEEDS "Decisions made by editor on a rolling basis. Poems judged purely on merit." Sometimes acceptance conditional on minor edits. Often comments on rejected poems. Accepts submissions via mail or e-mail, however e-mail is preferred. "Does *not* want epigrams, musings, and overt emotion poured into 17 syllables; surreal, science fiction, or political commentary 'ku;' strong puns or raunchy humor. A 5-7-5 syllable count is not necessary or encouraged." Length: 1-5 lines; 17 or fewer syllables.

TIPS "This is primarily a journal for those with a focused interest in *haiku*. It is a much richer genre than one might surmise from many of the recreational websites that claim to promote '*haiku*.'"

ACUMEN MAGAZINE

Ember Press, 6 The Mount, Higher Furzeham, Brixham, South Devon TQ5 8QY, United Kingdom. **E-mail:** patriciaoxley6@gmail.com. **Website:** www.acumen-poetry.co.uk. **Contact:** Patricia Oxley, general editor. *Acumen*, published 3 times/year in January, May, and September, is "a general literary magazine with emphasis on good poetry." Wants "well-crafted, high-quality, imaginative poems showing a sense of form." Does not want "experimental verse of an obscene type." Has published poetry by Ruth Padel, William Oxley, Hugo Williams, Peter Porter, Danielle Hope, and Leah Fritz. Responds in 3 months. Submission guidelines online at website.

○ *Acumen* is 120 pages, A5, perfect-bound.

MAGAZINES NEEDS Submit 5-6 poems at a time. All submissions should be accompanied by SASE. Include name and address on each separate sheet. Accepts e-mail submissions, but see guidelines on the website. Will send rejections, acceptances, proofs, and other communications via e-mail overseas to dispense with IRCs and other international postage. Any poem that may have chance of publication is shortlisted, and from list final poems are chosen. All other poems returned within 2 months. "If a reply is required, please send IRCs. One IRC for a decision, 3 IRCs if work is to be returned." Willing to reply by e-mail to save IRCs. Pays "by negotiation" and 1 contributor's copy.

TIPS "Read *Acumen* carefully to see what kind of poetry we publish. Also, read widely in many poetry magazines, and don't forget the poets of the past—they can still teach us a great deal."

THE ADIRONDACK REVIEW

Black Lawrence Press, 8405 Bay Parkway, Apt C8, Brooklyn NY 11214. **E-mail:** editors@theadirondackreview.com. **Website:** www.adirondackreview.homestead.com. **Contact:** Angela Leroux-Lindsey, editor; Amanda Himmelmann, fiction editor; Nicholas Samaras, poetry editor. *The Adirondack Review*, published quarterly online, is a literary journal dedicated to quality free verse poetry and short fiction as well as book and film reviews, art, photography, and interviews. "We are open to both new and established writers. Our only requirement is excellence. We would like to publish more French and German poetry translations as well as original poems in these languages. We publish an eclectic mix of voices and styles, but all poems should show attention to craft. We are open to beginners who demonstrate talent, as well as established voices. The work should speak for itself." Acquires first rights. Rights revert to author upon publication. Responds to queries in 1-2 months; in 2-4 months.

MAGAZINES NEEDS Submit 2-5 poems at a time; include brief bio. Submit via online submissions manager. Does not want "religious, overly sentimental, horror/gothic, rhyming, greeting card, pet-related, humor, or science fiction poetry."

TIPS "*The Adirondack Review* accepts submissions all year long, so send us your poetry, fiction, nonfiction, translation, reviews, interviews, and art and photography."

ADVOCATE, PKA'S PUBLICATION

1881 Little Westkill Rd., Prattsville NY 12468. (518)299-3103. **Website:** advocatepka.weebly.com; www.facebook.com/Advocate/PKAPublications; www.facebook.com/GaitedHorseAssociation. advoad@localnet.com. **Contact:** Patricia Keller, publisher. *Advocate, PKA's Publication*, published bimonthly, is an advertiser-supported tabloid using "original, previously unpublished works, such as feature stories, essays, 'think' pieces, letters to the editor, profiles, humor, fiction, poetry, puzzles, cartoons, or line drawings. Advocates for good writers and quality writings. We publish art, fiction, photos and poetry. *Advocate*'s submitters are talented people of all ages who do not earn their livings as writers. We wish to promote the arts and to give those we publish the opportunity to be published." Acquires first rights for mss, artwork, and photographs. Pays on publication with contributor's copies. Publishes ms 2-18 months after acceptance. Responds to queries in 6 weeks; mss in 2 months. Sample copy: $5 (includes guidelines). Subscription: $18.50 (6 issues). Previous 6 issues are on our website.

○ "This publication has a strong horse orientation." Includes Gaited Horse Association newsletter. Horse-oriented stories, poetry, art and photos are currently needed.

MAGAZINES NEEDS "Poetry ought to speak to people and not be so oblique as to have meaning only to the poet. If I had to be there to understand the poem, don't send it. Also looking for horse-related poems, stories, drawings, and photos." Considers poetry by children and teens (when included with release form signed by adult). Accepts about 25% of poems received. Wants "nearly any kind of poetry, any length." Occasionally comments on rejected poems. Submit any number of poems at a time. No religious or pornographic poetry. Pays contributor copies.

TIPS "Please, no simultaneous submissions, work that has appeared on the Internet, pornography, overt religiosity, anti-environmentalism, or gratuitous violence. Artists and photographers should keep in mind that we are a b&w paper. Please do not send postcards. Use envelope with SASE."

AFRICAN VOICES

African Voices Communications, Inc., 270 W. 96th St., New York NY 10025. (212)865-2982. **Fax:** (212)316-3335. **E-mail:** info@africanvoices.com. **Website:** www.africanvoices.com. **Contact:** Maitefa Angaza, managing editor; Mariahadessa Ekere Tallie, poetry editor. *African Voices*, published quarterly, is an "art and literary magazine that highlights the work of people of color. We publish ethnic literature and poetry on any subject. We also consider all themes and styles: avant-garde, free verse, haiku, light verse, and traditional. We do not wish to limit the reader or author." Buys first North American serial rights. Pays on publication. Publishes ms an average of 3-6 months after acceptance. Responds in 3 months to queries. Editorial lead time 3 months. Sample copy: $6. Subscription: $20.

○ *African Voices* is about 48 pages, magazine-sized, professionally printed, saddle-stapled, with paper cover. Receives about 100 submissions/year, accepts about 30%. Press run is 20,000.

MAGAZINES NEEDS Submit no more than 2 poems at a time. Accepts submissions by e-mail (in text box), by fax, and by postal mail. Cover letter and SASE required. Seldom comments on rejected poems. Reviews books of poetry in 500-1,000 words. Send materials for review consideration to Ekere Tallie. Considers poetry written by children. Has published poetry by Reg E. Gaines, Maya Angelou, Jessica Care Moore, Asha Bandele, Tony Medina, and Louis Reyes Rivera. Length: 5-100 lines. Pays 2 contributor copies.

ALSO OFFERS Sponsors periodic poetry contests and readings. Send SASE for details.

TIPS "A manuscript stands out if it is neatly typed with a well-written and interesting storyline or plot. Originality is encouraged. We are interested in more horror, erotic, and drama pieces. *AV* wants to highlight the diversity in our culture. Stories must touch the humanity in us all. We strongly encourage new writers/poets to send in their work. Accepted contributors are encouraged to subscribe."

AGNI

Creative Writing Program, Boston University, 236 Bay State Rd., Boston MA 02215. (617)353-7135. **Fax:** (617)353-7134. **E-mail:** agni@bu.edu. **Website:** www.agnimagazine.org. **Contact:** Sven Birkerts, editor. "Eclectic literary magazine publishing first-rate poems, essays, translations, and stories." Buys serial rights, rights to reprint in *AGNI* anthology (with author's consent). Pays on publication. Publishes ms an average of 6 months after acceptance. Responds in 2 weeks to queries; in 4 months to mss. Editorial lead time 1 year. Sample copy: $10 or online. Guidelines available online.

Reading period is September 1-May 31 only. Online magazine carries original content not found in print edition. All submissions are considered for both. Founding editor Askold Melnyczuk won the 2001 Nora Magid Award for Magazine Editing. Work from *AGNI* has been included and cited regularly in the *Pushcart Prize* and *Best American* anthologies.

MAGAZINES NEEDS Submit no more than 5 poems at a time. No e-mail submissions. Cover letter is required ("brief, sincere"). "No fancy fonts, gimmicks. Include SASE or e-mail address; no preformatted reply cards." Pays $20/page up to $150.

TIPS "We're also looking for extraordinary translations from little-translated languages. It is important to read work published in *AGNI* before submitting, to see if your own might be compatible."

AGNIESZKA'S DOWRY (AGD)

A Small Garlic Press (ASGP), 5445 N. Sheridan Rd., #3003, Chicago IL 60640. **E-mail:** marek@enteract.com; ketzle@ketzle.net. **Website:** asgp.org. **Contact:** Marek Lugowski and Katrina Grace Craig Valvis, co-editors. "*Agnieszka's Dowry (AgD)* is an innovative installation of mostly contemporary and mostly not-yet-famous literary texts (poems, letters to Ag-

nieszka, occasional short short stories), computer and freehand art, photography, and more. The magazine is published both in print and online. The print version consists of professionally crafted chapbooks. The online version comprises fast-loading pages employing an intuitive, if uncanny, navigation in an interesting space, all conducive to fast and comfortable reading. No restrictions on form or type. We use contextual and juxtapositional tie-ins with other material in making choices, so visiting the online *AgD* or reading a chapbook of an *AgD* issue is required of anyone making a submission." Acquires one-time rights where applicable. Responds in 2 months. Single copy: $2 plus $8 s&h. Make checks payable to A Small Garlic Press.

Agnieszka's Dowry is 5.5x8.5, stapled, 20-60 pages, heavy opaque white laser paper, cardstock cover, saddle-stitched (stapled), with cover art and often with internal art, in grayscale.

MAGAZINES NEEDS Submit 5-10 poems at a time. Accepts e-mail submissions only (pasted into body of message in plain text, sent to both editors simultaneously; no attachments). "We ask you to read well into *Agnieszka's Dowry* and to fit your submissions to the partially filled content of its open issues." Pays 1 contributor's copy.

ALASKA QUARTERLY REVIEW

University of Alaska Anchorage, 3211 Providence Dr. (ESH 208), Anchorage AK 99508. **Fax:** 907-786-6916. **E-mail:** aqr@uaa.alaska.edu. **Website:** www.uaa.alaska.edu/aqr. **Contact:** Ronald Spatz, editor in chief. "*Alaska Quarterly Review* is a literary journal devoted to contemporary literary art, publishing fiction, short plays, poetry, photo essays, and literary nonfiction in traditional and experimental styles. The editors encourage new and emerging writers, while continuing to publish award-winning and established writers." Buys first North American serial rights. Upon request, rights will be transferred back to author after publication. Publishes ms an average of 6 months after acceptance. Responds in 4 months to queries; in 6 weeks-4 months to mss. Sample copy: $6. Guidelines online.

Magazine: 6×9; 232-300 pages; 60 lb. Glatfelter paper; 12 pt. C15 black ink or 4-color; varnish cover stock; photos on cover and photo essays. Reads mss August 15-May 15.

MAGAZINES NEEDS Submit poetry by postal mail. Include cover letter with contact information and SASE for return of ms. No light verse. Length: up to 20 pages. Pays contributor's copies and honoraria when funding is available.

ALSO OFFERS Guest poetry editors have included Stuart Dybek, Jane Hirshfield, Stuart Dischell, Maxine Kumin, Pattiann Rogers, Dorianne Laux, Peggy Shumaker, Olena Kalytiak Davis, Nancy Eimers, Michael Ryan, and Billy Collins.

TIPS "Although we respond to e-mail queries, we cannot review electronic submissions."

ALBATROSS

The Anabiosis Press, 2 South New St., Bradford MA 01835. (978)469-7085. **E-mail:** rsmyth@anabiosispress.org. **Website:** www.anabiosispress.org. **Contact:** Richard Smyth, editor. *Albatross*, published "as soon as we have accepted enough quality poems to publish an issue—about 1 per year," considers the albatross "to be a metaphor for the environment. The journal's title is drawn from Coleridge's *The Rime of the Ancient Mariner* and is intended to invoke the allegorical implications of that poem. This is not to say that we publish only environmental or nature poetry but that we are biased toward such subject matter. We publish mostly free verse, and we prefer a narrative style." Acquires all rights. Returns rights provided that "previous publication in *Albatross* is mentioned in all subsequent reprintings." Time between acceptance and publication is 6 months to a year. Responds in 2-3 months to poems. Sample copy for $5. Subscription: $8 for 2 issues. Guidelines available online.

○   *Albatross* is 28 pages, digest-sized, laser-typeset, with linen cover.

MAGAZINES NEEDS Submit 3-5 poems at a time. Accepts e-mail submissions if included in body of message (but is "sometimes quicker at returning mailed submissions"). Name and address must accompany e-mail submissions. Cover letter is not required. "We do, however, need bio notes and SASE for return or response. Poems should be typed single-spaced, with name, address, and phone number in upper left corner." Has published poetry by Richard Brobst, Mary Fitzpatrick, Stephen Malin, Janet McCann, and John McKernan. Wants "poetry written in a strong, mature voice that conveys a deeply felt experience or makes a powerful statement." Does not want "rhyming poetry, prose poetry, or haiku." Length: up to 100 lines/poem. Pays 1 contributor's copy.

ALBERTA VIEWS

Alberta Views, Ltd., Suite 208, 320 23rd Ave. SW, Calgary AB T2S 0J2, Canada. (403)243-5334; (877)212-5334. **Fax:** (403)243-8599. **E-mail:** queries@albertaviews.ab.ca. **Website:** www.albertaviews.ab.ca. **Contact:** Evan Osenton, editor. "We are a regional magazine providing thoughtful commentary and background information on issues of concern to Albertans. Most of our writers are Albertans." Buys first North American serial rights, electronic rights. Pays on publication. Publishes ms an average of 3 months after acceptance. Responds in 6 weeks to queries; 2 months to mss. Editorial lead time 4 months. Sample copy free. "If you are a writer, illustrator, or photographer interested in contributing to *Alberta Views*, please see our contributor's guidelines online."

○   No phone queries.

MAGAZINES NEEDS Accepts unsolicited poetry. Submit complete ms.

THE ALEMBIC

Providence College, English Dept., Attn: The Alembic Editors, 1 Cunningham Square, Providence RI 02918-0001. **Website:** www.providence.edu/english/creative-writing/Pages/alembic.aspx. **Contact:** Magazine has revolving editor. Editorial term: 1 year. "*The Alembic* is an international literary journal featuring the work of both established and student writers and photographers. It is published each April by Providence College in Providence, Rhode Island." Acquires first rights. Publication is not copyrighted. Responds in 1 month to queries; in 8 months to mss. Sample: $15. Subscription: $25/2years.

○   Magazine: 6×9, 80 pages. Contains illustrations, photographs.

MAGAZINES NEEDS Submit up to 5 poems. Does not accept online submissions. Has published poems by Tara McLaughlin, Melanie Souchet, Jackleen Holton, Peter Mishler, Dennis Rhodes, Donna Pucciani, and Sarah O'Brien.

TIPS "We're looking for stories that are wise, memorable, grammatical, economical, poetic in the right places, and end strongly. Take Heraclitus' claim that 'character is fate' to heart and study the strategies, styles, and craft of such masters as Anton Chekov, J. Cheever, Flannery O'Connor, John Updike, Rick Bass, Phillip Roth, Joyce Carol Oates, William Treavor, Lorrie Moore, and Ethan Canin."

ALIMENTUM, THE LITERATURE OF FOOD

P.O. Box 210028, Nashville TN 37221. **E-mail:** editor@ alimentumjournal.com. **Website:** www.alimentum-journal.com. **Contact:** Peter Selgin, fiction and non-fiction editor; Cortney Davis, poetry editor. "*Alimentum* celebrates the literature and art of food. We welcome work from like-minded writers, musicians, and artists." Acquires First North American serial rights. Rights revert to authors upon publication. Pays on publication. Manuscript published 1-2 years after acceptance. Responds in 3 months to mss. Sample copy: $10. Guidelines available online. "We do not read year round. Check website for reading periods."

Semiannual. *Alimentum* is 128 pages, perfect-bound, with matte coated cover with 4-color art, interior b&w illustration, includes ads. Contains illustrations. Essays appearing in *Alimentum* have appeared in *Best American Essays* and *Best Food Writing*.

MAGAZINES NEEDS Send up to 5 poems with cover letter (postal mail only). Send either SASE (or IRC) for return of ms or disposable copy of ms and #10 SASE for reply only. Has published poetry by Dick Allen, Stephen Gibson, Carly Sachs, Jen Karetnik, and Virginia Chase Sutton. Pays 1 contributor's copy.

ALSO OFFERS Publishes an annual broadside of "menupoems" for restaurants during National Poetry Month in April.

TIPS "No e-mail submissions, only snail mail. Mark outside envelope to the attention of Poetry, Fiction, or Nonfiction Editor."

ALIVE NOW

1908 Grand Ave., P.O. Box 340004, Nashville TN 37203. (615)340-7254. **E-mail:** alivenow@upper-room.org. **Website:** www.alivenow.org; alivenow. upperroom.org. **Contact:** Beth A. Richardson, editor. *Alive Now,* published bimonthly, is a devotional magazine that invites readers to enter an ever-deepening relationship with God. "*Alive Now* seeks to nourish people who are hungry for a sacred way of living. Submissions should invite readers to see God in the midst of daily life by exploring how contemporary issues impact their faith lives. Each word must be vivid and dynamic and contribute to the whole. We make selections based on a list of upcoming themes. Manuscripts which do not fit a theme will be returned." Pays on acceptance. Subscription: $17.95/year (6 issues); $26.95 for 2 years (12 issues). Additional subscription information, including foreign rates, available on website. Guidelines online at website. Submissions should invite readers to seek God in the midst of daily life by exploring how contemporary issues impact their faith lives. If ms does not fit a theme, it will not be considered. Themes can be found on website. Prefers electronic submissions attached as Word document. Postal submissions should include SASE. Include name, address, theme on each sheet. Payment will be made at the time of acceptance for publication.

MAGAZINES NEEDS Pays $35 or more on acceptance.

ALLIGATOR JUNIPER

(928)350-2012. **Website:** alligatorjuniper.wordpress. com. "*Alligator Juniper* features contemporary poetry, fiction, creative nonfiction, and b&w photography. We encourage submissions from writers and photographers at all levels: emerging, early career, and established." Annual magazine comprised of the winners and finalists of national contests. "All entrants pay an $18 submission fee and receive a complementary copy of that year's issue in the spring. First-place winning writers in each genre recieve a $1,000 prize. The first-place winner in photography receives a $500 award. Finalists in writing and images are published and paid in contributor copies. There is currently no avenue for submissions other than the annual contest." Usually responds in January to mss. Always comments on mss. Sample: $5. Guidelines online.

MAGAZINES NEEDS Accepts submissions only through annual contest. If submitting by regular mail, include $18 entry fee payable to *Alligator Juniper* for each set of up to 5 poems. Include cover letter with name, address, phone number, and e-mail. Include author's name on first page. "Double-sided submissions are encouraged." No e-mail submissions. Length: open.

AMBIT

Staithe House, Main Road, Brancaster Staithe, Norfolk PE31 8PB, United Kingdom. **E-mail:** info@ambitmagazine.co.uk. **Website:** www.ambitmagazine. co.uk. **Contact:** Briony Bax, editor; Liz Berry and Declan Ryan, poetry editors. *Ambit* magazine is a literary and artwork quarterly published in the U.K. and read internationally. *Ambit* is put together entirely from unsolicited, previously unpublished poetry and short fiction submissions. Responds in 2-3 months. Sample copy: £9. Submit using Submittable portal on website on www.ambitmagazine.co.uk. There are 2 windows for submissions: February 1-April 1 and September 1-November 1. Please only submit during these windows. No e-mail submissions. Guidelines available in magazine or online.

MAGAZINES NEEDS Submit 3-6 poems via Submittable. No previously published poems (including on websites or blogs). Poems should be typed, double-spaced. Never comments on rejected poems. Does not want "indiscriminately centre-justified poems, jazzy fonts, or poems all in italics for the sake of it." Payment details on website.

TIPS "Read a copy of the magazine before submitting!"

THE AMERICAN DISSIDENT: A JOURNAL OF LITERATURE, DEMOCRACY & DISSIDENCE

217 Commerce Rd., Barnstable MA 02630. **E-mail:** todslone@hotmail.com. **Website:** www.theamericandissident.org. **Contact:** G. Tod Slone, editor. Reviews books/chapbooks of poetry and other magazines in 250 words, single-book format. Send materials for review consideration. Journal, published 2 times/year, provides "a forum for, amongst other things, criticism of the academic/literary established order, which clearly discourages vigorous debate, cornerstone of democracy, to the evident detriment of American Literature. The Journal seeks rare poets daring to risk going against that established-order grain." Wants "poetry, reviews, artwork, and short (1,000 words) essays in English, French, or Spanish, written on the edge with a dash of personal risk and stemming from personal experience, conflict with power, and/or involvement." Submissions should be "iconoclastic and parrhesiastic in nature." Acquires first North American serial rights. Publishes ms 2 months after acceptance. Responds in 1 month. Guidelines available for SASE.

Magazine: 56-64 pages, digest-sized, offset-printed, perfect-bound, with card cover. Press run is 200. Single copy: $9; subscriptions: individuals, $18; institutions $20. Almost always comments on rejected poems.

MAGAZINES NEEDS Submit 3 poems at a time. E-mail submissions from subscribers only. "Far too many poets submit without even reading the guidelines. Include SASE and cover letter containing not credits, but rather personal dissident information, as well as incidents that provoked you to 'go upright and vital, and speak the rude truth in all ways' (Emerson)." Pays 1 contributor's copy.

TIPS "Every poet knows what he or she should not write about to avoid upsetting those in positions of literary, cultural, and/or academic power. *The American Dissident* seeks to publish those poets who now and then will break those taboos and thus raise truth telling above getting published, funded, invited, tenured, nominated, and/or anointed. *The American Dissident* is, by the way, one of the very few literary journals encouraging and publishing in each issue criticism with its regard."

AMERICAN LITERARY REVIEW

University of North Texas, P.O. Box 311307, Denton TX 76203-1307. (940)565-2755. **E-mail:** americanliteraryreview@gmail.com. **Website:** www.americanliteraryreview.com. **Contact:** Bonnie Friedman, editor in chief. "The *American Literary Review* publishes "excellent poetry, fiction, and nonfiction by writers at all stages of their careers." Beginning in fall 2013, *ALR* became an online publication." Publishes ms within 2 years of acceptance. Responds in 3-5 months to mss. Guidelines online.

Reading period is from October 1-May 1.

MAGAZINES NEEDS "Poetry selections are made by a widely read group with eclectic tastes who look for the best poems, regardless of form or subject matter." Has published poetry by Kathleen Pierce, Mark Irwin, Stephen Dunn, William Olsen, David St. John, and Cate Marvin. Submit up to 5 poems online through submission manager for a fee of $3. Does not accept submissions via e-mail or postal mail.

TIPS "We encourage writers and artists to examine our journal."

THE AMERICAN POETRY JOURNAL

P. O. Box 2080, Aptos CA 95001-2080. **E-mail:** editor@americanpoetryjournal.com. **Website:** http://home.comcast.net/~jpdancingbear/apj.html. **Contact:** J.P. Dancing Bear, senior editor. *The American Poetry Journal*, published annually (July), seeks to publish work using poetic device, favoring image, metaphor, and good sound. Likes alliteration, extended metaphors, image, movement, and poems that can pass the "so what" test. *The American Poetry Journal* has in mind the reader who delights in discovering what a poem can do to the tongue and what the poem paints on the cave of the mind. Wants poems that exhibit strong, fresh imagery, metaphor, and good sound. Does not want narratives about family, simplistic verse, annoying word hodge-podges. Acquires first rights. Publishes ms 2-6 months after acceptance. Responds in 3 months. Guidelines available on website.

○ Accepts submissions through online submission form only.

MAGAZINES NEEDS Submit 3-5 poems at a time. Electronic submissions only. Cover letter is preferred. Considers unsolicited submissions February 1-May 31. All decisions made no later than June 30. Poets may submit no more than twice during the reading period. Poems are read first for clarity and technique, then read aloud for sound quality. Pays 1 contributor's copy.

TIPS "Know the magazine you are submitting to, before you commit your work and yourself. It's not that difficult, but it helps your odds when the editor can tell that you get what the magazine is about. Reading an issue is the easiest way to do this."

THE AMERICAN POETRY REVIEW

The University of the Arts, 320 S. Broad St., Hamilton #313, Philadelphia PA 19102. **E-mail:** sberg@aprweb. org. **Website:** www.aprweb.org. **Contact:** Stephen Berg, editor. "*The American Poetry Review* is dedicated to reaching a worldwide audience with a diverse array of the best contemporary poetry and literary prose. *APR* also aims to expand the audience interested in poetry and literature, and to provide authors, especially poets, with a far-reaching forum in which to present their work." Acquires first serial rights. Responds in 6 months. Sample: $4.50. Guidelines online.

○ *APR* has included the work of over 1,500 writers, among whom there are 9 Nobel Prize laureates and 33 Pulitzer Prize winners.

MAGAZINES NEEDS Submit up to 5 poems via online submissions manager. Has published poetry by D.A. Powell, James Franco, Dean Faulwell, and Caroline Pittman.

AMERICAN TANKA

E-mail: editor@americantanka.com. **Website:** www. americantanka.com. "*American Tanka* seeks to present the best and most well-crafted English-language tanka being written today, in a visually calm space that allows the reader's eye to focus on the single poem and linger in the moment it evokes." Wants "concise and vivid language, good crafting, and echo of the original Japanese form but with unique and contemporary content." Does not want "anything that's not tanka. No sequences or titled groupings."

Acquires first North American serial rights. Responds in 3 months.

MAGAZINES NEEDS Submit up to 5 poems. Accepts submissions by online submission form found on website or by e-mail (pasted into body). Welcomes submissions from anyone who has been writing tanka: experienced tanka poets, experienced poets in other forms, and novices. Seeks concise, well-crafted, 5-line tanka that evoke a specific moment in time. Has published poetry by Sanford Goldstein, Marianne Bluger, Jeanne Emrich, Tom Hartman, Larry Kimmel, Pamela Miller Ness, George Swede, and many others.

🅢 ANALOG SCIENCE FICTION & FACT

Dell Magazines, 44 Wall St., Suite 904, New York NY 10005-2401. **E-mail:** analog@dellmagazines.com. **Website:** www.analogsf.com. **Contact:** Trevor Quachri, editor. *Analog* seeks "solidly entertaining stories exploring solidly thought-out speculative ideas. But the ideas, and consequently the stories, are always new. Real science and technology have always been important in *ASF*, not only as the foundation of its fiction but as the subject of articles about real research with big implications for the future." Buys first North American serial rights, buys nonexclusive foreign serial rights. Pays on acceptance. Publishes ms an average of 10 months after acceptance. Responds in 2-3 months to mss. Sample copy: $5 and SASE. Guidelines online.

○ Fiction published in *Analog* has won numerous Nebula and Hugo Awards.

MAGAZINES NEEDS Send poems via online submissions manager (preferred) or postal mail. Does not accept e-mail submissions. Length: up to 40 lines/poem. Pays $1/line.

TIPS "I'm looking for irresistibly entertaining stories that make me think about things in ways I've never done before. Read several issues to get a broad feel for our tastes, but don't try to imitate what you read."

🅢 ANCIENT PATHS

E-mail: skylarburris@yahoo.com. **Website:** www.editorskylar.com/magazine/table.html. **Contact:** Skylar H. Burris, Editor. *Ancient Paths* provides "a forum for quality Christian poetry and flash fiction. All works should have a spiritual theme. The theme may be explicitly Christian or broadly religious. Works published in *Ancient Paths* explore themes such as redemption, sin, forgiveness, doubt, faith, gratitude for the ordinary blessings of life, spiritual struggle, and spiritual growth. Please, no overly didactic works. Subtlety is preferred." Acquires electronic rights. Author is free to republish work elsewhere. Responds in 4-6 weeks "if rejected; longer if being seriously considered." Single past printed sample copy: $9. Make checks payable to Skylar Burris. Guidelines available on website.

O New issues of *Ancient Paths* are no longer being produced in print. *Ancient Paths* online is published as a regularly updated Facebook page.

MAGAZINES NEEDS E-mail all submissions. Paste poems in e-mail message. Use the subject heading "AP Online Submission (title of your work)." Include your name and e-mail address at the top of your e-mail. Poems may be rhymed, unrhymed, free verse, or formal. Does not want "preachy" poetry, inconsistent meter, or forced rhyme; no stream of conscious or avant-garde work; no esoteric academic poetry. Length: no more than 60 lines. Pays $1.25 per poem. Published poets also receive discount code for $3 off 2 past printed issues.

TIPS "Read the great religious poets: John Donne, George Herbert, T.S. Eliot, Lord Tennyson. Remember not to preach. This is a literary magazine, not a pulpit. This does not mean you do not communicate morals or celebrate God. It means you are not overbearing or simplistic when you do so."

ANDERBO.COM

Anderbo Publishing, 270 Lafayette St., Suite 705, New York NY 10012-3364. **E-mail:** editors@anderbo.com. **Website:** www.anderbo.com. **Contact:** Rick Rofihe, editor-in-chief. Online literary magazine/journal. "Quality fiction, poetry, 'fact' and photography on a website with 'print-feel' design." Member CLMP. Acquires first rights, first North American serial rights, one-time rights, electronic rights. Publication is copyrighted. Publishes ms 1 month after acceptance. Responds to queries in 2 weeks. Responds to mss in 1-4 weeks. Considers simultaneous submissions. Editorial lead time 1-2 months. Guidelines available on website.

MAGAZINES Needs "We are looking for serious, affecting work." Publishes 40 poems/year. Submit up to 6 poems. Send complete ms. "We prefer your poems to be in the e-mail or together as a single attachment." Length: 6-60 lines. Does not pay.

TIPS "We are looking for fiction that is unique, urgent, accessible and involving. Look at our site and read what we've already published."

⊙⊙ THE ANTIGONISH REVIEW

St. Francis Xavier University, P.O. Box 5000, Antigonish NS B2G 2W5, Canada. (902)867-3962. **Fax:** (902)867-5563. **E-mail:** tar@stfx.ca. **Website:** www. antigonishreview.com. **Contact:** Bonnie McIsaac, office manager. *The Antigonish Review*, published quarterly, tries "to produce the kind of literary and visual mosaic that the modern sensibility requires or would respond to." Rights retained by author. Pays on publication. Publishes ms an average of 8 months after acceptance. Responds in 1 month to queries; in 6 months to mss. Editorial lead time 4 months. Sample copy: $7 or online. Guidelines for #10 SASE or online.

MAGAZINES NEEDS Open to poetry on any subject written from any point of view and in any form. However, writers should expect their work to be considered within the full context of old and new poetry in English and other languages. Has published poetry by Andy Wainwright, W.J. Keith, Michael Hulse, Jean McNeil, M. Travis Lane, and Douglas Lochhead. Submit 6-8 poems at a time. A preferable submission would be 3-4 poems. Lines/poem: not over 80, i.e., 2 pages. Pays $10/page to a maximum of $50 and 2 contributor's copies.

TIPS "Send for guidelines and/or sample copy. Send ms with cover letter and SASE with submission."

⊙ ANTIOCH REVIEW

P.O. Box 148, Yellow Springs OH 45387-0148. **E-mail:** mkeyes@antiochreview.org. **Website:** www.antiochreview.org. **Contact:** Robert S. Fogarty, editor; Judith Hall, poetry editor. Literary and cultural review of contemporary issues and literature for general readership. *The Antioch Review* "is an independent quarterly of critical and creative thought. For well over 70 years, creative authors, poets, and thinkers have found a friendly reception—regardless of formal reputation. We get far more poetry than we can possibly accept, and the competition is keen. Here, where form and content are so inseparable and reaction is so personal, it is difficult to state requirements or limitations. Studying recent issues of *The Antioch Review* should be helpful." Pays on publication. Publishes ms an average of 10 months after acceptance. Responds in 3-6 months to mss. Sample copy: $7. Guidelines available online.

O Work published in *The Antioch Review* has been included frequently in *The Best American Stories*, *Best American Essays*, and *The Best*

American Poetry. Finalist for National Magazine Award for essays in 2009 and 2011, and for fiction in 2010.

MAGAZINES NEEDS Has published poetry by Richard Howard, Jacqueline Osherow, Alice Fulton, Richard Kenney, and others. Receives about 3,000 submissions/year. Submit 3-6 poems at a time. No previously published poems or simultaneous submissions. Include SASE with all submissions. No light or inspirational verse. Poetry submissions are not accepted between between May 1-September 1. Pays $20/printed page, plus 2 contributor's copies.

APALACHEE REVIEW

Apalachee Press, P.O. Box 10469, Tallahassee FL 32302. (850)644-9114. **E-mail:** arsubmissions@gmail.com (for queries outside the U.S.). **Website:** apalacheereview.org. **Contact:** Michael Trammell, editor; Kathleen Laufenberg, nonfiction editor; Mary Jane Ryals, fiction editor; Jay Snodgrass and Dominika Wrozynski, poetry editors. "At *Apalachee Review*, we are interested in outstanding literary fiction, but we especially like poetry, fiction, and nonfiction that addresses intercultural issues in a domestic or international setting/context." Annual. Acquires one-time rights, electronic rights. Publication is copyrighted. Pays on publication. Publishes mss 1 year after acceptance. Responds to queries in 4-6 weeks. Responds to mss in 3-14 months. Sometimes comments on/critiques rejected mss. Sample copy: $8 for current issue; $5 for back issue. Subscription: $15 for 2 issues ($30 foreign). Guidelines available for SASE or on website.

○   *Apalachee Review* is 120 pages, digest-sized, professionally printed, perfect-bound, with card cover. Press run is 400-500. Includes photographs. Member CLMP.

MAGAZINES NEEDS Submit 3-5 poems at a time. Accepts submissions by postal mail only. "Submit clear copies, with name and address on each." SASE required. Reads submissions year round. Staff reviews books of poetry. Send materials for review consideration. Has published poetry by Rita Mae Reese and Charles Harper Webb. Pays 2 contributor's copies.

APPALACHIAN HERITAGE

CPO 2166, Berea KY 40404. (859)985-3699. **Fax:** (859)985-3903. **E-mail:** appalachianheritage@berea.edu. **Website:** pub.berea.edu/appalachian-heritage. **Contact:** George Brosi. "We are seeking poetry, short fiction, literary criticism and biography, book reviews, and creative nonfiction, including memoirs, opinion pieces, and historical sketches. Unless you request not to be considered, all poems, stories, and articles published in *Appalachian Heritage* are eligible for our annual Plattner Award. All honorees are rewarded with a sliding bookrack with an attached commemorative plaque from Berea College Crafts, and First Place winners receive an additional stipend of $200." Acquires first print and electronic rights. Responds in 1 month to queries; 3-5 months to mss. Guidelines available online at website.

○   Submission period: August 1-February 27.

MAGAZINES NEEDS Length: up to 42 lines. "One-page poems cannot exceed 42 lines, and two-page poems cannot exceed 84 lines." Pays 3 contributor's copies.

TIPS "Sure, we are *Appalachian Heritage* and we do appreciate the past, but we are a forward-looking contemporary literary quarterly, and, frankly, we receive too many nostalgic submissions. Please spare us the 'Papaw Was Perfect' poetry and the 'Mamaw Moved Mountains' manuscripts and give us some hard-hitting prose, some innovative poetry, some inventive photography, and some original art. Help us be the ground-breaking, stimulating kind of quarterly we aspire to be."

APPARATUS MAGAZINE

E-mail: submissions@apparatusmagazine.com; editor@apparatusmagazine.com. **Website:** www.apparatusmagazine.com. **Contact:** Adam W. Hart, publisher/editor. "*Apparatus Magazine* strives to bring readers poetry and fiction from around the world that explores the mythos of 'man (or woman) vs. machine,' that conjures up words from the inner machine, and more. Each issue features work from around the world, bringing the reader literary updates from the *internal machine*." Buys first North American serial rights, first rights, and electronic rights; retains right to archive material on website. No payment offered. Publishes 1-3 months after acceptance. Responds in 1 week to queries; 2-3 months to mss. Editorial lead time is 3 months. Sample copy available online at website. Guidelines are available by e-mail or on website.

MAGAZINES NEEDS Prefers shorter poetry, free verse. Attention given to poems with a strong, natural voice. Submit 3-5 poems at a time via e-mail; no postal submissions. Send complete ms with a cover letter including estimated word count, brief bio, list of publications. Label subject line with "poetry submission." Has published poetry by Rayne Arroyo, Anne Brooke, Lesley Dame, Gregg Shapiro, Inara Cedrins, and Chanming Yuan. No overtly inspirational poetry, poetry aimed at children, or confessional poetry. Length: 2 pages/poem.

TIPS "Be sure to read the guidelines as posted. Submit more than just 1 poem, so I can get a feel for your work. Be sure to read back issues of the magazine. The journal tends to select work that focuses on specific themes and usually tries to pick work that will complement/contrast with other pieces selected for the issue. Send your best work, and don't be afraid of trying again. I often suggest other publications/markets if a piece is not a good match for the journal. Do not submit additional new material until you've heard back from us, though."

APPLE VALLEY REVIEW: A JOURNAL OF CONTEMPORARY LITERATURE

88 South 3rd St., Suite 336, San Jose CA 95113. E-mail: editor@leahbrowning.net. **Website:** www.applevalleyreview.com. **Contact:** Leah Browning, editor. *Apple Valley Review: A Journal of Contemporary Literature*, published semiannually online, features "beautifully crafted poetry, short fiction, and essays." Acquires first rights and first serial rights, and retains the right to archive the work online for an indefinite period of time. "As appropriate, we may also choose to nominate published work for awards or recognition. Author retains all other rights." Time between acceptance and publication is 1-6 months. Sometimes comments on rejected poems and mss. Responds to mss in 1 week-2 months. Guidelines available on website.

MAGAZINES NEEDS Wants "work that has both mainstream and literary appeal. All work must be original, previously unpublished, and in English. Translations are welcome if permission has been granted. Preference is given to short (under 2 pages), nonrhyming poetry." Considers poetry by children and teens: "Our audience includes teens and adults of all ages." Has published poetry by Laura Lee Beasley, Cameron Conaway, Robert Lavett Smith, Sharlene Teo, Donna Vorreyer, Do-hyeon Ahn, and Susan Johnson. Receives about 5,000+ poems/year, accepts less than 1%. Accepts e-mail submissions (pasted into body of message, with "poetry" in subject line); no disk submissions. Reads submissions year round. Does not want "erotica, work containing explicit language or violence, or work that is scholarly, criti-cal, inspirational, or intended for children." Length: "No line limit, though we prefer short poems (under 2 pages)."

CONTEST/AWARD OFFERINGS Offers the annual *Apple Valley Review* Editor's Prize. Award is $100 and a gift of a book. Submit 1-6 poems. **Entry fee:** none. **Deadline:** rolling; all submissions to the *Apple Valley Review* and all work published during a given calendar year will be considered for the prize.

ARC

Arc Poetry Society, P.O. Box 81060, Ottawa ON K1P 1B1, Canada. **E-mail:** managingeditor@arcpoetry.ca; coordinatingeditor@arcpoetry.ca. **Website:** www.arcpoetry.ca. **Contact:** Monty Reid, managing editor; Chris Johnson, coordinating editor. Focus is poetry, and Canadian poetry in general, although *Arc* publishes writers from elsewhere. Looking for the best poetry from new and established writers. Often have special issues. Send a SASE for upcoming special issues and contests. Buys one-time rights. Pays on publication. Publishes ms an average of 6 months after acceptance. Responds in 4 months. Guidelines for #10 SASE.

Only accepts submissions via online submissions manager. Include brief biographical note with submission. Accepts unsolicited mss each year from September 1-May 31.

MAGAZINES NEEDS Pays $40/printed page (Canadian).

ARC POETRY MAGAZINE

P.O. Box 81060, Ottawa ON K1P 1B1, Canada. **E-mail:** arc@arcpoetry.ca. **Website:** www.arcpoetry.ca. **Contact:** Monty Reid, managing editor. *Arc Poetry Magazine* has been publishing the best in contemporary Canadian and international poetry and criticism for over 30 years. *Arc* is published 3 times/year, including an annual themed issue each fall. Canada's poetry magazine publishes poetry, poetry-related articles, interviews, and book reviews, and also publishes on its website; *Arc* also runs a Poet-in-Residence program. Acquires first Canadian serial rights. Responds in 4-6 months. Subscriptions: 1 year: $35 CDN; 2 years: $60 CND (in Canada). U.S. subscriptions: 1 year: $45 CAD; 2 years: $80 CAD. International subscriptions: 1 year: $55 CDN; 2 year: $90 CDN. Online ordering available for subscriptions and single copies (with occasional promotions). Guidelines available online.

Arc is 130-160 pages, perfect-bound, printed on matte white stock with a crisp, engaging design and a striking visual art portfolio in each issue. Receives over 2,500 submissions/year; accepts about 40-50 poems. Press run is 1,500.

MAGAZINES NEEDS *Arc* accepts unsolicited submissions of previously unpublished poems from September 1-May 31; maximum of 3 poems, 1 submission per year per person. Use online submissions manager. Has published poetry by Don Coles, Karen Solie, Nicole Brossard, Christian Bok, Elizabeth Bachinsky, George Elliott Clarke, Ken Babstock, Michael Ondaatje, Stephanie Bolster, and Don Domanski. Pays $40 CAD/page, plus contributor's copy.

CONTEST/AWARD OFFERINGS Poem of the Year Contest—**Deadline:** February 1; $5,000 grand prize; entry fee includes one-year subscription. Confederation Poets Prize and Critic's Desk Award for best poem and reviews published in *Arc* in the preceding year. Other awards include the Archibald Lampman Award and the Diana Brebner Prize.

ARDENT!

Poetry in the Arts, Inc., 302 Cripple Creek, Cedar Park TX 78613. **E-mail:** rimer777@gmail.com. **Website:** www.poetryinarts.org/publishing/ardent.html. **Contact:** Dillon McKinsey, executive editor. *Ardent!*, published semiannually in April and October, is a journal of poetry and art. All forms and styles are considered. *Ardent!* is perfect-bound.

MAGAZINES NEEDS Submit up to 3 poems by e-mail (pasted in body) or postal mail. "Include a statement giving Poetry in the Arts, Inc. your permission to use your work." Provide brief bio.

ARIES: A JOURNAL OF CREATIVE EXPRESSION

c/o Dr. Price McMurray, General Editor, School of Aries and Letters, 1201 Wesleyan St., Fort Worth TX 76105. **E-mail:** aries@txwes.edu; ariesjournal1@gmail.com. **Website:** ariesjournal.wix.com/aries. **Contact:** Rolandra West, managing editor; Price McMurray, general editor. *Aries: A Journal of Creative Expression*, is published annually by the Department of Languages and Literature at Texas Wesleyan University. Accepting poetry, short fiction, creative nonfiction, short plays, and b&w photography. Reads submissions August 15-December 15. Responds to mss in summer. Sample submissions available on website. Guidelines available on website.

MAGAZINES NEEDS Submit by mail or e-mail. Include cover letter and SASE. Do not include name or contact info on ms. Length: up to 60 lines each.

TIPS "*Aries* is open to a wide variety of perspectives, ideas, and theoretical approaches; however, at the heart of all editorial decisions is the overall quality of the work submitted."

ARKANSAS REVIEW: A JOURNAL OF DELTA STUDIES

Department of English and Philosophy, P.O. Box 1890, Office: Wilson Hall, State University AR 72467-1890. (870) 972-3043; (870)972-2210. **Fax:** (870)972-3045. **E-mail:** mtribbet@astate.edu. **E-mail:** jcollins@astate.edu; arkansasreview@astate.edu. **Website:** altweb.astate.edu/arkreview. **Contact:** Dr. Marcus Tribbett, general editor. "All material, creative and scholarly, published in the *Arkansas Review* must evoke or respond to the natural and/or cultural experience of the Mississippi River Delta region." Buys first North American serial rights. Time between acceptance and publication is about 6-12 months. Occasionally publishes theme issues. Responds in 2 weeks to queries; in 4 months to mss. Editorial lead time 4 months. Sample copy for $7.50. Subscription: $20. Make checks payable to ASU Foundation. Guidelines available online.

⚲ *Arkansas Review* is 92 pages, magazine-sized, photo offset-printed, saddle-stapled, with 4-color cover. Press run is 600; 50 distributed free to contributors.

MAGAZINES NEEDS Receives about 500 poems/year; accepts about 5%. Accepts e-mail and disk submissions. Cover letter is preferred. Include SASE. Has published poetry by Greg Fraser, Jo McDougall, and Catherine Savage Brosman. Length: 1-100 lines. Pays 3 contributor's copies.

ALSO OFFERS Staff reviews books/chapbooks of poetry "that are relevant to the Delta" in 500 words, single- and multibook format. Send materials for review consideration to Janelle Collins ("inquire in advance").

TIPS "Immerse yourself in the literature of the Delta, but provide us with a fresh and original take on its land, its people, its culture. Surprise us. Amuse us. Recognize what makes this region particular as well as universal, and take risks. Help us shape a new Delta literature."

ARSENIC LOBSTER

E-mail: lobster@magere.com. **Website:** arseniclobster.magere.com. **Contact:** Susan Yount, poetry editor. Guidelines online.

MAGAZINES NEEDS Submit 3-5 poems by e-mail. "Poems should be timeless, rich in imagery, and edgy; seeking elegant emotion, articulate experiment. Be compelled to write." "We do not want political rants or Hallmark poetry."

TIPS "All works must be previously unpublished. Include a lively, short biography. Poetry topics, reviews and criticism, and art/photographs (.pdf or .jpg attachment only) are also welcome."

ARTFUL DODGE

Dept. of English, College of Wooster, Wooster OH 44691. (330)263-2577. **E-mail:** artfuldodge@wooster. edu. **Website:** www.wooster.edu/artfuldodge. **Contact:** Daniel Bourne, editor-in-chief; Karin Lin-Greenberg, fiction editor; Marcy Campbell, associate fiction editor; Carolyne Wright, translation editor. *Artful Dodge* is an Ohio-based literary magazine that publishes "work with a strong sense of place and cultural landscape. Besides new American fiction, poetry, and narrative essay, we're also interested in contemporary translation—from all over the globe. There is no theme in this magazine, except literary power. We also have an ongoing interest in translations from Central/Eastern Europe and elsewhere." Buys first North American serial rights. Responds in 1-6 months to mss. Sample copy for $7. Guidelines for #10 SASE.

MAGAZINES NEEDS "We are interested in poems that utilize stylistic persuasions both old and new to good effect. We are not afraid of poems which try to deal with large social, political, historical, and even philosophical questions—especially if the poem emerges from one's own life experience and is not the result of armchair pontificating." "We don't want cute, rococo surrealism, someone's warmed-up, left-over notion of an avant-garde that existed 10-100 years ago, or any last bastions of rhymed verse in the civilized world." Pays at least 2 contributor's copies.

TIPS "Poets may send books for review consideration; however, there is no guarantee we can review them."

⬣ ARTS & LETTERS JOURNAL OF CONTEMPORARY CULTURE

Georgia College & State University, Milledgeville GA 31061. (478)445-1289. **E-mail:** al.journal@gcsu. edu. **Website:** al.gcsu.edu. *Arts & Letters Journal of Contemporary Culture*, published semiannually, is devoted to contemporary arts and literature, featuring ongoing series such as The World Poetry Translation Series and The Mentors Interview Series. Wants work that is of the highest literary and artistic quality. Acquires one-time rights. Pays on publication. Responds in 1-2 months to mss. Guidelines online at artsandletters.gcsu.edu/submit.

⬤ Work published in *Arts & Letters Journal* has received the Pushcart Prize.

MAGAZINES NEEDS Submit via online submissions manager (fee). Include cover letter. "Poems are screened, discussed by group of readers, then if approved, submitted to poetry editor for final approval." Has published poetry by Margaret Gibson, Marilyn Nelson, Stuart Lishan, R.T. Smith, Laurie Lamon, and Miller Williams. No light verse. Pays $10 per printed page (minimum payment: $50) and 1 contributor's copy.

ALSO OFFERS Offers the annual Arts & Letters/Rumi Prize for Poets (see separate listing in Contests & Awards).

⬣ ART TIMES

A Literary Journal and Resource for All the Arts, P.O. Box 730, Mount Marion NY 12456. (845)246-6944. **Fax:** (845)246-6944. **E-mail:** info@ArtTimesJournal. com. **Website:** www.arttimesjournal.com. **Contact:** Raymond J. Steiner, editor. "*Art Times* covers the art fields and is distributed in locations most frequented by those enjoying the arts. Our copies are distributed throughout the lower part of the northeast as well as the metropolitan New York area; locations include theaters, galleries, museums, schools, art clubs, cultural centers, and the like. Our readers are mostly over 40, affluent, art-conscious and sophisticated. Subscribers are located across US and abroad (Italy, France, Germany, Greece, Russia, etc.)." Buys first North American serial rights, buys first rights. Pays on publication. Publishes ms an average of 3 years after acceptance. Responds in 6 months; in 6 months to mss. Sample copy for SAE with 9x12 envelope and 6 first-class stamps. Writer's guidelines for #10 SASE or online.

MAGAZINES NEEDS Wants "poetry that strives to express genuine observation in unique language. All topics, all forms. We prefer well-crafted 'literary' poems. No excessively sentimental poetry." Publishes 2-3 poems each issue. Length: no more than 20 lines. Offers contributor copies and one-year subscription.

TIPS "Competition is greater (more submissions received), but keep trying. We print new as well as published writers. Be advised that we are presently on an approximate three-year lead for short stories, two-year lead for poetry. We are now receiving 300-400 poems and 40-50 short stories per month. Be familiar with *Art Times* and its special audience."

ASCENT ASPIRATIONS

1560 Arbutus Dr., Nanoose Bay BC C9P 9C8, Canada. **E-mail:** ascentaspirations@shaw.ca. **Website:** www. ascentaspirations.ca. **Contact:** David Fraser, editor. "*Ascent Aspirations* magazine publishes monthly online and once in print. The print issues are operated as contests. Please refer to current guidelines before submitting. *Ascent Aspirations* is a quality electronic publication dedicated to the promotion and encouragement of aspiring writers of any genre. The focus, however, is toward interesting experimental writing in dark mainstream, literary, science fiction, fantasy, and horror. Poetry can be on any theme. Essays need to be unique, current, and have social, philosophical commentary." Rights remain with author. Responds in 1 week to queries; 3 months to mss. Sometimes comments on rejected mss. Guidelines by e-mail or on website. Accepts multiple submissions and reprints.

Magazine: 40 electronic pages; illustrations; photos. Receives 100-200 unsolicited mss/month. Accepts 40 mss/issue; 240 mss/year. Publishes ms 3 months after acceptance. Publishes 10-50 new writers/year. Has published work by Taylor Graham, Janet Buck, Jim Manton, Steve Cartwright, Don Stockard, Penn Kemp, Sam Vargo, Vernon Waring, Margaret Karmazin, Bill Hughes, and recently spokenword artists Sheri-D Wilson, Missy Peters, Ian Ferrier, Cathy Petch, and Bob Holdman.

MAGAZINES NEEDS Submit 1-5 poems at a time. Prefers e-mail submissions (pasted into body of message or as attachment in Word); no disk submissions. "If you must submit by postal mail because it is your only avenue, provide a SASE with IRCs or Canadian stamps." Reads submissions on a regular basis year round. "We accept all forms of poetry on any theme. Poetry needs to be unique and touch the reader emotionally with relevant human, social, and philosophical imagery." Considers poetry by children and teens. Does not want poetry "that focuses on mainstream, overtly religious verse." "No payment at this time."

TIPS "Short fiction should first of all tell a good story, take the reader to new and interesting imaginary or real places. Short fiction should use language lyrically and effectively, be experimental in either form or content, and take the reader into realms where they can analyze and think about the human condition. Write with passion for your material, be concise and economical, and let the reader work to unravel your story. In terms of editing, always proofread to the point where what you submit is the best it possibly can be. Never be discouraged if your work is not accepted; it may just not be the right fit for a current publication."

ASHEVILLE POETRY REVIEW

P.O. Box 7086, Asheville NC 28802. (828)450-0357. **E-mail:** editor@ashevillereview.com. **Website:** www. ashevillereview.com. **Contact:** Keith Flynn, founder/managing editor. *Asheville Poetry Review*, published annually, prints "the best regional, national, and international poems we can find. We publish translations, interviews, essays, historical perspectives, and book reviews as well." Wants "quality work with well-crafted ideas married to a dynamic style. Any subject matter is fit to be considered so long as the language is vivid with a clear sense of rhythm. We subscribe to the Borges dictum that great poetry is a combination of 'algebra and fire.'" Rights revert back to author upon publication. Up to 1 year from acceptance to publishing time. Responds in up to 4 months. Sample: $13. "We prefer poets purchase a sample copy prior to submitting." Guidelines available for SASE or on website.

Asheville Poetry Review is 160-300 pages, digest-sized, perfect-bound, laminated, with full-color cover. Receives about 8,000 submissions/year, accepts about 5%. Press run is 3,000. Subscription: $22.50 for 2 years, $43.50 for 4 years. Occasionally publishes theme issues. Reviews books/chapbooks of poetry. Send materials for review consideration. Has published poetry by Sherman Alexie, Eavan Boland, Gary Snyder, Colette Inez, Robert Bly, and Fred Chappell.

MAGAZINES NEEDS Submit 3-5 poems at a time. No e-mail submissions. Cover letter is required. Include comprehensive bio, recent publishing credits, and SASE. Reads submissions January 15-July 15. Poems are circulated to an editorial board. Seldom comments on rejected poems. Pays 1 contributor's copy.

CONTEST/AWARD OFFERINGS Sponsors the William Matthews Poetry Prize: $1,000 awarded for a single poem, reads submissions September 15-January 15. See website for complete guidelines.

ASININE POETRY

E-mail: editor@asininepoetry.com. **Website:** www. asininepoetry.com. **Contact:** Shay Tasaday, editor.

Humorous poetry and prose, published quarterly online, "features 8-9 new works each issue. We specialize in poetry that does not take itself seriously." Wants "any form of poetry, but for us the poetry must be in a humorous, parodic, or satirical style. We prefer well-crafted poems that may contain serious elements or cover serious subjects—but which are also amusing, absurd, or hilarious."

MAGAZINES NEEDS Does not want serious, straightforward poems. Has published poetry by Hal Sirowitz, William Trowbridge, Elizabeth Swados, Daniel Thomas Moran, and Colonel Drunky Bob. Receives about 800 poems/year, accepts about 2%. Submit 3-4 poems at a time. Lines/poem: 50 maximum. Considers previously published poems and simultaneous submissions. Accepts e-mail (pasted into body of message). Length: 50 lines max.

CONTEST/AWARD OFFERINGS Guidelines available on website.

ATLANTA REVIEW

P.O. Box 8248, Atlanta GA 31106. **E-mail:** atlanta.review@yahoo.com. **Website:** www.atlantareview.com. **Contact:** Dan Veach, editor/publisher. *Atlanta Review*, published semiannually, is devoted primarily to poetry but occasionally features interviews and b&w artwork. Publishes ms 6 months after acceptance. Responds in 1 month. Sample copy: $5. Single copy: $10; subscription: $15. Guidelines available online at website.

○ Work published in *Atlanta Review* has been included in *The Best American Poetry* and *The Pushcart Prize*. *Atlanta Review* is 128 pages, digest-sized, professionally printed on acid-free paper, flat-spined, with glossy color cover. Receives about 10,000 poems/year, accepts about 1%. Press run is 1,000.

MAGAZINES NEEDS Wants "quality poetry of genuine human appeal." Submit up to 5 poems at a time. No e-mail submissions from within the U.S.; postal submissions only. Include SASE for reply. Authors living outside the U.S. and Canada may submit work via e-mail. Cover letter is preferred. Include brief bio. Put name and address on each poem. Reads submissions according to the following deadlines: June 1 for Fall; December 1 for Spring. Has published poetry by Seamus Heaney, Billy Collins, Derek Walcott, Maxine Kumin, Alicia Stallings, Gunter Grass, Eugenio Montale, and Thomas Lux. Pays in contributor's copies.

THE ATLANTIC MONTHLY

The Watergate, 600 New Hampshire Ave., NW, Washington DC 20037. **E-mail:** submissions@theatlantic.com; pitches@theatlantic.com. **Website:** www.theatlantic.com. **Contact:** Scott Stossel, magazine editor; Ann Hulbert, literary editor. General magazine for an educated readership with broad cultural and public-affairs interests. "*The Atlantic* considers unsolicited mss, either fiction or nonfiction. A general familiarity with what we have published in the past is the best guide to our needs and preferences." Buys first North American serial rights. Pays on acceptance. Responds in 4-6 weeks to mss. Guidelines online.

MAGAZINES NEEDS "Interest is in the broadest possible range of work: traditional forms and free verse, the meditative lyric and the 'light' or comic poem, the work of the famous and the work of the unknown. We have long been committed to the discovery of new poets. Our 1 limitation is length; we are unable to publish very long poems." *The Atlantic Monthly* publishes some of the most distinguished poetry in American literature. "We read with interest and attention every poem submitted to the magazine and, quite simply, we publish those that seem to us to be the best." Has published poetry by Maxine Kumin, Stanley Plumly, Linda Gregerson, Philip Levine, Ellen Bryant Voigt, and W.S. Merwin. Receives about 60,000 poems/year. Submit 2-6 poems by e-mail or mail.

TIPS "Writers should be aware that this is not a market for beginner's work (nonfiction and fiction), nor is it truly for intermediate work. Study this magazine before sending only your best, most professional work. When making first contact, cover letters are sometimes helpful, particularly if they cite prior publications or involvement in writing programs. Common mistakes: melodrama, inconclusiveness, lack of development, unpersuasive characters and/or dialogue."

THE AVALON LITERARY REVIEW

CCI Publishing, P.O. Box 780696, Orlando FL 32878. (407)574-7355. **E-mail:** submissions@avalonliteraryreview.com. **Website:** www.avalonliteraryreview.com. **Contact:** Valerie Rubino, managing editor. "*The Avalon Literary Review* welcomes work from both published and unpublished writers and poets. We accept submissions of poetry, short fiction, and personal essays. While we appreciate the genres of fantasy, historical romance, science fiction, and horror, our magazine is not the forum for such work." Quarterly magazine. Buys one-time rights. Pays on publication. Publishes ms an average of 6 months after acceptance. Editorial lead time is 3-6 months. Sample copy: $10, by e-mail or on website. Writer's guidelines available online at website or by e-mail.

MAGAZINES NEEDS Accepts 40-60 poems/year. Electronic submissions only. No rhyming verse. Length: no more than 50 lines. Pays 5 contributor's copies.

TIPS "The author's voice and point of view should be unique and clear. We seek pieces which spring from the author's life and experiences. Fiction submissions which explore both the sweet and bitter of life, with a touch of humor, and poetry with vivid imagery, are a good fit for our review."

THE AVOCET, A JOURNAL OF NATURE POETRY

P.O. Box 19186, Fountain Hills AZ 85269. **E-mail:** cportolano@hotmail.com. **Website:** www.avocetreview.com. **Contact:** Charles Portolano, editor. *The Avocet, a Journal of Nature Poetry*, published quarterly, is "looking for poetry that moves the reader through the beauty, the peace, and the fury of nature in all its glory. We want poems that have people interacting with nature, animals in their element, poems that have a message on the importance of Mother Nature and our life on this magical planet. Think of the season when sending your submission." Time between acceptance and publication is up to 3 months. Responds to submissions in 2 months. Single copy: $7.50. Subscription: $24. Make checks payable to *The Avocet*.

○ *The Avocet* is 64 pages, 5.5x8.5, professionally printed, perfect-bound, with glossy cover.

MAGAZINES NEEDS Submit up to 4 poems at a time. Considers previously published poems, if acknowledged. Include cover letter with e-mail. No SASE if you have an e-mail address; mss will not be returned.

THE AWAKENINGS REVIEW

P.O. Box 177, Wheaton IL 60187. **E-mail:** ar@awakeningsproject.org. **Website:** www.awakeningsproject.org. **Contact:** Robert Lundin, editor. *The Awakenings Review* is published by the Awakenings Project. Begun in cooperation with the University of Chicago Center for Psychiatric Rehabilitation in 2000, *The Awakenings Review* has been acclaimed internationally and draws writers from all over the United States and from several other countries including Israel, South Africa, Australia, Finland, Switzerland, the United Kingdom, and Canada. Acquires first rights. Publishes ms 8 months after acceptance. Responds in 1 month. Guidelines available in magazine, for SASE, by e-mail, or on website.

MAGAZINES NEEDS Submit 5 poems at a time. No e-mail submissions. Cover letter is preferred. Include SASE and short bio. Poems are read by a board of editors. Often comments on rejected poems. Occasionally publishes theme issue. Pays 1 contributor's copy, plus discount on additional copies.

BABEL: THE MULTILINGUAL, MULTICULTURAL ONLINE JOURNAL AND COMMUNITY OF ARTS AND IDEAS

E-mail: submissions@towerofbabel.com. **Website:** towerofbabel.com. **Contact:** Malcolm Lawrence, editor in chief. *Babel* publishes regional reports from international stringers all over the planet, as well as features, round-table discussions, fiction, columns, poetry, erotica, travelogues, and reviews of all the arts and editorials. "Our bloggers include James Schwartz, the first out gay poet raised in the Old Order Amish community in Southwestern Michigan and author of the book *The Literary Party*; Susanna Zaraysky, author of the book *Language Is Music: Making People Multilingual*; James Rovira, Assistant Professor of English and Program Chair of Humanities at Tiffin University and author of the book *Blake & Kierkegaard: Creation and Anxiety*; and Paul B. Miller, Assistant Professor Department of French and Italian at Vanderbilt University. We're interested in fiction, nonfiction, and poetry from all over the world, including multicultural or multilingual work." Cover letter is required. Reviews books/chapbooks of poetry and other magazines, single- and multibook format. Open to unsolicited reviews. Send materials for review consideration. Publishes ms 1-2 months after acceptance. Responds in 2-4 weeks. Guidelines available on website.

○ *Babel* is recognized by the U.N. as one of the most important social and human sciences online periodicals.

MAGAZINES NEEDS "We are currently looking for WordPress bloggers in the following languages: Arabic, Bulgarian, Bengali, Catalan, Czech, Welsh, Danish, German, English, Esperanto, Spanish, Persian, Finnish, Faroese, French, Hebrew, Croatian, Indonesian, Italian, Japanese, Korean, Latvian, Malay,

Dutch, Polish, Portuguese, Russian, Albanian, Serbian, Swedish, Tamil, Thai, Ukrainian, Urdu, Uzbek, Vietnamese, and Chinese."

HOW TO CONTACT Accepts e-mail submissions only. Cover letter is required. "Please send submissions with a résumé or bio as a Microsoft Word or RTF document attached to e-mail."

TIPS "We would like to see more fiction with first-person male characters written by female authors, as well as more fiction first-person female characters written by male authors. We would also like to see that dynamic in action when it comes to other languages, cultures, races, classes, sexual orientations, and ages. Know what you are writing about, and write passionately about it."

⊛ BABYBUG

Cricket Magazine Group, 70 East Lake St., Suite 800, Chicago IL 60601. **E-mail:** babybug@babybugmag-kids.com. **Website:** www.cricketmag.com/babybug; www.babybugmagkids.com. **Contact:** submissions editor. *Babybug* is a look-and-listen magazine for babies and toddlers ages 6 months-3 years. Publishes 9 issues per year. Rights vary. Pays on publication. Responds in 3-6 months to mss. Guidelines available online: www.cricketmag.com/submissions.

MAGAZINES NEEDS "We are especially interested in rhythmic and rhyming poetry. Poems may explore a baby's day, or they may be more whimsical." Pays up to $3/line; $25 minimum.

TIPS "Imagine having to read your story or poem—out loud—50 times or more! That's what parents will have to do. Babies and toddlers demand, 'Read it again!' Your material must hold up under repetition. And humor is much appreciated by all."

BABYSUE®

babysue ATTN: LMNOP aka dONW7, P.O. Box 15749, Chattanooga TN 373415. **E-mail:** LMNOP@babysue.com. **Website:** www.babysue.com; www.LM-NOP.com. **Contact:** Don W. Seven, editor/publisher. *babysue* is an ongoing online magazine featuring continually updated cartoons, poems, literature, and reviews. It is also published twice/year and offers obtuse humor for the extremely open-minded. Responds "immediately, if we are interested." Seldom comments on rejected poems. Sample: $7; cash only (no checks or money orders).

MAGAZINES NEEDS "We are open to all styles but prefer short poems." No restrictions. "We print prose, poems, and cartoons. We usually accept about 5% of what we receive." Has published poetry by Edward Mycue, Susan Andrews, and Barry Bishop. Pays 1 contributor's copy.

TIPS "We do occasionally review other magazines."

THE BALTIMORE REVIEW

E-mail: editor@baltimorereview.org. **Website:** www.baltimorereview.org. **Contact:** Barbara Westwood Diehl, senior editor; Kathleen Hellen, senior editor. *The Baltimore Review* publishes poetry, fiction, and creative nonfiction from Baltimore and beyond. Submission periods are August 1-November 30 and February 1-May 31. Buys first North American serial rights. Publishes ms an average of 6 months after acceptance. Responds in 3 months or less. Guidelines available online.

💭   In 2012, *The Baltimore Review* began its new life as a quarterly, online literary. Also prints annual anthology.

MAGAZINES NEEDS Submit 1-3 poems. See editor preferences on submission guidelines on website. Pays in web exposure and 1 copy of annual anthology.

CONTEST/AWARD OFFERINGS Sponsors 2 theme contests per year, $500, $200, and $100 prizes; all entries considered for publication. See website for themes and guidelines.

TIPS "See editor preferences on staff page of website."

◉ THE BANGALORE REVIEW

The Purple Patch Foundation, No. 149, 2nd Floor, 4th Cross, Kasturi Nagar, Bangalore Karnataka , India. **E-mail:** info@bangalorereview.com. **E-mail:** submissions@bangalorereview.com. **Website:** www.banga-lorereview.com. **Contact:** Arvind Radhakrishnan, editor; Suhail Rasheed, managing editor. *The Bangalore Review* is a monthly online magazine aimed at promoting literature, arts, culture, criticism, and philosophy at a deeper level. Strives to inculcate the habit of not just reading but the reading of good literature in the youth of today while also aspiring to be an unbiased, nonrestrictive platform for young and promising independent writers. The editorial team seeks to strike a balance between the old and the young, the published and the unpublished, the known and the unknown, and the mainstream and the unconventional, while curating the articles for each edition. Copyrights for articles, artwork, and photographs published in the magazine rest with the authors, with first publication rights to *The Bangalore*

Review. Does not offer payment. Posts mss an average of 2 months after acceptance. Editorial lead time is 2 months. Guidelines available online.

MAGAZINES NEEDS Length: Must be at least 5 lines. Does not offer payment.

BARKING SYCAMORES

1601 W. Fifth Ave., #247, Columbus OH 43212. E-mail: barkingsycamores@gmail.com. **Website:** www.barkingsycamores.wordpress.com. **Contact:** Nicole Nicholson, editor-in-chief; V. Solomon Maday, assistant editor-in-chief. "*Barking Sycamores*' primary mission is to publish poetry, short fiction (as of issue 3), and artwork by emerging and established writers who are neurodivergent—this includes autism, the state of being currently known as AD(H)D, Bipolar, synesthesia, and so on. We also seek to add positively to the public discussion about neurodivergence as a whole in the form of essays on the creation of literature and the interrelationship between alternative kinds of neurology and the creative process." Holds one-time rights and electronic rights, exclusively for 60 days from date of publication. Publishes ms 2 weeks after acceptance. Responds in 3 weeks to queries and mss. Sample copy available online. Guidelines available online.

◑   This is a non-paying market.

MAGAZINES NEEDS Does not want polemic, preachy, or rant-like poetry.

BARN OWL REVIEW

Olin Hall 342, The University of Akron, Akron OH 44325. **E-mail:** info@barnowlreview.com. **Website:** www.barnowlreview.com. **Contact:** Mary Biddinger and Jay Robinson, editors-in-chief. A handsomely designed print journal looking for work that takes risks while still connecting with readers. Aims to publish the highest quality poetry from both emerging and established writers.

◑   Uses online submissions manager. Open annually for submissions from June 1-November 1.

MAGAZINES NEEDS Barn Owl Review favors no particular poetic school or style; "however, we look for innovation and risk-taking in the poems that we publish." Submit 3-5 poems (in single attachment) via Submittable. Contributors receive 2 copies of the issue.

BARROW STREET

71 First Ave., Suite 12, New York NY 10003. **E-mail:** submissions@barrowstreet.org; journal@barrowstreet.org. **Website:** www.barrowstreet.org. **Contact:** Lorna Blake, Patricia Carlin, Peter Covino, and Melissa Hotchkiss, editors. *Barrow Street*, published annually, "is dedicated to publishing new and established poets." Wants "poetry of the highest quality; open to all styles and forms." Has published poetry by Molly Peacock, Lyn Hejinian, Carl Phillips, Marie Ponsot, Charles Bernstein, and Stephen Burt. Acquires first rights. Responds in 1 week-4 months. Sample copy: $10. Subscription: $18 for 2 years, $25 for 3 years. Guidelines online.

◑   Poetry published in *Barrow Street* is often selected for *The Best American Poetry*. *Barrow Street* is 96-120 pages, digest-sized, professionally printed, perfect-bound, with glossy cardstock cover with color or b&w photography. Receives about 3,000 poems/year, accepts about 3%. Press run is 1,000. Reading period: December 1-March 15.

MAGAZINES NEEDS Submit 3-5 poems via online submissions manager. Please always check our website to confirm submission guidelines. Does not accept hard copy submissions. Cover letter is preferred. Include brief bio. Must have name, address, e-mail, and phone on each page submitted or submission will not be considered. Pays 2 contributor's copies.

BATEAU

P.O. Box 1584, Northampton MA 01061. (413)586-2494. **E-mail:** jgrin@mac.com. **Website:** www.bateaupress.org. **Contact:** James Grinwis, editor. "*Bateau*, published annually, subscribes to no trend but serves to represent as wide a cross-section of contemporary writing as possible. For this reason, readers will most likely love and hate at least something in each issue. We consider this a good thing. To us, it means *Bateau* is eclectic, open-ended, and not mired in a particular strain." Acquires first North American serial rights, electronic rights. Publishes ms 3-8 months after acceptance. Responds in 1-6 months. Single copy: $15. Make checks payable to Bateau Press. Guidelines for SASE or on website. Submissions closed June-August.

◑   *Bateau* is around 80 pages, digest-sized, offset print, perfect-bound, with a 100% recycled letterpress cover. Press run is 250.

MAGAZINES NEEDS Submit via online submission form. Cover letter not necessary. Has published poetry by Tomaz Salamun, John Olsen, Michael Burkhardt, Joshua Marie Wilkinson, Allison Titus, Allan Peterson, and Dean Young. Receives about 5,000 poems/year, accepts about 60. Length: up to 5 pages. Pays in contributor's copies.

BAYOU

Dept. of English, University of New Orleans, 2000 Lakeshore Dr., New Orleans LA 70148. (504)280-5423. **E-mail:** bayou@uno.edu. **Website:** bayoumagazine. org. **Contact:** Joanna Leake, editor in chief. "A nonprofit journal for the arts, each issue of *Bayou* contains beautiful fiction, nonfiction, and poetry. From quirky shorts to more traditional stories, we are committed to publishing solid work. Regardless of style, at *Bayou* we are always interested first in a well-told tale. Our poetry and prose are filled with memorable characters observing their world, acknowledging both the mundane and the sublime, often at once, and always with an eye toward beauty. *Bayou* is packed with a range of material from established, award-winning authors as well as new voices on the rise. Recent contributors include Eric Trethewey, Virgil Suarez, Marilyn Hacker, Sean Beaudoin, Tom Whalen, Mark Doty, Philip Cioffari, Lyn Lifshin, Timothy Liu, and Gaylord Brewer. In 1 issue every year, *Bayou* features the winner of the annual Tennessee Williams/New Orleans Literary Festival One-Act Play Competition." Responds in 4-6 months. Guidelines available online at website.

○ Does not accept e-mail submissions. Reads submissions from September 1-June 1.

MAGAZINES NEEDS Submit via online submission system or postal mail. Length: "We have no strict length restrictions, though obviously it is harder to fit in very long poems." Pays 2 contributor's copies.

TIPS "Do not submit in more than 1 genre at a time. Don't send a second submission until you receive a response to the first."

BEAR CREEK HAIKU

P.O. Box 3787, Boulder CO 80307. **Website:** bearcreekhaiku.blogspot.com. **Contact:** Ayaz Daryl Nielsen, editor. Acquires first rights. Acceptance to publication time varies. Response time varies. Sample copy for SASE. Subscriptions: One year $5, renewed for free yearly if subscriber asks.

○ Reads submissions year-round.

MAGAZINES NEEDS Submit 5-20 poems at a time by mail. Length: 11 lines or less or haiku. Pays 2 contributor's copies if 24-page issue; 1 copy if 36-page issue.

THE BEAR DELUXE MAGAZINE

Orlo, 240 N. Broadway, #112, Portland OR 97227. **E-mail:** bear@orlo.org. **Website:** www.orlo.org. **Con-**

tact: Tom Webb, editor in chief; Kristin Rogers Brown, art director. "*The Bear Deluxe Magazine* is a national independent environmental arts magazine publishing significant works of reporting, creative nonfiction, literature, visual art, and design. Based in the Pacific Northwest, it reaches across cultural and political divides to engage readers on vital issues effecting the environment. Published twice per year, *The Bear Deluxe* includes a wider array and a higher percentage of visual artwork and design than many other publications. Artwork is included both as editorial support and as standalone or independent art. It has included nationally recognized artists as well as emerging artists. As with any publication, artists are encouraged to review a sample copy for a clearer understanding of the magazine's approach. Unsolicited submissions and samples are accepted and encouraged." Buys first rights, buys one-time rights. Pays on publication. Publishes ms an average of 6 months after acceptance. Responds in 3-6 months to mail queries. Only responds to e-mail queries if interested. Editorial lead time 6 months. Sample copy: $5. Guidelines online.

MAGAZINES NEEDS Submit 3-5 poems at a time. Poems are reviewed by a committee of 3-5 people. Publishes 1 theme issue per year. Length: up to 50 lines/poem. Pays $20, subscription, and contributor's copies.

TIPS "Offer to be a stringer for future ideas. Get a copy of the magazine and guidelines, and query us with specific nonfiction ideas and clips. We're looking for original, magazine-style stories, not fluff or PR. Fiction, essay, and poetry writers should know we have an open and blind review policy and they should keep sending their best work even if rejected once. Be as specific as possible in queries."

BELLEVUE LITERARY REVIEW

NYU Langone Medical Center, Department of Medicine, 550 First Ave., OBV-A612, New York NY 10016. (212)263-3973. **E-mail:** info@BLReview.org. **E-mail:** stacy.bodziak@nyumc.org. **Website:** www.blreview. org. **Contact:** Stacy Bodziak, managing editor. *Bellevue Literary Review*, published semiannually, prints "works of fiction, nonfiction, and poetry that touch upon relationships to the human body, illness, health, and healing." Acquires first North American serial rights. Sends galleys to author. Publishes ms 3-6 months after acceptance. Responds in 3-6 months to mss. Sample copy: $7. Single copy: $12; subscription:

$20/year, $35/2 years; $48/3 years (plus $5/year postage to Canada, $8/year postage foreign). Make checks payable to *Bellevue Literary Review*. Guidelines for SASE or on website.

○ Work published in *Bellevue Literary Review* has appeared in *The Pushcart Prize* and *Best American Short Stories*. Recently published work by Linda Pastan, Rachel Hadas, and Tom Sleigh.

MAGAZINES NEEDS Submit up to 3 poems at a time. Prefers poems of 1 page or less. No previously published poems; work published on personal blogs or websites will be considered on a case-by-case basis. No e-mail or disk submissions. "We accept poems via regular mail and through our website; when submitting via postal mail, please include SASE." Cover letter is preferred. Reads submissions year round. "Poems are reviewed by 2 independent readers, then sent to an editor." Sometimes comments on rejected poems. Sometimes publishes theme issues. Upcoming themes available on website. Receives about 1,800 poetry mss/year; accepts about 3%. Has published poetry by Edward Hirsch, Naomi Shihab Nye, Cornelius Eady, and David Wagoner. Pays 2 contributor's copies and one-year subscription for author, plus one-year gift subscription for friend.

BELLINGHAM REVIEW

Mail Stop 9053, Western Washington University, Bellingham WA 98225. (360)650-4863. **E-mail:** bellingham.review@wwu.edu. **Website:** wwww.bhreview.org. **Contact:** Brenda Miller, editor in chief; Kaitlyn Teer, managing editor. Nonprofit magazine published once/year in the spring. Seeks "literature of palpable quality: poems, stories, and essays so beguiling they invite us to touch their essence. *Bellingham Review* hungers for a kind of writing that nudges the limits of form or executes traditional forms exquisitely." Buys first North American serial rights. Pays on publication when funding allows. Publishes ms an average of 6 months after acceptance. Responds in 1-6 months to mss. Editorial lead time 6 months. Sample copy: $12. Guidelines online.

○ The editors are actively seeking submissions of creative nonfiction, as well as stories that push the boundaries of the form. Open submission period is from September 15-December 1.

MAGAZINES NEEDS Wants "well-crafted poetry, but is open to all styles." Has published poetry by David Shields, Tess Gallagher, Gary Soto, Jane Hirshfield,

Albert Goldbarth, and Rebecca McClanahan. Submit up to 3 poems via online submissions manager. Will not use light verse. Pays as funds allow, plus contributor's copies.

TIPS "The *Bellingham Review* holds 3 annual contests: the 49th Parallel Award for poetry, the Annie Dillard Award for Nonfiction, and the Tobias Wolff Award for Fiction. See the individual listings for these contests under Contests & Awards for full details."

BELL'S LETTERS POET

P.O. Box 14319 N. Swan Rd., Gulfport MS 39503. **E-mail:** jimbelpoet@aol.com. **Contact:** Jim Bell, editor/publisher. *Bell's Letters Poet*, published quarterly, **must be purchased by contributors before they can be published.** Wants "clean writing in good taste; no vulgarity, no artsy vulgarity." Guidelines available online or for SASE.

○ Has published poetry by Betty Wallace, C. David Hay, Mary L. Ports, and Tgrai Warden. *Bell's Letters Poet* is about 60 pages, digest-sized, photocopied on plain bond paper (including cover), saddle-stapled. Single copy: $7; subscription: $28. Sample: $5. "Send a poem (20 lines or under, in good taste) with your sample order, and we will publish it in our next issue."

MAGAZINES NEEDS Submit 4 poems at a time. Lines/poem: 4-20. Considers previously published poems "if cleared by author with prior publisher"; no simultaneous submissions. Accepts submissions by postal mail or e-mail. Submission deadline is 2 months prior to publication. Accepted poems by subscribers are published immediately in the next issue. Reviews chapbooks of poetry by subscribers. No payment for accepted poetry, but "many patrons send cash awards to the poets whose work they especially like."

TIPS "The Ratings" is a competition in each issue. Readers are asked to vote on their favorite poems, and the "Top 40" are announced in the next issue, along with awards sent to the poets by patrons. News releases are then sent to subscriber's hometown newspaper. *Bell's Letters Poet* also features a telephone and e-mail exchange among poets, a birth-date listing, and a profile of its poets." Tired of seeing no bylines this year? Subscription guarantees a byline in each issue."

BELOIT POETRY JOURNAL

Beloit Poetry Journal, P.O. Box 151, Farmington ME 04938. (207)778-0020. **E-mail:** bpj@bpj.org. **Website:**

www.bpj.org. **Contact:** John Rosenwald and Lee Sharkey, editors. *Beloit Poetry Journal*, published quarterly, prints "the most outstanding poems we receive, without bias as to length, school, subject, or form. For more than 60 years of continuous publication, we have been distinguished for the extraordinary range of our poetry and our discovery of strong new poets." Wants "visions broader than the merely personal; language that makes us laugh and weep, recoil, resist—and pay attention. We're drawn to poetry that grabs hold of the whole body, not just the head." Responds in 4 months to mss. Sample copy for $5. Guidelines available on website.

○ Has published poetry by Sherman Alexie, Mark Doty, Albert Goldbarth, Sonia Sanchez, A.E. Stallings, Janice Harrington, Douglas Kearney, Susan Tichy, and Eduardo Corral.

MAGAZINES NEEDS Submit via online submission manager or postal mail. Limit submissions to 5 pages or a single long poem. Pays 3 contributor's copies.

ALSO OFFERS The Chad Walsh Poetry Prize is awarded to the author of the poem or group of poems that the editorial board judges to be outstanding among those we published in the previous year.

TIPS "We seek only unpublished poems or translations of poems not already available in English. Poems may be submitted electronically on our website Submission Manager, or by postal mail. Before submitting, please buy a sample issue or browse our website archive."

⑤ BELTWAY POETRY QUARTERLY

E-mail: info@beltwaypoetry.com. **Website:** www.beltwaypoetry.com. **Contact:** Kim Roberts, editor. *Beltway Poetry Quarterly*, published online, "features poets who live or work in the greater Washington, D.C., metro region. *Beltway* showcases the richness and diversity of Washington, D.C., authors, with poets from different backgrounds, races, ethnicities, ages, and sexual orientations represented. We have included Pulitzer Prize winners and those who have never previously published. We publish academic, spoken word, and experimental authors—and those whose work defies categorization." Themes change annually; check website for details.

MAGAZINES NEEDS "Other than 1 annual themed issue, we are a curated journal and consider poems by invitation only. Themed issues and their open reading periods change each year; check website for guidelines. Themed issues have included prose poems, poems about working for the Federal government, and poems celebrating immigrant roots. Two issues per year feature portfolios, a larger group of poems than most journals generally include, up to 8 poems each by 5-7 authors from the greater-D.C. region, and these issues are open only by invitation. Most featured authors are found through earlier participation in themed issues; featured authors are paid a stipend."

⑤ BEYOND CENTAURI

White Cat Publications, LLC, 33080 Industrial Rd., Suite 101, Livonia MI 48150. **E-mail:** beyondcentauri@whitecatpublications.com. **Website:** www.whitecatpublications.com/guidelines/beyond-centauri. *Beyond Centauri*, published quarterly, contains fantasy, science fiction, sword and sorcery, very mild horror short stories, poetry, and illustrations for readers ages 10 and up. Publishes ms 1-2 months after acceptance. Responds in 2-3 months. Single copy: $7.

○ *Beyond Centauri* is 44 pages, magazine-sized, offset printed, perfect-bound, with paper cover for color art, includes ads. Receives about 200 poems/year, accepts about 50 (25%). Press run is 100; 5 distributed free to reviewers.

MAGAZINES NEEDS Wants fantasy, science fiction, spooky horror, and speculative poetry for younger readers. Considers poetry by children and teens. Has published poetry by Bruce Boston, Bobbi Sinha-Morey, Debbie Feo, Dorothy Imm, Cythera, and Terrie Leigh Relf. Looks for themes of science fiction and fantasy. Poetry should be submitted in the body of an e-mail, or as an RTF attachment. Does not want horror with excessive blood and gore. Length: up to 50 lines/poem. Pays $2/original poem, $1/reprints, $1/scifaiku and related form, plus 1 contributor's copy.

⑤ BIBLE ADVOCATE

Bible Advocate, Church of God (Seventh Day), P.O. Box 33677, Denver CO 80233. (303)452-7973. **E-mail:** bibleadvocate@cog7.org. **Website:** baonline.org. **Contact:** Sherri Langton, associate editor. "Our purpose is to advocate the Bible and represent the Church of God (Seventh Day) to a Christian audience." Buys first rights, second serial (reprint) rights, electronic rights. Pays on publication. Publishes ms an average of 9 months after acceptance. Responds in 2 months to queries. Editorial lead time 3 months. Sample copy for SAE with 9x12 envelope and 3 first-class stamps. Guidelines online.

MAGAZINES NEEDS Prefers e-mail submissions. Cover letter is preferred. "No handwritten submissions, please. I read them first and reject those that won't work for us. I send good ones to editor for approval." Seldom comments on rejected poems. No avant-garde. Length: 5-20 lines. Pays $20 and 2 contributor's copies.

TIPS "Be fresh, not preachy! Articles must be in keeping with the doctrinal understanding of the Church of God (Seventh Day). Therefore, the writer should become familiar with what the Church generally accepts as truth as set forth in its doctrinal beliefs. We reserve the right to edit mss to fit our space requirements, doctrinal stands, and church terminology. Significant changes are referred to writers for approval. No fax or handwritten submissions, please."

BIG BRIDGE

E-mail: walterblue@bigbridge.org. **Website:** www.bigbridge.org. **Contact:** Michael Rothenberg and Terri Carrion, editors. "*Big Bridge* is a webzine of poetry and everything else. If we like it, we'll publish it. We're interested in poetry, fiction, nonfiction essays, journalism, and art (photos, line drawings, performance, installations, siteworks, comics, graphics)." Guidelines available online.

MAGAZINES NEEDS Only accepts electronic submissions. Submit via e-mail.

TIPS "We are guided by whimsy and passion and urgency. Each issue will feature an online chapbook."

BIG MUDDY: A JOURNAL OF THE MISSISSIPPI RIVER VALLEY

Southeast Missouri State University Press, One University Plaza, MS 2650, Cape Girardeau MO 63701. (573)651-2044. **Website:** www6.semo.edu/universitypress/bigmuddy. **Contact:** Susan Swartwout, publisher/editor. "*Big Muddy* explores multidisciplinary, multicultural issues, people, and events mainly concerning, but not limited to, the 10-state area that borders the Mississippi River. We publish fiction, poetry, historical essays, creative nonfiction, environmental essays, biography, regional events, photography, art, etc." Acquires first North American serial rights. Publishes ms 6-12 months after acceptance. Responds in 12 weeks to mss. Send SASE for return of ms or send a disposable copy of ms and #10 SASE for reply only. Sample copy: $6. Guidelines for SASE, e-mail, fax, or on website.

MAGAZINES NEEDS Receives 50 unsolicited mss/month. Accepts 20-25 mss/issue. Accepts multiple submissions. Pays 2 contributor's copies; additional copies $5.

TIPS "We look for clear language, avoidance of clichés except in necessary dialogue, a fresh vision of the theme or issue. Find some excellent and honest readers to comment on your work-in-progress and final draft. Consider their viewpoints carefully. Revise if needed."

⑤ BIG PULP

Exter Press, P.O. Box 92, Cumberland MD 21501. **E-mail:** editors@bigpulp.com. **Website:** www.bigpulp.com. **Contact:** Bill Olver, editor. *Big Pulp* defines "pulp fiction" very broadly: It's lively, challenging, thought-provoking, thrilling, and fun, regardless of how many or how few genre elements are packed in. Doesn't subscribe to the theory that genre fiction is disposable; a great deal of literary fiction could easily fall under one of their general categories. Places a higher value on character and story than genre elements. Acquires one-time and electronic rights. Pays on publication. Publishes ms 1 year after acceptance. Responds in 2 months to mss. Sample copy: $10; excerpts available online at no cost. Guidelines available online at website.

○ Currently accepting submissions for themed collections only. See website for details on current needs. Submissions are only accepted during certain reading periods; check website to see if magazine is currently open.

MAGAZINES NEEDS All types of poetry are considered, but poems should have a genre connection. Length: up to 100 lines/poem. Pays $5/poem.

TIPS "We like to be surprised, and we have few boundaries. Fantasy writers may focus on the mundane aspects of a fantastical creature's life or the magic that can happen in everyday life. Romances do not have to be requited or have happy endings, and the object of one's obsession may not be a person. Mysteries need not focus on 'whodunit?' We're always interested in science or speculative fiction focusing on societal issues, but writers should avoid being partisan or shrill. We also like fiction that crosses genre; for example, a science fiction romance or a fantasy crime story. We have an online archive for fiction and poetry and encourage writers to check it out. That said, *Big Pulp* has a strong editorial bias in favor of stories with monkeys. Especially talking monkeys."

BILINGUAL REVIEW

Arizona State University, Hispanic Research Center, P.O. Box 875303, Tempe AZ 85287-5303. (480)965-3867. **Fax:** (480)965-0315. **E-mail:** brp@asu.edu. **Website:** www.asu.edu/brp/submit. **Contact:** Gary Francisco Keller, publisher. *Bilingual Review* is "committed to publishing high-quality writing by both established and emerging writers." Acquires all rights (50% of reprint permission fees given to author as matter of policy). Publishes ms 1 year after acceptance. Responds in 2-3 months. Often comments on rejected mss.

- Magazine: 7×10; 96 pages; 55 lb. acid-free paper; coated cover stock.

MAGAZINES NEEDS Submit via postal mail. Send 2 copies of poetry with SAE and loose stamps. Does not usually accept e-mail submissions except through special circumstance/prior arrangement.

THE BITTER OLEANDER

4983 Tall Oaks Dr., Fayetteville NY 13066. **Fax:** (315)637-5056. **E-mail:** info@bitteroleander.com. **Website:** www.bitteroleander.com. **Contact:** Paul B. Roth, editor and publisher. "We're reading to find a language uncommitted to the commonplace and more integrated with the natural world. A language that helps define the same particulars in nature that exist in us but have not been socialized out of us." Publishes ms an average of 1-6 months after acceptance. Editorial lead time is 6 months. Sample copy: $10. Guidelines available online.

- *The Bitter Oleander* is 6×9, 128 pages, 55 lb. paper, 12 pt. CIS cover stock, contains photos. Biannual.

MAGAZINES NEEDS Seeks "highly imaginative poetry whose language is serious. Particularly interested in translations." Has published poetry by Alberto Blanco (Mexico), José-Flore Tappy (Switzerland), Ana Minga (Ecuador), Károly Bari (Hungary), Astrid Cabral (Brazil), and numerous well-known and not so well-known U.S. poets. Does not want rhyme and meter or most traditional forms. Length: 1-60 lines. Pays contributor's copies.

TIPS "If you are writing poems or short fiction in the tradition of 98% of all journals publishing in this country, then your work will usually not fit for us. If within the first 400 words my mind drifts, the rest

rarely makes it. Be yourself, and listen to no one but yourself."

BLACKBIRD

Virginia Commonwealth University Department of English, P.O. Box 843082, Richmond VA 23284. (804)827-4729. **E-mail:** blackbird@vcu.edu. **Website:** www.blackbird.vcu.edu. *Blackbird* is published twice a year. Responds in 6 months. Guidelines online at website.

MAGAZINES NEEDS Submit 2-6 poems at a time. "If submitting online, put all poems into 1 document."

TIPS "We like a story that invites us into its world, that engages our senses, soul, and mind. We are able to publish long works in all genres, but query *Blackbird* before you send a prose piece over 8,000 words or a poem exceeding 10 pages."

💲 BLACK LACE

P.O. Box 83912, Los Angeles CA 90083. (310)410-0808. **Fax:** (310)410-9250. **E-mail:** newsroom@blk. com. **Website:** www.blacklace.org. "*Black Lace* seeks stories, articles, photography, models, illustration, and a very limited amount of poetry all related to black women unclothed or in erotic situations." Acquires first North American rights; acquires rights to anthologize accepted work. Responds in 1 month. Guidelines online.

MAGAZINES NEEDS Submit by postal mail (include SASE if you want your work returned), fax, or e-mail.

TIPS "*Black Lace* seeks erotic material of the highest quality, but it need not be written by professional writers. The most important thing is that the work be erotic and that it feature black women in the life or ITL themes. We are not interested in stories that demean black women or place them in stereotypical situations."

💲 BLACK WARRIOR REVIEW

P.O. Box 862936, Tuscaloosa AL 35486. (205)348-4518. **E-mail:** interns.bwr@gmail.com. **Website:** www.bwr. ua.edu. **Contact:** Kirby Johnson, editor. "We publish contemporary fiction, poetry, reviews, essays, and art for a literary audience. We publish the freshest work we can find." Buys first rights. Pays on publication. Publishes ms 6 months after acceptance. Responds in 3-6 months. Sample copy: $10. Guidelines available online.

- Work that appeared in the *Black Warrior Review* has been included in the *Pushcart Prize* anthology, *Harper's Magazine, Best American Short Stories, Best American Poetry,* and *New Stories from the South.*

MAGAZINES NEEDS "We welcome most styles and forms, and we favor poems that take risks—whether they be quiet or audacious." Submit poems in 1 document. Accepts up to 5 poems per submission at a maximum of 10 pages. "*BWR* pays a one-year subscription and a nominal lump-sum fee for all works published."

TIPS "We look for attention to language, freshness, honesty, a convincing and sharp voice. Send us a clean, well-printed, proofread manuscript. Become familiar with the magazine prior to submission."

BLOOD LOTUS

E-mail: bloodlotusjournal@gmail.com. **Website:** www.bloodlotusjournal.com. **Contact:** Bethany Brownholtz, art director and co-editor. *Blood Lotus,* published quarterly online, publishes "poetry, fiction, and anything in between!" Wants "fresh language, memorable characters, strong images, and vivid artwork." Will not open attachments. Reads submissions year round. Acquires first North American rights, electronic archival rights. Guidelines online.

MAGAZINES NEEDS Send "3-5 crafted, polished, image-centric, language-innovating poems, e-mailed to bloodlotuspoetry@gmail.com." No attachments.

TIPS "Don't be boring."

THE BLOOMSBURY REVIEW

1245 E. Colfax, Suite 304, Denver CO 80218. (303)455-3123. **Fax:** (303)455-7039. **E-mail:** info@bloomsburyreview.com. **E-mail:** editors@bloomsburyreview.com. **Website:** www.bloomsburyreview.com. **Contact:** Marilyn Auer, editor-in-chief/publisher. Publishes book reviews, interviews with writers and poets, literary essays, and original poetry. Audience consists of educated, literate, general readers. Buys first rights, asks for non-exclusive electronic rights. Pays on publication. Publishes ms an average of 4-6 months after acceptance. Responds in 4 months to queries. Sample copy for $5 and 9x12 SASE. Guidelines for #10 SASE or online.

MAGAZINES NEEDS Pays $5-10.

TIPS "We appreciate receiving published clips and/or completed mss. Please, no rough drafts. Book reviews should be of new books (within 6 months of publication)."

BLUE COLLAR REVIEW

Partisan Press, P.O. Box 11417, Norfolk VA 23517. **E-mail:** red-ink@earthlink.net. **Website:** www.partisanpress.org. **Contact:** A. Markowitz, editor; Mary Franke, co-editor. *Blue Collar Review (Journal of Progressive Working Class Literature),* published quarterly, contains poetry, short stories, and illustrations "reflecting the working-class experience—a broad range from the personal to the societal. Our purpose is to promote and expand working-class literature and an awareness of the connections between workers of all occupations and the social context in which we live. Also to inspire the creativity and latent talent in 'common' working people." Sample copy: $7. Subscription: $15 for 1 year; $25 for 2 years. Make checks payable to Partisan Press.

○ *Blue Collar Review* is 60 pages, digest-sized, offset-printed, saddle-stapled, with colored card cover, includes ads. Receives hundreds of poems/year, accepts about 15%. Press run is 500.

MAGAZINES NEEDS Send up to 5 poems. Include name and address on each page. Cover letter is helpful, though not required. Include SASE for response. Has published poetry by Simon Perchik, Jim Daniels, Mary McAnally, Marge Piercy, Alan Catlin, and Rob Whitbeck.

ALSO OFFERS Partisan Press looks for "poetry of power that reflects a working-class consciousness and moves us forward as a society. Must be good writing reflecting social realism including but not limited to political issues." Publishes about 3 chapbooks/year; not presently open to unsolicited submissions. "Submissions are requested from among the poets published in the *Blue Collar Review.*" Has published *A Possible Explanation* by Peggy Safire and *American Sounds* by Robert Edwards. Chapbooks are usually 20-60 pages, digest-sized, offset-printed, saddle-stapled or flat-spined, with card or glossy covers. Sample chapbooks are $7 and listed on website.

BLUELINE

120 Morey Hall, Dept. of English and Communication, Postdam NY 13676. (315)267-2044. **E-mail:** blueline@potsdam.edu. **Website:** bluelinemagadk.com. **Contact:** Donald McNutt, editor; Caroline Downing, art editor; Donald McNutt, nonfiction editor; Stephanie Coyne-Deghett, fiction editor; Rebecca Lehmann, poetry editor. "*Blueline* seeks poems, stories, and essays relating to the Adiron-

dacks and regions similar in geography and spirit, or focusing on the shaping influence of nature. Submission period is July-November. *Blueline* welcomes electronic submissions as Word document (.doc or .docx) attachments. Please identify genre in subject line. Please avoid using compression software." Acquires first North American serial rights. Publishes ms 3-6 months after acceptance. Responds in up to 3 months to mss. "Decisions in early February." Occasionally comments on rejected mss. Sample copy: $9. Guidelines available on our website, SASE, or by e-mail. Please visit www.bluelinemagadk.com.

⭕ "Proofread all submissions. It is difficult for our editors to get excited about work containing typographical and syntactic errors."

MAGAZINES NEEDS Submit 3-5 poems at a time. Submit July 1-November 30 only. Include short bio. Poems are circulated to an editorial board. Has published poetry by M.J. Iuppa, Alice Wolf Gilborn, Lyn Lifshin, Todd Davis, Maurice Kenny, Randy Lewis, and Kaye Bache-Snyder. Reviews books of poetry in 500-750 words, single- or multibook format. "We are interested in both beginning and established poets whose poems evoke universal themes in nature and show human interaction with the natural world. We look for thoughtful craftsmanship rather than stylistic trickery." Does not want "sentimental or extremely experimental poetry." Lines/poem: 75 maximum; "occasionally we publish longer poems." Pays 1 contributor's copy.

TIPS "We look for concise, clear, concrete prose that tells a story and touches upon a universal theme or situation. We prefer realism to romanticism but will consider nostalgia if well done. Pay attention to grammar and syntax. Avoid murky language, sentimentality, cuteness, or folkiness. We would like to see more good, creative nonfiction centered on the literature and/or culture of the Adirondacks, Northern New York, New England, or Eastern Canada. If ms has potential, we work with author to improve and reconsider for publication. Our readers prefer fiction to poetry (in general) or reviews. Write from your own experience, be specific and factual (within the bounds of your story), and if you write about universal features such as love, death, change, etc., write about them in a fresh way. You'll catch our attention if your writing is interesting, vigorous, and polished."

BLUE MESA REVIEW

700 Lomas NE, Suite 108, Albuquerque NM 87102. **E-mail:** bmreditr@unm.edu. **Website:** bluemesareview.org. **Contact:** Has rotating editorial board; see website for current masthead. "Originally founded by Rudolfo Anaya, Gene Frumkin, David Johnson, Patricia Clark Smith, and Lee Bartlette in 1989, the *Blue Mesa Review* emerged as a source of innovative writing produced in the Southwest. Over the years the magazine's nuance has changed, sometimes shifting towards more craft-oriented work, other times realigning with its original roots." Requests first North American serial rights for print and nonexclusive electronic rights for website. Responds in 2-6 months.

⭕ Open for submissions from September 30-March 31. Contest: June 1-August 31. Only accepts submissions through online submissions manager, available through website.

MAGAZINES NEEDS Submit 3-5 poems via online submissions manager.

TIPS "In general, we are seeking strong voices and lively, compelling narrative with a fine eye for craft. We look forward to reading your best work!"

BLUESTEM

E-mail: info@bluestemmagazine.com. **Website:** www.bluestemmagazine.com. **Contact:** Lania Knight, editor. *Bluestem*, formerly known as *Karamu*, produces a quarterly online issue (December, March, June, September) and an annual print issue. Submissions are accepted September 1-May 1. There is no compensation for online contributors but we will promote your work enthusiastically and widely. Past issues have included themes such as: The Humor Issue, The Music Issue, The Millennium. Produced by the English Department at Eastern Illinois University. Responds in 6-8 weeks. "Sample back issues of *Bluestem (Karamu)* are available for $5 for each issue you would like."

⭕ Only accepts submissions through online submissions manager.

MAGAZINES NEEDS Submit using online submissions manager. Include bio (less than 100 words) with submission. Pays 1 contributor's copy and discount for additional copies.

BOMBAY GIN

Writing and Poetics Dept., Jack Kerouac School, Naropa University, 2130 Arapahoe Ave., Boulder CO 80302. (303)245-4669. **Fax:** (303)546-5297. **E-mail:** bgin@naropa.edu. **Website:** www.bombayginjournal.

com. **Contact:** Jade Lascelles. *Bombay Gin*, published annually, is the literary journal of the Jack Kerouac School of Disembodied Poetics at Naropa University. Produced and edited by MFA students, *Bombay Gin* publishes established writers alongside unpublished and emerging writers. We have a special interest in works that push conventional literary boundaries. Submissions of poetry, prose, visual art, translation, and works involving hybrid forms and cross-genre exploration are encouraged. Translations are also considered. Guidelines are the same as for original work. Translators are responsible for obtaining any necessary permissions." One-year subscription: $10 + $3 shipping.

○ *Bombay Gin* is 150-200 pages, digest-sized, professionally printed, perfect-bound, with color card cover. Has published work by Amiri Baraka, Lisa Robertson, CA Conrad, Sapphire, Fred Moten, Anne Waldman, Diane di Prima and bell hooks, among others.

MAGAZINES NEEDS Please see website for current details on submission time frames and guidelines. Pays 1 contributor's copies.

⊖ BOMB MAGAZINE

New Arts Publications, 80 Hanson Place, Suite 703, Brooklyn NY 11217. (718)636-9100. **Fax:** (718)636-9200. **E-mail:** generalinquiries@bombsite.com. **Website:** www.bombmagazine.com. **Contact:** Mónica de la Torre, senior editor. "Written, edited, and produced by industry professionals and funded by those interested in the arts, *BOMB Magazine* publishes work which is unconventional and contains an edge, whether it be in style or subject matter." Buys first rights, buys one-time rights. Pays on publication. Publishes ms an average of 3-6 months after acceptance. Responds in 3-5 months to mss. Editorial lead time 3-4 months. Sample copy: $10. Guidelines by e-mail.

MAGAZINES NEEDS *BOMB Magazine* accepts unsolicited poetry and prose submissions for our literary supplement *First Proof* by online submission manager in January and August. Submissions sent outside these months will not be read. Submit 4-6 poems via online submission manager. E-mailed submissions will not be considered. Pays $100 and contributor's copies.

TIPS "Manuscripts should be typed, double-spaced, and proofread, and should be final drafts. Purchase a sample issue before submitting work."

BORDERLANDS: TEXAS POETRY REVIEW

P.O. Box 33096, Austin TX 78764. **E-mail:** borderlandspoetry@gmail.com. **Website:** www.borderlands.org. *Borderlands: Texas Poetry Review*, published semiannually, prints high-quality, outward-looking poetry by new and established poets, as well as brief reviews of poetry books and critical essays. Cosmopolitan in content, but particularly welcomes Texas and Southwest writers. Wants outward-looking poems that exhibit social, political, geographical, historical, feminist, or spiritual awareness coupled with concise artistry. Does not want introspective work about the speaker's psyche, childhood, or intimate relationships. Has published poetry by Walter McDonald, Naomi Shihab Nye, Mario Susko, Wendy Barker, Larry D. Thomas, Reza Shirazi, and Scott Hightower. Guidelines available online.

○ *Borderlands* is 100-150 pages, digest-sized, offset-printed, perfect-bound, with 4-color cover. Receives about 2,000 poems/year, accepts about 120. Press run is 1,000. Sample: $12. Submissions accepted via Submittable.

MAGAZINES NEEDS Submit 5 typed poems at a time. Include cover letter. Include SASE with sufficient return postage. Open to traditional and experimental forms. Submit outwardly directed poetry that exhibits social, political, geographical, historical or spiritual awareness.

TIPS "Editors read year round in two cycles. Submissions postmarked by June 15 will be considered for the Fall/Winter issue, and submissions postmarked by December 15 will be considered for the Spring/Summer issue. Occasionally, work may be held for publication in the following issue. Note that response times may be slower for work received immediately after a deadline. Do not submit work while we are considering a previous submission."

⊖ BOSTON REVIEW

PO Box 425786, Cambridge MA 02142. (617)324-1360. **Fax:** (617)452-3356. **E-mail:** review@bostonreview.net. **Website:** www.bostonreview.net. "The editors are committed to a society and culture that foster human diversity and a democracy in which we seek common grounds of principle amidst our many differences. In the hope of advancing these ideals, the *Review* acts as a forum that seeks to enrich the language of public debate." Buys first North American serial rights, buys first rights. Publishes ms an average of 4 months after acceptance. Responds in 4 months to queries. Sample copy for $6.95 plus shipping or online. Guidelines available online.

○ *Boston Review* is a recipient of the Pushcart Prize in Poetry.

MAGAZINES NEEDS "We are open to both traditional and experimental forms. What we value most is originality and a strong sense of voice." Send materials for review consideration. Reads poetry between September 15 and May 15 each year. Payment varies.

TIPS "The best way to get a sense of the kind of material *Boston Review* is looking for is to read the magazine."

⊕ BOULEVARD

Opojaz, Inc., 6614 Clayton Rd., Box 325, Richmond Heights MO 63117. (314)324-3351. **Fax:** (314)862-2982. **E-mail:** richardburgin@netzero.com; jessicarogen@ boulevardmagazine.org. **E-mail:** https://boulevard. submittable.com/submit. **Website:** www.boulevardmagazine.org. **Contact:** Richard Burgin, editor; Jessica Rogen, managing editor. "*Boulevard* is a diverse literary magazine presenting original creative work by well-known authors, as well as by writers of exciting promise." Triannual magazine featuring fiction, poetry, and essays.Sometimes comments on rejected mss. *Boulevard* has been called 'one of the half-dozen best literary journals' by Poet Laureate Daniel Hoffman in *The Philadelphia Inquirer*. We strive to publish the finest in poetry, fiction, and nonfiction. We frequently publish writers with previous credits, we are very interested in publishing less experienced or unpublished writers with exceptional promise. We've published everything from John Ashbery to Donald Hall to a wide variety of styles from new or lesser known poets. We're eclectic. We are interested in original, moving poetry written from the head as well as the heart. It can be about any topic." Buys first North American serial rights. Rights revert to author upon publication. Pays on publication. Publishes ms an average of 9 months after acceptance. Responds in 2 weeks to queries; 4-5 months to mss. Sample copy: $10. Subscription: $15 for 3 issues, $27 for 6 issues, $30 for 9 issues. Foreign subscribers, please add $10. Make checks payable to Opojaz, Inc. Subscriptions are available online at www.boulevardmagazine.org/subscribe. html. Publishes short fiction, poetry, and nonfiction, including critical and culture essays. Submit by mail or via Submittable. Accepts multiple submissions.

Does not accept mss between May 1 and October 1. SASE for reply.

○ *Boulevard* is 175-250 pages, digest-sized, flat-spined, with glossy card cover. Receives over 600 unsolicited mss/month. Accepts about 10 mss/issue. Publishes 10 new writers/year. Recently published work by Joyce Carol Oates, Floyd Skloot, John Barth, Stephen Dixon, David Guterson, Albert Goldbarth, Molly Peacock, Bob Hicok, Alice Friman, Dick Allen, and Tom Disch.

MAGAZINES NEEDS Does not consider book reviews. "Do not send us light verse." Does not want "poetry that is uninspired, formulaic, self-conscious, unoriginal, insipid." Length: up to 200 lines/poem. Pays $25-250.

ALSO OFFERS The Poetry Contest for Emerging Writers: $1,000 and publication in *Boulevard*, awarded to the winning group of 3 poems. Postmark deadline is June 1. Entry fee is $15 for each group of three poems, with no limit per author. It includes a one-year subscription to *Boulevard*. For contests, make check payable to *Boulevard* or submit online at https://boulevard.submittable.com/submit.

TIPS "Read the magazine first. The work *Boulevard* publishes is generally recognized as among the finest in the country. We continue to seek more good literary or cultural essays. Send only your best work."

THE BREAKTHROUGH INTERCESSOR

Breakthrough, Inc., P.O. Box 121, Lincoln VA 20160. **Fax:** (540)338-1934. **E-mail:** breakthrough@intercessors.org. **Website:** intercessors.org. *The Breakthrough Intercessor*, published quarterly, focuses on "encouraging people in prayer and faith; preparing and equipping those who pray." Accepts multiple articles per issue: 300- to 1,000-word true stories on prayer, or poems on prayer. Time between acceptance and publication varies. Subscription: $18. Make checks payable to Breakthrough, Inc. Guidelines available on website.

○ *The Breakthrough Intercessor* is 36 pages, magazine-sized, professionally printed, saddle-stapled with self-cover, includes art/graphics. Press run is 4,000.

MAGAZINES NEEDS Send poem, along with title, author's name, address, phone number, and e-mail. Accepts fax, e-mail (pasted into body of message or attachment), and mailed hard copy. Length: 12 lines/poem minimum.

THE BRIAR CLIFF REVIEW

3303 Rebecca St., Sioux City IA 51104. (712)279-5477. **E-mail:** tricia.currans-sheehan@briarcliff.edu (editor); jeanne.emmons@briarcliff.edu (poetry). **Website:** bcreview.org. **Contact:** Tricia Currans-Sheehan, Jeanne Emmons, Phil Hey, Paul Weber, editors. *The Briar Cliff Review,* published annually in April, is "an attractive, eclectic literary/art magazine." It focuses on (but is not limited to) "Siouxland writers and subjects. We are happy to proclaim ourselves a regional publication. It doesn't diminish us; it enhances us." Acquires first serial rights. Time between acceptance and publication is up to 6 months. Responds in 4-5 months to mss; in 6-8 months to poems. Sample copy: $15, plus 9x12 SAE. Guidelines available on website or for #10 SASE.

○ Magazine: 8.5×11; 125 pages; 70 lb. 100# Altima Satin Text; illustrations; photos; perfect-bound, with 4-color cover on dull stock. Member: CLMP, Humanities International Complete. Reads submissions August 1-November 1 only.

MAGAZINES NEEDS Wants quality poetry with strong imagery and tight, well-wrought language. Especially interested in, but not limited to, regional, Midwestern content. Receives about 1,000 poems/year; accepts about 30. Considers simultaneous submissions but expects prompt notification of acceptance elsewhere. Submit by postal mail (send SASE for return of ms) or via Submittable. No e-mail submissions, unless from overseas. Cover letter is required. "Include short bio. Submissions should be typewritten or letter quality, with author's name and address on each page. No mss returned without SASE." Seldom comments on rejected poems. Pays with 2 contributor's copies.

TIPS "So many stories are just telling. We want some action. It has to move. We prefer stories in which there is no gimmick, no mechanical turn of events, no moral except the one we would draw privately."

BRILLIANT CORNERS: A JOURNAL OF JAZZ & LITERATURE

Lycoming College, 700 College Place, Williamsport PA 17701. **Website:** www.lycoming.edu/brilliantcorners. **Contact:** Sascha Feinstein. "We publish jazz-related literature—fiction, poetry, and nonfiction. We are open as to length and form." Semiannual. Acquires first North American serial rights. Publishes ms 4-12 months after acceptance. Responds in 2 weeks to queries; 1-2 months to mss. Rarely comments on rejected mss. Sample copy: $7. Guidelines available online.

○ Does not read mss May 15-September 1.

MAGAZINES NEEDS Submit 3-5 poems at a time. No e-mail or fax submissions. Cover letter is preferred. Staff reviews books of poetry. Send materials for review consideration. Wants "work that is both passionate and well crafted—work worthy of our recent contributors." Has published poetry by Amiri Baraka, Jayne Cortez, Yusef Komunyakaa, Philip Levine, Sonia Sanchez, and Al Young. Does not want "sloppy hipster jargon or improvisatory nonsense."

TIPS "We look for clear, moving prose that demostrates a love of both writing and jazz. We primarily publish established writers, but we read all submissions carefully and welcome work by outstanding young writers."

BRYANT LITERARY REVIEW

Faculty Suite F, Bryant University, 1150 Douglas Pike, Smithfield RI 02917. **E-mail:** blr@bryant.edu. **Website:** http://bryantliteraryreview.org. **Contact:** Tom Chandler, editor; Kimberly Keyes, managing editor; Jeff Cabusao, fiction editor; Lucie Koretsky, associate editor. *Bryant Literary Review* is an international magazine of poetry and fiction published annually in May. Features poetry, fiction, photography, and art. "Our only standard is quality." Acquires one-time rights. Publishes ms 5 months after acceptance. Responds in 3 months. Single copy: $8; subscription: $8. To submit work, please review the submission guidelines on our website.

○ *Bryant Literary Review* is 125 pages, digest-sized, offset-printed, perfect-bound, with 4-color cover with art or photo. Has published poetry by Michael S. Harper, Mary Crow, Denise Duhamel, and Baron Wormser. Reading period: September 1-December 1.

MAGAZINES NEEDS Submit 3-5 poems at a time. Cover letter is required. "Include SASE; please submit only once each reading period." Pays contributor's copies.

TIPS "We expect readers of the *Bryant Literary Review* to be sophisticated, educated, and familiar with the conventions of contemporary literature. We see our purpose to be the cultivation of an active and growing connection between our community and the larger literary culture. Our production values are of the highest caliber, and our roster of published authors includes major award and fellowship winners. The *BLR* provides a respected venue for creative writing of every kind from around the world. Our only standard is quality. No abstract expressionist poems, please. We prefer accessible work of depth and quality."

BURNSIDE REVIEW

P.O. Box 1782, Portland OR 97207. **E-mail:** sid@burnsidereview.org. **Website:** www.burnsidereview.org. **Contact:** Sid Miller, founder and editor; Dan Kaplan, managing editor. *Burnside Review*, published every 9 months, prints "the best poetry and short fiction we can get our hands on." Each issue includes 1 featured poet with an interview and new poems. "We tend to publish writing that finds beauty in truly unexpected places; that combines urban and natural imagery; that breaks the heart." Acquires first rights. Pays on publication. Publishes ms 9 months after acceptance. Responds in 1-6 months. Submit seasonal poems 3-6 months in advance. Single copy: $8; subscription: $13. Make checks payable to *Burnside Review* or order online.

○ *Burnside Review* is 80 pages, 6x6, professionally printed, perfect-bound. Charges a $3 submission fee to cover printing costs.

MAGAZINES NEEDS Has published poetry by Linda Bierds, Dorianne Laux, Ed Skoog, Campbell McGrath, Paul Guest, and Larissa Szporluk. Reads submissions year-round. "Editors read all work submitted." Seldom comments on rejected work. Submit electronically on website. Pays $25 plus 1 contributor's copy.

TIPS "*Burnside Review* accepts submissions of poetry and fiction. If you have something else that you think would be a perfect fit for our journal, please query the editor before submitting. We like work that breaks the heart. That leaves us in a place that we don't expect to be. We like the lyric. We like the narrative. We like when the two merge. We like whiskey. We like hourglass figures. We like crying over past mistakes. We like to be surprised. Surprise us. Read a past issue and try to understand our tastes. At the least, please read the sample poems that we have linked from our prior issues."

⑤ BUTTON

P.O. Box 77, Westminster MA 01473. **E-mail:** sally@moonsigns.net. **Website:** www.moonsigns.net. "*But-

ton* is New England's tiniest magazine of poetry, fiction, and gracious living, published once a year. As 'gracious living' is on the cover, we like wit, brevity, cleverly-conceived essays/recipes, poetry that isn't sentimental, or song lyrics. I started *Button* so that a century from now, when people read it in landfills or, preferably, libraries, they'll say, 'Gee, what a great time to have lived. I wish I lived back then." Buys first North American serial rights. Pays on publication. Publishes ms 3-9 months after acceptance. Responds in 1 month to queries. Responds in 2 months to mss. Sometimes comments on rejected mss. Editorial lead time 6 months. Subscription: $5 for 4 issues. Sample copy for $2.50. Guidelines available online. "We don't take e-mail submissions, unless you're living overseas, in which case we respond electronically. But we strongly suggest you request writers' guidelines (send an SASE)."

○ Receives 20-40 unsolicited mss/month. Accepts 3-6 mss/issue; 3-6mss/year. *Button* is 16-24 pages, saddle-stapled, with cardstock offset cover with illustrations that incorporate 1 or more buttons. Has published poetryby Amanda Powell, Brendan Galvin, Jean Monahan, Mary Campbell, KevinMcGrath, and Ed Conti.

MAGAZINES NEEDS Wants quality poetry; "poetry that incises a perfect figure-8 on the ice, but also cuts beneath that mirrored surface. Minimal use of vertical pronoun. Do not submit more than twice in 1 year." Cover letter is required. Does not want "sentiment; no 'musing' on who or what done ya wrong." Pays honorarium and at least 2 contributor's copies.

TIPS "*Button* writers have been widely published elsewhere, in virtually all the major national magazines. They include Ralph Lombreglia, Lawrence Millman, They Might Be Giants, Combustible Edison, Sven Birkerts, Stephen McCauley, Amanda Powell, Wayne Wilson, David Barber, Romayne Dawnay, Brendan Galvin, and Diana DerHovanessian. Follow the guidelines, make sure you read your work aloud, and don't inflate or deflate your publications and experience. We've published plenty of new folks, but on the merits of the work."

CAKETRAIN

P.O. Box 82588, Pittsburgh PA 15218. **E-mail:** editors@caketrain.org. **Website:** www.caketrain.org. **Contact:** Amanda Raczkowski and Joseph Reed, editors. "All rights revert to author upon publication." Responds in 6 months, but often much shorter. Sample copy: $9. Guidelines available on website.

MAGAZINES NEEDS Submit via e-mail; no postal submissions. Include cover letter with titles of pieces and brief bio. Please do not submit any additional work until a decision has been made regarding your current submission. Pays 1 contributor's copy.

CALIFORNIA QUARTERLY

P.O. Box 7126, Orange CA 92863. The California State Poetry Society is dedicated to the advancement of poetry and its dissemination. Although located in California, its members are from all over the U.S. and abroad. Levels of membership/dues: $35/year for an individual, $39/year for a family or library, $51/year foreign. Benefits include membership in the National Federation of State Poetry Societies (NFSPS); 4 issues of California Quarterly, *Newsbriefs*, and *The Poetry Letter*. Sponsors monthly and annual contests. Additional information available for SASE. Acquires first rights. Rights revert to poet after publication.

MAGAZINES NEEDS Submit up to 6 poems maximum, 1 page preferred, name, address, e-mail on each sheet. Submit original poems only; no previously published poems. Foreign poems with translations welcome. Mail with SASE to *CQ* editors. Pays 1 contributor's copy.

CALLALOO: A JOURNAL OF AFRICAN DIASPORA ARTS & LETTERS

Texas A&M University, 249 Blocker Hall, College Station TX 77843-4227. (979)458-3108. **Fax:** (979)458-3275. **E-mail:** callaloo@tamu.edu. **Website:** callaloo. tamu.edu. *Callaloo: A Journal of African Diaspora Arts & Letters*, published quarterly, is devoted to poetry dealing with the African Diaspora, including North America, Europe, Africa, Latin and Central America, South America, and the Caribbean. Features about 15-20 poems (all forms and styles) in each issue along with short fiction, interviews, literary criticism, and concise critical book reviews. Responds in 6 months. Single copy: $20 for individuals; $50 for institutions. Subscription: $63 for individuals; $205 for institutions.

MAGAZINES NEEDS Submit no more than 5 poems at a time; no more than 10 per calendar year. Submit using online submissions manager only. Has published poetry by Aimeé Ceésaire, Lucille Clifton,

Rita Dove, Yusef Komunyakaa, Natasha Tretheway, and Carl Phillips.

TIPS "We look for freshness of both writing and plot, strength of characterization, plausibility of plot. Read what's being written and published, especially in journals such as *Callaloo*."

CALYX

Calyx, Inc., P.O. Box B, Corvallis OR 97339. (541)753-9384. **Fax:** (541)753-0515. **E-mail:** info@calyxpress. org; editor@calyxpress.org. **Website:** www.calyxpress. org. **Contact:** Brenna Crotty, senior editor. *"CALYX* exists to publish fine literature and art by women and is committed to publishing the work of all women, including women of color, older women, working-class women and other voices that need to be heard. We are committed to discovering and nurturing developing writers." Publishes ms an average of 6-12 months after acceptance. Responds in 4-8 months to mss. Sample copy: $10 plus $4 postage and handling.

Annual open submission period is October 1-December 31.

MAGAZINES NEEDS "When submitting through our online submissions manager, please put all poems in the same document." Wants "excellently crafted poetry that also has excellent content." Pays in contributor's copies and one-volume subscription.

TIPS "A forum for women's creative work—including work by women of color, lesbian and queer women, young women, old women—*CALYX* breaks new ground. Each issue is packed with new poetry, short stories, full-color artwork, photography, essays, and reviews."

CANADIAN WRITER'S JOURNAL

Box 1178, New Liskeard ON P0J 1P0, Canada. (705)647-5424. **Fax:** (705)647-8366. **E-mail:** cwj@cwj. ca. **Website:** www.cwj.ca. **Contact:** Deborah Ranchuk, editor. Digest-size magazine for writers emphasizing short "how-to" articles, which convey easily understood information useful to both apprentice and professional writers. General policy and postal subsidies require that the magazine must carry a substantial Canadian content. "We try for about 90% Canadian content but prefer good material over country of origin or how well you're known. Writers may query, but unsolicited mss are welcome." Buys one-time rights. Pays on publication. Publishes ms an average of 2-9 months after acceptance. Responds in 3 months to queries and mss. Sample copy: $8, including postage. Guidelines available online.

MAGAZINES NEEDS Poetry must be unpublished elsewhere; short poems or extracts used as part of articles on the writing of poetry. Accepts e-mail submissions (pasted into body of message, with 'Submission' in the subject line). Include SASE with postal submissions. "U.S. postage accepted; do not affix to envelope. Poems should be titled." Pays $2-5 per poem published (depending on length) and 1 contributor's copy. SASE required for response and payment.

TIPS "We prefer short, tightly written, informative how-to articles. U.S. writers: note that U.S. postage cannot be used to mail from Canada. Obtain Canadian stamps, use IRCs, or send small amounts in cash."

THE CAPILANO REVIEW

2055 Purcell Way, North Vancouver BC V7J 3H5, Canada. (604)984-1712. **E-mail:** tcr@capilanou.ca. **Website:** www.thecapilanoreview.ca. **Contact:** Todd Nickel, managing editor. Triannual visual and literary arts magazine that "publishes only what the editors consider to be the very best fiction, poetry, drama, or visual art being produced. *TCR* editors are interested in fresh, original work that stimulates and challenges readers. Over the years, the magazine has developed a reputation for pushing beyond the boundaries of traditional art and writing. We are interested in work that is new in concept and in execution." Buys first North American serial rights. Pays on publication. Publishes ms an average of within 1 year after acceptance. Responds in 4-6 months to mss. Sample copy: $10 (outside of Canada, USD). Guidelines with #10 SASE with IRC or Canadian stamps.

MAGAZINES NEEDS Submit up to 8 pages of poetry. Pays $50-300.

THE CARIBBEAN WRITER

University of the Virgin Islands, RR 1, P.O. Box 10,000, Kingshill, St. Croix USVI 00850. (340)692-4152. **Fax:** (340)692-4026. **E-mail:** info@thecaribbeanwriter. org. **E-mail:** submit@thecaribbeanwriter.org. **Website:** www.thecaribbeanwriter.org. **Contact:** Alscess Lewis-Brown, editor. "*The Caribbean Writer* features new and exciting voices from the region and beyond that explore the diverse and multi-ethnic culture in poetry, short fiction, personal essays, creative nonfiction, and plays. Social, cultural, economic and sometimes controversial issues are also explored, employing a wide array of literary devices." Acquires first

North American serial rights. Single copy: $25; subscription: $30/2 years.

Poetry published in *The Caribbean Writer* has appeared in *The Pushcart Prize*. *The Caribbean Writer* is 300+ pages, digest-sized, handsomely printed on heavy stock, perfect-bound, with glossy card cover. Press run is 1,200.

MAGAZINES NEEDS Reviews books of poetry and fiction in 1,000 words. Send materials for review consideration. Submit up to 6 poems at a time. E-mail as attachment; no fax submissions. Name, address, phone number, e-mail address, and title of ms should appear in cover letter along with brief bio. Title only on ms. Guidelines available by e-mail or on website. Has published poetry by Edwidge Danticat, Geoffrey Philp, and Thomas Reiter. Pays 1 contributor's copy.

ALSO OFFERS All submissions are eligible for the Daily News Prize ($300) for poetry, The Marguerite Cobb McKay Prize to a Virgin Island author ($200), the David Hough Literary Prize to a Caribbean author ($500), the Canute A. Brodhurst Prize for Fiction ($400), the Cecile Dejongh Literary Prize to an author whose work best expresses the spirit of the Caribbean ($500), and the Marvin Williams Literary Prize for first-time publication in the Caribbean ($500).

THE CAROLINA QUARTERLY

510 Greenlaw Hall, CB #3520, University of North Carolina, Chapel Hill NC 27599-3520. (919)408-7786. **E-mail:** carolina.quarterly@gmail.com. **Website:** www.thecarolinaquarterly.com. *The Carolina Quarterly*, published 3 times/year, prints fiction, poetry, reviews, nonfiction, and visual art. No specifications regarding form, length, subject matter, or style of poetry. Considers translations of work originally written in languages other than English. Acquires first rights. Responds in 4-6 months. Sample copy: $9.

Has published poetry by Denise Levertov, Richard Wilbur, Robert Morgan, Ha Jin, and Charles Wright. *The Carolina Quarterly* is about 100 pages, digest-sized, professionally printed, perfect-bound, with glossy cover, includes ads. Receives about 6,000 poems/year, accepts about 1%. Press run is 1,000. Subscription: $24 for individuals, $30 for institutions.

MAGAZINES NEEDS Submit 1-6 poems at a time. No previously published poems. (Simultaneous submissions welcome with nonficton.) No e-mail submissions. SASE required. Electronic submissions accepted, see website for details. "All mss are read by an editor. Poems that make it to the meeting of the full poetry staff are discussed by all. Poems are accepted by majority consensus informed by the poetry editor's advice." Seldom comments on rejected poems. "Poets are welcome to write or e-mail regarding their submission's status, but please wait about four months before doing so." Reviews books of poetry. Send materials for review consideration (attn: Editor). Pays 2 contributor's copies.

CARUS PUBLISHING COMPANY

30 Grove St., Suite C, Peterborough NH 03458. **Website:** www.cricketmag.com. See listings for *Babybug*, *Cicada*, *Click*, *Cricket*, *Ladybug*, *Muse*, *Spider*, and *Ask*. Carus Publishing owns Cobblestone Publishing, publisher of *AppleSeeds*, *Calliope*, *Cobblestone*, *Dig*, *Faces*, and *Odyssey*.

CAVEAT LECTOR

400 Hyde St., #606, San Francisco CA 94109. (415)928-7431. **Fax:** (415)928-7431. **E-mail:** editors@caveat-lector.org. **E-mail:** caveatlectormagazine@gmail.com. **Website:** www.caveat-lector.org. **Contact:** Christopher Bernard, co-editor. *Caveat Lector*, published 2 times/year, is devoted to the arts and cultural and philosophical commentary. As well as literary work, they publish art, photography, music, streaming audio of selected literary pieces, and short films. Poetry, fiction, artwork, music, and short films are posted on website. "Don't let those examples limit your submissions. Send what you feel is your strongest work, in any style and on any subject." Acquires first rights.

○ All submissions should be sent with a brief bio and SASE, or submitted electronically (poetry submissions only accepted through postal mail). Reads poetry submissions February 1-June 30; reads all other submissions year round.

MAGAZINES NEEDS Wants poetry on any subject, in any style, as long as the work is authentic in feeling and appropriately crafted. Looking for accomplished poems, something that resonates in the mind long after the reader has laid the poem aside. Wants work that has authenticity of emotion and high craft; poems that, whether raw or polished, ring true; and if humorous, are actually funny, or at least witty. Classical to experimental. Note: Sometimes request authors for audio of work to post on website. Has published poetry by Joanne Lowery, Simon Perchik, Les Murray, Alfred Robinson, and Ernest Hilbert. **Submit poetry**

through postal mail only. Send brief bio and SASE with submission. Pays contributor's copies.

CC&D: CHILDREN, CHURCHES & DADDIES

Scars Publications and Design, 829 Brian Court, Gurnee IL 60031. (847)281-9070. **E-mail:** ccandd96@scars.tv. **Website:** scars.tv/ccd. **Contact:** Janet Kuypers. "Our biases are works that relate to issues such as politics, sexism, society, and the like, but are definitely not limited to such. We publish good work that makes you think, that makes you feel like you've lived through a scene instead of merely reading it. If it relates to how the world fits into a person's life (political story, a day in the life, coping with issues people face), it will probably win us over faster. We have received comments from readers and other editors saying that they thought some of our stories really happened. They didn't, but it was nice to know they were so concrete, so believable that people thought they were nonfiction. Do that to our readers." Publishes every other month online and in print; issues sold via Amazon.com throughout the U.S., U.K., and continental Europe. Publishes short shorts, essays, and stories. Also publishes poetry. Always comments on/critiques rejected mss if asked. Ms published 1 year after acceptance. Responds to queries in 2 weeks; mss in 2 weeks. "Responds much faster to e-mail submissions and queries." Sample copy: $6 for issues before 2010. Guidelines available for SASE, via e-mail, on website.

○ Has published Mel Waldman, Kenneth DiMaggio, Linda Webb Aceto, Brian Looney, Joseph Hart, Fritz Hamilton, G.A. Scheinoha, and Ken Dean.

MAGAZINES NEEDS If you do not have e-mail and want to snail-mail a poetry submission, we do not accept poetry snail-mail submissions longer than 10 lines.

CEREMONY, A JOURNAL OF POETRY

Dance of My Hands Publishing, 120 Vista Dr., Warminster PA 18974. **E-mail:** danceofmyhands@aol.com. **Website:** www.danceofmyhands.com. *Ceremony, a Journal of Poetry*, published biannually, encourages "all expression and creativity. Beginning poets are especially encouraged." Wants poetry, short pieces of prose. Publishes ms 1-2 years after acceptance. E-mail poetry submissions to danceofmyhands@aol.com.

○ *Ceremony* is digest-sized, home-printed on recycled paper, single-sided, and staple-bound. Receives about 200 submissions/year.

MAGAZINES NEEDS Poems of shorter length preferred. Accepts e-mail submissions only. Reads submissions year round. Pays 1 contributor's copy. Each additional copy and sample copies: $4. Please make checks payable to Melanie Eyth.

CHAFFIN JOURNAL

English Department, Eastern Kentucky University, Richmond KY 40475-3102. (859)622-3080. **E-mail:** robert.witt@eku.edu. **Website:** www.english.eku.edu/chaffin_journal. **Contact:** Robert Witt, editor. *The Chaffin Journal*, published annually in December, prints quality short fiction and poetry by new and established writers/poets. "We publish fiction on any subject; our only consideration is the quality." Pays on publication for one-time rights. Publishes 6 months after acceptance. Send SASE for return of ms. Responds in 1 week to queries; in 3 months to mss. Sample copy: $6.

○ Receives 20 unsolicited mss/month. Accepts 6-8 mss/year. Does not read mss October 1-May 31. Publishes 2-3 new writers/year. Has published work by Meridith Sue Willis, Marie Manilla, Raymond Abbott, Marjorie Bixler, Chris Helvey.

MAGAZINES NEEDS Submit 5 poems per submission period. Considers simultaneous submissions (although not preferred); no previously published poems. No e-mail or disk submissions. Cover letter is preferred. "Submit typed pages with only 1 poem per page. Enclose SASE." Wants any form, subject matter, or style of poetry. Has published poetry by Taylor Graham, Diane Glancy, Judith Montgomery, Simon Perchik, Philip St. Clair, and Virgil Suárez. Does not want "poor quality." Pays 1 contributor's copy.

TIPS "All mss submitted are considered."

CHANTARELLE'S NOTEBOOK

E-mail: chantarellesnotebook@yahoo.com. **Website:** www.chantarellesnotebook.com. **Contact:** Kendall A. Bell and Christinia Bell, editors. *Chantarelle's Notebook*, published quarterly online, seeks "quality work from undiscovered poets. We enjoy poems that speak to us—poems with great sonics and visuals." Acquires one-time rights. Rights revert to poets upon publication. Responds in 6-8 weeks. Never comments on rejected poems. Sample: See website for latest issue. Guidelines available on website. "Please follow the guidelines—all the information is there!"

MAGAZINES NEEDS Receives about 500 poems/year, accepts about 20%. Submit 3-5 poems at a time. Accepts e-mail submissions (pasted into body of message; "we will not open any attachments—they will be deleted"). Cover letter is required. "Please include a short bio of no more than 75 words, should we decide to accept your work." Reads submissions year round. "The editors will review all submissions and make a decision within a week's time." Has published poetry by Emily Brogan, Heather Cadenhead, Taylor Copeland, Amber Decker, Taylor Graham, and Donna Vorreyer. Does not want "infantile rants, juvenile confessionals, greeting card-styled verse, political posturing, or religious outpourings." Considers poetry by children and teens. "There are no age restrictions, but submissions from younger people will be held to the same guidelines and standards as those from adults." Length: "shorter poems have a better chance, but long poems are fine."

THE CHARITON REVIEW

Truman State University Press, 100 E Normal Ave., Kirksville MO 63501. (660)785-8336. **E-mail:** chariton@truman.edu. **Website:** http://tsup.truman.edu/aboutChariton.asp. **Contact:** James D'Agostino, editor; Barbara Smith-Mandell and Jen Creer, managing editors. *The Chariton Review* is an international literary journal publishing the best in short fiction, essays, poetry, and translations in 2 issues each year. Guidelines available on website. Send a printout of the submission via snail mail; overseas authors may send submissions as email attachments. See also *The Chariton Review* Short Fiction Prize at http://tsup.truman.edu/prizes.asp.

MAGAZINES NEEDS Poetry collections are published through TSUP's annual T.S. Eliot Prize for Poetry. Deadline is October 31 of each year. See competition guidelines at http://tsup.truman.edu/prizes.asp.

⑤ THE CHATTAHOOCHEE REVIEW

555 N. Indian Creek Dr., Clarkston GA 30021. **E-mail:** gpccr@gpc.edu. **Website:** thechattahoocheereview.gpc.edu. **Contact:** Lydia Ship, managing editor. *The Chattahoochee Review*, published quarterly, prints poetry, short fiction, essays, reviews, and interviews. "We publish a number of Southern writers, but *The Chattahoochee Review* is not by design a regional magazine. All themes, forms, and styles are considered as long as they impact the whole person: heart, mind, intuition, and imagination." Acquires

first rights. Publishes ms 6 months after acceptance. Responds in 1 week-6 months. Sample copy: $6. Subscription: $20/year. Guidelines for SASE or on website.

○ Has recently published work by George Garrett, Jim Daniels, Jack Pendarvis, Ignacio Padilla, and Kevin Canty. *The Chattahoochee Review* is 160 pages, digest-sized, professionally printed, flat-spined, with four-color silk-matte card cover. Press run is 1,250; 300 are complimentary copies sent to editors and "miscellaneous VIPs." No e-mail submissions.

MAGAZINES NEEDS "*TCR* publishes excellent poetry of all types, including informal personal narratives, prose poems, and formal poems." Submit 3-5 poems via online submissions manager. Pays 2 contributor's copies.

CHAUTAUQUA LITERARY JOURNAL

Dept. of Creative Writing, University of North Carolina at Wilmington, 601 S. College Rd., Wilmington NC 28403. **E-mail:** clj@uncw.edu. **Website:** www.ci-web.org/literary-journal. **Contact:** Jill Gerard and Philip Gerard, editors. *Chautauqua*, published annually in June, prints poetry, short fiction, and creative nonfiction. The editors actively solicit writing that expresses the values of Chautauqua Institution broadly construed: a sense of inquiry into questions of personal, social, political, spiritual, and aesthetic importance, regardless of genre. Considers the work of any writer, whether or not affiliated with Chautauqua Institution. Looking for a mastery of craft, attention to vivid and accurate language, a true lyric "ear," an original and compelling vision, and strong narrative instinct. Above all, it values work that is intensely personal, yet somehow implicitly comments on larger public concerns, like work that answers every reader's most urgent question: Why are you telling me this? Acquires first rights plus one-time nonexclusive rights to reprint accepted work in an anniversary issue. Publishes ms 1 year after acceptance. Responds in 3-6 months. Guidelines online.

○ Reads submissions February 15-April 15 and August 15-November 15.

MAGAZINES NEEDS Submit up to 3 poems at a time. Submit online through submissions manager or postal mail (include SASE). Sometimes comments on rejected poems. Poetry published in *Chautauqua* has been included in *The Pushcart Prize* anthology. Pays 2 contributor's copies.

CHEST

CHEST Global Headquarters, 2595 Patriot Blvd., Glenview IL 60026. 800-343-2222. **E-mail:** poetrychest@aol.com. **Website:** www.chestjournal.org. **Contact:** Michael Zack, M.D., poetry editor. *CHEST*, published monthly, "is the official medical journal of the American College of Chest Physicians, the world's largest medical journal for pulmonologists, sleep, and critical care specialists, with over 30,000 subscribers." Wants "poetry with themes of medical relevance." Retains all rights. Responds in 2 months; always sends prepublication galleys. Subscription: $276. Make checks payable to American College Chest Physicians.

○ *CHEST* is approximately 300 pages, magazine-sized, perfect-bound, with a glossy cover, and includes ads. Press run is 22,000. Number of unique visitors: 400,000 to website.

MAGAZINES NEEDS Only accepts e-mail submissions (as attachment or in body of e-mail); no fax or disk submissions. Brief cover letter preferred. Reads submissions year round. Poems are circulated to an editorial board. Sometimes comments on rejected poems. Never publishes theme issues. Guidelines available in magazine and on website. Length: up to 350 words.

CHICAGO QUARTERLY REVIEW

Website: www.chicagoquarterlyreview.com. **Contact:** Syed Afzal Haider and Elizabeth McKenzie, editors. "The *Chicago Quarterly Review* is a nonprofit, independent literary journal publishing the finest short stories, poems, translations, and essays by both emerging and established writers. We hope to stimulate, entertain, and inspire." Acquires one-time rights. Responds in 6-8 months to mss. Sometimes comments on rejected mss. Sample copy: $14. Submissions accepted ONLINE ONLY at www.chicagoquarterlyreview.com. Up to 5 poems in a single submission; does not accept multiple short story submissions.

○ The *Chicago Quarterly Review* is 6x9; 225 pages; illustrations; photos. Receives 250 unsolicited mss/month. Accepts 10-15 mss/issue; 20-30 mss/year. Publishes ms 6 months-1 year after acceptance. Agented fiction 5%. **Publishes 8-10 new writers/year.**

MAGAZINES NEEDS Submit 3-5 poems through online submissions manager only. Pays 2 contributor's copies; additional copies $14.

TIPS "The writer's voice ought to be clear and unique and should explain something of what it means to be human. We want well-written stories that reflect an appreciation for the rhythm and music of language, work that shows passion and commitment to the art of writing."

⑤ CHICKEN SOUP FOR THE SOUL PUBLISHING, LLC

E-mail: webmaster@chickensoupforthesoul.com (for all inquires). **Website:** www.chickensoup.com. Buys one-time rights. Pays on publication. Responds upon consideration. Guidelines available online.

⚪   "Stories must be written in the first person."

MAGAZINES NEEDS No controversial poetry.

TIPS "We no longer accept submissions by mail or fax. Stories and poems can only be submitted on our website. Select the 'Submit Your Story' tab on the left toolbar. The submission form can be found there."

CHIRON REVIEW

522 E. South Ave., St. John KS 67576. **E-mail:** editor@chironreview.com. **Website:** chironreview.com. **Contact:** Michael Hathaway, editor. *Chiron Review*, published quarterly, presents the widest possible range of contemporary creative writing—fiction and nonfiction, traditional and off-beat—in an attractive, perfect-bound digest, including artwork and photographs. No taboos. Has published poetry by Charles Bukowski, Charles Harper Webb, Edward Field, Wanda Coleman, and Marge Piercy. Press run is about 1,000. Acquires first-time rights. Responds in 2-6 weeks. Subscription: $60, ppd/year (4 issues) and $80 ppd overseas. Single issue: $20 ppd and $27 ppd overseas. Guidelines available for SASE or on website.

MAGAZINES NEEDS Submit up to 3 poems or 1 long poem at a time. Only submit 4 times a year. Accepts e-mail and postal mail submissions. "Send all poems in ONE MS Word or translatable attachment. Complete postal address must accompany every single submission regardless of how many times you have submitted in the past. It helps if you put your name and genre of submission in subject line." Include SASE via postal mail. Pays 1 contributor's copy.

ADDITIONAL INFORMATION Will also publish occasional chapbooks; see website for details.

TIPS "Please visit our website for updates."

⑤ CHRISTIAN COMMUNICATOR

9118 W. Elmwood Dr., Suite 1G, Niles IL 60714-5820. (847)296-3964. **Fax:** (847)296-0754. **E-mail:** ljohnson@wordprocommunications.com. **Website:** acwriters.com. **Contact:** Lin Johnson, managing editor; Sally Miller, poetry editor (sallymiller@ameritech.net). Buys first rights, buys second serial (reprint) rights. Pays on publication. Publishes ms an average of 6-12 months after acceptance. Responds in 6-8 weeks to queries; in 8-12 weeks to mss. Editorial lead time 3 months. Sample copy for SAE and 5 first-class stamps. Writer's guidelines by e-mail or on website.

MAGAZINES NEEDS Length: 4-20 lines. Pays $5.

TIPS "We primarily use how-to articles and profiles of editors. However, we're willing to look at any other pieces geared to the writing life."

CHRISTIANITY AND LITERATURE

Pepperdine University, Humanities Division, 24255 Pacific Coast Hwy., Malibu CA 90263-7232. **E-mail:** jordan.hardman@pepperdine.edu. **E-mail:** christianityandliterature@pepperdine.edu. **Website:** www.pepperdine.edu/sponsored/ccl/journal. Poetry submissions: Tulane University, Dept. of English, Norman Mayer 122, New Orleans, LA 70118. **Contact:** Jordan Hardman, managing editor; Prof. Peter Cooley, poetry editor. "*Christianity & Literature* is devoted to the scholarly exploration of how literature engages Christian thought, experience, and practice. The journal presupposes no particular theological orientation but respects an orthodox understanding of Christianity as a historically defined faith. Contributions appropriate for submission should demonstrate a keen awareness of the author's own critical assumptions in addressing significant issues of literary history, interpretation, and theory." Rights to republish revert to poets upon written request. Time between acceptance and publication is 6-12 months. "Poems are chosen by our poetry editor." Responds within 4 months. Sample copy: $10 (back issue) .Subscription: $25 for 1 year; $45 for 2 years. Guidelines available on website.

MAGAZINES NEEDS Submit up to 6 poems. Accepts submissions by surface mail only. Cover letter is required. Submissions must be accompanied by SASE. Reviews collections of literary, Christian poetry occasionally in some issues (no chapbooks). Pays 1 contributor's copy and 5 offprints of poem.

TIPS "We look for poems that are clear and surprising. They should have a compelling sense of voice, formal sophistication (though not necessarily rhyme and meter), and the ability to reveal the spiritual through concrete images. We cannot return submissions that are not accompanied by SASE."

⑤ CHRISTIAN LIVING IN THE MATURE YEARS

The United Methodist Publishing House, 2222 Rosa L. Parks Blvd., P.O. Box 17890, Nashville TN 37228-7890. (615)749-6474. **Fax:** (615)749-6512. **E-mail:** matureyears@umpublishing.org. Buys first North American serial rights. Pays on acceptance. Publishes ms an average of 1 year after acceptance. Responds in 6-7 months to mss. Sample copy: $6, plus 9x12 SAE. Writer's guidelines for #10 SASE or by e-mail.

MAGAZINES NEEDS Submit seasonal and nature poems for spring from December through February; for summer from March through May; for fall from June through August; and for winter from September through November. Accepts fax and e-mail submissions (e-mail preferred). Length: 3-16 lines of up to 50 characters maximum. Pays $5-20.

TIPS "Practice writing dialogue! Listen to people talk; take notes; master dialogue writing! Not easy but well worth it! Most inquiry letters are far too long. If you can't sell me an idea in a brief paragraph, you're not going to sell the reader on reading your finished article or story."

⑤ THE CHRISTIAN SCIENCE MONITOR

210 Massachussetts Ave., Boston MA 02115. **E-mail:** homeforum@csmonitor.com. **Website:** www.csmonitor.com; http://www.csmonitor.com/About/Contributor-guidelines. *The Christian Science Monitor*, an international daily newspaper, regularly features poetry in The Home Forum section. Wants finely crafted poems that explore and celebrate daily life; that provide a respite from daily news and from the bleakness that appears in so much contemporary verse. Considers free verse and fixed forms. Has published poetry by Diana Der-Hovanessian, Marilyn Krysl, and Michael Glaser. Publishes 1-2 poems/week.

MAGAZINES NEEDS Submit up to 5 poems at a time. Accepts submissions via online form. Pays $20/haiku; $40/poem. Does not want "work that presents people in helpless or hopeless states; poetry about death, aging, or illness; or dark, violent, sensual poems. No poems that are overtly religious or falsely sweet." Length: under 20 lines.

⑤ CICADA MAGAZINE

Cricket Magazine Group, 70 E. Lake St., Suite 800, Chicago IL 60601. **E-mail:** cicada@cicadamag.com.

Website: www.cricketmag.com/cicada. **Contact:** submissions editor. "*Cicada* is a YA lit/comics magazine fascinated with the lyric and strange and committed to work that speaks to teens' truths. We publish poetry, realistic and genre fiction, essay, and comics by adults and teens. (We are also inordinately fond of Viking jokes.) Our readers are smart and curious; submissions are invited but not required to engage young adult themes." Bimonthly literary magazine for ages 14 and up. Publishes 6 issues/year. Pays after publication. Responds in 3-6 months to mss. Guidelines available online at submittable.cricketmag.com or www.cricketmag.com/submissions.

MAGAZINES NEEDS Reviews serious, humorous, free verse, rhyming. Length: up to 25 lines/poem. Pays up to $3/line ($25 minimum).

TIPS "Favorite writers, YA and otherwise: Bennett Madison, Sarah McCarry, Leopoldine Core, J. Hope Stein, José Olivarez, Sofia Samatar, Erica Lorraine Scheidt, David Levithan, Sherman Alexie, Hilary Smith, Nnedi Okorafor, Teju Cole, Anne Boyer, Malory Ortberg. @cicadamagazine; cicadamagazine.tumblr.com."

CIDER PRESS REVIEW

P.O. Box 33384, San Diego CA 92163. **Website:** ciderpressreview.com. **Contact:** Caron Andregg, publisher/editor in chief; Ruth Foley, managing editor. *Cider Press Review*, published quarterly online and annually in print, features "the best new work from contemporary poets." It was founded by co-publishers/editors Caron Andregg and Robert Wynne. Since its inception, *CPR* has published thousands of poems by over 500 authors. "Our reading period is from January 1-May 31 each year, and full mss (in conjunction with the *CPR* Annual Book Award) between September 1-November 30 and again between April 1 and June 30 each calendar year." Acquires first North American serial rights. Publishes ms 3-12 months after acceptance. Responds in 1-6 months. Single copy: $14.95; subscription: $24 for 2 issues (1 journal, 1 book from the *Cider Press Review* Book Award). Sample: $12 (journal). Guidelines online.

○ *Cider Press Review* is 128 pages, digest-sized, offset-printed, perfect-bound, with 4-color coated card cover. Receives about 2,500 poems/year, accepts about 3%. Press run for print edition is 500.

MAGAZINES NEEDS Wants "thoughtful, well-crafted poems with vivid language and strong images. We prefer poems that have something to say. We would like to see more well-written humor. We also encourage translations." Does not want "didactic, inspirational, greeting card verse, empty word play, therapy, or religious doggerel." Always sends prepublication galleys. Has published poetry by Robert Arroyo, Jr., Virgil Suárez, Linda Pastan, Kathleen Flenniken, Tim Seibles, Joanne Lowery, Thomas Lux, and Mark Cox. Submit up to 5 poems at a time. Strongly prefers submissions through online submissions manager, but accepts postal mail submissions. Cover letter is preferred. Include short bio (25 words maximum). SASE or valid e-mail address required for reply. Poems are circulated to an editorial board. Pays 1 contributor's copy.

ALSO OFFERS Also welcomes reviews under 500 words of current full-length books of poetry.

TIPS Each year, Cider Press publishes an annual journal of poetry and the winning mss from the *Cider Press Review* Book Award and the Editors' Prize for a first or second book. Mss entries must be accompanied by a required entry fee. Prize is $1,000 or $1,500 and publication for a full-length book of poetry and 25 copies.

CIMARRON REVIEW

205 Morrill Hall, English Department, Oklahoma State University, Stillwater OK 74078. **E-mail:** cimarronreview@okstate.edu. **Website:** cimarronreview.com. **Contact:** Toni Graham, editor; Lisa Lewis, poetry editor. "We want strong literary writing. We are partial to fiction in the modern realist tradition and distinctive poetry—lyrical, narrative, etc." Buys first North American serial rights. Publishes ms 2-6 months after acceptance. Responds in 3-6 months to mss. Sample copy: $9. Guidelines available on website.

⬤ *Cimarron Review* is 6.5×8.5; 110 pages. Accepts 3-5 mss/issue; 12-15 mss/year. Publishes 2-4 new writers/year. Eager to receive mss from both established and less experienced writers "who intrigue us with their unusual perspective, language, imagery, and character." Has published work by Molly Giles, Gary Fincke, David Galef, Nona Caspers, Robin Beeman, Edward J. Delaney, William Stafford, John Ashbery, Grace Schulman, Barbara Hamby, Patricia Fargnoli, Phillip Dacey, Holly Prado, and Kim Addonizio.

MAGAZINES NEEDS Submit 3-6 poems at a time with SASE, or submit online through submission manager; include cover letter. No restrictions as to

subject matter. Wants "poems whose surfaces and structures risk uncertainty and which display energy, texture, intelligence, and intense investment." Pays 2 contributor's copies.

TIPS "All postal submissions must come with SASE. A cover letter is encouraged. No e-mail submissions from authors living in North America. Query first and follow guidelines. In order to get a feel for the kind of work we publish, please read an issue or two before submitting."

💲 THE CINCINNATI REVIEW

P.O. Box 210069, Cincinnati OH 45221-0069. (513)556-3954. **E-mail:** editors@cincinnatireview.com. **Website:** www.cincinnatireview.com. **Contact:** Michael Griffith, fiction editor; Don Bogen, poetry editor. A journal devoted to publishing the best new literary fiction, creative nonfiction, and poetry, as well as book reviews, essays, and interviews. Buys first North American serial rights; buys electronic rights. All rights revert to author/poet upon publication. Pays on publication. Publishes ms an average of 6 months after acceptance. Responds in 6 weeks-4 months to mss. Always sends prepublication galleys. Sample: $7 (back issue). Single copy: $9 (current issue). Subscription: $15. Guidelines available on website. Considers submissions by mail and through online submission manager at cincinnatireview.com/submissions. Reads submissions August 15-March 15; mss arriving outside that period will not be read.

⬤ *The Cincinnati Review* is 180-200 pages, digest-sized, perfect-bound, with matte paperback cover with full-color art. Press run is 1,000.

MAGAZINES NEEDS Submit up to 10 pages of poetry at a time via submission manager at cincinnatireview.com/submissions; no e-mail or disk submissions. Cover letter is preferred. SASE required for print submissions. Considers simultaneous submissions with notification; no multiple submissions or previously published poems. Open to any schools, styles, forms—as long as the poem is well made and sophisticated in its language use and subject matter. Reviews books of poetry in 1,500 words, single-book format. Pays $30/page and 2 contributor's copies.

TIPS "Each issue includes a translation feature. For more information on translations, please see our website."

☉ THE CLAREMONT REVIEW

Suite 101, 1581-H Hillside Ave., Victoria V8T 2C1, B.C. (250)216-4248. **E-mail:** claremontreview@gmail.com.

Website: www.theclaremontreview.ca. **Contact:** Jody Carrow, editor in chief. "We publish anything from traditional to postmodern but with a preference for works that reveal something of the human condition. By this we mean stories that explore real characters in modern settings. Who are we, what are we doing to the planet, what is our relationship to one another, the earth, or God? Also, reading samples on the website or from past issues will give you a clearer indication of what we are looking for." Responds in 10-12 weeks. Guidelines available on website.

MAGAZINES NEEDS Submit complete poems on separate pages. Include SASE. Does not want rhyming poetry.

TIPS "Read guidelines before submitting."

CLARK STREET REVIEW

P.O. Box 1377, Berthoud CO 80513. **E-mail:** clarkreview@earthlink.net. **Contact:** Ray Foreman, editor. *Clark Street Review*, published 6 times/year, uses narrative poetry and short shorts. Tries "to give writers and poets cause to keep writing by publishing their best work." Press run is 200. Acquires one-time rights. Publishes ms 2 months after acceptance. Responds in 3 weeks. Single copy: $2; subscription: $6 for 6 issues postpaid for writers only. Make checks payable to R. Foreman. Guidelines for SASE or by e-mail.

○ "Editor reads everything with a critical eye of 30 years of experience in writing and publishing small-press work."

MAGAZINES NEEDS Wants "narrative poetry under 100 lines that reaches readers who are mostly published poets and writers. Subjects are open." Does not want "obscure or formalist work." Has published poetry by Alan Catlin, Charles Porto Lano, David Ochs, Rex Sexton, Jennifer Lagier, Cathy Porter, Charles Ries, Anselm Brocki, Ed Galling, Ellaraine Lockie, and J. Glenn Evans. Receives about 1,000 poems/year, accepts about 10%. Submit narrative poems (human condition poetry only). Send disposable sharp hard copies. Include SASE for reply. No cover letter. No limit on submissions. Maximum 55 characters in width. Flush left.

CLOUDBANK: JOURNAL OF CONTEMPORARY WRITING

P.O. Box 610, Corvallis OR 97339. **E-mail:** michael@cloudbankbooks.com. **Website:** www.cloudbankbooks.com. **Contact:** Michael Malan, editor. *Cloudbank* publishes poetry, short prose, and book reviews.

Acquires one-time rights. Rights revert to poets upon publication. Responds in 4 months to poems. Single copy: $8; subscription: $15. Make checks payable to *Cloudbank*. Guidelines available in magazine, for SASE, by e-mail, or on website.

○ *Cloudbank* is digest-sized, 84 pages of print, perfect-bound; color artwork on cover, includes ads. Press run is 400. Subscribers: 300; shelf sales: 100 distributed free.

MAGAZINES NEEDS Submit 5 poems or less at a time by mail with SASE. Cover letter is preferred. Does not accept fax, e-mail, or disk submissions from USA; overseas e-mail submissions accepted. Reads year round. Rarely sends prepublication galleys. Receives 1,600 poems/year; accepts about 8%. Has published poetry by Dennis Schmitz, Christopher Buckley, Stuart Friebert, Dore Kiesselbach, Karen Holmberg, and Vern Rutsala. Pays $200 prize for 1 poem or flash fiction piece per issue.

ALSO OFFERS *Cloudbank* Contest for $200 prize. $15 entry fee. See website for guidelines.

TIPS "Please consider reading a copy of *Cloudbank* before submitting."

CLOUD RODEO

E-mail: editors@cloudrodeo.org. **E-mail:** submit@cloudrodeo.org. **Website:** cloudrodeo.org. "We want your problems deploying a term liek nonelen. We want your isolated photographs of immense locomotives slogged down by the delirium of drunken yet pristine jungles. We want the one eye you caught on fire doing alchemy. The world you collapsed playing architect. We want what you think is too. We want you to anesthetize this aesthetic. Your Enfer, your Ciel, your Qu'importe. We want all your to to sound out." Acquires first electronic publishing rights. Guidelines available online.

MAGAZINES NEEDS Submit up to 5 poems via e-mail as a .doc or .docx attachment.

TIPS "Let's get weird."

COAL CITY REVIEW

Coal City Press, English Department, University of Kansas, Lawrence KS 66045. **E-mail:** briandal@ku.edu. **Website:** coalcitypress.wordpress.com. **Contact:** Brian Daldorph, editor. "*Coal City Review*, published annually, usually late in the year, publishes poetry, short stories, reviews: "The best material I can find." Responds in 3 months.

MAGAZINES NEEDS "Check out a copy to see what we like." Pays in contributor copies.

COBBLESTONE

Cobblestone Publishing, 30 Grove St., Suite C, Peterborough NH 03458. **Website:** www.cobblestonepub.com. **Contact:** Meg Chorlian. "*Cobblestone* is interested in articles of historical accuracy and lively, original approaches to the subject at hand." American history magazine for ages 8-14. Buys all rights. Pays on publication. Sample copy: $6.95, plus $2 s&h. Guidelines online.

○ "*Cobblestone* stands apart from other children's magazines by offering a solid look at one subject and stressing strong editorial content, color photographs throughout, and original illustrations." *Cobblestone* themes and deadline are available on website or with SASE.

MAGAZINES NEEDS Serious and light verse considered. Must have clear, objective imagery. Length: up to 100 lines/poem. Pays on an individual basis.

TIPS "Review theme lists and past issues to see what we're looking for."

COLD MOUNTAIN REVIEW

Department of English, Appalachian State University, ASU Box 32052, Boone NC 28608. **E-mail:** coldmountain@appstate.edu. **Website:** www.coldmountain.appstate.edu. **Contact:** Betty Miller Conway, managing editor. *Cold Mountain Review*, published twice/year (Spring and Fall), features poetry, interviews with poets, poetry book reviews, and b&w graphic art. Has published poetry by Sarah Kennedy, Robert Morgan, Susan Ludvigson, Aleida Rodriíguez, R.T. Smith, and Virgil Suaárez. Responds in 3 months. Guidelines for SASE.

○ *Cold Mountain Review* is about 72 pages, digest-sized, neatly printed with 1 poem/page (or 2-page spread), perfect-bound, with light cardstock cover. Publishes only 10-12 poems/issue; "hence, we are extremely competitive: send only your best." Reading period is August-May.

MAGAZINES NEEDS Include short bio and SASE. "Please include name, address, phone number, and (if available) e-mail address on each poem. Poems should be single-spaced on 1 side of the page." Pays in contributor's copies.

⑤ COLORADO REVIEW

Center for Literary Publishing, Colorado State University, 9105 Campus Delivery, Fort Collins CO 80523.

(970)491-5449. **E-mail:** creview@colostate.edu. **Website:** coloradoreview.colostate.edu. **Contact:** Stephanie G'Schwind, editor in chief and nonfiction editor; Steven Schwartz, fiction editor; Don Revell, Sasha Steensen, and Matthew Cooperman, poetry editors; Dan Beachy-Quick, book review editor. Literary magazine published 3 times/year. Buys first North American serial rights. Rights revert to author upon publication. Pays on publication. Publishes ms an average of 6 months after acceptance. Responds in 2 months to mss. Editorial lead time 1 year. Sample copy: $10. Guidelines available online.

○ Work published in *Colorado Review* has been included in *Best American Poetry*, *Best New American Voices*, *Best Travel Writing*, *Best Food Writing*, and the *Pushcart Prize Anthology*.

MAGAZINES NEEDS Considers poetry of any style. Poetry mss are read August 1-April 30. Mss received May 1-July 31 will be returned unread. Has published poetry by Sherman Alexie, Laynie Browne, John Gallaher, Mathias Svalina, Craig Morgan Teicher, Pam Rehm, Elizabeth Robinson, Elizabeth Willis, and Rosmarie Waldrop. Pays minimum of $30 or $10/page for poetry.

COLUMBIA: A JOURNAL OF LITERATURE AND ART

Columbia University, New York NY 10027. **E-mail:** columbia.editor@gmail.com. **Website:** columbiajournal.org. **Contact:** Mary Jean Murphy, managing editor. "*Columbia: A Journal of Literature and Art* is an annual publication that features the very best in poetry, fiction, nonfiction, and art. We were founded in 1977 and continue to be one of the few national literary journals entirely edited, designed, and produced by students. You'll find that our minds are open, our interests diverse. We solicit mss from writers we love and select the most exciting finds from our virtual submission box. Above all, our commitment is to our readers—to producing a collection that informs, surprises, challenges, and inspires."

○ Reads submissions March 1-September 15.

MAGAZINES NEEDS Submit poetry via online submissions manager.

COMMON GROUND REVIEW

Western New England University, H-5132, Western New England University, 1215 Wilbraham Rd., Springfield MA 01119. **E-mail:** editors@cgreview.org. **Website:** cgreview.org. **Contact:** Janet Bowdan, editor. *Common Ground Review*, published semiannually (Spring/Summer, Fall/Winter), prints poetry and 1 short nonfiction piece in the Fall issue and 1 short fiction piece in the Spring issue. "This is the official literary journal of Western New England." Acquires one-time rights. Publishes ms 4-6 months after acceptance. Responds in 2 months to mss. Submit seasonal poems 6 months in advance. Guidelines and Submittable link available on submissions page of website: www.cgreview.org.

MAGAZINES NEEDS Cover letter and biography are required. "Poems should be single-spaced indicating stanza breaks; include name, address, phone number, e-mail address, brief bio, and SASE (submissions without SASE will not be notified)." Reads submissions year round, but deadlines for noncontest submissions are August 31 and March 1. "Editor reads and culls submissions. Final decisions made by editorial board." Seldom comments on rejected poems. Has published poetry by James Doyle, B.Z. Niditch, Ann Lauinger, Kathryn Howd Machan, and Sheryl L. Nelms. Does not want "greeting card verse, overly sentimental, or stridently political poetry." Length: up to 60 lines/poem. Pays 1 contributor's copy.

ALSO OFFERS Sponsors an annual poetry contest. Offers 1st Prize: $500; 2nd Prize: $200; 3rd Prize: $100; Honorable Mentions. **Entry fee:** $15 for 1-3 unpublished poems. **Deadline:** March 1 for contest submissions only. All contest submissions are considered for publication in *Common Ground Review*.

TIPS "For poems, use a few good images to convey ideas. Poems should be condensed and concise, free from words that do not contribute. The subject matter should be worthy of the reader's time and should appeal to a wide range of readers. Sometimes the editors may suggest possible revisions."

COMMON THREADS

6519 Crab Apple Dr., Canal Winchester OH 43110. (614)829-5040. **E-mail:** team@ohiopoetryassn.org. **Website:** www.ohiopoetryassn.com. **Contact:** Chuck Salmons, OPA president. *Common Threads*, published annually in autumn, is the Ohio Poetry Association's member journal. **Submissions limited to OPA members.** "We accept poems from both beginners and accomplished writers. We like poems to make us think as well as feel. We are uninterested in work that is highly sentimental, overly morbid, religiously coercive, or pornographic. Poetry by students will also

be considered and prioritized if student is an OPA high school contest winner." While devoted primarily to members' poetry, *Common Threads* can include book reviews, essays on craft, interviews, and other articles related to poetry as an art. All rights revert to poet upon publication. Single copy: $5. Subscription ($20; $15 for seniors 65+) in the form of annual OPA membership dues includes annual issue of *Common Threads*. Visit www.ohiopoetryassn.org for membership applications and additional information on submissions.

MAGAZINES NEEDS Previously published poems are considered if first publisher is noted on submission. Submit up to 3 poems at a time to editor@ohiopoetryassociation.org (preferred) or as hard copies c/o 91 E. Duncan St., Columbus OH 43202 (w/SASE or e-mail address) throughout the year, with August 31 deadline for consideration. Length: up to 50 lines/poem.

COMMONWEAL

Commonweal Foundation, 475 Riverside Dr., Room 405, New York NY 10115. (212)662-4200. **Fax:** (212)662-4183. **E-mail:** editors@commonwealmagazine.org. **Website:** www.commonwealmagazine.org. **Contact:** Paul Baumann, editor; Tiina Aleman, production editor. Buys all rights. Pays on publication. Responds in 2 months to queries. Sample copy free. Guidelines available online.

MAGAZINES NEEDS *Commonweal*, published every 2 weeks, is a Catholic general interest magazine for college-educated readers. Does not publish inspirational poems. Length: no more than 75 lines. Pays 75¢/line plus 2 contributor's copies. Acquires all rights. Returns rights when requested by the author.

TIPS "Articles should be written for a general but well-educated audience. While religious articles are always topical, we are less interested in devotional and churchy pieces than in articles which examine the links between 'worldly' concerns and religious beliefs."

THE COMSTOCK REVIEW

4956 St. John Dr., Syracuse NY 13215. **Website:** www.comstockreview.org. **Contact:** Georgia A. Popoff, managing editor. *The Comstock Review* accepts "poetry strictly on the basis of quality, not reputation. We publish both noted and mid-career poets as well as those who are new to publishing. It is the quality of the poem that is the decisive factor. We do not accept overly sexual material, sentimental or "greeting card" verse, and very few haiku." Responds in 3 months.

○ *The Comstock Review* is 5.25x8.35, perfect-bound.

MAGAZINES NEEDS "We look for well-crafted poetry, either free or formal verse, with attention paid to the beauty of language, exceptional metaphor, unique voice, and fresh, vivid imagery. Poems may reflect any subject, although we have a slight bias toward poems dealing with the human condition in all its poignancy and humor." Accepts submissions of 4-5 poems, with SASE, for the Open Reading Period postmarked from January 1-March 31. Length: up to 38 lines/poem.

CONCHO RIVER REVIEW

Angelo State University, ASU Station #10894, San Angelo TX 76909. (325)486-6137. **E-mail:** crr@angelo. edu. **Website:** conchoriverreview.org. **Contact:** R. Mark Jackson, general editor. "*CRR* aims to provide its readers with escape, insight, laughter, and inspiration for many years to come. We urge authors to submit to the journal and readers to subscribe to our publication." Requests first print and electronic rights. Responds in 1-2 months for poetry and 2-6 months for fiction and nonfiction. Guidelines available online.

MAGAZINES NEEDS Welcomes original poetry submissions from all poets, established or emerging. Submit 3-5 poems at a time. Electronic submissions preferred. See website for appropriate section editor. Length: "Length and form are open, but shorter poems (1 page or less) are preferred."

⑤ CONFRONTATION

English Department, LIU Post, Brookville NY 11548. (516)299-2720. **E-mail:** confrontationmag@ gmail.com. **Website:** www.confrontationmagazine. org. **Contact:** Jonna Semeiks, editor in chief; Belinda Kremer, poetry editor. "*Confrontation* has been in continuous publication since 1968. Our taste and our magazine is eclectic, but we always look for excellence in style, an important theme, a memorable voice. We enjoy discovering and fostering new talent. Each issue contains work by both well-established and new writers. We read August 16-April 15. Do not send mss or e-mail submissions between April 16 and August 15." Buys first North American serial rights; electronic rights; first rights; one-time rights; all rights. Pays on publication. Publishes work in the first or second issue after acceptance. Responds in 8-10 weeks to mss. "We prefer single submissions. Clear copy. No

e-mail submissions unless writer resides outside the U.S. Mail submissions with a SASE."

○ *Confrontation* has garnered a long list of awards and honors, including the Editor's Award for Distinguished Achievement from CLMP (given to Martin Tucker, the founding editor of the magazine) and NEA grants. Work from the magazine has appeared in numerous anthologies, including the *Pushcart Prize*, *Best Short Stories*, and *The O. Henry Prize Stories*.

MAGAZINES NEEDS "*Confrontation* is interested in all poetic forms. Our only criterion is high literary merit. We think of our audience as an educated, lay group of intelligent readers." Has published poetry by David Ray, T. Alan Broughton, David Ignatow, Philip Appleman, Jane Mayhall, and Joseph Brodsky. Submit no more than 12 pages at a time (up to 6 poems). *Confrontation* also offers the annual Confrontation Poetry Prize. No sentimental verse. No previously published poems. Length should generally be kept to 2 pages. Pays $25-75; more for commissioned work.

TIPS "We look for literary merit. Keep honing your skills and keep trying."

CONGRUENT SPACES

820 Taylor St. #5, Medford OR 97504. **E-mail:** congruentspacesmag@gmail.com. **Website:** www.congruentspaces.com. **Contact:** Michael Camarata. "*Congruent Spaces* was developed as a common ground for a diverse variety of voices and writing styles within the writing community. In keeping with this sense of community, all submissions are posted directly to the slush pile in our Writer's Lair, where our community of writers and readers come together to read and rate these submissions. For each issue we then select from the top-rated submissions which stories and poems appear within the pages of our magazine. Our magazine covers fantasy, horror, literary/mainstream fiction, poetry, and science fiction." Purchases one-time rights. Submissions are currently accepted online only. For current guidelines, visit congruentspaces. com/home/submission. For general inquiries, contact congruentspacesmag@gmail.com.

MAGAZINES NEEDS Submit complete ms. No erotic or pornographic poetry. Length: less than 120 lines. Pays contributor's copies.

TIPS "Don't submit your work unless you truly believe it is ready for publication. Be sure to proof your formatting for readability before posting the manuscript for our ratings process. The most common error is failing to adequately separate paragraphs after copying and pasting the submission in the submission form. The easier it is to read your ms, the better your chances of receiving a quality rating and being published."

THE CONNECTICUT RIVER REVIEW

P.O. Box 516, Cheshire CT 06410. **E-mail:** patricia-mottola@yahoo.com. **Website:** www.ct-poetry-society.org/publications.htm. **Contact:** Pat Mottola, editor. *Connecticut River Review*, published annually in July or August by the Connecticut Poetry Society, prints original, honest, diverse, vital, well-crafted poetry. Wants any form, any subject. Translations and long poems welcome. Has published poetry by Marilyn Nelson, Jack Bedell, Maria Mazziotti Gillan, and Vivian Shipley. Poet retains copyright. Responds in up to 8 weeks. Guidelines available for SASE or on website.

○ Accepts submissions from January 1-April 15. *Connecticut River Review* is digest-sized, attractively printed, perfect-bound. Receives about 2,000 submissions/year, accepts about 100. Press run is about 300. Membership in the Connecticut Poetry Society is $30 per year and includes *Connecticut River Review* and *Long River Run*, a members-only magazine.

MAGAZINES NEEDS Submit no more than 3-5 poems at a time. Considers simultaneous submissions if notified of acceptance elsewhere; no previously published poems. Cover letter is preferred. Include bio. Complete contact information typed in upper right corner; SASE required. Pays 1 contributor's copy.

CONTEMPORARY HAIBUN

P.O. Box 2461, Winchester VA 22604-1661. (540)722-2156. **E-mail:** bob.lucky01@yahoo.com. **Website:** www.contemporaryhaibunonline.com; www.redmoonpress.com. **Contact:** Bob Lucky, content editor. contemporary haibun, published annually in April, is the first Western journal dedicated to haibun. Considers poetry by children and teens. Acquires first North American serial rights. Time between acceptance and publication varies according to time of submission. Sample available for SASE or by e-mail.

○ contemporary haibun is 128 pages, digest-sized, offset-printed on quality paper, with 4-color heavy-stock cover. Receives several hundred submissions/year, accepts about 5%. Print run

is 1,000. Subscription: $17 plus $5 p&h. Has published poetry by J. Zimmerman, Chen-ou Liu, Renée Owen, and Matthew Caretti.

MAGAZINES NEEDS Submit up to 3 haibun at a time. Accepts e-mail submissions. Include SASE for postal submissions. Poems are circulated to an editorial board.

⑤ CONTRARY

PO Box 806363, Chicago IL 60616-3299 (no submissions). **E-mail:** chicago@contrarymagazine.com (no submissions). **Website:** www.contrarymagazine.com. **Contact:** Jeff McMahon, editor; Frances Badgett, fiction editor; Shaindel Beers, poetry editor. *Contrary* publishes fiction, poetry, and literary commentary, and prefers work that combines the virtues of all those categories. Founded at the University of Chicago, it now operates independently and not-for-profit on the South Side of Chicago. "We like work that is not only contrary in content, but contrary in its evasion of the expectations established by its genre. Our fiction defies traditional story form. For example, a story may bring us to closure without ever delivering an ending. We don't insist on the ending, but we do insist on the closure. And we value fiction as poetic as any poem." Quarterly. Member CLMP. Acquires first rights and perpetual archive and anthology rights. Publication is copyrighted. Pays on publication. Mss published no more than 21 days after acceptance. Responds to queries in 2 weeks; 3 months to mss. Rarely comments on/critiques rejected mss. Guidelines available on website.

MAGAZINES NEEDS No mail or e-mail submissions; submit work via the website. Considers simultaneous submissions; no previously published poems. Accepts submissions through online form only. Often comments on rejected poems. $20 per byline, $60 for featured work."Upon acceptance, *Contrary* acquires the following rights: (1) exclusive rights for the three-month period that the accepted work appears in the current issue of *Contrary* magazine, (2) the right to permanent inclusion of the work in *Contrary's* electronic archive, and (3) the right to reproduce the work in print and electronic collections of our content. After the current issue expires, the author is free to seek republication elsewhere, but *Contrary* must be credited upon republication."

TIPS "Beautiful writing catches our eye first. If we realize we're in the presence of unanticipated meaning, that's what clinches the deal. Also, we're not fond of expository fiction. We prefer to be seduced by beauty, profundity, and mystery than to be presented with the obvious. We look for fiction that entrances, that stays the reader's finger above the mouse button. That is, in part, why we favor microfiction, flash fiction, and short shorts. Also, we hope writers will remember that most editors are looking for very particular species of work. We try to describe our particular species in our mission statement and our submission guidelines, but those descriptions don't always convey nuance. That's why many editors urge writers to read the publication itself, in the hope that they will intuit an understanding of its particularities. If you happen to write that particular species of work we favor, your submission may find a happy home with us. If you don't, it does not necessarily reflect on your quality or your ability. It usually just means that your work has a happier home somewhere else."

CONVERGENCE: AN ONLINE JOURNAL OF POETRY AND ART

E-mail: clinville@csus.edu. **Website:** www.convergence-journal.com. **Contact:** Cynthia Linville, managing editor. "We look for well-crafted work with fresh images and a strong voice. Work from a series or with a common theme has a greater chance of being accepted. Seasonally-themed work is appreciated (spring and summer for the January deadline, fall and winter for the June deadline). Please include a 75-word bio with your work (bios may be edited for length and clarity). A cover letter is not needed. Absolutely no simultaneous or previously published submissions."

⬚   Deadlines are January 5 and June 5.

MAGAZINES NEEDS New interpretations of the written word by pairing poems and flash fiction with complementary art. "We are open to many different styles, but we do not often publish formal verse. Read a couple of issues to get a sense of what we like; namely, well-crafted work with fresh images and a strong voice." *Convergence* is published quarterly online, Has published poetry by Oliver Rice, Simon Perchik, Mary Ocher. Receives about 800 poems/year, accepts about 10 per issue plus monthly selections for "Editor's Choice." Has about 200 online subscribers. Guidelines available on website. Does not often publish formal verse. Does not want "poetry with trite, unoriginal language or unfinished work." Length: 60 max. No payment.

HOW TO CONTACT No simultaneous or previously published submissions. Accepts e-mail submissions only. Reads submissions year round. Time between acceptance and publication is 1-2 months. Poems are circulated to an editorial board. Responds in 6 months. Acquires first rights.

TIPS "We look for freshness and originality and a mastery of the craft of flash fiction. Working with a common theme has a greater chance of being accepted."

COTTONWOOD

Room 400 Kansas Union, 1301 Jayhawk Blvd., University of Kansas, Lawrence KS 66045. **E-mail:** tlorenz@ku.edu. **Website:** www2.ku.edu/~englishmfa/cottonwood. **Contact:** Tom Lorenz, fiction editor. "Established in the 1960s, *Cottonwood* is the nationally circulated literary review of the University of Kansas. We publish high-quality literary work in poetry, fiction, and creative nonfiction. Over the years authors such as William Stafford, Rita Dove, Connie May Fowler, Virgil Suarez, and Cris Mazza have appeared in the pages of *Cottonwood*, and recent issues have featured the work of Kim Chinquee, Quinn Dalton, Carol Lee Lorenzo, Jesse Kercheval, Joanne Lowery, and Oliver Rice. We welcome submissions from new and established writers. New issues appear once yearly, in the fall." Acquires one-time rights. Responds in 6 months. Guidelines available online at website.

MAGAZINES NEEDS Wants poems "on daily experience, perception; strong narrative or sensory impact, nonderivative." Pays in contributor's copies.

TIPS "We're looking for depth and originality of subject matter, engaging voice and style, emotional honesty, command of the material and the structure. *Cottonwood* publishes high-quality literary fiction, but we are very open to the work of talented new writers. Write something honest and that you care about, and write it as well as you can. Don't hesitate to keep trying us. We sometimes take a piece from a writer we've rejected a number of times. We generally don't like clever, gimmicky writing. The style should be engaging but not claim all the the attention itself."

CRAB CREEK REVIEW

7315 34th Ave. NW, Seattle WA 98117. **E-mail:** crabcreekreview@gmail.com. **Website:** www.crabcreekreview.org. **Contact:** Sayantani Dasgupta, nonfiction editor; Martha Silano, poetry editor. *Crab Creek Review* is an 80- to 120-page, perfect-bound paperback.

"We are an international journal based in the Pacific Northwest that is looking for poems, stories, and essays that pay attention to craft while still surprising us in positive ways with detail and content. We publish well-known and emerging writers." Buys first North American rights. Responds in 2-4 months to mss. Sample copy: $6. Subscription: $15/year, $28/2 year. Accepts submissions via Submittable only. Guidelines online.

○ Nominates for the Pushcart Prize and offers annual *Crab Creek Review* Editors' Prize of $100 for the best poem, essay, or short story published in the previous year. Annual *Crab Creek Review* poetry prize: $500.

MAGAZINES NEEDS Submit via online submission form. Has published poetry by Oliver de la Paz, Dorianne Laux, Denise Duhamel, and translations by Ilya Kaminsky and Matthew Zapruder. Pays 1 contributor's copy.

⑤ CRAB ORCHARD REVIEW

Dept. of English, Southern Illinois University Carbondale, Faner Hall 2380, Mail Code 4503, 1000 Faner Dr., Carbondale IL 62901. (618)453-6833. **Fax:** (618)453-8224. **Website:** www.craborchardreview.siu.edu. **Contact:** Jon Tribble, managing editor. "We are a general-interest literary journal published twice/year. We strive to be a journal that writers admire and readers enjoy. We publish fiction, poetry, creative nonfiction, fiction translations, interviews, and reviews." Buys first North American serial rights. Publishes ms an average of 9-12 months after acceptance. Responds in 3 weeks to queries. Responds in 9 months to mss. Always comments on rejected work. Sample copy for $12. Guidelines available online.

○ Reads submissions February 15-April 1(Winter/Spring issue) and October-November 15 (special Summer/Fall issue).

MAGAZINES NEEDS Wants all styles and forms from traditional to experimental. Does not want greeting card verse; literary poetry only. Has published poetry by Luisa A. Igloria, Erinn Batykefer, Jim Daniels, and Bryan Tso Jones. Postal submissions only. Cover letter is preferred. "Indicate stanza breaks on poems of more than 1 page. Poems that are under serious consideration are discussed and decided on by the managing editor and poetry editor." Pays $25/published magazine page, $50 minimum, 2 contributor's copies and 1-year subscription.

CRAZYHORSE

College of Charleston, Department of English, 66 George St., Charleston SC 29424. (843)953-4470. **E-mail:** crazyhorse@cofc.edu. **Website:** http://crazyhorse.cofc.edu. **Contact:** Jonathan Bohr Heinen, managing editor; Emily Rosko, poetry editor; Anthony Varallo, fiction editor; Bret Lott, nonfiction editor. "We like to print a mix of writing regardless of its form, genre, school, or politics. We're especially on the lookout for original writing that doesn't fit the categories and that engages in the work of honest communication." Buys first North American serial rights. Publishes ms an average of 6-12 months after acceptance. Responds in 1 week to queries. Responds in 3-4 months to mss. Sample copy for $5. Guidelines for SASE or by e-mail.

○ Reads submissions September 1-May 31.

MAGAZINES NEEDS Submit 3-5 poems at a time. No fax, e-mail or disk submissions. Cover letter is preferred. Pays $20 per page ($200 maximum) and 2 contributor's copies.

TIPS "Write to explore subjects you care about. The subject should be one in which something is at stake. Before sending, ask, 'What's reckoned with that's important for other people to read?'"

CREAM CITY REVIEW

E-mail: info@creamcityreview.org. **Website:** www.creamcityreview.org. **Contact:** Ching-In Chen, editor in chief; Loretta McCormick, managing editor. *Cream City Review* publishes "memorable and energetic fiction, poetry, and creative nonfiction. Features reviews of contemporary literature and criticism as well as author interviews and artwork. We are interested in camera-ready art depicting themes appropriate to each issue." Responds in 2-8 months to mss. Sample back issue: $7. Guidelines available online at www.creamcityreview.org/submit. Check for regular updates at www.facebook.com/creamcityreview. Submit using online submissions manager ONLY.

MAGAZINES NEEDS Submit poems via online submissions manager only.

TIPS "Please include a few lines about your publication history. *CCR* seeks to publish a broad range of writings and a broad range of writers with diverse backgrounds. We accept submissions for our annual theme issue from August 1-November 1 and general submissions from December 1-April 1. No e-mail submissions, please."

CREATIVE WITH WORDS PUBLICATIONS

P.O. Box 223226, Carmel CA 93922. **Fax:** (831)655-8627. **E-mail:** geltrich@mbay.net. **Website:** creativewithwords.tripod.com. **Contact:** Brigitta Gisella Geltrich-Ludgate, publisher and editor. *Creative With Words* publishes "poetry, prose, illustrations, photos by all ages." Publishes ms 1-2 months after acceptance. Responds in 2-4 weeks. Guideline online.

MAGAZINES NEEDS Submit up to 5 poems by mail or e-mail. Always include SASE and legitimate address with postal submissions. Cover letter preferred.

TIPS "We offer a great variety of themes. We look for clean family-type fiction/poetry. Also, we ask the writer to look at the world from a different perspective, research topic thoroughly, be creative, apply brevity, tell the story from a character's viewpoint, tighten dialogue, be less descriptive, proofread before submitting, and be patient. We will not publish every ms we receive. It has to be in standard English, well written, proofread. We do not appreciate receiving mss where we have to do the proofreading and correct the grammar."

CRUCIBLE

Barton College, Wilson NC 27893. **E-mail:** crucible@barton.edu. **Website:** www.barton.edu/crucible. *Crucible*, published annually in the fall, publishes poetry and fiction as part of its Poetry and Fiction Contest run each year. Deadline for submissions: May 1. Acquires first rights. Notifies winners by October each year. Sample: $8. Guidelines online.

⬤ *Crucible* is under 100 pages, digest-sized, professionally printed on high-quality paper, with matte card cover. Press run is 500.

MAGAZINES NEEDS Submit "poetry that demonstrates originality and integrity of craftsmanship as well as thought. Traditional metrical and rhyming poems are difficult to bring off in modern poetry. The best poetry is written out of deeply felt experience which has been crafted into pleasing form." Wants "free verse with attention paid particularly to image, line, stanza, and voice." Does not want "very long narratives, poetry that is forced." Has published poetry by Robert Grey, R.T. Smith, and Anthony S. Abbott. Submit up to 5 poems by e-mail. Ms accepted only through May 1. Do not include name on poems. Include separate bio. Pays $150 for 1st prize, $100 for 2nd prize, contributor's copies.

CURA: A LITERARY MAGAZINE OF ART AND ACTION

441 E. Fordham Rd., English Department, Dealy 541W, Bronx NY 10548. **E-mail:** curamag@fordham.edu. **Website:** www.curamag.com. **Contact:** Sarah Gambito, managing editor. *CURA: A Literary Magazine of Art and Action* is a multi-media initiative based at Fordham University committed to integrating the arts and social justice. Featuring creative writing, visual art, new media and video in response to current news, we seek to enable an artistic process that is rigorously engaged with the world at the present moment. *CURA* is taken from the Ignatian educational principle of "cura personalis," care for the whole person. On its own, the word "cura" is defined as guardianship, solicitude, and significantly, written work. Acquires first rights. Publishes ms 5 months after acceptance. Editorial lead time is 5 months. Sample copy online. Guidelines online.

⬤ Reading period: October 1-March 15.

MAGAZINES NEEDS Pays 1 contributor's copy.

CURRENT ACCOUNTS

Current Accounts, Apt. 2D, Bradshaw Hall, Hardcastle Gardens, Bolton BL2 4NZ, UK. **E-mail:** bswscribe@gmail.com. **E-mail:** fjameshartnell@aol.com. **Website:** for Bank Street Writers: sites.google.com/site/bankstreetwriters. **Contact:** Rod Riesco. *Current Accounts*, an online publication, prints poetry, drama, fiction, and nonfiction by members of Bank Street Writers, and other contributors. Acquires first rights. Uploads ms up to 6 months after acceptance. Responds ASAP. Guidelines available for SASE, by fax, by e-mail or on website.

⬤ Receives about 200 poems and stories/plays per year; accepts about 5%.

MAGAZINES NEEDS Open to all types of poetry. No requirements, although some space is reserved for members. Considers poetry by children and teens. Has published poetry by Pat Winslow, M.R. Peacocke, and Gerald England.pen to all types of poetry. No requirements, although some space is reserved for members. Considers poetry by children and teens. Has published poetry by Pat Winslow, M.R. Peacocke, and Gerald England. E-mail submissions only. Doesn't mind rhyming poetry. Travel or tourist poetry needs to be more than just exotic names and places. Titles need care. Poetry should be poetic in some form. Experimental work is welcome. Lines/poem: 40 maximum. Pays 1 contributor's copy.

TIPS Bank Street Writers meets once/month and offers workshops, guest speakers, and other activities. E-mail for details."We like originality of ideas, images, and use of language. No inspirational or religious verse unless it's also good in poetic terms."

CURRICULUM VITAE

Simpson Publications, 342 Aiken Rd., Trumansburg NY 14886. **E-mail:** simpub@hotmail.com. **Contact:** Amy Dittman, managing editor. *Curriculum Vitae*, published semiannually in January and July, is a zine where quality work is always welcome. Time between acceptance and publication is 8 months. Responds within 1 month. Guidelines available for SASE or by e-mail.

MAGAZINES NEEDS *Curriculum Vitae*, published semiannually in January and July, is "a zine where quality work is always welcome. We'd like to see more metrical work, especially more translations, and well-crafted narrative free verse is always welcome. We do not want to see rambling Bukowski-esque free verse or poetry that overly relies on sentimentality." *Curriculum Vitae* is 40 pages, digest-sized, photocopied, saddle-stapled, with 2-color cardstock cover. Receives about 500 poems/year, accepts about 75. Press run is 1,000. Subscription: $6 for 4 issues. Sample: $4. Submit 3 poems at a time. Considers previously published poems and simultaneous submissions. Cover letter is preferred ("to give us an idea of who you are"). "Submissions without a SASE cannot be acknowledged due to postage costs." Poetry is circulated among 3 board members. Often comments on rejected poems. Publishes theme issues. "We're also interested in expanding our list of innovative side projects, books, graphic novels, chapbooks like *The Iowa Monster*, and the CV Poetry Postcard Project." Simpson Publications publishes about 5 chapbooks/year. Query with full mss or well-thought-out plans with clips. Include SASE. Pays 2 contributor's copies plus one-year subscription.

TIPS "We are currently looking for poets who would like to be part of our Poetry Postcard series."

CUTTHROAT, A JOURNAL OF THE ARTS

P.O. Box 2414, Durango CO 81302. (970)903-7914. **E-mail:** cutthroatmag@gmail.com. **Website:** www.cutthroatmag.com. **Contact:** William Luvaas, fiction editor; William Pitt Root, poetry editor. "We publish only high-quality fiction and poetry. We are looking for the cutting edge, the endangered word, fiction with wit, heart, soul, and meaning." *CUTTHROAT* is a literary magazine/journal and "one separate online edition of poetry, translations, short fiction and book reviews yearly." Acquires first North American serial rights. Sends galleys to author. Publication is copyrighted. Responds in 1-2 weeks to queries; 6-8 months to mss. Sometimes comments on/critiques rejected mss. Sample copy available for $10. Guidelines available for SASE, on website.

Member CCLMP.

MAGAZINES NEEDS Submit 3-5 poems. Reading periods for online editions are March 15-June 1; for print editions, July 15-October 10. "We prefer online submissions through our submission manager! If submitting by mail, please include cover letter and SASE for response only; mss are recycled." Has published Joy Harjo, Linda Hogan, Patricia Smith, Wendell Berry, Marvin Bell, Richard Jackson, Sean Thomas Dougherty, Doug Anderson, Dan Vera, Martin Espada, TR Hummer, Naomi Shihab Nye, Daniel Nathan Terry, and many more.

TIPS "Read our magazine and see what types of work we've published. The piece must have heart and soul, excellence in craft. "

THE DALHOUSIE REVIEW

Dalhousie University, Halifax NS B3H 4R2, Canada. **E-mail:** dalhousie.review@dal.ca. **Website:** dalhousiereview.dal.ca. **Contact:** Carrie Dawson, editor. *Dalhousie Review*, published 3 times/year, is a journal of criticism publishing poetry and fiction. Considers poetry from both new and established writers. Responds in 3-9 months. Subscription: $25 CAD, $30 USD. Make checks payable to *Dalhousie Review*.

Dalhousie Review is 144 pages, digest-sized. Accepts about 5% of poems received. Press run is 500.

MAGAZINES NEEDS Submit via postal mail only. Reads year round. Length: up to 40 lines/poem. Pays 2 contributor's copies and 10 offprints.

THE DARK

311 Fairbanks Ave., Northfield NJ 08225. **E-mail:** thedarkmagazine@gmail.com. **Website:** www.thedarkmagazine.com. **Contact:** Jack Fisher and Sean Wallace, editors. Buys first North American serial rights; buys electronic rights. Pays on publication. Publishes ms an average of 6 months after acceptance. Responds in 1-2 weeks to mss. Always sends prepublication galleys. 1 month editorial lead time. Sample: $2.99 (back issue). Guidelines available on website.

TIPS "All fiction must have a dark, surreal, fantastical bend to it. It should be out of the ordinary and/or experimental. Can also be contemporary."

DARKLING MAGAZINE

Darkling Publications, 28780 318th Avenue, Colome SD 57528. (605)455-2892. **E-mail:** darkling@mitchelltelecom.net; jvanoort@darklingpublications.com. **Website:** http://darklingpublications.com. **Contact:** James C. Van Oort, editor-in-chief. *Darkling Magazine*, published annually in late summer, is "primarily interested in poetry. All submissions should be dark in nature and should help expose the darker side of man. Dark nature does not mean whiny or overly murderous, and being depressed does not make an artist's work dark." Has published poems by Robert Cooperman, Kenneth DiMaggio, Arthur Gottlieb, Simon Perchik, Cathy Porter and Susanna Rich, among others.

⌕   Reading period: October1-May 15.

MAGAZINES NEEDS Guidelines available online. Submit via e-mail. Length: any length is acceptable, but epic length poetry must be of exceptional quality and content to be considered.

THE DEAD MULE SCHOOL OF SOUTHERN LITERATURE

E-mail: deadmule@gmail.com. **E-mail:** submit. mule@gmail.com. **Website:** www.deadmule.com. Robert MacEwan, technical and design. **Contact:** Valerie MacEwan, publisher and editor. "No good southern fiction is complete without a dead mule." *The Dead Mule* is one of the oldest, if not *the* oldest, continuously published online literary journals alive today. Publisher and editor Valerie MacEwan welcomes submissions. *The Dead Mule School of Southern Literature* wants flash fiction, visual poetry, essays, and creative nonfiction. "We usually publish new work on the 1st and 15th of the month, depending on whims, obligations, and mule jumping contest dates." Acquires first electronic rights and indefinite archival rights. All other rights revert to author upon publication. Submissions handled through the website, not via e-mail. We use Submittable. Go to deadmule.com/submissions for the link. Please do not query the editor directly.

⌕   "*The Dead Mule School of Southern Literature* Institutional Alumni Association recruits year round. Want to join the freshman class of 2018? Submit today.

MAGAZINES NEEDS Check the *Mule* for poetry information.

TIPS "Read the site to get a feel for what we're looking to publish. Read the guidelines. We look forward to hearing from you. We are nothing if not for our writers. *The Dead Mule* strives to deliver quality writing in every issue. It is in this way that we pay tribute to our authors. Send us something original."

DENVER QUARTERLY

University of Denver, 2000 E. Asbury, Denver CO 80208. (303)871-2892. **E-mail:** denverquarterly@gmail.com. **Website:** www.du.edu/denverquarterly/. **Contact:** Laird Hunt, editor. Publishes fiction, articles, and poetry for a generally well-educated audience, primarily interested in literature and the literary experience. Audience reads *DQ* to find something a little different from a stictly academic quarterly or a creative writing outlet. Quarterly. Reads between September 15 and May 15. Acquires first North American serial rights. Publishes ms 1 year after acceptance. Responds in 3 months. Sample copy for $10.

⌕   *Denver Quarterly* received an Honorable Mention for Content from the American Literary Magazine Awards and selections have been anthologized in the *Pushcart Prize* anthologies.

MAGAZINES NEEDS Poetry submissions should be comprised of 3-5 poems. Submit ms by mail, include SASE. Pays $5/page for fiction and poetry and 2 contributor's copies.

TIPS "We look for serious, realistic, and experimental fiction; stories which appeal to intelligent, demanding readers who are not themselves fiction writers. Nothing so quickly disqualifies a manuscript as sloppy proofreading and mechanics. Read the magazine before submitting to it. We try to remain eclectic, but the odds for beginners are bound to be small considering the fact that we receive nearly 10,000 mss per year and publish only about 10 short stories."

THE DERONDA REVIEW

E-mail: derondareview@att.net. **Website:** www.derondareview.org; www.pointandcircumference.com. Mindy Aber Barad, co-editor for Israel, P.O. Box 1299, Efrat 90435, Israel. **E-mail:** maber4kids@yahoo.com. **Contact:** Esther Cameron, editor in chief; Mindy Aber Barad (Israel only), co-editor. Semiannual literary journal publishing poetry and seeking to "promote a literature of introspection, dialogue, and social concern." Acquires first rights. Publishes ms 1 year after acceptance. Responds in up to 4 months; "if longer, please query via the website."

○ Now mainly a digital publication, with print copies for libraries.

MAGAZINES NEEDS Cover letter is unnecessary. E-mail submissions preferred. "Do include SASE with sufficient postage to return all mss or with 'Reply Only' clearly indicated. Poets whose work is accepted will be asked for URLS and titles of books available to be published in the online contributors exchange."

TIPS "Longer selections of poets frequently published in the magazine are posted on www.pointandcircumference.com."

☺ DESCANT

P.O. Box 314, Station P, Toronto ON M5S 2S8, Canada. (416)593-2557. **Fax:** (416)593-9362. **E-mail:** info@descant.ca. **E-mail:** submit@descant.ca; managingeditor@descant.ca. **Website:** www.descant.ca. **Contact:** Karen Mulhallen, editor-in-chief; Vera DeWaard, managing editor. *Descant* is a quarterly journal publishing new and established contemporary writers and visual artists from Canada and around the world. *Descant* is devoted to the discovery and development of new writers, and to placing their work in the company of celebrated writers. Pays on publication. Publishes ms an average of 16 months after acceptance. Editorial lead time 1 year. Sample copy for $8.50 plus postage. Guidelines available online.

○ Pays $100 honorarium, plus 1-year's subscription for accepted submissions of any kind.

MAGAZINES NEEDS "*Descant* seeks high quality poems and stories in both traditional and innovative form." Member CLMP. Literary. Pays $100.

CONTEST/AWARD OFFERINGS Several stories first published by *Descant* have appeared in *Best American Short Stories*.

TIPS "Familiarize yourself with our magazine before submitting."

DESCANT: FORT WORTH'S JOURNAL OF POETRY AND FICTION

TCU Department of English, Box 297270, Ft. Worth TX 76129. (817)257-5907. **Fax:** (817)257-6239. **E-mail:** descant@tcu.edu; m.pitt@tcu.edu. **Website:** www.descant.tcu.edu. **Contact:** Matt Pitt, editor-in-chief. "*descant* seeks high-quality poems and stories in both traditional and innovative form." Member CLMP. Magazine: 6×9; 120-150 pages; acid-free paper; paper cover. Pays on publication for one-time rights. Pays 2

contributor's copies; additional copies $6. Responds in 6-8 weeks to mss. Sample copy for $15. SASE, e-mail, or fax.

○ Reading period: Septmeber 1-April 1. Offers 4 cash awards: The $500 Frank O'Connor Award for the best story in an issue; the $250 Gary Wilson Award for an outstanding story in an issue; the $500 Betsy Colquitt Award for the best poem in an issue; and the $250 Baskerville Publishers Award for outstanding poem in an issue. Several stories first published by *descant* have appeared in *Best American Short Stories*.

MAGAZINES NEEDS Length: 60 lines or fewer.

TIPS "We look for character and quality of prose. Send your best short work."

⊗ DEVOZINE

1908 Grand Ave., P.O. Box 340004, Nashville TN 37203-0004. **E-mail:** devozine@upperroom.org. **Website:** www.devozine.org. **Contact:** Sandi Miller, editor. *devozine,* published bimonthly, is an 80-page devotional magazine for youth (ages 12-18) and adults who care about youth. Offers meditations, scripture, prayers, poems, stories, songs, and feature articles to "aid youth in their prayer life, introduce them to spiritual disciplines, help them shape their concept of God, and encourage them in the life of discipleship."

MAGAZINES NEEDS Considers poetry by teens. Submit by postal mail with SASE or by e-mail. Include name, age/birth date (if younger than 25), mailing address, e-mail address, phone number, and fax number (if available). Always publishes theme issues (available for SASE or online). Indicate theme you are writing for. Length: 10-20 lines/poem. Pays $25.

DIAGRAM

Department of English, University of Arizona, P.O. Box 210067, Tucson AZ 85721-0067. **E-mail:** editor@thediagram.com. **Website:** www.thediagram.com. **Contact:** Ander Monson, editor; T. Fleischmann and Nicole Walker, nonfiction editors; Sarah Blackman and Lauren Slaughter, fiction editors; Heidi Gotz and E.A. Ramey, poetry editors. "*DIAGRAM* is an electronic journal of text and art, found and created. We're interested in representations, naming, indicating, schematics, labeling and taxonomy of things; in poems that masquerade as stories; in stories that disguise themselves as indices or obituaries. We specialize in work that pushes the boundaries of traditional genre or work that is in some way schematic. We do publish traditional fiction and poetry, too, but hybrid forms (short stories, prose poems, indexes, tables of contents, etc.) are particularly welcome! We also publish diagrams and schematics (original and found)." Buys first North American serial rights. Time between acceptance and publication is 1-10 months. Responds in 2 weeks to queries; 1-2 months to mss. Often comments on rejected mss. Print version sample copy: $12. Writer's guidelines online.

- Publishes 6 new writers/year. Bimonthly. Member CLMP. "We sponsor yearly contests for unpublished hybrid essays and innovative fiction. Guidelines on website."

MAGAZINES NEEDS Submit 3-6 poems at a time. Electronic submissions accepted through submissions manager; no e-mail, disk, or fax submissions. Electronic submissions much preferred; print submissions must include SASE if response is expected. Cover letter is preferred. Reads submissions year round. Poems are circulated to an editorial board. Sometimes comments on rejected poems. Sometimes publishes theme issues. Receives about 1,000 poems/year, accepts about 5%. Does not want light verse. Length: no limit.

ADDITIONAL INFORMATION *DIAGRAM* also publishes periodic perfect-bound print anthologies.

TIPS "Submit interesting text, images, sound, and new media. We value the insides of things, vivisection, urgency, risk, elegance, flamboyance, work that moves us, language that does something new, or does something old—well. We like iteration and reiteration. Ruins and ghosts. Mechanical, moving parts, balloons, and frenzy. We want art and writing that demonstrates interaction; the processes of things; how functions are accomplished; how things become or expire, move or stand. We'll consider anything."

DIODE POETRY JOURNAL

Website: www.diodepoetry.com. **Contact:** Patty Paine, editor. "*Diode* is looking for 'electropositive' poetry. What is electropositive poetry? It's poetry that excites and energizes. It's poetry that uses language that crackles and sparks. We're looking for poetry from all points on the arc, from formal to experimental." Acquires one-time rights. Rights revert to poet upon publication. Time between acceptance and publication varies. Responds in 3-5 weeks. Always sends prepublication galleys. Guidelines available on website.

- Does not want "light verse, erotic." Receives about 6,000 poems/year; accepts about 3%.

MAGAZINES NEEDS Submit 3-5 poems at a time. Accepts submissions by e-mail; attach document. Cover letter is required. Reads submissions year round. Sometimes comments on rejected poems. Considers reviews and essays. Has published poetry by Bob Hicok, Beckian Fritz Golberg, G.C. Waldrep, Dorianne Laux, David Wojahn, and Rae Armantrout.

DMQ REVIEW

E-mail: editors@dmqreview.com. **Website:** www. dmqreview.com. **Contact:** Sally Ashton, editor in chief; Marjorie Manwaring, assistant editor. *DMQ Review* seeks work that represents the diversity of contemporary poetry and demonstrates literary excellence, whether it be lyric, free verse, prose, or experimental form. Buys first North American serial rights. Publishes ms 1-3 months after acceptance. Responds in 3 months. Guidelines online.

MAGAZINES NEEDS Has published poetry by David Lehman, Ellen Bass, Amy Gerstler, Bob Hicok, Ilya Kaminsky, and Jane Hirshfield. Receives about 3,000-5,000 poems/year, accepts about 1%. E-mail submissions only; no attachments. Include a brief bio, 50 words max. Type "Poetry Submission," followed by your name, in the subject line of your e-mail.

ALSO OFFERS Nominates for the Pushcart Prize. Also considers submissions of visual art, which is published with the poems in the magazine, with links to the artists' websites.

TIPS "Check our current and past issues, and read and follow submission guidelines closely. Important: Copy and include the permission statement with your submission (it's in our guidelines online)."

DOWN IN THE DIRT

829 Brian Court, Gurnee IL 60031-3155. (847)281-9070. **E-mail:** dirt@scars.tv. **Website:** www.scars.tv/dirt. **Contact:** Janet Kuypers, editor. *Down in the Dirt*, published every other month online and in print issues sold via Amazon.com throughout the U.S., U.K., and continental Europe, prints "good work that makes you think, that makes you feel like you've lived through a scene instead of merely read it." Also considers poems. *Down in the Dirt* is published "electronically as well as in print, either as printed magazines sold through our printer over the Internet, on the Web (Internet web pages), or sold through our printer." Publishes ms within 1 year after acceptance.

Responds in 1 month to queries; 1 month to mss. If asked, always comments on rejected mss. Sample copy: $6 for issues before 2010. Samples from 2010 and beyond do not exist; you can just directly purchase the issues online any time. Guidelines for SASE, e-mail, or on website.

Literary magazine/journal. Has published work by Mel Waldman, Ken Dean, Jon Brunette, John Ragusa, and Liam Spencer.

MAGAZINES NEEDS Accepts e-mail submissions (vastly preferred to snail mail; pasted into body of message or as Microsoft Word .doc file attachment) and disk submissions (formatted for Macintosh). "If you do not have e-mail and want to snail-mail a poetry submission, we do not accept poetry snail-mail submissions longer than 10 lines. Currently, accepted writings get their own web page in the 'writings' section at scars.tv/dirt, and samples of accepted writings are placed into an annual collection book that Scars Publications produces." Has published work by I.B. Rad, Pat Dixon, Mel Waldman, and Brian Looney. Does not want smut, rhyming poetry, or religious writing. Lines/poem: any length is appreciated. No payment.

TIPS Scars Publications sponsors a contest "where accepted writing appears in a collection book. Write or e-mail (dirt@scars.tv) for information." Also able to publish electronic chapbooks. Write for more information.

DRUNKEN BOAT

119 Main St., Chester CT 06412. **E-mail:** editor@drunkenboat.com. **Website:** www.drunkenboat.com. *Drunken Boat*, published 3 times/year online, is a multimedia publication reaching an international audience with an extremely broad aesthetic. Considers poetry by teens. "We judge by quality, not age. However, most poetry we publish is written by published poets with training in creative writing." Has published more than 500 poets, including Heather McHugh, Jane Hirshfield, Alfred Corn, Alice Fulton, Ron Silliman, and Roseanna Warren. Received about 3,000 poems/year, accepts about 5%. To cover operational costs, charges a $3 fee for each submission. Responds in 3 months to mss. Guidelines available online.

MAGAZINES NEEDS "Submit no more than 3 poems, in a single document. Our aesthetic is very broad. We welcome work ranging from received form to the cutting edge avant-garde, from one line to the multipage, from collaborations to hybridizations and cut-ups as well as works that use other media in their composition, originality and in translation (with the writer's permission), American and from around the globe."

TIPS "Submissions should be submitted in Word and .rtf format only. (This does not apply to audio, visual, and Web work.) Accepts chapbooks. See our submissions manager system."

DUCTS

E-mail: vents@ducts.org. **Website:** www.ducts.org. **Contact:** Jonathan Kravetz, editor-in-chief. *DUCTS* is a semi-annual webzine of personal stories, fiction, essays, memoirs, poetry, humor, profiles, reviews and art. "*DUCTS* was founded in 1999 with the intent of giving emerging writers a venue to regularly publish their compelling, personal stories. The site has been expanded to include art and creative works of all genres. We believe that these genres must and do overlap. *DUCTS* publishes the best, most compelling stories and we hope to attract readers who are drawn to work that rises above." Pays on publication. Responds in 1-6 months. Guidelines available on website.

MAGAZINES NEEDS Submit 3-5 poems to poetry@ducts.org.

TIPS "We prefer writing that tells a compelling story with a strong narrative drive."

EARTHSHINE

c/o Ruminations, P.O. Box 245, Hummelstown PA 17036. **E-mail:** poetry@earthshinepoetry.org. **Website:** www.earthshinepoetry.org. **Contact:** Sally Zaino and Julie Moffitt, poetry editors. *Earthshine*, published irregularly in print, and constantly online, features poetry and 1-2 pieces of cover art per volume. "When the online journal is full, a printed volume is produced and offered for sale. Subscriptions will be available as the publication becomes regular. The voice of *Earthshine* is one of illumination, compassion, humanity, and reason. Please see submission guidelines webpage for updated information. Poems are the ultimate rumination, and if the world is to be saved, the poets will be needed; they are who see the connections between all things, and the patterns shared. We seek poetry of high literary quality which will generate its own light for our readers." Acquires first rights and requests ongoing electronic rights. Time between acceptance and publication is "almost immediate" for online publication and "TBD" for printed publication. Responds in 1-2 months. Guidelines available in magazine, for SASE, and on website.

○ Has published poetry by Richard Schiffman, Anne Pierson Wiese, Steven Keletar, Mario Susko, and Daniel J. Langton.

MAGAZINES NEEDS Accepts e-mail submissions (pasted into body of message); no fax or disk submissions. Cover letter is preferred. "Please let us know where you heard about *Earthshine*. If submitting by mail, please include an SASE for reply only. Please do not send the only copy of your work." Reads submissions year round. Sometimes comments on rejected poems. Never publishes theme issues. Pays 2 contributor's copies.

ECLECTICA

E-mail: editors@eclectica.org. **Website:** www.eclectica.org. **Contact:** Tom Dooley, managing editor. "A sterling-quality literary magazine on the World Wide Web. Not bound by formula or genre, harnessing technology to further the reading experience and dynamic and interesting in content. *Eclectica* is a quarterly online journal devoted to showcasing the best writing on the Web, regardless of genre. 'Literary' and 'genre' work appear side-by-side in each issue, along with pieces that blur the distinctions between such categories. Pushcart Prize, National Poetry Series, and Pulitzer Prize winners, as well as Nebula Award nominees, have shared issues with previously unpublished authors." Buys first world electronic (online/Internet) rights. All rights revert to author upon publication, except for anthology rights. Guidelines online.

○ Submission deadlines: December 1 for January/February issue; and March 1 for April/May issue.

MAGAZINES NEEDS Seeks "outstanding poetry." Submit using online submissions manager.

TIPS "We pride ourselves on giving everyone (high schoolers, convicts, movie executives, etc.) an equal shot at publication, based solely on the quality of their work. Because we like eclecticism, we tend to favor the varied perspectives that often characterize the work of international authors, people of color, women, alternative lifestylists—but others who don't fit into these categories often surprise us."

ECOTONE

Department of Creative Writing, University of North Carolina Wilmington, 601 S. College Rd., Wilmington NC 28403. (910)962-2547. **Fax:** (910)962-7461. **E-mail:** info@ecotonejournal.com. **Website:** www.ecotonejournal.com. **Contact:** Kate O'Reilly, managing editor; Peter Kusnic, nonfiction editor; Ryan Kaune, fiction editor; Laurel Jones, poetry editor. "*Ecotone* is a literary journal of place that seeks to publish creative works about the environment and the natural world while avoiding the hushed tones and clichés of much of so-called nature writing. Responds in 3-6 months to mss.

○ Reading period is August 15-April 15."

MAGAZINES NEEDS Send poems via postal mail or online submission manager.

EKPHRASIS

Frith Press, P.O. Box 161236, Sacramento CA 95816-1236. **E-mail:** frithpress@aol.com. **Website:** ekphrasisjournal.com. **Contact:** Laverne Frith and Carol Frith, editors. *Ekphrasis*, published semiannually in March and September, is an "outlet for the growing body of poetry focusing on individual works from any artistic genre. Poetry should transcend mere description. Open to all forms." Acquires first North American serial rights or one-time rights. Publishes ms 1 year after acceptance. Responds in 4 months. Seldom comments on rejected poems. Sample: $6. Subscription: $12/year. Make checks payable, in U.S. funds, to Laverne Frith. Guidelines available for SASE or on website.

○ *Ekphrasis* is 32-50 pages, digest-sized, photocopied, saddle-stapled. Poems from *Ekphrasis* have been featured on *Poetry Daily*. Nominates for the Pushcart Prize.

MAGAZINES NEEDS Submit 3-5 poems at a time. Considers previously published poems "infrequently; must be credited." Cover letter is required, including short bio with representative credits and phone number. Include SASE. Until further notice, Frith Press will publish **occasional chapbooks by invitation only**. Has published poetry by Jeffrey Levine, Peter Meinke, David Hamilton, Barbara Lefcowitz, Molly McQuade, Alice Friman, and Annie Boutelle. Does not want "poetry without ekphrastic focus. No poorly crafted work. No archaic language." Pays 1 contributor's copy.

⑤ ELLERY QUEEN'S MYSTERY MAGAZINE

Dell Magazines, 267 Broadway, 4th Floor, New York NY 10017. (212)686-7188. **Fax:** (212)686-7414. **E-mail:** elleryqueenmm@dellmagazines.com. **Website:** www.

themysteryplace.com/eqmm. **Contact:** Jackie Sherbow, assistant editor. *"Ellery Queen's Mystery Magazine* welcomes submissions from both new and established writers. We publish every kind of mystery short story: the psychological suspense tale, the deductive puzzle, the private eye case—the gamut of crime and detection from the realistic (including the policeman's lot and stories of police procedure) to the more imaginative (including 'locked rooms' and 'impossible crimes'). We look for strong writing, an original and exciting plot, and professional craftsmanship. We encourage writers whose work meets these general criteria to read an issue of *EQMM* before making a submission." Buys first North American serial rights. Pays on acceptance. Publishes ms an average of 6-12 months after acceptance. Responds in 3 months to mss. Sample copy for $6.50. Guidelines online.

○ Magazine: 5⅞×8⅝, 112 pages with special 192-page combined March/April and September/October issues.

MAGAZINES NEEDS Wants short mystery verses, limericks. *EQMM* uses an online submission system (eqmm.magazinesubmissions.com) that has been designed to streamline our process and improve communication with authors. We ask that all submissions be made electronically, using this system, rather than on paper. All stories should be in standard manuscript format and submitted in .DOC format. We cannot accept .DOCX, .RTF, or .TXT files at this time. For detailed submission instructions, see eqmm.magazinesubmissions.com or our writers guidelines page (www.themysteryplace.com/eqmm/guidelines). Length: up to 1 page, double-spaced.

TIPS "We have a Department of First Stories to encourage writers whose fiction has never before been in print. We publish an average of 10 first stories every year. Mark subject line Attn: Dept. of First Stories."

🌀 ELLIPSIS MAGAZINE

(801)832-2321. **E-mail:** ellipsis@westminstercollege.edu. **Website:** www.westminstercollege.edu/ellipsis. *Ellipsis*, published annually in April, needs good literary poetry, fiction, essays, plays, and visual art. Has published poetry by Allison Joseph, Molly McQuade, Virgil Suaárez, Maurice Kilwein-Guevara, Richard Cecil, and Ron Carlson. Buys first North American serial rights. Pays on publication. Publishes ms an average of 3 months after acceptance. Responds in

6 months to mss. Sample copy for $7.50. Guidelines available online.

○ Reads submissions August 1-November 1. Staff changes from year to year. Check website for an updated list of editors. *Ellipsis* is 120 pages, digest-sized, perfect-bound, with color cover. Accepts about 5% of submissions received. Press run is 2,000; most distributed free through college.

MAGAZINES NEEDS No fax or e-mail submissions. Submit through Submittable. One poem per page, with name and contact information on every page. Include SASE and brief bio No previously published poems. Pays $10/poem, plus 2 contributor's copies.

CONTEST/AWARD OFFERINGS All accepted poems are eligible for the *Ellipsis* Award which includes a $100 prize. Past judges have included Jorie Graham, Sandra Cisneros, and Stanley Plumly.

EPOCH

251 Goldwin Smith Hall, Cornell University, Ithaca NY 14853-3201. (607)255-3385. **Fax:** (607)255-6661. **Website:** http://english.arts.cornell.edu/publications/epoch. **Contact:** Michael Koch, editor; Heidi E. Marschner, managing editor. Looking for well-written literary fiction, poetry, personal essays. Newcomers welcome. Open to mainstream and avant-garde writing. Buys first North American serial rights. Pays on publication. Publishes ms an average of 6 months after acceptance. Responds in 2 weeks to queries. Responds in 6 weeks to mss. Sometimes comments on rejected mss. Editorial lead time 6 months. Sample copy for $5. Guidelines online and for #10 SASE.

○ Magazine: 6×9; 128 pages; good quality paper; good cover stock. Receives 500 unsolicited mss/month. Accepts 15-20 mss/issue. Reads submissions September 15-April 15. Publishes 3-4 new writers/year. Has published work by Antonya Nelson, Doris Betts, Heidi Jon Schmidt.

MAGAZINES NEEDS Mss not accompanied by SASE will be discarded unread. Occasionally provides criticism on poems. Considers poetry in all forms. Pays $5 and up/printed page (maximum of $50/poem).

TIPS "Tell your story, speak your poem, straight from the heart. We are attracted to language and to good writing, but we are most interested in what the good writing leads us to, or where."

ESSAYS & FICTIONS

(914)572-7351. **E-mail:** essaysandfictions@gmail.com. **Website:** essaysandfictions.com. **Contact:** David Pollock and Danielle Winterton, co-founding editors. "*Essays & Fictions* publishes fictional essay, reflective essay, academic rhetorical essay, literary narrative essay, lyric essay, linear fiction, nonlinear fiction, essayistic fiction, fictionalized memoir, questionable histories, false historical accounts, botched accounts, cultural analysis, criticism or commentary, compositional analysis, criticism or commentary, or any blend thereof. We do not differentiate between essay and fiction in the table of contents because we consciously challenge the validity of genre boundaries and definitions. We believe language is not fixed and neither is truth. As art, forms of literature have varying degrees of truth value. Many writers have recently chosen to compose works that blend or subvert the genres of short fiction and essay. We are particularly interested in publishing these kinds of writers. We encourage writers to experiment with hybrid forms that lead to literary transcendence." Semiannual. Acquires first and electronic rights. Publication is copyrighted. Publishes ms 3-8 months after acceptance. Responds to mss in 1-8 months. Sample copy: $15. Guidelines available by e-mail or on website.

MAGAZINES NEEDS Contributors get 1 free copy and 15% off additional copies of the issue in which they are published.

TIPS "We look for confident work that uses form/structure and voice in interesting ways without sounding overly self-conscious or deliberate. We encourage rigorous excellence of complex craft in our submissions and discourage bland reproductions of reality. Read the journal. Be familiar with the *Essays & Fictions* aesthetic. We are particularly interested in writers who read theory and/or have multiple intellectual and artistic interests, and who set high intellectual standards for themselves and their work."

EUROPEAN JUDAISM

LBC, The Sternberg Centre, 80 East End Rd., London N3 2SY, England. **E-mail:** european.judaism@lbc.ac.uk. **Website:** www.journals.berghahnbooks.com/ej. **Contact:** managing editor. "For over 40 years, *European Judaism* has provided a voice for the postwar Jewish world in Europe. It has reflected the different realities of each country and helped to rebuild Jewish consciousness after the Holocaust. It is a peer-reviewed journal with emphasis on European Jewish theology, philosophy, literature, and history. Each issue includes a poetry and book reviews section." *Eu-

ropean Judaism is available online. Individual Rate (Online Only): $34.95/£21.95/€24.95. Student Rate (Online Only): $19.95/ £12.95/ €14.95. Please visit the website for institutional pricing. Guidelines available online.

MAGAZINES NEEDS Submit by e-mail, accompanied by 1 double-spaced copy and a brief biographical note on the author. Please visit the website for further details.

EVANGEL

Light and Life Communications, 770 N. High School Rd., Indianapolis IN 46214. (317)244-3660. **Contact:** Julie Innes, editor. *Evangel,* published quarterly, is an adult Sunday School paper. "Devotional in nature, it lifts up Christ as the source of salvation and hope. The mission of *Evangel* is to increase the reader's understanding of the nature and character of God and the nature of a life lived for Christ. Material fitting this mission and not longer than 1,200 words will be considered." Press run is less than 10,000. Buys second serial (reprint) or one-time rights. Pays on publication. Publishes ms 18-36 months after acceptance. Responds in 6-10 weeks to submissions. Seldom comments on rejected poems. Sample copy and writer's guidelines for #10 SASE. Subscription: $2.69/quarter (13 weeks). "Write 'guidelines request' on your envelope to separate it from the submissions."

MAGAZINES NEEDS Submit no more than 5 poems at a time. Cover letter is preferred. "Poetry must be typed on 8.5x11 white paper. In the upper left corner of each page, include your name, address, and phone number. In the upper right corner of cover page, specify what rights you are offering. One-eighth of the way down the page, give the title. All subsequent material must be double-spaced with 1-inch margins." Accepts about 5% of poetry received. Rarely uses rhyming work. Pays $10/poem plus 2 contributor's copies.

TIPS Desires concise, tight writing that supports a solid thesis and fits the mission expressed in the guidelines.

EVANSVILLE REVIEW

University of Evansville Creative Writing Deptartment, 1800 Lincoln Ave., Evansville IN 47722. (812)488-1042. **E-mail:** evansvillereview@evansville.edu. **Website:** http://evansvillereview.evansville.edu. **Contact:** Jessica Ingle, editor-in-chief. *The Evansville Review* is an annual literary journal published at the University of Evansville. Past contributors include

Arthur Miller, Joseph Brodsky, John Updike, Rita Dove, Willis Barnstone, W.D. Snodgrass, Edward Albee, Dana Gioia, and Marjorie Agosin. Acquires one-time rights. Pays on publication. Responds in 3 months. Sample copy for $5. Guidelines available online at website.

○ Reading period: September 1-December 1.

MAGAZINES NEEDS Submit no more than 5 poems at a time. No fax or e-mail submissions; postal submissions only. Cover letter is required. Include brief bio. Pays in contributor's copies.

TIPS "Because editorial staff rolls over every 1-2 years, the journal always has a new flavor."

EXIT 13 MAGAZINE, "THE CROSSROADS OF POETRY SINCE 1988"

P.O. Box 423, Fanwood NJ 07023-1162. **E-mail:** exit-13magazine@yahoo.com. **Contact:** Tom Plante, editor. *Exit 13*, published annually, uses poetry that is short, to the point, with a sense of geography. It features poets of all ages, writing styles and degrees of experience, focusing on where and how we live and what's going on around us. The emphasis is on geography, travel, adventure, and the fertile ground of the imagination. It's a travelogue in poetry, a reflection of the world we see, and a chronicle of the people we meet along the way. Acquires one-time and possible anthology rights. Pays 1 contributor's copy. Responds in 4 months. Sample copy: $10. Guidelines available in magazine or for SASE.

○ *Exit 13* is about 76 pages. Press run is 300.

MAGAZINES NEEDS Submit through postal mail or e-mail. Paste in body of e-mail. Has published poetry by Carole Stone, Wanda Praisner, Nancy Scott, Sander Zulauf, Paul Sohar, and Charles Rammelkamp.

EYE ON LIFE ONLINE MAGAZINE

38 Linden St., Unit 5, Brookline MA 02445. **E-mail:** eyeonlife.ezine@gmail.com. **Website:** eyeonlifemag.com. **Contact:** Tom Rubenoff, senior poetry editor. Poets keep all rights. Responds in 4-6 weeks.

MAGAZINES NEEDS Publishes up to 5 poems/week. Online submissions only. Seeking poems 400 words or less with vivid imagery that either works well within its form or transcends it. Does not pay for poetry at this time. See submission guidelines online or e-mail poetry editor (trubenoff@gmail.com) for guidelines.

Ⓢ FACES MAGAZINE

Cobblestone Publishing, Editorial Dept., 30 Grove St., Peterborough NH 03458. (603)924-7209. **E-mail:**

ecarpentiere@caruspub.com. **Website:** www.cricket-mag.com. **Contact:** Elizabeth Crooker, Carpentiere. *FACES Magazine*, published 9 times/year, features cultures from around the globe for children ages 9-14. "Readers learn how other kids live around the world and about the important inventions and ideas that a particular culture has given to the world. All material must relate to the theme of a specific upcoming issue in order to be considered." Wants "clear, objective imagery. Serious and light verse considered. Must relate to theme." Acquires all rights. Responds to queries in "several months." Does not respond for unused queries. Sample copy: $6.95, plus $2 s&h.

○ Publishes theme issues; visit website for details.

FAULTLINE

University of California at Irvine, Dept. of English, 435 Humanities Instructional Building, Irvine CA 92697. (949)824-1573. **E-mail:** faultline@uci.edu. **Website:** faultline.sites.uci.edu. Buys first North American serial rights. Publishes ms an average of 5 months after acceptance. Responds in 4 weeks to queries; in 4 months to mss. Editorial lead time 4 months. Sample copy: $5 or online. Writer's guidelines online.

○ Reading period is August 15-January 15. Submissions sent at any other time will not be read. Editors change in September of each year.

MAGAZINES NEEDS Submit up to 5 poems via online submissions manager or postal mail. Pays contributor copies.

TIPS "Our commitment is to publish the best work possible from well-known and emerging authors with vivid and varied voices."

FEELINGS OF THE HEART

c/o Feelings of the Heart, 3637 SE 6th St. N6, Topeka KS 66607. **E-mail:** aliceharnisch@yahoo.com. **Website:** www.freewebs.com/feelingsoftheheartliterary-journal. **Contact:** Alice M. Harnisch, editor/publisher/poet/writer. "*Feelings of the Heart* is seeking poetry, writings, and any other work that you wish to submit for publication in a small print journal. *FOTH* accepts all types of works as long as they are in good taste." Sample: $6. Subscription: $20/year (4 issues); $40/2 years (8 issues). Please make checks/money orders out to Ms. Alice M. Harnisch and send to address above.

MAGAZINES NEEDS Submit by mail (please send SASE for reply) or e-mail. Considers all lengths; no word count limits.

TIPS "Check out our Facebook page: www.facebook.com/feelingsoftheheartliteraryjournal."

FICKLE MUSES

E-mail: editor@ficklemuses.com. **Website:** www.ficklemuses.com. "*Fickle Muses* is an online journal of poetry and fiction engaged with myth and legend. A poet or fiction writer is featured each week, with new selections posted on Sundays. Art is updated monthly." Publishes ms 3 months after acceptance. Responds in 2-4 months. Guidelines online.

MAGAZINES NEEDS Open to all kinds of poetry. No limits on length.

TIPS Seeks "originality. An innovative look at an old story. I'm looking to be swept away. Get a feel from our website."

○⑤ THE FIDDLEHEAD

University of New Brunswick, Campus House, 11 Garland Court, Box 4400, Fredericton NB E3B 5A3, Canada. (506)453-3501. **Fax:** (506) 453-5069. **E-mail:** fiddlehd@unb.ca. **Website:** www.thefiddlehead.ca. Mark Anthony Jarman and Gerard Beirne, fiction editors; Phillip Crymble, Claire Kelly, and Ian LeTourneau, poetry editors. **Contact:** Kathryn Taglia, managing editor. "Canada's longest living literary journal, *The Fiddlehead* is published 4 times/year at the University of New Brunswick, with the generous assistance of the University of New Brunswick, the Canada Council for the Arts, and the Province of New Brunswick. It is experienced, wise enough to recognize excellence, and always looking for freshness and surprise. *The Fiddlehead* publishes short stories, poems, book reviews, and a small number of personal essays. Our full-color covers have become collectors' items and feature work by New Brunswick artists and from New Brunswick museums and art galleries. The journal is open to good writing in English from all over the world, looking always for freshness and surprise. Our editors are always happy to see new unsolicited works in fiction and poetry. Work is read on an ongoing basis; the acceptance rate is around 1-2%. Apart from our annual contest, we have no deadlines for submissions." Pays on publication for first or one-time serial rights. Responds in 3-9 months to mss. Occasionally comments on rejected mss. Sample copy: $15 (U.S.).

○ "No criteria for publication except quality. For a general audience, including many poets and writers." Has published work by George Elliott Clarke, Kayla Czaga, Daniel Woodrell, and Clea Young. *The Fiddlehead* also sponsors an annual writing contest.

MAGAZINES NEEDS Send SASE and *Canadian* stamps or IRCs for return of mss. No e-mail, fax, or disc submissions. Simultaneous submissions only if stated on cover letter; must contact immediately if accepted elsewhere. Pays up to $40 (Canadian)/published page and 2 contributor's copies.

CONTEST/AWARD OFFERINGS Sponsors poetry contest.

TIPS "If you are serious about submitting to *The Fiddlehead*, you should subscribe or read several issues to get a sense of the journal. Contact us if you would like to order sample back issues ($10-15 plus postage)."

FIELD: CONTEMPORARY POETRY & POETICS

Oberlin College Press, 50 N. Professor St., Oberlin OH 44074-1095. (440)775-8408. **Fax:** (440)775-8124. **E-mail:** oc.press@oberlin.edu. **Website:** www.oberlin.edu/ocpress. **Contact:** Marco Wilkinson, managing editor. *FIELD: Contemporary Poetry and Poetics*, published semiannually in April and October, is a literary journal with "emphasis on poetry, translations, and essays by poets. See electronic submission guidelines." Buys first rights. Pays on publication. Responds in 6-8 weeks to mss. Editorial lead time 4 months. Sample copy for $8. Guidelines available online and for #10 SASE.

○ *FIELD* is 100 pages, digest-sized, printed on rag stock, flat-spined, with glossy color card cover. Subscription: $16/year, $28 for 2 years. Sample: $8 postpaid. Has published poetry by Michelle Glazer, Tom Lux, Carl Phillips, Betsy Sholl, Charles Simic, Jean Valentine and translations by Marilyn Hacker and Stuart Friebert.

MAGAZINES NEEDS Submissions are read August 1 through May 31. Submit 2-6 of your best poems. No e-mail submissions. Include cover letter and SASE. Submit using submission manager. Pays $15/page and 2 contributor's copies.

TIPS "Keep trying!"

⑤ THE FIFTH DI...

E-mail: thefifthdi@yahoo.com. **Website:** www.nomadicdeliriumpress.com/fifth.htm. *The Fifth Di...*, published quarterly online, features fiction from the science fiction and fantasy genres. Acquires first rights. Publishes ms 3 months after acceptance. Responds in 2 months to mss. Guidelines online.

⟳ FILLING STATION

P.O. Box 22135, Bankers Hall, Calgary AB T2P 4J5, Canada. **E-mail:** mgmt@fillingstation.ca; poetry@fillingstation.ca; fiction@fillingstation.ca; nonfiction@fillingstation.ca. **Website:** www.fillingstation.ca. **Contact:** Paul Zits, managing editor. *filling Station*, published 3 times/year, prints contemporary poetry, fiction, visual art, interviews, reviews, and articles. "We are looking for all forms of contemporary writing, but especially that which is original and/or experimental." Responds in 3-4 months. "After your work is reviewed by our Collective, you will receive an e-mail from an editor to let you know if your work has been selected for publication. If selected, you will later receive a second e-mail to let you know which issue your piece has been selected to appear in. Note that during the design phase, we sometimes discover the need to shuffle a piece to a future issue instead. In the event your piece is pushed back, we will inform you." Sample: $8.

◖   Has published poetry by Fred Wah, Larissa Lai, Margaret Christakos, Robert Kroetsch, Ron Silliman, Susan Holbrook, and many more. *filling Station* is 64 pages, 8.5×11, perfect-bound, with card cover, includes photos and artwork. Receives about 100 submissions for each issue, accepts approximately 10%. Press run is 700. Subscription: $20/3 issues; $36 for 6 issues.

MAGAZINES NEEDS Up to 6 pages of poetry may be sent to poetry@fillingstation.ca. A submission lacking mailing address and/or bio will be considered incomplete.

TIPS "*filling Station* accepts singular or simultaneous submissions of previously unpublished poetry, fiction, creative nonfiction, nonfiction, or art. We are always on the hunt for great writing!"

FLINT HILLS REVIEW

Dept. of English, Modern Languages, and Journalist (Box 4019), Emporia State University, 1200 Commercial St., Emporia KS 66801. **Website:** www.emporia.edu/fhr. **Contact:** Kevin Rabas. *Flint Hills Review*, published annually in December, is "a regionally focused journal presenting writers of national distinction alongside new authors. *FHR* seeks work informed by a strong sense of place or region, especially Kansas and the Great Plains region. We seek to provide a publishing venue for writers of the Great Plains and Kansas while also publishing authors whose work evidences a strong sense of place, writing of literary quality, and accomplished use of language and depth of character development." Acquires one-time rights. Publishes ms 4-12 months after acceptance. Responds in 6-9 months to mss. Sample copy: $5.50 Guidelines online.

◖   Magazine: 9×6; 120-200 pages; perfect-bound; 60 lb. paper; glossy cover; illustrations; photos. Has published work by Elizabeth Dodds, Kim Stafford, and Brian Daldorph. Reads mss January to mid-March.

MAGAZINES NEEDS Wants all forms of poetry except rhyming. Does not want sentimental or gratuitous verse. Has published poetry by E. Ethelbert Miller, Elizabeth Dodd, Walt McDonald, and Gwendolyn Brooks. Submit 3-6 poems by postal mail. Cover letter is required. Include SASE. Reads submissions January-March only. Pays 1 contributor's copy; additional copies at discounted price.

TIPS Submit writing that has "strong imagery and voice, writing that is informed by place or region, writing of literary quality with depth of character development. Hone the language down to the most literary depiction possible in the shortest space that still provides depth of development without excess length."

THE FLORIDA REVIEW

Department of English, University of Central Florida, P.O. Box 161346, Orlando FL 32816. **E-mail:** flreview@mail.ucf.edu. **Website:** http://floridareview.cah.ucf.edu/. **Contact:** Jocelyn Bartkevicius, editor. "We publish fiction and essays of high 'literary' quality—stories that delight, instruct, and take risks. Our audience consists of avid readers of fiction, poetry, graphic narrative, and creative nonfiction." Responds in 2-4 weeks to queries about reviews or interviews; 3-8 months to mss. Sample copy: $10. Writer's guidelines for #10 SASE or online.

◖   Recently published work by Gerald Vizenor, Billy Collins, Sherwin Bitsui, Kelly Clancy, Denise Duhamel, Tony Hoagland, Baron Wormser, Marcia Aldrich, and Patricia Foster.

MAGAZINES NEEDS "We look for clear, strong poems, filled with real people, emotions, and objects. Any style will be considered."

TIPS "We're looking for writers with fresh voices and original stories. We like risk."

FLOYD COUNTY MOONSHINE

720 Christiansburg Pike, Floyd VA 24091. (540)745-5150. **E-mail:** floydshine@gmail.com. **Website:** www.floydcountymoonshine.org. **Contact:** Aaron Lee Moore, editor in chief. *Floyd County Moonshine*, published biannually, is a "literary and arts magazine in Floyd, Virginia, and the New River Valley. We accept poetry, short stories, and essays addressing all manner of themes; however, preference is given to those works of a rural or Appalachian nature. *Floyd County Moonshine* publishes a variety of home-grown Appalachian writers in addition to writers from across the country. The mission of *Floyd County Moonshine* is to publish thought-provoking, well-crafted, free-thinking, uncensored prose and poetry. Our literature explores the dark and Gothic as well as the bright and pleasant in order to give an honest portrayal of the human condition. We aspire to publish quality literature in the local color genre, specifically writing that relates to Floyd, Virginia, and the New River Valley. Floyd and local Appalachian authors are given priority consideration; however, to stay versatile we also aspire to publish some writers from all around the country in every issue. We publish both well-established and beginning writers." Single copy: $10. Subscription: $20/1 year, $38/2 years. Accepts e-mail (preferred). Submit a Word document as attachment. Accepts previously published works and simultaneous submissions on occasion. Cover letter is unnecessary. Include brief bio. Reads submissions year round.

○ Wants "literature addressing rural or Appalachian themes." Has published poetry by Steve Kistulentz, Louis Gallo, Ernie Wormwood, R.T. Smith, Chelsea Adams, and Justin Askins.

TIPS "If we favor your work, it may appear in several issues, so prior contributors are also encouraged to re-submit. Every year we choose at least 1 featured author for an issue. We also nominate for *Pushcart* prizes, and we will do book reviews if you mail us the book."

FLYWAY

Department of English, 206 Ross Hall, Iowa State University, Ames IA 50011-1201. **E-mail:** flywayjournal@gmail.com; flyway@iastate.edu. **Website:** www.flyway.org. **Contact:** Elizabeth A. Giorgi, managing editor. Based out of Iowa State University, *Flyway: Journal of Writing and Environment* publishes poetry, fiction, nonfiction, and visual art exploring the many complicated facets of the word environment—at once rural, urban, and suburban—and its social and political implications. Also open to all different interpretations of environment. Acquires first North American serial rights, electronic rights, and future anthology rights. Publishes ms 4 months after acceptance. Often comments on rejected mss. Sample copy and guidelines on website.

○ Reading period is September 15-May 15. Has published work by Rick Bass, Jacob M. Appel, Madison Smartt Bell, Jane Smiley. Also sponsors the annual fall "Notes from the Field" nonfiction contest, and the spring "Sweet Corn Prize in Fiction" short story contest. Details on website.

MAGAZINES NEEDS Submit up to 5 poems (combined in 1 document) only via online submission manager. Pays one-year subscription to *Flyway*.

TIPS "For *Flyway*, there should be tension between the environment or setting of the story and the characters in it. A well-known place should appear new, even alien and strange through the eyes and actions of the characters. We want to see an active environment, too—a setting that influences actions, triggers it's one events.'"

⊘⑤ FOGGED CLARITY

(231)670-7033. **E-mail:** editor@foggedclarity.com. **E-mail:** submissions@foggedclarity.com. **Website:** www.foggedclarity.com. **Contact:** Editors. "*Fogged Clarity* is an arts review that accepts submissions of poetry, fiction, nonfiction, music, visual art, and reviews of work in all mediums. We seek art that is stabbingly eloquent. Our print edition is released once every year, while new issues of our online journal come out at the beginning of every month. Artists maintain the copyrights to their work until they are monetarily compensated for said work. If your work is selected for our print edition and you consent to its publication, you will be compensated." Acquires first North American serial rights. Rights revert to author upon publication. Averages 1-2 months from acceptance to publishing. Responds in 3 months to mss. Accepts queries by e-mail only. Sample copy online. Guidelines available at www.foggedclarity.com/submissions.

○ "By incorporating music and the visual arts and releasing a new issue monthly, *Fogged Clarity* aims to transcend the conventions of a typical literary journal. Our network is extensive, and our scope is as broad as thought itself;

we are, you are, unconstrained. With that spirit in mind, *Fogged Clarity* examines the work of authors, artists, scholars, and musicians, providing a home for exceptional art and thought that warrants exposure."

MAGAZINES NEEDS Submit up to 5 poems by e-mail (submissions@foggedclarity.com) as attached .DOC or .DOCX file. Subject line should be formatted as: "Last Name: Medium of Submission." For example, "Evans: Poetry." Include brief cover letter, complete contact information, and a third-person bio.

TIPS "The editors appreciate artists communicating the intention of their submitted work and the influences behind it in a brief cover letter. Any artists with proposals for features or special projects should feel free to contact Ben Evans directly at editor@fogged-clarity.com."

FOLIATE OAK LITERARY MAGAZINE

University of Arkansas-Monticello, Arts & Humanities, 562 University Dr., Monticello AR 71656. E-mail: foliateoak@gmail.com. Website: www.folia-teoak.com. Contact: Diane Payne, faculty advisor. "The *Foliate Oak Literary Magazine* is a student-run magazine accepting wonderful works of prose, poetry, and artwork." Acquires one-time, nonexclusive rights. Publishes ms an average of 1 month after acceptance. Responds in 1 week to queries; 1 month to mss. Editorial lead time 1 month. Guidelines online.

○ "After you receive a rejection/acceptance notice, please wait 1 month before submitting new work. **Submission Period: August 1-April 24**. We do not read submissions during summer break. If you need to contact us for anything other than submitting your work, please write to: foliateoak@gmail.com." No e-mail submissions.

MAGAZINES NEEDS Submit poems via online submission manager. "We enjoy poems that we understand, preferably not rhyming poems, unless you make the rhyme so fascinating we'll wonder why we ever said anything about avoiding rhymes. Give us something fresh, unexpected, and that will make us say, 'Wow!'" "No homophobic, religious rants, or pornographic, violent poems. Please avoid using offensive language."

ALSO OFFERS "At the end of the year, we'll use selected works from our website for the annual print anthology."

TIPS "Please submit all material via our online submission manager. Read our guidelines before submitting. We are eager to include multimedia submissions of videos, music, and collages. Submit your best work."

FOLIO, A LITERARY JOURNAL AT AMERICAN UNIVERSITY

Department of Literature, American University, Washington DC 20016. (202)885-2971. **Fax:** (202)885-2938. **E-mail:** folio.editors@gmail.com. **Website:** www.american.edu/cas/literature/folio. "*Folio* is a nationally recognized literary journal sponsored by the College of Arts and Sciences at American University in Washington, DC. Since 1984, we have published original creative work by both new and established authors. Past issues have included work by Michael Reid Busk, Billy Collins, William Stafford, and Bruce Weigl, and interviews with Michael Cunningham, Charles Baxter, Amy Bloom, Ann Beattie, and Walter Kirn. We look for well-crafted poetry and prose that is bold and memorable." Acquires first North American serial rights. Single copy: $7.50. Make checks payable to *Folio* at American University. Guidelines available on website.

○ Poems and prose are reviewed by editorial staff and senior editors. Press run is 250; 50-60 distributed free to the American University community and contributors. Reads submissions September 1-January 1.

MAGAZINES NEEDS Submit via the online submission form at https://foliolitjournal.submittable.com/submit. Considers simultaneous submissions "with notice." No fax, e-mail, or disk submissions. Cover letter is preferred. Include name, address, e-mail address, brief bio, and phone number. Receives about 1,000 poems/year, accepts about 25. Pays $50 and 2 contributor's copies.

FOOTHILL: A JOURNAL OF POETRY

165 E. 10th St., Claremont CA 91711. (909)607-3962. **Fax:** (909)621-8029. **E-mail:** foothill@cgu.edu. **Website:** www.cgu.edu/foothill. **Contact:** Kevin Riel; editor in chief. Directed by students at Claremont Graduate University, *Foothill: a journal of poetry*, a biannual journal, is the only literary journal devoted exclusively to poetry written by graduate students who are based in the United States. *Foothill* acquires electronic rights as well as right to print poem in year-end print journal. Rights revert to poets upon publication. Responds in 5 weeks. Sometimes comments on

rejected poems. Single copy: $25. Subscription: $25. Make checks payable to CGU. Guidelines available in magazine, by e-mail, and on website.

○ Published online quarterly, with 1 print edition each year. Digest-sized, 72 pages, digital press, perfect bound. Press run is 500. No ads. Never publishes theme issues.

MAGAZINES NEEDS Accepts any poetry by graduate students (currently enrolled or recently graduated) from anywhere in the world. Students do not need to be enrolled in an MFA or writing program. Welcomes poetry submissions from those in other disciplines. Submit via e-mail. Include document as attachment in e-mail. Cover letter preferred. Poems are circulated to an editorial board. Accepts submissions year round. Welcomes submissions from beginning poets. Does not consider poetry by children or teens. No limit for poem length.

FORPOETRY.COM

E-mail: editors@forpoetry.com. **E-mail:** sub@forpoetry.com. **Website:** www.forpoetry.com. **Contact:** Jackie Marcus, editor. *ForPoetry.Com*, published online with daily updates, wants "lyric poetry, vivid imagery, open form, natural landscape, philosophical themes—but not at the expense of honesty and passion." Does not want "city punk, corny sentimental fluff, or academic workshop imitations." Has published poetry by Sherod Santos, John Koethe, Robert Hass, Kim Addonizio, and Brenda Hillman. Time between acceptance and publication is 2 weeks-1 month. Responds in 2 weeks to submissions.

○ Not currently accepting unsolicited poems.

MAGAZINES NEEDS Submit up to 2 poems at a time. Accepts e-mail submissions only (pasted into body of message; no attachments). Cover letter is preferred. Does not read submissions May 1-August 15.

FOURTEEN HILLS

Dept. of Creative Writing, San Francisco State University, 1600 Holloway Ave., San Francisco CA 94132. **Website:** www.14hills.net. "*Fourteen Hills* publishes the highest-quality innovative fiction and poetry for a literary audience." Editors change each year. Always sends prepublication galleys. Acquires one-time rights. Responds in 4-9 months to mss. Sometimes comments on rejected mss. SASE for return of ms. Sample copy: $10. Guidelines online.

○ Semiannual magazine: 6×9; 200 pages; 60 lb. paper; 10-point C15 cover. Reading periods:

September 1-December 1 for summer issue; March 1-June 1 for winter issue.

MAGAZINES NEEDS Submit up to 3 poems via online submissions manager. Length: up to 70 lines/poem; ideally 30-35 lines/poem. Pays 2 contributor's copies and discount on additional copies.

TIPS "Please read an issue of *Fourteen Hills* before submitting."

THE FOURTH RIVER

Chatham College, Woodland Rd., Pittsburgh PA 15232. **E-mail:** 4thriver@gmail.com. **Website:** fourthriver.chatham.edu. *The Fourth River*, an annual publication of Chatham University's MFA in Creative Writing Programs, features literature that engages and explores the relationship between humans and their environments. Wants writings that are richly situated at the confluence of place, space, and identity, or that reflect upon or make use of landscape and place in new ways. Buys first North American serial rights. Pays with contributor copies only. Publishes mss in 5-8 months after acceptance. Responds in 3-5 months to mss. Sample copy: $5 (back issue). Single copy: $10; subscription: $16 for 2 years. Guidelines online.

○ *The Fourth River* is digest-sized, perfect-bound, with full-color cover by various artists. *The Fourth River*'s contributors have been published in *Glimmer Train, Alaska Quarterly Review, The Missouri Review, The Best American Short Stories, The O. Henry Prize Stories*, and *The Best American Travel Writing*.

MAGAZINES NEEDS Submit 3-5 poems via online submissions manager.

○⑤ FREEFALL MAGAZINE

Freefall Literary Society of Calgary, 922 Ninth Ave. SE, Calgary AB T2G 0S4, Canada. **E-mail:** editors@freefallmagazine.ca. **Website:** www.freefallmagazine.ca. **Contact:** Ryan Stromquist, managing editor. "Magazine published triannually containing fiction, poetry, creative nonfiction, essays on writing, interviews, and reviews. We are looking for exquisite writing with a strong narrative." Buys first North American serial rights (ownership reverts to author after one-time publication). Pays on publication. Guidelines and submission forms on website.

MAGAZINES NEEDS Submit 2-5 poems via website. Attach submission file (file name format is lastname_firstname_storytitle.doc or .docx or .pdf). Accepts any style of poetry. Length: no more than 6 pages. Pays $25 per poem and 1 contributor's copy.

TIPS "Our mission is to encourage the voices of new, emerging, and experienced Canadian writers and provide a platform for their quality work."

🌀 FREEXPRESSION

P.O. Box 4, West Hoxton NSW 2171, Australia. **E-mail:** editor@freexpression.com.au. **Website:** www. freexpression.com.au. **Contact:** Peter F. Pike, managing editor. *FreeXpresSion*, published monthly, contains "creative writing, how-to articles, short stories, and poetry, including cinquain, haiku, etc., and bush verse." Open to all forms. "Christian themes OK. Humorous material welcome. No gratuitous sex; bad language OK. We don't want to see anything degrading." Purchases first Australian rights. Publishes ms 2 months after acceptance. Responds in 2 months. Subscription: $15 AUS/3 months, $32 AUS/6 months, $60 AUS/1 year. Guidelines available in magazine, for SAE and IRC, or by fax or e-mail.

🗨 *FreeXpresSion* also publishes books up to 200 pages **through subsidy arrangements with authors**. Some poems published throughout the year are used in *Yearbooks* (annual anthologies). *FreeXpresSion* is 32 pages, magazine-sized, offset-printed, saddle-stapled, full color. Receives about 3,500 poems/year, accepts about 30%.

MAGAZINES NEEDS Submit 3-4 poems at a time. Accepts e-mail (pasted into body of message) and disk submissions. Cover letter is preferred. Has published poetry by many prize-winning poets like Ron Stevens, Ellis Campbell, Brenda Joy, David Campbell, Max and Jacqui Merckenschlager. Length: "Very long poems are not desired but would be considered."

ALSO OFFERS Sponsors an annual contest with 3 categories for poetry: blank verse (up to 120 lines); traditional verse (up to 120 lines), and haiku. 1st Prize in blank verse: $250 AUS; 2nd Prize: $100 AUS; 1st Prize in traditional rhyming poetry: $250 AUS; 2nd Prize: $100 AUS. Haiku, 1st Prize $120 AUS; 2nd Prize $80 AUS; 3rd Prize $50 AUS. Guidelines and entry form available by e-mail or download from website.

🌀 THE FRIEND

The Friend Publications Ltd, 173 Euston Rd., London England NW1 2BJ, United Kingdom. (44)(207)663-1010. **Fax:** (44)(207)663-1182. **E-mail:** editorial@the-friend.org. **Website:** www.thefriend.org. **Contact:**

Ian Kirk Smith. Completely independent, *The Friend* brings readers news and views from a Quaker perspective, as well as from a wide range of authors whose writings are of interest to Quakers and non-Quakers alike. There are articles on issues such as peace, spirituality, Quaker belief, and ecumenism, as well as news of Friends from Britain and abroad. Guidelines available online.

🗨 Prefers queries, but sometimes accepts unsolicited mss.

MAGAZINES NEEDS There are no rules regarding poetry, but doesn't want particularly long poems.

THE FRIEND MAGAZINE

The Church of Jesus Christ of Latter-day Saints, 50 E. North Temple St., Salt Lake City UT 84150. (801)240-2210. **Fax:** (801)240-2270. **E-mail:** friend@ldschurch.org. **Website:** www.lds.org/friend. **Contact:** Paul B. Pieper, editor; Mark W. Robison, art director. "The *Friend* is published by The Church of Jesus Christ of Latter-day Saints for boys and girls up to 3-12 years of age." Buys all rights. "Authors may request rights to have their work reprinted after their ms is published." Pays on acceptance. Responds in 2 months to mss. Sample copy for $1.50, 9x12 envelope, and 4 first-class stamps.

MAGAZINES NEEDS "We are looking for easy-to-illustrate poems with catchy cadences. Poems should convey a sense of joy and reflect gospel teachings. Also brief poems that will appeal to preschoolers." Pays $30 for poems.

🌀 THE FROGMORE PAPERS

21 Mildmay Rd., Lewes, East Sussex BN7 1PJ, England. **Website:** www.frogmorepress.co.uk. **Contact:** Jeremy Page, editor. *The Frogmore Papers*, published semiannually, is a literary magazine with emphasis on new poetry and short stories. Responds in 6 months. Subscription: £10/1 year (2 issues); £15/2 years (4 issues). Guidelines online.

🗨 *The Frogmore Papers* is 46 pages, photocopied in photo-reduced typescript, saddle-stapled, with matte card cover. Accepts 2% of poetry received. Press run is 500. Reading periods: October 1-31 for March issue and April 1-30 for September issue.

MAGAZINES NEEDS "Poems where the form drives the meaning are unlikely to find favour. Poems written by people who clearly haven't read any poetry since Wordsworth will not find favour. Prose may be experimental or traditional, but is unlikely to be accepted if it's either very experimental or very traditional." Has published poetry by Marita Over, Brian Aldiss, Carole Satyamurti, John Mole, Linda France, and Tobias Hill. Submit 4-6 poems by e-mail or mail (postal submissions only accepted from within the U.K.). Length: 20-80 lines/poem. Pays 1 contributor's copy.

ALSO OFFERS Sponsors the annual Frogmore Poetry Prize. Write for information.

FROGPOND: JOURNAL OF THE HAIKU SOCIETY OF AMERICA

Haiku Society of America, 985 S. Grandview Ave., Dubuque IA 52003. **E-mail:** fnbanwarth@yahoo. com. **Website:** www.hsa-haiku.org/frogpond. **Contact:** Francine Banwarth, editor. *Frogpond*, published triannually, is the international journal of the Haiku Society of America, an affiliate of the American Literature Association. Its primary function is to "publish the best in contemporary English-language haiku and senryu, linked forms including sequences, renku, rengay, and haibun, essays and articles on these forms, and book reviews." Responds at the end of each submission period (June 1-August 1; September 15-November 15; February 15-April 15). Single issue: $14. Subscription: USA, $35/year; Canada/Mexico, $37/ year; for seniors and students in North America, $30; elsewhere, $47/year. Guidelines available for SASE or on website. Detailed instructions on website.

MAGAZINES NEEDS Submissions to *Frogpond* by e-mail are preferred. "Postal submissions should be accompanied by SASE with sufficient U.S. postage to reach your location. Submit to fnbanwarth@yahoo. com or 985 S. Grandview, Dubuque, IA."

ALSO OFFERS The "Best of Issue" prize is awarded to a poem from each issue of *Frogpond* through a gift from the Museum of Haiku Literature, located in Tokyo. The Haiku Society of America also sponsors a number of other contests, most of which have cash prizes: The Harold G. Henderson Haiku Award Contest, the Gerald Brady Senryu Award Contest, the Bernard Lionel Einbond Memorial Renku Contest, the HSA Haibun Contest, the Nicholas A. Virgilio Memorial Haiku Competition for High School Students, the Mildred Kanterman Merit Book Awards for outstanding books in the haiku field. Guidelines available on website.

FUGUE LITERARY MAGAZINE

200 Brink Hall, University of Idaho, P.O. Box 44110, Moscow ID 83844. **E-mail:** fugue@uidaho.edu. **Website:** www.fuguejournal.org. **Contact:** Alexandra Teague, faculty advisor. Biannual literary magazine. "Submissions are accepted online only. Poetry, fiction, and nonfiction submissions are accepted September 1-April 1. All material received outside of this period will not be read." $3 submission fee per entry. See website for submission instructions. Responds in 3-6 months to mss. Sample copy: $8. Guidelines online.

 Work published in *Fugue* has won the Pushcart Prize and has been cited in *Best American Essays*.

MAGAZINES NEEDS Submit up to 3 poems using online submissions manager. Pays 2 contributor's copies and additional payment.

ALSO OFFERS "For information regarding our annual prose and poetry contest, please visit our website."

TIPS "The best way, of course, to determine what we're looking for is to read the journal. As the name *Fugue* indicates, our goal is to present a wide range of literary perspectives. We like stories that satisfy us both intellectually and emotionally, with fresh language and characters so captivating that they stick with us and invite a second reading. We are also seeking creative literary criticism which illuminates a piece of literature or a specific writer by examining that writer's personal experience."

GARBANZO LITERARY JOURNAL

Seraphemera Books, 211 Greenwood Ave., Suite 224, Bethel CT 06801. **E-mail:** storyteller@garbanzoliteraryjournal.org. **Website:** www.garbanzoliteraryjournal.org. **Contact:** Marc Moorash and Ava Dawn Heydt, co-editors. Limited-edition handmade book, also available at iBookstore. "We are calling out to all who have placed word on page (and even those who still carry all their works in the mind). Stories of up to 1,172 words, poems of up to 43 lines, micro-fiction, macro-fiction, limericks, villanelles, cinquains, couplets, couplings, creative nonfiction, noncreative fictions ... and whatever form your moving, thoughtful, memorable tale wishes to take (which means disregard the rules, punk-rock style). In our specific instance, there is always a light that shines through these works, always a redemption that happens in the end. We're whimsical and full of light, even though some of the subject matter and form is dark. If your work is full of sarcasm and cynicism, if your cover letter is full of the same, we're probably not a good fit to work with each other. We somewhat consider each issue of *Garbanzo* to be a moment in infinite space when a group of mostly disparate people wind up in the same room due to some strange space/time glitch. We're not all going to agree on everything, and we probably wouldn't all get along, but we're not going to waste that moment together in complaint ... We're going to celebrate each picking up a feather and causing this massive bird to fly ..." Pays on publication. Publishes ms 3 months after acceptance. "We respond once the submission period closes for each volume." Sample copy: $20.00 + shipping. Guidelines free by e-mail or online at website.

MAGAZINES NEEDS Length: 1-1,247 lines. Pays contributor's copies.

TIPS "Read our website and the various suggestions therein. We're not much for rules—so surprise us. In that same regard, if you send us certain things it will be immediately obvious that you are sending to us another long list and haven't bothered to learn about us. Those who pay attention to detail are far more interesting to work with—as we're very interactive with our published authors. We want people who want to work and play with our style of publishing as much as we want good writing."

GARGOYLE

Paycock Press, 3819 N. 13th St., Arlington VA 22201. (703)525-9296. **E-mail:** rchrdpeabody9@gmail.com. **E-mail:** gargoyle@gargoylemagazine.com. **Website:** www.gargoylemagazine.com. **Contact:** Richard Peabody, editor, Lucinda Ebersole, co-editor. "*Gargoyle* has always been a scallywag magazine, a maverick magazine, a bit too academic for the underground and way too underground for the academics. We are a writer's magazine in that we are read by other writers and have never worried about reaching the masses." Annual. Acquires first North American serial and first British rights. Publishes ms 1 year after acceptance. Responds in 1 month to queries, proposals, and mss. Sample copy: $12.95. Catalog available online at FAQ link. "We don't have guidelines; we have never believed in them." Query in an e-mail. "We prefer electronic submissions. Please use submission engine online." For snail mail, send SASE for reply and return of ms, or send a disposable copy of ms.

Accepts submissions from February 1 until full; in 2014 that was by February 14. Recently published work by Shane Allison, Rafael Alvarez, Carolyn Banks, Alison Bundy, Sophy Burnham, Valentina Cano, Theodore Carter, James Cervantes, Peter Cherches, Kelly Cherry, Joan Colby, Anne Colwell, Michael Daley, William Virgil Davis, Trevor Dodge, Sarah Einstein, Angela Featherstone, Thalia Field, Gary Fincke, Andy Fogle, Jesse Glass, Myronn Hardy, Lola Haskins, Allison Hedge-Coke, Wayne Karlin, Eurydice Kamyvisseli, W.F. Lantry, Nathan Leslie, Melvin E. Lewis, Lyn Lifshin, Adrian C. Louis, Mary Mackey, Nick Mamatas, David McAleavey, Margaret McCarthy, Franetta McMillian, Dora E. McQuaid, Mark Melnicove, Stephen C. Middleton, Roberto Montes, Samina Najmi, Amelie Olaiz, Jose Padua, Ted Pelton, Deborah Pintonelli, Shelley Puhak, Carol Quinn, Misti Rainwater-Lites, Kit Reed, Doug Rice, Lou Robinson, Stuart Ross, Tomaz Salamun, Lynda Schor, E.M. Schorb, Helen Maryles Shankman, Gregg Shapiro, Rose Solari, Marilyn Stablein, D.E. Steward, Art Taylor, David A. Taylor, An Tran, Michael Waters, Paul West, Tom Whalen, and Paula Whyman.

MAGAZINES NEEDS Pays contributor's copies.

TIPS "We have to fall in love with a particular fiction."

A GATHERING OF THE TRIBES

P.O. Box 20693, Tompkins Square Station, New York NY 10009. (212)777-2038. **E-mail:** gatheringofthetribes@gmail.com. **E-mail:** tribes.editor@gmail.com. **Website:** www.tribes.org. **Contact:** Steve Cannon. *A Gathering of the Tribes* is a multicultural and multigenerational publication featuring poetry, fiction, interviews, essays, visual art, and musical scores. Audience is anyone interested in the arts from a diverse perspective." Publishes ms 3-6 months after acceptance. "Due to the massive number of submissions we receive, we do not guarantee responses or return work that is not accepted for publication." Sample copy: $15. Guidelines on website.

Magazine: 8.5x10; 130 pages; glossy paper and cover; illustrations; photos. Receives 20 unsolicited mss/month. Publishes 40% new writers/year. Has published work by Carl Watson, Ishle Park, Wang Pang, and Hanif Kureishi. Sponsors awards/contests.

MAGAZINES NEEDS Submit up to 5 poems by postal mail or e-mail. No metrical or rhyming poetry, "unless it is exceedingly contemporary/experimental." Pays 1 contributor's copy.

TIPS "Make sure your work has substance."

THE GEORGIA REVIEW

The University of Georgia, Main Library, Room 706A, 320 S. Jackson St., Athens GA 30602. (706)542-3481. **Fax:** (706)542-0047. **E-mail:** garev@uga.edu. **Website:** thegeorgiareview.com. **Contact:** Stephen Corey, editor. "Our readers are educated, inquisitive people who read a lot of work in the areas we feature, so they expect only the best in our pages. All work submitted should show evidence that the writer is at least as well educated and well read as our readers. Essays should be authoritative but accessible to a range of readers." Buys first North American serial rights. Pays on publication. Publishes ms an average of 6 months after acceptance. Responds in 2 weeks to queries; in 2-3 months to mss. Sample copy: $10. Guidelines available online.

○ Electronic submissions available for $3 fee. Reading period: August 15-May 15.

MAGAZINES NEEDS "We seek original, excellent poetry. Submit 3-5 poems at a time." Pays $4/line.

GERTRUDE

P.O. Box 28281, Portland OR 97228. **E-mail:** editor@gertrudepress.org. *Gertrude*, the annual literary arts journal of Gertrude Press, is a "publication featuring the voices and visions of the gay, lesbian, bisexual, transgender, and supportive community." Responds in 9-12 months to mss. Sample copy: $8. Subscription: $18 for 1 year, $32 for 2 years.

MAGAZINES NEEDS Has published poetry by Judith Barrington, Deanna Kern Ludwin, Casey Charles, Michael Montlack, Megan Kruse, and Noah Tysick. Submit up to 6 poems via online submissions manager. Length: open, but "poems less than 60 lines are preferable."

TIPS "We look for strong characterization and imagery, and new, unique ways of writing about universal experiences. Follow the construction of your work until the ending. Many stories start out with zest, then flipper and die. Show us, don't tell us."

THE GETTYSBURG REVIEW

Gettysburg College, Gettysburg PA 17325. (717)337-6770. **Fax:** (717)337-6775. **E-mail:** pstitt@gettysburg.edu; mdrew@gettysburg.edu. **Website:** www.gettys-burgreview.com. **Contact:** Peter Stitt, editor; Ellen Hathaway, managing editor; Mark Drew, assistant editor. Published quarterly, *The Gettysburg Review* considers unsolicited submissions of poetry, fiction, and essays. "Our concern is quality. Manuscripts submitted here should be extremely well written. Reading period September 1-May 31." Buys first North American serial rights. Pays on publication. Publishes ms an average of 6 months after acceptance. Responds in 1 month to queries; in 3-5 months to mss. Editorial lead time 1 year. Sample copy: $10. Guidelines available online.

MAGAZINES NEEDS Considers "well-written poems of all kinds." Has published poetry by Rita Dove, Alice Friman, Philip Schultz, Michelle Boisseau, Bob Hicok, Linda Pastan, and G.C. Waldrep. Pays $2.50/line and 1 contributor's copy.

GINOSKO LITERARY JOURNAL

P.O. Box 246, Fairfax CA 94978. **E-mail:** editorginosko@aol.com. **Website:** www.ginoskoliteraryjournal.com. **Contact:** Robert Paul Cesaretti, editor. "*Ginosko* (ghin-océ-koe): To perceive, understand, realize, come to know; knowledge that has an inception, a progress, an attainment. The recognition of truth by experience." Accepting short fiction and poetry, creative nonfiction, interviews, social justice concerns, and literary insights for www.GinoskoLiteraryJournal.com. Copyright reverts to author. Editorial lead time 1-2 months. Guidelines available online at website.

○ Reads year round. Length of articles flexible; accepts excerpts. Publishing as semiannual ezine. Check downloadable issues on website for tone and style. Downloads free; accepts donations. Also looking for books, art, and music to post on website, and links to exchange. Member CLMP.

MAGAZINES NEEDS Submit via postal mail, e-mail (prefers attachments: .wps, .doc, or .rtf), or online submissions manager (https://ginosko.submittable.com/submit).

○ ○ GRAIN

P.O. Box 67, Saskatoon SK S7K 3K1, Canada. (306)244-2828. **Fax:** (306)565-8554. **E-mail:** grainmag@skwriter.com. **Website:** www.grainmagazine.ca. **Contact:** Rilla Friesen, editor. "*Grain, The Journal Of Eclectic Writing* is a literary quarterly that publishes engaging, diverse, and challenging writing and art by some of the best Canadian and international writers and artists. Every issue features superb new writing from both developing and established writers. Each issue also highlights the unique artwork of a different visual artist. *Grain* has garnered national and international recognition for its distinctive, cutting-edge content and design." Acquires first Canadian serial rights. Pays on publication. Typically responds in 3-6 months. Sample: $13 CAD. Subscription: $35 CAD/year, $55 CAD for 2 years. (See website for U.S. and foreign postage fees.) Guidelines available by SASE (or SAE and IRC), e-mail, or on website.

○ *Grain* is 112-128 pages, digest-sized, professionally printed. Press run is 1,100. Receives about 3,000 submissions/year. Submissions are read September-May only. Mss postmarked between June 1 and August 31 will not be read.

MAGAZINES NEEDS Has published poetry by Lorna Crozier, Don Domanski, Cornelia Haeussler, Patrick Lane, Karen Solie, and Monty Reid. Wants "high-quality, imaginative, well-crafted poetry." Submit up to 12 pages of poetry, typed in readable font on 1 side only. No fax or e-mail submissions; postal submissions only. Cover letter with all contact information, title(s), and genre of work is required. "No staples. Your name and address must be on every page. Pieces of more than 1 page must be numbered. Please only submit work in 1 genre at a time." Pays $50-250 CAD (depending on number of pages) and 2 contributor's copies.

TIPS "Only work of the highest literary quality is accepted. Read several back issues."

THE GREAT AMERICAN POETRY SHOW

P.O. Box 691197, West Hollywood CA 90069. (323)424-4943. **E-mail:** info@tgaps.net. **Website:** www.tgaps.net. **Contact:** Larry Ziman, editor/publisher. *The Great American Poetry Show*, published about every 3-5 years, is a hardcover serial-poetry anthology. "For Volume 1, we read over 8,000 poems from about 1,400 poets and accepted only 113 poems from 83 poets. For Volume 2, we read over 15,000 poems and accepted 134 poems from 92 poets." Press run for Volumes 1 and 2 was 1,000. Responds usually within 1-2 weeks ("depends on how busy we are"). Single copy: $35 (print), $.99 (e-book, download only).

○ *The Great American Poetry Show* is 150 pages, sheet-fed offset-printed, perfect-bound, with cloth cover and art/graphics.

MAGAZINES NEEDS Submit any number of poems at a time. Accepts e-mail submissions in body of e-mail or as attachment. Cover letter is optional. Include SASE. "If we reject a submission of your work, please send us another group to go through." Has published poetry by Carol Carpenter, Philip Wexler, Fredrick Zydek, Patrick Polak, Steve De France, Lois Swann, Alan Catlin, Kevin Pilkington, and Julie M. Tate. Wants poems on any subject, in any style, of any length. Pays 1 contributor's copy.

TIPS "Please visit our website with over 10,000 links to articles, essays, interviews, reviews, magazines, publishers, and blogs."

GREEN HILLS LITERARY LANTERN

Truman State University, Dept. of English, Truman State University, Kirksville MO 63501. **E-mail:** adavis@truman.edu. **Website:** ghll.truman.edu. **Contact:** Adam Brooke Davis, managing editor; Joe Benevento, poetry editor. *Green Hills Literary Lantern* is published annually, in June, by Truman State University. Historically, the print publication ran between 200-300 pages, consisting of poetry, fiction, reviews, and interviews. The digital magazine is of similar proportions and artistic standards. Open to the work of new writers, as well as more established writers. Holds all rights, but returns rights to author on request. Does not provide payment. Publishes ms an average of 6 months after acceptance. Responds in 2 months to mss; in 2 months on queries. Sample copies available online. Guidlines available online.

MAGAZINES NEEDS "We prefer poetry written by poets who are more interested in communicating something that seems important, beautiful, funny, or interesting to them than they are in making themselves seem erudite, clever, or in the know. We pay attention to all the usual things—command of line; attention to the sound, rhythm, and imagery; arresting figurative language—but we also seek poetry that has some investment of real feeling rather than bloodless exhibitions of technical talent." Length: No more than 60 lines/poem. No payment provided.

GREEN MOUNTAINS REVIEW

Johnson State College, 337 College Hill, Johnson VT 05656. (802)635-1350. **E-mail:** gmr@jsc.edu. **Website:** http://greenmountainsreview.com/. **Contact:** Elizabeth Powell, editor. The editors are open to a wide rane of styles and subject matter. Acquires first North American serial rights. Rights revert to author upon request. Publishes ms 6-12 months after acceptance. Responds in 1 month to queries; 6 months to mss. Sample copy for $7. Guidelines available free.

○ Open reading period: September 1-May 15.

MAGAZINES NEEDS Has published poetry by Carol Frost, Sharon Olds, Carl Phillips, David St. John, and David Wojahn.

TIPS "We encourage you to order some of our back issues to acquaint yourself with what has been accepted in the past."

THE GREENSBORO REVIEW

MFA Writing Program, 3302 HHRA Building, UNC-Greensboro, Greensboro NC 27402. (336)334-5459. **E-mail:** jlclark@uncg.edu. **Website:** tgronline.net. **Contact:** Jim Clark, editor. "A local lit mag with an international reputation. We've been 'old school' since 1965." Acquires first North American serial rights. Responds in about 4 months. Sample copy: $8. Guidelines online.

○ Stories for *the Greensboro Review* have been included in *Best American Short Stories, The O. Henry Awards Prize Stories, New Stories from The South* and *Pushcart Prize*. Does not accept e-mail submissions.

MAGAZINES NEEDS Submit via online submission form or postal mail. Include cover letter. Length: no length limit. Pays in contributor's copies.

TIPS "We want to see the best being written regardless of theme, subject, or style."

THE GRIFFIN

Gwynedd Mercy College, 1325 Sumneytown Pike, P.O. Box 901, Gwynedd Valley PA 19437-0901. (215)641-5518. **Fax:** (215)641-5552. **E-mail:** allego.d@gmercy. edu. **Website:** www.gmercyu.edu/about-gwynedd-mercy/publications/griffin. **Contact:** Dr. Donna M. Allego, editor. Published by Gwynedd Mercy University, *The Griffin* is a literary journal for the creative writer—subscribing to the belief that improving the human condition requires dedication to and respect for the individual and the community. Seeks works which explore universal qualities—truth, justice, integrity, compassion, mercy... Publishes poetry, short stories, short plays, and reflections. Does not buy rights. No payment. Writer can add publication to his/her cv. Publishes an average of 12 months after acceptance. Responds in 9 months to ms. Sample copy available on website. Guidelines available on website.

MAGAZINES NEEDS Any style of well-crafted verse considered. Submit complete poems via e-mail or on disk with a hard copy. Include short author bio. Length: up to 30 lines.

TIPS "Pay attention to the word length requirements, the mission of the magazine, and how to submit ms as set forth. These constitute the writer's guidelines listed online."

GUERNICA MAGAZINE

112 W. 27th St., Suite 600, New York NY 10001. **E-mail:** editors@guernicamag.com; art@guernicamag. com; publisher@guernicamag.com. **Website:** www. guernicamag.com. **Contact:** See masthead online for specific editors. "*Guernica* is called a 'great online literary magazine' by *Esquire*. *Guernica* contributors come from dozens of countries and write in nearly as many languages." Publishes mss 3-4 months from acceptance. Responds in 2 months. Guidelines online.

○ Received Caine Prize for African Writing, Best of the Net.

MAGAZINES NEEDS Submit 3-5 poems via online submissions manager. Accepts 15-20 poems/year. Has published James Galvin, Barbara Hamby, Terrance Hayes, Richard Howard.

TIPS "Please read the magazine first before submitting. Most stories that are rejected simply do not fit our approach. Submission guidelines available online."

GULF COAST: A JOURNAL OF LITERATURE AND FINE ARTS

4800 Calhoun Road, Houston TX 77204-3013. (713)743-3223. **E-mail:** editors@gulfcoastmag.org. **Website:** www.gulfcoastmag.org. **Contact:** Adrienne Perry, editor; Martin Rock, managing editor; Carlos Hernandez, digital editor; Conor Bracken, Katie Condon, Sam Mansfield, poetry editors; Julia Brown, Laura Jok, Dino Piacentini, fiction editors; Talia Mailman, Steve Sanders, nonfiction editors; Matthew Salesses, online fiction editor; Christopher Murray, online poetry editor; Talia Mailman, online nonfiction editor. Buys first North American serial rights. Publishes ms 6 months-1 year after acceptance. Responds in 4-6 months to mss. Sometimes comments on rejected mss. Back issue: $8, plus 7x10 SASE with 4 first-class stamps. Writer's guidelines for #10 SASE or on website.

○ Magazine: 7x9; approximately 300 pages; stock paper, gloss cover; illustrations; photos.

MAGAZINES NEEDS Submit up to 5 poems at a time. Considers simultaneous submissions with notification; no previously published poems. Cover letter is required. List previous publications and include a brief bio. Reads submissions September-April. Pays $50/page.

TIPS "Submit only previously unpublished works. Include a cover letter. Online submissions are strongly preferred. Stories or essays should be typed, double-spaced, and paginated with your name, address, and phone number on the first page and the title on subsequent pages. Poems should have your name, address, and phone number on the first page of each." The Annual Gulf Coast Prizes award publication and $1,500 each in poetry, fiction, and nonfiction; opens in December of each year. Honorable mentions in each category will receive a $250 second prize. Postmark/online entry deadline: March 22 of each year. Winners and honorable mentions will be announced in May. **Entry fee:** $23 (includes one-year subscription). Make checks payable to *Gulf Coast*. Guidelines available on website.

GULF STREAM MAGAZINE

English Department, FIU, Biscayne Bay Campus, 3000 NE 151 St., North Miami FL 33181. **E-mail:** gulfstreamfiu@yahoo.com. **Website:** www.gulfstreamlitmag.com. **Contact:** Paul Christiansen, editor-in-chief. "*Gulf Stream Magazine* has been publishing emerging and established writers of exceptional fiction, nonfiction, and poetry since 1989. We also publish interviews and book reviews. Past contributors include Sherman Alexie, Steve Almond, Jan Beatty, Lee Martin, Robert Wrigley, Dennis Lehane, Liz Robbins, Stuart Dybek, David Kirby, Ann Hood, Ha Jin, B.H. Fairchild, Naomi Shihab Nye, F. Daniel Rzicznek, and Connie May Fowler. *Gulf Stream Magazine* is supported by the Creative Writing Program at Florida International University in Miami, Florida. Each year we publish 2 online issues." Acquires first serial rights. Responds in 6 months. Guidelines online.

MAGAZINES NEEDS "Submit online only. Please read guidelines on website in full. Submissions that do not conform to our guidelines will be discarded. We do not accept e-mailed or mailed submissions. We read from September 1-November 1 and January 1-March 1." Cover letter is required. Wants "poetry of any style and subject matter as long as it's of high literary quality." Has published poetry by Robert Wrigley, Jan Beatty, Jill Bialosky, and Catherine Bowman.

TIPS "Looks for fresh, original writing—well-plotted stories with unforgettable characters, fresh poetry, and experimental writing. Usually longer stories do not get accepted. There are exceptions, however."

HAIGHT ASHBURY LITERARY JOURNAL

558 Joost Ave., San Francisco CA 94127. (415)584-8264. **E-mail:** haljeditor@gmail.com. **Website:** haightashburyliteraryjournal.wordpress.com; www.facebook.com/pages/Haight-Ashbury-Literary-Journal/365542018331. **Contact:** Alice Rogoff and Cesar Love, editors. *Haight Ashbury Literary Journal*, publishes "well-written poetry and fiction. *HALJ*'s voices are often of people who have been marginalized, oppressed, or abused. *HALJ* strives to bring literary arts to the general public, to the San Francisco community of writers, to the Haight Ashbury neighborhood, and to people of varying ages, genders, ethnicities, and sexual preferences. The Journal is produced as a tabloid to maintain an accessible price for low-income people." Rights revert to author. Responds in 4 months. Sample: $6. Subscription: $14 for 2 issues, $28 for 4 issues; $75 for back issues and future issues. Guidelines available for SASE.

MAGAZINES NEEDS Submit up to 6 poems at a time. Submit only once every 6 months. No e-mail submissions (unless overseas); postal submissions only. "Please type 1 poem to a page, put name and address on every page, and include SASE. No bio." Sometimes publishes theme issues (each issue changes its theme and emphasis). Has published poetry by Dan O'Connell, Diane Frank, Dancing Bear, Lee Herrick, Al Young, and Laura Beausoleil.

HANGING LOOSE

Hanging Loose Press, 231 Wyckoff St., Brooklyn NY 11217. **E-mail:** editor@hangingloosepress.com. **Website:** www.hangingloosepress.com. **Contact:** Robert Hershon, Dick Lourie, and Mark Pawlak, poetry editors. *Hanging Loose*, published in April and October, concentrates on the work of new writers. Wants excellent, energetic poems. Responds in 3 months. Sample: $14.

Hanging Loose is 120 pages, offset-printed on heavy stock, flat-spined, with 4-color glossy card cover. Considers poetry by teens (one section contains poems by high-school-age poets).

MAGAZINES NEEDS Submit up to 6 poems at a time. No fax or e-mail submissions; postal submissions only. "Would-be contributors should read the magazine first." Has published poetry by Sherman Alexie, Paul Violi, Donna Brook, Kimiko Hahn, Harvey Shapiro, and Ha Jin. Pays small fee and 2 contributor's copies.

ALSO OFFERS Hanging Loose Press does not consider unsolicited book mss or artwork.

HARPUR PALATE

English Department, P.O. Box 6000, Binghamton University, Binghamton NY 13902-6000. **E-mail:** harpur.palate@gmail.com. **Website:** harpurpalate. blogspot.com. **Contact:** Melanie J. Cordova, editor. *Harpur Palate*, published biannually, is "dedicated to publishing the best poetry and prose, regardless of style, form, or genre. We have no restrictions on subject matter or form. Quite simply, send us your highest-quality fiction and poetry." Buys first North American serial rights; buys electronic rights. Publishes ms an average of 1-2 months after acceptance. Responds in 1-3 week to queries; 2-4 months to mss. No response without SASE. Sometimes comments on rejected mss. Accepts simultaneous submissions if stated in the cover letter. Sample: $8. Current issue: $12. Subscription: $18/year (2 issues). Make checks payable to *Harpur Palate*. Guidelines available online.

⬤ Submission periods are September 1-November 15 for the Winter issue and February 1-April 15 for the Summer issue.

MAGAZINES NEEDS Submit no more than 10 pages total, and no more than 5 poems. No response without SASE. Considers simultaneous submissions, "but we must be notified immediately if the piece is taken somewhere else"; no previously published poems. Submissions can be made via submittable.com or by post. No e-mail submissions. Cover letter and SASE is required. Reads submissions during open submission period only. Poems are circulated to an editorial board. Seldom comments on rejected poems. Has published poetry by Sherman Alexie, Tess Gallagher, Alex Lemon, Marvin Bell, Ryan G. Van Cleave, Sascha Feinstein, Allison Joseph, Neil Shepard, and Ruth Stone. Pays 2 contributor copies.

TIPS "We are interested in high-quality writing of all genres but especially literary poetry and fiction. We also sponsor a fiction contest for the Summer issue

and a poetry and nonfiction contest for the Winter issue with $500 prizes."

HARTWORKS

D.C. Creative Writing Workshop, 601 Mississippi Ave. SE, Washington DC 20032. (202)445-4280. **E-mail:** nschwalb@dccww.org; info@dccww.org. **Website:** www.dccww.org. **Contact:** Nancy Schwalb, artistic director. *hArtworks* appears 3 times/year. "We publish the poetry of Hart Middle School students (as far as we know, Hart may be the only public middle school in the U.S. with its own poetry magazine) and the writing of guest writers such as Nikki Giovanni, Alan Cheuse, Arnost Lustig, Henry Taylor, Mark Craver, and Cornelius Eady, along with interviews between the kids and the grown-up pros. We also publish work by our writers-in-residence, who teach workshops at Hart, and provide trips to readings, slams, museums, and plays." Wants "vivid, precise, imaginative language that communicates from the heart as well as the head." Does not want "poetry that only 'sounds' good; it also needs to say something meaningful." Has published poetry by Maryum Abdullah, Myron Jones, Nichell Kee, Kiana Murphy, James Tindle, and Sequan Wilson. Single copy: $12; subscription: $30. Make checks payable to D.C. Creative Writing Workshop.

⬤ Although this journal doesn't accept submissions from the general public, it's included here as an outstanding example of what a literary journal can be (for anyone of any age). *hArtworks* is 92 pages, magazine-sized, professionally printed, perfect bound, with card cover. Receives about 1,000 poems/year, accepts about 20%. Press run is 500; 100 distributed free to writers, teachers.

MAGAZINES NEEDS "Writers-in-residence solicit most submissions from their classes, and then a committee of student editors makes the final selections. Each year, our second issue is devoted to responses to the Holocaust."

HARVARD REVIEW

Houghton Library of the Harvard College Library, Lamont Library, Harvard University, Cambridge MA 02138. (617)495-9775. **Fax:** (617)496-3692. **E-mail:** info@harvardreview.org. **Website:** harvardreview.fas. harvard.edu. **Contact:** Christina Thompson, editor; Suzanne Berne, fiction editor; Major Jackson, poetry editor. Semiannual magazine covering poetry, fiction, essays, drama, graphics, and reviews in the spring and fall by an eclectic range of international writers. "Previous contributors include John Updike, Alice Hoffman, Joyce Carol Oates, Miranda July, and Jim Crace. We also publish the work of emerging and previously unpublished writers." Responds in 6 months to mss.

○ Does not accept e-mail submissions. Reading period: September 1-May 31.

MAGAZINES NEEDS Submit up to 5 poems via online submissions manager or postal mail.

TIPS "Writers at all stages of their careers are invited to apply, however, we can only publish a very small fraction of the material we receive. We recommend that you familiarize yourself with *Harvard Review* before you submit your work."

HAWAI'I PACIFIC REVIEW

1060 Bishop St., Honolulu HI 96813. (808)544-1108. **Fax:** (808)544-0862. **Website:** hawaiipacificreview. org. **Contact:** Tyler McMahon, editor; Bianca Flores, managing editor. "*Hawai'i Pacific Review* is the online literary magazine of Hawai'i Pacific University. It features poetry and prose by authors from Hawai'i, the mainland, and around the world. *HPR* was started as a print annual in 1987. In 2013, it began to publish exclusively online. *HPR* publishes work on a rolling basis. Poems, stories, and essays are posted one piece at a time, several times a month. All contents are archived on the site." Acquires online rights. All other rights remain with the author.

MAGAZINES NEEDS Submit up to 5 poems at a time via online submissions manager (each poem should be a separate submission).

TIPS "We look for the unusual or original plot; prose with the texture and nuance of poetry. Character development or portrayal must be unusual/original; humanity shown in an original insightful way (or characters); sense of humor where applicable. Be sure it's a draft that has gone through substantial changes, with supervision from a more experienced writer, if you're a beginner. Write about intense emotion and feeling, not just about someone's divorce or shaky relationship. No soap-opera-like fiction."

HAWAII REVIEW

University of Hawaii Board of Publications, 2445 Campus Rd., Hemenway Hall 107, Honolulu HI 96822. (808)956-3030. **Fax:** (808)956-3083. **E-mail:** hawaiireview@gmail.com. **Website:** www.kaleo.org/hawaii_review. *Hawai'i Review* is a student run biannual literary and visual arts print journal featuring national and international writing and visual art, as well as regional literature and visual art of Hawai'i and the Pacific. Buys first North American serial rights, archive rights. Publishes ms an average of 3 months after acceptance. Responds in 3 months to mss. Sample copy: free, plus $5 shipping (back issue). Single copy: $12.50. Guidelines available online.

○ Accepts submissions online through Submittable only. Offers yearly award with $500 prizes in poetry and fiction.

MAGAZINES NEEDS Submit up to 6 poems via online submission manager. Length: up to 500 lines/poem (though space limitations are taken into account for longer poems).

TIPS "Make it new."

⑤ HAYDEN'S FERRY REVIEW

c/o Dept. of English, Arizona State University, P.O. Box 870302, Tempe AZ 85287. **E-mail:** hfr@asu.edu. **Website:** www.haydensferryreview.org. **Contact:** Editorial staff changes every year; see website for current masthead. "*Hayden's Ferry Review* publishes the best quality fiction, poetry, and creative nonfiction from new, emerging, and established writers." Buys first North American serial rights. No honorarium. Publishes ms an average of 6 months after acceptance. Responds in 1 week or less to e-mail queries; 3-4 months to mss. Editorial lead time 5 months. Sample copy: $13. Guidelines online.

○ Work from *Hayden's Ferry Review* has been selected for inclusion in *Pushcart Prize* anthologies and *Best Creative Nonfiction*. No longer accepts postal mail submissions.

MAGAZINES NEEDS Submit up to 6 poems via online submissions manager. Pays 2 contributor's copies and one-year subscription.

◑⊘ THE HELIX

E-mail: helixmagazine@gmail.com. **Website:** helixmagazine.org. **Contact:** See masthead online for current editorial staff. "*The Helix* is a Central Connecticut State University publication, and it puts out an issue every semester. It accepts submissions from all over the globe. The magazine features writing from CCSU students, writing from the Hartford County community, and an array of submissions from all over the world. The magazine publishes multiple genres of literature and art including: poetry, fiction, drama, nonfiction, paintings, photography, watercolor, collage, stencil, and computer-generated artwork. It is a student-run publication, and is funded by the university." Acquires first North American serial rights. All rights revert to author upon publication. Guidelines online. **MAGAZINES NEEDS** Submit by online submissions manager.

TIPS "Please see our website for specific deadlines, as it changes every semester based on a variety of factors, but we typically leave the submission manager open sometime starting in the summer to around the end of October for the Fall issue, and during the winter to late February or mid-March for the Spring issue. Contributions are invited from all members of the campus community, as well as the literary community at large."

HELLOHORROR

Houston TX **E-mail:** info@hellohorror.com. **E-mail:** submissions@hellohorror.com. **Website:** www.hellohorror.com. **Contact:** Brent Armour, editor-in-chief. "*HelloHorror* is an online literary magazine and blog. We are currently in search of literary pieces, photography, and visual art including film from writers and artists that have a special knack for inducing goose bumps and raised hairs. This genre has become, especially in film, noticeably saturated in gore and high shock-value aspects as a crutch to avoid the true challenge of bringing about real, psychological fear to an audience that's persistently more and more numb to its tactics. While we are not opposed to the extreme, blood and guts need bones and cartilage. Otherwise it's just a sloppy mess." Buys first serial rights. Publishes ms 3 months after acceptance. Responds in 1-6 months to queries and mss. Sample copy and guidelines available online at website. **MAGAZINES NEEDS** Submit poems via e-mail. "All types are accepted so long as they are of the horror genre."

TIPS "We like authors that show consideration for their readers. A great horror story leaves an impression on the reader long after it is finished. The motivation behind creating the site was the current saturation of gore and shock-value horror. A story that gives you goosebumps is a much greater achievement than a story that just grosses you out. We have television for that. Consider your reader and consider yourself. What really scares you as opposed to what's stereotypically supposed to scare you? Bring us and our readers into that place of fear with you."

HIGHLIGHTS FOR CHILDREN

803 Church St., Honesdale PA 18431. (570)253-1080. **Fax:** (570)251-7847. **Website:** www.highlights.com. **Contact:** Christine French Cully, editor-in-chief. "This book of wholesome fun is dedicated to helping children grow in basic skills and knowledge, in creativeness, in ability to think and reason, in sensitivity to others, in high ideals, and worthy ways of living—for children are the world's most important people. We publish stories for beginning and advanced readers. Up to 500 words for beginning readers, up to 800 words for advanced readers." Buys all rights. Pays on acceptance. Responds in 2 months to queries. Sample copy free. Guidelines on website in "Company" area. **MAGAZINES NEEDS** Lines/poem: 16 maximum ("most poems are shorter"). Considers simultaneous submissions ("please indicate"); no previously published poetry. No e-mail submissions. "Submit typed manuscript with very brief cover letter." Occasionally comments on submissions "if manuscript has merit or author seems to have potential for our market." Guidelines available for SASE. Responds "generally within 2 months." Always sends prepublication galleys. Pays 2 contributor's copies; "money varies." Acquires all rights.

TIPS "Know the magazine's style before submitting. Send for guidelines and sample issue if necessary." Writers: "At *Highlights* we're paying closer attention to acquiring more nonfiction for young readers than we have in the past." Illustrators: "Fresh, imaginative work encouraged. Flexibility in working relationships a plus. Illustrators presenting their work need not confine themselves to just children's illustrations as long as work can translate to our needs. We also use animal illustrations, real and imaginary. We need crafts, puzzles and any activity that will stimulate children mentally and creatively. Know our publication's standards and content by reading sample issues, not just the guidelines. Avoid tired themes, or put a fresh twist on an old theme so that its style is fun and lively. Write what inspires you, not what you think the market needs. We are pleased that many authors of children's literature report that their first published work was in the pages of *Highlights*. It is not our policy to consider fiction on the strength of the reputation of the author. We judge each submission on its own merits. Query with simple letter to establish whether the nonfiction subject is likely to be of interest. Expert reviews and complete bibliography required for nonfiction. A beginning writer should first become familiar with the type of material that *Highlights* publishes. Include special qualifications, if any, of author. Write for the child, not the editor. Write in a voice that children understand and relate to. Speak to today's kids, avoiding didactic, overt messages. Even though our general principles haven't changed over the years, we are contemporary in our approach to issues. Avoid worn themes."

HOLINESS TODAY

Nazarene Global Ministry Center, 17001 Prairie Star Pkwy., Lenexa KS 66220. (913)577-0500. **E-mail:** holinesstoday@nazarene.org. **Website:** www.holinesstoday.org. **Contact:** Carmen J. Ringhiser, managing editor; Frank M. Moore, editor in chief. *Holiness Today*, published bimonthly online and in print, is the primary print voice of the Church of the Nazarene, with articles geared to enhance holiness living by connecting Nazarenes with our heritage, vision, and mission through real-life stories of God at work in the world. *Holiness Today* (print) is 40 pages. Subscription: $12/year U.S.

THE HOLLINS CRITIC

P.O. Box 9538, Hollins University, Roanoke VA 24020-1538. **E-mail:** acockrell@hollins.edu. **Website:** www.hollins.edu/who-we-are/news-media/hollins-critic. **Contact:** Cathryn Hankla. *The Hollins Critic*, published 5 times a year, presents the first serious surveys of the whole bodies of contemporary writers' work, with complete checklists. In past issues, you'll find essays on such writers as John Engels (by David Huddle), James McCourt (by David Rollow), Jane Hirshfield (by Jeanne Larsen), Edwidge Danticat (by Denise Shaw), Vern Rutsala (by Lewis Turco), Sarah Arvio (by Lisa Williams), and Milton Kessler (by Liz Rosenberg). Buys first North American serial rights. Pays on publication. Publishes ms an average of 1 year after acceptance. Responds in 2 months to mss. Sample copy for $3. Guidelines for #10 SASE.

○ Uses a few short poems in each issue, interesting in form, content, or both. *The Hollins Critic* is 24 pages, magazine-sized. Press run is 500. Subscription: $12/year ($17 outside US). No postal or e-mail submissions. Has published poetry by Natasha Trethewey, Carol Moldaw, David Huddle, Margaret Gibson, and Julia Johnson.

MAGAZINES NEEDS Submit up to 5 poems at a time using the online submission form at www.

hollinscriticsubmissions.com, available September 15-December 1. Submissions received at other times will be returned unread. Reading period: September 15-December 15. Publishes 16-20 poems/year. Pays $25/poem plus 5 contributor's copies.

TIPS "We accept unsolicited poetry submissions; all other content is by prearrangement."

HOME PLANET NEWS

P.O. Box 455, High Falls NY 12440. (845)687-4084. **E-mail:** homeplanetnews@gmail.com. **Website:** www.homeplanetnews.org. **Contact:** Donald Lev, editor. Triannual. *Home Planet News* publishes mainly poetry along with some fiction, as well as reviews (books, theater, and art) and articles of literary interest. Acquires one-time rights. Publishes ms 1 year after acceptance. Responds in 6 months to mss. Sample copy: $4. Guidelines available for SASE or on website. Usually best to just send work.

○ *HPN* has received a small grant from the Puffin Foundation for its focus on AIDS issues. Receives 12 unsolicited mss/month. Accepts 1 mss/issue; 3 mss/year. Has published work by Hugh Fox, Walter Jackman, and Jim Story. "Our spin-off publication, *Home Planet News Online*, can be found at homeplanetnews.org/AOnLine.html. We urge everyone to check it out."

MAGAZINES NEEDS Submit 3-6 poems at a time. Cover letter is preferred. Send SASE. Seldom comments on rejected poems. Occasionally publishes theme issues. Upcoming themes available in magazine. Reviews books/chapbooks of poetry and other magazines in 1,200 words, single- and multibook format. Send materials for review consideration to Donald Lev. "Note: We do have guidelines for book reviewers; please write for them or check website. Magazines are reviewed by a staff member." Length: no limit, but shorter poems (under 30 lines) stand a better chance. Pays one-year gift subscription plus 3 contributor's copies.

TIPS "We use very little fiction, and a story we accept just has to grab us. We need short pieces of some complexity, stories about complex people facing situations which resist simple resolutions."

HOMESTEAD REVIEW

Box A-5, 156 Homestead Ave., Hartnell College, Salinas CA 93901. (831)755-6700. **E-mail:** thehomesteadreview@gmail.com. **Website:** http://old-www.hartnell.edu/homestead_review/. *Homestead Review* is published twice a year by the Department of Language Arts, Hartnell College. The spring issue is published in both print and online versions. The fall issue is published online only. Acquires one-time rights. Publishes ms 6 months after acceptance. Responds in 5 months. Guidelines for SASE.

○ Reading Period: February 1-June 1 for online fall issue, September 1-December 1 for spring online/print issue.

MAGAZINES NEEDS Submit 3-5 poems at a time. Include a biographical sketch, e-mail, and mailing addresses. Pays 1 contributor's copy.

ⓢ HOOT

A postcard review of {mini} poetry and prose, 1413 Academy Lane, Elkins Park PA 19027. **E-mail:** info@hootreview.com. **E-mail:** onlinesubmissions@hoot-review.com. **Website:** www.hootreview.com. **Contact:** Amanda Vacharat and Dorian Geisler, editors/co-founders. *HOOT* publishes 1 piece of writing, designed with original art/photographs, on the front of a postcard every month, as well as 2-3 pieces online. The postcards are intended for sharing, to be hung on the wall, etc. Therefore, *HOOT* looks for very brief, surprising-yet-gimmick-free writing that can stand on its own, that also follows "The Refrigerator Rule"—something that you would hang on your refrigerator and would want to read and look at for a whole month. This rule applies to online content as well. Buys first North American serial rights and electronic rights. Pays on publication. Publishes ms 2 months after acceptance. Sample copy: $2. Writer's guidelines available on website.

○ Costs $2 to submit up to 2 pieces of work. Submit through online submissions manager.

MAGAZINES NEEDS Length: up to 10 lines. Pays $10-100 for print publication.

TIPS "We look for writing with audacity and zest from authors who are not afraid to take risks. We appreciate work that is able to go beyond mere description in its 150 words. We offer free online workshops every otherWednesday for authors who would like feedback on their work from the *HOOT* editors. We also often give feedback with our rejections. We publish roughly 6-10 new writers each year."

HORIZONS

100 Witherspoon St., Louisville KY 40202-1396. (844)797-2872. **E-mail:** yvonne.hileman@pcusa.org. **Website:** www.pcusa.org/horizons. **Contact:**

Yvonne Hileman, assistant editor. *Horizons* magazine provides information, inspiration, and education from the perspectives of women who are committed to Christ, the church and faithful discipleship. *Horizons* brings current issues dealing with family life, the mission of the church and the challenges of culture and society to its readers. Interviews, feature articles, Bible study resources, and departments offer help and insight for up-to-date, day-to-day concerns of the church and individual Christians. Buys all rights. Pays on publication. Publishes ms an average of 4 months after acceptance. Sample copy for $4 and 9x12 SAE. Guidelines for writers are on the *Horizons* website.

MAGAZINES NEEDS Accepts poems of varying themes and topics.

HOTEL AMERIKA

Columbia College, English Department, 600 S. Michigan Ave., Chicago IL 60605. (312)369-8175. **E-mail:** editors@hotelamerika.net. **Website:** www.hotelamerika.net. **Contact:** David Lazar, editor; Adam McOmber, managing editor. *Hotel Amerika* is a venue for both well-known and emerging writers. Publishes exceptional writing in all forms. Strives to house the most unique and provocative poetry, fiction, and nonfiction available. Guidelines online.

○ Mss will be considered between September 1 and May 1. Materials received after May 1 and before September 1 will be returned unread. Send submissions only via mail, with SASE. Work published in *Hotel Amerika* has been included in *The Pushcart Prize* and *The Best American Poetry* and featured on *Poetry Daily*.

MAGAZINES NEEDS Welcomes submissions in all genres.

HUBBUB

5344 SE 38th Ave., Portland OR 97202. **E-mail:** lisa.steinman@reed.edu. **Website:** www.reed.edu/hubbub. J. Shugrue and Lisa M. Steinman, co-editors. *Hubbub*, published once/year, is designed "to feature a multitude of voices from interesting, contemporary American poets." Wants "poems that are well crafted, with something to say. We have no single style, subject, or length requirement and in particular will consider long poems." Acquires first North American serial rights. Responds in 4 months. Sample copy: $3.35 (back issues), $7 (current issue). Subscription: $7/year. Guidelines available for SASE.

Hubbub is 50-70 pages, digest-sized, offset-printed, perfect-bound, with cover art. Receives about 1,200 submissions/year, accepts up to 2%. Press run is 350.

MAGAZINES NEEDS Submit 3-6 typed poems at a time. Include SASE. "We review 2-4 poetry books/year in short (3-page) reviews; all reviews are solicited. We do, however, list books received/recommended." Send materials for review consideration. Has published poetry by Madeline DeFrees, Cecil Giscombe, Carolyn Kizer, Primus St. John, Shara McCallum, and Alice Fulton. Does not want light verse. Pays $20/poem.

ALSO OFFERS Outside judges choose poems from each volume for 4 awards: Vern Rutsala Award ($1,000), Vi Gale Award ($500), Stout Award ($75), and Kenneth O. Hanson Award ($100). There are no special submission procedures or entry fees involved.

THE HUDSON REVIEW

The Hudson Review, Inc., 684 Park Ave., New York NY 10065. (212)650-0020. **E-mail:** info@hudsonreview.com. **Website:** hudsonreview.com. **Contact:** Paula Deitz, editor. Pays on publication. Publishes ms an average of 6 months after acceptance. Responds in 6 months to mss. Editorial lead time 3 months. Sample copy: $11. Guidelines online.

Send with SASE. Mss sent outside accepted reading period will be returned unread if SASE contains sufficient postage.

MAGAZINES NEEDS Submit up to 7 poems by postal mail between **April 1-June 30** only.

TIPS "We do not specialize in publishing any particular 'type' of writing; our sole criterion for accepting unsolicited work is literary quality. The best way for you to get an idea of the range of work we publish is to read a current issue. Unsolicited mss submitted outside of specified reading times will be returned unread. Do not send submissions via e-mail."

🟢 HUNGER MOUNTAIN

Vermont College of Fine Arts, 36 College St., Montpelier VT 05602. (802)828-8517. **E-mail:** hungermtn@vcfa.edu. **Website:** www.hungermtn.org. **Contact:** Miciah Bay Gault, editor. Accepts high-quality work from unknown, emerging, or successful writers. No genre fiction, drama, or academic articles, please. Buys first worldwide serial rights. Pays on publication. Publishes ms an average of 1 year after acceptance. Responds in 4 months to mss. Single copy: $10; subscrip-

tion: $12/year, $22 for 2 years. Make checks payable to Vermont College of Fine Arts. Guidelines online.

Hunger Mountain is about 200 pages, 7x10, professionally printed, perfect-bound, with full-bleed color artwork on cover. Press run is 1,000; 10,000 visits online monthly. Uses online submissions manager. Member: CLMP.

MAGAZINES NEEDS Submit 3-10 poems at a time. All poems should be in **1** file. "We look for poetry that is as much about the world as about the self, that's an invitation, an opening out, a hand beckoning. We like poems that name or identify something essential that we may have overlooked. We like poetry with acute, precise attention to both content and diction." Submit using online submissions manager. No light verse, humor/quirky/catchy verse, greeting card verse.

ALSO OFFERS Annual contests: Ruth Stone Poetry Prize; The Howard Frank Mosher Short Fiction Prize; the Katherine Paterson Prize for Young Adult and Children's Writing; The Hunger Mountain Creative Nonfiction Prize. Visit www.hungermtn.org for information about prizes.

TIPS "Mss must be typed, prose double-spaced. Poets submit at least 3 poems. No multiple genre submissions. Fresh viewpoints and human interest are very important, as is originality. We are committed to publishing an outstanding journal of the arts. Do not send entire novels, mss, or short story collections. Do not send previously published work."

HYDE PARK LIVING

(859)291-1412. **E-mail:** hydepark@livingmagazines.com. **Website:** www.livingmagazines.com. **Contact:** Grace DeGregorio. Buys all rights. Pays on publication. Editorial lead time 2 months. Guidelines by e-mail.

MAGAZINES NEEDS Please query.

I-70 REVIEW

Writing From the Middle and Beyond, 913 Joseph Dr., Lawrence KS 66044. **E-mail:** i70review@gmail.com. **Website:** www.fieldinfoserv.com. **Contact:** Gary Lechliter, editor; Maryfrances Wagner, editor; Greg Field, editor; Jan Duncan-O'Neal, editor. *I-70 Review* is an annual literary magazine. "Our interests lie in writing grounded in fresh language, imagery, and metaphor. We prefer free verse in which the writer pays attention to the sound and rhythm of the language. We appreciate poetry with individual voice and a good lyric or a strong narrative. In fiction, we like short pieces that are surprising and uncommon. We want writing that captures the human spirit with unusual topics or familiar topics with different perspective or approaches. We reject stereotypical and clichéd writing, as well as sentimental work or writing that summarizes and tells instead of shows. We look for writing that pays attention to wrds, sentences, and style. We publish literary writing. We do not publish anything erotic, religious, or political." All submissions should be typed and submitted in a single document via e-mail. See website for complete guidelines. Open submission period is July 1-December 1. Buys one-time, first North American serial rights. Pays with contributor copies only. Publishes annually in September. Responds in 4-6 weeks, sometime sooner, on queries. Sample poetry available online. Sample copy available for SASE and $13.50 (issue plus postage/handling). Guidelines available online or by e-mail.

MAGAZINES NEEDS "We publish a variety of literary styles but prefer lyric and narrative. We want nothing sentimental, nothing with sing-songy rhyme, nothing abstract or clichéd or predictable. Nothing political, religious, didactic, or erotic. We accept some experimental as long as it is well-crafted and accessible. We reject writing that makes no sense or provides no meaning for the reader, and we rarely publish work difficult to format." Line length: 3-40 maximum. Pays in contributor copies.

IBBETSON ST. PRESS

25 School St., Somerville MA 02143-1721. **E-mail:** dougholder@post.harvard.edu. **Website:** ibbetsonpress.com. **Contact:** Doug Holder, editor; Rene Schwiesow and Lawrence Kessenich, managing editors; Harris Gardner, poetry editor. *Ibbetson St. Press*, published semiannually in June and November, prints "down-to-earth" poetry that is well written and has clean, crisp images with a sense of irony and humor. Wants mostly free verse but is open to rhyme. Does not want maudlin, trite, overly political, vulgar-for-vulgar's-sake work. Acquires one-time rights. Time between acceptance and publication is up to 8 months. Responds in 2 months. Single copy: $8; subscription: $13. Make checks payable to *Ibbetson St. Press*. Guidelines available for SASE.

○ *Ibbetson St. Press* is 50 pages, magazine-sized, desktop-published, with glossy white cover; includes ads. Receives about 1,000 poems/year, accepts up to 10%. Press run is 200. Also archived at Harvard, Brown, University of Wisconsin, Poets House-NYC, Endicott College, and Buffalo University Libraries.

MAGAZINES NEEDS Submit 3-5 poems at a time. E-mail submissions only. Cover letter is required. Three editors comment on submissions. Has published poetry by Marge Piercy, X.J. Kennedy, Ted Kooser, Elizabeth Swados, Teisha Twomey, Gloria Mindock, Harris Gardner, Diana-der Hovanessian, Michael Todd Steffan, and Gary Metras. Does not accept unsolicited chapbook mss. Has published *Dead Beats* by Sam Cornish, *On the Wings of Song* by Molly Lynn Watt, *Fairytales and Misdemeanors* by Jennifer Matthews, *Steerage* by Bert Stern, *From the Paris of New England* by Doug Holder, *Ti and Blood Soaked*; *East of the Moon* by Ruth Kramer Baden, and *Lousia Solano: The Grolier Poetry Book Shop* edited by Steve Glines and Doug Holder. Pays 1 contributor's copy.

ALSO OFFERS Reviews books/chapbooks of poetry and other magazines in 250-500 words. Send materials for review consideration.

☉ ICONOCLAST

1675 Amazon Rd., Mohegan Lake NY 10547-1804. **Website:** www.iconoclastliterarymagazine.com. **Contact:** Phil Wagner, editor and publisher. *Iconoclast Magazine* seeks and chooses the best new writing and poetry available—of all genres and styles and entertainment levels. Its mission is to provide a serious publishing opportunity for unheralded, unknown but deserving creators, whose work is often overlooked or trampled in the commercial, university, or Internet marketplace. Buys first North American serial rights. Responds in 6 weeks to mss. Sample copy: $5. Subscription: $20 for 6 issues.

MAGAZINES NEEDS "Try for originality; if not in thought than expression. No greeting card verse or noble religious sentiments. Look for the unusual in the usual, parallels in opposites, the capturing of what is unique or often unnoticed in an ordinary or extraordinary moment. What makes us human—and the resultant glories and agonies. The universal usually wins out over the personal. Rhyme isn't as easy as it looks—especially for those unversed in its study." Submit by postal mail; include SASE. Cover letter not necessary. Length: up to 2 pages. Pays $2-6/poem and 1 contributor's copy per page or work. Contributors get 40% discount on extra copies.

TIPS "Please don't send preliminary drafts—rewriting is half the job. If you're not sure about the story, don't truly believe in it, or are unenthusiastic about the subject (we will not recycle your term papers or thesis), then don't send it. This is not a lottery (luck has nothing to do with it)."

THE IDAHO REVIEW

Dept. of English, Boise State University, 1910 University Dr., Boise ID 83725. (208)426-1002. **Fax:** (208)426-4373. **E-mail:** idahoreview@boisestate.edu; mwieland@boisestate.edu. **Website:** idahoreview.org. **Contact:** Mitch Wieland, editor. *The Idaho Review* is the literary journal of Boise State University. Acquires one-time rights. Pays on publication. Publishes ms 1 year after acceptance. Responds in 3-5 months. Guidelines available online.

Recent stories reprinted in *The Best American Short Stories, The O. Henry Prize Stories, The Pushcart Prize*, and *New Stories from The South*.

MAGAZINES NEEDS Submit up to 5 poems. Prefers submissions using online submissions manager, but will accept submissions by postal mail.

TIPS "We look for strongly crafted work that tells a story that needs to be told. We demand vision and intelligence and mystery in the fiction we publish."

IDIOM 23

Central Queensland University, Idiom 23 Literary Magazine, Rockhampton QLD 4702, Australia. **E-mail:** idiom@cqu.edu.au. **Website:** www.cqu.edu.au/idiom23. **Contact:** *Idiom 23* editorial board. *Idiom 23*, published annually, is "named for the Tropic of Capricorn and is dedicated to developing the literary arts throughout the Central Queensland region. Submissions of original short stories, poems, articles, and b&w drawings and photographs are welcomed by the editorial collective. *Idiom 23* is not limited to a particular viewpoint but, on the contrary, hopes to encourage and publish a broad spectrum of writing. The collective seeks out creative work from community groups with as varied backgrounds as possible." Single copy: $20, available at bookshop.cqu.edu.au. See website for submission details. Electronic submissions only.

ILLUMINATIONS

Dept. of English, College of Charleston, 66 George St., Charleston SC 29424-0001. (843)953-4972. **E-mail:** illuminations@cofc.edu. **Website:** illuminations.cofc.edu. **Contact:** Simon Lewis, editor. "Over these many years *Illuminations* has remained consistently true to its mission statement to publish new writers alongside some of the world's finest, including Nadine Gordimer, James Merrill, Carol Ann Duffy, Dennis Brutus, Allen Tate, interviews with Tim O'Brien, and letters from Flannery O'Connor and Ezra Pound. A number of new poets whose early work appeared in *Illuminations* have gone on to win prizes and accolades, and we at *Illuminations* sincerely value the chance to promote the work of emerging writers." Returns rights on request. Sample copy: $10.

MAGAZINES NEEDS Open to any form and style, and to translations. Does not want to see anything "bland or formally clunky." Has published poetry by Brenda Marie Osbey, Geri Doran, Dennis Brutus, and Carole Satyamurti. Submit up to 6 poems at a time. Pays 2 contributor's copies of current issue; 1 of subsequent issue.

IMAGE

3307 Third Ave. W., Seattle WA 98119. (206)281-2988. **Fax:** (206)281-2979. **E-mail:** image@imagejournal.org. **Website:** www.imagejournal.org. **Contact:** Gregory Wolfe, publisher and editor in chief. "*Image* is a unique forum for the best writing and artwork that is informed by—or grapples with—religious faith. We have never been interested in art that merely regurgitates dogma or falls back on easy answers or didacticism. Instead, our focus has been on writing and visual artwork that embody a spiritual struggle, that seek to strike a balance between tradition and a profound openness to the world. Each issue explores this relationship through outstanding fiction, poetry, painting, sculpture, architecture, film, music, interviews, and dance. *Image* also features 4-color reproductions of visual art." Buys first North American serial rights. Pays on acceptance. Publishes ms an average of 8 months after acceptance. Responds in 1 month to queries; in 5 months to mss. Sample copy: $16 or available online. Guidelines online.

Magazine: 7×10; 136 pages; glossy cover stock; illustrations; photos.

MAGAZINES NEEDS Wants poems that grapple with religious faith, usually Judeo-Christian. Submit by mail. Send SASE for reply, return of ms, or send disposable copy of ms. Does not accept e-mail submissions. Pays $2/line ($150 maximum) and 4 contributor's copies.

TIPS "Fiction must grapple with religious faith, though subjects need not be overtly religious."

INDEFINITE SPACE

P.O. Box 40101, Pasadena CA 91114. **E-mail:** indefinitespace@yahoo.com. **Website:** www.indefinitespace.net. "Published annually. From minimalist to avant garde, *Indefinite Space* is open to innovative, imagistic, philosophical, experimental creations: poetry, drawings, collage, photography. Reads year round." Poet retains copyright. Responds in 3 months. Seldom comments on rejected poems. Single copy: $8; subscription: $14 for 2 issues. Make checks payable to Marcia Arrieta.

○ *Indefinite Space* is 48 pages, digest-sized.

MAGAZINES NEEDS No rhyming poetry. Has published poetry by Andrea Moorhead, Rob Cook, Linda King, Bob Heman, Khat Xiong, and Guy R. Beining. Pays 1 contributor's copy.

$ INDIANA REVIEW

Ballantine Hall 465, 1020 E. Kirkwood, Indiana University, Bloomington IN 47405. (812)855-3439. **E-mail:** inreview@indiana.edu. **Website:** indianareview.org. **Contact:** Britt Ashley, editor; Justin Wolfe, nonfiction editor; Joe Hiland, fiction editor; Michael Mlekoday, poetry editor. "*Indiana Review*, a nonprofit organization run by IU graduate students, is a journal of previously unpublished poetry and fiction. Literary interviews and essays are also considered. We publish innovative fiction, nonfiction, and poetry. We're interested in energy, originality, and careful attention to craft. While we publish many well-known writers, we also welcome new and emerging poets and fiction writers." Buys first North American serial rights. Pays on publication. Publishes ms an average of 3-6 months after acceptance. Responds in 2 or more weeks to queries; in 4 or more months to mss. Sample copy: $12. Guidelines available online. "We no longer accept hard-copy submissions. All submissions must be made online."

MAGAZINES NEEDS "We look for poems that are skillful and bold, exhibiting an inventiveness of language with attention to voice and sonics." Wants experimental, free verse, prose poem, traditional form, lyrical, narrative. Length: 5 lines minimum. Pays $5/page ($10 minimum), plus 2 contributor's copies.

CONTEST/AWARD OFFERINGS Holds yearly poetry and prose poem contests.

TIPS "We're always looking for nonfiction essays that go beyond merely autobiographical revelation and utilize sophisticated organization and slightly radical narrative strategies. We want essays that are both lyrical and analytical where confession does not mean nostalgia. Read us before you submit. Often reading is slower in summer and holiday months. Only submit work to journals you would proudly subscribe to, then subscribe to a few. Take care to read the latest 2 issues and specifically mention work you identify with and why. Submit work that 'stacks up' with the work we've published. Offers annual poetry, fiction, short short/prose poem prizes. See website for full guidelines."

$ INDIA-USA PUNJABI ENGLISH MAGAZINE

22619 97th Ave. S., Kent WA 98031. **E-mail:** aasra@q.com. **Contact:** Sarab Singh, editor. *India-USA Punjabi English Magazine*, formerly *Aasra Punjabi English Magazine*, published bimonthly, features current events mainly Indian, but has featured others, too, of interest. Also features interviews, yoga, and other articles, and poetry. Acquires one-time rights. Rights revert to poet upon publication. Time between acceptance and publication is 2 months. Sometimes comments on rejected poems. Single copy: $3 (postage); subscription: $20/year. "The magazine is distributed free in the Seattle area and available through other libraries. We charge $3 per copy for p&h or $2 per copy if you purchase more than 10 copies. Back issue: $2." Guidelines in magazine. "We will print 1 poem per issue. We usually charge $4 to print a small poem and more for long poems. (Please note we do not send a free copy in which your poem is printed. The money usually goes to cover p&h.)"

○ Magazine: Measures approximately 8.5x11, press printed, staple bound, includes ads. Page count varies.

MAGAZINES NEEDS Submit 1-2 small poems at a time. Cover letter is required. Include SASE, name, address, telephone number, and e-mail address with age and gender on cover letter. Include a short bio. "If interested we can print 'About the Poet' along with the poem." Reads submissions year round. Sometimes publishes theme issues. Has published poetry by Tripat Singh, Elizabeth Tallmadge, and Carmen Arhiveleta.

CONTEST/AWARD OFFERINGS Best Poem of the Year is awarded one-year free subscription.

INNISFREE POETRY JOURNAL

E-mail: editor@innisfreepoetry.org. **Website:** www.innisfreepoetry.org. **Contact:** Greg McBride, editor.

Innisfree Poetry Journal "welcomes original, previously unpublished poems year round. We accept poems only via e-mail from both established and new writers whose work is excellent. We publish well-crafted poems, poems grounded in the specific which speak in fresh language and telling images. And we admire musicality. We welcome those who, like the late Lorenzo Thomas, 'write poems because I can't sing.'" Acquires first North American serial rights. "Acquires first publication rights, including the right to publish it online and maintain it there as part of the issue in which it appears, to make it available in a printer-friendly format, to make the issue of *Innisfree* in which it appears downloadable as a PDF document and available as a printed volume. All other rights revert to the poet after online publication of the poem in *The Innisfree Poetry Journal*." Guidelines available on website.

MAGAZINES NEEDS Submit up to 5 poems by e-mail; single Word attachment. "Include your name as you would like it to appear in *Innisfree* in the subject line of your submission. Format all poems flush with the left margin—no indents other than any within the poem itself. Simultaneous submissions are welcome. If a poem is accepted elsewhere, however, please be sure to notify us immediately."

⊖ INTERPRETER'S HOUSE

Tryst Cottage, 16 Main Street, Monks Kirby, Nr Rugby Warwickshire CV23 0QX, England. **E-mail:** theinterpretershouse@aol.com. **Website:** www.theinterpretershouse.com. **Contact:** Martin Malone, editor. *The Interpreter's House*, published 3 times/year in February, June, and October, prints short stories and poetry. Responds in 3 months. Sample copy: £5 plus £1.20 postage. Guidelines for SASE.

○ Submission windows: October for the Spring issue, February for the Summer issue, June for the Autumn issue.

MAGAZINES NEEDS Submit by mail (include SASE) or e-mail (as a single Word attachment). Wants "good poetry, not too long." Does not want "Christmas-card verse or incomprehensible poetry." Has published poetry by Dannie Abse, Tony Curtis, Pauline Stainer, Alan Brownjohn, Peter Redgrove, and R.S. Thomas. "All work is dealt with swiftly. Usually no more than 1 poem is accepted, and writers who have already appeared in the magazine are asked to wait for at least a year before submitting again." Pays in contributor's copies.

IODINE POETRY JOURNAL

P.O. Box 18548, Charlotte NC 28218. (704)595-9526. **E-mail:** iodineopencut@aol.com. **Website:** www.iodinepoetryjournal.com. **Contact:** Jonathan K. Rice, editor/publisher. *Iodine Poetry Journal*, published semiannually, provides "a venue for both emerging and established poets." Acquires first North American serial rights. Time between acceptance and publication is 6 months to 1 year. Responds in 2-3 months. Single copy: $8; subscription: $14/year (2 issues) $26 for 2 years (4 issues). Sample: "Back issues vary in price." Make checks payable to *Iodine Poetry Journal*. Guidelines available in magazine, for SASE, or on website.

○ Poetry published in *Iodine Poetry Journal* has been selected for inclusion in *The Best American Poetry*. *Iodine Poetry Journal* is 84 pages, digest-sized, perfect-bound, with full-color laminated cover; includes ads. Receives about 2,000 poems/year, accepts about 75 poems/issue. Press run is 350.

MAGAZINES NEEDS Submit 3-5 poems at a time. Accepts e-mail submissions from international poets only; no disk submissions. Cover letter is preferred. "Always include SASE, and specify if SASE is for return of ms or reply only. I like a brief introduction of yourself in the cover letter." Reads submissions year round. Poems are circulated to an editorial board. Associate editors assist in the selection process. Sometimes comments on rejected poems. Sometimes sends prepublication galleys. Has published poetry by Fred Chappell, Colette Inez, Ron Koertge, Dorianne Laux, and R.T. Smith. Length: 40 lines/poem or less preferred, "but not totally averse to longer poems." Pays 1 contributor's copy and discounts extra copies of the issue in which work appears.

TIPS "We no longer publish our broadside, *Open Cut*."

⊖ IOTA

P.O. Box 7721, Matlock, Derbyshire DE4 9DD, England. (44)01629 582500. **E-mail:** info@iotamagazine.co.uk. **E-mail:** submissions@templarpoetry.co.uk. **Website:** www.iotamagazine.co.uk. **Contact:** Nigel McLoughlin, editor. *Iota* considers "any style and subject; no specific limitations as to length." Has published poetry by Jane Kinninmont, John Robinson, Tony Petch, Chris Kinsey, Christopher James, and

Michael Kriesel. Responds in 3 months (unless production of the next issue takes precedence).

○ *Iota* is 120 or more pages, professionally printed, litho stitched, with full-color cover. Receives 6,000 poems/year, accepts about 300. Press run is around 1,000. Single copy: £6.99 UK; subscription: £18 UK, £25 outside UK.

MAGAZINES NEEDS Submit up to 6 poems at a time. No previously published poems or simultaneous submissions. Cover letter is required. Prefers name and address on each poem, typed. "No SAE, no reply." Online submissions now accepted; see details at www.iotamagazine.co.uk/submissions." Reviews books of poetry. Send materials for review consideration. There is a $1 administration fee for submitting online. Pays 1 contributor's copy.

ADDITIONAL INFORMATION The editors also publish Templar Poetry (www.templarpoetry.co.uk), sponsor the annual Derwent Poetry Festival, and host an online poetry bookshop of their titles at www.templarpoetry.com. "Templar Poetry is a major UK poetry publisher and publishes poetry collections, nonfiction, and an annual anthology of poetry linked to international pamphlet and collection awards. Details at www.templarpoetry.co.uk/awards.

CONTEST/AWARD OFFERINGS Sponsors an annual poetry Pamphlet/Chapbook-Iota Shot Award, offering 2-3 awards of £100, plus publication of *ishot* chapbook. Submission fee: £15.50 online. Worldwide submissions in English welcome. **Deadline:** November 19.

○ THE IOWA REVIEW

308 EPB, The University of Iowa, Iowa City IA 52242. (319)335-0462. **Website:** www.iowareview.org. **Contact:** Harilaos Stecopoulos. *The Iowa Review*, published 3 times/year, prints fiction, poetry, essays, reviews, and, occasionally, interviews. Receives about 5,000 submissions/year, accepts up to 100. Press run is 2,900; 1,500 distributed to stores. Subscription: $25. Stories, essays, and poems for a general readership interested in contemporary literature. Buys first North American serial rights; buys nonexclusive anthology, classroom, and online serial rights. Pays on publication. Publishes ms an average of 12-18 months after acceptance. Responds in 4 months to mss. Sample copy for $9.95 and online. Guidelines available online.

○ This magazine uses the help of colleagues and graduate assistants. Its reading period for unsolicited work is September 1-December 1.

From January through April, they read entries to their annual Iowa Awards competition. Check the website for further information.

MAGAZINES NEEDS Submit up to 8 pages at a time. Online submissions accepted, but no e-mail submissions. Cover letter (with title of work and genre) is encouraged. SASE required. Reads submissions "only during the fall semester, September through November, and then contest entries in the spring." Time between acceptance and publication is "around a year." Occasionally comments on rejected poems or offers suggestions on accepted poems. "We simply look for poems that, at the time we read and choose, we find we admire. No specifications as to form, length, style, subject matter, or purpose. Though we print work from established writers, we're always delighted when we discover new talent." Pays $1.50/line of poetry, $40 minimum.

TIPS "We publish essays, reviews, novel excerpts, stories, poems, and photography. We have no set guidelines as to content or length but strongly recommend that writers read a sample issue before submitting."

○ ISLAND

P.O. Box 4703, Bathurst St. Post Office, Hobart Tasmania 7000, Australia. **E-mail:** matthew@islandmag.com. **Website:** www.islandmag.com. **Contact:** Matthew Lamb, editorial director and features editor. *Island* seeks quality fiction, poetry, and essays. It is "one of Australia's leading literary magazines, tracing the contours of our national, and international culture, while still retaining a uniquely Tasmanian perspective." Buys one-time rights. Subscriptions and sample copies available for purchase online. Guidelines available online.

○ Only publishes the work of subscribers; you can submit if you are not currently a subscriber, but if your piece is chosen, the subscription will be taken from the fee paid for the piece.

MAGAZINES NEEDS Pay varies.

ITALIAN AMERICANA

University of Rhode Island, Alan Shawn Feinstein College of Continuing Education, 80 Washington St., Providence RI 02903. (401)277-5306. **Fax:** (401)277-5100. **E-mail:** it.americana@yahoo.com. **Website:** www.uri.edu/prov/research/italianamericana/italianamericana.html. **Contact:** Carol Bonomo Albright, editor-in-chief. A semi-annual historical and cultural journal devoted to the Italian experience in America.

Italian Americana, in cooperation with the American Italian Historical Association, is the first and only cultural as well as historical review dedicated to the Italian experience in the New World. Responds in 1-2 months.

○ Offers annual prizes: $1,000 John Ciardi Poetry Prize, $500 Massaro Prize for the best critical essay, $250 Bruno Arcudi Short Fiction Award, and $250 A. William Salamone History Award. See website for details.

MAGAZINES NEEDS Send poems (in triplicate) with SASE and cover letter. Include 3-5 line bio, list of publications. Length: no more than 3 pages. Pays in contributor's copies.

JABBERWOCK REVIEW

Department of English, Mississippi State University, Drawer E, Mississippi State MS 39762. **E-mail:** jabberwockreview@english.msstate.edu. **Website:** www.jabberwockreview.org.msstate.edu. **Contact:** Becky Hagenston, editor. *"Jabberwock Review* is a literary journal published semi-annually by students and faculty of Mississippi State University. The journal consists of art, poetry, fiction, and nonfiction from around the world. Funding is provided by the Office of the Provost, the College of Arts & Sciences, the Shackouls Honors College, the Department of English, fundraisers, and subscriptions." Rights revert to author upon publication. Responds in 3-5 months. "If you have not heard from us in 5 months, feel free to contact us about the status of your submission." Guidelines available online at website.

○ Submissions will be accepted from August 15-October 20 and January 15-March 15.

MAGAZINES NEEDS "Poems of multiple pages should indicate whether or not stanza breaks accompany page breaks."

TIPS "It might take a few months to get a response from us, but your manuscript will be read with care. Our editors enjoy reading submissions (really!) and will remember writers who are persistent and committed to getting a story 'right' through revision."

⑤ JACK AND JILL

U.S. Kids, P.O. Box 567, Indianapolis IN 46206. (317)634-1100. **E-mail:** jackandjill@uskidsmags.com. **Website:** www.jackandjillmag.org. Buys all rights. Pays on publication. Publishes ms an average of 8 months after acceptance. Responds to mss in 3 months. Guidelines available online.

○ "Please do not send artwork. We prefer to work with professional illustrators of our own choosing."

MAGAZINES NEEDS Submit via postal mail; no e-mail submissions. Wants light-hearted poetry appropriate for the age group. Mss must be typewritten with poet's contact information in upper right-hand corner of each poem's page. SASE required. Length: up to 30 lines/poem. Pays $25 and up.

TIPS "We are constantly looking for new writers who can tell good stories with interesting slants—stories that are not full of outdated and time-worn expressions. We like to see stories about kids who are smart and capable but not sarcastic or smug. Problem-solving skills, personal responsibility, and integrity are good topics for us. Obtain current issues of the magazine and study them to determine our present needs and editorial style."

JERRY JAZZ MUSICIAN

2207 NE Broadway, Portland OR 97232. (503)287-5570. **Fax:** (801)749-9896. **E-mail:** jm@jerryjazz.com. **Website:** www.jerryjazzmusician.com. *"Jerry Jazz Musician's* mission is to explore the culture of 20th-century America with, as noted jazz critic Nat Hentoff wrote, 'jazz as the centerpiece.' We focus on publishing content geared toward readers with interests in jazz music, its rich history, and the culture it influenced—and was influenced by. We regularly publish original interviews, poetry, literature, and art, and encourage readers to share their own perspectives."

MAGAZINES NEEDS Submit 1-2 poems at a time. Length: 6-100 lines.

JEWISH CURRENTS

P.O. Box 111, Accord NY 12404. (845)626-2427. **E-mail:** editor@jewishcurrents.org. **Website:** www.jewishcurrents.org. *Jewish Currents*, published 4 times/year, is a progressive Jewish bimonthly magazine that carries on the insurgent tradition of the Jewish left through independent journalism, political commentary, and a 'countercultural' approach to Jewish arts and literature. Publishes mss 6-9 months after acceptance. Responds in 3 months. Subscription: $30/year.

○ *Jewish Currents* is 80 pages, magazine-sized, offset-printed, saddle-stapled with a full-color arts section, "Jcultcha & Funny Pages." "Our Winter issue is a 12-month arts calendar."

MAGAZINES NEEDS Submit 4 poems at a time with a cover letter. "Writers should include brief bio-

graphical information." Poems should be typed, double-spaced; include SASE. Pays contributor's copies.
ALSO OFFERS "We also run a national poetry contest October 15-January 15."

💲 JEWISH WOMEN'S LITERARY ANNUAL
Eleanor Leff Jewish Women's Resource Center, 241 W. 72nd St., New York NY 10023. (212)687-5030. E-mail: info@ncjwny.org. **Website:** www.ncjwny.org/services_annual.htm. **Contact:** Henny Wenkart, editor. *Jewish Women's Literary Annual*, published in April, prints poetry, fiction, and creative nonfiction by Jewish women. Sample copy: $15. Subscription: $48 for 3 issues. Make checks payable to NCJW New York Section.

○ *Jewish Women's Literary Annual* is 230 pages, digest-sized, perfect-bound, with laminated card cover. Press run is 1,500.

MAGAZINES NEEDS Submit poems by postal mail. Receives about 1,500 poems/year, accepts about 10%. Has published poetry by Linda Zisquit, Merle Feld, Helen Papell, Enid Dame, Marge Piercy, and Lesléa Newman.

TIPS "Send only your very best. We are looking for humor, as well as other things, but nothing cutesy or smart-aleck. We do no politics and prefer topics other than 'Holocaust'."

J JOURNAL: NEW WRITING ON JUSTICE
524 West 59th St., 7th Floor, New York NY 10019. (212)237-9697. **E-mail:** jjournal@jjay.cuny.edu. **Website:** www.jjournal.org. **Contact:** Adam Berlin and Jeffrey Heiman, editors. "*J Journal* publishes literary fiction, creative nonfiction, and poetry on the justice theme. Subjects often include crime, criminal justice, law, law enforcement, and prison writing. While the theme is specific, it need not dominate the work. We're interested in questions of justice from all perspectives. Tangential connections to justice are often better than direct." Acquires first rights. Publication is copyrighted. Pays on publication. Ms published 6 months after acceptance. Responds to queries in 4 weeks; mss in 12 weeks. Sometimes comments on/critiques rejected mss. Send recyclable copy of ms and e-mail for reply. Sample copy: $10. Guidelines available online.

MAGAZINES NEEDS Submit up to 3 poems. Include brief bio and list of publications. Writers receive 2 contributor's copies. Additional copies $10.

TIPS "We're looking for literary fiction/memoir/personal narrative poetry with a connection, direct or tangential, to the theme of justice."

JOURNAL OF NEW JERSEY POETS
English Department, County College of Morris, 214 Center Grove Rd., Randolph NJ 07869-2086. (973)328-5460. **Fax:** (973)328-5425. **E-mail:** ebirx@ccm.edu. **Contact:** Emily Birx, editor; Matthew Ayres, Debra DeMattio, Philip Chase, Dee McAree, associate editors. *Journal of New Jersey Poets*, published annually in April, is "not necessarily about New Jersey—but of, by, and for poets from New Jersey." Wants "serious work that conveys the essential, real, whole emotional moment of the poem to the reader without sentimentality." Acquires first North American serial rights. Time between acceptance and publication is within 1 year. Responds in up to 1 year. Sample: $10 (includes postage and handling). Subscription: $16 for 2 issues ($16/issue for institutions). Guidelines available for SASE or by e-mail.

○ *Journal of New Jersey Poets* is about 90 pages, perfect-bound, offset-printed on recycled stock. Press run is 500.

MAGAZINES NEEDS All reviews are solicited. Send 2 copies of books for review consideration. Poets who live or work in New Jersey (or who formerly lived or worked here) are invited to submit up to 3 poems with their New Jersey bio data mentioned in the cover letter. Accepts fax and e-mail submissions, "but they will not be acknowledged nor returned. Include SASE with sufficient postage for return of ms, or provide instructions to recycle." Annual deadline for submissions: September 1. Has published poetry by X.J. Kennedy, Allen Ginsberg, Amiri Baraka, Gerald Stern, Kenneth Burke, Stephen Dobyns, Thomas Edison, Ruth Moon Kempher, Joe Weil, Joe Salerno, and Catherine Doty. Pays 2 contributor's copies and a one-year subscription.

ALSO OFFERS Awarded first New Jersey poets prize to Stephen Dobyns in 2010. For prize guidelines, e-mail editor Matthew Ayres.

JOURNAL OF THE AMERICAN MEDICAL ASSOCIATION (JAMA)
(312)464-4444. **E-mail:** jamams@jamanetwork.com. **Website:** www.jama.com. **Contact:** Howard Bauchner, editor-in-chief; Phil B. Fontanarosa, executive editor. *JAMA* is an international peer-reviewed general medical journal published 48 times/year. It is the

most widely circulated journal in the world. *JAMA* publishes Original Investigations, Reviews, Brief Reports, Special Communications, Viewpoints, and other categories of articles. Publishes mss 1 month after acceptance. Guidelines available online.

◯ Receives about 6,000 mss annually. Publishes 9% of mss.

MAGAZINES NEEDS *JAMA* includes a poetry and medicine column and publishes poetry in some way related to a medical experience, whether from the point of view of a health care worker or patient, or simply an observer. Has published poetry by Jack Coulehan, Floyd Skloot, and Walt McDonald. *JAMA* is magazine-sized, flat-spined, with glossy paper cover. Receives about 750 poems/year, accepts about 7%. Length: no longer than 50 lines.

⑤ THE JOURNAL

(614)292-6065. **Fax:** (614)292-7816. **E-mail:** managingeditor@thejournalmag.org. **Website:** thejournalmag.org. "We are interested in quality fiction, poetry, nonfiction, art, and reviews of new books of poetry, fiction, and nonfiction. We impose no restrictions on category, type, or length of submission for fiction, poetry, and nonfiction. We are happy to consider long stories and self-contained excerpts of novels. Please double-space all prose submissions. Please send 3-5 poems in 1 submission. We only accept online submissions and will not respond to mailed submissions." Buys first North American serial rights. Payment for art contributors only. All other contributors receive 2 contributor's copies and a one-year subscription. Publishes ms an average of 1 year after acceptance. Responds in 3-4 months to mss. Sample copy: $8 on Submittable or free online spring and fall issues. Guidelines available online: thejournalmag.org/submit. Submit online only at thejournal.submittable.com/submit.

◯ "We're open to all forms; we tend to favor work that gives evidence of a mature and sophisticated sense of the language."

MAGAZINES NEEDS "However else poets train or educate themselves, they must do what they can to know our language. Too much of the writing we see indicates poets do not, in many cases, develop a feel for the possibilities of language and do not pay attention to craft. Poets should not be in a rush to publish—until they are ready." Publishes about 100 poems/year.

⑨ THE JOURNAL

Original Plus Press, 17 High St., Maryport Cumbria CA15 6BQ, United Kingdom. 01900 812194. **E-mail:** smithsssj@aol.com. **Website:** http://thesamsmith.webs.com. *The Journal*, published 3 times/year, features English poetry/translations, reviews, and articles. Wants "new poetry howsoever it comes; translations and original English-language poems." Does not want "staid, generalized, all form/no content." Buys all rights. Pays on publication. Publishes ms an average of 6 months after acceptance. Responds in 4 weeks to queries. Often comments on rejected poems. Editorial lead time 6 months.

◯ Since 1997, Original Plus Press has been publishing collections of poetry. Has recently published books by Grahaeme Barrasford Young, Dina Kafiris, Alfred Todd, Fiona Sinclair, Neil Leadbeater, Janette Ayachi, Paul Lee, Kate Ruse, and Chris Deakins. "From now on we will be publishing mainly chapbooks. Send SASE (or SAE and IRC) or e-mail for details."

MAGAZINES NEEDS Submit up to 6 poems at a time. Accepts e-mail submissions. Cover letter is preferred. "Please send 2 IRCs with hard-copy submissions." Always sends prepublication galleys. Pays 1 contributor's copy "only to U.K. contributors. Contributors outside of the U.K. receive PDF copy of that issue."

TIPS "Send 6 poems; I'll soon let you know if it's not *Journal* or Original Plus material."

KAIMANA: LITERARY ARTS HAWAI'I

Hawai'i Literary Arts Council, P.O. Box 11213, Honolulu HI 96828. **E-mail:** reimersa001@hawaii.rr.com. **Website:** www.hawaii.edu/hlac. *Kaimana: Literary Arts Hawai'i*, published annually, is the magazine of the Hawai'i Literary Arts Council. Wants submissions with "some Pacific reference—Asia, Polynesia, Hawai'i—but not exclusively." Responds with "reasonable dispatch." Subscription: $15, includes membership in HLAC. Sample: $10.

◯ *Kaimana* is 64-76 pages, 7.5x10, saddle-stapled, with high-quality printing. Press run is 1,000. "Poets published in *Kaimana* have received the Pushcart Prize, the Hawaii Award for Literature, the Stefan Baciu Award, the Cades Award, and the John Unterecker Award."

MAGAZINES NEEDS Submit poems with SASE. No e-mail submissions. Cover letter is preferred. Sometimes comments on rejected poems. Has published poetry by Kathryn Takara, Howard Nemerov, Anne Waldman, Reuel Denney, Haunani-Kay Trask, and Simon Perchik. Pays 2 contributor's copies.

TIPS "Hawai'i gets a lot of 'travelling regionalists,' visiting writers with inevitably superficial observations. We also get superb visiting observers who are careful craftsmen anywhere. *Kaimana* is interested in the latter, to complement our own best Hawai'i writers."

🟢 KALEIDOSCOPE

Kaleidoscope, 701 S. Main St., Akron OH 44311-1019. (330)762-9755. **Fax:** (330)762-0912. **E-mail:** kaleidoscope@udsakron.org. **Website:** www.kaleidoscope-online.org. **Contact:** Gail Willmott, editor in chief. "*Kaleidoscope* magazine creatively focuses on the experiences of disability through literature and the fine arts. Unique to the field of disability studies, this award-winning publication expresses the diversity of the disablity experience from a variety of perspectives including: individuals, families, friends, caregivers, educators, and healthcare professionals, among others." Buys first rights. Rights return to author upon publication. Pays on publication. Responds within 6-9 months. Guidelines available online. Submissions and queries electronically via website and e-mail.

⭕ *Kaleidoscope* has received awards from the Great Lakes Awards Competition and Ohio Public Images; received the Ohioana Award of Editorial Excellence.

MAGAZINES NEEDS Wants poems that have strong imagery, evocative language. Submit up to 5 poems. "Do not get caught up in rhyme scheme. We want high quality with strong imagery and evocative language." Reviews any style.

TIPS "The material chosen for *Kaleidoscope* challenges and overcomes stereotypical, patronizing, and sentimental attitudes about disability. We accept the work of writers with and without disabilities; however the work of a writer without a disability must focus on some aspect of disability. The criteria for good writing apply: effective technique, thought-provoking subject matter, and, in general, a mature grasp of the art of storytelling. Writers should avoid using offensive language and always put the person before the disability."

THE KELSEY REVIEW

Liberal Arts Division, Mercer County Community College, P.O. Box 17202, Trenton NJ 08690. **E-mail:** kelsey.review@mccc.edu. **Website:** www.mccc.edu/

community_kelsey-review.shtml. **Contact:** Ed Carmien. *The Kelsey Review*, published annually online in September by Mercer County Community College, serves as "an outlet for literary talent of people living and working in Mercer County, New Jersey only." Rights revert to author on publication. Responds no later than September 1 to mss. Electronic submissions only. Sample copy free online. Guidelines online.

MAGAZINES NEEDS Deadline is May 15. Submissions are limited to people who live, work, or give literary readings in the Mercer County, New Jersey area. Decisions on which material will be published are made by the 4-person editorial board in June and July. Contributors will be notified of submission acceptance determination(s) by the second week of August. Has no specifications as to form, subject matter, or style. Submit up to 6 pages. Has published poetry by Vida Chu, Dan O'Brien, and Carolina Morales. Does not want to see poetry "about kittens and puppies."

TIPS "See *The Kelsey Review* website for current guidelines. Note: We only accept submissions from the Mercer County, New Jersey area."

🟢 THE KENYON REVIEW

Finn House, 102 W. Wiggin, Gambier OH 43022. (740)427-5208. **Fax:** (740)427-5417. **E-mail:** kenyon-review@kenyon.edu. **Website:** www.kenyonreview.org. **Contact:** Marlene Landefeld. "An international journal of literature, culture, and the arts, dedicated to an inclusive representation of the best in new writing (fiction, poetry, essays, interviews, criticism) from established and emerging writers." Buys first rights. Pays on publication. Publishes ms an average of 1 year after acceptance. Responds in 4 months to mss. Editorial lead time 1 year. Sample copy: $10; includes postage and handling. Call or e-mail to order. Guidelines available online.

⭕ *The Kenyon Review* receives about 8,000 submissions/year. Also now publishes *KR Online*, a separate and complementary literary magazine.

MAGAZINES NEEDS Features all styles, forms, lengths, and subject matters. Considers translations. Has published poetry by Billy Collins, D.A. Powell, Jamaal May, Rachel Zucker, Diane di Prima, and Seamus Heaney. Submit up to 6 poems at a time. No previously published poems. Only accepts mss via online submissions program; visit website for instructions.

Do not submit via e-mail or snail mail. Reads submissions September 15-January 15. Pays $40/page.

TIPS "We no longer accept mailed or e-mailed submissions. Work will only be read if it is submitted through our online program on our website. Reading period is September 15-January 15. We look for strong voice, unusual perspective, and power in the writing."

THE KERF

College of the Redwoods, 883 W. Washington Blvd., Crescent City CA 95531. **E-mail:** ken-letko@redwoods.edu. **Website:** www.redwoods.edu/Departments/english/poets&writers/clm.htm. **Contact:** Ken Letko. *The Kerf*, published annually in fall, features "poetry that speaks to the environment and humanity." Wants "poetry that exhibits an environmental consciousness." Considers poetry by children and teens. Sample copy: $5. Make checks payable to College of the Redwoods.

○ *The Kerf* is 54 pages, digest-sized, printed via Docutech, saddle-stapled, with CS2 coverstock. Receives about 1,000 poems/year, accepts up to 3%. Press run is 350-400; 100 distributed free to contributors and writing centers.

MAGAZINES NEEDS Submit up to 5 poems (7 pages maximum) at a time. Reads submissions January 15-March 31 only. Has published poetry by Marsha de la O, James Grabill, George Keithley, Carol Tyx, and Paul Willis.

💲 LADYBUG

Cricket Magazine Group, 700 E. Lake St., Suite 800, Chicago IL 60601. **Website:** www.cricketmag.com/ladybug; ladybugmagkids.com. **Contact:** submissions editor. *Ladybug* magazine is an imaginative magazine with art and literature for young children (ages 3-6). Publishes 9 issues per year. Pays on publication. Responds in 6 months to mss. Guidelines available online at submittable.cricketmag.com or www.cricketmag.com/submissions.

MAGAZINES NEEDS Wants poetry that is "rhythmic, rhyming; serious, humorous." Submit via online submissions manager: cricket.submittable.com. Length: up to 20 lines/poem. Pays up to $3/line ($25 minimum).

💲 LADY CHURCHILL'S ROSEBUD WRISTLET

150 Pleasant St., #306, Easthampton MA 01027. **E-mail:** smallbeerpress@gmail.com. **Website:** www.smallbeerpress.com/lcrw. **Contact:** Gavin Grant, editor. *Lady Churchill's Rosebud Wristlet* accepts fiction, nonfiction, poetry, and b&w art. "The fiction we publish tends toward, but is not limited to, the speculative. This does not mean only quietly desperate stories. We will consider items that fall out with regular categories. We do not accept multiple submissions." Pays on publication for first serial, nonexclusive anthology, and nonexclusive electronic rights. Publishes ms 6-12 months after acceptance. Responds in 6 months to mss. Sometimes comments on rejected mss. Sample copy: $5. Guidelines online.

○ Semiannual.

MAGAZINES NEEDS Send complete ms with a cover letter. Include estimated word count. Send SASE (or IRC) for return of ms, or send a disposable copy of ms and #10 SASE for reply only. Pays $5/poem.

TIPS "We recommend you read *Lady Churchill's Rosebud Wristlet* before submitting. You can procure a copy from us or from assorted book shops."

LA FOVEA

E-mail: editors@lafovea.org. **Website:** www.lafovea.org. **Contact:** Frank Giampietro, creator; Virginia McLure, editor. Published 20 times/year online. "Each Nerve editor (found on the main page of www.lafovea.org) is in charge of a nerve. The nerves are made up of poets who are invited to submit to *La Fovea*. Click on the editor's name to see all the poets and poems in his or her nerve. The nerve editor asks a poet to submit 2 poems. After that poet has had his or her poems on *La Fovea*, he or she will ask another poet to submit poems. If the last poet on the nerve does not find a poet to submit poems for whatever reason, the nerve is dead. It's okay to have a dead nerve. The most important thing is for the nerve editor to notice a nerve has died and begin a new nerve from their first page of poems."

MAGAZINES NEEDS Wants any poetry. "If a poet wants to submit to *La Fovea* but has not been invited, he or she may submit to *La Fovea* and choose the editor whom the poet believes most matches his or her family of aesthetic style. The editor of the nerve may choose to send these poems to the current nerve editor and ask if he or she wishes to publish the poet's work. If the poet does not wish to publish the work, than the work will be returned to the submitter." Has published poetry by Denise Duhamel, Campbell McGrath, and Julianna Baggott. Submit ONLY 3 poems at a time by e-mail, along with short bio.

LAKE EFFECT: A JOURNAL OF THE LITERARY ARTS

School of Humanities & Social Sciences, Penn State Erie, 4951 College Dr., Erie PA 16563-1501. (814)898-6281. **Fax:** (814)898-6032. **E-mail:** gol1@psu.edu. **Website:** www.pserie.psu.edu/lakeeffect. **Contact:** George Looney, editor in chief. *Lake Effect* is a publication of the School of Humanities and Social Sciences at Penn State Erie, The Behrend College. Sample copy: $6. Guidelines online at website.

MAGAZINES NEEDS *"Lake Effect* is looking for poems that demonstrate an original voice and that use multilayered, evocative images presented in a language shaped by an awareness of how words sound and what they mean. Each line should help to carry the poem. *Lake Effect* seeks poems from both established poets and from new and emerging voices." Length: open.

LANDFALL: NEW ZEALAND ARTS AND LETTERS

Otago University Press, P.O. Box 56, Dunedin , New Zealand. (64)(3)479-4155. **Fax:** (64)(3)479-8385. **E-mail:** landfall@otago.ac.nz. **Website:** www.otago.ac.nz/press/landfall. *Landfall: New Zealand Arts and Letters* contains literary fiction and essays, poetry, extracts from work in progress, commentary on New Zealand arts and culture, work by visual artists including photographers and reviews of local books. (*Landfall* does not accept unsolicited reviews.) Guidelines for SASE or on website.

○ Deadlines for submissions: January 10 for the May issue, June 10 for the November issue.

MAGAZINES NEEDS Prefers e-mail submissions. Accepts postal mail submissions, but must include SASE. Include contact information and brief bio. Publishes theme issues. Reads year-round.

LEADING EDGE

4087 JKB, Provo UT 84602. **E-mail:** editor@leadingedgemagazine.com; fiction@leadingedgemagazine.com; art@leadingedgemagazine.com. **Website:** www.leadingedgemagazine.com. **Contact:** Kenna Blaylock, editor in chief. *"Leading Edge* is a magazine dedicated to new and upcoming talent in the fields of science fiction and fantasy. We strive to encourage developing and established talent and provide high-quality speculative fiction to our readers." Does not accept mss with sex, excessive violence, or profanity. Buys first North American serial rights. Pays on publication. Publishes ms an average of 2-4 months after acceptance. Responds in 2-4 months to mss. Single copy: $5.95. "We no longer provide subscriptions, but *Leading Edge* is now available on Amazon Kindle, as well as print-on-demand." Guidelines available online at website.

○ Accepts unsolicited submissions.

MAGAZINES NEEDS "Publishes 2-4 poems per issue. Poetry should reflect both literary value and popular appeal and should deal with science fiction- or fantasy-related themes." Submit 1 or more poems at a time. No e-mail submissions. Cover letter is preferred. Include name, address, phone number, length of poem, title, and type of poem at the top of each page. Please include SASE with every submission." Pays $10 for first 4 pages; $1.50/each subsequent page.

TIPS "Buy a sample issue to know what is currently selling in our magazine. Also, make sure to follow the writer's guidelines when submitting."

LEFT CURVE

P.O. Box 472, Oakland CA 94604-0472. (510)763-7193. **E-mail:** editor@leftcurve.org. **Website:** www.leftcurve.org. **Contact:** Csaba Polony, editor. *"Left Curve* is an artist-produced journal addressing the problem(s) of cultural forms emerging from the crises of modernity that strive to be independent from the control of dominant institutions, based on the recognition of the destructiveness of commodity (capitalist) systems to all life." Published irregularly. Rights revert to author. Publishes ms 6-12 months after acceptance. Responds in 6 months to mss and poems. Sometimes comments on rejected mss. Sample copy for $12; back copies $10. Guidelines available for SASE, by e-mail, or on website.

○ Magazine: 8.5×11; 144 pages; 60 lb. paper; 100 pt. C1S gloss layflat lamination cover; illustrations; photos. Receives 50 unsolicited mss/month. Accepts 3-4 mss/issue. Has published work by Mike Standaert, Ilan Pappe, Terrence Cannon, John Gist.

MAGAZINES NEEDS Submit up to 5 poems at a time. Accepts e-mail or postal submissions. Cover letter is required. "Explain why you are submitting." Publishes theme issues. Lines/poem: "Most of our published poetry is 1 page in length, though we have published longer poems of up to 8 pages." Pays 2-3 contributor's copies.

TIPS "We look for continuity, adequate descriptive passages, endings that are not simply abandoned (in both meanings). Dig deep; no superficial personalisms, no corny satire. Be honest, realistic, and gouge out the truth you wish to say. Understand yourself and the world. Have writing be a means to achieve or realize what is real."

LILITH MAGAZINE: INDEPENDENT, JEWISH & FRANKLY FEMINIST

Attn: Submissions, 250 W. 57th St., Suite 2432, New York NY 10107. (212)757-0818. **Fax:** (212)757-5705. **E-mail:** info@lilith.org; naomi@lilith.org. **Website:** www.lilith.org. **Contact:** Susan Weidman Schneider, editor in chief; Naomi Danis, managing editor. *Lilith Magazine: Independent, Jewish & Frankly Feminist*, published quarterly, welcomes submissions of high-quality, lively writing: reportage, opinion pieces, memoirs, fiction, and poetry on subjects of interest to Jewish women. Responds in 3 months. Sample copy: $7. Guidelines online.

O   *Lilith Magazine* is 48 pages, magazine-sized, with glossy color cover. Press run is about 10,000 (about 6,000 subscribers). Subscription: $26/year. For all submissions: Make sure name and contact information appear on each page of mss. Include a short bio (1-2 sentences), written in third person. Accepts submissions year round.

MAGAZINES NEEDS Has published poetry by Irena Klepfisz, Lyn Lifshin, Marcia Falk, Adrienne Rich, and Muriel Rukeyser. Send up to 3 poems at a time via online submissions form or mail; no e-mail submissions. Copy should be neatly typed and proofread for typos and spelling errors.

TIPS "Read a copy of the publication before you submit your work. Please be patient."

LILLIPUT REVIEW

282 Main St., Pittsburgh PA 15201-2807. **E-mail:** lilliputreview@gmail.com. **Website:** https://sites.google.com/site/lilliputreview/home; Blog:lilliputreview.blogspot.com. *Lilliput Review*, published irregularly, is "shipped 2 issues at a time, every fourth issue being a broadside that features the work of a single poet." Wants poems in any style or form, no longer than 10 lines. Has published poetry by Roberta Beary, Albert Huffstickler, Charlie Mehrhoff, and John Martone. Acquires first rights. Responds in 6 months. Sample: $1 or SASE. Subscription: $5 for 6 issues, $10 for 15 issues; $12 for institutions (12 issues). Make checks payable to Don Wentworth or make a payment to

Paypal on the blog. Guidelines available for SASE or on website.

O   *Lilliput Review* is 12-16 pages, 4.25x3.5, laserprinted on colored paper, stapled. Press run is 400.

MAGAZINES NEEDS Submit up to 3 poems at a time. SASE required. Considers previously published poems if noted as such. Editor comments on submissions "occasionally; I always try to establish human contact." Length: up to 10 lines/poem. Pays 2 contributor's copies/poem.

ALSO OFFERS The Modest Proposal Chapbook Series began in 1994, publishing 1 chapbook/year, 18-24 pages in length. Has published *Now Now* by Cid Corman. **Chapbook submissions are by invitation only.** Query with standard SASE. Sample chapbook: $3.

LINEBREAK

333 Kimpel Hall, University of Arkansas, Fayetteville AR 72701. **E-mail:** editors@linebreak.org. **Website:** http://linebreak.org. **Contact:** Johnathon Williams, founding editor; Ash Bowen. "Linebreak is a weekly online magazine of original poetry. Each poem we publish is read and recorded by another working poet selected by the editors." Has published Dorianne Laux, Bob Hicok, D.A. Powell, C. Dale Young, Richard Siken, Sandra Beasley. Publishes ms 4 months after acceptance. Responds in 6 weeks. Guidelines available on website.

O   Poems published on Linebreak have been selected for the Best New Poets anthology and nominated for the Pushcart Prize.

MAGAZINES NEEDS Submit up to 5 poems at a time through upload form on website. Considers simultaneous submissions. Reads submissions year round. Poems are circulated to an editorial board. Sometimes comments on rejected poems. Guidelines available on website. Sometimes sends prepublication galleys. Acquires electronic rights: "We require the rights to publish and archive the work indefinitely on our website, and the right to create an audio recording of each poem, which is also archived indefinitely. Copyright remains with the author."

LIPS

P.O. Box 616, Florham Park NJ 07392. (201)724-8500. **E-mail:** LBoss79270@aol.com. **Contact:** Laura Boss, poetry editor. *Lips*, published twice/year, takes pleasure "in publishing previously unpublished poets as well as the most established voices in contemporary poetry. We look for quality work: the strongest work of a poet; work that moves the reader; poems that take risks that work. We prefer clarity in the work rather than the abstract. Poems longer than 6 pages present a space problem." Acquires first rights. Responds in 1 month (but has gotten backlogged at times). Sometimes sends prepublication galleys. Sample: $10, plus $2.50 for postage. Guidelines available for SASE.

◯ *Lips* is about 150 pages, digest-sized, flat-spined. Has published poetry by Robert Bly, Allen Ginsberg, Michael Benedikt, Ruth Stone, Maria Mazziotti Gillan, Stanley Barkan, Lyn Lifshin, and Ishmael Reed.

MAGAZINES NEEDS Submit 6 pages maximum at a time. Poems should be typed. Reads submissions September-March only. Receives about 16,000 submissions/year, accepts about 1%. Pays 1 contributor's copy.

THE LISTENING EYE

Kent State University Geauga Campus, 14111 Claridon-Troy Rd., Burton OH 44021. (440)286-3840. **E-mail:** grace_butcher@msn.com. **Contact:** Grace Butcher, editor. "We look for powerful, unusual imagery, content, and plot in our short stories. In poetry, we look for tight lines that don't sound like prose, unexpected images or juxtapositions, the unusual use of language, noticeable relationships of sounds, a twist in viewpoint, an ordinary idea in extraordinary language, an amazing and complex idea simply stated, play on words and with words, an obvious love of language. Poets need to read the 'Big Three'—Cummings, Thomas, Hopkins—to see the limits to which language can be taken. Then read the 'Big Two'—Dickinson to see how simultaneously tight, terse, and universal a poem can be, and Whitman to see how sprawling, cosmic, and personal. Then read everything you can find that's being published in literary magazines today, and see how your work compares to all of the above." Acquires first or one-time rights. Time between acceptance and publication is up to 6 months. Responds in 4 weeks to queries; 4 months to mss. Sample copy: $3, plus $1 postage. Writer's guidelines for SASE.

◯ Magazine: 5.5×8.5; 60 pages; photographs. "We publish the occasional very short stories (750 words/3 pages double-spaced) in any subject and any style, but the language must be strong, unusual, free from cliché and vagueness. We are a shoestring operation from a small cam-

pus, but we publish high-quality work." Reads submissions January 1-April 15 only.

MAGAZINES NEEDS Submit up to 4 poems at a time. Accepts previously published poems "occasionally"; no simultaneous submissions. No e-mail submissions "unless from overseas." Cover letter is required. Poems should be typed, single-spaced, with 1 poem/page—name, address, phone number, and e-mail address in upper left corner of each page with SASE for return of work. Poems are circulated to the editor and 2 assistant editors who read and evaluate work separately, then meet for final decisions. Length: Prefers shorter poems (less than 2 pages), but will consider longer if space allows. Pays 2 contributor's copies.

ALSO OFFERS Awards $30 to the best sports poem in each issue.

LITERAL LATTÉ

200 E. 10th St., Suite 240, New York NY 10003. (212)260-5532. **E-mail:** litlatte@aol.com. **Website:** www.literal-latte.com. **Contact:** Jenine Gordon Bockman, editor and publisher. Bimonthly online publication with an annual print anthology featuring the best of the website. "We want great writing in all styles and subjects. A feast is made of a variety of flavors." Buys first rights and requests permission for use in anthology. Responds in 6 months to mss. Editorial lead time 3 months. Writer's guidelines online, via e-mail, or for #10 SASE

MAGAZINES NEEDS "We want any poem that captures the magic of the form." Length: no more than 4,000 words.

ADDITIONAL INFORMATION "We will publish an anthology in book form at the end of each year, featuring the best of our Web magazine."

TIPS "Keeping free thought free and challenging entertainment are not mutually exclusive. Words make a manuscript stand out, words beautifully woven together in striking and memorable patterns."

LITERARY JUICE

Sammamish WA 98075. **E-mail:** info@literaryjuice.com. **E-mail:** srajan@literaryjuice.com. **Website:** www.literaryjuice.com. **Contact:** Sara Rajan, editor-in-chief; Andrea O'Connor and Dinesh Rajan, managing editors. Bimonthly online literary magazine. "*Literary Juice* publishes original works of short fiction, flash fiction, and poetry. We do not publish nonfiction material, essays, or interviews, nor do we accept previously published works." Acquires electronic rights.

Responds in 1-3 months to mss. Guidelines available on website.

MAGAZINES NEEDS Length: 2-20 lines.

TIPS "It is crucial that writers read our submission guidelines, which can be found on our website. Most important, send us your very best writing. We are looking for works that are not only thought provoking but venture into unconventional territory as well. For instance, avoid sending mainstream stories and poems (stories about wizards or vampires fall into this category). Instead, take the reader to a new realm that has yet to be explored."

LITERARY MAMA

E-mail: lminfo@literarymama.com. **Website:** www.literarymama.com. **Contact:** Maria Scala, editor-in-chief. Website offering writing about the complexities and many faces of motherhood in a variety of genres. "Departments include columns, creative nonfiction, fiction, Literary Reflections, poetry, and Profiles & Reviews. We are interested in reading pieces that are long, complex, ambiguous, deep, raw, irreverent, ironic, and body conscious." Responds in 3 weeks-3 months to mss. "We correspond via e-mail only." Guidelines available at www.literarymama.com/submissions.

TIPS "We seek top-notch creative writing. We also look for quality literary criticism about mother-centric literature and profiles of mother writers. We publish writing with fresh voices, superior craft, and vivid imagery. Please send submission (copied into e-mail) to appropriate departmental editors. Include a brief cover letter. We tend to like stark revelation (pathos, humor, and joy); clarity; concrete details; strong narrative development; ambiguity; thoughtfulness; delicacy; irreverence; lyricism; sincerity; the elegant. We need the submissions 3 months before the following months: October (Desiring Motherhood); May (Mother's Day Month); and June (Father's Day Month)."

THE LITERARY REVIEW

Fairleigh Dickinson University, 285 Madison Ave., Madison NJ 07940. (973)443-8564. **Fax:** (973)443-8364. **E-mail:** info@theliteraryreview.org. **Website:** www.theliteraryreview.org. **Contact:** Minna Proctor, editor. *The Literary Review,* published quarterly, seeks "work by new and established poets that reflects a sensitivity to literary standards and the poetic form." No specifications as to form, length, style, subject matter,

or purpose. Acquires first rights. Responds in 8-12 months.

○ *TLR Online,* available on the website, features original work not published in the print edition. *The Literary Review* is about 200 pages, digest-sized, professionally printed, flat-spined, with glossy color cover. Receives about 1,200 submissions/year, accepts 100-150. Press run is 2,000 (800 subscribers, one-third are overseas). Sample: $8 domestic, $8 + $3.99 shipping outside U.S.; request a "general issue." Has published poetry by Albert Goldbarth, Mary Jo Bang, David Citino, Rick Mulkey, Virgil Suárez and Gary Fincke.

MAGAZINES NEEDS Accepts only online submissions through Submittable. Pays 2 contributor's copies plus 1 year free subscription.

LITTLE PATUXENT REVIEW

P.O. Box 6084, Columbia MD 21045. **E-mail:** editor@littlepatuxentreview.org. **Website:** www.littlepatuxentreview.org. **Contact:** Steven Leyva, editor. "*Little Patuxent Review* (*LPR*) is a community-based, biannual print journal devoted to literature and the arts, primarily in the Mid-Atlantic region. We profile the work of a major poet or fiction writer and a visual artist in each issue. We celebrate the launch of each issue with a series of readings and broadcast highlights on *LPR*'s YouTube channel. All forms and styles considered. Please see our website for the current theme." Buys first rights. Responds in 3-5 months to mss. Sample copy: $10. Guidelines available in magazine and on website.

○ *LPR* is about 120 pages; digest-sized; 100# finch cover; artwork (varies depending on featured artist). Has published poetry by Lucille Clifton, Martín Espada, Donald Hall, Joy Harjo, Marie Howe, Myra Sklarew, Clarinda Harriss, and Alan King. 2011 Pushcart Prize for "Patronized" by Tara Hart.

MAGAZINES NEEDS Submit up to 3 poems by online submissions manager; no mail or e-mail submissions. Include word count and 75-word bio. Length: up to 100 lines/poem. Pays 1 contributor's copy.

ALSO OFFERS "*LPR* co-sponsors monthly arts Salon Series events in conjunction with the Columbia Art Center, featuring literary readings, art presentations, and musical performances. Events are free and open to the public. Contributors are invited to participate in reading series and literary festivals, such as the Baltimore Book Festival. As part of our outreach effort, the *LPR* in the Classroom Program provides *LPR* issues to high schools and colleges at a discounted rate."

TIPS "Please see our website for the current theme. Poetry and prose must exhibit the highest quality to be considered. Please read a sample issue before submitting."

⚭⑤ THE LONDON MAGAZINE

11 Queen's Gate, London SW7 5EL, England. (44) (0)20 7584 5977. **E-mail:** admin@thelondonmagazine.org. **E-mail:** submissions@thelondonmagazine.org. **Website:** www.thelondonmagazine.org. **Contact:** Steven O'Brien, editor. "We publish literary writing of the highest quality. We look for poetry and short fiction that startles and entertains us. Reviews, essays, memoir pieces, and features should be erudite, lucid, and incisive. We are obviously interested in writing that has a London focus, but not exclusively so, since London is a world city with international concerns." Buys first rights. Pays on publication. Published ms an average of 4 months after acceptance. Responds in 1 month to queries; 3 months to mss. Editorial lead time 3 months. Sample copy: £6.95. Guidelines online.

MAGAZINES NEEDS "Abstraction is the enemy of good poetry. Poetry should display a commitment to the ultra specificities of language and show a refined sense of simile and metaphor. The structure should be tight and exact." Submit up to 6 poems via online submissions manager, e-mail (as an attachment), or postal mail (enclose SASE). "We do not publish long, loose poems." Length: up to 40 lines/poem.

TIPS "Please look at *The London Magazine* before you submit work so that you can see the type of material we publish."

LONE STARS MAGAZINE

4219 Flint Hill St., San Antonio TX 78230-1619. **E-mail:** lonestarsmagazine@yahoo.com. **Website:** www.lonestarsmagazine.net. **Contact:** Milo Rosebud, editor/publisher. *Lone Stars*, published 3 times/year, features contemporary poetry. Acquires one-time publication rights. Authors retain all rights. Time between acceptance and publication is 3-6 months. Responds within 3 months. Sample (past issues): $5.50. Single copy: $6. Subscription: $20 for 4 issues. Guidelines available for SASE.

🖵 *Lone Stars* is 25+ pages, magazine-sized, photocopied, saddle-stapled, bound with tape. Press run is 200.

MAGAZINES NEEDS Wants poetry "that holds a continuous line of thought." Does not want profanity. Considers poetry by children and teens. Submit 3-5 poems at a time. Cover letter is preferred. Submit poems on any subject, formatted and "typed the way you want them in print." **Charges reading fee of $1 per poem.** Has published poetry by Terry Lee, Eve J. Blohm, Linda Amos, and many more.

ALSO OFFERS Sponsors Annual Songbook Lyric Poetry Contest, Annual Light of the Stars Poetry Contest, The Write Idea Interactive Poem Contests, and Great "One-Liner" Contributions. Details available with e-mail or SASE.

TIPS "Submit poetry that expresses a reasonable train of thought."

LONG LIFE

Longevity through Technology, The Immortalist Society, 1437 Pineapple Ave., Melbourne FL 32935. **E-mail:** porter@kih.net. **Website:** www.cryonics.org/resources/long-life-magazine. **Contact:** York Porter, executive editor. "*Long Life* magazine is a publication for people who are particularly interested in cryonic suspension: the theory, practice, legal problems, etc. associated with being frozen when you die in the hope of eventual restoration to life and health. Many people who receive the publication have relatives who have undergone cryonic preparation or have made such arrangements for themselves or are seriously considering this option. Readers are also interested in other aspects of life extension such as anti-aging research and food supplements that may slow aging. Articles we publish include speculation on what the future will be like; problems of living in a future world, and science in general, particularly as it may apply to cryonics and life extension." Publication is copyrighted. Responds in 1 month to queries and mss. Sample copy is free for SASE.

MAGAZINES NEEDS "Poems are welcomed, especially short, humorous poems with a cryonics or life-extension theme." Pays 1 contributor's copy.

TIPS "We are a small magazine but with a highly intelligent and educated readership which is socially and economically diverse. We currently don't pay for material but are seeking new authors and provide contributors with copies of the magazine with the contributor's published works. Look over a copy of *Long Life*, or talk with the editor to get the tone of the publication. There is an excellent chance that your ms will be accepted if it is well written and 'on theme.' Pictures to accompany the article are always welcome, and we like to publish photos of the authors with their first ms."

LONG STORY SHORT, AN E-ZINE FOR WRITERS

P.O. Box 475, Lewistown MT 59457. **E-mail:** alongstory_short@aol.com. **Website:** www.alongstoryshort. net. **Contact:** Anisa Claire, Kim Bussey, editors; Amy Pacini, poetry editor. *Long Story Short, An E-zine for Writers,* published monthly online, is "eclectic—open to all forms and styles" of poetry. Does not want "profanity; overly explicit sex." Considers poetry by children (ages 10 and up) and teens. Has published poetry by Michael Lee Johnson, Maria Ercilla, Shonda Buchanan, Patricia Wellingham-Jones, Floriana Hall, and Russell Bittner. Time between acceptance and publication is up to 6 months, depending on theme. Guidelines available on website. "Read them!"

O   Free newsletter with poetry of the month chosen by poetry editor; includes author's bio and web page listed in the e-zine. Offers light critique of submissions upon request and a free writing forum.

MAGAZINES NEEDS Accepts poetry up to 32 lines. Considers previously published poems and simultaneous submissions. Accepts e-mail submissions only ("paste poems in the body of your e-mail; no attachments will be opened"). Include a brief bio and permission to use e-mail address for reader contact. Reads submissions year-round. "Poems are reviewed and chosen by the poetry editor." Often comments on rejected poems. All rights reserved by author.

LOS

150 N. Catalina St., No. 2, Los Angeles CA 90004. **E-mail:** lospoesy@earthlink.net. **Website:** home.earthlink.net/~lospoesy. *Los,* published 4 times/year, features poetry. Has published poetry by John P. Campbell, George J. Farrah, Peter Layton, Rich Murphy, Ed Orr, Anis Shivani, and Robert Wooten. *Los* is digest-sized and saddle-stapled. Press run is 100. Publishes ms 1 month after acceptance. Responds in 3 months. Guidelines available online.

MAGAZINES NEEDS Accepts e-mail submissions (pasted into body of message or as attachment).

LOST LAKE FOLK OPERA

Shipwreckt Books Publishing Company, 309 W. Stevens Ave., Rushford MN 55971. **E-mail:** contact@

shipwrecktbooks.com. **Website:** www.shipwrecktbooks.com. **Contact:** Tom Driscoll, managing editor. *Lost Lake Folk Opera* magazine is the arts heartbeat and journalistic pulse of rural Mid-America. Currently accepting submissions of critical journalism, short fiction, poetry, and graphic art. Published 3 times annually. Retains one-time rights. Pays on acceptance; offers honorarium, contributor copies, and discount contributor copy price. Publishes ms 3-6 months after acceptance. Responds in 6 weeks on queries; 3 months on mss. Editorial lead time: 3 months. Sample copy available for cover price with SASE. Guidelines available by e-mail.

MAGAZINES NEEDS Length: 1-250 lines. Does not offer payment.

TIPS "Send clean copies of your work. When in doubt, edit and cut."

LOUISIANA LITERATURE

SLU Box 10792, Hammond LA 70402. **E-mail:** lalit@ selu.edu. **Website:** www.louisianaliterature.org. **Contact:** Jack B. Bedell, editor. "Since 1984, *Louisiana Literature* has featured some of the finest writing published in America. The journal has always striven to spotlight local talent alongside nationally recognized authors. Whether it's work from established writers or from first-time publishers, *Louisiana Literature* is always looking to print the finest poetry and fiction available. Acquires one-time rights. Publishes ms 6-12 after acceptance. Responds in 1-3 months to mss. Sometimes comments on rejected mss. Sample copy: $8. Guidelines for SASE or online.

O   Biannual magazine: 6×9; 150 pages; 70 lb. paper; card cover; illustrations. Receives 100 unsolicited mss/month. May not read mss June-July. Publishes 4 new writers/year. Publishes theme issues. Has published work by Anthony Bukowski, Aaron Gwyn, Robert Phillips, R.T. Smith. Work first published in *Louisiana Literature* is regularly reprinted in collections and is nominated for prizes from the National Book Awards for both genres and the Pulitzer. Recently, stories by Aaron Gwyn and Robert Olen Butler were selected for inclusion in *New Stories from the South.*

MAGAZINES NEEDS Submit 3-5 poems at a time via online submissions manager. Reads submissions year round, "although we work more slowly in summer." Sometimes sends prepublication galleys. Send materials for review consideration; include cover letter." Pays 2 contributor's copies.

TIPS "Cut out everything that is not a functioning part of the story. Make sure your ms is professionally presented. Use relevant, specific detail in every scene. We love detail, local color, voice, and craft. Any professional ms stands out."

THE LOUISIANA REVIEW

Division of Liberal Arts, Louisiana State University Eunice, P.O. Box 1129, Eunice LA 70535. (337)550-1315. **E-mail:** bfonteno@lsue.edu. **Website:** web.lsue.edu/la-review. **Contact:** Dr. Billy Fontenot, fiction editor; Dr. Jude Meche, poetry editor; Dr. Diane Langlois, art editor. *The Louisiana Review*, published annually during the fall or spring semester, offers "Louisiana poets, writers, and artists a place to showcase their most beautiful pieces. Others may submit Louisiana- or Southern-related poetry, stories, and art, as well as interviews with Louisiana writers. We want to publish the highest-quality poetry, fiction, and art." Wants "strong imagery, metaphor, and evidence of craft." Pays on publication for one-time rights. Not copyrighted, but has an ISSN number. Publishes ms 6-12 months after acceptance. Responds in 5 weeks to queries; 10 weeks to mss. Sometimes comments on rejected mss. Single copy: $5

○ *The Louisiana Review* is 100 pages, digest-sized, professionally printed, perfect-bound. Press run is 300-600.

MAGAZINES NEEDS Submit up to 5 poems at a time. No previously published poems. No fax or e-mail submissions. "Include cover letter indicating your association with Louisiana, if any. Has published poetry by Gary Snyder, Antler, and David Cope. Receives up to 2,000 poems/year, accepts 30-50. Does not want "sing-song rhymes, abstract, religious, or overly sentimental work." Pays 1 contributor's copy.

TIPS "We do like to have fiction play out visually as a film would, rather than bestatic and undramatized. Louisiana or Gulf Coast settings and themes preferred."

THE LOUISVILLE REVIEW

Spalding University, 851 S. Fourth St., Louisville KY 40203. (502)873-4398. **Fax:** (502)992-2409. **E-mail:** louisvillereview@spalding.edu. **Website:** www.louisvillereview.org. **Contact:** Ellyn Lichvar, assistant managing editor. *The Louisville Review*, published twice/year, prints all kinds of poetry. Has a section devoted to poetry by children and teens (grades K-12) called The Children's Corner. Sample: $5. Single copy: $8. Subscription: $14/year, $27/2 years, $40/3 years (foreign subscribers add $6/year for s&h).

○ *The Louisville Review* is 150 pages, digest-sized, flat-spined. Receives about 700 submissions/year, accepts about 10%.

MAGAZINES NEEDS Accepts submissions via online manager; please see website for more information. "Poetry by children must include permission of parent to publish if accepted. Address those submissions to The Children's Corner." Reads submissions year round. Has published poetry by Wendy Bishop, Gary Fincke, Michael Burkard, and Sandra Kohler. Pays in contributor's copies.

LULLWATER REVIEW

Lullwater Review, P.O. Box 122036, Atlanta GA 30322. **E-mail:** emorylullwaterreview@gmail.com. **Website:** www.lullwaterreview.wordpress.com. **Contact:** Aneyn M. O'Grady, editor-in-chief; Gabriel Unger, managing editor. "We're a small, student-run literary magazine published out of Emory University in Atlanta, Georgia with 2 issues yearly—once in the fall and once in the spring. You can find us in the *Index of American Periodical Verse*, the *American Humanities Index* and as a member of the Council of Literary Magazines and Presses. We welcome work that brings a fresh perspective, whether through language or the visual arts." Buys first North American serial rights. Pays on publication. Publishes ms an average of 1-2 months after acceptance. Responds in 1-3 months to queries; 3-6 months to mss. Sample copy for $5. Guidelines with #10 SASE.

MAGAZINES NEEDS *Lullwater Review*, published in May and December, prints poetry, short fiction, and artwork. Wants poetry of any genre with strong imagery, original voice, on any subject. Has published poetry by Amy Greenfield, Peter Serchuk, Katherine McCord, and Ha Jin. Submit 6 or fewer poems at a time. Considers simultaneous submissions; no previously published poems. Cover letter is preferred. Prefers poems single-spaced with name and contact info on each page. "Poems longer than 1 page should include page numbers. We must have a SASE with which to reply." Reads submissions September 1-May 15 only. Poems are circulated to an editorial board. Seldom comments on rejected poems. No profanity or pornographic material. Pays 3 contributor's copies.

TIPS "We at the *Lullwater Review* look for clear cogent writing, strong character development and an engaging approach to the story in our fiction submissions. Stories with particularly strong voices and well-developed central themes are especially encouraged. Be sure that your manuscript is ready before mailing it off to us. Revise, revise, revise! Be original, honest, and of course, keep trying."

LUNGFULL! MAGAZINE

316 23rd St., Brooklyn NY 11215. **E-mail:** editor@ lungfull.org. **E-mail:** lungfull@rcn.com. **Website:** lungfull.org. **Contact:** Brendan Lorber, editor/publisher. "*LUNGFULL!* Magazine World Headquarters in Brooklyn is home to a team of daredevils who make it their job to bring you only the finest in typos, misspellings, and awkward phrases. That's because *LUNGFULL!magazine* is the only literary and art journal in America that prints the rough drafts of people's work so you can see the creative process as it happens." Responds in 1 year to mss. Submit by postal mail. Include SASE. If sending by e-mail (not preferred) do NOT send attachments and put "Submission by [Your Name]" in the subject line.

◑ *LUNGFULL!* was the recipient of a grant from the New York State Council for the Arts.

MAGAZINES NEEDS Submit up to 8 poems. Include cover letter.

THE LUTHERAN DIGEST

The Lutheran Digest, Inc., 6160 Carmen Ave., Inver Grove Heights MN 55076. (952)933-2820. **Fax:** (952)933-5708. **E-mail:** editor@lutherandigest.com. **Website:** www.lutherandigest.com. **Contact:** Lori Rosenkvist, editor. Articles frequently reflect a Lutheran Christian perspective but are not intended to be sermonettes. Popular stories show how God has intervened in a person's life to help solve a problem. Buys first rights, buys second serial (reprint) rights. Pays on publication. Publishes ms an average of 6 months after acceptance. Responds in 1 month to queries; in 4 months to mss. No response to e-mailed mss unless selected for publication. Editorial lead time 9 months. Sample copy: $3.50. Subscription: $16/year, $22/2 years. Guidelines available online.

◑ *The Lutheran Digest* is 64 pages, digest-sized, offset-printed, saddle-stapled, with 4-color paper cover, includes local ads. Receives about 200 poems/year, accepts 10-20%. Press run is 60,000-65,000; most distributed free to Lutheran churches.

MAGAZINES NEEDS Submit up to 3 poems at a time. Prefers e-mail submissions but also accepts mailed submissions. Cover letter is preferred. Include SASE only if return is desired. Poems are selected by editor and reviewed by publication panel. Length: up to 25 lines/poem. Pays 1 contributor's copy.

TIPS "Reading our writers' guidelines and sample articles online is encouraged and is the best way to get a feel for the type of material we publish."

THE LYRIC

P.O. Box 110, Jericho Corners VT 05465. **E-mail:** themuse@thelyricmagazine.com. **Website:** www.thelyricmagazine.com. *The Lyric*, published quarterly, is the oldest magazine in North America in continuous publication devoted to traditional poetry. Responds in 3 months ("average; inquire after 6 months"). Sample: $5, available in Europe through the Rome office for 18 euros/year sent to Nancy Mellichamp-Savo, Via Lola Montez, #14, Rome, Italy 00135. Subscription: $15/year, $28/2 years, $38/3 years (U.S.), $17/year for Canada and other countries (in U.S. funds only). Guidelines available for SASE or by e-mail.

◑ *The Lyric* is 32 pages, digest-sized, professionally printed with varied typography, with matte card cover. Receives about 3,000 submissions/year, accepts 5%.

MAGAZINES NEEDS Submit by postal service; out-of-country poems may be submitted by e-mail. Considers simultaneous submissions (although not preferred); no previously published poems. Cover letter is often helpful, but not required. Has published poetry by Michael Burch, Gail White, Constance Rowell Mastores, Ruth Harrison, Barbara Loots, Tom Riley, Catherine Chandler, and Glenna Holloway. "Our themes are varied, ranging from religious ecstasy to humor to raw grief, but we feel no compulsion to shock, embitter, or confound our readers. We also avoid poems about contemporary political or social problems—'grief but not grievances,' as Frost put it. Frost is helpful in other ways: If yours is more than a lover's quarrel with life, we are not your best market. And most of our poems are accessible on first or second reading." Length: up to 40 lines. Pays 1 contributor's copy.

TIPS All contributors are eligible for quarterly and annual prizes totaling $650. Also offers *The Lyric* College Contest, open to undergraduate students in the U.S. Awards prize of $500; 2nd Place: $100. **Deadline:** December 1. Send entries by e-mail September 1-December 1: tanycim@aol.com, or to Tanya Cimonetti, 1393 Spear St., S, Burlington, VT 05403."Our *raison d'etre* has been the encouragement of form, music, rhyme, and accessibility in poetry. As we witness the growing tide of appreciation for traditional/lyric poetry, we are proud to have stayed the course for 94 years, helping keep the roots of poetry alive."

⑤ LYRICAL PASSION POETRY E-ZINE

P.O. Box 17331, Arlington VA 22216. **Website:** lyrical-passionpoetry.yolasite.com. **Contact:** Raquel D. Bailey, founding editor. Founded by award-winning poet Raquel D. Bailey, *Lyrical Passion Poetry E-Zine* is an attractive monthly online literary magazine specializing in Japanese short-form poetry. Publishes quality artwork, well-crafted short fiction, and poetry in English by emerging and established writers. Literature of lasting literary value will be considered. Welcomes the traditional to the experimental. Poetry works written in German will be considered if accompanied by translations. Offers annual short-fiction and poetry contests. Acquires first-time rights, electronic rights (must be the first literary venue to publish online or in any electronic format). Rights revert to poets upon publication. Publishes ms 1 month after acceptance. Responds in 2 months. Guidelines and upcoming themes available on website.

MAGAZINES NEEDS Multiple submissions are permitted, but no more than 3 submissions in a 6-month period. Does not want dark, cliché, limerick, erotica, extremely explicit, violent, or depressing literature. Length: 1-40 lines (free verse).

THE MACGUFFIN

18600 Haggerty Rd., Livonia MI 48152. (734)462-4400, ext 5327. **E-mail:** macguffin@schoolcraft.edu. **Website:** www.macguffin.org. **Contact:** Steven A. Dolgin, editor; Gordon Krupsky, managing editor;. "Our purpose is to encourage, support and enhance the literary arts in the Schoolcraft College community, the region, the state, and the nation. We also sponsor annual literary events and give voice to deserving new writers as well as established writers." Acquires first rights. Once published, rights revert back to author. Responds in 2-4 months to mss. Guidelines available online.

MAGAZINES NEEDS Poetry should be typed, single-spaced, only one poem per page. Pays 2 contributor's copies.

HOW TO CONTACT For mail submissions, do not staple work. Include name, e-mail, address and the page no. on each page. Include SASE for reply only. For e-mail, submit each work (single story or five-poem submission) as a Word .doc attachment.

CONTEST/AWARD OFFERINGS "We also sponsor the National Poet Hunt Contest. See contest rules online."

THE MADISON REVIEW

University of Wisconsin, 600 N, Park St., 6193 Helen C. White Hall, Madison WI 53706. **E-mail:** madisonrevw@gmail.com. **Website:** www.english.wisc.edu/madisonreview. **Contact:** Will Conley and Sam Zisser, fiction editors; Mckenna Kohlenberg and Cody Dunn, poetry editors. *The Madison Review* is a student-run literary magazine that looks to publish the best available fiction and poetry. Buys one-time rights. Publishes ms an average of 9 months after acceptance. Responds in 4 weeks to queries; in 6 months to mss. Editorial lead time 6 months. Sample copy: $3. Guidelines free online.

🎧 Does not publish unsolicited interviews or genre fiction. Send all submissions through online submissions manager.

MAGAZINES NEEDS Cover letter is preferred. Does not want religious or patriotic dogma and light verse. Pays 2 contributor's copies.

TIPS "Our editors have very eclectic tastes, so don't specifically try to cater to us. Above all, we look for original, high-quality work."

⑤ THE MAGAZINE OF FANTASY & SCIENCE FICTION

P.O. Box 3447, Hoboken NJ 07030. (201) 876-2551. **E-mail:** fandsf@aol.com. **Website:** www.fandsf.com. **Contact:** C.C. Finlay, editor. *"The Magazine of Fantasy and Science Fiction* publishes various types of science fiction and fantasy short stories and novellas, making up about 80% of each issue. The balance of each issue is devoted to articles about science fiction, a science column, book and film reviews, cartoons, and competitions." Bimonthly. Buys first North American serial rights, buys foreign serial rights. Pays on acceptance. Publishes ms an average of 9-12 months after acceptance. Responds in 2 months to queries.

Sample copy: $6. Guidelines for SASE, by e-mail, or on website.

○ The *Magazine of Fantasy and Science Fiction* won a Nebula Award for Best Novelet for *What We Found* by Geoff Ryman in 2012. Also won the 2012 World Fantasy Award for Best Short Story for *The Paper Menagerie* by Ken Liu.

MAGAZINES NEEDS Wants only poetry that deals with the fantastic or the science fictional. Has published poetry by Rebecca Kavaler, Elizabeth Bear, Sophie M. White, and Robert Frazier. Pays $50/poem and 2 contributor's copies.

TIPS "Good storytelling makes a submission stand out. Regarding manuscripts, a well-prepared manuscript (i.e., one that follows the traditional format, like that describted here: www.sfwa.org/writing/vonda/vonda.htm) stands out more than any gimmicks. Read an issue of the magazine before submitting. New writers should keep their submissions under 15,000 words—we rarely publish novellas by new writers."

MAGMA POETRY

23 Pine Walk, Carshalton Surrey SM5 4ES, United Kingdom. **E-mail:** contributions@magmapoetry.com; info@magmapoetry.com. **Website:** www.magmapoetry.com. **Contact:** Laurie Smith. *Magma* appears 3 times/year and contains modern poetry, reviews and interviews with poets. Wants poetry that is modern in idiom and shortish (2 pages maximum). Nothing sentimental or old fashioned. Has published poetry by Thomas Lynch, Thom Gunn, Michael Donaghy, John Burnside, Vicki Feaver, and Roddy Lumsden. Guidelines available online.

○ Only accepts contributions from the UK. *Magma* is 64 pages, 8×8, photocopied and stapled, includes b&w illustrations. Receives about 3,000 poems/year, accepts 4-5%. Press run is about 500. Single copy: £5.70 UK and Ireland, £6.15 rest of Europe, £7.50 airmail ROW. Subscription: £14.50 UK and Ireland, £18 rest of Europe, £20.50 airmail ROW. Make checks payable to *Magma*. For subscriptions, contact Helen Nicholson, distribution secretary, Flat 2, 86 St. James's Dr., London SW17 7RR England.

MAGAZINES NEEDS Accepts submissions by post (with SAE and IRCs). Cover letter is preferred. Deadlines for submissions: end of January, May, and September. Poems are considered for one issue only. Each issue has an editor who submits his/her selections to a board for final approval. Editor's selection very rarely changed. Occasionally publishes theme issues. Pays 1 contributor's copy.

ALSO OFFERS "We hold a public reading in London three times/year, to coincide with each new issue, and poets in the issue are invited to read."

TIPS "See 'About Magma' and the contents of our website to gain an idea of the type of work we accept." Keep up with the latest news and comment from *Magma Poetry* by receiving free updates via e-mail. Sign up online to receive the Magma Blog and/or the *Magma* newsletter.

THE MAGNOLIA QUARTERLY

P.O. Box 10294, Gulfport MS 39505. **E-mail:** writerpllevin@gmail.com. **Website:** www.gcwriters.org. **Contact:** Phil Levin, editor. *The Magnolia Quarterly* publishes poetry, fiction, nonfiction, and reviews. **For members of GCWA only.** Returns rights to author upon publication. Time between acceptance and publication varies. Single copy: $3; subscription: included in $30 GCWA annual dues. Make checks payable to Gulf Coast Writers Association. Guidelines available in magazine or on website.

○ *The Magnolia Quarterly* is 40 pages, pocket-sized, stapled, with glossy cover, includes ads. Editing service offered on all prose.

MAGAZINES NEEDS Submit 1-3 poems at a time. Prefers e-mail submissions. Reads submissions year round. Has published poetry by Leonard Cirino, Catharine Savage Brosman, Angela Ball, Jack Bedell, and Larry Johnson. Will consider all styles of poetry. Does not want "pornography, racial or sexist bigotry, far-left or far-right political poems." Length: up to 40 lines/poem. No payment.

ALSO OFFERS Holds the "Let's Write" contest, with cash prizes for poetry and prose. Additional information available on website.

THE MAIN STREET RAG

P.O. Box 690100, Charlotte NC 28227-7001. (704)573-2516. **E-mail:** editor@mainstreetrag.com. **Website:** www.mainstreetrag.com. **Contact:** M. Scott Douglass, editor/publisher. *The Main Street Rag*, published quarterly, prints "poetry, short fiction, essays, interviews, reviews, photos, and art. We like publishing good material from people who are interested in more than notching another publishing credit, people who support small independent publishers like ourselves." Will consider "almost anything," but prefers "writing with an edge—either gritty or bitingly humorous. Contributors are advised to visit our website prior to submission to confirm current needs." Acquires first North American print rights. Time between acceptance and publication is up to 1 year. Responds in 6 weeks. Single copy: $8. Subscription: $24/year, $45 for 2 years. E-mail submissions only. Detailed guidelines and current needs available on website.

○ *The Main Street Rag* receives about 5,000 submissions/year; publishes 50+ poems and 3-5 short stories per issue, a featured interview, photos, and an occasional nonfiction piece. Press run is about 500 (250 subscribers, 15 libraries).

MAGAZINES NEEDS Submit 6 pages of poetry at a time; no more than 1 poem per page. E-mail submissions only. Cover letter is preferred. "No bios or credits—let the work speak for itself." Pays 1 contributor's copy.

○⑤ THE MALAHAT REVIEW

The University of Victoria, P.O. Box 1700, STN CSC, Victoria BC V8W 2Y2, Canada. (250)721-8524. **E-mail:** malahat@uvic.ca (for queries only). **Website:** www.malahatreview.ca. **Contact:** John Barton, editor. Quarterly magazine covering poetry, fiction, creative nonfiction, and reviews. "We try to achieve a balance of views and styles in each issue. We strive for a mix of the best writing by both established and new writers." Buys first world rights. Pays on acceptance. Publishes ms an average of 6 months after acceptance. Responds in 2 weeks to queries; in 3-10 months to mss. Sample copy: $16.95 (US). Guidelines available online.

MAGAZINES NEEDS Submit 3-5 poems via online submissions manager: malahatreview.ca/submission_guidelines.html#submittable. Length: up to 6 pages. Pays $50/magazine page.

CONTEST/AWARD OFFERINGS Presents the P.K. Page Founders' Award for Poetry, a $1,000 prize to the author of the best poem or sequence of poems to be published in *The Malahat Review*'s quarterly issues during the previous calendar year. Also offers the Open Season Awards, biennial Long Poem Prize, biennial Novella Prize, Constance Rooke Creative Nonfiction Prize, the biennial Far Horizons Award for Short Fiction, and the biennial Far Horizons Award for Poetry.

TIPS "Please do not send more than 1 submission at a time: 3-5 poems, 1 piece of creative nonfiction, or 1 short story (do not mix poetry and prose in the same submission). See *The Malahat Review*'s Open Season Awards for poetry and short fiction, creative nonfiction, long poem, and novella contests in the Awards section of our website."

THE MANHATTAN REVIEW

440 Riverside Dr., #38, New York NY 10027. **E-mail:** phfried@gmail.com. **Website:** themanhattanreview. com. **Contact:** Philip Fried. *The Manhattan Review* publishes only poetry, reviews of poetry books, and poetry-related essays. The editor reads unsolicited submissions year round but requests that you observe the guidelines. *The Manhattan Review* acquires first North American serial rights only for the work it publishes. Responds in 3 months if possible. Guidelines online.

MAGAZINES NEEDS Send 3-5 poems with SASE and brief bio. Read magazine before submitting. Pays contributor's copies.

⑤ MANOA

English Dept., University of Hawaii, Honolulu HI 96822. (808)956-3070. **Fax:** (808)956-3083. **E-mail:** mjournal-l@lists.hawaii.edu. **Website:** manoajournal. hawaii.edu. **Contact:** Frank Stewart, editor. *Manoa* is seeking "high-quality literary fiction, poetry, essays, and personal narrative. In general, each issue is devoted to new work from Pacific and Asian nations. Our audience is international. U.S. writing need not be confined to Pacific settings or subjects. Please note that we seldom publish unsolicited work." Buys first North American serial rights, buys nonexclusive, one-time print rights. Pays on publication. Responds in 3 weeks to queries. Editorial lead time 9 months. Sample copy: $15 (U.S.). Guidelines available online.

○ *Manoa* has received numerous awards, and work published in the magazine has been selected for prize anthologies. See website for recently published issues.

MAGAZINES NEEDS No light verse. Pays $25 per poem.

TIPS "Not accepting unsolicited mss at this time because of commitments to special projects. Please query before sending mss as e-mail attachments."

⑤ THE MASSACHUSETTS REVIEW

University of Massachusetts, Photo Lab 309, Amherst MA 01003. (413)545-2689. **E-mail:** massrev@external. umass.edu. **Website:** www.massreview.org. **Contact:** Emily Wojcik, managing editor. Seeks a balance between established writers and promising new ones. Interested in material of variety and vitality relevant to the intellectual and aesthetic questions of our time. Aspire to have a broad appeal. Buys first North American serial rights. Pays on publication. Publishes ms an average of 18 months after acceptance. Responds in 6 months to mss. Sample copy: $8 for back issue, $10 for current issue. Guidelines available online.

O Does not respond to mss without SASE.

MAGAZINES NEEDS Has published poetry by Catherine Barnett, Billy Collins, and Dara Wier. Include your name and contact on every page. Length: There are no restrictions for length, but generally poems are less than 100 lines. Pays $50/publication.

TIPS "No manuscripts are considered May-September. Electronic submission process can be found on website. No fax or e-mail submissions. No simultaneous submissions. Shorter rather than longer stories preferred (up to 28-30 pages)." Looks for works that "stop us in our tracks." Manuscripts that stand out use "unexpected language, idiosyncrasy of outlook, and are the opposite of ordinary."

MEASURE: A REVIEW OF FORMAL POETRY

526 S. Lincoln Park Dr., Evansville IN 47714. (812)488-2963. **E-mail:** editors@measurepress.com. **Website:** www.measurepress.com/measure. *Measure*, an international journal of formal poetry, began in 2005 in conjunction with the University of Evansville. Measure Press is a new enterprise by editors Rob Griffith and Paul Bone. The goal is to continue bringing readers the best new poetry from both established and emerging writers through the biannual journal. *Measure* has a mission not only to publish the best new poetry from both established and emerging writers but also to reprint a small sampling of poems from books of metrical poetry published the previous year. Likewise, each issue includes interviews with some of the most important contemporary poets and also offers short critical essays on the poetry that has helped to shape the craft. Responds in 3 months. Guidelines online at website.

MAGAZINES NEEDS Send no more than 3 to 5 poems at a time. Poems must be metrical. Include poet's name and phone number. Submit electronically on website.

THE MENNONITE

718 N. Main St., Newton KS 67114-1703. (866)866-2872 ext. 34398. **Fax:** (316)283-0454. **E-mail:** gor-donh@themennonite.org. **Website:** www.themennonite.org. **Contact:** Gordon Houser, associate editor. *The Mennonite*, published monthly, seeks "to help readers glorify God, grow in faith, and become agents of healing and hope in the world. Our readers are primarily people in Mennonite churches." Acquires first or one-time rights. Publishes ms up to 1 year after acceptance. Responds in 2 weeks. Single copy: $4; subscription: $46 U.S. Guidelines online.

TIPS "Writing should be concise, accessible to the general reader, and with strong lead paragraphs. This last point cannot be overemphasized. The lead paragraph is the foundation of a good article. It should provide a summary of the article. We are especially interested in personal stories of Mennonites exercising their faith."

MENSBOOK JOURNAL

CQS Media, Inc., P.O. Box 418, Sturbridge MA 01566. **Fax:** (508)347-8150. **E-mail:** features@mensbook.com. **Website:** www.mensbook.com. **Contact:** P.C. Carr, editor/publisher. "We target bright, inquisitive, discerning gay men who want more noncommercial substance from gay media. We seek primarily first-person autobiographical pieces—then: biographies, political and social analysis, cartoons, short fiction, commentary, travel, and humor." Responds in 8 weeks to queries. Editorial lead time 4 months. Sample copy sent free by PDF. Publisher splits download fee with authors 50/50. Submit finished material anytime by e-mail. Do not call. Guidelines online at www.mensbook.com/writersguidelines.htm.

TIPS "Be a tight writer with a cogent, potent message. Structure your work with well-organized progressive sequencing. Edit everything down before you send it over so we know it is the best you can do, and we'll work together from there."

MERIDIAN

University of Virginia, P.O. Box 400145, Charlottesville VA 22904-4145. **E-mail:** meridianuva@gmail.com; meridianpoetry@gmail.com; meridianfiction@gmail.com. **Website:** www.readmeridian.org. *Meridian*, published semiannually, prints poetry, fiction, nonfiction, interviews, and reviews. "*Meridian* is interested in writing that is vibrant, moving, and alive, and welcomes contributions from a variety of aesthetic approaches. Has published such poets as Alexandra Teague, Gregory Pardlo, Sandra Meek, and Bob Hicok, and such fiction writers as Matt Bell, Kate

Milliken, and Ron Carlson. Has recently interviewed C. Michael Curtis, Ann Beatty, and Claire Messud, among other luminaries. Also publishes a recurring feature called 'Lost Classic,' which resurrects previously unpublished work by celebrated writers and which has included illustrations from the mss of Jorge Luis Borges, letters written by Elizabeth Bishop, Stephen Crane's deleted chapter from *The Red Badge of Courage*, and a letter written by Flannery O'Connor about her novel *Wise Blood*." Time between acceptance and publication is 1-2 months. Seldom comments on rejected poems and mss. Responds in 1-4 months. Always sends prepublication galleys and author contracts. Sample copy: $6 (back issue). Single print copy: $7. Print subscription: $12 for 1 year; $22 for 2 years. Single digital copy: $3. Digital subscription: $4 for 1 year; $7 for 2 years. Buy subscriptions online via credit card, or mail an order form with a check made out to *Meridian*. Guidelines online.

- *Meridian* is 130 pages, digest-sized, offset-printed, perfect-bound, with color cover. Receives about 2,500 poems/year, accepts about 40 (less than 1%). Press run is 1,000 (750 subscribers, 15 libraries, 200 shelf sales); 150 distributed free to writing programs. Work published in *Meridian* has appeared in *The Best American Poetry* and *The Pushcart Prize Anthology*.

MAGAZINES NEEDS Submit up to 5 poems via online submissions manager or postal mail. Length: up to 10 pages total. Pays 2 contributor's copies (additional copies available at discount).

ALSO OFFERS *Meridian* Editors' Prize Contest offers annual $1,000 award. Submit online only; see website for formatting details. **Entry fee:** $8.50, includes one-year subscription to *Meridian* for all U.S. entries or 1 copy of the prize issue for all international entries. **Deadline:** December or January; see website for current deadline.

🄢 MICHIGAN QUARTERLY REVIEW

0576 Rackham Bldg., 915 E. Washington, Ann Arbor MI 48109-1070. (734)764-9265. **E-mail:** mqr@umich.edu. **Website:** www.michiganquarterlyreview.com. **Contact:** Jonathan Freedman, editor; Vicki Lawrence, managing editor. *MQR* is an eclectic interdisciplinary journal of arts and culture that seeks to combine the best of poetry, fiction, and creative nonfiction with outstanding critical essays on literary, cultural, social,

and political matters. The flagship journal of the University of Michigan, *MQR* draws on lively minds here and elsewhere, seeking to present accessible work of all varieties for sophisticated readers from within and without the academy. Buys first serial rights. Pays on publication. Publishes ms an average of 1 year after acceptance. Responds in 2 months to queries. Responds in 2 months to mss. Sample copy for $4. Guidelines available online.

- The Laurence Goldstein Award is a $500 annual award to the best poem published in *MQR* during the previous year. The Lawrence Foundation Award is a $1,000 annual award to the best short story published in *MQR* during the previous year. The Page Davidson Clayton Award for Emerging Poets is a $500 annual award given to the best poet appearing in *MQR* during the previous year who has not yet published a book.

MAGAZINES NEEDS No previously published poems or simultaneous submissions. No e-mail submissions. Cover letter is preferred. "It puts a human face on the ms. A few sentences of biography is all I want, nothing lengthy or defensive." Prefers typed mss. Reviews books of poetry. "All reviews are commissioned." Length: should not exceed 8-12 pages. Pays $8-12/published page.

TIPS "Read the journal and assess the range of contents and the level of writing. We have no guidelines to offer or set expectations; every manuscript is judged on its unique qualities. On essays—query with a very thorough description of the argument and a copy of the first page. Watch for announcements of special issues, which are usually expanded issues and draw upon a lot of freelance writing. Be aware that this is a university quarterly that publishes a limited amount of fiction and poetry and that it is directed at an educated audience, one that has done a great deal of reading in all types of literature."

MID-AMERICAN REVIEW

Bowling Green State University, Dept. of English, Bowling Green OH 43403. (419)372-2725. **E-mail:** mar@bgsu.edu. **E-mail:** marsubmissions.bgsu.edu. **Website:** www.bgsu.edu/midamericanreview. **Contact:** Abigail Cloud, editor in chief; Laura Walter, fiction editor. "We aim to put the best possible work in front of the biggest possible audience. We publish contemporary fiction, poetry, creative nonfiction, translations, and book reviews." Buys first North American serial rights. Publishes mss an average of 6 months after acceptance. Responds in 5 months to mss. Sample copy: $9 (current issue), $5 (back issue), $10 (rare back issues). Guidelines available online.

○ Contests: The Fineline Competition for Prose Poems, Short Shorts, and Everything In Between (June 1 deadline, $10 per 3 pieces, limit 500 words each); The Sherwood Anderson Fiction Award (November 1 deadline, $10 per piece); and the James Wright Poetry Award (November 1 deadline, $10 per 3 pieces).

MAGAZINES NEEDS Submit by mail with SASE or with online submission manager. Publishes poems with "textured, evocative images, an awareness of how words sound and mean, and a definite sense of voice. Each line should help carry the poem, and an individual vision must be evident." Recently published work by Mary Ann Samyn, G.C. Waldrep, and Daniel Bourne.

TIPS "We are seeking translations of contemporary authors from all languages into English; submissions must include the original and proof of permission to translate. We would also like to see more creative nonfiction."

THE MIDWEST QUARTERLY

406b Russ Hall, Pittsburg State University, Pittsburg KS 66762. (620)235-4369; (620)235-4317. **E-mail:** midwestq@pittstate.edu; smeats@pittstate.edu. **Website:** www.pittstate.edu/department/english/midwest-quarterly. **Contact:** Dr. Jonathan Dresner, editor. *The Midwest Quarterly* publishes "articles on any subject of contemporary interest, particularly literary criticism, political science, philosophy, education, biography, and sociology. Each issue contains a section of poetry usually 12 poems in length. We seek discussions of an analytical and speculative nature and well-crafted poems." For publication in *MQ* and eligibility for the annual Emmett Memorial Prize competition, the editors invite submission of articles on any literary topic but preferably on Victorian or Modern British Literature, Literary Criticism, or the Teaching of Literature. The winner receives an honorarium and invitation to deliver the annual Emmett Memorial Lecture. Contact Dr. Stephen Meats, English Department, Pittsburg State University, Pittsburg, KS 66762. Acquires first serial rights. Responds in 2 months to

mss. Sample copy: $5. Subscription: $15 US; $25 foreign. Guidelines available on website.

○ *The Midwest Quarterly* is 130 pages, digest-sized, professionally printed, flat-spined, with matte cover. Press run is 650 (600 subscribers, 500 are libraries).

MAGAZINES NEEDS Submit up to 5 poems at a time. No fax or e-mail submissions. "Mss should be typed with poet's name on each page. Include e-mail address for notification of decision. SASE only for return of poem." Comments on rejected poems "if the poet or poem seems particularly promising." Occasionally publishes theme issues or issues devoted to the work of a single poet. Receives about 3,500-4,000 poems/year, accepts about 50. Has published poetry by Peter Cooley, Lyn Lifshin, Judith Skillman, Naomi Shihab Nye, Jonathan Holden, and Ted Kooser. Wants "well-crafted poems, traditional or untraditional, that use intense, vivid, concrete, and/or surrealistic images to explore the mysterious and surprising interactions of the natural and inner human worlds." Does not want "'nature poems,' per se, but if a poem doesn't engage nature in a significant way, as an integral part of the experience it is offering, I am unlikely to be interested in publishing it." Length: up to 60 lines/poem ("occasionally longer if exceptional"). Pays 2 contributor's copies.

⑤ MILLER'S POND

E-mail: mail@handhpress.com (C.J. Houghtaling); mpwebeditor@yahoo.com (Julie Damerell). **Website:** www. millerspondpoetry.com. **Contact:** C.J. Houghtaling, publisher; Julie Damerell, editor. *miller's pond* is exclusively an e-zine and does not publish in hard copy format. Web version is published 3 times/year. Submissions accepted year round but read in December, April, and August. Responses sent only in December, April, and August. "Current guidelines, updates, and changes are always available on our website. Check there first before submitting anything."

MAGAZINES NEEDS Submit poems to Julie Damerell, editor. All submissions must be sent in the body of an e-mail. Mail sent through the post office will be discarded. No payment for accepted poems or reviews.

TIPS "Follow submission guidelines on the website. Submissions that do not fulfill the guidelines are deleted without comment. Read the website to see the kind of poetry we like."

MINAS TIRITH EVENING-STAR: JOURNAL OF THE AMERICAN TOLKIEN SOCIETY

American Tolkien Society, P.O. Box 97, Highland MI 48357-0097. **E-mail:** editor@americantolkiensociety. org; americantolkiensociety@yahoo.com. **Website:** www.americantolkiensociety.org. **Contact:** Amalie A. Helms, editor. *Minas Tirith Evening-Star: Journal of the American Tolkien Society*, published quarterly, publishes poetry, book reviews, essays, and fan fition. *Minas Tirith Evening-Star* is digest-sized, offset-printed from typescript, with cartoon-like b&w graphics. Press run is 400. Single copy: $3.50; subscription: $12.50. Sample: $3. Make checks payable to American Tolkien Society. Responds in 2 weeks. Guidelines for SASE or by e-mail.

MAGAZINES NEEDS Uses poetry of fantasy about Middle-earth and Tolkien. Considers poetry by children and teens. Has published poetry by Thomas M. Egan, Anne Etkin, Nancy Pope, and Martha Benedict. Submit by mail or e-mail. Reviews related books of poetry; length depends on the volume ("a sentence to several pages"). Send materials for review consideration. Pays 1 contributor's copy.

ALSO OFFERS Membership in the American Tolkien Society is open to all, regardless of country of residence, and entitles one to receive the quarterly journal. Dues are $12.50/year to addresses in U.S., Canada, and Mexico, and $15 elsewhere. Sometimes sponsors contests.

THE MINNESOTA REVIEW

Virginia Tech, ASPECT, 202 Major Williams Hall (0192), Blacksburg VA 24061. **E-mail:** editors@theminnesotareview.org. **Website:** http://minnesotareview.wordpress.com. **Contact:** Janell Watson, editor. *The Minnesota Review*, published biannually, is a journal featuring creative and critical work from writers on the rise or who are already established. Each issue is about 200 pages, digest-sized, flat-spined, with glossy card cover. Press run is 1,000 (400 subscribers). Also available online. Subscription: $30/2 years for individuals, $60/year for institutions. Sample: $15. Guidelines available online.

Open to submissions August 1-November 1 and January 1-April 1. Accepts submissions via online submissions manager.

MAGAZINES NEEDS Submit up to 5 poems every 3 months online. Pays 2 contributor's copies.

M.I.P. COMPANY

P.O. Box 27484, Minneapolis MN 55427. (763)544-5915. **Website:** www.mipco.com. **Contact:** Michael Peltsman, editor. The publisher of controversial Russian literature (erotic poetry). Responds to queries in 1 month. Seldom comments on rejected poems.

MAGAZINES NEEDS Considers simultaneous submissions; no previously published poems.

MISSISSIPPI REVIEW

University of Southern Mississippi, 118 College Dr., #5144, Hattiesburg MS 39406-0001. (601)266-4321. **Fax:** (601)266-5757. **E-mail:** msreview@usm.edu. **Website:** www.usm.edu/mississippi-review. **Contact:** Andrew Malan Milward, editor in chief; Caleb Tankersley and Allison Campbell, associate editors. *Mississippi Review* "is one of the most respected literary journals in the country. Raymond Carver, an early contributor to the magazine, once said that *Mississippi Review* 'is one of the most remarkable and indispensable literary journals of our time.' Well-known and established writers have appeared in the pages of the magazine, including Pulitzer and Nobel Prize winners, as well as new and emerging writers who have gone on to publish books and to receive awards." Buys first North American serial rights. Sample copy for $10. "We do not accept unsolicited manuscripts except under the rules and guidelines of the *Mississippi Review* Prize Competition. See website for guidelines."

Publishes 25-30 new writers/year. Annual fiction and poetry competition: $1,000 awarded in each category, plus publication of all winners and finalists. Fiction entries: 8,000 words or less. Poetry entries: 1-5 poems; page limit is 10. $15 entry fee includes copy of prize issue. No limit on number of entries. Deadline December 1. No mss returned.

THE MISSOURI REVIEW

357 McReynolds Hall, University of Missouri, Columbia MO 65211. (573)882-4474. **Fax:** (573)884-4671. **E-mail:** question@moreview.com. **Website:** www.missourireview.com. **Contact:** Speer Morgan, editor; Michael Nye, managing editor. Publishes contemporary fiction, poetry, interviews, personal essays, cartoons, special features—such as History as Literature series and Found Text series—for the literary and the general reader interested in a wide range of subjects. Offers signed contract. Responds in 2 weeks to queries.

Responds in 10-12 weeks to mss. Editorial lead time 6 months. Sample copy for $8.95 or online Guidelines available online.

MAGAZINES NEEDS *TMR* publishes poetry features only—6-14 pages of poems by each of 3-5 poets per issue. Keep in mind the length of features when submitting poems. Typically, successful submissions include 8-20 pages of unpublished poetry (note: do not send complete mss—published or unpublished—for consideration). Pays $40/printed page and 3 contributor's copies.

ADDITIONAL INFORMATION The Tom McAfee Discovery Feature is awarded at least once/year to showcase an outstanding young poet who has not yet published a book; poets are selected from regular submissions at the discretion of the editors.

TIPS "Send your best work."

MOBIUS

149 Talmadge, Madison WI 53704. (608)335-9340. E-mail: fmschep@charter.net. **Website:** www.mobius-magazine.com. **Contact:** Fred Schepartz, publisher and executive editor. *Mobius: The Journal of Social Change* became an online-only journal, published quarterly in March, June, September, and December, in 2009. Publishes ms 3-6 months after acceptance. Responds in 1 month. Guidelines available online.

MAGAZINES NEEDS Submit poetry dealing with themes of social change. Accepts e-mailed poetry submissions only. "We have a marked distate for prosaic didacticism (but a weakness for prose poems)." DO NOT submit poems by postal mail.

TIPS "We like high impact. We like plot- and character-driven stories that function like theater of the mind. We look first and foremost for good writing. Prose must be crisp and polished; the story must pique my interest and make me care due to a certain intellectual, emotional aspect. *Mobius* is about social change. We want stories that make some statement about the society we live in, either on a macro or micro level. Not that your story needs to preach from a soapbox (actually, we prefer that it doesn't), but your story needs to have something to say."

THE MOCCASIN

The League of Minnesota Poets, 427 N. Gorman St., Blue Earth MN 56013. (507)526-5321. **Website:** www.mnpoets.com. **Contact:** Meredith R. Cook, editor. *The Moccasin*, published annually in October, is the literary magazine of The League of Minnesota Poets. Membership is required to submit work.

The Moccasin is 40 pages, digest-sized, offset-printed, stapled, with 80 lb. linen-finish text cover with drawing and poem. Receives about 190 poems/year, accepts about 170. Press run is 200. Single copy: $6.25; subscription: free with LOMP membership.

MAGAZINES NEEDS Send submissions by mid-July each year. Looking for all forms of poetry. Prefer strong short poems. Considers poetry by children and teens who are student members of The League of Minnesota Poets (write grade level on poems submitted). Has published poetry by Diane Glancy, Laurel Winter, Susan Stevens Chambers, Doris Stengel, Jeanette Hinds, and Charmaine Donovan. Does not want profanity or obscenity. Do not use inversions or archaic language. Length: 24 lines max.

TIPS To become a member of The League of Minnesota Poets, send $20 ($10 if high school student or younger) to Angela Foster, LOMP Treasurer, 30036 St. Croix Rd, Pine City MN 55063. Make checks payable to LOMP. You do not have to live in Minnesota to become a member of LOMP. "Membership in LOMP automatically makes you a member of the National Federation of State Poetry Societies, which makes you eligible to enter its contests at a cheaper (members') rate."

THE MOCHILA REVIEW

Missouri Western State University, 4525 Downs Dr., St. Joseph MO 64507. **E-mail:** mochila@missouri-western.edu. **Website:** www.missouriwestern.edu/orgs/mochila/homepage.htm. **Contact:** Marianne Kunkel, editor. "We are looking for writing that has a respect for the sound of language. We value poems that have to be read aloud so your mouth can feel the shape of the words. Send us writing that conveys a sense of urgency, writing that the writer can't *not* write. We crave fresh and daring work." Responds in 3-4 months to mss. Guidelines available online.

MAGAZINES NEEDS Submit no more than 5 poems at a time by postal mail. Include cover letter, contact information, SASE. Pays in contributor's copies.

TIPS "Manuscripts with fresh language, energy, passion, and intelligence stand out. Study the craft and be entertaining and engaging."

MODERN HAIKU

P.O. Box 930, Portsmouth RI 02871. **E-mail:** modernhaiku@gmail.com. **Website:** modernhaiku.org.

Modern Haiku is the foremost international journal of English-language haiku and criticism and publishes high-quality material only. Haiku and related genres, articles on haiku, haiku book reviews, and translations comprise its contents. It has an international circulation; subscribers include many university, school, and public libraries. Acquires first North American serial rights, first international serial rights. Publishes ms an average of 6 months after acceptance. Responds in 1 week to queries; in 6-8 weeks to mss. Editorial lead time 4 months. Sample copy: $15 in North America, $16 in Canada, $20 in Mexico, $22 overseas. Subscription: $35 ppd by regular mail in the U.S. Payment possible by PayPal on the *Modern Haiku* website. Guidelines available for SASE or on website.

○ *Modern Haiku* is 140 pages (average), digest-sized, printed on heavy-quality stock, with full-color cover illustrations, 4-page full-color art sections. Receives about 15,000 submissions/year, accepts about 1,000. Press run is 700.

MAGAZINES NEEDS Postal submissions: "Send 5-15 haiku on 1 or 2 letter-sized sheets. Put name and address at the top of each sheet. Include SASE." E-mail submissions: "May be attachments (recommended) or pasted in body of message. Subject line must read: MH Submission. Adhere to guidelines on the website. No payment for haiku sent/accepted by e-mail." Publishes 750 poems/year. Has published haiku by Roberta Beary, Billy Collins, Lawrence Ferlinghetti, Carolyn Hall, Sharon Olds, Gary Snyder, John Stevenson, George Swede, and Cor van den Heuvel. Does not want "general poetry, tanka, renku, linked-verse forms. No special consideration given to work by children and teens." No payment.

ALSO OFFERS Reviews of books of haiku by staff and freelancers by invitation in 350-1,000 words, usually single-book format. Send materials for review consideration with complete ordering information. Sponsors the annual Robert Spiess Memorial Haiku Competition. Guidelines available for SASE or on website.

TIPS "Study the history of haiku, read books about haiku, learn the aesthetics of haiku and methods of composition. Write about your sense perceptions of the suchness of entities; avoid ego-centered interpretations. Be sure the work you send us conforms to the definitions on our website."

MUDFISH

Box Turtle Press, 184 Franklin St., New York NY 10013. (212)219-9278. **E-mail:** mudfishmag@aol.com. **Website:** www.mudfish.org. **Contact:** Jill Hoffman, editor. *Mudfish*, a journal of art and poetry (and some fiction), takes its title from the storyteller's stool in Nigerian art. The poems each tell a story. They are resonant, and visceral, encapsulating the unique human experience. There is a wide range to the subject matter and style, but the poems all have breath and life, a living voice. *Mudfish* has featured work from the best established and emerging artists and poets—including John Ashbery, Charles Simic, and Frank Stella—since it burst onto the poetry scene. Responds in 3 months.

MAGAZINES NEEDS Wants free verse with energy, intensity, and originality of voice, mastery of style, the presence of passion. Submit 5 or 6 poems at a time. No e-mail submissions; postal submissions only. Pays 1 contributor's copy.

CONTEST/AWARD OFFERINGS Sponsors the Mudfish Poetry Prize Award of $1,000. **Entry fee:** $15 for up to 3 poems, $3 for each additional poem. **Deadline:** varies. Guidelines available for SASE.

MUDLARK: AN ELECTRONIC JOURNAL OF POETRY & POETICS

Department of English, University of North Florida, Jacksonville FL 32224-2645. (904)620-2273. **Fax:** (904)620-3940. **E-mail:** mudlark@unf.edu. **Website:** www.unf.edu/mudlark. **Contact:** William Slaughter, editor and publisher. *Mudlark: An Electronic Journal of Poetry & Poetics*, published online "irregularly, but frequently," offers 3 formats: Issues of *Mudlark* "are the electronic equivalent of print chapbooks; posters are the electronic equivalent of print broadsides; and flash poems are poems that have news in them, poems that feel like current events. The poem is the thing at *Mudlark*, and the essay about it. As our full name suggests, we will consider accomplished work that locates itself anywhere on the spectrum of contemporary practice. We want poems, of course, but we want essays, too, that make us read poems (and write them?) differently somehow. Although we are not innocent, we do imagine ourselves capable of surprise. The work of hobbyists is not for *Mudlark*. As for representative authors: No naming names here. If we are, as we imagine ourselves, capable of surprise, then there is no such thing as a 'representative author' in the *Mudlark* archive, which is 'never in and never out of print.' The *Mudlark* archive, going back to 1995, is as wide as it is deep, as rich and various as it is full." *Mudlark* is archived and permanently on view at www.unf.edu/mudlark. Acquires one-time rights. No payment; however, "one of the things we can do at *Mudlark* to 'pay' our authors for their work is point to it here and there. We can tell our readers how to find it, how to subscribe to it, and how to buy it—if it is for sale. Toward that end, we maintain A-Notes on the authors we publish. We call attention to their work." Publishes ms no more than 3 months after acceptance. Responds in "1 day to 1 month, depending." Guidelines for SASE, by e-mail, or on website.

MAGAZINES NEEDS Submit any number of poems at a time. "Prefers not to receive multiple submissions but will consider them if informed of the fact, up front, and if notified immediately when poems are accepted elsewhere. Considers previously published work only as part of a *Mudlark* issue, the electronic equivalent of a print chapbook, and only if the previous publication is acknowledged in a note that covers the submission. Only poems that have not been previously published will be considered for *Mudlark* posters, the electronic equivalent of print broadsides, or for *Mudlark* flashes." Accepts e-mail or USPS submissions with SASE; no fax submissions. Cover letter is optional. Seldom comments on rejected poems. Always sends prepublication galleys "in the form of inviting the author to proof the work on a private website that *Mudlark* maintains for that purpose."

🚫 MYTHIC DELIRIUM

3514 Signal Hill Ave. NW, Roanoke VA 24017-5148. **E-mail:** mythicdelirium@gmail.com. **Website:** www.mythicdelirium.com. **Contact:** Mike Allen, editor. "*Mythic Delirium* is an online and e-book venue for fiction and poetry that ranges through science fiction, fantasy, horror, interstitial, and cross-genre territory—we love blurred boundaries and tropes turned on their heads. We are interested in work that demonstrates ambition, that defies traditional approaches to genre, that introduces readers to the legends of other cultures, that re-evaluates the myths of old from a modern perspective, that twists reality in unexpected ways. We are committed to diversity and are open to and encourage submissions from people of every race, gender, nationality, sexual orientation, political affiliation and religious belief. We publish 12 short stories and 24 poems a year. Our quarterly ebooks

in PDF, EPUB, and MOBI formats, published in July, October, January, and April, will each contain 3 stories and 6 poems. We will also publish 1 story and 2 poems on our website each month." Reading period: August 1-October 1 annually. Responds in 2 months. Accepts electronic submissions only to mythicdelirium@gmail.com.

MAGAZINES NEEDS "No unsolicited reprints. Please use the words 'poetry submission' in the e-mail subject line. Poems may be included in the e-mail as RTF or DOC attachments." Length: open. Pays $5 flat fee.

TIPS "*Mythic Delirium* isn't easy to get into, but we publish newcomers in every issue. Show us how ambitious you can be, and don't give up."

NARRATIVE MAGAZINE

2443 Fillmore St. #214, San Francisco CA 94115. **Website:** www.narrativemagazine.com. **Contact:** Michael Croft, senior editor; Mimi Kusch, managing editor; Michael Wiegers, poetry editor. "*Narrative* publishes high-quality contemporary literature in a full range of styles, forms, and lengths. Submit poetry, fiction, and nonfiction, including stories, short shorts, novels, novel excerpts, novellas, personal essays, humor, sketches, memoirs, literary biographies, commentary, reportage, interviews, and short audio recordings of short-short stories and poems. We welcome submissions of previously unpublished mss of all lengths, ranging from short-short stories to complete book-length works for serialization. In addition to submissions for issues of *Narrative* itself, we also encourage submissions for our Story of the Week, literary contests, and Readers' Narratives. Please read our Submission Guidelines for all information on ms formatting, word lengths, author payment, and other policies. We accept submissions only through our electronic submission system. We do not accept submissions through postal services or e-mail. You may send us mss for the following submission categories: General Submissions, Narrative Prize, Story of the Week, Readers' Narrative, iPoem, iStory, Six-Word Story, or a specific Contest. Your ms must be in one of the following file forms: .doc, .rtf, .pdf, .docx, .txt, .wpd, .odf, .mp3, .mp4, .mov, or .flv." Buys exclusive first North American serial rights in English for 90 days, and thereafter, for nonexclusive rights "to maintain the work in our online library." Responds in 4-14 weeks to queries. Guidelines available online. Charges $20 reading fee except for 2 weeks in April.

○ *Narrative* has received recognitions in *New Stories from the South*, *Best American Mystery Stories*, *O. Henry Prize Stories*, *Best American Short Stories*, *Best American Essays*, and the *Pushcart Prize Collection*. In their first quarterly issue of 2010, the National Endowment for the Arts featured an article on the business of books, with *Narrative*'s digital publishing model a key focus. Providing a behind-the-scenes look at the way in which *Narrative* functions and thrives, it is an essential read for anyone looking to learn more about the current state of publishing both in the print and digital arenas.

TIPS "Log on and study our magazine online. Narrative fiction, graphic art, and multimedia are selected, first and foremost, for quality."

NASSAU REVIEW

Nassau Community College, State University of New York, English Dept., 1 Education Dr., Garden City NY 11530. **E-mail:** nassaureview@ncc.edu. **Website:** www.ncc.edu/nassaureview. **Contact:** Christina Rau, editor in chief and poetry editor; Beth Beatrice Smith, fiction editor; Emily Hegarty, creative nonfiction editor. *The Nassau Review* welcomes submissions of many genres, preferring work that is "innovative, captivating, well-crafted, and unique, work that crosses boundaries of genre and tradition. You may be serious. You may be humorous. You may be somewhere in between. We are looking simply for quality. New and seasoned writers are welcome." Acquires first North American serial rights "and the right to archive your work online for an indefinite period of time." Submit via online submissions system only. Please read all guidelines and details on the website: www.ncc.edu/nassaureview.

○ All open submissions are under consideration for the Writer Awards.

MAGAZINES NEEDS Accepts simultaneous submissions: "Please let us know they are simultaneous when you submit them." Submit via online submissions manager. Include title, word count, and bio of up to 100 words. Length: 50 lines/poem. Pays 1 contributor's copy.

⊙ THE NATION

33 Irving Place, 8th Floor, New York NY 10003. **E-mail:** submissions@thenation.com. **Website:** www.

thenation.com. Steven Brower, art director. **Contact:** Roane Carey, managing editory; Ange Mlinko, poetry editor. *The Nation*, published weekly, is a journal of left/liberal opinion, with arts coverage that includes poetry. The only requirement for poetry is excellence. Guidelines available online.

○ Poetry published by *The Nation* has been included in *The Best American Poetry*. Has published poetry by W.S. Merwin, Maxine Kumin, James Merrill, May Swenson, Edward Hirsch, and Charles Simic.

MAGAZINES NEEDS Submit poems only via mail. Send no more than 8 poems in a calendar year. Include a SASE.

HOW TO CONTACT *The Nation* welcomes unsolicited poetry submissions. You may send up to three poems at a time, and no more than eight poems during a calendar year. Send poems by first-class mail, accompanied by a SASE. Does not reply to or return poems sent by fax or e-mail or submitted without an SASE. Submissions are not accepted from June 1 to September 15. Manuscripts may be mailed to: Ange Mlinko, poetry editor.

THE NATIONAL POETRY REVIEW

P.O. Box 2080, Aptos CA 95001-2080. **E-mail:** editor@nationalpoetryreview.com; nationalpoetryreview@yahoo.com. **Website:** www.nationalpoetryreview.com. **Contact:** C.J. Sage, editor. *The National Poetry Review* seeks "distinction, innovation, and *joie de vivre*. We agree with Frost about delight and wisdom. We believe in rich sound. We believe in the beautiful—even if that beauty is not in the situation of the poem but simply the sounds of the poem, the images, or (and, ideally) the way the poem stays in the reader's mind long after it's been read." *TNPR* considers both experimental and 'mainstream' work." Does not want "overly self-centered or confessional poetry." Acquires first rights. Time between acceptance and publication is no more than 1 year. "The editor makes all publishing decisions." Sometimes comments on rejected poems. Usually responds in about 1-12 weeks. Guidelines available in magazine or on website.

○ *The National Poetry Review* is 80 pages, perfect-bound, with full-color cover. Accepts less than 1% of submissions received. Single copy: $15; subscription: $15/year. Make checks payable to *TNPR* only. Poetry appearing in *The National Poetry Review* has also appeared in *The Push-*

cart Prize. Has published poetry by Bob Hicok, Jennifer Michael Hecht, Larissa Szplorluk, Martha Zweig, Nance Van Winkel, William Waltz, and Ted Kooser.

MAGAZINES NEEDS Submit 3-5 poems at a time by e-mail only to address below; postal submissions will be recycled unread. Considers simultaneous submissions "with notification only. Submit only between December 1 and February 28 unless you are a subscriber or benefactor. Put your name in the subject line of your e-mail and send to tnprsubmissions@yahoo.com." Bio is required. Subscribers and benefactors may submit any time during the year ("please write 'subscriber' or 'benefactor' in the subject line"). See website before submitting. Pays 1 contributor's copy and small honorarium when funds are available.

NATURAL BRIDGE

Dept. of English, University of Missouri-St. Louis, One University Blvd., St. Louis MO 63121. (314)516-7327. **E-mail:** natural@umsl.edu. **Website:** www.umsl.edu/~natural. *Natural Bridge*, published biannually in May and December, invites submissions of poetry, fiction, personal essays, and translations. Acquires first North American rights. Publishes ms 9 months after acceptance. Responds in 4-8 months. Guidelines available online at website.

○ No longer accepts submissions via e-mail. Accepts submissions through online submission form and postal mail only.

MAGAZINES NEEDS Seeks "fresh, innovative poetry, both free and formal, on any subject. We want poems that work on first and subsequent readings—poems that entertain and resonate and challenge our readers." Submit 4-6 poems at a time. "Submissions should be typewritten, with name and address on each page. Do not staple manuscripts. Send SASE." Submit year round; however, "we do not read May 1-August 1. Work is read and selected by the guest-editor and editor, along with editorial assistants made up of graduate students in our MFA program. We publish work by both established and new writers." Length: no limit. Pays 2 contributor's copies and one-year subscription.

NATURALLY

Internaturally, Inc., P.O. Box 317, Newfoundland NJ 07435. (973)697-3552. **Fax:** (973)697-8313. **E-mail:** naturally@internaturally.com. **Website:** www.internaturally.com. "A full-color, glossy magazine with on-line editions, and the foremost naturist/nudist magazine in the U.S. with international distribution, *Naturally* focuses on the clothes-free lifestyle, publishing articles about worldwide destinations, first-time nudist experiences, and news information pertaining to the clothes-free lifestyle. Our mission is to demystify the human form and allow each human to feel comfortable in their own skin, in a nonsexual environment. We offer a range of books, DVDs, magazines, and other products useful to naturists/nudists in their daily lives and for the education of nonnaturists. Travel DVDs featuring resorts to visit; books on Christianity and nudity, nudist plays, memoirs, cartoons, and novellas; and also towels, sandals, calendars, and more." Buys first North American serial rights, first rights, one-time rights, second serial (reprint) rights, simultaneous rights, electronic rights. Makes work-for-hire assignments. Pays on publication. Publishes ms an average of 3 months after acceptance. Responds in 2 weeks to queries; in 3 months to mss. Editorial lead time 3-6 months. Sample copy available online.

○ Write about nudists and naturists. Wants more people stories than travel.

TIPS "Become a nudist/naturist. Appreciate human beings in their natural state."

NAUGATUCK RIVER REVIEW

P.O. Box 368, Westfield MA 01085. **E-mail:** naugatuckriver@aol.com. **Website:** naugatuckriverreview.wordpress.com. **Contact:** Lori Desrosiers, publisher. *Naugatuck River Review*, published semiannually, "is a literary journal for great narrative poetry looking for narrative poetry of high caliber, where the narrative is compressed with a strong emotional core." Acquires first North American serial rights. Responds in 1-4 months. Always sends prepublication galleys. Guidelines available in magazine and on website.

○ Accepts submissions through online submission form only.

MAGAZINES NEEDS Submit up to 3 poems. Prefers unpublished poems. Accepts online submissions through submission manager only; no e-mail, fax, or disk submissions. Include a brief bio and mailing information. Reads submissions January 1-March 1 and July 1-September 1 for contest (fee). Length: up to 50 lines.

TIPS "WHAT IS NARRATIVE POETRY? What *NRR* is looking for are poems that tell a story or have a strong sense of story. They can be stories of a moment or an experience and can be personal or historical. A good narrative poem that would work for our journal has a compressed narrative, and we prefer poems that take up 2 pages or less of the journal (50 lines max). We are looking above all for poems that are well crafted, have an excellent lyric quality, and contain a strong emotional core. Any style of poem is considered, including prose poems. Poems with very long lines don't fit well in the 6x9 format."

NEBO

Arkansas Tech University, Department of English, Russellville AR 72801. (501)968-0256. **E-mail:** nebo@ atu.edu. **Website:** www.atu.edu/worldlanguages/ Nebo.php. **Contact:** Editor. "*Nebo* routinely publishes Arkansas Tech students and unpublished writers alongside nationally known writers." Acquires one-time rights. Publishes mss 3-6 months after acceptance. Responds in 2 weeks to 4 months to mss. Occasionally comments on rejected mss. Sample copy: $6. Subscriptions: $10. Guidelines available on website.

Literary journal: 5x8; 50-60 pages. For general, academic audience. Receives 20-30 unsolicited mss per month. *Nebo* is published in the spring and fall.

MAGAZINES NEEDS Accepts all forms of poetry. Contact editor for specifics. Submit by mail. Reads mss August 15-January 31. Pays 1 contributor's copy.

TIPS "Avoid pretentiousness. Write something you genuinely care about. Please edit your work for spelling, grammar, cohesiveness, and overall purpose. Many of the mss we receive should be publishable with a little polishing. Mss should never be submitted handwritten or on 'onion skin' or colored paper."

NEON MAGAZINE

E-mail: info@neonmagazine.co.uk. **Website:** www. neonmagazine.co.uk. **Contact:** Krishan Coupland. Quarterly website and print magazine covering alternative work of any form of poetry and prose, short stories, flash fiction, artwork and reviews. "Genre work is welcome. Experimentation is encouraged. We like stark poetry and weird prose. We seek work that is beautiful, shocking, intense, and memorable. Darker pieces are generally favored over humorous ones." Buys one-time rights. "After publication all rights revert back to you." Responds in 1 month. Query if you have received no reply after 6 weeks. Guidelines available online.

Neon was previously published as *FourVolts Magazine*.

MAGAZINES NEEDS "No nonsensical poetry; we are not appreciative of sentimentality. Rhyming poetry is discouraged." No word limit. Pays royalties.

TIPS "Send several poems, 1 or 2 pieces of prose or several images via form e-mail. Include the word 'submission' in your subject line. Include a short biographical note (up to 100 words). Read submission guidelines before submitting your work."

NEW AMERICAN WRITING

369 Molino Ave., Mill Valley CA 94941. **Website:** www.newamericanwriting.com. Editors: Maxine Chernoff and Paul Hoover. New American Writing is a literary magazine emphasizing contemporary American poetry. The magazine is distinctive for publishing a range of contemporary innovative poetry. Sample copies available for $15. Guidelines online.

MAGAZINES NEEDS Reading period September 1 to January 15. Submit via postal mail. Response time varies between 2 weeks to 6 months.

THE NEW CRITERION

Website: www.newcriterion.com. **Contact:** Roger Kimball, editor and publisher. "A monthly review of the arts and intellectual life, *The New Criterion* began as an experiment in critical audacity—a publication devoted to engaging, in Matthew Arnold's famous phrase, with 'the best that has been thought and said.' This also meant engaging with those forces dedicated to traducing genuine cultural and intellectual achievement, whether through obfuscation, politicization, or a commitment to nihilistic absurdity. We are proud that *The New Criterion* has been in the forefront both of championing what is best and most humanely vital in our cultural inheritance and in exposing what is mendacious, corrosive, and spurious. Published monthly from September through June, *The New Criterion* brings together a wide range of young and established critics whose common aim is to bring you the most incisive criticism being written today."

Has published poetry by Donald Justice, Andrew Hudgins, Elizabeth Spires, and Herbert Morris. *The New Criterion* is 90 pages, 7x10, flat-spined. Single copy: $12.

NEW ENGLAND REVIEW

Middlebury College, Middlebury VT 05753. (802)443-5075. **E-mail:** nereview@middlebury.edu. **Website:** www.nereview.com. **Contact:** Carolyn Kuebler, editor. *New England Review* is a prestigious, nationally distributed literary journal. Reads September 1-May 31 (postmarked dates). Buys first North American serial rights, buys first rights, buys second serial (reprint) rights. Sends galleys to author. Pays on publication. Publishes ms an average of 6 months after acceptance. Responds in 2 weeks to queries; in 3 months to mss. Sometimes comments on rejected mss. Sample copy: $10 (add $5 for overseas). Subscription: $30. Overseas shipping fees add $25 for subscription, $12 for Canada. Guidelines available online.

○ *New England Review* is 200+ pages, 7x10, printed on heavy stock, flat-spined, with glossy cover with art. Receives 3,000-4,000 poetry submissions/year, accepts about 70-80 poems/year. Receives 550 unsolicited mss/month, accepts 6 mss/issue, 24 fiction mss/year. Does not accept mss June-August. Agented fiction less than 5%.

MAGAZINES NEEDS Submit up to 6 poems at a time. No previously published or simultaneous submissions for poetry. Accepts submissions by postal mail or online submission manager only; accepts questions by e-mail. "Cover letters are useful." Address submissions to "Poetry Editor." Pays $20/page ($20 minimum), and 2 contributor's copies.

ALSO OFFERS *NER* pays $50 per published online essay in their series "Confluences," works of 500-1,000 words. Submission details appear online.

TIPS "We consider short fiction, including short shorts, novellas, and self-contained extracts from novels in both traditional and experimental forms. In nonfiction, we consider a variety of general and literary but not narrowly scholarly essays; we also publish long and short poems, screenplays, graphics, translations, critical reassessments, statements by artists working in various media, testimonies, and letters from abroad. We are committed to exploration of all forms of contemporary cultural expression in the U.S. and abroad. With few exceptions, we print only work not published previously elsewhere."

⑤ NEW LETTERS

University of Missouri-Kansas City, 5101 Rockhill Rd., Kansas City MO 64110. (816)235-1168. **Fax:** (816)235-2611. **E-mail:** newletters@umkc.edu. **Website:** www.newletters.org. **Contact:** Robert Stewart, editor in chief. "*New Letters* continues to seek the best new writing, whether from established writers or those ready and waiting to be discovered. In addition, it supports those writers, readers, and listeners who want to experience the joy of writing that can both

surprise and inspire us all." Buys first North American serial rights. Pays on publication. Publishes ms an average of 6 months after acceptance. Responds in 1 month to queries; in 5 months to mss. Editorial lead time 6 months. Sample copy: $10 or sample articles on website. Guidelines available online.

○ Submissions are not read May 1-October 1.

MAGAZINES NEEDS No light verse. Length: open. Pays $10-25.

TIPS "We aren't interested in essays that are footnoted or essays usually described as scholarly or critical. Our preference is for creative nonfiction or personal essays. We prefer shorter stories and essays to longer ones (an average length is 3,500-4,000 words). We have no rigid preferences as to subject, style, or genre, although commercial efforts tend to put us off. Even so, our only fixed requirement is good writing."

NEW MADRID

Murray State University, Department of English and Philosophy, 7C Faculty Hall, Murray KY 42071-3341. (270)809-4730. **E-mail:** msu.newmadrid@murraystate.edu. **Website:** newmadridjournal.org. **Contact:** Ann Neelon, editor. "*New Madrid* is the national journal of the low-residency MFA program at Murray State University. It takes its name from the New Madrid seismic zone, which falls within the central Mississippi Valley and extends through western Kentucky." Acquires first North American serial rights. Publication is copyrighted. Responds at the close of each reading period. Guidelines available on website.

○ See website for guidelines and upcoming themes. "We have 2 reading periods, one from August 15-October 15, and one from January 15-March 15." Also publishes poetry and creative nonfiction. Rarely comments on/critiques rejected mss.

MAGAZINES NEEDS Accepts submissions by online submissions manager only. Include brief bio, list of publications. Considers multiple submissions.

TIPS "Quality is the determining factor for breaking into *New Madrid*. We are looking for well-crafted, compelling writing in a range of genres, forms, and styles."

⑤ NEW MILLENNIUM WRITINGS

New Messenger Writing and Publishing, P.O. Box 2463, Knoxville TN 37901. (865)428-0389. **Website:** newmillenniumwritings.com. **Contact:** Elizabeth Petty, submissions editor. Only accepts general submissions January-April, but holds 4 contests twice each year for all types of fiction, nonfiction, short-short fiction, and poetry. Publishes mss 6 months to 1 year after acceptance. Rarely comments on/critiques rejected mss.

○ Annual anthology. 6x9, 204 pages, 50 lb. white paper, glossy 4-color cover. Contains illustrations and photographs.

MAGAZINES NEEDS Submit 3 poems, up to 5 pages total.

NEW OHIO REVIEW

English Department, 360 Ellis Hall, Ohio University, Athens OH 45701. (740)597-1360. **E-mail:** noreditors@ohio.edu. **Website:** www.ohiou.edu/nor. **Contact:** Jill Allyn Rosser, editor. *New Ohio Review*, published biannually in spring and fall, publishes fiction, nonfiction, and poetry. Responds in 2-4 months. Single copy: $9. Subscription: $16. Guidelines available on website.

○ Member CLMP. Reading period is September 15-December 15 and January 15-April 1.

MAGAZINES NEEDS "Please do not submit more than once every 6 months."

⊙ NEW ORLEANS REVIEW

Box 195, Loyola University, New Orleans LA 70118. (504)865-2295. **E-mail:** noreview@loyno.edu. **Website:** neworleansreview.org. **Contact:** Heidi Braden, managing editor. *New Orleans Review* is a biannual journal of contemporary literature and culture, publishing new poetry, fiction, nonfiction, art, photography, film and book reviews. Buys first North American serial rights. Pays on publication. Responds in 4 months to mss. Sample copy: $5.

○ The journal has published an eclectic variety of work by established and emerging writers including Walker Percy, Pablo Neruda, Ellen Gilchrist, Nelson Algren, Hunter S. Thompson, John Kennedy Toole, Richard Brautigan, Barry Spacks, James Sallis, Jack Gilbert, Paul Hoover, Rodney Jones, Annie Dillard, Everette Maddox, Julio Cortazar, Gordon Lish, Robert Walser, Mark Halliday, Jack Butler, Robert Olen Butler, Michael Harper, Angela Ball, Joyce Carol Oates, Diane Wakoski, Dermot Bolger, Roddy Doyle, William Kotzwinkle, Alain Robbe-Grillet, Arnost Lustig, Raymond Queneau, Yusef Komunyakaa, Michael Martone, Tess Gallagher, Matthea Harvey, D. A. Powell, Rikki Ducornet, and Ed Skoog.

TIPS "We're looking for dynamic writing that demonstrates attention to the language and a sense of the medium, writing that engages, surprises, moves us. We're not looking for genre fiction or academic articles. We subscribe to the belief that in order to truly write well, one must first master the rudiments: grammar and syntax, punctuation, the sentence, the paragraph, the line, the stanza. We receive about 3,000 manuscripts a year and publish about 3% of them. Check out a recent issue, send us your best, proofread your work, be patient, be persistent."

⊙⊙ THE NEW QUARTERLY

St. Jerome's University, 290 Westmount Rd. N., Waterloo ON N2L 3G3, Canada. (519)884-8111, ext. 28290. **E-mail:** editor@tnq.ca; info@tnq.ca. **Website:** www.tnq.ca. "Emphasis on emerging writers and genres, but we publish more traditional work as well if the language and narrative structure are fresh." Buys first Canadian rights. Pays on publication. Responds in early January to submissions received March 1-August 31; in early June to submissions received September 1-February 28. Editorial lead time 6 months. Sample copy: $16.50 (cover price, plus mailing). Guidelines online.

○ Open to Canadian writers only. Reading periods: March 1-August 31; September 1-February 28.

MAGAZINES NEEDS *Canadian work only.* Pays $40/poem.

TIPS "Reading us is the best way to get our measure. We don't have preconceived ideas about what we're looking for other than that it must be Canadian work (Canadian writers, not necessarily Canadian content). We want something that's fresh, something that will repay a second reading, something in which the language soars and the feeling is complexly rendered."

NEW SOUTH

English Dept., Georgia State University, P.O Box 3970, Atlanta GA 30302-3970. (404)413-5874. **E-mail:** newsoutheditors@gmail.com. **Website:** www.newsouthjournal.com. Semiannual magazine dedicated to finding and publishing the best work from artists around the world. Wants original voices searching to rise above the ordinary. Seeks to publish high-quality work, regardless of genre, form, or regional ties. Acquires first North American serial rights. Time between acceptance and publication is 3-5 months. Responds in 3-5 months. Sample: $3 (back issue). Single copy: $5; subscription: $8 for 1 year. Guidelines available online.

○ *New South* is 160+ pages. Press run is 2,000; 500 distributed free to students. The *New South* Annual Writing Contest offers $1,000 for the best poem and $1,000 for the best story or essay; one-year subscription to all who submit. Submissions must be unpublished. Submit up to 3 poems, 1 story, or 1 essay on any subject or in any form. Specify "poetry" or "fiction" on outside envelope. Guidelines available by e-mail or on website. Competition receives 300 entries. Past judges include Sharon Olds, Jane Hirschfield, Anthony Hecht, Phillip Levine, and Jake Adam York. Winner will be announced in the Fall issue.

MAGAZINES NEEDS Submit up to 5 poems at a time through Submittable. Pays 2 contributor's copies.

TIPS "We want what's new, what's fresh, and what's different—whether it comes from the Southern United States, the South of India, or the North, East or West of Anywhere."

● THE NEW VERSE NEWS

Tangerang , Indonesia. **E-mail:** nvneditor@gmail.com. **Website:** www.newversenews.com. **Contact:** James Penha, editor. *The New Verse News*, published online and updated "every day or 2," has "a clear liberal bias but will consider various visions and views." Acquires first rights. Rights revert to poet upon publication. "Normally, poems are published immediately upon acceptance." Responds in 1-3 weeks. Does not comment on rejected poems. Guidelines available on website.

MAGAZINES NEEDS Wants "previously unpublished poems, both serious and satirical, on current events and topical issues; will also consider prose poems." Does not want "work unrelated to the news." Submit 1-5 poems at a time. Accepts only e-mail submissions (pasted into body of message); use "Verse News Submission" as the subject line; no disk or postal submissions. Send brief bio. Reads submissions year round. Poems are circulated to an editorial board. Receives about 1,200 poems/year; accepts about 300. No length restrictions.

● NEW WELSH REVIEW

P.O. Box 170, Aberystwyth, Ceredigion Wa SY23 1 WZ, United Kingdom. 01970-626230. **E-mail:** editor@newwelshreview.com. **E-mail:** submissions@newwelshreview.com. **Website:** www.newwelshreview.com. **Contact:** Gwen Davies, editor. "*NWR*, a literary quarterly ranked in the top 5 of British literary magazines, publishes stories, poems, and critical essays. The best of Welsh writing in English, past and present, is celebrated, discussed, and debated. We seek poems, short stories, reviews, special features/articles, and commentary." Quarterly.

● THE NEW YORKER

1 World Trade Center, New York NY 10007. **Website:** www.newyorker.com. **Contact:** David Remnick, editor in chief. A quality weekly magazine of distinct news stories, articles, essays, and poems for a literate audience. Pays on acceptance. Responds in 3 months to mss. Subscription: $59.99/year (47 issues), $29.99 for 6 months (23 issues).

○ *The New Yorker* receives approximately 4,000 submissions per month.

MAGAZINES NEEDS Submit up to 6 poems at a time by e-mail (as PDF attachment) or mail (address to Poetry Department). Pays top rates.

TIPS "Be lively, original, not overly literary. Write what you want to write, not what you think the editor would like."

NIMROD: INTERNATIONAL JOURNAL OF POETRY AND PROSE

University of Tulsa, 800 S. Tucker Dr., Tulsa OK 74104-3189. (918)631-3080. **Fax:** (918)631-3033. **E-mail:** nimrod@utulsa.edu. **Website:** www.utulsa.edu/nimrod. **Contact:** Eilis O'Neal, editor-in-chief. "*Nimrod*'s mission is the discovery and support of new writing of vigor and quality from this country and abroad. The journal seeks new, unheralded writers; writers from other lands who become accessible to the English-speaking world through translation, and established authors who have vigorous new work to present that has not found a home within the establishment. We believe in a living literature; that it is possible to search for, recognize, and reward contemporary writing of content and vigor, without reliance on a canon." Responds in 3 months to mss. Sample copy: $11. Subscription: $18.50/year U.S., $20 foreign. Guidelines online or for SASE.

○ Semiannual magazine: 200 pages; perfect-bound; 4c cover. Receives 120 unsolicited mss/month. **Publishes 5-10 new writers/year.** Reading period: January 1-November 30. Does not accept submissions by e-mail unless the writer is living outside the U.S. Poetry published in *Nimrod* has been included in *The Best American Poetry.*

MAGAZINES NEEDS Submit poems by mail. Length: 3-10 pages. Pays 2 contributor's copies.

ALSO OFFERS Sponsors the annual *Nimrod* Literary Awards, including The Pablo Neruda Prize for Poetry (see separate listing in Contests & Awards). "During the months that the *Nimrod* Literary Awards competition is being conducted, reporting time on noncontest mss will be longer."

NINTH LETTER

Department of English, University of Illinois, 608 S. Wright St., Urbana IL 61801. (217)244-3145. **E-mail:** info@ninthletter.com; editor@ninthletter.com. **Website:** www.ninthletter.com. **Contact:** Jodee Stanley, editor. "*Ninth Letter* accepts submissions of fiction, poetry, and essays from September 1-February 28 (postmark dates). *Ninth Letter* is published semiannually at the University of Illinois, Urbana-Champaign. We are interested in prose and poetry that experiment with form, narrative, and nontraditional subject matter, as well as more traditional literary work." Pays on publication.

Ninth Letter won Best New Literary Journal 2005 from the Council of Editors of Learned Journals (CELJ) and has had poetry selected for *The Pushcart Prize, Best New Poets,* and *The Year's Best Fantasy and Horror.*

MAGAZINES NEEDS Submit 3-6 poems (no more than 10 pages) at a time. "All mailed submissions must include an SASE for reply." Pays $25 per printed page and 2 contributor's copies.

ALSO OFFERS Member: CLMP; CELJ.

NITE-WRITER'S INTERNATIONAL LITERARY ARTS JOURNAL

158 Spencer Ave., Suite 100, Pittsburgh PA 15227. (412)668-0691. **E-mail:** nitewritersliteraryarts@gmail.com. **Website:** nitewritersinternational.webs.com. **Contact:** John Thompson. *Nite-Writer's International Literary Arts Journal* is an online literary arts journal. "We are 'dedicated to the emotional intellectual' with a creative perception of life." Retains first North American serial rights. Copyright reverts to author upon publication. Guidelines available on website. Does not pay authors but offers international exposure to the individual artist.

Journal is open to beginners as well as professionals.

MAGAZINES NEEDS Wants strong imagery in everything you write. Considers previously published poems and simultaneous submissions (let us know when and where your work has been published). Cover letter is preferred. "Give brief bio, state where you heard of us, state if material has been previously published and where." Receives about 1,000 poems/year, accepts about 10-15%. Has published poetry by Lyn Lifshin, Rose Marie Hunold, Peter Vetrano, Carol Frances Brown, and Richard King Perkins II. Does not want porn or violence. Open to length.

TIPS "Read a lot of what you write—study the market. Don't fear rejection, but use it as a learning tool to strengthen your work before resubmitting."

NON + X: AN EXPERIMENTAL JOURNAL OF BUDDHIST THOUGHT

E-mail: admin@nonplusx.com. **E-mail:** wtompepper@att.net. **Website:** www.nonplusx.com. **Contact:** Tom Pepper, editor. "*non + x* is an experimental e-journal dedicated to the critique of Buddhist and other contemporary cultural materials. Our goal 'consists in wresting vital potentialities of humans from the artificial forms and static norms that subjugate them' (Marjorie Gracieuse)." Buys one-time rights. Responds in 2 weeks to queries. Editorial lead time is 4 months. Sample copy online at website or for SASE. Guidelines available online at website (www.nonplusx.com/contribute) or for SASE.

THE NORMAL SCHOOL

The Press at the California State University - Fresno, 5245 North Backer Ave., M/S PB 98, Fresno CA 93740-8001. **E-mail:** editors@thenormalschool.com. **Website:** http://thenormalschool.com. **Contact:** Steven Church, editor. Semiannual magazine that accepts outstanding work by beginning and established writers. Acquires first North American serial rights. Publication is copyrighted. Publishes ms 3-6 months after acceptance. Responds to stories in 2 months. Sample copy available for $7 on website or via e-mail. For guidelines, send check and address or visit website.

Mss are read from September 1 to December 1 and from January 15 to April 15. Address submissions to the appropriate editor. Charges $3 fee for each online submission, due to operational costs.

MAGAZINES NEEDS Considers poetry of any style. Limit the number of cat poems.

⑤ NORTH AMERICAN REVIEW

University of Northern Iowa, 1222 W. 27th St., Cedar Falls IA 50614. (319)273-6455. **Fax:** (319)273-4326. **E-mail:** nar@uni.edu. **Website:** northamericanreview. wordpress.com. **Contact:** Kim Groninga, nonfiction editor. "The *NAR* is the oldest literary magazine in America and one of the most respected; though we have no prejudices about the subject matter of material sent to us, our first concern is quality." Buys first North American serial rights, buys first rights. Publishes ms an average of 1 year after acceptance. Responds in 3 months to queries; 4 months to mss. Sample copy: $7. Guidelines available online.

- This is the oldest literary magazine in the country and one of the most prestigious. Also one of the most entertaining—and a tough market for the young writer.

MAGAZINES NEEDS No restrictions; highest quality only.

TIPS "We like stories that start quickly and have a strong narrative arc. Poems that are passionate about subject, language, and image are welcome, whether they are traditional or experimental, whether in formal or free verse (closed or open form). Nonfiction should combine art and fact with the finest writing."

⑤ NORTH CAROLINA LITERARY REVIEW

East Carolina University, Mailstop 555 English, Greenville NC 27858-4353. (252)328-1537. **Fax:** (252)328-4889. **E-mail:** nclrsubmissions@ecu.edu. **Website:** www.nclr.ecu.edu. **Contact:** Margaret Bauer. "Articles should have a North Carolina slant. Fiction, creative nonfiction, and poetry accepted through yearly contests. First consideration is always for quality of work. Although we treat academic and scholarly subjects, we do not wish to see jargon-laden prose; our readers, we hope, are found as often in bookstores and libraries as in academia. We seek to combine the best elements of a magazine for serious readers with the best of a scholarly journal." Acquires first North American serial rights. Rights returned to writer on request. Publishes ms an average of 1 year after acceptance. Responds in 1 month to queries; in 6 months to mss. Editorial lead time 6 months. Sample copy: $5-25. Guidelines available online.

- Accepts submissions through Submittable.

MAGAZINES NEEDS Submit poetry for the James Applewhite Poetry Prize competition via Submittable. Submit up to 3 poems for $15 entry fee or up to 5 poems for $20 entry fee. Published writers paid in copies of the journal. First-place winners of contests receive a prize of $250.

TIPS "By far the easiest way to break in is with special issue sections. We are especially interested in reports on conferences, readings, meetings that involve North Carolina writers, and personal essays or short narratives with a strong sense of place. See back issues for other departments. Interviews are probably the other easiest place to break in; no discussions of poetics/theory, etc., except in reader-friendly (accessible) language. Interviews should be personal, more like conversations, that explore connections between a writer's life and his/her work."

NORTH CENTRAL REVIEW

North Central College, CM #235, 30 N. Brainard St., Naperville IL 60540. (630)637-5291. **E-mail:** nccreview@noctrl.edu. **Website:** http://orgs.noctrl.edu/review. **Contact:** Heather M. Placko, editor; Kelly Noel Rasmussen, editor. *North Central Review*, published semiannually, considers work in all literary genres, including occasional interviews, from undergraduate writers globally. The journal's goal is for college-level, emerging creative writers to share their work publicly and create a conversation with each other. All styles and forms are welcome as submissions. The readers tend to value attention to form (but not necessarily fixed form), voice, and detail. Very long poems or sequences (running more than 4 or 5 pages) may require particular excellence because of the journal's space and budget constraints. Does not want overly sentimental language and hackneyed imagery. These are all-too-common weaknesses that readers see in submissions; recommends revision and polishing before sending work. Considers poetry by teens (undergraduate writers only). Acquires first rights. Publishes ms 1-4 months after acceptance. Responds in 1-4 months. Guidelines for SASE, by e-mail, online and in magazine.

- *North Central Review* is 120 pages, digest-sized, perfect-bound, with cardstock cover with 4-color design. Press run is about 750, distributed free to contributors and publication reception attendees. Single copy: $5; subscription: $10. Make checks payable to North Central College.

MAGAZINES NEEDS Accepts e-mail submissions (as Word attachments only); no fax submissions. Cover letter is preferred. Include name, postal address, phone number, and e-mail address (.edu address as proof of student status). If necessary (i.e., .edu address not available), include a photocopy of student ID with number marked out as proof of undergraduate status. Reads submissions September-March, with deadlines in February and October. Poems are circulated to an editorial board. All submissions are read by at least 3 staff members, including an editor. Rarely comments on rejected poems. No line limit. Pays 2 contributor's copies.

TIPS "Don't send anything you just finished moments ago—rethink, revise, and polish. Avoid sentimentalitity and abstraction. That said, the *North Central Review* publishes beginners, so don't hesitate to submit and, if rejected, submit again."

NORTH DAKOTA QUARTERLY

276 Centennial Dr. Stop 7209, Merrifield Hall Room 15, Grand Forks ND 58202. (701)777-3322. **Website:** www.und.edu/org/ndq. **Contact:** Kate Sweney, managing editor. "*North Dakota Quarterly* strives to publish the best fiction, poetry, and essays that in our estimation we can. Our tastes and interests are best reflected in what we have been recently publishing, and we suggest that you look at some current issues for guidance." Requires first serial rights. Guidelines available online.

◑ Only reads fiction and poetry between September 1-May 1. Work published in *North Dakota Quarterly* was selected for inclusion in *The O. Henry Prize Stories*, *The Pushcart Prize Series*, and *Best American Essays*.

MAGAZINES NEEDS Submit up to 5 poems as hard copy.

⑤ NOTRE DAME REVIEW

University of Notre Dame, B009C McKenna Hall, Notre Dame IN 46556. **Website:** ndreview.nd.edu. "The *Notre Dame Review* is an indepenent, noncommercial magazine of contemporary American and international fiction, poetry, criticism, and art. Especially interested in work that takes on big issues by making the invisible seen, that gives voice to the voiceless. In addition to showcasing celebrated authors like Seamus Heaney and Czelaw Milosz, the *Notre Dame Review* introduces readers to authors they may have never encountered before but who are doing

innovative and important work. In conjunction with the *Notre Dame Review*, the online companion to the printed magazine, the *nd[re]view* engages readers as a community centered in literary rather than commercial concerns, a community we reach out to through critique and commentary as well as aesthetic experience." Buys first North American serial rights. Pays on publication. Publishes ms an average of 6 months after acceptance. Responds in 4 or more months to mss. Sample copy: $6. Guidelines online.

◑ Does not accept e-mail submissions. Only reads hardcopy submissions September-November and January-March.

MAGAZINES NEEDS Send complete ms with cover letter. Include 4-sentence bio. Send SASE for response, return of ms, or send a disposable copy of ms.

TIPS "We're looking for high-quality work that takes on big issues in a literary way. Please read our back issues before submitting."

NOW & THEN: THE APPALACHIAN MAGAZINE

East Tennessee State University, Box 70556, Johnson City TN 37614-1707. (423)439-5348. **Fax:** (423)439-6340. **E-mail:** nowandthen@etsu.edu. **E-mail:** sandersr@etsu.edu. **Website:** www.etsu.edu/cass/nowandthen. **Contact:** Randy Sanders, managing editor; Wayne Winkler, music editor; Charlie Warden, photo editor. Literary magazine published twice/year. "*Now & Then* accepts a variety of writing genres: fiction, poetry, nonfiction, essays, interviews, memoirs, and book reviews. All submissions must relate to Appalachia and to the issue's specific theme. Our readership is educated and interested in the region." Buys first North American serial rights. Rights revert back to author after publication. Responds in 5 months to queries; 5 months to mss. Sample copy: $8 plus $3 shipping. Guidelines and upcoming themes available on website.

◑ *Now & Then* tells the stories of Appalachia and presents a fresh, revealing picture of life in Appalachia, past and present, with engaging articles, personal essays, fiction, poetry, and photography.

MAGAZINES NEEDS Submit up to 5 poems, with SASE and cover letter including "a few lines about yourself for a contributor's note and whether the work has been published or accepted elsewhere." Will consider simultaneous submissions; occasionally accepts previously published poems. Put name, address, and phone number on every poem. Deadlines: last work-day in February (spring/summer issue) and August 31 (fall/winter issues). Publishes theme issues. Pays $25 for each accepted poem. Pays on publication.

TIPS "Keep in mind that *Now & Then* only publishes material related to the Appalachian region. Plus we only publish fiction that has some plausible connection to a specific issue's themes. We like to offer first-time publication to promising writers."

NTH DEGREE

E-mail: submissions@nthzine.com. **Website:** www.nthzine.com. **Contact:** Michael Pederson. Free online fanzine to promote up-and-coming new science fiction and fantasy authors and artists. Also supports the world of fandom and conventions. Acquires one-time rights. Responds in 2 weeks to queries; 3 months to mss. Online e-zine; copies available upon request. Guidelines available online.

No longer accepts hard copy submissions.

MAGAZINES NEEDS Submit through e-mail. Looking for poetry about science fiction, fantasy, horror, alternate history, well-crafted mystery, and humor. Pays in contributor's copies.

TIPS "Don't submit anything that you may be ashamed of 10 years later."

NTHPOSITION

E-mail: val@nthposition.com. **Website:** www.nthposition.com. **Contact:** Val Stevenson, managing editor. *nthposition*, published monthly online, is an eclectic, London-based journal with politics and opinion, travel writing, fiction and poetry, art reviews and interviews, and some high weirdness. Does not request rights but expects proper acknowledgement if poems are reprinted later. Time between acceptance and publication is 4 months. Responds in 6 weeks. Never comments on rejected poems. Guidelines available online.

TIPS "Submit as text in the body of an e-mail, along with a brief bio note (2-3 sentences). If your work is accepted, it will be archived into the British Library's permanent collection."

NUTHOUSE

Website: www.nuthousemagazine.com. *Nuthouse*, published every 3 months, uses humor of all kinds, including homespun and political. Acquires one-time rights. Publishes ms 6-12 months after acceptance. Responds in 1 month. Sample: $1.50. Make checks payable to Twin Rivers Press. Guidelines for #10 SASE.

Nuthouse is 12 pages, digest-sized, photocopied from desktop-published originals. Receives about 500 poems/year, accepts about 100. Press run is 100. Subscription: $5 for 4 issues.

MAGAZINES NEEDS Wants "humorous verse; virtually all genres considered." Has published poetry by Holly Day, Daveed Garstenstein-Ross, and Don Webb. Send complete ms with SASE and cover letter. Include bio (paragraph) and list of publications. No e-mail submissions. Pays 1 contributor's copy per poem.

OBSIDIAN

North Carolina State University, Department of English, Box 8105, Raleigh NC 27695. **E-mail:** obsidianatbrown@gmail.com. **Website:** obsidian-magazine.tumblr.com. **Contact:** Maya Finoh, managing editor. *Obsidian* is a "literary and visual space to showcase the creativity and experiences of black people, specifically at Brown University, formed out of the need for a platform made for us, by us." It is "actively intersectional, safe, and open: a space especially for the stories and voices of black women, black queer and trans people, and black people with disabilities." Acquires one-time rights.

MAGAZINES NEEDS Submit by e-mail. Include brief bio up to 3 sentences.

TIPS "Following proper format is essential. Your title must be intriguing and text clean. Never give up. Some of the writers we publish were rejected many times before we published them."

OFF THE COAST

Resolute Bear Press, P.O. Box 14, Robbinston ME 04671. (207)454-8026. **E-mail:** poetrylane2@gmail.com. **Website:** www.off-the-coast.com. **Contact:** Valerie Lawson, editor/publisher. Quarterly journal with deadlines of March, June, September and December 15. *Off the Coast* is accepting submissions of poetry (any subject or style; please use our submission manager: www.offthecoast.submittable.com/submit; postal submissions OK with SASE), photography, graphics, and books for review (books only, no chapbooks). Subscriptions are $35 for 1 year, $60 for 2 years. Single issue: $10. *Off the Coast* prints all styles and forms of poetry. Considers poetry by children and teens. Has published poetry by Wes McNair, Kate Barnes, Henry Braun, Baron Wormser, Betsy Sholl, David Wagoner, Diana DerHovanessian, Simon Perchik, and Rhina Espaillat. *Off the Coast* is 80-100+ pages, perfect-bound, with stock cover with original art. Receives about 5,000 poems/year, accepts about 250. Press run is 300; occasional complimentary copies offered. Make checks payable to *Off the Coast*. Editorial decisions are not made until after the deadline for each issue. Notifications go out the first two weeks of the month following the deadline date eg: early April for March 15 deadline. **For samples of poetry, art and reviews, visit our website** www.off-the-coast.com. "The mission of *Off the Coast* is to become recognized around the world as Maine's international poetry journal, a publication that prizes quality, diversity and honesty in its publications and in its dealings with poets. *Off the Coast*, a quarterly print journal, publishes poetry, artwork and reviews. Arranged much like an anthology, each issue bears a title drawn from a line or phrase from one of its poems." The rights to each individual poem and print are retained by each individual artist. Publishes mss 1-2 months after acceptance. Responds in 1-3 months. Editorial decisions are not made until after the deadline for each issue. Notifications go out the first two weeks of the month following the deadline date, e.g. early April for March 15 deadline. For samples of poetry, art and reviews, visit our website: www.off-the-coast.com. Contributors receive one free copy. Additional copies of the issue their work appears in available for $5, half the cover price. Sample issue for $10. Guidelines available in magazine.

HOW TO CONTACT "Send 1-3 previously unpublished poems, any subject or style, using our submission manager: www.offthecoast.submittable.com/submit. We accept postal submissions with SASE with sufficient postage for return. Please include contact information and brief bio with submission. We accept simultaneous submissions, but please inform us if your work is accepted elsewhere. Pays one contributor's copy. "The rights to each individual poem and print are retained by each individual artist." For reviews, send a single copy of a newly published poetry book. Please send bound books only, we do not review chapbooks."

OHIO TEACHERS WRITE

1209 Heather Run, Wilmington OH 45177. **E-mail:** ohioteacherswrite@octela.org. **Website:** www.octela.org/OTW.html. **Contact:** Eimile Máiréad Green, editor. "*Ohio Teachers Write* is a literary magazine published annually by the Ohio Council of Teachers of English Language Arts. This publication seeks to promote both poetry and prose of Ohio teachers and to provide an engaging collection of writing for our readership of educators and other like-minded adults. Invites electronic submissions from both active and retired Ohio educators for our annual literary print magazine."

MAGAZINES NEEDS Submit up to 4 poems by e-mail. Pays 2 contributor's copies.

TIPS Check website for yearly theme.

OLD RED KIMONO

Georgia Highlands College, 3175 Cedartown Highway SE, Rome GA 30161. **E-mail:** napplega@highlands.edu. **Website:** www.highlands.edu/site/ork. **Contact:** Dr. Nancy Applegate, professor of English; Thomas Dobson, literary editor. *Old Red Kimono*, published annually, prints original, high-quality poetry and fiction. Has published poetry by Walter McDonald, Peter Huggins, Ruth Moon Kempher, John Cantey Knight, Kirsten Fox, and Al Braselton. Acquires one-time rights. Responds in 3 months. Accepts e-mail submissions. Reads submissions September 1-February 15 only. Guidelines available for SASE or on website for more submission information.

Old Red Kimono is 72 pages, magazine-sized, professionally printed on heavy stock, with colored matte cover with art. Receives about 500 submissions/year, accepts about 60-70. Sample: $3.

MAGAZINES NEEDS Submit 3-5 poems at a time. Pays 2 contributor's copies.

ON SPEC

P.O. Box 4727, Station South, Edmonton AB T6E 5G6, Canada. (780)628-7121. **E-mail:** onspec@onspec.ca. **Website:** www.onspec.ca. "We publish speculative fiction and poetry by new and established writers, with a strong preference for Canadian-authored works." Buys first North American serial rights. Pays on acceptance. Publishes ms an average of 6-18 months after acceptance. Responds in 2 weeks to queries; in 6 months after deadline to mss. Editorial lead time 6 months. Sample copy: $8. Guidelines on website.

See website guidelines for submission announcements. "Please refer to website for information regarding submissions, as we are not open year round."

MAGAZINES NEEDS No rhyming or religious material. Length: 4-100 lines. Pays $50 and 1 contributor's copy.

TIPS "We want to see stories with plausible characters, a well-constructed, consistent, and vividly described setting, a strong plot, and believable emotions; characters must show us (not tell us) their emotional responses to each other and to the situation and/or challenge they face. Also: Don't send us stories written for television. We don't like media tie-ins, so don't watch TV for inspiration! Read instead! Strong preference given to submissions by Canadians."

⚙ OPEN MINDS QUARTERLY

Northern Initiative for Social Action, 36 Elgin St., 2nd Floor, Sudbury ON P3C 5B4, Canada. (705)675-9193, ext. 8286. **E-mail:** openminds@nisa.on.ca. **Website:** www.openmindsquarterly.com. **Contact:** Dinah Laprairie, editor. *Open Minds Quarterly* provides a venue for individuals who have experienced mental illness to express themselves via poetry, short fiction, essays, first-person accounts of living with mental illness, and book/movie reviews. Wants unique, well-written, provocative poetry. Does not want overly graphic or sexual violence. Time between acceptance and publication is 6-18 months. Responds in up to 4 months. Single copy: $7 CAD, $7 USD; subscription: $24.95 CAD and USD (special rates also available). Make checks payable to NISA/Northern Initiative for Social Action. Guidelines available for SASE, by fax, e-mail, or on website.

○ *Open Minds Quarterly* is 24 pages, magazine-sized, saddle-stapled, with 100 lb. stock cover with original artwork, includes ads. Press run is 550; 100 distributed free to potential subscribers, published writers, advertisers, and conferences and events.

MAGAZINES NEEDS Submit 1-5 poems at a time. Accepts e-mail and postal submissions. Cover letter is required. Info in cover letter: indication as to "consumer/survivor" of the mental health system status. Reads submissions year round. Poems are first reviewed by poetry editor, then accepted/rejected by the editor. Sometimes, submissions are passed on to a third party for input or a third opinion. Seldom comments on rejected poems. Rarely sends prepublication galleys. Considers poetry by teens. Has published poetry by Beth Brown Preston, Sophie Soil, Ky Perraun, and Kurt Sass.

ALSO OFFERS The Brainstorm Poetry Contest runs in first 2 months of each year. Contact the editor for information.

◑ ORBIS

17 Greenhow Ave., West Kirby Wirral CH48 5EL, UK. **E-mail:** carolebaldock@hotmail.com. **Website:** www.orbisjournal.com. **Contact:** Carole Baldock, editor; Noel Williams, reviews editor. "*Orbis* has long been considered one of the top 20 small-press magazines in the UK. We are interested in social inclusion projects and encouraging access to the Arts, young people, Under 20s, and 20-somethings. Subjects for discussion: 'day in the life,' technical, topical." Responds in 3 months.

○ Please see guidelines on website before submitting.

MAGAZINES NEEDS Readers' Award: £50 for piece receiving the most votes in each issue. Four winners selected for submissions to Forward Poetry Prize, Single Poem category. Plus £50 split between 4 or more runners-up. Feature Writer receives £50. NB, work commissioned: 3-4 poems or 1,500 words.

TIPS "Any publication should be read cover to cover because it's the best way to improve your chances of getting published. Enclose SAE with all correspondence. Overseas: 2 IRCs, 3 if work is to be returned."

OSIRIS

P.O. Box 297, Deerfield MA 01342. **E-mail:** amoorhead@deerfield.edu. **Website:** www.facebook.com/osiris.poetry. **Contact:** Andrea Moorhead, editor. *Osiris*, published semiannually, prints contemporary poetry in English, French, and Italian without translation, and in other languages with translation, including Polish, Danish, and German. Responds in 1 month. Sometimes sends prepublication galleys. Sample: $15.

MAGAZINES NEEDS Wants poetry that is "lyrical, non-narrative, post-modern. Also looking for translations from non-Indo-European languages." Has published poetry by Abderrahmane Djelfaoui (Algeria); George Moore, Rob Cook, Simon Perchik, Ingrid Swanberg (USA); Flavio Ermini (Italy); Denise Desautels (Quebec); Yves Broussard (France); and Frances Presley (UK). Submit 4-6 poems at a time. "Poems should be sent by postal mail. Include short bio and SASE with submission. Translators should include a letter of permission from the poet or publisher as well as copies of the original text." Pays 3 contributor's copies.

OVER THE TRANSOM

120 San Lorenzo Blvd., #3, Santa Cruz CA 95060. (415)678-9554. **E-mail:** jsh619@earthlink.net. **Con-**

tact: Jonathan Hayes, editor. *Over the Transom*, published 2 times/year, is a free publication of poetry and prose. Open to all styles of poetry. "We look for the highest-quality writing that best fits the issue." Publishes ms 2-6 months after acceptance. Responds in 2 months. Sample copy: $10. Single copy: free. Make checks payable to Jonathan Hayes.

○ *Over The Transom* is 32 pages, magazine-sized, saddle-stapled, with cardstock cover. Receives about 1,000 poems/year, accepts about 5%. Press run is 300 (100 subscribers); 150 distributed free to cafés, bookstores, universities, and bars.

MAGAZINES NEEDS Submit up to 5 poems at a time. Accepts e-mail submissions; no disk submissions. Must include an SASE with postal submissions. Reads submissions year round. Never comments on rejected poems. Occasionally publishes theme issues. Considers poetry by children and teens. Has published poetry by Klipschutz, Richard Lopez, Glen Chesnut, Peter Cherches, and Don Skiles. Pays 1 contributor's copy.

OXFORD MAGAZINE

Miami University, Oxford OH 45056. **Website:** www.oxfordmagazine.org. *Oxford Magazine*, published annually online in May, is open in terms of form, content, and subject matter. "Since our premiere in 1984, our magazine has received Pushcart Prizes for both fiction and poetry and has published authors such as Charles Baxter, William Stafford, Robert Pinsky, Stephen Dixon, Helena Maria Viramontes, Andre Dubus, and Stuart Dybek." Acquires first North American serial rights, one-time anthology rights, online serial rights. Responds in 6 months, starting in September.

○ Work published in *Oxford Magazine* has been included in the *Pushcart Prize* anthology. Does not read submissions June through August.

MAGAZINES NEEDS Submit 3-5 poems via online submissions manager.

OYEZ REVIEW

Roosevelt University, Dept. of Literature & Languages, 430 S. Michigan Ave., Chicago IL 60605. **E-mail:** oyezreview@roosevelt.edu. **Website:** oyezreview.wordpress.com. Annual magazine of the Creative Writing Program at Roosevelt University, publishing fiction, creative nonfiction, poetry, and art. There are no restrictions on style, theme, or subject matter. Buys first North American serial rights. Publishes ms an average of 2-3 months after acceptance. Responds by mid-December each year. Sample copies available by request, or using e-book retailers. Guidelines online.

○ Reading period is August 1-October 1. Each issue has 104 pages: 92 pages of text and an 8-page spread of 1 artist's work (in color or b&w). Work by the issue's featured artist also appears on the front and back cover, totaling 10 pieces. The journal has featured work from such writers as Charles Bukowski, James McManus, Carla Panciera, Michael Onofrey, Tim Foley, John N. Miller, Gary Fincke, and Barry Silesky, and visual artists Vivian Nunley, C. Taylor, Jennifer Troyer, and Frank Spidale. Accepts queries by e-mail.

MAGAZINES NEEDS Send up to 5 poems via online submissions manager or postal mail. Length: up to 10 pages total.

OYSTER BOY REVIEW

P.O. Box 1483, Pacifica CA 94044. **E-mail:** email_2015@oysterboyreview.com. **Website:** www.oysterboyreview.com. **Contact:** Damon Suave, editor/publisher. Electronic and print magazine. *Oyster Boy Review*, published annually, is interested in "the underrated, the ignored, the misunderstood, and the varietal. We'll make some mistakes." Publishes ms 12 months after acceptance. Responds in 6 months. Guidelines by e-mail or online at website.

MAGAZINES NEEDS Submit by postal mail or e-mail. Pays 2 contributor's copies.

TIPS "Keep writing, keep submitting, keep revising."

PACIFICA LITERARY REVIEW

E-mail: pacificalitreview@gmail.com. **Website:** www.pacificareview.com. **Editor-in-Chief:** Matt Muth. **Managing Editor:** Courtney Johnson. *Pacifica Literary Review* is a small literary arts magazine based in Seattle. Our print editions are published biannually in winter and summer. *PLR* is now accepting submissions of poetry, fiction, creative nonfiction, author interview, and b&w photography. Submission period: September 15-May 7. Acquires first North American rights. Guidelines available online.

MAGAZINES NEEDS Submit poems via onlline submission form.

PACKINGTOWN REVIEW

111 S. Lincoln St., Batavia IL 60510. **E-mail:** editors@packingtownreview.com. **Website:** www.packingtownreview.com. *Packingtown Review* publishes

imaginative and critical prose and poetry by emerging and established writers. Welcomes submissions of poetry, scholarly articles, drama, creative nonfiction, fiction, and literary translation, as well as genre-bending pieces. Acquires first North American serial rights. Sends galleys to author. Publication is copyrighted. Pays on publication. Publishes ms a maximum of 1 year after acceptance. Responds in 3 weeks to queries; in 3 months to mss. Single copy: $10 (back issue). Guidelines available on website.

⚲ Literary magazine/journal. 8½x11, 250 pages. Press run: 500.

MAGAZINES NEEDS Wants well-crafted poetry. Open to most styles and forms. Looking for poetry that takes risks and does so successfully. Send 3-5 poems with cover letter. Include estimated word count, brief bio, SASE. Does not want uninspired or unrevised work. Length: up to 10 pages of single-spaced verse. Pays 2 contributor's copies.

TIPS "We are looking for well-crafted prose. We are open to most styles and forms. We are also looking for prose that takes risks and does so successfully. We will consider articles about prose."

⊖ PAINTED BRIDE QUARTERLY

Drexel University, Department of English and Philosophy, 3141 Chestnut St., Philadelphia PA 19104. **E-mail:** pbq@drexel.edu. **Website:** pbq.drexel.edu. *Painted Bride Quarterly* seeks literary fiction (experimental and traditional), poetry, and artwork and photographs. Buys first North American serial rights. Responds in 6 months to mss. Guidelines available online and by e-mail.

MAGAZINES NEEDS Submit via postal mail. Does not accept e-mail submissions. "We have no specifications or restrictions. We'll look at anything."

ALSO OFFERS Sponsors an annual poetry contest and a chapbook competition. Guidelines available for SASE or on website.

TIPS "We look for freshness of idea incorporated with high-quality writing. We receive an awful lot of nicely written work with worn-out plots. We want quality in whatever—we hold experimental work to as strict standards as anything else. Many of our readers write fiction; most of them enjoy a good reading. We hope to be an outlet for quality. A good story gives, first, enjoyment to the reader. We've seen a good many of them lately, and we've published the best of them."

PALABRA

P.O. Box 86146, Los Angeles CA 90086. **E-mail:** info@palabralitmag.com. **Website:** www.palabra-litmag.com. "*PALABRA* is about exploration, risk, and ganas—the myriad intersections of thought, language, story, and art—*el mas alla of letters*, symbols and spaces into meaning." Acquires first serial rights, electronic promotional rights, and nonexclusive print anthology rights. Responds in 3-4 months to mss. Guidelines online.

⚲ Reading period: September 1-April 30.

MAGAZINES NEEDS Submit up to 5 poems via postal mail. Include brief cover letter and SASE. Pays $25-40.

PANK

Website: www.pankmagazine.com. **Contact:** M. Bartley Seigel, editor. "*PANK* Magazine fosters access to emerging and experimental poetry and prose, publishing the brightest and most promising writers for the most adventurous readers. To the end of the road, up country, a far shore, the edge of things, to a place of amalgamation and unplumbed depths, where the known is made and unmade, and where unimagined futures are born, a place inhabited by contradictions, a place of quirk and startling anomaly. *PANK*, no soft pink hands allowed." Buys first North American serial rights and electronic rights. Publishes ms and average of 3-12 months after acceptance. Writer's guidelines are free and online at website.

MAGAZINES NEEDS Submit through online submissions manager. Pays $20, a one-year subscription, and a *PANK* t-shirt.

TIPS "To read *PANK* is to know *PANK*. Or, read a lot within the literary magazine and small press universe—there's plenty to choose from. Unfortunately, we see a lot of submissions from writers who have clearly read neither *PANK* nor much else. Serious writers are serious readers. Read. Seriously."

♻ PAPERPLATES

19 Kenwood Ave., Toronto ON M6C 2R8, Canada. (416)651-2551. **E-mail:** magazine@paperplates.org. **Website:** www.paperplates.org. **Contact:** Bernard Kelly, publisher. *paperplates* is a literary quarterly published in Toronto. "We make no distinction between veterans and beginners. Some of our contributors have published several books; some have never before published a single line." Acquires first North

American serial rights. Responds in 4-6 months. Guidelines available online at website.

○ No longer accepts IRCs.

MAGAZINES NEEDS Submit no more than 5 poems via surface mail or e-mail with short bio. Length: no more than 1,500 words.

⑤ THE PARIS REVIEW

544 West 27th St., New York NY 10001. (212)343-1333. **E-mail:** queries@theparisreview.org. **Website:** www.theparisreview.org. **Contact:** Lorin Stein, editor; Robyn Creswell, poetry editor. *The Paris Review* publishes "fiction and poetry of superlative quality, whatever the genre, style, or mode. Our contributors include prominent, as well as less well-known and previously unpublished writers. The Writers at Work interview series includes important contemporary writers discussing their own work and the craft of writing." Buys all rights, buys first English-language rights. Pays on publication. Responds in 4 months to mss. Guidelines available online.

○ Address submissions to proper department. Do not make submissions via e-mail.

MAGAZINES NEEDS Submit no more than 6 poems at a time. Poetry can be sent to the poetry editor (please include a self-addressed, stamped envelope). Poets receive $100/poem.

PARNASSUS: POETRY IN REVIEW

Poetry in Review Foundation, 205 W. 89th St., #8F, New York NY 10024. (212)362-3492. **E-mail:** parnew@aol.com. **Website:** www.parnassusreview.com. **Contact:** Herbert Leibowitz, editor and publisher. *Parnassus: Poetry in Review* provides "a forum where poets, novelists, and critics of all persuasions can gather to review new books of poetry, including translations—international poetries have occupied center stage from our very first issue—with an amplitude and reflectiveness that Sunday book supplements and even the literary quarterlies could not afford. Our editorial philosophy is based on the assumption that reviewing is a complex art. Like a poem or a short story, a review essay requires imagination, scrupulous attention to rhythm, pacing, and supple syntax; space in which to build a persuasive, detailed argument; analytical precision and intuitive gambits; verbal play, wit, and metaphor. We welcome and vigorously seek out voices that break aesthetic molds and disturb xenophobic habits." Buys one-time rights. Pays on publication. Publishes ms an average of 12-14 months after acceptance. Responds in 2 months to mss. Sample copy: $15.

MAGAZINES NEEDS Accepts most types of poetry.

TIPS "Be certain you have read the magazine and are aware of the editor's taste. Blind submissions are a waste of everybody's time. We'd like to see more poems that display intellectual acumen and curiosity about history, science, music, etc., and fewer trivial lyrical poems about the self, or critical prose that's academic and dull. Prose should sing."

PASSAGER

Passager Press, 1420 N. Charles St., Baltimore MD 21201. **E-mail:** editors@passagerbooks.com. **Website:** www.passagerbooks.com. **Contact:** Mary Azrael and Kendra Kopelke, editors. "*Passager* has a special focus on older writers. Its mission is to encourage, engage, and strengthen the imagination well into old age and to give mature readers oppertunities that are sometimes closed off to them in our youth-oriented culture. We are dedicated to honoring the creativity that takes hold in later years and to making public the talents of those over the age of 50." Passager publishes 2 issues/year, an Open issue (fall/winter) and a Poetry Contest issue (spring/summer). Acquires first North American serial rights. Publication is copyrighted. Responds in 5 months to mss. Sample copy: $10. Guidelines online.

○ Literary magazine/journal. 8.25x8.25, 84 pages, recycled paper.

MAGAZINES NEEDS Publishes poetry as part of annual poetry contest. **Deadline:** April 15. Send up to 5 poems with cover letter. Include estimated word count, brief bio, list of publications. Send either SASE (or IRC) for return of ms or disposable copy of ms and #10 SASE for reply only. **Reading fee:** $20 (includes one-year subscription). Length: up to 40 lines/poem.

TIPS "Stereotyped images of old age will be rejected immediately. Write humorous, tongue-in-cheek essays. Read the publication, or at least visit the website."

PASSAGES NORTH

English Department, Northern Michigan University, 1401 Presque Isle Ave., Marquette MI 49855. (906)227-1203. **E-mail:** passages@nmu.edu. **Website:** www.passagesnorth.com. **Contact:** Jennifer A. Howard, editor in chief; Matt Weinkam and Robin McCarthy, managing editors; Matthew Gavin Frank, nonfiction editor; Martin Achatz, poetry editor; Timston Johnston, fiction editor. *Passages North*, published annually in spring, prints poetry, short fiction, creative nonfiction, essays, and interviews. Sample: $3 (back issue). Single copy: $13; subscription: $13/year, $23 for 2 years. Guidelines available for SASE, by e-mail, or on website.

○ Magazine: 7×10; 200-300 pgs; 60 lb. paper. Publishes work by established and emerging writers.

MAGAZINES NEEDS "We're looking for poems that give us pause, poems that surprise us, poems that keep us warm during long northern nights. We want them to sing and vibrate with energy. We're open to all forms and aesthetics." Submit up to 5 poems together in 1 document. Has published poetry by Moira Egan, Frannie Lindsay, Ben Lerner, Bob Hicok, Gabe Gudding, John McNally, Steve Almond, Tracy Winn, and Midge Raymond.

TIPS "We look for voice, energetic prose, writers who take risks. We look for an engaging story in which the author evokes an emotional response from the reader through carefully rendered scenes, complex characters, and a smart, narrative design. Revise, revise. Read what we publish."

● PASSION

Crescent Moon Publishing, P.O. Box 1312, Maidstone Kent ME14 5XU, United Kingdom. (44)(162)272-9593. **E-mail:** cresmopub@yahoo.co.uk. **Website:** www.crmoon.com. *Passion*, published quarterly, features poetry, fiction, reviews, and essays on feminism, art, philosophy, and the media. Single copy: £2.50 ($4 USD); subscription: £10 ($17 USD). Make checks payable to Crescent Moon Publishing.

○ Wants "thought-provoking, incisive, polemical, ironic, lyric, sensual, and hilarious work." Does not want "rubbish, trivia, party politics, sport, etc."

MAGAZINES NEEDS Submit 5-10 poems at a time. Cover letter is required. Include brief bio and publishing credits ("and please print your address in capitals"). Wants "poetry that is passionate and authentic. Any form or length." Does not want "the trivial, insincere, or derivative." Has published poetry by Jeremy Reed, Penelope Shuttle, Alan Bold, D.J. Enright, and Peter Redgrove. Pays 1 contributor's copy.

ALSO OFFERS *Crescent Moon* publishes about 25 books and chapbooks/year on arrangements **subsidized by the poet.** "We are also publishing 2 anthologies of new American poetry each year titled *Pagan America.*"

THE PATERSON LITERARY REVIEW

Passaic County Community College, Cultural Affairs Dept., One College Blvd., Paterson NJ 07505-1179. (973)684-6555. **Fax:** (973)523-6085. **E-mail:** mGillan@pccc.edu. **Website:** www.pccc.edu/poetry. **Contact:** Maria Mazziotti Gillan, editor/executive director. *Paterson Literary Review*, published annually, is produced by the The Poetry Center at Passaic County Community College. Wants poetry of "high quality; clear, direct, powerful work." Acquires first North American serial rights. Publishes ms 6-12 months after acceptance. Reads submissions December 1-March 31 only. Responds within 1 year. Sample cop: $13 plus $1.50 postage.

○ Work for *PLR* has been included in the *Pushcart Prize* anthology and *Best American Poetry.*

MAGAZINES NEEDS Submit up to 5 poems at a time. Has published poetry and work by Diane di Prima, Ruth Stone, Marge Piercy, Laura Boss, Robert Mooney, and Abigail Stone. Lines/poem: 100 maximum.

ALSO OFFERS Publishes *The New Jersey Poetry Resource Book* ($5 plus $1.50 p&h) and *The New Jersey Poetry Calendar.* The Distinguished Poets Series offers readings by poets of international, national, and regional reputation. Poetryworks/USA is a series of programs produced for UA Columbia-Cablevision. See website for details about these additional resources.

TIPS Looks for "clear, moving, and specific work."

THE PAUMANOK REVIEW

E-mail: editor@paumanokreview.com. **E-mail:** submissions@paumanokreview.com. **Website:** www.paumanokreview.com. "*The Paumanok Review* is a quarterly Internet literary magazine dedicated to promoting and publishing the best in contemporary art, music, and literature. *TPR* is published exclusively on the Web and is available free of charge. Acquires one-time and nonexclusive anthology rights. "Rights revert to the individual creator of a work with the exception of an option to publish the work, whole or in part, in a future electronic or print anthology edition of *The Paumanok Review.*" Responds in 1 month. Guidelines available online at website.

MAGAZINES NEEDS Wants all forms of poetry. Submit up to 5 poems per submission via e-mail (submissions@paumanokreview.com). Include cover letter. Length: up to 100 lines.

TIPS "*TPR* does not accept multiple submissions. The best statement of *TPR*'s publishing preferences is the magazine itself. Please read at least 1 issue before submitting."

PAVEMENT SAW

Pavement Saw Press, 321 Empire St., Montpelier OH 43543. **E-mail:** editor@pavementsaw.org. **Website:** pavementsaw.org. **Contact:** David Baratier, editor. *Pavement Saw*, published annually in August, wants "letters, short fiction, and poetry on any subject, especially work." Dedicates 15-20 pages of each issue to a featured writer. Acquires first rights. Responds in 4 months. Sometimes sends prepublication galleys. Seldom comments on rejected poems. Sample: $7. Subscription: $14. Guidelines available in magazine or for SASE.

◯ *Pavement Saw* is 88 pages, digest-sized, perfect-bound. Press run is 550.

MAGAZINES NEEDS Receives about 9,000 poems/year, accepts less than 1%. Submit 5 poems at a time. Considers simultaneous submissions, "as long as poet has not published a book with a press run of 1,000 or more." No e-mail submissions; postal submissions only. Cover letter is required. "No fancy typefaces." Does not want "poems that tell; no work by a deceased writer, and no translations." Length: up to 1-2 pages. Pays at least 2 contributor's copies.

ALSO OFFERS "Pavement Saw Press has been publishing steadily since the fall of 1993. Each year since 1999, we have published at least 4 full-length paperback poetry collections, with some printed in library edition hard covers, 1 chapbook and a yearly literary journal anthology. We specialize in finding authors who have been widely published in literary journals but have not published a chapbook or full-length book."

PEACE & FREEDOM

Peace & Freedom Press, 17 Farrow Rd., Whaplode Drove, Spalding, Lincs PE12 0TS, England. **Website:** http://pandf.booksmusicfilmstv.com/index.htm. Published semiannually; emphasizes social, humanitarian, and environmental issues. Considers submissions from subscribers only. Those new to poetry are welcome. The poetry published is pro-animal rights/welfare, anti-war, environmental; poems reflecting love; erotic, but not obscene; humorous; spiritual, humanitarian; with or without rhyme/meter. Considers poetry by children and teens. Has published poetry by Dorothy Bell-Hall, Freda Moffatt, Andrew Bruce, Bernard Shough, Mona Miller, and Andrew Savage. Responds to submissions in less than a month usually, with SAE/IRC. Submissions from subscribers only.

◯ Peace & Freedom has a varied format. Subscription: $20 U.S., £10 UK for 6 issues. Sample: $5 U.S., £1.75 UK. Sample copies can be purchased only from the above address. Advisable to buy a sample copy before submitting. Banks charge the equivalent of $5 to cash foreign checks in the UK, so please only send bills, preferably by registered post.

MAGAZINES NEEDS No previously published poems or simultaneous submissions. Accepts e-mail submissions (pasted into body of message, no attachments; no more than 3 poems/e-mail); no fax submissions. Include bio. Reads submissions year round. Publishes theme issues. Upcoming themes available in magazine, for SAE with IRC, by e-mail, or on website. "Work without correct postage will not be responded to or returned until proper postage is sent." Pays one contributor's copy. Reviews books of poetry. Lines/poem: 32 max.

CONTEST/AWARD OFFERINGS "*Peace & Freedom* holds regular poetry contests as does one of our other publications, *Eastern Rainbow*, which is a magazine concerning 20th-century popular culture using poetry up to 32 lines." Subscription: $20 U.S., £10 UK for 6 issues. Further details of competitions and publications available for SAE with IRC or on website.

TIPS "Too many writers have lost the personal touch that editors generally appreciate. It can make a difference when selecting work of equal merit."

⊙ THE PEDESTAL MAGAZINE

6815 Honors Court, Charlotte NC 28210. **E-mail:** pedmagazine@carolina.rr.com. **Website:** www.the-pedestalmagazine.com. **Contact:** John Amen, editor in chief. Committed to promoting diversity and celebrating the voice of the individual. Buys first rights. All rights revert back to the author/artist upon publication. Retains the right to publish the piece in any subsequent issue or anthology without additional payment. Publishes ms 2-4 weeks after acceptance. Responds in 1-2 months to mss. Guidelines available online.

See website for reading periods for different forms. Member: CLMP.

MAGAZINES NEEDS Open to a wide variety of poetry, ranging from the highly experimental to the traditionally formal. Submit all poems in 1 form. No need to query before submitting. No length restriction.

TIPS "If you send us your work, please wait for a response to your first submission before you submit again."

PENNINE INK MAGAZINE

1 Neptune St., Burnley BB11 1SF, England. **E-mail:** sheridansdandl@yahoo.co.uk. **Website:** pennineink. weebly.com. **Contact:** Laura Sheridan, editor. *Pennine Ink*, published annually in January, prints poems and short prose pieces. Responds to submissions in 3 months.

Pennine Ink is 48 pages, A5, with b&w illustrated cover. Receives about 400 poems/year, accepts about 40. Press run is 200. "Contributors wishing to purchase a copy of *Pennine Ink* should enclose £4 ($8 USD) per copy."

MAGAZINES NEEDS Submit up to 6 poems at a time. Accepts e-mail submissions. Seldom comments on rejected poems. Length: up to 40 lines/poem; up to 1,000 words for prose. Pays 1 contributor's copy.

PENNSYLVANIA ENGLISH

(814)375-4785. **Fax:** (814)375-4785. **E-mail:** avallone@ psu.edu. **Website:** www.english.iup.edu/pcea/publications.htm. **Contact:** Dr. Jess Haggerty, editor; Dr. Michael Cox, nonfiction and fiction editor (mwcox@ pitt.edu). *Pennsylvania English*, published annually, is "sponsored by the Pennsylvania College English Association. Our philosophy is quality. We publish literary fiction (and poetry and nonfiction). Our intended audience is literate, college-educated people." Acquires first North American serial rights. Pays upon publication. Publishes ms up to 12 months after acceptance. Responds in up to 12 months to mss. Sometimes comments on rejected mss. Sample copy: $10. Guidelines available on website.

Pennsylvania English is 5.25×8.25, up to 200 pages, perfect-bound, full-color cover featuring the artwork of a Pennsylvania artist. Reads mss during the summer. Publishes 4-6 new writers/year. Has published work by Dave Kress, Dan Leone, Paul West, Liz Rosenberg,

Walt MacDonald, Amy Pence, Jennifer Richter, and Jeff Schiff.

MAGAZINES NEEDS Submit 3 or more poems at a time via the online submission manager at https://paenglish.submittable.com/submit. "For all submissions, please include a brief bio for the contributors' page. Be sure to include your name, address, phone number, e-mail address, institutional affiliation (if you have one), the title of your poem(s), and any other relevant information. We will edit if necessary for space." Wants poetry of "any length, any style."

TIPS "Quality of the writing is our only measure. We're not impressed by long-winded cover letters detailing awards and publications we've never heard of. Beginners and professionals have the same chance with us. We receive stacks of competently written but boring fiction. For a story to rise from the rejection pile, it takes more than the basic competence."

PENNSYLVANIA LITERARY JOURNAL

Anaphora Literary Press, 1803 Treehills Parkway, Stone Mountain GA 30088. (520)425-4266. **E-mail:** director@anaphoraliterary.com. **Website:** anaphoraliterary.com. **Contact:** Anna Faktorovich, editor/director. "*Pennsylvania Literary Journal* is a printed, peer-reviewed journal that publishes critical essays, book reviews, short stories, interviews, photographs, art, and poetry. Published triannually, most are special issues with room for random projects in a wide variety of different fields. These special issues can be used to present a set of conference papers, so feel free to apply on behalf of a conference you are in charge of, if you think attending writers might be interested in seeing their revised conference papers published." Does not provide payment. Publishes ms an average of 2 months after acceptance. Responds in 1 day to queries and ms. Sample copy: $15. Guidelines available online. Accepts queries and ms submissions by e-mail at director@anaphoraliterary.com.

MAGAZINES NEEDS No line limit. Does not provide payment.

TIPS "We are just looking for great writing. Send your materials; if they are good and you don't mind working for free, we'll take it."

PENNY DREADFUL: TALES & POEMS OF FANTASTIC TERROR

P.O. Box 719, Radio City Station, Hell's Kitchen NY 10101-0719. **E-mail:** mmpendragon@aol.com. **Website:** www.mpendragon.com. *Penny Dreadful: Tales &*

Poems of Fanastic Terror, published irregularly (about once a year), features goth-romantic poetry and prose. Publishes poetry, short stories, essays, letters, listings, reviews, and b&w artwork "which celebrate the darker aspects of Man, the World, and their Creator." Wants "literary horror in the tradition of Poe, M.R. James, Shelley, M.P. Shiel, and LeFanu—dark, disquieting tales and verses designed to challenge the reader's perception of human nature, morality, and man's place within the Darkness. Stories and poems should be set prior to 1910 and/or possess a timeless quality." Does not want "references to 20th- and 21st-century personages/events, graphic sex, strong language, excessive gore and shock elements." Acquires one-time rights. Sample: $10. Subscription: $25/3 issues. Make checks payable to Michael Pendragon. Guidelines online.

○   "Works appearing in *Penny Dreadful* have been reprinted in *The Year's Best Fantasy and Horror*." *Penny Dreadful* nominates best tales and poems for Pushcart Prizes. *Penny Dreadful* is over 100 pages, digest-sized, desktop-published, perfect-bound. Press run is 200.

MAGAZINES NEEDS Submit by mail or e-mail. Rhymed, metered verse preferred. Has published poetry by Nancy Bennett, Michael R. Burch, Lee Clark, Louise Webster, K.S. Hardy, and Kevin N. Roberts. Length: up to 5 pages. Pays 1 contributor's copy.

ALSO OFFERS *Penny Dreadful* "includes market listings for, and reviews of, kindred magazines." Pendragon Publications also publishes *Songs of Innocence & Experience*.

THE PENWOOD REVIEW

P.O. Box 862, Los Alamitos CA 90720. **E-mail:** lcameron65@verizon.net. **E-mail:** submissions@penwoodreview.com. **Website:** www.penwoodreview.com. **Contact:** Lori Cameron, editor. *The Penwood Review* has been established to embrace high-quality poetry of all kinds and to provide a forum for poets who want to write intriguing, energetic, and disciplined poetry as an expression of their faith in God. We encourage writing that elevates the sacred while exploring its mystery and meaning in our lives. Semiannual. Wants "disciplined, high-quality, well-crafted poetry on any subject. Rhyming poetry must be written in traditional forms (sonnets, tercets, villanelles, sestinas, etc.)." Acquires one-time and electronic rights. Publishes ms 1 year after acceptance. Responds

in up to 3 months. Sample copy: $6. Single copy: $8. Subscription: $16.

○   *The Penwood Review* is about 40 pages, magazine-sized, saddle-stapled, with heavy card cover. Press run is 50-100.

MAGAZINES NEEDS Submit 3-5 poems at a time. Prefers e-mail submissions (pasted into body of message). Cover letter is optional. One poem to a page with the author's full name, address, and phone number in the upper right corner. "Submissions are circulated among an editorial staff for evaluations." Never comments on rejected poems. Has published poetry by Kathleen Spivack, Anne Babson, Hugh Fox, Anselm Brocki, Nina Tassi, and Gary Guinn. Does not want "light verse, doggerel, or greeting card-style poetry. Also, nothing racist, sexist, pornographic, homophobic, or blasphemous." Length: less than 2 pages preferred. Pays with subscription discount of $12 and, with subscription, 1 additional contributor's copy.

PEREGRINE

Amherst Writers & Artists Press, P.O. Box 1076, Amherst MA 01004. (413)253-3307. **Fax:** (413)253-7764. **E-mail:** peregrine@amherstwriters.com. **Website:** www.amherstwriters.com. **Contact:** Jan Haag, editor. *Peregrine*, published annually, features poetry and fiction. "*Peregrine* has provided a forum for national and international writers since 1983 and is committed to finding excellent work by emerging as well as established writers. We welcome work reflecting diversity of voice. We like to be surprised. We look for writing that is honest, unpretentious, and memorable. All decisions are made by the editors." Acquires first rights. Sample copy: $12. Guidelines online.

○   Magazine: 6x9; 100+ pages; 60 lb. white offset paper; glossy cover. Member: CLMP. Reading period: March 15-May 15.

MAGAZINES NEEDS Submit 3 single-spaced, one-page poems. "We seek poems that inform and surprise us. We appreciate fresh and specific imagery and layered metaphors, but not excessive verbiage, abstractions, or clichés." "We will not consider inspirational poetry, greeting-card verse, religious tirades, or nostalgia." Length: up to 40 lines and spaces/poem. Pays in contributor's copies.

TIPS "Check guidelines before submitting your work. Familiarize yourself with *Peregrine*. We look for heart and soul as well as technical expertise. Trust your own voice."

PERMAFROST: A LITERARY JOURNAL

c/o English Dept., Univ. of Alaska Fairbanks, P.O. Box 755720, Fairbanks AK 99775. **E-mail:** editor@permafrostmag.com. **Website:** permafrostmag.com. *Permafrost: A Literary Journal*, published in May/June, contains poems, short stories, creative nonfiction, b&w drawings, photographs, and prints. "We survive on both new and established writers, hoping and expecting to see the best work out there. We have published work by E. Ethelbert Miller, W. Loran Smith, Peter Orlovsky, Jim Wayne Miller, Allen Ginsberg, and Andy Warhol." Responds in 3 months to mss. Subscription: $10/year, $18/2 years. Back issues $5. Guidelines available on website. Reads submissions September 1-December 1 for print edition, February 5-April 30 for summer online edition.

○ *Permafrost* is about 200 pages, digest-sized, professionally printed, flat-spined. Also publishes summer online edition.

MAGAZINES NEEDS We publish any style of poetry provided it is conceived, written, and revised with care. While we encourage submissions about Alaska and by Alaskans, we also welcome poems about anywhere, from anywhere. Submit up to 5 poems via online submissions manager at permafrostmag.submittable.com; "e-mail submissions will not be read." Sometimes comments on poems. Pays 1 contributor's copy. Reduced contributor rate of $5 on additional copies.

PERSPECTIVES

4500 60th St. SE, Grand Rapids MI 49512. **E-mail:** submissions@perspectivesjournal.org. **Website:** perspectivesjournal.org. "*Perspectives* is a journal of theology in the broad Reformed tradition. We seek to express the Reformed faith theologically; to engage issues that Reformed Christians meet in personal, ecclesiastical, and societal life; and thus to contribute to the mission of the church of Jesus Christ. The editors are interested in submissions that contribute to a contemporary Reformed theological discussion. Our readers tend to be affiliated with the Presbyterian Church (USA), the Reformed Church in America, and the Christian Reformed Church. Some of our subscribers are academics or pastors, but we also gear our articles to thoughtful, literate laypeople who want to engage in Reformed theological reflection on faith and culture." Acquires first rights. Time between acceptance and publication is 3-12 months. Responds in 3-6 months. Sample: $3.50. Subscription: $30.

○ *Perspectives* is 24 pages, magazine-sized, Web offset-printed, saddle-stapled, with paper cover containing b&w illustration. Receives about 300 poems/year, accepts 6-20. Press run is 3,300.

MAGAZINES NEEDS Wants "poems excellent in craft and significant in subject, both traditional and free in form. We publish 1-2 poems every other issue." Has published poetry by Ann Hostetler, Paul Willis, and Priscilla Atkins. Submit poems via e-mail. Pays 5 contributor's copies.

PHILADELPHIA STORIES

Fiction/Art/Poetry of the Delaware Valley, 93 Old York Rd., Suite 1/#1-753, Jenkintown PA 19046. (215) 551-5889. **E-mail:** christine@philadelphiastories.org; info@philadelphiastories.org. **Website:** www.philadelphiastories.org. Carla Spataro, editorial director/co-publisher. **Contact:** Christine Weiser, executive director/co-publisher. *Philadelphia Stories*, published quarterly, publishes "fiction, poetry, essays, and art written by authors living in, or originally from, Pennsylvania, Delaware, or New Jersey. "*Philadelphia Stories* also hosts 2 national writing contests: The Marguerite McGlinn Short Story Contest ($2,000 first-place prize; $500 second-place prize; $250 third-place prize) and the Sandy Crimmins National Poetry Contest ($1,000 first-place prize, 3 $100 runner-up prizes). Visit our website for details. "*Philadelphia Stories* also launched a "junior" version in 2012 for Philadelphia-area writers ages 18 and younger. Visit www.philadelphiastories.org/junior for details. Acquires one-time rights. Publication is copyrighted. Publishes ms 1-2 months after acceptance. Responds in 6 months. Rarely comments on/critiques rejected mss. Sample copy available for $5, and on website. Guidelines available on website. Send complete ms with cover letter via online submission form only. Include estimated word count, list of publications, and affiliation to the Philadelphia area.

○ Literary magazine/journal. 8.5×11; 24 pages; 70# matte text, all 4-color paper; 70# matte text cover. Contains illustrations, photographs. Subscription: "We offer $20 memberships that include home delivery." Make checks payable to *Philadelphia Stories*. Member: CLMP.

MAGAZINES NEEDS Submit 3 poems at a time. No previously published poems. Cover letter is preferred. Reads submissions year round. "Each poem is reviewed by a preliminary board that decides on a final list; the entire board discusses this list and chooses the mutual favorites for print and Web. We send a layout proof to check for print poems." Receives about 600 poems/year, accepts about 15%. Considers poetry by teens. Has published poetry by Daniel Abdal-Hayy Moore, Scott Edward Anderson, Sandy Crimmins, Liz Dolan, Alison Hicks, and Margaret A. Robinson. Wants "polished, well-crafted poems." Does not want "first drafts." Lines/poem: 36.

TIPS "We look for exceptional, polished prose, a controlled voice, strong characters and place, and interesting subjects. Follow guidelines. We cannot stress this enough. Read every guideline carefully and thoroughly before sending anything out. Send out only polished material. We reject many quality pieces for various reasons; try not to take rejection personally. Just because your piece isn't right for one publication doesn't mean it's bad. Selection is an extremely subjective process."

PHOEBE: A JOURNAL OF LITERATURE AND ART

MSN 2C5, George Mason University, 400 University Dr., Fairfax VA 22030. **E-mail:** phoebeliterature@gmail.com. **Website:** www.phoebejournal.com. Publishes poetry, fiction, nonfiction, and visual art. "*Phoebe* prides itself on supporting up-and-coming writers, whose style, form, voice, and subject matter demonstrate a vigorous appeal to the senses, intellect, and emotions of our readers." Responds in 4-6 months. Guidelines available on website.

MAGAZINES NEEDS Submit 3-5 poems via online submission manager. Pays 2 contributor's copies.

PILGRIMAGE MAGAZINE

E-mail: info@pilgrimagepress.org. **Website:** www.pilgrimagepress.org. **Contact:** Juan Morales, editor. Serves an eclectic fellowship of readers, writers, artists, naturalists, contemplatives, activists, seekers, adventurers, and other kindred spirits. Guidelines available online. Submit via online submissions manager (https://pilgrimagemagazine.submittable.com/submit) or snail mail (with SASE for reply only).

MAGAZINES NEEDS Fit poetry on 1 page.

TIPS "Our interests include wildness in all its forms; inward and outward explorations; home ground, the open road, service, witness, peace, and justice; symbols, story, and myth in contemporary culture; struggle and resilience; insight and transformation; wisdom wherever it is found; and the great mystery of it all. We like good storytellers and a good sense of humor. No e-mail submissions, please."

THE PINCH

English Department, University of Memphis, Memphis TN 38152. (901)678-4591. **E-mail:** editor@pinchjournal.com. **Website:** www.pinchjournal.com. **Contact:** Tim Johnston, editor in chief; Matthew Gallant, managing editor. Semiannual literary magazine. "We publish fiction, creative nonfiction, poetry, and art of literary quality by both established and emerging artists." Acquires first North American serial rights. Publication is copyrighted. Responds in 3 months to mss. Sample copy: $5. Guidelines available on website.

○ "The Pinch Literary Awards in Fiction, Poetry, and Nonfiction offer a $1,000 prize and publication. Check our website for details."

MAGAZINES NEEDS "We do NOT accept submissions via e-mail. Submissions sent via e-mail will not receive a response. To submit, see guidelines." Submit through mail or via online submissions manager.

ALSO OFFERS Offers an annual award in poetry. 1st Prize: $1,000 and publication; 2nd and 3rd Prize poems may also be published. Any previously unpublished poem of up to 2 pages is eligible. No simultaneous submissions. Poems should be typed and accompanied by a cover letter. Author's name should not appear anywhere on ms. Mss will not be returned. Guidelines available for SASE, by e-mail, or on website. **Entry fee:** $20 for up to 3 poems (includes one-year subscription). **Deadline:** March 15 (inclusive postmark dates). Winners will be notified in July and published in subsequent issue.

TIPS "We have a new look and a new edge. We're soliciting work from writers with a national or international reputation as well as strong, interesting work from emerging writers."

THE PINK CHAMELEON

E-mail: dpfreda@juno.com. **Website:** www.thepinkchameleon.com. **Contact:** Dorothy Paula Freda, editor/publisher. *The Pink Chameleon*, published annually online, contains "family-oriented, upbeat poetry, stories, essays, and articles, any genre in good taste that gives hope for the future." Acquires one-time rights for 1 year. Time between acceptance and publication is up to 1 year, depending on date of acceptance. Responds in 1 month to ms. Sometimes comments on rejected mss. Sample copy and writer's guidelines online.

○ Reading period is January 1-April 30 and September 1-October 31.

MAGAZINES NEEDS Also considers poetry by children and teens. Submit 1-4 poems at a time. Accepts e-mail submissions only (pasted into body of message; no attachments.) Use plain text and include a brief bio. Often comments on rejected poems. Receives about 50 poems/year, accepts about 50%. Does not want "pornography, cursing, swearing; nothing evoking despair." Length: 6-24 lines. No payment.

TIPS Wants "simple, honest, evocative emotion; upbeat fiction and nonfiction submissions that give hope for the future; well-paced plots; stories, poetry, articles, essays that speak from the heart. Read guidelines carefully. Use a good, but not ostentatious, opening hook. Stories should have a beginning, middle, and end that make the reader feel the story was worth his or her time. This also applies to articles and essays. In the latter 2, wrap your comments and conclusions in a neatly packaged final paragraph. Turnoffs include violence and bad language. Simple, genuine, and sensitive work does not need to shock with vulgarity to be interesting and enjoyable."

PINYON POETRY

Mesa State College, Languages, Literature and Mass Communications, Mesa State College, Grand Junction CO 81502. **E-mail:** rphillis@mesa5.mesa. colorado.edu. **Website:** http://org.coloradomesa. edu/~rphillis/. **Contact:** Randy Phillis, editor. *Pinyon Poetry*, published annually in June, prints "the best available contemporary American poetry. No restrictions other than excellence. We appreciate a strong voice." Subscription: $8/year. Sample: $5. Make checks payable to Pinyon Poetry. Guidelines for SASE or online.

○ Literary magazine/journal: 8.5×5.5, 120 pages, heavy paper. Contains illustrations and photographs. Press run is 300; 100 distributed free to contributors, friends, etc.

MAGAZINES NEEDS Does not want "inspirational, light verse, or sing-song poetry." Has published poetry by Mark Cox, Barry Spacks, Wendy Bishop, and Anne Ohman Youngs. Receives about 4,000 poems/year, accepts 2%. Submit 3-5 poems at a time. Cover letter is preferred. "Name, address, e-mail, and phone number on each page. SASE required." Reads submissions August 1-December 1. "Three groups of assistant editors, led by an associate editor, make recommendations to the editor." Seldom comments on rejected poems. Pays 2 contributor's copies.

TIPS "Ask yourself if the work is something you would like to read in a publication."

PIRENE'S FOUNTAIN

E-mail: pirenesfountain@gmail.com. **Website:** pirenesfountain.com. **Contact:** Elizabeth Nichols, editor; Lark Vernon, editor in chief; Ami Kaye, publisher and managing editor. *Pirene's Fountain* is published annually in November. Reading period: August 15-March 1. Poets retain copyright to their own work; rights revert to poets upon publication. Publishes ms 1-3 months after acceptance. Responds in 1-4 months. Guidelines available online.

○ Receives about 1,500 poems/year, accepts about 20%.

MAGAZINES NEEDS Submit 3-8 poems at a time. Poems are circulated to an editorial board. Never comments on rejected poems. Sometimes publishes theme issues. A 50-100 word bio note is required with submissions. Has published work by Lisel Mueller, Linda Pastan, J.P. Dancing Bear, Alison Croggon, Dorianne Laux, Rebecca Seiferle, Joseph Millar, Kim Addonizio, Jane Hirshfeld, and Jim Moore, among others. Does not want "anything obscene, pornographic, or discriminatory in nature."

ALSO OFFERS "Poets whose work has been selected for publication in our journal during the past calendar year (with the exception of staff /featured poets) are automatically entered for the annual Liakoura Poetry award. Our editors will each choose 1 poem from all of the selections. The 5 nominated poems will be sent "blind" to an outside editor/publisher for the final decision. The winning poet will be awarded a certificate and a $100 Amazon gift card via e-mail. Pushcart and Best of the Net nominations: Editors select the best work published by PF during the year. This is open to all submitting and featured poets. Only previously unpublished poems will be considered; please indicate that in your submission. Nominated poets are notified after selections have been sent in."

TIPS "Please read submission guidelines carefully and send in at least 3 poems. We offer a poetry discussion group on Facebook, titled Pirene's Fountain Poetry."

PISGAH REVIEW

Division of Humanities, Brevard College, 1 Brevard College Dr., Brevard NC 28712. (828)577-8324. **E-mail:** tinerjj@brevard.edu. **Website:** www.pisgahreview.com. **Contact:** Jubal Tiner, editor. "*Pisgah Review* publishes primarily literary short fiction, creative nonfiction, and poetry. Our only criteria is quality of work; we look for the best." Acquires first North American serial rights. Publication is copyrighted. Pays on publication. Sends galleys to author. Publishes mss 6-9 months after acceptance. Responds to mss in 4-6 months. Sometimes comments on/critiques rejected mss. Sample copy: $7. Guidelines available on website.

Has published Ron Rash, Thomas Rain Crowe, Joan Conner, Gary Fincke, Steve Almond, and Fred Bahnson.

MAGAZINES NEEDS "Send complete ms to our submission manager on our website."

TIPS "We select work of only the highest quality. Grab us from the beginning and follow through. Engage us with your language and characters. A clean ms goes a long way toward acceptance. Stay true to the vision of your work, revise tirelessly, and submit persistently."

PLAINSONGS

Department of Languages and Literature, Hastings NE 68901. (402)461-7343. **Fax:** (402)461-7756. **E-mail:** plainsongs@hastings.edu. **Contact:** Laura Marvel Wunderlich, editor. *Plainsongs*, published 3 times/ year, considers poems on any subject, in any style, but free verse predominates. *Plainsongs'* title suggests not only its location on the great plains, but its preference for the living language, whether in free or formal verse. Acquires first rights. Responds 2 months after deadline. Sample: $5. Subscription: $15 for 3 issues.

MAGAZINES NEEDS Submit up to 6 poems at a time. No fax, e-mail, or disk submissions. Postal submissions only. Reads submissions according to the following deadlines: August 15 for winter issue; November 15 for spring issue; March 15 for fall issue. Pays 2 contributor's copies and one-year subscription.

CONTEST/AWARD OFFERINGS Three poems in each issue receive a $25 prize. "A short essay in appreciation accompanies each award poem."

PLANET-THE WELSH INTERNATIONALIST

P.O. Box 44, Aberystwyth Ceredigion SY23 3ZZ, United Kingdom. **E-mail:** emily.trahair@planet-magazine.org.uk. **Website:** www.planetmagazine.org.uk. **Contact:** Emily Trahair, editor. A literary/ cultural/political journal centered on Welsh affairs but with a strong interest in minority cultures in Europe and elsewhere. *Planet: The Welsh Internationalist*, published quarterly, is a cultural magazine "centered on Wales, but with broader interests in arts, sociology, politics, history, and science." Publishes ms 4-6 months after acceptance. Responds in 3 months. Single copy: £6.75; subscription: £22 (£40 overseas). Sample copy: £5. Guidelines online.

Planet is 128 pages, A5, professionally printed, perfect-bound, with glossy color card cover. Receives about 500 submissions/year, accepts about 5%. Press run is 1,550 (1,500 subscribers, about 10% libraries, 200 shelf sales).

MAGAZINES NEEDS Wants "good poetry in a wide variety of styles. No limitations as to subject matter; length can be a problem." Has published poetry by Nigel Jenkins, Anne Stevenson, and Les Murray. Submit 4-6 poems via mail or e-mail (with attachment). For postal submissions, no submissions returned unless accompanied by an SASE. Writers submitting from abroad should send at least 3 IRCs for return of typescript; 1 IRC for reply only. Pays £30/poem.

TIPS "We do not look for fiction that necessarily has a 'Welsh' connection, which some writers assume from our title. We try to publish a broad range of fiction, and our main criterion is quality. Try to read copies of any magazine you submit to. Don't write out of the blue to a magazine which might be completely inappropriate for your work. Recognize that you are likely to have a high rejection rate, as magazines tend to favor writers from their own countries."

PLEIADES

Pleiades Press, Department of English, University of Central Missouri, Martin 336, Warrensburg MO 64093. (660)543-8106. **E-mail:** pleiades@ucmo.edu. **Website:** www.ucmo.edu/pleiades. **Contact:** Kevin Prufer, editor-at-large. "We publish contemporary fiction, poetry, interviews, literary essays, special-interest personal essays, and reviews for a general and literary audience from authors from around the world." Reads August 15-May 15. Buys first North American serial rights, buys second serial (reprint) rights. Occasionally requests rights for TV, radio reading, website. Pays on publication. Publishes ms an average of 9 months after acceptance. Responds in 2 months to queries. Responds in 1-4 months to mss. Editorial lead time 9 months. Sample copy for $5 (back issue); $6 (current issue) Guidelines available online.

MAGAZINES NEEDS Submit 3-5 poems at a time via online submission manager. "Nothing didactic, pretentious, or overly sentimental." Pays $3/poem, and contributor copies.

ALSO OFFERS "Also sponsors the Lena-Miles Wever Todd Poetry Series competition, a contest for the best book ms by an American poet. The winner receives $2,000, publication by Pleiades Press (1,000 copies), and distribution by Louisiana State University Press. Check website for deadline and details."

TIPS "Submit only 1 genre at a time to appropriate editors. Show care for your material and your readers—submit quality work in a professional format. Include cover letter with brief bio and list of publications. Include SASE. Cover art is solicited directly from artists. We accept queries for book reviews."

PLOUGHSHARES

Emerson College, 120 Boylston St., Boston MA 02116. (617)824-3757. **E-mail:** pshares@pshares.org. **Website:** www.pshares.org. **Contact:** Ladette Randolph, editor in chief/executive director; Andrea Martucci, managing editor. *Ploughshares*, published 3 times/year, is "a journal of new writing guest-edited by prominent poets and writers to reflect different and contrasting points of view. Translations are welcome if permission has been granted. Our mission is to present dynamic, contrasting views on what is valid and important in contemporary literature and to discover and advance significant literary talent. Each issue is guest-edited by a different writer. We no longer structure issues around preconceived themes." Editors have included Carolyn Forché, Gerald Stern, Rita Dove, Chase Twichell, and Marilyn Hacker. "We do accept electronic submissions—there is a $3 fee per submission, which is waived if you are a subscriber." Buys first North American serial rights. Pays on publication. Publishes ms an average of 6 months after acceptance. Responds in 3-5 months to mss. Sample copy: $14 current issue, $7 back issue; please inquire for shipping rates. Subscription: $30 domestic, $30 plus shipping (see website) foreign. Guidelines online.

○ *Ploughshares* is 200 pages, digest-sized. Receives about 11,000 poetry, fiction, and essay submissions/year. Reads submissions June 1-January 15 (postmark); mss submitted January 16-May 31 will be returned unread.

MAGAZINES NEEDS Submit up to 5 poems via online submissions form or by mail. Has published poetry by Donald Hall, Li-Young Lee, Robert Pinsky, Brenda Hillman, and Thylias Moss. Pays $25/printed page ($50 minimum, $250 maximum); 2 contributor's copies; and one-year subscription.

PMS

University of Alabama at Birmingham, HB 217, 1530 3rd Ave. S, Birmingham AL 35294. (205)934-2641. **Fax:** (205)975-8125. **E-mail:** poemmemoirstory@gmail.com. **Website:** pms-journal.org. **Contact:** Kerry Madden, editor in chief. "*PMS poemmemoirstory* appears once a year. We accept unpublished, original submissions of poetry, memoir, and short fiction during our January 1-March 31 reading period. We accept simultaneous submissions; however, we ask that you please contact us immediately if your piece is published elsewhere so we may free up space for other authors. While *PMS* is a journal of exclusively women's writing, the subject field is wide open." Copyright returns to author after publication, but work published elsewhere should acknowledge first publication in *PMS poemmemoirstory*. Sample copy: $10. Subscription: $10 for 1 year, $15 for 2 years, $18 for 3 years. Guidelines online.

○ *PMS* has gone all-digital on Submittable. "There is now a $3 fee, which covers costs associated with our online submissions system. Please send all submissions to https://poemmemoirstory.submittable.com/submit."

MAGAZINES NEEDS Submit up to 5 poems through online submissions manager. Pays 2 contributor's copies.

TIPS "We strongly encourage you to familiarize yourself with *PMS* before submitting. You can find links to some examples of what we publish in the pages of *PMS* 8 and *PMS* 9. We look forward to reading your work."

POCKETS

The Upper Room, P.O. Box 340004, Nashville TN 37203. (615)340-7333. **E-mail:** pockets@upperroom.org. **Website:** pockets.upperroom.org. **Contact:** Lynn W. Gilliam, editor. Magazine published 11 times/year. "*Pockets* is a Christian devotional magazine for children ages 6-12. All submissions should address the broad theme of the magazine. Each issue is built around a theme with material which can be used by children in a variety of ways. Scripture stories, fiction, poetry, prayers, art, graphics, puzzles and activities are included. Submissions do not need to be overtly religious. They should help children experience a Christian lifestyle that is not always a neatly wrapped moral package but is open to the continuing revelation of God's will. Seasonal material, both secular and liturgical, is desired." Buys first North American serial rights. Pays on acceptance. Publishes ms an average of 1 year after acceptance. Responds in 8 weeks to mss. Each issue reflects a specific theme. Guidelines online.

○ Does not accept e-mail or fax submissions.

MAGAZINES NEEDS Both seasonal and theme poems needed. Considers poetry by children. Length: up to 20 lines. Pays $25 minimum.

TIPS "Theme stories, role models, and retold scripture stories are most open to freelancers. Poetry is also open. It is very helpful if writers read our writers' guidelines and themes on our website."

POEM

Huntsville Literary Association, P.O. Box 2006, Huntsville AL 35804. **E-mail:** poem@hlahsv.org. **Website:** www.hlahsv.org/POEM. **Contact:** Rebecca Harbor, editor; Harry V. Moore and Peggy Brosious, assistant editors. *Poem*, published twice/year in the spring and fall, consists entirely of poetry. Welcomes submissions from established poets as well as from less-known and beginning poets. Acquires first serial rights. Responds in 1-3 months. Sample copy: $7 (back issue). Single copy: $10. Subscription: $20.

○ *Poem* is 90 pages, digest-sized, flat-spined, printed on good stock paper, with a clean design and a matte cover. Prints more than 60 poems/issue, generally featured 1 per page. Press run is 500.

MAGAZINES NEEDS Wants poems characterized by compression, rich vocabulary, significant content, and evidence of a tuned ear and a practiced pen. Wants coherent work that moves through the particulars of the poem to make a point. Submit poems with a cover letter. Place name, address, telephone number, and e-mail address on cover letter and on each poem. Include SASE with sufficient postage. Submissions are read year round. Has published poetry by Ronald Wallace, Bill Brown, and Margaret Holley. Does not want translations, greeting card verse, or "proselytizing or didactic poems." Pays 2 contributor's copies.

POEMELEON: A JOURNAL OF POETRY

E-mail: editor@poemeleon.org. **Website:** www.poemeleon.org. **Contact:** Cati Porter, editor. Each issue of *Poemeleon* is devoted to a specific kind of poetry. Previous emphases include: poetry of place, ekphrastic poetry, poems in form, prose poems, persona poems, humor, gender, and collaboration. Acquires one-time, non-exclusive rights. Responds in 1-3 months after close of submissions.

MAGAZINES NEEDS Submit 1-5 poems using online submission manager. Include a brief third-person bio in cover letter.

POESY MAGAZINE

P.O. Box 458, Santa Cruz CA 95061. **E-mail:** info@poesy.org; submissions@poesy.org. **Website:** www.poesy.org. **Contact:** Brian Morrisey, editor in chief. *POESY Magazine*, published biannually, is "an anthology of American poetry. *POESY*'s main concentrations are Boston, Massachusetts, and Santa Cruz, California, 2 thriving homesteads for poets, beats, and artists of nature. Our goal is to unite the 2 scenes, updating poets on what's happening across the country." Wants to see "original poems that express observational impacts with clear and concise imagery. Acceptence is based on creativity, composition, and relation to the format of *POESY*." Does not want "poetry with excessive profanity. We would like to endorse creativity beyond the likes of everyday babble." Has published poetry by Lawrence Ferlinghetti, Jack Hirschman, Edward Sanders, Todd Moore, Diane Di Prima, and Julia Vinograd. Acquires first rights. Publishes ms 1 month after acceptance. Responds in 4-6 weeks. Guidelines available online.

○ *POESY* is 16 pages, magazine-sized, newsprint, glued/folded, includes ads. Receives about 1,000 poems/year, accepts about 10%. Press run is 1,000; most distributed free to local venues.

MAGAZINES NEEDS Submit up to 5 poems by e-mail or postal mail. Cover letter is preferred. Reads submissions year round. Indicate if you want your poems returned, and include SASE. "We encourage poems ... that create an image, stop moments in time, and leave your reader with a lasting impression. Please no poems about dogs, cats, angels, or the food you ate recently." Length: up to 32 lines/poem. Pays 3 contributor's copies.

TIPS "Our main focus is on Santa Cruz and Boston poetry, but we also accept submissions across the country. We see the poem as something to immerse the reader into a welcomed world of arresting images that jerks the eyes onto the page and leaves the reels of the mind turning long after the poem is finished. We see the poem as a work of art; save the narrative voice for the enlightenment of prose. We see the poem as a camera documenting a moment in time seen before the lens, rather than from the eyes of its beholder behind the lens. To accomplish this goal, we have to be very precise that everything we publish falls within our portrayal of the poem."

POETALK

Bay Area Poets Coalition, 1791 Solano Ave. #A11, Berkeley CA 94707-2209. **E-mail:** poetalk@aol.com. **Website:** www.bayareapoetscoalition.org. **Contact:** John Rowe, acquisitions. *POETALK*, currently published 1-2 issues/year, is the poetry journal of the Bay Area Poets Coalition (BAPC) and publishes 60-plus poets in each issue. "*POETALK* is open to all. No particular genre. Rhyme must be well done." All rights revert to author upon publication. Usually responds in up to 6 months. Guidelines available early summer for SASE, by e-mail, or see posting on website.

○ *POETALK* is 36 pages, digest-sized, photocopied, saddle-stapled, with heavy card cover. Press run is 400. Subscription: $5/2 issues. Sample copy: $2. Submissions are read year-round.

MAGAZINES NEEDS In general, poets may submit 3-5 poems at a time, no more than twice/year. Lines/poem: under 35 preferred; longer poems of "outstanding quality" considered. Considers previously published poems and simultaneous submissions, but must be noted. Cover letter is preferred. Include SASE. Mss should be clearly typed, single-spaced, and include author's name and mailing address on every page. Provide an e-mail address. Pays 1 contributor's copy.

CONTEST/AWARD OFFERINGS Sponsors yearly contest.

TIPS "If you don't want suggested revisions, you need to say so clearly in your cover letter or indicate on each poem submitted." Bay Area Poets Coalition holds monthly readings (in Berkeley, CA). BAPC has 150 members; membership is $15/year (includes subscription to *POETALK* and other privileges); extra outside U.S.

POETICA MAGAZINE, CONTEMPORARY JEWISH WRITING

P.O. Box 11014, Norfolk VA 23517. **E-mail:** poetica-publishing@aol.com. **Website:** www.poeticamagazine.com. *Poetica Magazine, Contemporary Jewish Writing*, published in print 3 times/year, offers "an outlet for the many writers who draw from their Jewish backgrounds and experiences to create poetry/prose/short stories, giving both emerging and recognized writers the opportunity to share their work with the larger community." Poets retain all rights. Publishes ms 4 months after acceptance. Responds in 1 month. Single copy: $10; subscription: $21.50 individual; $24.95 libraries and Canada; $28.95 international.

○ *Poetica* is 70 pages, perfect-bound, full-color cover, includes some ads. Receives about 500 poems/year, accepts about 60%. Press run is 350.

MAGAZINES NEEDS Submit ms through online submissions manager. Include e-mail, bio, and mailing address. Pays 1 contributor's copy.

TIPS "We publish original, unpublished works by Jewish and non-Jewish writers alike. We are interested in works that have the courage to acknowledge, challenge, and celebrate modern Jewish life beyond distinctions of secular and sacred. We like accessible works that find fresh meaning in old traditions that recognize the challenges of our generation. We evaluate works on several levels, including its skillful use of craft, its ability to hold interest, and layers of meaning."

POET LORE

The Writer's Center, 4508 Walsh St., Bethesda MD 20815. **E-mail:** genevieve.deleon@writer.org. **Website:** http://poetlore.com; www.writer.org. **Contact:** Genevieve DeLeon, managing editor; Jody Bolz, editor; E. Ethelbert Miller, editor. *Poet Lore*, published semiannually, is dedicated to the best in American and world poetry as well as timely reviews and commentary. Wants fresh uses of traditional forms and devices. Has published poetry by Ai, Denise Duhamel, Jefferey Harrison, Eve Jones, Carl Phillips, and Ronald Wallace. Responds in 3 months. Guidelines for SASE or online at website.

○ *Poet Lore* is 144 pages, digest-sized, professionally printed, perfect-bound, with glossy card cover. Receives about 4,200 poems/year, accepts 125. Press run is at least 800. Single copy: $8; subscription: $18/nonmember, $12/member. "Add $1/single copy for shipping; add $5 postage for subscriptions outside U.S."

MAGAZINES NEEDS Considers simultaneous submissions with notification in cover letter. No e-mail or disk submissions. Submit typed poems, with author's name and address on each page; SASE is required. Pays 2 contributor's copies and a one-year subscription.

⑤ POETRY

The Poetry Foundation, 61 W. Superior St., Chicago IL 60654. (312)787-7070. **Fax:** (312)787-6650. **E-mail:** editors@poetrymagazine.org. **Website:** www.poetry-magazine.org. Don Share, editor. **Contact:** Don Share, editor. *Poetry*, published monthly by The Poetry Foundation (see separate listing in Organizations), "has no special ms needs and no special requirements as to form: We examine in turn all work received and accept that which seems best." Has published poetry by the major voices of our time as well as new talent. Buys first serial rights. Pays on publication. Publishes ms an average of 9 months after acceptance. Responds in 2 months to mss and queries. Guidelines online.

○ *Poetry's* website offers featured poems, letters, reviews, interviews, essays, and web-exclusive features. *Poetry* is elegantly printed, flat-spined. Receives 100,000 submissions/year, accepts about 300-350. Press run is 16,000.

MAGAZINES NEEDS Accepts all styles and subject matter. Submit up to 4 poems via online submissions manager. Reviews books of poetry in multibook formats of varying lengths. Does not accept unsolicited reviews. Length: up to 10 pages total. Pays $10 line (minimum payment of $300).

ALSO OFFERS Offers 8 prizes (Bess Hokin Prize, Levinson Prize, Frederick Bock Prize, J. Howard and Barbara M.J. Wood Prize, John Frederick Nims Memorial Prize for Translation, Friends of Literature Prize, Editors Prize for Feature Article, Editors Prize for Reviewing) ranging from $500-5,000 are awarded annually to poets whose work has appeared in the magazine that year. Only work already published in *Poetry* is eligible for consideration; no formal application is necessary.

POETRYBAY

P.O. Box 114, Northport NY 11768. (631)427-1950. **E-mail:** poetrybay@aol.com. **E-mail:** info@poetrybay.com. **Website:** www.poetrybay.com. **Contact:** George Wallace, editor. *Poetrybay*, published semiannually online, seeks "to add to the body of great contemporary American poetry by presenting the work of established and emerging writers. Also, we consider essays and reviews." Has published poetry by Robert Bly, Yevgeny Yevtushenko, Marvin Bell, Diane Wakoski, Cornelius Eady, and William Heyen.

MAGAZINES NEEDS Open to format, length, and style. Works previously published in magazine or online publications will not be considered. Submit 3-5 poemts in the body of an e-mail, with name, a brief bio, and address. Or submit poems via snail mail with a cover letter and SASE for reply.

POETRY INTERNATIONAL

San Diego State University, 5500 Campanile Dr., San Diego CA 92182-6020. (619)594-1522. **Fax:** (619)594-4998. **E-mail:** poetryintl@gmail.com. **Website:** http://poetryinternational.sdsu.edu. **Contact:** Jenny Minniti-Shippey, managing editor. *Poetry International*, published annually in November, is "an eclectic poetry magazine intended to reflect a wide range of poetry being written today." Wants "a wide range of styles and subject matter. We're particularly interested in translations." Does not want "cliché-ridden, derivative, or obscure poetry." Has published poetry by Adrienne Rich, Robert Bly, Hayden Carruth, Kim Addonizio, Maxine Kumin, and Gary Soto. "We intend to continue to publish poetry that makes a difference in people's lives, and startles us anew with the endless capacity of language to awaken our senses and expand our awareness." Responds in 6-8 months to mss. Subscription: $19.95/1 year. Sample: $15.

○ *Poetry International* is 200 pages, perfect-bound, with coated cardstock cover. Features the Poetry International Prize ($1,000) for best original poem. Submit up to 3 poems with a $15 entry fee.

MAGAZINES NEEDS Features the poetry of a different nation of the world as a special section in each issue. Does not accept e-mail submissions. Pays in contributor's copies.

TIPS "Seeks a wide range of styles and subject matter. We read unsolicited mss only between September

1-December 31 of each year. Manuscripts received any other time will be returned unread."

POETRY KANTO

Kanto Gakuin University, 3-22-1 Kamariya-Minami Kanazawa-ku, Yokohama 236-8502, Japan. **E-mail:** alan@kanto-gakuin.ac.jp. **Website:** poetrykanto.com. **Contact:** Alan Botsford, editor. *Poetry Kanto*, published annually in November by the Kanto Gakuin University, is a journal bridging east and west, featuring (as *Mythic Imagination Magazine* wrote) "outstanding poetry that navigates the divide of ocean and language from around the world." They seek exciting, well-crafted contemporary poetry in English and also encourage and publish high-quality English translations of modern and emerging Japanese poets. All translations must be accompanied by the original poems. Guidelines available on website.

After 35 years as a print publication, *Poetry Kanto* is now an online digital publication available worldwide. See website for sample poems.

MAGAZINES NEEDS Submit up to 5 poems at a time. Queries welcome. Send e-mail submissions (as attachment in Word). Cover letter is required. Include brief bio. Reads submissions December-June. Has published poetry by Jane Hirshfield, Ilya Kaminsky, Beth Ann Fennelly, Vijay Seshadri, Michael S. Collins, Mari L'Esperance, Michael Sowder, Alicia Ostriker, and Sarah Arvio.

POETRY NORTHWEST

Everett Community College, 2000 Tower St., Everett WA 98201. (425)388-9395. **E-mail:** editors@poetrynw. org; pnw@poetrynw.org. **Website:** www.poetrynw. org. **Contact:** Kevin Craft, editor. *Poetry Northwest* is published semiannually in June and December. "The mission of *Poetry Northwest* is to publish poetry with a vibrant sense of language at play in the world and a strong presense of the physical world in language. We publish new, emerging, and established writers. In the words of founding editor Carolyn Kizer, we aim to 'encourage the young and the inexperienced, the neglected mature, and the rough major talents and the fragile minor ones.' All styles and aesthetics will find consideration." Acquires all rights. Returns rights to poets upon publication. Pays 2 contributor's copies. Time between acceptance and publication is 3-12 months. Sometimes comments on rejected poems. Responds in 8-12 weeks. Single copy: $10. Sample: $10. Make checks payable to *Poetry Northwest*. Guidelines available on website. Submit by regular mail or online submission form only; no e-mail or disk submissions. Cover letter is required.

Has published poetry by Theodore Roethke, Czeslaw Milosz, Anne Sexton, Harold Pinter, Thom Gunn, Philip Larkin, Heather McHugh, and Richard Kenney. *Poetry Northwest* is 40+ pages, magazine-sized, Web press-printed, saddle-stapled, with 4-color cover, includes ads. Receives about 10,000 poems/year; accepts about 1%. Press run is 2,000.

MAGAZINES NEEDS Submit 3-5 poems at a time once per submission period. Sometimes publishes theme issues. Upcoming themes available in magazine or on website. Reading period is September 15-March 15. Mss sent outside reading period will be returned unread. Always sends prepublication galleys. Reviews books of poetry in single- and multi-book format.

POETRY SALZBURG REVIEW

University of Salzburg, Department of English and American Studies, Unipark Nonntal, Erzabt-Klotz-Strasse 1, Salzburg A-5020, Austria. (43)(662)8044-4424. **Fax:** (43)(662)8044-167. **E-mail:** editor@poetrysalzburg.com. **Website:** www.poetrysalzburg.com. **Contact:** Dr. Wolfgang Goertschacher and Mag. Andreas Schachermayr, editors. *Poetry Salzburg Review*, published twice/year, contains "articles on poetry, mainly contemporary, and 70% poetry. Also includes long poems, sequences of poems, essays on poetics, review-essays, interviews, artwork, and translations. We tend to publish selections by authors who have not been taken up by the big poetry publishers. Nothing of poor quality." Acquires first rights. Time between acceptance and publication is 3-6 months. Responds in 2-4 months. Single copy: $13; subscription: $25 (cash preferred; subscribers can also pay with PayPal).

Poetry Salzburg Review is about 200 pages, A5, professionally printed, perfect-bound, with illustrated card cover. Receives about 10,000 poems/year; accepts 3%. Press run is 500.

MAGAZINES NEEDS Accepts e-mail submissions (as attachment). Seldom comments on rejected poems. Has published poetry by Brian W. Aldiss, Rae Armantrout, Paul Muldoon, Alice Notley, Samuel Menashe, Jerome Rothenberg, Michael Heller, and Nathaniel Tarn. No payment.

ALSO OFFERS Reviews books/chapbooks of poetry as well as books on poetics. Send materials for review consideration.

TIPS "No requirements, but it's a good idea to subscribe to *Poetry Salzburg Review*."

POETS AND ARTISTS (O&S)

E-mail: unitguesteditors@gmail.com. **Website:** www.poetsandartists.com. **Contact:** Didi Menendez, publisher; Luke Brekke, poetry editor. Reviews books of poetry, chapbooks of poetry, and other magazines/journals. Reads poetry submissions year round. Sometimes upcoming themes are available online at website. Authors published include Denise Duhamel, Bob Hicok, Billy Collins, Ron Androla, Blake Butler, and Matthew Hittinger. Rights revert to poets upon publication. Time between acceptance and publication is 1½ months. Sample copy for $25.

O   Prefers submissions from skilled, experienced poets; will consider work from beginning poets.

MAGAZINES NEEDS Paste submissions into body of e-mail message. Cover letter is unnecessary. Does not like "weird" formats.

TIPS Publisher also publishes *MiPOesias Magazine*, which has been featured in Best American Poetry, and OCHO, which has received Pushcart Prize and has been featured in *Best American Poetry*.

THE POET'S ART

171 Silverleaf Lane, Islandia NY 11749. (631)439-0427. **E-mail:** davidirafox@yahoo.com. **E-mail:** ipoetdavid@gmail.com. **Contact:** David Fox, editor. *The Poet's Art*, published quarterly, is "a family-style journal, accepting work from the unpublished to the well known and all levels in between." Wants "family-friendly, positive poetry; any form considered. Topics include humor, nature, inspirational, children's poetry, or anything else that fits the family-friendly genre." Does not want "violent, vulgar, or overly depressing work. Work is read and accepted by the mentally-ill population, but they should keep in mind this is a family-friendly journal." Considers poetry by children and teens, "any age, as long as it's good quality; if under 18, get parents' permission."

O   *The Poet's Art* is 40 or more pages, magazine-sized, photocopied, paper-clipped or stapled, with computer cover, includes ads. Receives about 100 poems a year; accepts about 50%. Press run is 30+.

MAGAZINES NEEDS Submit "as many poems that will fit on 1 page" at a time. Considers simultaneous submissions; "list any other small press journals (if any) poem titles." No e-mail or disk submissions; postal submissions only. Cover letter is preferred: "It's only polite. And include an SASE—a must! (I have been lax in this rule about SASEs, but I will now throw away any submissions without a SASE!)." Reads submissions year round. "I review all poems submitted and then decide what I wish to publish." Always comments on rejected poems. Has published poetry by Linda Amos, Frank De Canio, Shirley Smothers, Gerald Zipper, and Rev. Maurice J. Reynolds. Length: rarely accepts anything over 1 page. "I have had to institute a $5 charge per accepted page of poetry, which will be used for 1 or more issues to cover postage and photocopying."

ALSO OFFERS Reviews chapbooks of poetry and other magazines/journals, "but editors and authors must write reviews themselves. After all, who knows your magazine/journal or chapbook better than you? (Little-known/newer journals sent in by editors or contributors get first consideration for reviews)." Send to David Fox.

POETS' ESPRESSO REVIEW

E-mail: poetsespressoreview@gmail.com. Donald Anderson, layout consultant. **Contact:** Patricia Mayorga, editor-in-chief. *Poets' Espresso Review*, published quarterly online and in print, is "a small b&w publication of poetry, art, photography, recipes, and local events." Sponsored by the Writers' Guild, a club of San Joaquin Delta College. "We value variety, appropriateness for most age groups, and poetry that goes well with the season of the issue, visual and bilingual poetry (side by side with translation), and of length that will fit on our half-sheet pages." Does not want "profanity, racially prejudiced, otherwise offensive material, porn, submissions that are excessively long, illegible writing, nor your only copy of the poem." Considers poetry by all ages. "Please include contact info of parent if from a minor." Has published poetry by David Humphreys, Nikki Quismondo, Susan Richardson Harvey, Marie J. Ross, Christine Stoddard, Michael C. Ford, and Allen Field Weitzel.

O   *Poets' Espresso Review* (print edition) is 24-28 pages, digest-sized, printed "on College's industrial printers," stapled, with color card stock cover with b&w photograph/artwork, might include ads. Accepts about 100 poems/year. Number of unique visitors (online): "small count with rapid growth." Single copy: $3; subscription: $15/year (4 issues). Sample: free in return for review or swap for a desired publication. Make checks payable to Patricia Mayorga.

MAGAZINES NEEDS Length: 50 lines per page or less including stanza breaks.

ADDITIONAL INFORMATION "We occasionally publish anthologies. For info on other works we have published, please visit the websites for the books *Sun Shadow Mountain* and *Moon Mist Valley*. Other projects linked on the project page at www.rainflowers. org."

THE POET'S HAVEN

Website: www.poetshaven.com. **Contact:** Vertigo Xavier, publisher. *The Poet's Haven* publishes poetry, artwork, stories, essays, and more. Acquires rights to publish on the website permanently. Poet retains rights to have poems published elsewhere, "provided the other publishers do not require first-time or exclusive rights." Time between acceptance and publication is about 2 weeks. Never comments on rejected poems. Guidelines available on website.

Work published in *The Poet's Haven* online galleries is left on the website permanently. Receives about 1,000 poems/year, accepts about 50%.

MAGAZINES NEEDS Accepts submissions through online form ONLY. Wants work that is "emotional, personal, and intimate with the author or subject. Topics can cover just about anything." Has published poetry by Mark Sebastian Jordan, Lori Ann Kusterbeck, Kenneth Pobo, Jennifer Polhemus, and AKeemjamal Rollins. Does not publish religious material. No payment for online publication.

ALSO OFFERS Also publishes chapbooks, anthologies, and audio podcasts. Check website for themed calls and submission information.

POINTED CIRCLE

Portland Community College, Cascade Campus, SC 206, 705 N. Killingsworth Street, Portland OR 97217. **E-mail:** wendy.bourgeois@pcc.edu. **Website:** http://www.pcc.edu/about/literary-magazines/pointed-circle. **Contact:** Wendy Bourgeois, faculty advisor. Publishes "anything of interest to educationally/culturally mixed audience. We will read whatever is sent, but we encourage writers to remember we are a quality literary/arts magazine intended to promote the arts in the community. No pornography, nothing trite. Be mindful of deadlines and length limits." Accepts submissions by e-mail, mail; artwork in high-resolution digital form. Acquires one-time rights.

Reading period: October 1-February 7. Magazine: 80 pages; b&w illustrations; photos.

MAGAZINES NEEDS Submit up to 6 pages of poetry. Submitted materials will not be returned; SASE for notification only. Accepts multiple submissions. No pornography, nothing trite. Pays 2 contributor's copies.

POLYPHONY H.S.

An International Student-Run Literary Magazine for High School Writers and Editors, Polyphony High School, 1514 Elmwood Ave., Suite 2, Evanston IL 60201. (847)910-3221. **E-mail:** info@polyphonyhs. com; billy@polyphonyhs.com. **Website:** www.polyphonyhs.com. **Contact:** Billy Lombardo, co-founder and managing editor. "Our mission is to create a high-quality literary magazine written, edited, and published by high school students. We believe that when young writers put precise and powerful language to their lives it helps them better understand their value as human beings. We believe the development of that creative voice depends upon close, careful, and compassionate attention. Helping young editors become proficient at providing thoughtful and informed attention to the work of their peers is essential to our mission. We believe this important exchange between young writers and editors provides each with a better understanding of craft, of the writing process, and of the value of putting words to their own lives while preparing them for participation in the broader literary community. We strive to build respectful, mutually beneficial writer-editor relationships that form a community devoted to improving students' literary skills in the areas of poetry, fiction, and creative nonfiction." Acquires first rights. Pays on publication. Responds in 2-3 months. No query letters. Sample copy: $10. Digital copies also available (see website for details). Guidelines online.

Does not accept hard-copy entries; submit only through online submissions form.

MAGAZINES NEEDS Submit poetry via online submissions form. "Avoid clichés. Please." Length: up to 80 lines/poem. Pays 1 contributor's copy.

TIPS "We manage the Claudia Ann Seaman Awards for Young Writers; cash awards for the best poem, best story, best essay. See website for details."

PORTLAND REVIEW

Portland State University, P.O. Box 751, Portland OR 97207. **Website:** portlandreview.org. **Contact:** Alex Dannemiller, editor in chief. Triannual magazine covering short prose, poetry, photography, and art. Press run is 1,000 for subscribers, libraries, and bookstores nationwide. Buys first North American serial rights. Publishes ms an average of 3-6 months after acceptance. Responds in 2-4 months to mss. Single copy: $12; subscription: $30/year, $54/2 years. Guidelines available online. "Automatic rejection of mss not following guidelines."

MAGAZINES NEEDS Submit up to 3 poems at a time, no more than 10 pages in length. No previously published poems. To submit, use submission manager on website. Include phone number, e-mail address, and other contact information in cover letter. Reads submissions year round, with reading periods for print publication. "Our website is a general introduction to our magazine, with samples of our poetry, fiction, and art. *Portland Review* will only consider 1 submission per writer, per reading period."

TIPS "View website for current guidelines."

THE POTOMAC

2020 Pennsylvania Ave., NW, Suite 443, Washington DC 20006. **E-mail:** potomac-politics@webdelsol.com. **E-mail:** charles.rammelkamp@ssa.gov. **Website:** http://thepotomacjournal.com. **Contact:** Charles Rammelkamp, editor; Michael Neff, publisher. *The Potomac*, published semiannually online, features political commentary, cutting-edge poetry, flash fiction, and reviews. Open to all forms of poetry by new and established writers. Acquires one-time rights. Time between acceptance and publication is 3 months. Responds in 2 months. Often comments on rejected poems. Sometimes sends prepublication galleys. Sample copy free online. Guidelines available on website.

Accepts submissions year round. Receives a variable number of poems/year, accepts about 30-40. Has published poetry and fiction by Robert Cooperman, Michael Salcman, Joanne Lowery, Roger Netzer, Pamela Painter, and L.D. Brodsky.

MAGAZINES NEEDS Submit any number of poems at a time. Considers simultaneous submissions; no previously published poems. Accepts e-mail submissions (as attachment) only; no postal or disk submissions. Cover letter is preferred. Reads submissions year round. Reviews books/chapbooks of poetry and other magazines/journals in up to 2,000 words, single- and multi-book format. Send materials for review consideration. No payment.

POTOMAC REVIEW: A JOURNAL OF ARTS & HUMANITIES

Montgomery College, 51 Mannakee St., MT/212, Rockville MD 20850. (240)567-4100. **E-mail:** PotomacReviewEditor@montgomerycollege.edu. **Website:** www.montgomerycollege.edu/potomacreview. **Contact:** Julie Wakeman-Linn, editor-in-chief; Kathleen Smith, poetry editor. *Potomac Review: A Journal of Arts & Humanities*, published semiannually in August and February, welcomes poetry from across the spectrum, both traditional and nontraditional poetry, free verse and in-form (translations accepted). Essays, fiction, and creative nonfiction are also welcome. Publishes ms in the next issue. Responds in 3-6 months. Sample: $10. Subscription: $24/year (includes 2 issues). Guidelines available on website.

Reading period: September 1-May 1. Has published work by David Wagoner, Jacob Appel, Sandra Beasley, and Amy Holman.

MAGAZINES NEEDS Submit up to 3 poems (5 pages maximum) at a time, electronically through website. Receives about 2,500 poems/year, accepts 3%. Poems are read "in house" and then sent to poetry editor for comments and dialogue. Does not publish theme issues. Pays 2 contributor's copies and offers 40% discount on additional copies.

CONTEST/AWARD OFFERINGS Sponsors an annual poetry contest and annual fiction contest. Guidelines available in magazine (fall/winter issue) for SASE.

THE PRAIRIE JOURNAL

P.O. Box 68073, 28 Crowfoot Terrace NW, Calgary AB Y3G 3N8, Canada. **E-mail:** editor@prairiejournal.org (queries only); prairiejournal@yahoo.com. **Website:** www.prairiejournal.org. **Contact:** A.E. Burke, literary editor. "The audience is literary, university, library, scholarly, and creative readers/writers." Buys first North American serial rights or buys electronic rights. In Canada, author retains copyright and owns permission to republish (with acknowledgement appreciated). Pays on publication. Publishes ms an average of 4-6 months after acceptance. Responds in 2 weeks to queries; 2-6 months to mss. Editorial lead time 2-6 months. Sample copy: $5. Guidelines available online.

○ "Use our mailing address for submissions and queries with samples or for clippings."

MAGAZINES NEEDS Seeks poetry "of any length; free verse, contemporary themes (feminist, nature, urban, nonpolitical), aesthetic value, a poet's poetry." Does not want to see "most rhymed verse, sentimentality, egotistical ravings. No cowboys or sage brush." Has published poetry by Liliane Welch, Cornelia Hoogland, Sheila Hyland, Zoe Lendale, and Chad Norman. Receives about 1,000 poems/year, accepts 10%. No heroic couplets or greeting card verse. Length: 3-50 lines. Pays $5-50.

TIPS "We publish many, many new writers and are always open to unsolicited submissions because we are 100% freelance. Do not send U.S. stamps; always use IRCs. We have poems, interviews, stories, and reviews online (query first)."

PRAIRIE SCHOONER

The University of Nebraska Press, Prairie Schooner, 123 Andrews Hall, University of Nebraska, Lincoln NE 68588. (402)472-0911. **Fax:** (402)472-1817. **E-mail:** PrairieSchooner@unl.edu. **Website:** prairieschooner. unl.edu. **Contact:** Ashley Strosnider, managing editor. "We look for the best fiction, poetry, and nonfiction available to publish, and our readers expect to read stories, poems, and essays of extremely high quality. We try to publish a variety of styles, topics, themes, points of view, and writers with a variety of backgrounds in all stages of their careers. We like work that is compelling—intellectually or emotionally—either in form, language, or content." Buys all rights, which are returned to the author upon request after publication. Pays on publication. Publishes ms an average of 1 year after acceptance. Responds in 1 week to queries; in 3-4 months to mss. Editorial lead time 6 months. Sample copy: $6. Guidelines for #10 SASE.

○ Submissions must be received between September 1 and May 1. Poetry published in *Prairie Schooner* has been selected for inclusion in *The Best American Poetry* and *The Pushcart Prize*.

MAGAZINES NEEDS Wants "poems that fulfill the expectations they set up." No specifications as to form, length, style, subject matter, or purpose. Has published poetry by Alicia Ostriker, Marilyn Hacker, D.A. Powell, Stephen Dunn, and David Ignatow. Pays 3 copies of the issue in which the writer's work is published.

CONTEST/AWARD OFFERINGS "All manuscripts published in *Prairie Schooner* will automatically be considered for our annual prizes." These include The Strousse Award for Poetry ($500), the Bernice Slote Prize for Beginning Writers ($500), the Hugh J. Luke Award ($250), the Edward Stanley Award for Poetry ($1,000), the Virginia Faulkner Award for Excellence in Writing ($1,000), the Glenna Luschei Prize for Excellence ($1,500), and the Jane Geske Award ($250). Also, each year 10 Glenna Luschei Awards ($250 each) are given for poetry, fiction, and nonfiction. All contests are open only to those writers whose work was published in the magazine the previous year. Editors serve as judges. Also sponsors The *Prairie Schooner* Book Prize.

TIPS "Send us your best, most carefully crafted work, and be persistent. Submit again and again. Constantly work on improving your writing. Read widely in literary fiction, nonfiction, and poetry. Read *Prairie Schooner* to know what we publish."

○ ⑤ PRISM INTERNATIONAL

Dept. of Creative Writing, Buch E462, 1866 Main Mall, University of British Columbia, Vancouver British Columbia V6T 1Z1, Canada. (604)822-2514. **Fax:** (604)822-3616. **E-mail:** prismcirculation@gmail. com. **Website:** www.prismmagazine.ca. **Buys 10 poems/issue.** A quarterly international journal of contemporary writing—fiction, poetry, drama, creative nonfiction and translation. *PRISM international* is 80 pages, digest-sized, elegantly printed, flat-spined, with original color artwork on a glossy card cover. Readership: public and university libraries, individual subscriptions, bookstores—a world-wide audience concerned with the contemporary in literature. "We have no thematic or stylistic allegiances: Excellence is our main criterion for acceptance of manuscripts." Receives 1,000 submissions/year, accepts about 80. Circulation is for 1,200 subscribers. Subscription: $35/year for Canadian subscriptions, $40/year for US subscriptions, $45/year for international. Sample: $13. Buys first North American serial rights. Pays on publication. Publishes ms an average of 4 months after acceptance. Responds in 4 months to queries. Responds in 3-6 months to mss. Sample copy for $13, more info online. Guidelines available online.

MAGAZINES NEEDS Wants "fresh, distinctive poetry that shows an awareness of traditions old and new. We read everything." Considers poetry by children and teens. "Excellence is the only criterion." Has published poetry by Margaret Avison, Elizabeth Bachinsky, John Pass, Warren Heiti, Don McKay, Bill Bissett, and Stephanie Bolster. Pays $40/printed page, and 2 copies of issue.

HOW TO CONTACT Submit up to 6 poems at a time. No previously published poems or simultaneous submissions. No e-mail submissions. Cover letter is required. Include brief introduction and list of previous publications. Poems must be typed or computer-generated (font and point size open). Include SASE (or SAE with IRCs). "Note: American stamps are not valid postage in Canada. No SASEs with U.S. postage will be returned. Translations must be accompanied by a copy of the original." Guidelines available for SASE (or SAE with IRCs), by e-mail, or on website. Responds in up to 6 months. Editors sometimes comment on rejected poems. Acquires first North American serial rights.

ADDITIONAL INFORMATION Sponsors annual Earle Birney Prize for Poetry. Prize awarded by the outgoing poetry editor to an outstanding poetry contributor published in *PRISM international*. Enter by regular submission only: no fee required. $500 prize.

CONTEST/AWARD OFFERINGS Annual Poetry Contest. First prize: $2,000; second prize: $300; third prize: $200. Entry fee: $35 for 3 poems; $5 per additional poem. Entry fee includes one-year subscription. Deadline: see website.

TIPS "We are looking for new and exciting fiction. Excellence is still our No. 1 criterion. As well as poetry, imaginative nonfiction and fiction, we are especially open to translations of all kinds, very short fiction pieces and drama which work well on the page. Translations must come with a copy of the original language work."

A PUBLIC SPACE

323 Dean St., Brooklyn NY 11217. (718)858-8067. **E-mail:** general@apublicspace.org. **Website:** www.apublicspace.org. **Contact:** Brigid Hughes, founding editor; Anne McPeak, managing editor. *A Public Space*, published quarterly, is an independent magazine of literature and culture. "In an era that has relegated literature to the margins, we plan to make fiction and poetry the stars of a new conversation. We believe that stories are how we make sense of our lives and how we learn about other lives. We believe that stories matter." Single copy: $15; subscription: $36/year or $60/2 years.

○ Accepts unsolicited submissions from September 15-April 15. Submissions accepted through Submittable or by mail (with SASE).

MAGAZINES NEEDS Submit via online submissions manager. No limit on line length.

PUDDING MAGAZINE: THE INTERNATIONAL JOURNAL OF APPLIED POETRY

(614)986-1881. **E-mail:** info@puddingmagazine.com. **E-mail:** connie@puddingmagazine.com. **Website:** www.puddingmagazine.com. **Contact:** Connie Willett Everett, editor. *Pudding Magazine: The International Journal of Applied Poetry*, published every couple of months, seeks what hasn't been said before. Speak the unspeakable. Long poems okay as long as it isn't windy. *Pudding* also serves as a forum for poems and articles by people who take poetry arts into the schools and the human services. Wants poetry on popular culture, rich brief narratives, i.e. virtual journalism (see website). Does not want preachments or sentimentality; obvious traditional forms without fresh approach. Has published poetry by Knute Skinner, David Chorlton, Mary Winters, and Robert Collins. Responds in 4-6 months. Sample copy: $8.95. Subscription: $29.95 for 4 issues. Guidelines online.

○ *Pudding* is 70 pages, digest-sized, offset-composed on Microsoft Word PC. Press run is 1,500.

MAGAZINES NEEDS Previously published submissions "respected, but include credits"; no simultaneous submissions. Cover letter is preferred ("cultivates great relationships with writers"). Submit poems by e-mail only. Pays 1 contributor's copy; discount on additional copies.

TIPS "Our website is one of the greatest poetry websites in the country—calls, workshops, publication list/history, online essays, games, guest pages, calendars, poem of the month, poet of the week, much more." The website also links to the site for The Unitarian Universalist Poets Cooperative and American Poets Opposed to Executions, both national organizations.

PUERTO DEL SOL

New Mexico State University, English Dept., P.O. Box 30001, MSC 3E, Las Cruces NM 88003. (505)646-3931. **E-mail:** puertodelsoljournal@gmail.com. **Website:**

www.puertodelsol.org. **Contact:** Carmen Giménez Smith, editor in chief and poetry editor; Lily Hoang, prose editor. Publishes innovative work from emerging and established writers and artists. Wants poetry, fiction, nonfiction, drama, theory, artwork, interviews, reviews, and interesting combinations thereof. Acquires one-time print and electronic rights and anthology rights. Rights revert to author after publication. Responds in 3-6 months to mss. Single copy: $10. Subscriptions: $20 for 1 year, $35 for 2 years, $45 for 3 years. Guidelines available online.

○ *Puerto del Sol* is 150 pages, digest-sized, professionally printed, flat-spined, with matte card cover with art. Press run is 1,250 (300 subscribers, 25-30 libraries). Reading period is September 15-December 1 and January 1-March 1.

MAGAZINES NEEDS Wants top-quality poetry, any style, from anywhere; excellent poetry of any kind, any form. Submit 3-5 poems at a time through online submission manager. Brief cover letter is welcome. Do not send publication vitae. One poem/page. Sometimes sends prepublication galleys. Has published poetry by Richard Blanco, Maria Ercilla, Pamela Gemin, John Repp, and Lee Ann Roripaugh. Pays 2 contributor's copies.

TIPS "We are especially pleased to publish emerging writers who work to push their art form or field of study in new directions."

● PULSAR POETRY MAGAZINE

Ligden Publishers, 34 Lineacre, Grange Park, Swindon, Wiltshire SN5 6DA, England. **E-mail:** pulsar.ed@btopenworld.com. **Website:** www.pulsarpoetry.com. **Contact:** David Pike, Editor. Acquires first rights. "Originators retain copyright of their poems." Publishes ms 1 year after acceptance. Responds in 1 month. Guidelines available for SASE (or SAE and IRC) or on website.

○ *Pulsar Poetry Magazine* is now a webzine only.

MAGAZINES NEEDS "We will publish poems on the *Pulsar* web on a quarterly basis, i.e. March, June, September, and December. The selection process for poems will not alter, and we will continue to publish on a merit basis only; be warned, the editor is very picky! See poem submission guidelines online. We encourage the writing of poetry from all walks of life." Wants "hard-hitting, thought-provoking work; interesting and stimulating poetry." Does not want "racist material. Not keen on religious poetry." Has

published poetry by Ann Egan, Mark Rutter, David Sapp, Julia Stothard, Stephen Komarnyckyi, Donna Pucciani, Sam Silva, Ian C. Smith, B. Diehl, Richard Dinges Jr., and Michael Jannings. Pays 1 contributor's copy.

TIPS "Give explanatory notes if poems are open to interpretation. Be patient, and enjoy what you are doing. Check grammar, spelling, etc. (should be obvious). Note: We are a nonprofit society."

◉ PURPOSE

718 N. Main St., Newton KS 67114. (316)281-4412. **Fax:** (316)283-0454. **E-mail:** CarolD@MennoMedia.org; info@MennoMedia.org. **Website:** www.faithandliferesources.org. **Contact:** Carol Duerksen, contract editor. *Purpose*, published monthly by Mennomedia, an imprint of the Mennonite Publishing Network (the official publisher for the Mennonite Church in the US and Canada), is a "religious young adult/adult monthly." Focuses on "action-oriented, discipleship living." Buys one-time rights. Pays upon publication. Publishes ms an average of 18 months after acceptance. Responds in 3 months to queries, responds in 6 months to mss. Sample (with guidelines): $2 and 9x12 SAE. Guidelines available online: www.faithandliferesources.org/periodicals/purpose.

○ *Purpose* is digest-sized with 4-color printing throughout. Receives about 2,000 poems/year, accepts 150.

MAGAZINES NEEDS Prefers e-mail submissions. Postal submissions should be double-spaced, typed on 1 side of sheet only. Length: 12 lines maximum. Pays $10-20/poem depending on length and quality, plus 2 contributor's copies.

TIPS "Many stories are situational, how to respond to dilemmas. Looking for first-person storylines. The story form is an excellent literary device to help readers explore discipleship issues. The first 2 paragraphs are crucial in establishing the mood/issue to be resolved in the story. Work hard on the development of these."

●◉ QUANTUM LEAP

York House, 15 Argyle Terrace, Rothesay, Isle of Bute PA20 0BD, Scotland. **Website:** www.qqpress.co.uk. *Quantum Leap*, published quarterly, uses "all kinds of poetry—free verse, rhyming, whatever—as long as it's well written and preferably well punctuated, too. We rarely use haiku." Has published poetry by Pamela Constantine, Ray Stebbing, Leigh Eduardo, Sky Higgins, Norman Bissett, and Gordon Scapens. Acquires first or second British serial rights. Time between acceptance and publication is usually 3 months "but can be longer now, due to magazine's increasing popularity." Responds in 3 weeks. Sometimes comments on rejected poems. Single copy: $13; subscription: $40. Sample: $10. Make checks payable to Alan Carter. Guidelines online.

○ *Quantum Leap* is 40 pages, digest-sized, desktop-published, saddle-stapled, with card cover. Receives about 2,000 poems/year, accepts about 15%. Press run is 200. "All things being equal in terms of a poem's quality, **I will sometimes favor that of a subscriber (or someone who has at least bought an issue) over a nonsubscriber,** as it is they who keep us solvent."

MAGAZINES NEEDS Submit 6 poems at a time. Cover letter is required. "Within the U.K., send a SASE; outside it, send IRCs to the return postage value of what has been submitted." Length: 20-40 lines/poem (likes a mix of lengths). Pays £2 sterling.

CONTEST/AWARD OFFERINGS Sponsors open poetry competitions as well as competitions for subscribers only. Send SAE and IRC for details.

QUARTER AFTER EIGHT

Ohio University, 360 Ellis Hall, Athens OH 45701. **Website:** www.quarteraftereight.org. **Contact:** Patrick Swaney and Brad Aaron, editors. "*Quarter After Eight* is an annual literary journal devoted to the exploration of innovative writing. We celebrate work that directly challenges the conventions of language, style, voice, or idea in literary forms. In its aesthetic commitment to diverse forms, *QAE* remains a unique publication among contemporary literary magazines." Acquires first North American serial rights. Rights revert to author upon publication. Publishes ms 6-12 months after acceptance. Responds in 3-5 months. Sample copy: $10. Subscriptions: one-year subscription (1 volume): $10; two-year subscription (2 volumes): $18; three-year subscription (3 volumes): $25. Guidelines available online at website.

○ Holds annual short prose (any genre) contest with grand prize of $1,000. Deadline is November 30.

MAGAZINES NEEDS Submit through online submissions manager.

TIPS "We look for prose and poetry that is innovative, exploratory, and—most importantly—well writ-

ten. Please subscribe to our journal and read what is published to get acquainted with the *QAE* aesthetic."

QUARTERLY WEST

University of Utah, 255 S. Central Campus Dr., Room 3500, Salt Lake City UT 84112. **E-mail:** quarterlywest@gmail.com. **Website:** www.quarterlywest.com. **Contact:** Lillian Bertram and Claire Wahmanholm, editors. "We publish fiction, poetry, nonfiction, and new media in long and short formats, and will consider experimental as well as traditional works." Buys first North American serial rights; buys all rights. Publishes ms an average of 6 months after acceptance. Responds in 3-4 months to mss. Guidelines available online.

○ *Quarterly West* was awarded first place for Editorial Content from the American Literary Magazine Awards. Work published in the magazine has been selected for inclusion in the *Pushcart Prize* anthology and *The Best American Short Stories* anthology.

MAGAZINES NEEDS Submit 3-5 poems at a time using online submissions manager only.

TIPS "We publish a special section of short shorts every issue, and we also sponsor an annual novella contest. We are open to experimental work—potential contributors should read the magazine! Don't send more than 1 story per submission. Novella competition guidelines available online. We prefer work with interesting language and detail—plot or narrative are less important. We don't do religious work."

QUEEN'S QUARTERLY

144 Barrie St., Queen's University, Kingston ON K7L 3N6, Canada. (613)533-2667. **Fax:** (613)533-6822. **E-mail:** queens.quarterly@queensu.ca. **Website:** www.queensu.ca/quarterly. **Contact:** Joan Harcourt, literary editor (fiction and poetry); Boris Castel, nonfiction editor (articles, essays and reviews). *Queen's Quarterly* is "a general interest intellectual review featuring articles on science, politics, humanities, arts and letters, extensive book reviews, and some poetry and fiction." Requires first North American serial rights. Pays on publication. Sends galleys to author. Publishes ms on average 6-12 months after acceptance. Responds in 2-3 months to queries; 1-2 months to ms. Sample: $6.50 U.S. Subscription: $20 Canadian, $25 US for U.S. and foreign subscribers. Guidelines on website.

○   Has published work by Gail Anderson-Dargatz, Tim Bowling, Emma Donohue, Viktor Carr, Mark Jarman, Rick Bowers, and Dennis Bock.

MAGAZINES NEEDS Receives about 400 submissions of poetry/year, accepts 40. Submissions can be sent on hard copy with a SASE (no replies/returns for foreign submissions unless accompanied by an IRC) or by e-mail and will be responded to by same. "We are especially interested in poetry by Canadian writers. Shorter poems preferred." Has published poetry by Evelyn Lau, Sue Nevill, and Raymond Souster. Each issue contains about 12 pages of poetry. Usually pays $50 (Canadian)/poem (but it varies), plus 2 copies.

QUIDDITY INTERNATIONAL LITERARY JOURNAL AND PUBLIC-RADIO PROGRAM

Benedictine University at Springfield, 1500 N. 5th St., Springfield IL 62702. **Website:** www.quidditylit.com. **Contact:** Joanna Beth Tweedy, founding editor; Jim Warner, managing editor. *Quiddity*, published semi-annually, is a print journal and public-radio program featuring poetry, prose, and artwork by new, emerging, and established contributors from around the world. Has published work by J.O.J. Nwachukwu-Agbada, Kevin Stein, Karen An-Hwei Lee, and Haider Al-Kabi. Publishes ms 6 months to 2 years after acceptance. Responds in 6 months. Guidelines available online.

○   *Quiddity* is 176 pages, 7X9, perfect-bound, with 60 lb. full color cover. Receives about 3,500 poems/year, accepts about 3%. Press run is 1,000. Single copy: $9; subscription: $15/year. Make checks payable to *Quiddity*. Each work selected is considered for public-radio program feature offered by NPR-member station. International submissions are encouraged.

MAGAZINES NEEDS Submit up to 5 poems (no more than 10 pages total) through snail mail (hard copy) or through submissions manager. Considers simultaneous submissions; no previously published poems (previously published includes work posted on a public website/blog/forum and on private, password-protected forums). Cover letter is preferred. Address to poetry editor, SASE required (except international). See website for reading dates. Pays 1 contributor's copy.

RADIX MAGAZINE

Radix Magazine, Inc., P.O. Box 4307, Berkeley CA 94704. (510)548-5329. **E-mail:** radixmag@aol.com.

Website: www.radixmagazine.com. **Contact:** Sharon Gallagher, editor. *Radix Magazine*, published quarterly, is named for the Latin word for "root" and "has its roots both in the 'real world' and in the truth of Christ's teachings." Wants poems that reflect a Christian world-view, but aren't preachy. Has published poetry by John Leax, Czeslaw Milosz, Madeleine L'Engle, and Luci Shaw. Interested in first North American serial rights. Publishes ms 3 months to 3 years after acceptance. Responds in 2 months to queries and to mss. Editorial lead time 6 months. Sample copy for $5. Guidelines by e-mail.

○   *Radix* is 32 pages, magazine-sized, offset-printed, saddle-stapled, with 60-lb. self cover. Receives about 120 poems/year, accepts about 10%. Press run varies. Subscription: $15. Sample: $5. Make checks payable to *Radix Magazine*."

MAGAZINES NEEDS Submit 1-4 poems at a time. Length: 4-20 lines. Pays 2 contributor copies.

TIPS "We accept very few unsolicited manuscripts. We do not accept fiction. All articles and poems should be based on a Christian world view. Freelancers should have some sense of the magazine's tone and purpose."

THE RAG

P.O. Box 17463, Portland OR 97217. **E-mail:** submissions@raglitmag.com. **Website:** raglitmag.com. **Contact:** Seth Porter, editor; Dan Reilly, editor. *The Rag* focuses on the grittier genres that tend to fall by the wayside at more traditional literary magazines. *The Rag*'s ultimate goal is to put the literary magazine back into the entertainment market while rekindling the social and cultural value short fiction once held in North American literature. Purchases first rights only. Pays prior to publication. Responds in 1 month or less for queries; in 1-2 months for mss. Editorial lead time 1-2 months.

○   Fee to submit online ($3) is waived if you subscribe or purchase a single issue.

MAGAZINES NEEDS Note: Not accepting poetry at this time. Accepts all themes and styles. Submit complete ms. Length: 5 poems or 2,000 words, whichever occurs first. Pays $20-100+.

TIPS "We like gritty material: material that is psychologically believable and that has some humor in it, dark or otherwise. We like subtle themes, original characters, and sharp wit."

THE RAINTOWN REVIEW

Central Ave. Press, 5390 Fallriver Row Court, Columbia MD 21044. **E-mail:** theraintownreview@gmail.com. **Website:** www.theraintownreview.com. **Contact:** John Oelfke, publisher; Anna Evans, editor-in-chief; Quincy R. Lehr, associate editor. *The Raintown Review*, published 2 times/year in Winter and Summer, contains poetry, reviews, and belletristic critical prose. Wants well-crafted poems. Primarily a venue for formal/metrical poetry. Has published poetry by Julie Kane, Alexandra Oliver, Rick Mullin, Annie Finch, Kevin Higgins, David Mason, A.E. Stallings, Richard Wilbur, and many others. Responds in 10-12 weeks. One can also subscribe online via our website preferred method.

○ *The Raintown Review* is 120 pages, perfect-bound. Receives about 2,500 poems/year, accepts roughly 5%. Press run is approximately 500. Subscription: $24/year, $45 for 2 years, $65 for 3 years. Sample: $12. Make checks/money orders payable to Central Ave Press.

MAGAZINES NEEDS Submit 3-5 poems at a time. Accepts e-mail submissions only (pasted into body of message); no postal submissions. Guidelines available on website. Strong bias toward formal/metrical poetry. No restrictions on length.

RALEIGH REVIEW LITERARY & ARTS MAGAZINE

P.O. Box 6725, Raleigh NC 27628-6725. **E-mail:** info@raleighreview.org. **Website:** www.raleighreview.org. Karin Wiberg, managing editor. **Contact:** Rob Greene, editor; Karin Wiberg, managing editor; Craig Lincoln and Landon Houle, fiction editors; Sierra Golden, poetry editor. "*Raleigh Review* is a national nonprofit magazine of poetry, short fiction (including flash), and art. We believe that great literature inspires empathy by allowing us to see the world through the eyes of our neighbors, whether across the street or across the globe. Our mission is to foster the creation and availability of accessible yet provocative contemporary literature. We look for work that is emotionally and intellectually complex without being unnecessarily 'difficult.'" Buys first North American serial rights. Publication is copyrighted. Pays on publication. Publishes ms 3-6 months after acceptance. Responds typically in 1-3 months, though sometimes up to 3-6 months. "Poetry and fiction submissions through Tell It Slant online system; no prior query

required." Sample copy: $13.50 hardcopy or $4.95 on Kindle. "Sample work also online at website." Guidelines available online at www.raleighreview.org.

MAGAZINES NEEDS Submit up to 5 poems. "If you think your poems will make a perfect stranger's toes tingle, heart leap, or brain sizzle, then send them our way. We typically do not publish avant garde, experimental, or language poetry. We *do* like a poem that causes—for a wide audience—a visceral reaction to intellectually and emotionally rich material." Length: open. Pays $10 maximum.

TIPS "Please be sure to read the guidelines and look at sample work on our website. Every piece is read for its intrinsic value, so new/emerging voices are often published alongside nationally recognized, award-winning authors."

RATTAPALLAX

Rattapallax Press, 217 Thompson St., Suite 353, New York NY 10012. **E-mail:** info@rattapallax.com. **Website:** www.rattapallax.com. **Contact:** Flávia Rocha, editor n chief. *Rattapallax*, published semiannually, is named for "Wallace Stevens's word for the sound of thunder. The magazine includes a DVD featuring poetry films and audio files. *Rattapallax* is looking for the extraordinary in modern poetry and prose that reflect the diversity of world cultures. Our goals are to create international dialogue using literature and focus on what is relevant to our society." Buys first North American serial rights, South American rights. Pays on publication. Publishes ms an average of 6 months after acceptance. Responds in 3 months to queries; in 3 months to mss. Editorial lead time 6 months. Sample copy: $7.95. Make checks payable to *Rattapallax*. Guidelines online.

○ *Rattapallax* is 112 pages, magazine-sized, off-set-printed, perfect-bound, with 12-pt. CS1 cover; some illustrations; photos. Press run is 2,000 (100 subscribers, 50 libraries, 1,200 shelf sales); 200 distributed free to contributors, reviews, and promos.

MAGAZINES NEEDS Submit via online submission manager at rattapallax.submittable.com/submit. Often comments on rejected poems. Length: 1 page per poem. Pays 2 contributor's copies.

RATTLE

12411 Ventura Blvd., Studio City CA 91604. (818)505-6777. **E-mail:** tim@rattle.com. **Website:** www.rattle.com. **Contact:** Timothy Green, editor. *RATTLE* "includes poems, essays, and interviews with poets, and tribute features dedicated to a specific ethnic or vocational group."

MAGAZINES NEEDS Wants "meaningful poetry in any form." Submit up to 5 poems at a time. Accepts e-mail submissions (pasted into body of message). Cover letter is required (with e-mail address, if possible).

ALSO OFFERS "All submissions are automatically considered for the Neil Postman Award for Metaphor, an annual $500 prize for the best use of metaphor as judged by the editors. No entry fee or special formatting is required; simply follow the regular guidelines." Also holds the *RATTLE* Poetry Prize (see separate listing in Contests & Awards). Also considers poetry by children and teens under the age of 16 for a separate annual anthology, *Rattle Young Poets Anthology*. Parents must submit through an online portal. See www.rattle.com/poetry/children for more information.

RATTLING WALL

c/o PEN USA, 269 S. Beverly Dr. #1163, Beverly Hills CA 90212. **E-mail:** michelle@penusa.org. **Website:** therattlingwall.com. **Contact:** Michelle Meyering, editor. Acquires first rights. Rights revert to author upon publication. Pays on publication. Publishes ms 2 months after acceptance. Responds in 6 months. Sample copy for $18.95. Guidelines online.

○ Magazine: 6x9, square bound.

MAGAZINES NEEDS Submit 3-5 poems at a time. Does not want sentimental love poetry or religious verse. Does not consider poetry by children or teens. Pays 2 contributor's copies.

THE RAVEN CHRONICLES

A Journal of Art, Literature, & the Spoken Word, 15528 12th Ave. NE, Shoreline WA 98155. (206)941-2955. **E-mail:** editors@ravenchronicles.org. **Website:** www.ravenchronicles.org. "*The Raven Chronicles* publishes work which reflects the cultural diversity of the Pacific Northwest, Canada, and other areas of America. We promote art, literature and the spoken word for an audience that is hip, literate, funny, informed, and lives in a society that has a multicultural sensibility. We publish fiction, talk art/spoken word, poetry, essays, reflective articles, reviews, interviews, and contemporary art. We look for work that reflects the author's experiences, perceptions, and insights." Responds in 3 months. Guidelines available online at website.

MAGAZINES NEEDS Send a maximum of 3 poems at a time via postal mail with SASE. Focus is on content that melds with form—whether traditional or experimental.

TIPS "In 2015 we will be changing to an online submission process. See our website for details."

THE READER

The Reader Organisation, Calderstones Mansion, Calderstones Park, Liverpool L18 3JB, United Kingdom. **E-mail:** magazine@thereader.org.uk; info@thereader.org.uk. **Website:** www.thereader.org.uk. **Contact:** Philip Davis, editor. "*The Reader* is a quarterly literary magazine aimed at the intelligent 'common reader'—from those just beginning to explore serious literary reading to professional teachers, academics, and writers. As well as publishing short fiction and poetry by new writers and established names, the magazine features articles on all aspects of literature, language, and reading; regular features, including a literary quiz and a section on the Reading Revolution, reporting on The Reader Organisation's outreach work; reviews; and readers' recommendations of books that have made a difference to them. *The Reader* is unique among literary magazines in its focus on reading as a creative, important, and pleasurable activity, and in its combination of high-quality material and presentation with a genuine commitment to ordinary but dedicated readers." Also publishes literary essays, literary criticism, poetry. Pays on publication. Publishes ms 16 months after acceptance. Responds to queries and mss in 2 months. Guidelines for SASE.

MAGAZINES NEEDS Submit up to 6 poems. No e-mail submissions. Send complete ms with cover letter. Include estimated word count, brief bio, list of publications.

TIPS "The style or polish of the writing is less important than the deep structure of the story (though, of course, it matters that it's well written). The main persuasive element is whether the story moves us—and that's quite hard to quantify. It's something to do with the force of the idea and the genuine nature of enquiry within the story. When fiction is the writer's natural means of thinking things through, that'll get us. "

READER'S CARNIVAL

317-7185 Hall Rd., Surrey BC V3W4X5, Canada. **E-mail:** info@readerscarnival.ca; readerscarnival@gmail.com. **Website:** www.readerscarnival.ca. **Con-**

tact: Doug Langille, editor; Anisa Irwin, managing editor. Purchases one-time print and electronic rights. Publishes mss 3 months after acceptance. Responds in 2 months to mss. Editorial lead time is 3 months. Sample copies available online for $7 CAD. Guidelines available online or via e-mail.

○ Must be an upgraded member of Writer's Carnival to submit to *Reader's Carnival*. Upgraded members can also enter contests on WC. Contests are every second month with $100 prize.

MAGAZINES NEEDS Length: 3-16 lines. Pays $7 (CAD) flat fee.

TIPS "Be open to writing all kinds of fiction. Call us Doug or Anisa, not 'To whom it may concern.' Writing is serious and fun. Edit your work to the best of your ability and write like you love it."

REAL: REGARDING ARTS & LETTERS

Stephen F. Austin State University, P.O. Box 13007, Nacogdoches TX 75962-3007. **E-mail:** brininsta@sfasu.edu. **Website:** regardingartsandletters.wordpress.com. **Contact:** Andrew Brininstool, editor. "*REAL: Regarding Arts & Letters* was founded in 1968 as an academic journal which occasionally published poetry. Now, it is an international creative magazine dedicated to publishing the best contemporary fiction, poetry, and nonfiction." Features both established and emerging writers. Responds in 3 months, though response time is slower in summer months.

○ Magazine: semiannual, 120 pages, perfect-bound.

MAGAZINES NEEDS Submit up to 5 poems at a time via online submissions manager. Include cover letter addressed to Dr. Christine Butterworth-Mc-Dermott.

TIPS "We are looking for the best work, whether you are established or not."

REALPOETIK

E-mail: realpoetikblog@gmail.com. **Website:** www.realpoetik.club. **Contact:** Thibault Raoult, editor. *RealPoetik* publishes innovative work. Poems are published online and also sent to subscribers via e-mail. "We provide a club/poem atmosphere." Publishes poetry 2-4 months after acceptance. Responds in 1 month to queries. Sometimes comments on rejected mss. Sample copy online.

○ Publishes 20-30 new poets/year.

MAGAZINES NEEDS Query first via e-mail with short bio, project description (if applicable), and any assertions/questions you might have.

REDACTIONS: POETRY, POETICS, & PROSE

604 N. 31st Ave., Apt. D-2, Hattiesburg MS 39401. **E-mail:** redactionspoetry@yahoo.com (poetry and essays on poetry); redactionsprose@yahoo.com (creative prose). **Website:** www.redactions.com. *Redactions*, released every 9 months, covers poems, reviews of new books of poems, translations, manifestos, interviews, essays concerning poetry, poetics, poetry movements, or concerning a specific poet or a group of poets; and anything dealing with poetry. "We now also publish fiction and creative nonfiction." All rights revert back to the author. Responds in 3 months.

MAGAZINES NEEDS "Anything dealing with poetry."

TIPS "We only accept submissions by e-mail. We read submissions throughout the year. E-mail us and attach submission into one Word, Wordpad, Notepad, .rtf, or .txt document, or place in the body of an e-mail. Include brief bio and your snail-mail address. Query after 90 days if you haven't heard from us. See website for full guidelines for each genre, including artwork."

THE RED CLAY REVIEW

Dr. Jim Elledge, Director, M. A. in Professional Writing Program, Department of English, Kennesaw State University, 1000 Chastain Rd., #2701, Kennesaw GA 30144. **E-mail:** redclay2013@gmail.com. **Website:** redclayreview.com. **Contact:** Javy Gwaltney, editor in chief. *The Red Clay Review* is supported by the Graduate Writers Association of Kennesaw State University. America's only literary magazine to feature exclusively the work of graduate and doctoral students. Publishes poetry, flash fiction, short fiction, creative nonfiction, and one-act/10-minute plays. Accepts new and established authors. Publishes ms 6 weeks after acceptance. Responds in 3-4 months. Guidelines online.

○ Submission period begins annually in August.

MAGAZINES NEEDS Submit complete ms with cover letter. A brief bio, list of publications, and an e-mail address must be supplied for the student, as well as the student's advisor's contact information (to verify student status). Length: up to 300 words. Pays in contributor's copies.

TIPS "Because the editors of *RCR* are graduate student writers, we are mindful of grammatical proficiency, vocabulary, and the organizational flow of the submissions we receive. We appreciate a heightened level of writing from fellow graduate writing students, but we also hold it to a standard to which we have learned in our graduate writing experience. Have your submission(s) proofread by a fellow student or professor."

REDHEADED STEPCHILD

E-mail: redheadedstepchildmag@gmail.com. **Website:** www.redheadedmag.com/poetry. **Contact:** Malaika King Albrecht. "*Redheaded Stepchild* only accepts poems that have been rejected by other magazines. We publish biannually, and we accept submissions in the months of August and February only. We do not accept previously published work. We do, however, accept simultaneous submissions, but please inform us immediately if your work is accepted somewhere else. We are open to a wide variety of poetry and hold no allegiance to any particular style or school. If your poem is currently displayed online on your blog or website or wherever, please do not send it to us before taking it down, at least temporarily." Acquires first rights. Rights revert to poets upon publication. Time between acceptance and publication is 3 months. Poems are circulated to an editorial board. Sometimes comments on rejected poems. Responds in 3 months. Guidelines on website.

○ Wants a wide variety of poetic styles.

MAGAZINES NEEDS "Submit 3-5 poems that have been rejected elsewhere with the names of the magazines that rejected the poems. We do not want multiple submissions, so please wait for a response to your first submission before you submit again. As is standard after publication, rights revert back to the author, but we request that you credit *Redheaded Stepchild* in subsequent republications. We do not accept e-mail attachments; therefore, in the body of your e-mail, please include the following: a brief bio, 3-5 poems, and the publication(s) that rejected the poems." Has published poetry by Kathryn Stripling Byer, Alex Grant, Amy King, Diane Lockward, Susan Yount, and Howie Good.

REDIVIDER

Department of Writing, Literature, and Publishing, Emerson College, 120 Boylston St., Boston MA 02116. **E-mail:** editor@redividerjournal.org. **Website:** www. redividerjournal.org. *Redivider*, a journal of literature and art, is published twice a year by students in the graduate writing, literature, and publishing department of Emerson College. Editors change each year. Prints high-quality poetry, art, fiction, and creative nonfiction. Pays on publication. Responds in 3-6 months. Sample copy $8. One-year subscription: $15; two-year subscription: $25. Make checks payable to *Redivider* at Emerson College. Guidelines available online at website.

○ Every spring, *Redivider* hosts the Beacon Street Prize Writing Contest, awarding a cash prize and publication to the winning submission in fiction, poetry, and nonfiction categories. See www.redividerjournal.org for details.

MAGAZINES NEEDS Wants "all styles of poetry. Most of all, we look for language that seems fresh and alive on the page, that tries to do something new. Read a sample copy for a good idea." Does not want "greeting card verse or inspirational verse." Submit 3-6 poems through online submissions manager. Pays 2 contributor's copies.

TIPS "Our deadlines are July 1 for the Fall issue and December 1 for the Spring issue."

🟢 RED LIGHTS TANKA JOURNAL

2740 Andrea Dr., Allentown PA 18103-4602. (212)875-9342. **E-mail:** marilynhazelton@rcn.com. **Website:** www.facebook.com/pages/Red-lights-tanka-journal/402853516419098. **Contact:** Marilyn Hazelton, editor. *Red Lights Tanka Journal*, published biannually in January and June, is devoted to English-language tanka and tanka sequences. Wants "print-only tanka, mainly 'free-form' but also strictly syllabic 5-7-5-7-7; will consider tanka sequences and tan-renga." Considers poetry by children and teens. Has published poetry by Sanford Goldstein, Michael McClintock, Laura Maffei, Linda Jeannette Ward, Jane Reichhold, and Michael Dylan Welch. Single copy: $10; subscription: $20 U.S., $25 USD Canada, $28 USD foreign. Make checks payable to *Red Lights* in the U.S.

○ *Red Lights* is 36-40 pages, offset-printed, saddle-stapled, with Japanese textured paper cover; copies are numbered. Receives about 1,200 poems/year, accepts about 20%. Press run is 180.

MAGAZINES NEEDS Submit up to 10 tanka or tanka sets or up to 2 tan renga (no longer than 5 stanzas each) by e-mail (preferred) or postal mail.

THE RED MOON ANTHOLOGY OF ENGLISH LANGUAGE HAIKU

P.O. Box 2461, Winchester VA 22604-1661. **E-mail:** jim.kacian@redmoonpress.com. **Website:** www.redmoonpress.com. **Contact:** Jim Kacian, editor/publisher. *The Red Moon Anthology of English Language Haiku*, published annually in February, is "a collection of the best haiku published in English around the world." Acquires North American serial rights. Sample available for SASE or by e-mail. Subscription: $17 plus $5 p&h. Guidelines available for SASE or by e-mail.

○ *The Red Moon Anthology of English Language Haiku* is 160 pages, digest-sized, offset-printed on quality paper, with 4-color heavy-stock cover. Receives several thousand submissions/year; accepts less than 2%. Print run is 1,000 for subscribers and commercial distribution. Considers poetry by children and teens.

MAGAZINES NEEDS "We do not accept direct submissions to the *Red Moon Anthology*. Rather, we employ an editorial board who are assigned journals and books from which they cull and nominate. Nominated poems are placed on a roster and judged anonymously by the entire editorial board twice a year." Has published haiku and related forms by Susan Diridoni, Dietmar Tauchner, Mike Dillon, and Fay Aoyagi.

RED RIVER REVIEW

E-mail: info@redriverreview.com. **Website:** www.redriverreview.com. **Contact:** Michelle Hartman, editor. "Our editorial philosophy is simple: It is the duty of the writer to accurately chronicle our times and to reflect honestly on how these events affect us. Poetry which strikes a truth, which artfully conveys the human condition, is most likely to be selected. Vulgarity and coarseness are part of our daily life and are thus valid. Life isn't always pretty. However, vulgarity and coarseness just for the sake of the exercise doesn't generally benefit anyone. *Red River Review* is open to all styles of writing. Abstract, beat, confessional, free verse, synthetic, formal—we will publish just about anything that has the authenticity and realism we're seeking. With this said, however, rhymed poetry of any nature is rarely accepted." Acquires first North American electronic rights and possible future anthology electronic rights. Rights revert to poets upon publication. Time between acceptance and publication is 2 weeks. Responds in 2 weeks to poems. Sometimes comments on rejected poems. **Charges criticism fee. Handled on individual basis.** Guidelines available on website.

○ "We are associated with the Dallas Poets Community and therefore recommend their workshops and events to poets in the North Texas area."

MAGAZINES NEEDS Submit 1 poem per page, up to 5 poems at a time via online submissions manager; no e-mail submissions. Receives about 2,000 poems/year. Does not consider previously published poems (poetry posted on a public website, blog, or forum). "Please be very sure you have entered your e-mail address correctly. If an acceptance comes back as bad mail, we pull the poem. Please include a serious bio. If you do not respect your work, why should we?" Has published poetry by Naomi Shihab Nye, Larry Thomas, Rob Walker, Alan Gann, Jerry Bradley, and Ann Howells. Rarely takes rhyming or form poems, "although we love a good sonnet every now and then."

RED ROCK REVIEW

College of Southern Nevada, CSN Department of English, J2A, 3200 E. Cheyenne Ave., North Las Vegas NV 89030. (702)651-4094. **Fax:** (702)651-4455. **E-mail:** redrockreview@csn.edu. **Website:** sites.csn.edu/english/redrockreview. **Contact:** Erica Vital-Lazare, senior editor; John Ziebell, fiction editor (john.ziebell@csn.edu);. Dedicated to the publication of fine contemporary literature. Buys first North American serial rights. All other rights revert to the authors and artists upon publication. Sample: $6.50. Subscriptions: $9.50/year. No longer accepting snail-mail submissions. Send all submissions as Word, RTF, or PDF file attachments. Guidelines available online. Occasionally comments on rejections.

○ Does not accept submissions during June, July, August, or December. Any files sent at this time will be deleted. *Red Rock Review* is about 130 pages, magazine-sized, professionally printed, perfect-bound, with 10-pt. CS1 cover. Accepts about 15% of poems received/year. Press run is 2,350.

MAGAZINES NEEDS Looking for the very best literature. Poems need to be tightly crafted, characterised by expert use of language. Submit 2-3 poems at a time. Length: up to 80 lines/poem. Pays 2 contributor's copies.

TIPS "Open to short fiction and poetry submissions from September 1-May 31. Include SASE and include brief bio. No general submissions between June 1 and August 31. See guidelines online."

RED WHEELBARROW

De Anza College, 21250 Stevens Creek Blvd., Cupertino CA 95014. **Website:** www.deanza.edu/redwheelbarrow. Buys first North American serial rights. Publishes ms an average of 2-4 months after acceptance. Responds in 2 weeks to queries; in 2-4 months to mss. Sample copy: $10 ($2.50 for back issues). Guidelines available online.

"We seek to publish a diverse range of styles and voices from around the country and the world." Publishes a student edition and a national edition.

MAGAZINES NEEDS Send up to 5 poems by mail (include SASE) or e-mail. Does not want excessively abstract or excessively sentimental poetry.

TIPS "Write freely, rewrite carefully. Resist clichés and stereotypes. We are not affiliated with Red Wheelbarrow Press or any similarly named publication.

REED MAGAZINE

San Jose State University, Dept. of English, One Washington Square, San Jose CA 95192. (408)924-4425. **E-mail:** reedmagazinesjsu@gmail.com; cathleen.miller@sjsu.edu. **Website:** www.reedmag.org. **Contact:** Cathleen Miller, editor in chief. *Reed Magazine* is the oldest literary journal west of the Mississippi. It publishes works of short fiction, nonfiction, poetry, and art, and offers nearly $4,000 in cash prizes. Pays on publication. Responds annually in December. Guidelines on website and through Submittable.

Accepts electronic submissions only.

MAGAZINES NEEDS Submit up to 5 poems in 1 attachment via online submissions manager. Include contact information on first page. Contest contributors receive 1 free copy; additional copies $10.

TIPS "Well-writen, original, clean grammatical prose is essential. We are interested in established authors as well as fresh new voices. Keep submitting!"

RENDITIONS: A CHINESE-ENGLISH TRANSLATION MAGAZINE

Research Centre for Translation, Chinese University of Hong Kong, Shatin, N.T. , Hong Kong. (852)3943-7399. **Fax:** (852)2603-5110. **E-mail:** renditions@cuhk.edu.hk; rct@cuhk.edu.hk. **Website:** www.renditions.org; www.cuhk.edu.hk/rct. *Renditions: A Chinese-English Translation Magazine*, published twice/year in May and November, uses "exclusively translations from Chinese, ancient and modern." Poems are printed with Chinese and English texts side by side. Has published translations of the poetry of Yang Lian, Gu Cheng, Shu Ting, Mang Ke, and Bei Dao. *Renditions* is about 132 pages, magazine-sized, elegantly printed, perfect-bound, with glossy card cover. Single copy: $21.90; subscription: $33.90/year, $59.90/2 years, $79.90/3 years. Responds in 2 months. Guidelines on website.

MAGAZINES NEEDS Submissions should be accompanied by Chinese originals. Accepts e-mail and fax submissions. "Submissions by postal mail should include two copies. Use British spelling." Sometimes comments on rejected translations. Publishes theme issues.

ADDITIONAL INFORMATION Also publishes a hardback series (Renditions Books) and a paperback series (Renditions Paperbacks) of Chinese literature in English translation. Will consider book mss; query with sample translations.

RHINO

The Poetry Forum, Inc., P.O. Box 591, Evanston IL 60204. **E-mail:** editors@rhinopoetry.org. **Website:** rhinopoetry.org. "This independent, eclectic annual journal of more than 35 years accepts poetry, flash fiction (750 words max), and poetry-in-translation from around the world that experiments, provokes, compels. More than 80 emerging and established poets are showcased." Accepts general submissions April 1-August 31 and Founders' Prize submissions September 1-October 31. Buys first North American serial rights. Response time may exceed 6 weeks. Single copy: $12. Sample copy: $6 plus $2.50 s/h (back issue). Guidelines available online.

MAGAZINES NEEDS Wants "work that reflects passion, originality, engagement with contemporary culture, and a love affair with language. We welcome free verse, formal poetry, innovation, humor, and risk-taking. All entries considered for the Editors' Prize." Submit no more than 5 poems (1 poem per page) via online submissions manager (preferred) or by postal mail. Include cover letter.

TIPS "Our diverse group of editors looks for the very best in contemporary writing, and we have created a dynamic process of soliciting and reading new work by local, national, and international writers. We are open to all styles and look for idiosyncratic, rigorous, well-crafted, lively, and passionate work."

◐ ⑤ THE RIALTO

P.O. Box 309, Alysham, Norwich NR11 6LN, England. **E-mail:** info@therialto.co.uk. **Website:** www.therialto.co.uk. **Contact:** Michael Mackmin, editor. *The Rialto*, published 3 times/year, seeks to publish the best new poems by established and beginning poets. Seeks excellence and originality. Has published poetry by Alice Fulton, Jenny Joseph, Les Murray, George Szirtes, Philip Gross, and Ruth Padel. Publishes ms 5 months after acceptance. Responds in 3-4 months.

○ *hhe Rialto* is 64 pages, A4, with full-color cover. Receives about 12,000 poems/year, accepts about 1%. Press run is 1,500. Single copy: £7.50; subscription: £23 (prices listed are for U.S. and Canada). Make checks payable to *The Rialto*. Checks in sterling only. Online payment also available on website.

MAGAZINES NEEDS Submit up to 6 poems at a time with a SASE. Does not accept e-mail submissions. Pays £20/poem on publication.

TIPS "*The Rialto* has recently commenced publishing first collections by poets. Please do not send book-length manuscripts. Query first." Sponsors an annual young poets competition. Details available in magazine and on website. Before submitting, "you will probably have read many poems by many poets, both living and dead. You will probably have put aside each poem you write for at least 3 weeks before considering it afresh. You will have asked yourself, 'Does it work technically?'; checked the rhythm, the rhymes (if used), and checked that each word is fresh and meaningful in its context, not jaded and tired. You will hopefully have read *The Rialto*."

RIBBONS: TANKA SOCIETY OF AMERICA JOURNAL

David Rice, *Ribbons* Editor, 1470 Keoncrest Dr., Berkley CA 94702. **E-mail:** drice2@comcast.net. **Website:** https://sites.google.com/site/tankasocietyofamerica/home. **Contact:** David Rice, editor. Published three times per year, seeks and regularly prints the best tanka poetry being written in English, together with reviews, critical and historical essays, commentaries, and translations. Wants poetry that exemplifies the very best in English-language tanka, having a significant contribution to make to the short poem in English. All schools and approaches are welcome. Tanka should reflect contemporary life, issues, values, and experience, in descriptive, narrative, and lyrical

modes. Does not want work that merely imitates the Japanese masters. Considers poetry by children and teens. Has published poetry by Cherie Hunter Day, Marianne Bluger, Sanford Goldstein, Larry Kimmel, John Stevenson, and George Swede. Publishes ms 2 months after acceptance. Respond in 1-2 months.

○ *Ribbons* is 60-72 pages, 6x9 perfect-bound, with color cover and art. Receives about 2,000 poems/year, accepts about 20%. Press run is 275; 15 distributed free. Single copy: $10; subscription: $30. Make checks payable to Tanka Society of America and contact Carole MacRury, Secretary/Treasurer (e-mail: macrury@whidbey.com; 1636 Edwards Dr., Point Roberts, WA 98281).

MAGAZINES NEEDS No previously published poems or simultaneous submissions. Prefers e-mail submissions (pasted into body of message); no disk submissions. Postal submissions must include SASE. Reads submissions year-round. See the publication or contact the editor for specific deadlines for each issue. Deadlines: April 30 (spring/summer issue), August 31 (fall issue), and December 31 (winter issue). Length: 5 lines. Sequences of up to 50 total lines considered.

TIPS "Work by beginning as well as established English-language tanka poets is welcome; first-time contributors are encouraged to study the tanka form and contemporary examples before submitting. No particular school or style of tanka is preferred over another; our publications seek to showcase the full range of English-language tanka expression and subject matter through the work of new and established poets in the genre from around the world."

RIO GRANDE REVIEW

University of Texas at El Paso, PMB 671, 500 W. University Ave., El Paso TX 79968-0622. **E-mail:** rgreditors@gmail.com. **Website:** www.utep.edu/rgr. *Rio Grande Review*, published in January and August, is a bilingual (English-Spanish) student publication from the University of Texas at El Paso. Contains poetry; flash, short, and nonfiction; short drama; photography and line art. Guidelines available for SASE, by e-mail, or on website.

○ *Rio Grande Review* is 168 pages, digest-sized, professionally printed, perfect-bound, with card cover with line art. Subscription: $8/year, $15/2 years.

MAGAZINES NEEDS Poetry has a limit of 10 pages. No simultaneous submissions. Accepts e-mail submissions only (as attachment). Include short bio. Any submissions received after a reception deadline will automatically be considered for the following edition. Permission to reprint material remains the decision of the author. However, *Rio Grande Review* does request it be given mention. Pays 2 contributor's copies.

RIVER STYX MAGAZINE

Big River Association, 3139A Grand Blvd., Suite 203, St. Louis MO 63118. (314)533-4541. **E-mail:** bigriver@riverstyx.org. **Website:** www.riverstyx.org. **Contact:** Richard Newman, editor. *"River Styx* publishes the highest-quality fiction, poetry, interviews, essays, and visual art. We are an internationally distributed multicultural literary magazine. Mss read May-November." Buys first North American serial rights, buys one-time rights. Pays on publication. Publishes ms an average of 6 months after acceptance. Responds in 6 months to mss. Sample copy: $9. Guidelines available online.

> Work published in *River Styx* has been selected for inclusion in past volumes of *New Stories from the South*, *The Best American Poetry*, *Best New Poets*, *New Poetry from the Midwest*, and *The Pushcart Prize Anthology*.

MAGAZINES NEEDS Wants "excellent poetry—original, energetic, musical, and accessible." Does not want "chopped prose or opaque poetry that isn't about anything." Has published poetry by Jennifer Perrine, Dorianne Laux, Ted Kooser, Louis Simpson, Molly Peacock, Marilyn Hacker, Yusef Komunyakaa, Andrew Hudgins, and Catie Rosemurgy. Include SASE. No religious poetry. Pays 2 contributor copies, plus one-year subscription. Cash payment as funds permit.

ALSO OFFERS Sponsors an annual poetry contest. Past judges include Terrance Hayes, Maxine Kumin, Stephen Dunn, Kim Addonizio, Alan Shapiro, Dorianne Laux, Ellen Bryant Voigt, Philip Levine, and Naomi Shihab Nye. Guidelines available for SASE or on website.

THE ROAD NOT TAKEN: A JOURNAL OF FORMAL POETRY

E-mail: kathryn.jacobs@tamuc.edu. **Website:** www.journalformalpoetry.com. **Contact:** Dr. Kathryn Jacobs, editor. *The Road Not Taken: A Journal of Formal Poetry*, published 3 times/year online. "Poetry should be metrical; rhyme is welcome but optional. *The Road*

Not Taken aims for a modern metrical style written in contemporary idiom on contemporary subjects. Please make only sparing use of end-stopped lines; this is the 21st century, not the 18th. Likewise, strive for flexible rhymes. In short, explore tradition but make it new." Responds in up to 4 months; "please wait until the next issue appears before querying." Sometimes comments on rejected poems.

MAGAZINES NEEDS Submit 3-5 poems by e-mail only. "Simultaneous submissions are acceptable, but contact me promptly if a poem is accepted elsewhere."

ROANOKE REVIEW

Roanoke College, 221 College Lane, Salem VA 24153-3794. **E-mail:** review@roanoke.edu. **Website:** http://roanokereview.wordpress.com. **Contact:** Paul Hanstedt, editor. "The *Roanoke Review* is an online literary journal that is dedicated to publishing accessible fiction, nonfiction, and poetry that is smartly written. Humor is encouraged; humility as well." Pays on publication for one-time rights. Publishes ms 6-9 months after acceptance. Responds in 1 month to queries; 6 months to mss; 3-6 months to poetry. Sometimes comments on rejected mss. Guidelines available on website.

> Has published work by Siobhan Fallon, Jacob M. Appel, and JoeAnn Hart.

MAGAZINES NEEDS Submit original typed mss; no photocopies. Pays "cash when budget allows."

TIPS "Pay attention to sentence-level writing—verbs, metaphors, concrete images. Don't forget, though, that plot and character keep us reading. We're looking for stuff that breaks the MFA story style. Be real. Know rhythm. Concentrate on strong images."

THE ROCKFORD REVIEW

The Rockford Writers Guild, P.O. Box 858, Rockford IL 61105. **E-mail:** rwg@rockfordwritersguild.com. **Website:** www.rockfordwritersguild.com. **Contact:** Connie Kluntz. "Published twice/year. Members only edition in summer-fall and winter-spring edition which is open to all writers. Open season to submit for the winter-spring edition of the Rock Review is August. If pubished in the winter-spring edition of the Rockford Review, payment is one copy of magazine and $5 per published piece. Credit line given. Check website for frequent updates. We are also on Facebook under Rockford Writers' Guild." Buys first North American serial rights. Pays on publication.

Sample copy available for $12. Guidelines available on website.

◯ Poetry 50 lines or less, prose 1,300 words or less.

MAGAZINES NEEDS Wants eclectic poetry. Length: up to 50 lines. If published in the winter-spring edition of the *Rockford Review*, payment is one copy of magazine and $5 per published piece. Pays on publication.

TIPS "We're wide open to new and established writers alike—particularly short satire."

◯⑤ ROOM

P.O. Box 46160, Station D, Vancouver BC V6J 5G5, Canada. **E-mail:** contactus@roommagazine.com. **Website:** www.roommagazine.com. "*Room* is Canada's oldest literary journal by, for, and about women. Published quarterly by a group of volunteers based in Vancouver, *Room* showcases fiction, poetry, reviews, art work, interviews, and profiles about the female experience. Many of our contributors are at the beginning of their writing careers, looking for an opportunity to get published for the first time. Some later go on to great acclaim. *Room* is a space where women can speak, connect, and showcase their creativity. Each quarter we publish original, thought-provoking works that reflect women's strength, sensuality, vulnerability, and wit." Buys first rights. Pays on publication. Responds in 6 months. Sample copy: $13 or online at website.

◯ *Room* is digest-sized; illustrations, photos. Press run is 1,000 (420 subscribers, 50-100 libraries, 350 shelf sales).

MAGAZINES NEEDS *Room* uses "poetry by and about women, written from a feminist perspective. Nothing simplistic, clichéd. We prefer to receive up to 5 poems at a time, so we can select a pair or group." Submit via online submissions manager. Pays $50-120 (Canadian), 2 contributor's copies, and a one-year subscription.

ROSEBUD

N3310 Asje Rd., Cambridge WI 53523. (608)423-9780. **Website:** www.rsbd.net. **Contact:** Roderick Clark, publisher/managing editor; John Lehman, founder/editor-at-large. *Rosebud*, published 3 times/year in April, August, and December, has presented many of the most prominent voices in the nation and has been listed as among the very best markets for writers. Responds in 45 days. Sample copy: $7.95. Subscription: $20 for 3 issues, $35 for 6 issues.

◯ *Rosebud* is elegantly printed with full-color cover. Press run is 10,000.

MAGAZINES NEEDS Wants poetry that avoids "excessive or well-worn abstractions, not to mention clichés. Present a unique and convincing world (you can do this in a few words!) by means of fresh and exact imagery, and by interesting use of syntax. Explore the deep reaches of metaphor. But don't forget to be playful and have fun with words." E-mail up to 3 poetry submissions to poetry editor John Smelcer at: jesmelcer@aol.com.

ALSO OFFERS Sponsors The William Stafford Poetry Award and the X.J. Kennedy Award for Creative Nonfiction. Guidelines for both available on website.

TIPS "Each issue has 6 or 7 flexible departments (selected from a total of 16 departments that rotate). We are seeking stories; articles; profiles; and poems of love, alienation, travel, humor, nostalgia and unexpected revelation. Something has to 'happen' in the pieces we choose, but what happens inside characters is much more interesting to us than plot manipulation. We like good storytelling, real emotion, and authentic voice."

SACRED CITY PRODUCTIONS

Sacred City Productions, Ltd., 5781 Springwood Ct., Mentor on the Lake OH 44060. (440)290-9325. **E-mail:** info@sacredcityproductions.com. **E-mail:** info@sacredcityproductions.com. **Website:** sacredcityproductions.com. **Contact:** Erin Garlock, editor/owner. Sacred City Productions is dedicated to creative endeavors that promote the ideals of a positive faith life. "We ask people to think about what they believe and to take action on those beliefs. Our own actions reflect our Christian beliefs as we reach out in ministry to extend an uplifting hand to those around us." Buys first print rights for 2 months. After that period, author is free to republish the story elsewhere. Please allow 2 weeks to review work. If you haven't heard back in that time, a single inquiry letter will suffice. Sacred City Productions guarantees a response of acceptance, rejection, or under consideration. Guidelines available online.

MAGAZINES NEEDS Submit 1-5 sample poems. Sacred City Productions tends to favor poetry with a formal structure (rhyme, meter, etc.) or poetry whose artistic visual layout is relevant to the piece. Poetry will be sparingly used with fiction anthologies.

TIPS "We are very interested in submissions from first-time authors and authors with a very limited record."

SALMAGUNDI

Skidmore College, 815 North Broadway, Saratoga Springs NY 12866. **Fax:** (518)580-5188. **E-mail:** salmagun@skidmore.edu. **E-mail:** ssubmit@skidmore.edu. **Website:** cms.skidmore.edu/salmagundi. "*Salmagundi* publishes an eclectic variety of materials, ranging from short-short fiction to novellas from the surreal to the realistic. Authors include Nadine Gordimer, Russell Banks, Steven Millhauser, Gordon Lish, Clark Blaise, Mary Gordon, Joyce Carol Oates, and Cynthia Ozick. Our audience is a generally literate population of people who read for pleasure." Acquires first rights, electronic rights. Publishes ms up to 2 years after acceptance. Responds in 2 months to mss. "If you do not hear back from us within 2 months, it means we did not find a space for your work in our magazine." Sample copy: $5. Guidelines on website.

Magazine: 8x5; illustrations; photos. *Salmagundi* authors are regularly represented in *Pushcart* collections and *Best American Short Story* collections. Reading period: November 1-December 1.

MAGAZINES NEEDS Submit up to 6 poems via e-mail. Pays 6-10 contributor's copies and one-year subscription.

TIPS "I look for excellence and a very unpredictable ability to appeal to the interests and tastes of the editors. Be brave. Don't be discouraged by rejection. Keep stories in circulation. Of course, it goes without saying: Work hard on the writing. Revise tirelessly. Study magazines and send only to those whose sensibility matches yours."

SALT HILL JOURNAL

Creative Writing Program, Syracuse University, English Deptartment, 401 Hall of Languages, Syracuse University, Syracuse NY 13244. **Website:** salthilljournal.net. **Contact:** Emma DeMilta and Jessica Poli, editors. "*Salt Hill* is published through Syracuse University's Creative Writing MFA program. We strive to publish a mix of the best contemporary and emerging talent in poetry, fiction, and nonfiction. Your work, if accepted, would appear in a long tradition of exceptional contributors, including Steve Almond, Mary Caponegro, Kim Chinquee, Edwidge Danticat, Denise Duhamel, Brian Evenson, B.H. Fairchild, Mary Gaitskill, Terrance Hayes, Bob Hicok, Laura Kasischke, Etgar Keret, Phil Lamarche, Dorianne Laux, Maurice Manning, Karyna McGlynn, Ander Monson, David Ohle, Lucia Perillo, Tomaž Šalamun, Zachary Schomburg, Christine Schutt, David Shields, Charles Simic, Patricia Smith, Dara Wier, and Raúl Zurita among many others." Guidelines available online.

Only accepts submissions by online submission form; does not accept unsolicited e-mail submissions.

MAGAZINES NEEDS Submit up to 5 poems via online submissions manager; contact poetry editor via e-mail for retractions and queries only.

THE SAME

P.O. Box 494, Mount Union PA 17066. **E-mail:** editors@thesamepress.com. **Website:** www.thesamepress.com. **Contact:** Nancy Eldredge, managing editor. *The Same*, published biannually, prints nonfiction (essays, reviews, literary criticism), poetry, and short fiction. Publishes ms 11 months after acceptance. Responds within 6 months. Single copy: $6; subscription: $12 for 2 issues, $20 for 4 issues.

The Same is 50-100 pages, desktop-published, and perfect-bound.

MAGAZINES NEEDS "We want eclectic poetry (formal to free verse, 'mainstream' to experimental, all subject matter.)" Submit 1-7 poems at a time. No previously published poems or simultaneous submissions without query. Prefers e-mail submissions as attachments. Cover letter is optional. Include SASE if you want a snail mail response. "If you don't want your manuscript returned, you may omit the SASE if we can respond by e-mail. Please query before submitting fiction and nonfiction. Submissions are read year round. Length: up to 120 lines/poem.

SAMSARA: THE MAGAZINE OF SUFFERING

P.O. Box 467, Ashburn VA 20147. **E-mail:** rdfsamsara@gmail.com. **Website:** www.samsaramagazine.net. **Contact:** R. David Fulcher, editor. *Samsara: The Magazine of Suffering*, published biannually, prints poetry and fiction dealing with suffering and healing. Acquires first rights. Publishes ms 3 months after acceptance. Responds in 2 months. Single copy: $5.50. Subscription: $10. Make checks payable to R. David Fulcher. Guidelines for SASE or on website.

Samsara is 80 pages, magazine-sized, desktop-published, with color cardstock cover. Receives about 200 poems/year, accepts about 15%. Press run is 300 (200 subscribers).

MAGAZINES NEEDS "Both metered-verse and free-verse poetry are welcome if dealing with the theme of suffering/healing." Has published poetry by Michael Foster, Nicole Provencher, and Jeff Parsley. Submit up to 5 poems at a time. Considers simultaneous submissions "if noted as such"; no previously published poems. Cover letter is preferred. Accepts e-mail submissions. Length: 3-100 lines/poem. Pays 1 contributor's copy.

THE SANDY RIVER REVIEW

University of Maine at Farmington, 114 Prescott St., Farmington ME 04938. **E-mail:** srreview@gmail.com. **Website:** sandyriverreview.com. **Contact:** Nicole Byrne, editor. "*The Sandy River Review* seeks prose, poetry, and art submissions twice a year for our Spring and Fall issues. Prose submissions may be either fiction or creative nonfiction and should be a maximum of 3,500 words in length, 12-point, Times New Roman font, and double-spaced. Most of our art is published in b&w and must be submitted as 300-dpi quality, CMYK color mode, and saved as a TIFF file. We publish a wide variety of work from students as well as professional, established writers. Your submission should be polished and imaginative with strongly drawn characters and an interesting, original narrative. The review is the face of the University of Maine at Farmington's venerable BFA Creative Writing program, and we strive for the highest quality prose and poetry standard." Rights for the work return to the writer once published. Pays on publication. Publishes ms 2 months after acceptance.

TIPS "We recommend that you take time with your piece. As with all submissions to a literary journal, submissions should be fully completed, polished final drafts that require minimal to no revision once accepted. Double-check your prose pieces for basic grammatical errors before submitting."

SANSKRIT LITERARY ARTS MAGAZINE

UNC Charlotte, 9201 University City Blvd., Student Union Room 045, Charlotte NC 28223. (704)687-7141. **E-mail:** sanskrit@uncc.edu; sanskritliteraryarts@gmail.com. **Website:** http://sanskrit.uncc.edu; www.facebook.com/SanskritLitArtMagazine. **Contact:** Joshua Wood, editor-in-chief. *Sanskrit* is a collection of poems, short stories, and art from people all around the world, including students. All of the

work goes through a selection process that includes staff and university professors. Finally, each year, the magazine has a theme. This theme is completely independent from the work and is chosen by the editor as a design element to unify the magazine. The theme is kept secret until the return of the magazine in April. Responds to mss and poems by February. Never comments on rejected mss. Guidelines available for SASE or by e-mail.

○ Submissions deadline: first Friday in November.

MAGAZINES NEEDS Submit up to 15 poems at a time. Considers simultaneous submissions. Accepts e-mail submissions. Cover letter is required. Include 30- to 70-word third-person bio. Do not list previous publications as a bio. Pays 1 contributor's copy.

SANTA CLARA REVIEW

Santa Clara Review, Santa Clara University, 500 El Camino Real, Box 3212, Santa Clara CA 95053-3212. (408)554-4484. **E-mail:** santaclarareview@gmail.com. **Website:** www.santaclarareview.com. "*SCR* is one of the oldest literary publications in the West. Entirely student-run by undergraduates at Santa Clara University, the magazine draws upon submissions from SCU affiliates as well as contributors from around the globe. The magazine is published in February and May each year. In addition to publishing the magazine, the Review staff organizes a writing practicum, open mic nights, and retreats for writers and artists, and hosts guest readers. Our printed magazine is also available to view free online. For contacts, queries, and general info, visit our website. *SCR* accepts submissions year round. Publishes ms an average of 2 months after acceptance. Guidelines online.

MAGAZINES NEEDS Submit up to 3 poems via online submissions manager or mail (include SASE for return of ms). Length: up to 10 pages.

THE SARANAC REVIEW

Dept. of English, Champlain Valley Hall, 101 Broad St., Plattsburgh NY 12901. **Website:** saranacreview.com. **Contact:** J.L. Torres, editor. "*The Saranac Review* is committed to dissolving boundaries of all kinds, seeking to publish a diverse array of emerging and established writers from Canada and the U.S. *The Saranac Review* aims to be a textual clearing in which a space is opened for cross-pollination between American and Canadian writers. In this way the magazine reflects the expansive, bright spirit of the etymology of its name, Saranac, meaning 'cluster of stars.'" Published annually. Purchases first North American serial rights. Pays on publication. Publishes ms 8 months after acceptance. Responds in 4-6 months to mss. Sample copy: $6.95. Guidelines online.

○ "*The Saranac Review* is digest-sized, with color photo or painting on cover, includes ads. Publishes both digital and print-on-demand versions. Has published Lawrence Raab, Jacob M. Appel, Marilyn Nelson, Tom Wayman, Colette Inez, Louise Warren, Brian Campbell, Gregory Pardlo, Myfanwy Collins, William Giraldi, Xu Xi, Julia Alvarez, and other fine emerging and established writers.

MAGAZINES NEEDS "We're open to most forms and styles. We want poetry that, to paragraph Dickinson, blows the top of your head off, and that, in Williams's view, prevents us from dying miserably every day." Submit 3-5 poems via online submissions manager. Length: up to 10 pages. Pays 2 contributor's copies and offers discount on additional copies.

SCIENCE EDITOR

Council of Science Editors, 10200 W. 44th Ave., Suite 304, Wheat Ridge CO 80033. (720)881-6046. **Fax:** (303)422-8894. **E-mail:** pkbaskin@gmail.com; cse@councilscienceeditors.org. **Website:** www.councilscienceeditors.org. **Contact:** Patty K. Baskin, editor in chief. *Science Editor*, published 3 times/year, is a forum for the exchange of information and ideas among professionals concerned with publishing in the sciences. Acquires one-time rights, electronic rights. Publishes ms 3-6 months after acceptance. Responds in 3-6 weeks. Guidelines by e-mail.

⊛ SCIFAIKUEST

P.O. Box 782, Cedar Rapids IA 52406. **E-mail:** gatrix65@yahoo.com. **Website:** albanlake.com/scifaikuest. **Contact:** Tyree Campbell, managing editor; Teri Santitoro, editor. *Scifaikuest*, published quarterly both online and in print, features "science fiction/fantasy/horror minimalist poetry, especially scifaiku, and related forms. We also publish articles about various poetic forms and reviews of poetry collections. The online and print versions of *Scifaikuest* are different." Acquires first North American serial rights. Time between acceptance and publication is 1-2 months. Responds in 6-8 weeks. Single copy: $7; subscription: $20/year, $37 for 2 years. Make checks payable to Tyree Campbell/Alban Lake Publishing. Guidelines available on website.

○ *Scifaikuest* (print edition) is 32 pages, digest-sized, offset-printed, perfect-bound, with color cardstock cover, includes ads. Receives about 500 poems/year, accepts about 160 (32%). Press run is 100/issue; 5 distributed free to reviewers. Member: The Speculative Literature Foundation. *Scifaikuest* was voted #1 poetry magazine in the 2004 Preditors & Editors poll.

MAGAZINES NEEDS Wants "artwork, scifaiku, and speculative minimalist forms such as tanka, haibun, ghazals, senryu. Submit 5 poems at a time. Accepts e-mail submissions (pasted into body of message). No disk submissions; artwork as e-mail attachment or inserted body of e-mail. "Submission should include snail-mail address and a short (1-2 lines) bio." Reads submissions year round. "Editor Teri Santitoro makes all decisions regarding acceptances." Often comments on rejected poems. Has published poetry by Tom Brinck, Oino Sakai, Deborah P. Kolodji, Aurelio Rico Lopez III, Joanne Morcom, and John Dunphy. "No 'traditional' poetry." Length: varies, depending on poem type. Pays $1/poem, $4/review or article, and 1 contributor's copy.

SCREAMINMAMAS

Harmoni Productions, LLC, 1911 Cleveland St., Hollywood FL 33020. **E-mail:** screaminmamas@gmail.com. **Website:** www.screaminmamas.com. **Contact:** Darlene Pistocchi, editor; Denise Marie, managing editor. "We are the voice of everyday moms. We share their stories, revelations, humorous rants, photos, talent, children, ventures, etc." Acquires one-time rights. Publishes ms 1-3 months after acceptance. Responds in 3-6 weeks to queries; 1-3 months on mss. Editorial lead time: 3 months. Sample copy online. Guidelines online.

MAGAZINES NEEDS Length: 2-20 lines.

TIPS "Visit our submissions page and themes page on our website."

THE SEATTLE REVIEW

Box 354330, University of Washington, Seattle WA 98195. (206)543-2302. **E-mail:** seaview@uw.edu. **Website:** www.seattlereview.org. **Contact:** Andrew Feld, editor in chief. *The Seattle Review* includes poetry, fiction, and creative nonfiction. Buys first North American serial rights. Pays on publication. Responds in 2-4 months to mss. Subscriptions: $20 for 3 issues,

$32 for 5 issues. Back issue: $6. Guidelines available online.

○ *The Seattle Review* will only publish long works. Poetry must be 10 pages or longer, and prose must be 40 pages or longer. *The Seattle Review* is 8x10; 175-250 pages. Receives 200 unsolicited mss/month. Accepts 10-15 mss/issue; 20-30 mss/year. Publishes ms 6 months-1 year after acceptance.

MAGAZINES NEEDS "We are looking for exceptional, risk-taking, intellectual, and imaginative poems between 10 and 30 pages in length." *The Seattle Review* will publish, and will only publish, long poems and novellas. The long poem can be a single long poem in its entirety, a self-contained excerpt from a book-length poem, or a unified sequence or series of poems. Accepts electronic submissions only. Pays 4 contributor's copies and one-year subscription.

TIPS "Know what we publish; no genre fiction. Look at our magazine and decide if your work might be appreciated. Beginners do well in our magazine if they send clean, well-written manuscripts. We've published a lot of 'first stories' from all over the country and take pleasure in discovery."

THE SECRET PLACE

P.O. Box 851, Valley Forge PA 19482. (610)768-2434. **E-mail:** thesecretplace@abc-usa.org. **Website:** www.judsonpress.com/catalog_secretplace.cfm. Buys first rights. Pays on acceptance. Editorial lead time 1 year. Guidelines online.

MAGAZINES NEEDS Submit up to 6 poems by mail or e-mail. Length: 4-30 lines/poem. Pays $20.

TIPS "Prefers submissions via e-mail."

SEEMS

P.O. Box 359, Lakeland College, Sheboygan WI 53082-0359. (920)565-1000 ext. 2295 or (920)565-3871. **E-mail:** elderk@lakeland.edu. **E-mail:** seems@lakeland.edu. **Website:** www.seems.lakeland.edu. *SEEMS*, published irregularly, prints poetry, fiction, and essays. Focuses on work that integrates economy of language, "the musical phrase," forms of resemblance, and the sentient. Will consider unpublished poetry, fiction, and creative nonfiction. See the editor's website at www.karlelder.com. "Links to my work and an interview may provide insight for the potential contributor." Acquires first North American serial rights and permission to publish online. Returns rights upon publication. Responds in 4 months (slower in the summer).

MAGAZINES NEEDS Now considers e-mail submissions. Cover letter is optional. Include biographical information, SASE. Reads submissions year round. There is a one- to two-year backlog. "People may call or fax with virtually any question, understanding that the editor may have no answer." Guidelines available on website. Length: open. Pays 1 contributor's copy.

SENECA REVIEW

Hobart and William Smith Colleges, Geneva NY 14456. (315)781-3392. **E-mail:** senecareview@hws.edu. **Website:** www.hws.edu/academics/senecareview/index.aspx. The editors have special interest in translations of contemporary poetry from around the world. Publisher of numerous laureates and award-winning poets, *Seneca Review* also publishes emerging writers and is always open to new, innovative work. Poems from *SR* are regularly honored by inclusion in *The Best American Poetry* and *Pushcart Prize* anthologies. Distributed internationally. Accepts queries by mail or via Submittable. Responds in 3 months. Guidelines available online. E-mail questions to senecareview@hws.edu.

○ Reading period is September 1-May 1.

SEQUESTRUM

E-mail: sequr.info@gmail.com. **Website:** www.sequestrum.org. **Contact:** R.M. Cooper, managing editor. All publications are cpaired with a unique visual component. Regularly holds contests and features well-known authors, as well as promising new and emerging voices. Buys first North American serial rights and electronic rights. Pays on acceptance. Publishs ms 2-3 months after acceptance. Editorial lead time: 3 months. Sample copy available for free online. Guidelines available for free online.

MAGAZINES NEEDS Length: 35 lines max. Pays $10/set of poems.

TIPS "Reading a past issue goes a long way; there's little excuse not to: Our entire archive is available online and subscribing is free. Send your best, most interesting work. General submissions are open, though we regularly hold contests and offer awards which are themed."

THE SEWANEE REVIEW

University of the South, 735 University Ave., Sewanee TN 37383-1000. (931)598-1000. **E-mail:** sreview@sewanee.edu. **Website:** review.sewanee.edu. **Contact:**

George Core, editor. *The Sewanee Review* is America's oldest continuously published literary quarterly. Publishes original fiction, poetry, essays on literary and related subjects, and book reviews for well-educated readers who appreciate good American and English literature. Only erudite work representing depth of knowledge and skill of expression is published. Buys first North American serial rights, buys second serial (reprint) rights. Pays on publication. Responds in 6-8 weeks to mss. Sample copy for $8.50 ($9.50 outside U.S.). Guidelines online.

Ⓞ Does not read mss June 1-August 31.

MAGAZINES NEEDS Submit up to 6 poems by postal mail. Keep in mind that for each poem published in *The Sewanee Review,* approximately 250 poems are considered. Length: up to 40 lines/poem. Pays $2.50/line, plus 2 contributor's copies (and reduced price for additional copies).

SHADOWS & LIGHT

E-mail: angelshadow7@msn.com. **Website:** angelshadowauthor.webs.com/shadowslight.htm. **Contact:** Shawna (Angel Shadow), editor. *Shadows & Light*, published as a yearly anthology, features short stories, flash fiction, poetry, nonfiction, memoir, and self-help articles. Author retains all rights. Sample copy: $8.50. Guidelines online.

MAGAZINES NEEDS Submit by e-mail. Include "Submission" in subject line. Pays 1 contributor's copy.

TIPS "A well-written story makes a ms stand out, as well as good character development. Just submit your story. All stories have the potential of being heard. Keep writing. Don't give up."

SHEARSMAN

Shearsman Books Ltd, Shearsman, 50 Westons Hill Drive, Emersons Green, Bristol Bristol BS16 7DF, England. **E-mail:** editor@shearsman.com. **Website:** www.shearsman.com/pages/magazine/home.html. "We are inclined toward the more exploratory end of the current spectrum. Notwithstanding this, however, quality work of a more conservative kind will always be considered seriously, provided that the work is well written. I always look for some rigour in the work, though I will be more forgiving of failure in this regard if the writer is trying to push out the boundaries." Guidelines available online.

MAGAZINES NEEDS Avoid sending attachments with your e-mails unless they are in PDF format. Include SASE; no IRCs. No sloppy writing of any kind.

TIPS "We no longer read through the year. Our reading window for magazines is March 1-March 31 for the October issue and September 1-September 30 for the April issue; this window is for magazine submissions only. See guidelines online."

Ⓞ SHEMOM

2486 Montgomery Ave., Cardiff CA 92007. **E-mail:** pdfrench@cox.net. **Contact:** Peggy French, editor. *Shemom*, published 3 times/year, is a zine that "showcases writers of all ages reflecting on life's varied experiences. We often feature haiku." Includes poetry, haiku, and occasional essays. Open to any style, but prefers free verse. "We like to hear from anyone who has a story to tell and will read anything you care to send our way." Acquires one-time rights. Publishes ms 3 months after acceptance. Responds in 1 month. Single copy: $4; subscription: $12/3 issues. Make checks payable to Peggy French. Guidelines for SASE.

Ⓞ *Shemom* is 20-30 pages. Receives about 200 poems/year, accepts 50%. Press run is 60 (30 subscribers).

MAGAZINES NEEDS Submit 3-10 poems at a time. Accepts e-mail submissions (as attachment or pasted into body of message). "Prefer e-mail submission, but not required; if material is to be returned, please include an SASE." Pays 1 contributor's copy.

SHENANDOAH

Washington and Lee University, Lexington VA 24450. (540)458-8908. **Fax:** (540)458-8461. **E-mail:** shenandoah@wlu.edu. **Website:** shenandoahliterary.org. **Contact:** R.T. Smith, editor. For over half a century, *Shenandoah* has been publishing splendid poems, stories, essays, and reviews which display passionate understanding, formal accomplishment, and serious mischief. Buys first North American serial rights, one-time rights. Pays on publication. Publishes ms an average of 10 months after acceptance. Responds in 4-6 weeks to mss. Sample copy: $12. Guidelines online.

MAGAZINES NEEDS Submit 3-5 poems via online submissions manager or postal mail. No inspirational, confessional poetry. Pays $2.50/line, one-year subscription, and 1 contributor's copy.

ALSO OFFERS Sponsors the annual James Boatwright III Prize for Poetry, a $1,000 prize awarded to the author of the best poem published in *Shenandoah* during a volume year.

THE SHEPHERD

1530 Seventh St., Rock Island IL 61201. (309)788-3980. **Contact:** Betty Mowery, poetry editor. *The Shepherd*, published quarterly, features inspirational poetry from all ages. Wants something with a message but not preachy. Subscription: $12. Sample: $4. Make all checks payable to *The Oak*.

MAGAZINES NEEDS Submit up to 5 poems at a time. Lines/poem: 35 maximum. Considers previously published poems. Include SASE with all submissions. Responds in one week. "*The Shepherd* does not pay in dollars or copies, but you need not purchase to be published." Acquires first or second rights. All rights revert to poet upon publication.

TIPS Sponsors poetry contest. Guidelines available for SASE.

SHIP OF FOOLS

Ship of Fools Press, University of Rio Grande, Box 1028, Rio Grande OH 45674. (740)992-3333. **Website:** meadhall.homestead.com/Ship.html. **Contact:** Jack Hart, editor. *Ship of Fools*, published "more or less quarterly," seeks "coherent, well-written, traditional or modern, myth, archetype, love—most types." Responds in 1 month to ms. "If longer than 6 weeks, write and ask why." Often comments on rejected poems. Sample copy: $3. Subscription: $10 for 4 issues. Guidelines available for SASE.

- Has published poetry by Rhina Espaillat and Gale White. *Ship of Fools* is digest-sized, saddle-stapled, includes cover art and graphics. Press run is 270.

MAGAZINES NEEDS Cover letter is preferred. Sometimes reviews books of poetry. Ship of Fools Press has "no plans to publish chapbooks in the next year due to time constraints." Does not want "concrete, incoherent, or greeting card poetry." Considers poetry by children and teens but judges it by the same standards as adult poetry. Pays 1-2 contributor's copies.

SIERRA NEVADA REVIEW

999 Tahoe Blvd., Incline Village NV 89451. **E-mail:** sncreview@sierranevada.edu. **Website:** www.sierranevada.edu/academics/humanities-social-sciences/english/the-sierra-nevada-review. "*Sierra Nevada Review*, published annually in May, features poetry, short fiction, and literary nonfiction by new and established writers. Wants "writing that leans toward the unconventional, surprising, and risky." Responds in 3 months. Guidelines available on website.

- Reads submissions September 1-February 15 only.

MAGAZINES NEEDS Submit up to 5 poems at a time or 5 pages, whichever comes first. Pays 2 contributor's copies.

SKIPPING STONES: A MULTICULTURAL LITERARY MAGAZINE

P.O. Box 3939, Eugene OR 97403-0939. (541)342-4956. **E-mail:** editor@skippingstones.org. **Website:** www.skippingstones.org. **Contact:** Arun Toké, editor. "*Skipping Stones* is an award-winning multicultural, nonprofit magazine designed to promote cooperation, creativity and celebration of cultural and ecological richness. We encourage submissions by children of color, minorities and under-represented populations. We want material meant for children and young adults/teenagers with multicultural or ecological awareness themes. Think, live and write as if you were a child, tween or teen. We want material that gives insight to cultural celebrations, lifestyle, customs and traditions, glimpse of daily life in other countries and cultures. Photos, songs, artwork are most welcome if they illustrate/highlight the points. Translations are invited if your submission is in a language other than English." Themes may include cultural celebrations, living abroad, challenging disability, hospitality customs of various cultures, cross-cultural understanding, African, Asian and Latin American cultures, humor, international understanding, turning points and magical moments in life, caring for the earth, spirituality, and multicultural awareness. *Skipping Stones* is magazine-sized, saddle-stapled, printed on recycled paper. Published quarterly during the school year (4 issues). Buys first North American serial rights, non-exclusive reprint, and electronic rights. Publishes ms an average of 4-8 months after acceptance. Responds only if interested. Send nonreturnable samples. Editorial lead time 3-4 months. Sample: $7. Subscription: $25. Guidelines available online or for SASE.

MAGAZINES NEEDS Submit up to 5 poems at a time. Considers simultaneous submissions; no previously published poems. Accepts e-mail submissions. Cover letter is preferred. "Include your cultural background, experiences, and the inspiration behind your creation." Time between acceptance and publication is 6-9 months. "A piece is chosen for publication when most of the editorial staff feel good about it." Seldom comments on rejected poems. Publishes multi-theme issues. Responds in up to 4 months. Length: 30 lines maximum. Pays 2 contributor's copies, offers 40% discount for more copies and subscription, if desired. **CONTEST/AWARD OFFERINGS** Sponsors annual youth honor awards for 7- to 17-year-olds. Theme is "multicultural, social, international, and nature awareness." Guidelines available for SASE or on website. Entry fee: $4 (entitles entrant to a free issue featuring the 10 winners). Deadline: June 25.

TIPS "Be original and innovative. Use multicultural, nature, or cross-cultural themes. Multilingual submissions are welcome."

SLANT: A JOURNAL OF POETRY

University of Central Arkansas, P.O. Box 5063, 201 Donaghey Ave., Conway AR 72035. (501)450-5107. **Website:** uca.edu/english/slant-a-journal-of-poetry. **Contact:** James Fowler, editor. *Slant: A Journal of Poetry*, published annually in May, aims "to publish a journal of fine poetry from all regions of the U.S. and beyond." Poet retains rights. Responds in 3-4 months from November 15 deadline. Sample: $10. Guidelines available in magazine, for SASE, or on website.

◯ *Slant* is 120 pages, professionally printed on quality stock, flat-spined, with matte card cover. Receives about 1,000 poems/year, accepts 70-75. Press run is 175 (70-100 subscribers). Accepts submissions September 1-November 15. Accepts submissions September 1-November 15.

MAGAZINES NEEDS Wants "traditional and 'modern' poetry, even experimental; moderate length, any subject on approval of Board of Readers." Doesn't want "haiku, translations." Submit up to 5 poems at a time. Submissions should be typed; include SASE. "Put name, address (including e-mail if available), and phone number at the top of each page." Comments on rejected poems "on occasion." Has published poetry by Richard Broderick, Linda Casebeer, Marc Jampole, Sandra Kohler, Charles Harper Webb, and Ellen Roberts Young. Poems should be of moderate length. Pays 1 contributor's copy.

SLIPSTREAM

P.O. Box 2071, Dept. W-1, Niagara Falls NY 14301. **E-mail:** editors@slipstreampress.org. **Website:** www. slipstreampress.org/index.html. **Contact:** Dan Sicoli, co-editor. Guidelines available online.

◯ Does not accept e-mail submissions.

MAGAZINES NEEDS Submit poetry via mail or online submission manager, Submittable. Prefers contemporary urban themes—writing from the grit that is not afraid to bark or bite. Shies away from pastoral, religious, and rhyming verse. Chapbook Contest prize is $1,000 plus 50 professionally printed copies of your chapbook.

SLOW TRAINS LITERARY JOURNAL

E-mail: editor@slowtrains.com. **Website:** www. slowtrains.com. **Contact:** Susannah Grace Indigo, editor. Looking for fiction, essays, and poetry that reflect the spirit of adventure, the exploration of the soul, the energies of imagination, and the experience of Big Fun. Music, travel, sex, humor, love, loss, art, spirituality, childhood/coming of age, baseball, and dreams, but most of all, *Slow Trains* wants to read about the things you are passionate about. Requests one-time electronic rights with optional archiving. Responds in 2 months. Guidelines online.

MAGAZINES NEEDS Also publishes online poetry chapbooks. Query with samples of poetry before submitting an entire chapbook. Review current issue before submitting. Submit via e-mail only. Length: up to 200 lines/poem.

SMARTISH PACE

P.O. Box 22161, Baltimore MD 21203. **E-mail:** sppoems@gmail.com. **Website:** www.smartishpace.com. **Contact:** Stephen Reichert, editor.

MAGAZINES NEEDS Smartish Pace, published in April, contains poetry and translations. "Smartish Pace is an independent poetry journal and is not affiliated with any institution." No restrictions on style or content of poetry. Has published poetry in the past year by Gerald Stern, Eamon Grennan, Katie Ford, Sherman Alexie, Carol Muske-Dukes, and Aram Saroyan. Smartish Pace is about 140 pages, digest-sized, professionally printed, perfect-bound, with full-color cover featuring contemporary artwork. Receives about 5,000 poems/year, accepts 1%. Press run is 1,100. Subscription: $20. Sample: $10.

HOW TO CONTACT Submit no more than 6 poems at a time via online submission form. Does not accept submissions by mail. Considers simultaneous submissions; no previously published poems. Responds in 1-6 months. Pays 1 contributor's copy. Acquires first rights. Encourages unsolicited reviews, essays, and interviews. Send materials for review consideration. All books received will also be listed in the Books Received section of each issue and on the website along with ordering information and a link to the publisher's website.

SNOW MONKEY

E-mail: snowmonkey.editor@comcast.net. **Website:** www.ravennapress.com/snowmonkey/. Seeks writing "that's like footprints of the Langur monkeys left at 11,000 feet on Poon Hill, Nepal. Open to most themes." Responds in 8-10 weeks to mss.

MAGAZINES NEEDS Submit via e-mail. Does not pay.

TIPS "Send submissions as text only in the body of your e-mail. Include your last name in the subject line. We do not currently use bios, but we love to read them."

⑤ SNOWY EGRET

The Fair Press, P.O. Box 9265, Terre Haute IN 47808. **Website:** www.snowyegret.net. *Snowy Egret*, published in spring and autumn, specializes in work that is nature-oriented. Features fiction, nonfiction, artwork, and poetry. Acquires first North American and one-time reprint rights. Pays on publication. Responds in 2 months to mss. Sample: $8; subscription: $15/year, $25 for 2 years. Guidelines online.

○ *Snowy Egret* is 60 pages, magazine-sized, offset-printed, saddle-stapled.

MAGAZINES NEEDS Wants poetry that celebrates the abundance and beauty of nature or explores the interconnections between nature and the human psyche. Has published poetry by Conrad Hilberry, Lyn Lifshin, Gayle Eleanor, James Armstrong, and Patricia Hooper. Submit poems with SASE. Cover letter optional: do not query. Pays $4/poem or $4/page and 2 contributor's copies.

TIPS Looks for "honest, freshly detailed pieces with plenty of description and/or dialogue which will allow the reader to identify with the characters and step into the setting; fiction in which nature affects character development and the outcome of the story."

SNREVIEW

197 Fairchild Ave., Fairfield CT 06825-4856. (203)366-5991. **E-mail:** editor@snreview.org. **Website:** www.snreview.org. **Contact:** Joseph Conlin, editor. "We search for material that not only has strong characters and plot but also a devotion to imagery." Quarterly. Acquires first electronic and print rights. Publishes ms 3 months after acceptance. Responds in 1 year to mss. Sample copy and guidelines online.

○ Also publishes literary essays, poetry. Print and Kindle edition is now available from an on-demand printer.

MAGAZINES NEEDS Submit via e-mail; label the e-mail "SUB: Poetry." Copy and paste work into the body of the e-mail. Don't send attachments. Include 100-word bio and list of publications. Length: up to 200 words/poem.

THE SOCIETY OF CLASSICAL POETS JOURNAL

The Society of Classical Poets, 11 Heather Ln., Mount Hope NY 10940. **E-mail:** submissions@classicalpoets.org. **Website:** www.classicalpoets.org. **Contact:** Evan Mantyk, president. Annual literary magazine, published in a book format, that features poetry, essays, and artwork. Interested in poetry with meter and rhyme. Believes in reviving classical poetry and classical arts. Purchases electronic and reprint rights. Publishes ms an average of 6 months after acceptance. Responds in 1 weeks to queries and 1 month to mss. Editorial lead time is 2 months. Sample copy available for free for SASE. Writer's guidelines available for free for SASE.

MAGAZINES NEEDS Some type of meter, such as iambic pentameter, is preferred but not absolutely required. If you want feedback on your submission, indicate it on the submission. Accepts poetry only on 5 themes (generally): beauty (in human nature, culture, the natural world, classical art forms, and the divine), great culture (good figures, stories, and other elements from classical history and literature), Falun Dafa, science (great technological and scientific achievements both ancient and modern), and human (clean humor only). Also will consider short stories, essays, art, news, and videos on the above themes. Does not want love, free verse, or any dark poetry. Does not offer payment.

SONG OF THE SAN JOAQUIN

P.O. Box 1161, Modesto CA 95353. **E-mail:** cleor36@yahoo.com. **Website:** www.chaparralpoets.org/SSJ.html. **Contact:** Cleo Griffith, editor. *Song of the San Joaquin*, published quarterly, features "subjects about or pertinent to the San Joaquin Valley of Central California. This is defined geographically as the region from Fresno to Stockton, and from the foothills on the west to those on the east." Acquires one-time rights. Publishes ms 3-6 months after acceptance. Responds in up to 3 months. Guidelines available for SASE or by e-mail.

○ Reads submissions "periodically throughout the year." Considers poetry by children and teens.

MAGAZINES NEEDS This is a quarterly; please keep in mind the seasons of the year. E-mail submissions are preferred; no disk submissions. Cover letter is preferred. "SASE required. All submissions must be typed on 1 side of the page only. Proofread submissions carefully. Name, address, phone number, and e-mail address should appear on all pages. Cover letter should include any awards, honors, and previous publications for each poem and a biographical sketch of 75 words or less." Has published poetry by Robert Cooperman, Taylor Graham, Dan Williams, Jennifer Fenn, and Charles Rammelkamp. Length: up to 40 lines. Pays 1 contributor's copy.

SO TO SPEAK

George Mason University, 4400 University Dr., MSN 2C5, Fairfax VA 22030-4444. **E-mail:** sts@gmu.edu (inquiries only). **Website:** sotospeakjournal.org. **Contact:** Jessie Szalay, editor in chief; Alex Ghaly, nonfiction editor; Robert Schuster, fiction editor; A.K. Padovich, poetry editor. *So to Speak*, published semi-annually, prints "high-quality work relating to feminism, including poetry, fiction, nonfiction (including book reviews and interviews), photography, artwork, collaborations, lyrical essays, and other genre-questioning texts." Wants "work that addresses issues of significance to women's lives and movements for women's equality. Especially interested in pieces that explore issues of race, class, and sexuality in relation to gender." Reads submissions August 20-October 25 for Spring issue and January 1-March 15 for Fall issue. Acquires first North American serial rights. Publishes ms 6-8 months after acceptance. Responds in 6 months to mss. Sample copy: $7; subscription: $12.

○ *So to Speak* is 100-128 pages, digest-sized, photo-offset-printed, perfect-bound, with glossy cover; includes ads. Press run is 1,000 (75 subscribers, 100 shelf sales); 500 distributed free to students/contributors.

MAGAZINES NEEDS Receives about 800 poems/year; accepts 10%. Accepts submissions only via submissions manager on website. No e-mail or paper submissions. "Please submit poems as you wish to see them in print. Be sure to include a cover letter with

full contact info, publication credits, and awards received." Poetry submitted during the August 20-October 25 reading period will be considered for our Spring annual poetry contest and must be accompanied by a $15 reading fee. Pays 2 contributor's copies.

TIPS "Every writer has something they do exceptionally well; do that and it will shine through in the work. We look for quality prose with a definite appeal to a feminist audience. We are trying to move away from strict genre lines. We want high-quality fiction, nonfiction, poetry, art, innovative and risk-taking work."

SOUL FOUNTAIN

E-mail: davault@aol.com. **Website:** www.thevault.org. **Contact:** Tone Bellizzi, editor. *Soul Fountain*, published 2-3 times/year, is produced by The Vault, a not-for-profit arts project of the Hope for the Children Foundation, committed to empowering young and emerging artists of all disciplines at all levels to develop and share their talents through performance, collaboration, and networking. Prints poetry, art, photography, short fiction, and essays. Open to all. Publishes quality submitted work, and specializes in emerging voices. Favors visionary, challenging, and consciousness-expanding material. Publishes ms 1 year after acceptance. Sample copy: $7. Subscription: $24. Make checks payable to Hope for the Children Foundation. Guidelines online.

○ *Soul Fountain* is 28 pages, magazine-sized, offset-printed, saddle-stapled.

MAGAZINES NEEDS Submit 2-3 poems by e-mail. No cover letters, please. Does not want poems about pets, nature, romantic love, or the occult. Sex and violence themes not welcome. Welcomes poetry by teens. Length: up to 1 page/poem. Pays 1 contributor's copy.

THE SOUTH CAROLINA REVIEW

Center for Electronic and Digital Publishing, Strode Tower Room 611, Box 340522, Clemson SC 29634-0522. (864)656-5399. **Fax:** (864)656-1345. **E-mail:** cwayne@clemson.edu. **Website:** www.clemson.edu/cedp/press/scr/index.htm. **Contact:** Wayne Chapman, editor. "Since 1968, *The South Carolina Review* has published fiction, poetry, interviews, unpublished letters and manuscripts, essays, and reviews from well-known and aspiring scholars and writers." Responds in 2 months.

○ *The South Carolina Review* is 6×9; 200 pages; 60 lb. cream white vellum paper; 65 lb. color cover stock. Semiannual. Does not read mss

June-August or December. Receives 50-60 unsolicited mss/month.

MAGAZINES NEEDS Submit 3-10 poems at a time. Cover letter is preferred. "Editor prefers a chatty, personal cover letter plus a list of publishing credits. Ms format should be according to new MLA Stylesheet." Submissions should be sent "in an 8x10 manila envelope so poems aren't creased." Do not submit during June, July, August, or December. Occasionally publishes theme issues.

SOUTH DAKOTA REVIEW

The University of South Dakota, Dept. of English, 414 E. Clark St., Vermillion SD 57069. (605)677-5184. **E-mail:** sdreview@usd.edu. **Website:** www.usd.edu/sdreview. **Contact:** Lee Ann Roripaugh, editor in chief. "*South Dakota Review*, published quarterly, is committed to cultural and aesthetic diversity. First and foremost, we seek to publish exciting and compelling work that reflects the full spectrum of the contemporary literary arts. Since its inception in 1963, *South Dakota Review* has maintained a tradition of supporting work by contemporary writers writing from or about the American West. We hope to retain this unique flavor through particularly welcoming works by American Indian writers, writers addressing the complexities and contradictions of the 'New West,' and writers exploring themes of landscape, place, and/or eco-criticism in surprising and innovative ways. At the same time, we'd like to set these ideas and themes in dialogue with and within the context of larger global literary communities. Single copy: $12; subscription: $40/year, $65/2 years. Sample: $8. Acquires first, second serial (reprint) rights. Publishes ms 1-6 months after acceptance. Responds in 10-12 weeks. Sample copy: $8.

○ Writing from *South Dakota Review* has appeared in *Pushcart* and *Best American Essays* anthologies. Press run is 500-600 (more than 500 subscribers, many of them libraries).

MAGAZINES NEEDS Submit up to 5 poems via online submissions manager. Include cover letter. *SDR* contributors include Norman Dubie, Tarfia Faizullah, Carol Guess and Daniela Olszewska, Megan Kaminski, Ted Kooser, Adrian C. Louis, Joseph Massey, Tiffany Midge, Ira Sukrungruang, Ocean Vuong, and Martha Zweig. Pays 2 contributor's copies.

THE SOUTHEAST REVIEW

Florida State University, Tallahassee FL 32306-1036. **Website:** southeastreview.org. **Contact:** Erin Hoover, editor. "The mission of *The Southeast Review* is to present emerging writers on the same stage as well-established ones. In each semi-annual issue, we publish literary fiction, creative nonfiction, poetry, interviews, book reviews, and art. With nearly 60 members on our editorial staff who come from throughout the country and the world, we strive to publish work that is representative of our diverse interests and aesthetics, and we celebrate the eclectic mix this produces. We receive approximately 400 submissions per month, and we accept less than 1-2% of them." Acquires first North America serial rights, which then revert to the author. Publishes ms 2-6 months after acceptance. Responds in 2-6 months.

○ Publishes 4-6 new writers/year. Has published work by Eduardo J. Astigarraga, Matthew Gavin Frank, Kent Shaw, Charles Harper Webb, and Leslie Wheeler.

MAGAZINES NEEDS Submit 3-5 poems at a time through online manager. Reviews books and chapbooks of poetry. "Please query the book review editor before submitting a book review." Pays 2 contributor's copies.

ALSO OFFERS Sponsors an annual poetry, nonfiction, and short fiction contest. Winner receives $500 and publication; 2-5 finalists will also be published in each category. **Entry fee:** $16 for 3 poems, 3 short stories, or 1 piece of narrative nonfiction. **Deadline:** March. Guidelines available on website.

TIPS "*The Southeast Review* accepts regular submissions for publication consideration year-round exclusively through the online submission manager. **Except in the case of contests, paper submissions sent through regular postal mail will not be read or returned**. Avoid trendy experimentation for its own sake (present-tense narration, observation that isn't also revelation). Fresh stories; moving, interesting characters; and a sensitivity to language are still fiction mainstays. We also publish the winner and runners-up of the World's Best Short Story Contest, Poetry Contest, and Creative Nonfiction Contest."

SOUTHERN CALIFORNIA REVIEW

University of Southern California, Master of Professional Writing Program, 3501 Trousdale Pkwy., Mark Taper Hall of Humanities, THH 355J, Los Angeles

CA 90089. **Website:** southerncaliforniareview.word-press.com. The *Southern California Review* encourages new, emerging, and established writers to submit previously unpublished work. Accepts fiction, poetry, nonfiction, comics, and dramatic forms (including one-act plays, scenes, and short films or screenplay excerpts). Different theme for each issue; check website for current/upcoming themes. Responds in 3-6 months. Sample copy: $15. Guidelines online.

○ Unsolicited mss are read September 1-December 1.

MAGAZINES NEEDS Submit up to 3 poems by mail or online submissions manager. Include cover letter. Pays 2 contributor's copies.

SOUTHERN HUMANITIES REVIEW

Auburn University, 9088 Haley Center, Auburn University AL 36849. (334)844-9088. **Fax:** (334)844-9027. **E-mail:** shr@auburn.edu. **Website:** www.southern-humanitiesreview.com. **Contact:** Aaron Alford, managing editor. *Southern Humanities Review* publishes fiction, nonfiction, and poetry. Acquires all rights. Copyright reverts to author after publication. Guidelines online.

ALSO OFFERS Sponsors the Theodore Christian Hoepfner Award, a $50 prize for the best poem published in a given volume of *Southern Humanities Review*.

SOUTHERN POETRY REVIEW

Dept. of LLP, Armstrong Atlantic State University, 11935 Abercorn St., Savannah GA 31419. (912)344-3196. **E-mail:** james.smith@armstrong.edu. **Website:** www.southernpoetryreview.org. **Contact:** James Smith, co-editor. *Southern Poetry Review*, published twice a year, is one of the oldest poetry journals in America. Acquires one-time rights. Publishes ms 6 months after acceptance. Responds in 3 months. Single copy: $7.00. Guidelines available in journal, by SASE, by e-mail, or on website.

○ Work appearing in *Southern Poetry Review* received 2005 and 2013 Pushcart Prizes. Often has poems selected for Poetry Daily (poems.com) and VerseDaily.org. Member: CLMP. *Southern Poetry Review* is 70-80 pages, digest-sized, perfect-bound, with 80 lb. matte card stock cover and b&w photography. Includes ads.

MAGAZINES NEEDS Wants "poetry eclectically representative of the genre; no restrictions on form, style, or content." Has published poetry by Claudia

Emerson, Carl Dennis, Robert Morgan, Linda Pastan, A.E. Stallings, R.T. Smith, and David Wagoner. Considers simultaneous submissions (with notification in cover letter); no previously published poems ("previously published" includes poems published or posted online). No e-mail submissions. Cover letter is preferred. "Include SASE for reply; ms returned only if sufficient postage is included. No international mail coupons. U.S. stamps only." Reads submissions year round. Sometimes comments on rejected poems. Sends pre-publication galleys. Does not want fiction, essays, reviews, or interviews. Pays 1-2 contributor's copies.

ALSO OFFERS Sponsors annual Guy Owen Contest. See website for guidelines.

THE SOUTHERN REVIEW

(225)578-5108. **Fax:** (225)578-5098. **E-mail:** southernreview@lsu.edu. **Website:** thesouthernreview.org. **Contact:** Jessica Faust, co-editor and poetry editor; Emily Nemens, co-editor and prose editor. "The *Southern Review* is one of the nation's premiere literary journals. Hailed by *Time* as 'superior to any other journal in the English language,' we have made literary history since our founding in 1935. We publish a diverse array of fiction, nonfiction, and poetry by the country's—and the world's—most respected contemporary writers." Reading period: September1-December 1. All mss submitted during outside the reading period will be recycled. Buys first North American serial rights. Pays on publication. Publishes ms an average of 6 months after acceptance. Responds in 6 months. Sample copy: $12. Guidelines available online.

MAGAZINES NEEDS Has published poetry by Aimee Baker, Wendy Barker, David Bottoms, Nick Courtright, Robert Dana, Oliver de la Paz, Ed Falco, Piotr Florczyk, Rigoberto Gonzalez, Ava Leavell Haymon, and Philip Schultz. Submit poems by mail. Length: 1-4 pages. Pays $25/printed page (max $125); 2 contributor's copies, and one-year subscription.

TIPS "Careful attention to craftsmanship and technique combined with a developed sense of the creation of story will always make us pay attention."

SOUTH POETRY MAGAZINE

PO BOX 4228, Bracknell RG42 9PX, England. **E-mail:** south@southpoetry.org. **Website:** www.southpoetry.org. *SOUTH Poetry Magazine*, published biannually in Spring and Autumn, is based in the southern counties of England. Poets from or poems about the South region are particularly welcome, but poets from all over the world are encouraged to submit work on all subjects. Has published poetry by Ian Caws, Stella Davis, Lyn Moir, Elsa Corbluth, Paul Hyland, and Sean Street. Publishes ms 2 months after acceptance. Guidelines available online.

○ *SOUTH* is 68 pages, digest-sized, litho-printed, saddle-stapled, with gloss-laminated duotone cover. Receives about 1,500 poems/year, accepts about 120. Press run is 350 (250 subscribers). Single copy: £5.80; subscription: £10/year, £18/2 years. Make cheques (in sterling) payable to *SOUTH Poetry Magazine.*

MAGAZINES NEEDS Send two copies of each poem submitted. Print submission form on website and submit via postal mail. Selection does not begin prior to the deadline and may take up to 8 weeks or more from that date. Deadlines are May 31 for the autumn issue and November 30 for the spring issue.

TIPS "Buy the magazine and read it. That way you will see the sort of work we publish, and whether your work is likely to fit in. You'll also be contributing to its continued success."

SOUTHWESTERN AMERICAN LITERATURE

Center for the Study of the Southwest, Texas State University, Brazos Hall, 601 University Dr., San Marcos TX 78666-4616. (512)245-2224. **Fax:** (512)245-7462. **E-mail:** swpublications@txstate.edu. **Website:** www.txstate.edu/cssw/publications/sal.html. **Contact:** William Jensen, editor. *Southwestern American Literature* is a biannual scholarly journal that includes literary criticism, fiction, poetry, and book reviews concerning the Greater Southwest. Responds in 2-4 months. "Please feel free to e-mail the editors after 6 months to check on the status of your work." Sample copy for $11. Guidelines online.

MAGAZINES NEEDS "Generally speaking, we seek material covering the Greater Southwest or material written by southwestern writers." Length: no more than 100 lines. Pays 2 contributor's copies.

TIPS "We look for crisp language, an interesting approach to material; a regional approach is desired but not required. Read widely, write often, revise carefully. We are looking for stories that probe the relationship between the tradition of Southwestern American literature and the writer's own imagination in creative ways. We seek stories that move beyond stereotype

and approach the larger defining elements and also ones that, as William Faulkner noted in his Nobel Prize acceptance speech, treat subjects central to good literature—the old verities of the human heart, such as honor and courage and pity and suffering, fear and humor, love and sorrow."

SOUTHWEST REVIEW

P.O. Box 750374, Dallas TX 75275-0374. (214)768-1037. **Fax:** (214)768-1408. **E-mail:** swr@smu.edu. **Website:** www.smu.edu/southwestreview. **Contact:** Willard Spiegelman, editor-in-chief. The majority of readers are well-read adults who wish to stay abreast of the latest and best in contemporary fiction, poetry, and essays in all but the most specialized disciplines. Published quarterly. Acquires first North American serial rights. Sends galleys to author. Publishes ms 6-12 months after acceptance. Responds in 1-4 months to mss. Occasionally comments on rejected mss. Sample copy: $6. Guidelines available for SASE or online.

○ Has published work by Alice Hoffman, Sabina Murray, Alix Ohlin. The Elizabeth Matchett Stover Memorial Award presents $250 to the author of the best poem or groups of poems (chosen by editors) published in the preceding year. Also offers The Morton Marr Poetry Prize and the David Nathan Meyerson Prize for Fiction.

MAGAZINES NEEDS Demands very high quality in poems. Accepts both traditional and experimental writing. Submissions accepted online for a $2 fee. No fee for submissions sent by mail. Reading period: September 1-May 31. No arbitrary limits on length. Accepted pieces receive nominal payment upon publication and copies of the issue.

TIPS "Despite the title, we are not a regional magazine. Before you submit your work, it's a good idea to take a look at recent issues to familiarize yourself with the magazine. We strongly advise all writers to include a cover letter. Keep your cover letter professional and concise, and don't include extraneous personal information, a story synopsis, or a résumé. When authors ask what we look for in a strong story submission, the answer is simple regardless of graduate degrees in creative writing, workshops, or whom you know: We look for good writing, period."

SOU'WESTER

Department of English, Box 1438, Southern Illinois University Edwardsville, Edwardsville IL 62026.

Website: http://souwester.org. **Contact:** Allison Funk poetry editor; Valerie Vogrin, prose editor. *Sou'wester* appears biannually in spring and fall. Leans toward poetry with strong imagery, successful association of images, and skillful use of figurative language. Has published poetry by Robert Wrigley, Beckian Fritz Goldberg, Eric Pankey, Betsy Sholl, and Angie Estes. Returns rights. Responds in 3 months. Sample: $8.

Uses online submission form. Open to submissions in mid-August for fall and spring issues. Close submissions in winter and early spring. *Sou'wester* has 30-40 pages of poetry in each digest-sized, 100-page issue. *Sou'wester* is professionally printed, flat-spined, with textured matte card cover, press run is 300 for 500 subscribers of which 50 are libraries. Receives 3,000 poems (from 600 poets) each year, accepts 36-40, has a 6-month backlog. Subscription: $15/2 issues.

MAGAZINES NEEDS Submit up to 5 poems. Editor comments on rejected poems "usually, in the case of those that we almost accept." Pays 2 contributor's copies and a 1-year subscription.

THE SOW'S EAR POETRY REVIEW

308 Greenfield Ave., Winchester VA 22602. **E-mail:** sowsearpoetry@yahoo.com; rglesman@gmail.com;. **Website:** www.sows-ear.kitenet.net. **Contact:** Kristin Camitta Zimet, editor; Robert G. Lesman, managing editor. *The Sow's Ear* prints fine poetry of all styles and lengths, complemented by b&w art. Also welcomes reviews, interviews, and essays related to poetry. Open to group submissions. "Crossover" section features poetry married to any other art form, including prose, music, and visual media. Acquires first publication rights. Publishes ms an average of 1-6 months after acceptance. Responds in 2 weeks to queries. Responds in 3 months to mss. Editorial lead time 1-6 months. Sample copy for $8. Guidelines available for SASE, by e-mail, or on website.

MAGAZINES NEEDS Considers simultaneous submissions "if you tell us promptly when work is accepted elsewhere"; no previously published poems, although will consider poems from chapbooks if they were never published in a magazine. Previously published poems may be included in Crossover if rights are cleared. No e-mail submissions, except for poets outside the US; postal submissions only. Include brief bio and SASE. Pays 2 contributor's copies. Inquire about reviews, interviews, and essays. Contest/Award offerings: *The Sow's Ear* Poetry Competition and *The Sow's Ear* Chapbook Contest. Open to any style or length. No limits on line length.

TIPS "We like work that is carefully crafted, keenly felt, and freshly perceived. We respond to poems with voice, a sense of place, delight in language, and a meaning that unfolds. We look for prose that opens new dimensions to appreciating poetry."

SPACE AND TIME

458 Elizabeth Ave., Somerset NJ 08873. **Website:** www.spaceandtimemagazine.com. **Contact:** Hildy Silverman, editor-in-chief. "We love stories that blend elements—horror and science fiction, fantasy with SF elements, etc. We challenge writers to try something new and send us their unclassifiable works-—what other publications reject because the work doesn't fit in their 'pigeonholes.'" Acquires first North American serial rights and one-time rights. Pays on publication. Publishes ms 3-6 months after acceptance. Sample copy available for $6. Guidelines available only on website.

MAGAZINES NEEDS "Multiple submissions are okay within reason (don't send an envelope stuffed with 10 poems). Submit embedded in an e-mail or as a Word doc or .rtf attacment." Pays $5/poem.

SPEEDPOETS ZINE

16 Cooradilla St., Jindalee QLD 4074, Australia. (61)(7)3420-6092. **E-mail:** speedpoets@yahoo.com.au; speedpoetszine@gmail.com. **Website:** speedpoets.com. **Contact:** John Wainwright, editor. *SpeedPoets Zine*, published monthly, showcases the community of poets that perform at the monthly SpeedPoets readings in Brisbane, as well as showcasing poets from all around the world. Publishes ms 2 weeks after acceptance. Responds in 2 weeks. Single copy: PDF for contributors upon request. Guidelines available by e-mail.

SpeedPoets Zine is up to 28 pages, digest-sized, photocopied, folded and stapled, with color cover. Press run is 100.

MAGAZINES NEEDS Submit 2 poems at a time. Accepts e-mail submissions (pasted into body of message, no attachments). Cover letter is preferred. Reads submissions year round. Does not want long submissions. Length: up to 25 lines/poem.

SPIDER

70 E. Lake St., Suite 800, Chicago IL 60601. **E-mail:** spider@spidermagkids.com. **Website:** www.cricketmag.com/spider; www.spidermagkids.com. **Contact:** Submissions editor. *SPIDER* is full-color, 8×10, 34 pages with a 4-page activity pullout for children ages 6-9. Features the world's best children's authors.

MAGAZINES NEEDS Poems should be succinct, imaginative, and accessible; tend to avoid long narrative poems. Length: no more than 20 lines. Pays up to $3/line, $25 minimum.

SPILLWAY

P.O. Box 7887, Huntington Beach CA 92615. (714)968-0905. **E-mail:** spillway2@spillway.org; mifanwy.kaiser@gmail.com. **Website:** http://www.spillway.org/index.html. **Contact:** Mifanwy Kaiser, publisher; Susan Terris, editor. Published semi-annually in June and December, *Spillway* celebrates "writing's diversity and power to affect our lives." Open to all voices, schools, and tendencies. Acquires one-time rights. Responds in up to 6 months.

Spillway is about 125 pages, digest-sized, attractively printed, perfect-bound, with full color card cover. Press run is 2,000. "We recommend ordering a sample copy before you submit, though acceptance does not depend upon purchasing a sample copy." Single copy is $13.50, includes shipping and handling; 1 year subscription is $23, includes shipping and handling; 2 year subscription is $40, includes shipping and handling. To order, visit the website and use PayPal.

MAGAZINES NEEDS Submit 3-5 poems at a time (in a single document). No fiction. For more complete information about upcoming themes and submission periods, check our website. E-mail submissions only to spillway2@spillway.org (MS Word attachment); no disk or fax submissions. Cover letter is required. Include brief bio. Responds in up to 6 months. Pays 1 contributor's copy.

SPINNING JENNY

c/o Black Dress Press, P.O. Box 1067, New York NY 10014. **E-mail:** editor@spinning-jenny.com. **Website:** www.spinning-jenny.com. **Contact:** C.E. Harrison, editor. *Spinning Jenny*, published once/year in the fall (usually September), has published poetry by Abraham Smith, Cynthia Cruz, Michael Morse, and Joyelle McSweeney. Authors retain rights. Responds

within 4 months. Single copy: $10; subscription: $20 for 2 issues. Guidelines available on website.

Spinning Jenny is 96 pages, digest-sized, perfect-bound, with heavy card cover. "We accept less than 5% of unsolicited submissions." Press run is 1,000.

MAGAZINES NEEDS "*Spinning Jenny* is an open forum for poetry. We are pleased to consider experimental writing and work by unpublished authors. However, writers are strongly encouraged to review a recent issue of the magazine before submitting their work." Submit via online submission form (submit.spinning-jenny.com). Pays in contributor's copies.

SPITBALL: THE LITERARY BASEBALL MAGAZINE

5560 Fox Rd., Cincinnati OH 45239. **E-mail:** spitball5@hotmail.com. **Website:** www.spitballmag.com. **Contact:** Mike Shannon, editor-in-chief. *Spitball: The Literary Baseball Magazine*, published semiannually, is a unique magazine devoted to poetry, fiction, and book reviews exclusively about baseball. Newcomers are very welcome, but they must know the subject. "Perhaps a good place to start for beginners is one's personal reactions to the game, a game, a player, etc., and take it from there." Writers submitting to *Spitball* for the first time must buy a sample copy (waived for subscribers). "This is a one-time-only fee, which we regret, but economic reality dictates that we insist those who wish to be published in *Spitball* help support it, at least at this minimum level."

Spitball is 96 pages, digest-sized, computer-typeset, perfect-bound. Receives about 1,000 submissions/year, accepts about 40. Press run is 1,000. Subscription: $12. Sample: $6.

MAGAZINES NEEDS Submit a "batch" of poems at a time ("we prefer to use several of same poet in an issue rather than a single poem"). Lines/poem: open. Cover letter is required. Include brif bio and SASE. "Many times we are able to publish accepted work almost immediately." All material published in *Spitball* will be automatically considered for inclusion in the next *Best of Spitball* anthology. Poems submitted to *Spitball* will be considered automatically for Poem of the Month, to appear on the website. "We sponsor the Casey Award (for best baseball book of the year) and hold the Casey Awards Banquet in late February or early March. Any chapbook of baseball poetry should be sent to us for consideration for the 'Casey' plaque that we award to the winner each year." Pays 2 contributor's copies.

TIPS "Take the subject seriously. We do. In other words, get a clue (if you don't already have one) about the subject and about the poetry that has already been done and published about baseball. Learn from it—think about what you can add to the canon that is original and fresh—and don't assume that just anybody with the feeblest of efforts can write a baseball poem worthy of publication. And most importantly, stick with it. Genius seldom happens on the first try."

🟢 SPOON

315 Eastern SE, Grand Rapids MI 49503. (616)245-8633; (616)328-4090. **E-mail:** edholman@rocketmail.com. **Contact:** Ed Holman, poetry editor. "A creative newsletter by and for homeless and disempowered people in the Heartside area of Grand Rapids. We accept material from everywhere." Publishes ms 2 months after acceptance. Responds in 1 month. Sometimes comments on rejected poems. Sample copy for $1.50. Guidelines available by e-mail.

⊙ Bimonthly. Magazine-size with offset printing, no binding; rarely includes ads. Receives 140 poems/year, accepts about 15-20%. Press run is 1,000. No reading fees. Never publishes theme issues. Never sends prepublication galleys. Single copy: $3; subscription: $15/year. Sample copy for $1.50. Make checks payable to: Cathy Needham, memo: *Spoon.* as published poetry by Edward Holman, Cathy Bousma Richa, Walter Mathews, Tammy Reindle. Considers poetry by children/teens. Reads submissions year round.

MAGAZINES NEEDS "Does not want vulgar poetry 'for shock value;' however, if a poem has a serious meaning we won't silence it." Pays $5 per accepted submission.

TIPS "Read, write, and be passionate."

SPOUT MAGAZINE

P.O. Box 581067, Minneapolis MN 55458. **E-mail:** editors@spoutpress.org. **Website:** www.spoutpress.org. **Contact:** Michelle Filkins. As the counterpart to Spout Press, *Spout Magazine* features poetry, art, fiction, and thought pieces with diverse voices and styles. Publishes ms 2-3 months after acceptance. Responds in 4 months. Guidelines online at website.

⊙ "We are currently accepting submissions of poetry, short stories, essays, opinion, art, and cartoons—*basically anything creative that can be affixed to an 8.5x11 page*—**for the upcoming issue of our magazine**. Follow our guidelines online."

MAGAZINES NEEDS Submit up to 5 poems at a time. Considers previously published poems and simultaneous submissions. Cover letter is preferred. "Poems are reviewed by 2 of 3 editors; those selected for final review are read again by all 3."

SPRING: THE JOURNAL OF THE E.E. CUMMINGS SOCIETY

129 Lake Huron Hall, Grand Valley State University, Allendale MI 49401. **E-mail:** websterm@gvsu.edu. **Website:** faculty.gvsu.edu/websterm/cummings. **Contact:** Michael Webster, editor. *Spring: The Journal of the E.E. Cummings Society*, published annually (usually in the fall), is designed "to broaden the audience for E.E. Cummings and to explore various facets of his life and art." **Contributors are required to subscribe.** Reads May-August. Responds in 6 months.

MAGAZINES NEEDS Wants poems in the spirit of Cummings, primarily poems of 1 page or less. Submit as e-mail attachment. Include cover letter. Does not want "amateurish" work.

SRPR (SPOON RIVER POETRY REVIEW)

4241 Department of English, Illinois State University, Normal IL 61790. **E-mail:** editors@srpr.org; contact@srpr.org. **Website:** http://srpr.org. **Contact:** Kirstin Hotelling Zona, editor. *SRPR (Spoon River Poetry Review)*, published biannually, is "one of the nation's oldest continuously published poetry journals. We seek to publish the best of all poetic genres, experimental as well as mainstream, and are proud of our commitment to regional as well as international poets and readers. *SRPR* includes, alongside poems from emerging and established poets, a chapbook-length selection of poetry by our featured *SRPR* poet, a substantial interview with the featured poet, and a long review-essay on books of recently published poetry written by established poet-critics. The Summer/Fall issue also spotlights the winner and runners-up of our highly competitive editor's prize contest." Acquires first North American serial rights. Responds in 2-6 months. Guidelines available in magazine or on website.

⊙ Accepts submissions from September 15-February 15 (postmarked).

MAGAZINES NEEDS "We publish the best of all poetic genres, including translations, and are proud of our commitment to regional as well as international poets. At *SRPR*, both innovative and mainstream poems are welcome, though all poetry we publish must be as intellectually and emotionally ambitious as it is formally attentive." Submit 3-5 poems at a time. Submit using online submission form or by postal mail with SASE. Pays 2 contributor's copies and a 1-year subscription.

STAND MAGAZINE

Leeds University, School of English, Leeds LS2 9JT, United Kingdom. (44)(113)233-4794. **Fax:** (44) (113)233-2791. **E-mail:** stand@leeds.ac.uk. **Website:** www.standmagazine.org. North American submissions: David Latané, Stand Magazine, Dept. of English, Virginia Commonwealth University, Richmond VA 23284. **Contact:** Jon Glover, managing editor. "*Stand Magazine* is concerned with what happens when cultures and literatures meet, with translation in its many guises, with the mechanics of language, with the processes by which the policy receives or disables its cultural makers. *Stand* promotes debate of issues that are of radical concern to the intellectual community worldwide. U.S. submissions can be made through the Virginia office (see separate listing). Guidelines online.

Does not accept e-mail submissions.

MAGAZINES NEEDS Submit through postal mail only. Include SASE.

ST. ANTHONY MESSENGER

Franciscan Media, 28 W. Liberty St., Cincinnati OH 45202-6498. (513)241-5615. **Fax:** (513)241-0399. **E-mail:** magazineeditors@franciscanmedia.org. **Website:** www.stanthonymessenger.org. **Contact:** John Feister, editor-in-chief. *St. Anthony Messenger* is a Catholic family magazine which aims to help its readers lead more fully human and Christian lives. "We publish articles that report on a changing church and world, opinion pieces written from the perspective of Christian faith and values, personality profiles, and fiction which entertains and informs." Buys first North American serial rights, buys electronic rights, buys first worldwide serial rights. Pays on acceptance. Publishes ms within an average of 1 year after acceptance. Responds in 3 weeks to queries. Responds in 2 months to mss. Sample copy for 9x12 SAE with 4 first-class stamps. Please study writers' guidelines at StAnthonyMessenger.org.

MAGAZINES NEEDS Submit a few poems at a time. "Please include your phone number and a SASE with your submission. Do not send us your entire collection of poetry. Poems must be original." Submit seasonal poems several months in advance. "Our poetry needs are very limited." Length: up to 20-25 lines; "the shorter, the better." Pays $2/line; $20 minimum.

TIPS "The freelancer should consider why his or her proposed article would be appropriate for us, rather than for *Redbook* or *Saturday Review*. We treat human problems of all kinds, but from a religious perspective. Articles should reflect Catholic theology, spirituality, and employ a Catholic terminology and vocabulary. We need more articles on prayer, scripture, Catholic worship. Get authoritative information (not merely library research); we want interviews with experts. Write in popular style; use lots of examples, stories, and personal quotes. Word length is an important consideration."

STAR*LINE

Science Fiction Poetry Association, W5679 State Rd. 60, Poynette WI 53955. **E-mail:** starline@sfpoetry.com. **Website:** www.sfpoetry.com. **Contact:** F.J. Bergmann, editor. *Star*Line*, published quarterly by the Science Fiction Poetry Association (see separate listing in Organizations), is a speculative poetry magazine. "Open to all forms as long as your poetry uses speculative motifs: science fiction, fantasy, or horror." Buys first North American serial rights. Responds in 3 days. Guidelines online.

MAGAZINES NEEDS Submit 3-5 poems at a time. Accepts e-mail submissions (preferred; pasted into body of message, no attachments). Pays $3 for 10 lines or less; 3¢/word rounded to the next dollar for 51+ lines.

ALSO OFFERS The Association also publishes *The Rhysling Anthology*, a yearly collection of nominations from the membership "for the best long and short speculative poetry of the preceding year, and *Dwarf Stars*, an annual collection of micro-poetry (ten lines or fewer)."

STEPPING STONES MAGAZINE

First Step Press, P.O. Box 902, Norristown PA 19404-0902. **E-mail:** info@ssmalmia.com. **Website:** http://ssmalmia.com. **Contact:** Trinae A. Ross, publisher. *Stepping Stones Magazine*, a Web publication with a rolling publication date, seeks "poetry as diverse as the authors themselves. Poems should have something to say other than, 'Hi, I'm a poem please publish me.'" Does not want "poems that promote intolerance for race, religion, gender, or sexual preference." Also accepts fiction and nonfiction. Responds in 2 months. Guidelines available for SASE, by sending an e-mail to info@ssmalmia.com, or on the website.

○   Has published poetry by Richard Fenwick, Karlanna Lewis, and Stephanie Kaylor. Receives about 600 poems/year, accepts about 10-15%.

MAGAZINES NEEDS Submit no more than 5 poems at a time. Prefers e-mail submissions; should include cover letter and formatted with a simple font and saved as .doc, .rtf, or .odf. Attach submissions and cover letter to e-mail and send to poetry@ssmalmia.com. Reads submissions year round. Length: up to 100 lines. Pays 1 contributor's copy. Free advertising space available.

ALSO OFFERS "The continuing goal of *Stepping Stones Magazine* is to provide sanctuary for new and established writers, to hone their skills and commune with one another within the comfort of our electronic pages."

STILL CRAZY

(614)746-0859. **E-mail:** editor@crazylitmag.com. **Website:** www.crazylitmag.com. **Contact:** Barbara Kussow, editor. *Still Crazy*, published biannually in January and July, features poetry, short stories, and essays written by or about people over age 50. The editor is particularly interested in material that challenges the stereotypes of older people and that portrays older people's inner lives as rich and rewarding. Wants writing by people over age 50 and writing by people of any age if the topic is about people over 50. Acquires one-time rights. Rights revert to author upon publication. Time between acceptance and publication is up to 1 year. Simultaneous submissions OK, but notify editor as soon as possible if work is accepted elsewhere. Previously published submissions are OK, but "author must make previous publication known at time of submission. We do not want materials that have appeared online elsewhere." Responds in 6 months to mss. Sometimes sends prepublication galleys. Sometimes comments on/critiques rejected mss. Single paper copy: $10. Subscriptions: $18 (2 issues per year). Downloads: $4. Sometimes publishes

theme issues. Guidelines on website. Submit via submissions manager on website.

○   Accepts 3-4 mss/issue; 6-8/year. Reads submissions year round.

MAGAZINES NEEDS Wants poems that tell a story. The editor is particularly interested in material that challenges the stereotypes of older people and that portrays older people's inner lives as rich and rewarding. Does not want "rhyming poetry, or poetry that is too sentimental." Lines/poem: up to 30. Pays 1 contributor's copy.

TIPS Looking for "interesting characters and interesting situations that might interest readers of all ages. Humor and lightness welcomed."

STIRRING: A LITERARY COLLECTION

c/o Erin Elizabeth Smith, Dept. of English, 301 McClung Tower, University of Tennessee, Knoxville TN 37996. **E-mail:** eesmith81@gmail.com. **E-mail:** stirring.fiction@gmail.com; stirring.poetry@gmail.com; stirring.nonfiction@gmail.com. **Website:** www.sundresspublications.com/stirring. **Contact:** Erin Elizabeth Smith, managing editor. "*Stirring* is one of the oldest continually-published literary journals on the web. *Stirring* is a monthly literary magazine that publishes poetry, short fiction, creative nonfiction, and photography by established and emerging writers." Acquires first North American serial rights. Publishes ms 1-2 weeks after acceptance. Responds in 3 months. E-mail for guidelines.

MAGAZINES NEEDS Wants free verse, formal poetry, etc. Doesn't want religious verse or children's verse. Has published poetry by Dorianne Laux, Sharon Olds, Patricia Smith, Chad Davidson. Receives about 1,500 poems/year, accepts 60. Submit up to 5 poems by e-mail to stirring.poetry@gmail.com. Length: 1-6 pages (most often accepts half- to full-page poems).

STONE SOUP

Children's Art Foundation, P.O. Box 83, Santa Cruz CA 95063-0083. (831)426-5557. **E-mail:** editor@stonesoup.com. **Website:** http://stonesoup.com. **Contact:** Ms. Gerry Mandel, editor. *Stone Soup* is 48 pages, 7x10, professionally printed in color on heavy stock, saddle-stapled, with coated cover with full-color illustration. Receives 5,000 poetry submissions/year, accepts about 12. Press run is 15,000. Subscription: $37/year (U.S.). "We have a preference for writing and art based on real-life experiences; no formula stories or poems. We only publish writing by children ages 8 to 13. We do not publish writing by adults." Buys all rights. Pays on publication. Publishes ms an average of 4 months after acceptance. Sample copy by phone only. Guidelines available online.

○ "Stories and poems from past issues are available online."

MAGAZINES NEEDS Wants free verse poetry. Does not want rhyming poetry, haiku, or cinquain. Pays $40/poem, a certificate, and 2 contributor's copies, plus discounts.

TIPS "All writing we publish is by young people ages 13 and under. We do not publish any writing by adults. We can't emphasize enough how important it is to read a couple of issues of the magazine. You can read stories and poems from past issues online. We have a strong preference for writing on subjects that mean a lot to the author. If you feel strongly about something that happened to you or something you observed, use that feeling as the basis for your story or poem. Stories should have good descriptions, realistic dialogue, and a point to make. In a poem, each word must be chosen carefully. Your poem should present a view of your subject, and a way of using words that are special and all your own."

STORYSOUTH

E-mail: terry@storysouth.com. **Website:** www.storysouth.com. **Contact:** Terry Kennedy, editor; Cynthia Nearman, creative nonfiction editor; Drew Perry, fiction editor; Julie Funderburk, poetry editor. "*storySouth* accepts unsolicited submissions of fiction, poetry, and creative nonfiction during 2 submission periods annually: March 15-June 15 and September 15-December 15. Long pieces are encouraged. Please make only 1 submission in a single genre per reading period." Acquires first serial rights. Publishes ms 1 month after acceptance. Responds in 2-6 months to mss. Guidelines online.

MAGAZINES NEEDS Submit 3-5 poems via online submissions manager. No word/line limit.

TIPS "What really makes a story stand out is a strong voice and a sense of urgency—a need for the reader to keep reading the story and not put it down until it is finished."

THE STORYTELLER

2441 Washington Rd., Maynard AR 72444. (870)647-2137. **E-mail:** storytellermag1@yahoo.com. **Website:** www.thestorytellermagazine.com. **Contact:** Regina Williams, editor. Buys first North American rights.

Publishes ms an average of 1-12 months after acceptance. Responds in 1 week to queries; in 2 weeks to mss. Editorial lead time 6 months. Guidelines online.

MAGAZINES NEEDS Submit up to 3 poems with SASE. Does not want long rambling. Length: up to 40 lines/poem.

ALSO OFFERS Sponsors a quarterly contest. "Readers vote on their favorite poems. Winners receive a copy of the magazine and a certificate. We also nominate for the Pushcart Prize." See website for yearly contest announcements and winners.

TIPS "*The Storyteller* is one of the best places you will find to submit your work, especially new writers. Our best advice, be professional. You have one chance to make a good impression. Don't blow it by being unprofessional."

🅢 STRANGE HORIZONS

E-mail: editor@strangehorizons.com. **Website:** strangehorizons.com. **Contact:** Niall Harrison, editor in chief. "*Strange Horizons* is a magazine of and about speculative fiction and related nonfiction. Speculative fiction includes science fiction, fantasy, horror, slipstream, and other flavors of fantastica." For nonfiction: buys exclusive online publication rights for 6 months and requests ongoing nonexclusive rights to display the work in archive. For fiction and poetry: buys first world exclusive English-language rights (including audio rights) for 2 months. Responds in 1-3 month to mss. Only responds if interested.

○ Work published in *Strange Horizons* has been shortlisted for or won Hugo, Nebula, Rhysling, Theodore Sturgeon, James Tiptree Jr., and World Fantasy Awards.

MAGAZINES NEEDS "We're looking for high-quality SF, fantasy, horror, and slipstream poetry. We're looking for modern, exciting poems that explore the possible and impossible: stories about human and nonhuman experiences, dreams and reality, past and future, the here-and-now and otherwhere-and-elsewhen. We want poems from imaginative and unconventional writers; we want voices from diverse perspectives and backgrounds." Submit up to 6 poems within 2 calendar months via e-mail; 1 poem per e-mail. Include "POETRY SUB: Your Poem Title" in subject line. Pays $30 per poem.

STRAYLIGHT

UW-Parkside, English Department, University of Wisconsin-Parkside, 900 Wood Rd., Kenosha WI

53141. **E-mail:** submissions@straylightmag.com. **Website:** www.straylightmag.com. *Straylight*, published biannually, seeks fiction and "poetry of almost any style as long as it's inventive." Acquires first North American serial rights. Publication is copyrighted. Pays on publication. Publishes ms 6 months after acceptance. Responds in 3 weeks to queries; in 3 months to mss. Rarely comments on/critiques rejected mss. Sample copy: $10; subscription: $18. Guidelines online.

○ Literary magazine/journal: 6x9, 115 pages, quality paper, uncoated index stock cover. Contains illustrations, photographs.

MAGAZINES NEEDS Submit 3-6 poems at a time. Send poems with cover letter. Accepts submissions by online submission manager or mail (send either SASE or IRC for return of ms, or disposable copy of ms and #10 SASE for reply only). Include brief bio, list of publications. Pays 2 contributor's copies.

TIPS "We tend to publish character-based and inventive fiction with cutting-edge prose. We are unimpressed with works based on strict plot twists or novelties. Read a sample copy to get a feel for what we publish."

STRIDE MAGAZINE

Stride Publications, 4b Tremayne Close, Devoran, Cornwall TR3 6QE, England. **E-mail:** editor@stridemagazine.co.uk. **E-mail:** submissions@stridemagazine.co.uk. **Website:** www.stridemagazine.co.uk. **Contact:** Rupert Loydell, editor. *Stride Magazine*, published online, is "a gathering of new poetry, prose poems, reviews, and whatever takes our fancy. *Stride* is regularly updated with new contributions."

MAGAZINES NEEDS Submit 4-5 poems at a time. Accepts e-mail submissions (pasted into body of message; no attachments). "Attachments or snail mail without SAEs will not be considered or replied to."

STRUGGLE: A MAGAZINE OF PROLETARIAN REVOLUTIONARY LITERATURE

P.O. Box 28536, Detroit MI 48228. (313)273-9039. **E-mail:** timhall11@yahoo.com. **Website:** www.strugglemagazine.net. **Contact:** Tim Hall, editor. "A quarterly magazine featuring African American, Latino and other writers of color, prisoners, disgruntled workers, activists in the anti-war, anti-racist and other mass movements, and many writers discontented with Obama and with the Republicans, their joint aus-

terity campaign against the workers and the poor, and their continuing aggressive wars and drone murders abroad. While we urge literature in the direction of revolutionary working-class politics and a vision of socialism as embodying a genuine workers' power, in distinction to the state-capitalist regimes of the former Soviet Union, present-day China, North Korea, Cuba, etc., we accept a broader range of rebellious viewpoints in order to encourage creativity and dialogue." No rights acquired. Responds in 3-4 months to queries generally. Sample copy: $5. Subscription: $10 for 4 issues; make checks payable to Tim Hall, Special Account, not to *Struggle*.

MAGAZINES NEEDS Submit up to 8 poems at a time. Accepts e-mail submissions (pasted into body of message, no attachments), but prefers postal mail. "Writers must include SASE. Name and address must appear on the opening page of each poem."

STUDIO, A JOURNAL OF CHRISTIANS WRITING

727 Peel St., Albury NS 2640, Australia. (61)(2)6021-1135. **E-mail:** studio00@bigpond.net.au. **Contact:** Paul Grover, publisher. *Studio, A Journal of Christians Writing*, published quarterly, prints "poetry and prose of literary merit, offering a venue for previously published, new, and aspiring writers and seeking to create a sense of community among Christians writing." Also publishes occasional articles as well as news and reviews of writing, writers, and events of interest to members. People who send material should be comfortable being published under this banner: *Studio, A Journal of Christians Writing*. Acquires first Australian rights. Time between acceptance and publication is 6-9 months. Responds in 2 months to poems; in 1 week to queries and mss. Editorial lead time is 3 months. Sample copy: $10 (AUD; airmail to U.S.). Subscription: $60 AUD for overseas members. Guidelines by e-mail.

○ *Studio* is 36 pages, digest-sized, professionally printed on high-quality recycled paper, saddle-stapled, with matte card cover. Press run is 300 (all subscriptions).

MAGAZINES NEEDS Wants shorter pieces (of poetry) but with no specification as to form or length (necessarily less than 200 lines), subject matter, style, or purpose. Cover letter is required. Include brief details of previous publishing history, if any. SAE with IRC required. "Submissions must be typed and double-spaced on 1 side of A4 white paper. Name and address must appear on the reverse side of each page submitted." Has published poetry by John Foulcher, Les Murray, and other Australian poets. Length: less than 200 lines/poem. Pays 1 contributor's copy.

ALSO OFFERS Reviews books of poetry in 250 words, single-book format. Send materials for review consideration. Conducts a biannual poetry and short story contest.

STUDIO ONE

Murray Hall 170, College of St. Benedict, 37 S. College Ave., St. Joseph MN 56374. **E-mail:** studio1@csbsju.edu. **Website:** http://digitalcommons.csbsju.edu/studio_one/. **Contact:** Nikki Orth, Dana Hicks, editors-in-chief. *Studio One* is a literary and visual arts magazine published each spring by the College of Saint Benedict/Saint John's University. Its mission is to give new and established writers alike a forum in which to present their works. The magazine's focus is poetry, short fiction, essays, and all forms of reproducible visual art works. *Studio One* is student-run, and the student editors change yearly. Submissions are open to all students on either Saint John's or Saint Benedict's campuses and to the general public regardless of regional, national, or international location. Sample copy can be obtained by sending a self-addressed, stamped manila envelope and $6.

🔾 Reading period: September-February.

MAGAZINES NEEDS Considers simultaneous submissions; no previously published poems. Accepts e-mail submissions (pasted into body of message); "clearly show page breaks and indentations." Seldom comments on rejected poems. Lines/poem: "poetry no more than 2 pages stands a better chance of publication."

🔾🔾🔾 SUBTERRAIN

Strong Words for a Polite Nation, P.O. Box 3008, MPO, Vancouver BC V6B 3X5, Canada. (604)876-8710. **Fax:** (604)879-2667. **E-mail:** subter@portal.ca. **Website:** www.subterrain.ca. **Contact:** Brian Kaufman, editor in chief. *"subTerrain* magazine is published 3 times/year from modest offices just off of Main Street in Vancouver, BC. We strive to produce a stimulating fusion of fiction, poetry, photography, and graphic illustration from uprising Canadian, U.S., and international writers and artists." Pays on publication for first North American serial rights. Publishes ms 4 months after acceptance. Responds in 2-4 months to

mss. Rarely comments on rejected mss. Sample copy: $5 (subterrain.ca/subscriptions). Writer's guidelines online (subterrain.ca/about/35/sub-terrain-writer-s-guidelines).

🔾 Magazine: 8.25×10.75; 72 pages; gloss stock paper; color gloss cover stock; illustrations; photos. "Strong words for a polite nation."

MAGAZINES NEEDS "We accept poetry, but we no longer accept unsolicited submissions, except when related to 1 of our theme issues." Pays $50/poem.

TIPS "Read the magazine first. Get to know what kind of work we publish."

🔾 SUBTROPICS

University of Florida, P.O. Box 112075, 4008 Turlington Hall, Gainesville FL 32611-2075. **E-mail:** subtropics@english.ufl.edu. **Website:** www.english.ufl.edu/subtropics. **Contact:** David Leavitt, editor. *Subtropics* seeks to publish the best literary fiction, essays, and poetry being written today, both by established and emerging authors. Will consider works of fiction of any length, from short shorts to novellas and self-contained novel excerpts. Gives the same latitude to essays. Appreciates work in translation and, from time to time, republishes important and compelling stories, essays, and poems that have lapsed out of print by writers no longer living. Member: CLMP. Buys first North American serial rights. Pays on acceptance for prose; pays on publication of the issue preceding the issue in which the author's work will appear for poetry. Publishes ms an average of 6 months after acceptance. Responds in 1 month to queries and mss. Rarely comments on/critiques rejected mss Sample copy: $12.95. Guidelines online.

🔾 Literary magazine/journal: 9x6, 160 pages. Includes photographs. Submissions accepted from September 1-April 15.

MAGAZINES NEEDS Submit up to 4 poems via online submissions manager. Pays $100 per poem.

TIPS "We publish longer works of fiction, including novellas and excerpts from forthcoming novels. Each issue includes a short-short story of about 250 words on the back cover. We are also interested in publishing works in translation for the magazine's English-speaking audience."

SUCCESS STORIES

Franklin Publishing Company, 2723 Steamboat Circle, Arlington TX 76006. (817)548-1124. **E-mail:** ludwigotto@sbcglobal.net. **Website:** www.franklinpublishing.net; www.londonpress.us. **Contact:** Dr. Ludwig Otto. Buys one-time rights. Does not pay, but offers 15% discount on issues purchased and one-year free membership in the International Association of Professionals. Publishes ms an average of 1 month after acceptance. Responds in 1 week to queries and mss. Editorial lead time 1 month. Guidelines available online.

THE SUN

107 N. Roberson St., Chapel Hill NC 27516. (919)942-5282. **Fax:** (919)932-3101. **Website:** www.thesunmagazine.org. **Contact:** Sy Safransky, editor. *The Sun* publishes essays, interviews, fiction, and poetry. "We are open to all kinds of writing, though we favor work of a personal nature." Buys first rights, buys one-time rights. Pays on publication. Publishes ms an average of 6-12 months after acceptance. Responds in 3-6 months to queries and mss. Sample copy: $7. Guidelines online.

Magazine: 8.5x11; 48 pages; offset paper; glossy cover stock; photos.

MAGAZINES NEEDS Submit up to 6 poems at a time. Considers previously published poems but strongly prefers unpublished work. "Poems should be typed and accompanied by a cover letter and SASE." Recently published poems by Tony Hoagland, Ellen Bass, Steve Kowit, Brian Doyle, and Alison Luterman. Rarely publishes poems that rhyme. Pays $100-500 on publication plus contributor's copies and subscription.

TIPS "Do not send queries except for interviews. We're open to unusual work. Read the magazine to get a sense of what we're about. Our submission rate is extremely high. Please be patient after sending us your work and include return postage."

SUNSTONE

343 N. Third W., Salt Lake City UT 84103-1215. (801)355-5926. **E-mail:** info@sunstonemagazine.com. **Website:** www.sunstonemagazine.com. *Sunstone*, published 6 times/year, prints scholarly articles of interest to an open, Mormon audience; personal essays; fiction (selected only through contests), and poetry. Has published poetry by Susan Howe, Anita Tanner, Robert Parham, Ryan G. Van Cleave, Robert Rees, and Virgil Suárez. Acquires first North American serial rights. Publishes ms 2 years after acceptance. Responds in 3 months. Sample copy: $10 postpaid. Subscription: $45 for 6 issues. Guidelines online.

Sunstone is 64 pages, magazine-sized, professionally printed, saddle-stapled, with semi-glossy paper cover. Receives more than 500 poems/year, accepts 40-50. Press run is 3,000.

MAGAZINES NEEDS Wants both lyric and narrative poetry that engages the reader with fresh, strong images; skillful use of language; and a strong sense of voice and/or place. Short poems, including haiku, limericks, couplets, and one liners, are welcome. Does not want didactic poetry, sing-song rhymes, or in-process work. Submit by mail or e-mail. Include name, address, and e-mail on each poem. Seldom comments on rejected poems. Length: up to 40 lines/poem. Pays 5 contributor's copies.

SYCAMORE REVIEW

Purdue University Department of English, 500 Oval Dr., West Lafayette IN 47907. (765) 494-3783. **Fax:** (765) 494-3780. **E-mail:** sycamore@purdue.edu. **Website:** www.sycamorereview.com. **Contact:** Kara Krewer, editor in chief; Bess Cooley, managing editor. *Sycamore Review* is Purdue University's internationally acclaimed literary journal, affiliated with Purdue's College of Liberal Arts and the Dept. of English. Strives to publish the best writing by new and established writers. Looks for well-crafted and engaging work, works that illuminate our lives in the collective human search for meaning. Would like to publish more work that takes a reflective look at national identity and how we are perceived by the world. Looks for diversity of voice, pluralistic worldviews, and political and social context. Buys first North American serial rights.

Reading period: September 1-March 31.

MAGAZINES NEEDS Submi via online submissions manager. Does not publish creative work by any student currently attending Purdue University. Former students should wait 1 year before submitting. Pays $25/poem.

TIPS "We look for originality, brevity, significance, strong dialogue, and vivid detail. We sponsor the Wabash Prize for Poetry (deadline: December 1) and Fiction (deadline: April 17). $1,000 award for each. All contest submissions will be considered for regular inclusion in the *Sycamore Review*."

TAB: THE JOURNAL OF POETRY & POETICS

Chapman University, One University Dr., Orange CA 92866. (714)997-6750. **E-mail:** poetry@chapman.edu;

leahy@chapman.edu. **Website:** http://journals.chap-man.edu/ojs/index.php/TAB-journal. **Contact:** Anna Leahy, director; Claudine Jaenichen, creative director. *TAB: A Journal of Poetry & Poetics* is a national and international journal of creative and critical writing. This literary journal's mission is to discover, support, and publish the contemporary poetry and writing about poetry; to provide a forum in which the poetic tradition is practiced, extended, challenged, and discussed by emerging and established voices; and to encourage wide appreciation of poetry and expand the audience for poems and writing about poetry. Welcomes submissions of poems from established and emerging poets as well as critical essays, creative nonfiction, interviews, and reviews. *TAB* will reach audience of poets, poetry readers and appreciators, poetry scholars and critics, and students of poetry. Buys first North American serial rights. Pays on publication. Publishes ms 2-6 months after acceptance. Responds in 2-4 months to mss. Sample copy for $4 s&h or online at website. Guidelines free online at website.

MAGAZINES NEEDS No greeting card poetry. No work by writers under 18 years of age. No work by students, faculty, or staff of Chapman University. No length restrictions.

TIPS "Read poetry and read it widely. Take a look at the range we publish. Work hard and revise."

●● ⊛ TAKAHE

P.O. Box 13-335, Christchurch 8001, New Zealand. (03)359-8133. **E-mail:** admin@takahe.org.nz. **Website:** www.takahe.org.nz/index.php. The Takahē Collective Trust is a nonprofit organization that aims to support emerging and published writers, poets, artists, and cultural commentators. The *Takahē* magazine appears 3 times/year and publishes short stories, poetry, and art by established and emerging writers and artists as well as essays and interviews (by invitation) and book reviews in these related areas. Acquires first rights. Responds in 4 months. Guidelines available online at www.takahe.org.nz.

MAGAZINES NEEDS No e-mail submissions. "**Please note:** U.S. stamps should not be used on SAEs. They do not work in New Zealand. Please enclose IRCs and supply e-mail address." Cover letter is required. " Submit up to 6 poems at a time. Pays 1 contributor's copy and free one-year subscription.

TIPS "We pay a flat rate to each writer/poet appearing in a particular issue regardless of the number/length

of items. Editorials and literary commentaries are by invitation only."

TALKING RIVER

Division of Literature and Languages, 500 8th Ave., Lewiston ID 83501. (208)792-2189. **Fax:** (208)792-2324. **E-mail:** talkingriver@lcmail.lcsc.edu. **Website:** www.lcsc.edu/talking-river. **Contact:** Kevin Goodan, editorial advisor. "We look for new voices with something to say to a discerning general audience." Wants more well-written, character-driven stories that surprise and delight the reader with fresh, arresting yet unselfconscious language, imagery, metaphor, revelation. Reads mss September 1-May 1 only. Recently published work by Chris Dombrowski, Sherwin Bitsui, and Lia Purpura. Acquires one-time rights. Publishes ms 1-2 years after acceptance. Responds in 6 months to mss. Sample copy: $6. Writer's guidelines for #10 SASE.

◯   Submission period runs August 1-April 1.

MAGAZINES NEEDS Submit via postal mail. Send SASE for reply and return of ms, or send disposable copy of ms. Pays contributor's copies; additional copies $4.

TIPS "We look for the strong, the unique; we reject clichéd images and predictable climaxes."

TARPAULIN SKY

P.O. Box 189, Grafton VT 05146. **E-mail:** editors@tarpaulinsky.com. **E-mail:** submissions@tarpaulinsky.com. **Website:** www.tarpaulinsky.com. **Contact:** Resh Daily, managing editor. *Tarpaulin Sky*, published biannually in print and online, features the highest-quality poetry, prose, cross-genre work, art, photography, interviews, and reviews. Open to all styles and forms, providing the forms appear inevitable and/or inextricable from the poems. Especially fond of inventive/experimental and cross-/trans-genre work. The best indication of aesthetic is found in the journal: Read it before submitting. Also, hardcopy submissions may be received by different editors at different times; check guidelines before submitting. Acquires first rights. Publishes ms 2-6 months after acceptance. Responds in 1-4 months.

MAGAZINES NEEDS Submit 4-6 poems at a time. Considers simultaneous submissions; no previously published poems. Accepts e-mail submissions ("best received as attachments in .rtf or .pdf formats"); no disk submissions. Cover letter is preferred. Reads submissions year round. Poems are read by all editors. Rarely comments on rejected poems. Guidelines available for SASE, by e-mail, or on website. Has published poetry by Jenny Boully, Matthea Harvey, Bin Ramke, Eleni Sikelianos, Juliana Spahr, and Joshua Marie Wilkinson. Receives about 3,000 poems/year. Pays in contributor's copies and by waiving readings fees for Tarpaulin Sky Press Open Reading Periods.

TAR RIVER POETRY

Mail Stop 159, Erwin Hall, East Fifth St., East Carolina University, Greenville NC 27858. **E-mail:** TarRiverPoetry@gmail.com. **Website:** www.tarriverpoetry.com. **Contact:** Luke Whisnant, editor. *Tar River Poetry*, published twice/year, is an all-poetry magazine that publishes 40-50 poems per issue, providing the talented beginner and experienced writer with a forum that features all styles and forms of verse. Wants skillful use of figurative language and poems that appeal to the senses. Does not want sentimental, flat-statement poetry. Acquires first rights and reassigns reprint rights after publication. Responds in 6 weeks. Rarely comments on rejections due to volume of submissions. Sample: $7, postage paid. Subscription: $12 for 1 year; $20 for 2 years. Guidelines available for SASE or on website.

○ Only considers submissions 2 months of the year—usually September and February; check website for reading periods before submitting. Work submitted at other times will not be considered. *Tar River Poetry* is 64 pages, 9x5, professionally printed with color cover. Receives 6,000-8,000 submissions/year, accepts 60-80. Press run is 900 (500 subscribers, 125 libraries).

MAGAZINES NEEDS Accepts e-mail submissions only; no print submissions; print submissions will be returned unread. Detailed submission instructions appear on the website along with writer's guidelines. Has published poetry by William Stafford, Sharon Olds, Carolyn Kizer, A.R. Ammons, and Claudia Emerson. Has also published many other well-known poets, as well as numerous new and emerging poets. Pays 2 contributor's copies.

ALSO OFFERS Reviews books of poetry in 4,000 words maximum, single- or multibook format. Query for reviews.

TIPS "We are usually not interested in obscure or abstract poetry, concrete poetry, or prose poems. We favor image-based narrative and lyric poetry that is accessible and meaningful without being simplistic,

sophisticated without being pretentious. We publish both free verse and formal poems; for samples, see our website. Writers of poetry should first be readers of poetry. Subscribers receive expedited editorial decisions on their submissions."

THE TEACHER'S VOICE

P.O. Box 150384, Kew Gardens NY 11415. **E-mail:** editor@the-teachers-voice.org. **Website:** www.the-teachers-voice.org. **Contact:** Andres Castro, founding/managing editor. *The Teacher's Voice*, was founded as an experimental hardcopy literary magazine and is now free and online. Publishes poetry, short stories, creative nonfiction, and essays that reflect the many different American teacher experiences. Wants all styles and forms. Asks to see critical creative writing that takes risks without being overly self-indulgent or inaccessible. Welcomes work that ranges from "art for art's sake" to radically social/political. Writing that illuminates the most pressing/urgent issues in American education and the lives of teachers gets special attention. Has published poetry by Edward Francisco, Sapphire, Hal Sirowitz, and Antler. Acquires first electronic rights. Guidelines on website.

○ Receives about 1,000 submissions/year. Accepts around 10%.

MAGAZINES NEEDS Cover letter is preferred. Does not accept responsibility for submissions or queries not accompanied by a SASE with adequate postage. Poems are circulated to an editorial board. Send up to 5 pages of poetry.

ADDITIONAL INFORMATION "Since we publish open as well as theme issues (that require enough thematic pieces to be compiled) and do rely on readership financial support, our publishing schedule and format may vary from year to year. We publish hardcopy limited press collections when funds allow. Our production goal is to showcase strong cohesive collections that support our mission and satisfy the needs of particular issues. For the moment, our new focus on electronic publishing is a matter of survival that offers many new possibilities and opportunities in keeping with the changing times."

CONTEST/AWARD OFFERINGS Sponsors *The Teacher's Voice* Annual Chapbook Contest and *The Teacher's Voice* Annual Poetry Contest for Unpublished Poets. Final contest judges have included, Sapphire, Jack Hirschman, and Taylor Mali. Guidelines for both contests available for SASE, by e-mail, or on website.

🌑 TEARS IN THE FENCE

Portman Lodge, Durweston, Blandford Forum, Dorset DT11 0QA, England. **E-mail:** tearsinthefence@gmail.com. **Website:** tearsinthefence.com. *Tears in the Fence*, published 3 times/year, is a "small-press magazine of poetry, fiction, interviews, essays, and reviews. We are open to a wide variety of poetic styles and work that shows social and poetic awareness whilst prompting close and divergent readings. However, we like to publish a variety of work." Time between acceptance and publication is 3 months. Sample: $13. Subscription: $60/3 (£40/3) issues.

🌑   *Tears in the Fence* is 176 pages, A5, digitally printed on 110-gms. paper, perfect-bound, with matte card cover. Press run is 600.

MAGAZINES NEEDS Books for review to Ian Brinton, Brescia House, 2 Capel Road, Faversham, Kent, ME13 8RL, England. Submit 6 poems at a time. Accepts e-mail (pasted into body of message). Cover letter with brief bio is required. Poems must be typed; include SASE. Has published Aidan Semmens, Hannah Silva, Jennifer K. Dick, Pansy Maurer-Alvarez, Carrie Etter, Nathaniel Tarn, Chris McCabe, Sheila E. Murphy, Robert Vas Dias, and Sarah Crewe. Pays 1 contributor's copy.

ALSO OFFERS The magazine runs a regular series of readings in Dorset and an annual international literary festival.

TERRAIN.ORG: A JOURNAL OF THE BUILT + NATURAL ENVIROMENTS

Terrain.org, P.O. Box 19161, Tucson AZ 85731-9161. **E-mail:** contact2@terrain.org. **Website:** www.terrain.org. Reviews Editor address: P.O. Box 51332, Irvine CA 92619-1332. **Contact:** Simmons B. Buntin, editor in chief. *Terrain.org* is based on, and thus welcomes quality submissions from, new and experienced authors and artists alike. Our online journal accepts only the finest poetry, essays, fiction, articles, artwork, and other contributions' material that reaches deep into the earth's fiery core, or humanity's incalculable core, and brings forth new insights and wisdom. *Terrain.org* is searching for that interface—the integration among the built and natural environments, that might be called the soul of place. The works contained within *Terrain.org* ultimately examine the physical realm around us and how those environments influ-

ence us and each other physically, mentally, emotionally, and spiritually." Acquires one-time rights. Sends galleys to author. Publication is copyrighted. Publishes mss 5 weeks-18 months after acceptance. Responds in 2 weeks to queries; in 2-3 months to mss. Sometimes comments on/critiques rejected mss. Guidelines available online.

🌑   Beginning March 2014, publication schedule is rolling; we will no longer be issue-based. Sends galleys to author. Publication is copyrighted. Sponsors *Terrain.org* Annual Contest in Poetry, Fiction, and Nonfiction. **Deadline:** August 1. Submit via online submissions manager.

MAGAZINES NEEDS Accepts submissions online at sub.terrain.org. Include brief bio. Send complete ms with cover letter. No erotica. Length: open.

TIPS "We have 3 primary criteria in reviewing fiction: (1) The story is compelling and well crafted. (2) The story provides some element of surprise; whether in content, form, or delivery we are unexpectedly delighted in what we've read. (3) The story meets an upcoming theme, even if only peripherally. Read fiction in the current issue and perhaps some archived work, and if you like what you read—and our overall enviromental slant—then send us your best work. Make sure you follow our submission guidelines (including cover note with bio), and that your mss is as error-free as possible."

TEXAS POETRY CALENDAR

Dos Gatos Press, 1310 Crestwood Rd., Austin TX 78722. (512)467-0678. **E-mail:** editors@dosgatospress.org; managingeditor@dosgatospress.org. **E-mail:** https://dosgatospress.submittable.com/submit. **Website:** www.dosgatospress.org. **Contact:** Scott Wiggerman and David Meischen, publishers. *Texas Poetry Calendar*, published annually in July, features a "week-by-week calendar side-by-side with poems with a Texas connection." Wants "a wide variety of styles, voices, and forms, including rhyme, though a Texas connection is preferred. Humor is welcome! Poetry only!" Does not want "children's poetry, erotic poetry, profanity, obscure poems, previously published work, or poems over 35 lines." Publishes 1-2 months after acceptance. Single copy: $13.95 plus $3 shipping. Make checks payable to Dos Gatos Press.

🌑   *Texas Poetry Calendar* is about 144 pages, digest-sized, offset-printed, spiral-bound, with full-color cardstock cover. Receives about 600 poems/year, accepts about 80-85. Press run is 1,000; 80-85 distributed free to contributors. Reads submissions February-May.

MAGAZINES NEEDS Submit 3 poems through Submittable: https://dosgatospress.submittable.com/submit. No fax, e-mail, or snail mail submissions; only electronic submissions via Submittable. Cover letter is required. "Include a short bio (100-200 words) and poem titles in cover letter. Also include e-mail address and phone number. Do not include poet's name on the poems themselves!" Never comments on rejected poems, but nominates poems for Pushcart Prizes each year. Deadline: February 21 (postmark). Length: up to 35 lines/poem, "including spaces and title."

TEXAS REVIEW

Texas Review Press, Department of English, Sam Houston State University, Box 2146, Huntsville TX 77341-2146. (936)294-1992. **Fax:** (936)294-3070. **E-mail:** eng_pdr@shsu.edu; cww006@shsu.edu. **Website:** www.shsu.edu/~www_trp. **Contact:** Dr. Paul Ruffin, editor/director; Greg Bottoms, essay editor; Eric Miles Williamson, fiction editor; Nick Lantz, poetry editor. "We publish top-quality poetry, fiction, articles, interviews, and reviews for a general audience." Semiannual. Pays on publication for first North American serial, one-time rights. Sends galleys to author. Publishes ms 6-12 months after acceptance. Responds in 2 weeks to queries; 3-6 months to mss. Sometimes comments on rejected mss. Sample copy: $5. Guidelines available on website: https://texasreview.submittable.com/submit.

○ *Texas Review* is 6×9; 148-190 pages; best quality paper; 70 lb. cover stock; illustrations; photos. Receives 40-60 unsolicited mss/month. Accepts 4 mss/issue; 6 mss/year. **Publishes some new writers/year.** Does not read mss May-September. A member of the Texas A&M University Press consortium.

MAGAZINES NEEDS No previously published poems or simultaneous submissions. Include SASE. Reads submissions September 1-April 30 only. Seldom comments on rejected poems. Pays one-year subscription and 1 contributor's copy (may request more).

ALSO OFFERS Sponsors the X.J. Kennedy Poetry Prize (for best full-length book of poetry), the Robert Phillips Poetry Chapbook Prize (for best poetry chapbook), the George Garrett Fiction Prize (for best book of stories or short novel), and the Clay Reynolds Novella Prize (for best novella.) Publication of winning mss and 50 copies of book. **Entry fee:** $20.

⊙ THEMA

Thema Literary Society, P.O. Box 8747, Metairie LA 70011-8747. **E-mail:** thema@cox.net. **Website:** http://themaliterarysociety.com. **Contact:** Gail Howard, poetry editor. "*THEMA* is designed to stimulate creative thinking by challenging writers with unusual themes, such as 'The Box Under the Bed' and 'Put It In Your Pocket, Lillian.' Appeals to writers, teachers of creative writing, and general reading audience." Acquires one-time rights. Pays on acceptance. Publishes ms, on average, within 6 months after acceptance. Responds in 1 week to queries. Responds in 5 months to mss. Sample $10 U.S./$15 foreign. Upcoming themes and guidelines available in magazine, for SASE, by e-mail, or on website.

○ *THEMA* is 100 pages, digest-sized professionally printed, with glossy card cover. Receives about 400 poems/year, accepts about 8%. Press run is 400 (230 subscribers, 30 libraries). Subscription: $20 U.S./$30 foreign. Has published poetry by Beverly Boyd, Elizabeth Creith, James Penha and Matthew J. Spireng.

MAGAZINES NEEDS Submit up to 3 poems at a time. Include SASE. "All submissions should be typewritten on standard 812x11 paper. Submissions are accepted all year, but evaluated after specified deadlines." Specify target theme. Editor comments on submissions. "Each issue is based on an unusual premise. Please send SASE for guidelines before submitting poetry to find out the upcoming themes." Does not want "scatologic language, alternate lifestyle, explicit love poetry." Pays $10/poem and 1 contributor's copy.

THINK JOURNAL

Western State Colorado University, Gunnison CO **E-mail:** drothman@western.edu; susandelaneyspear@msn.com. **Website:** www.western.edu/academics/graduate-programs/master-fine-arts-creative-writing/think-journal. **Contact:** Susan Spear, managing editor. "*Think Journal*, established in 2008 by Christine Yurick, was acquired by the graduate program in creative writing at Western State Colorado University in 2013. *Think* publishes twice yearly and focuses on words that have meaning, that are presented in a clear way, and that exhibit the skills demanded by craft. The journal prints work that achieves a balance between form and content. The most important traits considered are form, structure, clarity, content, imagination, and style." Responds in 2-4 weeks to queries. Editorial lead time 6 months. Yearly subscription: $15. Contact the webpage on Western's site at www.western.edu. Direct any questions to Susan Spear, managing editor, at susandelaneyspear@msn.com.

MAGAZINES NEEDS Submit up to 5 poems on https://think-journal.submittable.com/submit. Pays 1 contributor's copy.

THIRD COAST

Western Michigan University, English Dept., 1903 W. Michigan Ave., Kalamazoo MI 49008-5331. **Website:** www.thirdcoastmagazine.com. **Contact:** Laurie Ann Cedilnik, editor in chief. "*Third Coast* publishes poetry, fiction (including traditional and experimental fiction, shorts, and novel excerpts, but not genre fiction), creative nonfiction (including reportage, essay, memoir, and fragments), drama, and translations." Acquires first North American serial rights. Publishes ms an average of 6 months after acceptance. Responds in 4 months to queries and mss. Sample copy: $6 (back issue). Make checks payable to *Third Coast*. Guidelines available online at www.thirdcoastmagazine.com/submit. *Third Coast* only accepts submissions submitted to its online submission manager. All hard copy submissions will be returned unread.

⭕ *Third Coast* is 176 pages, digest-sized, professionally printed, perfect-bound, with 4-color cover with art. Reads mss from September through December of each year.

MAGAZINES NEEDS Has published poetry by Marianne Boruch, Terence Hayes, Alex Lemon, Philip Levine, David Shumate, Tomz Salamun, and Jean Valentine. Submit up to 5 poems via online submissions manager. No simple narratives or any simplistic poetry. Pays 2 contributor's copies and one-year subscription.

ALSO OFFERS Sponsors an annual poetry contest. 1st Prize: $1,000 and publication. Guidelines available on website. **Entry fee:** $16, includes one-year subscription to *Third Coast*.

TIPS "We will consider many different types of fiction and favor those exhibiting a freshness of vision and approach."

💲 THIRD WEDNESDAY: A LITERARY ARTS MAGAZINE

174 Greenside Up, Ypsilanti MI 48197. (734) 434-2409. **E-mail:** submissions@thirdwednesday.org; Laurence-WT@aol.com. **Website:** http://thirdwednesday.org. **Contact:** Laurence Thomas, editor. "*Third Wednesday* publishes quality (a subjective term at best) poetry, short fiction, and artwork by experienced writers and artists. We welcome work by established writers/artists, as well as those who are not yet well known but headed for prominence." Acquires first North American serial rights, electronic rights. "*TW* retains the right to reproduce accepted work as samples on our website." Rights revert to author upon publication. Pays on acceptance. Publishes ms 3 months after acceptance. Responds to mss in 6-8 weeks. Sometimes comments on/critiques rejected mss. Sample copy: $12; includes postage. Subscription: $40. Guidelines available for SASE, or via e-mail. Does not welcome submissions by snail mail.

MAGAZINES NEEDS Receives 800 poems/year. Has published poetry by Wanda Coleman, Philip Dacey, Richard Luftig, Simon Perchik, Marge Piercy, Charles Harper Webb. Submit 1-5 poems at a time. Wants "all styles and forms of poetry, from formal to experimental. Emphasis is placed on the ideas conveyed, craft and language, beauty of expression, and the picture that extends beyond the frame of the poem." Does not want "hate-filled diatribes, pornography (though eroticism is acceptable), prose masquerading as poetry, first drafts of anything." Pays $3 and 1 contributor's copy.

TIPS "Of course, originality is important, along with skill in writing, deft handling of language, and meaning, which goes hand in hand with beauty—whatever that is. Short fiction is specialized and difficult, so the writer should read extensively in the field."

34THPARALLEL MAGAZINE

P.O. Box 4823, Irvine CA 92623. **E-mail:** 34thParallel@gmail.com. **Website:** www.34thparallel.net. **Contact:** Tracey Swan, Martin Chipperfield, editors. *34thParallel Magazine*, published quarterly in digital and print editions, seeks "to promote and publish the exceptional writing of new and emerging writers overlooked by large commercial publishing houses and mainstream presses. Wants work that experiments with and tests boundaries: anything that communicates a sense of wonder, reality, tragedy, fantasy, and brilliance. Does not want historical romance, erotica, Gothic horror, or book reviews." Submit via online submissions manager (Submittable). Guidelines on website.

"Milan Kundera wrote that fiction is like a parallel reality (okay, so he didn't say that exactly). But reality and fiction mix up, don't you think? Our lives exist in words; it's how we make our reality. But maybe the fiction is truer? What if in our writing we reach out beyond the parallels of reality and fiction? Question life, challenge the boundaries, confront our perceptions and misconceptions. Welcome again to the *34thParallel*."

MAGAZINES NEEDS Pays 1 contributor's copy in PDF format and offers print-edition copy at cost from print-on-demand publisher Lulu.

TIPS "We want it all, but we don't want everything. Take a look at the mag to get a feel for our style."

THE THREEPENNY REVIEW

P.O. Box 9131, Berkeley CA 94709. (510)849-4545. **E-mail:** wlesser@threepennyreview.com. **Website:** www.threepennyreview.com. **Contact:** Wendy Lesser, editor. "We are a general-interest, national literary magazine with coverage of politics, the visual arts, and the performing arts." Reading period: January 1-June 30. Buys first North American serial rights. Pays on acceptance. Publishes ms an average of 1 year after acceptance. Responds in 1 month to queries; in 2 months to mss. Sample copy: $12, or online. Guidelines available online.

MAGAZINES NEEDS No poems without capital letters or poems without a discernible subject. Length: up to 100 lines/poem. Pays $200.

TIPS Nonfiction (political articles, memoirs, reviews) is most open to freelancers.

TIGER'S EYE

Tiger's Eye Press, P.O. Box 9723, Denver CO 80209. (541)285-8355. **E-mail:** tigerseyepoet@yahoo.com. **Website:** www.tigerseyejournal.com. **Contact:** Colette Jonopulos and JoAn Osborne, editors. *Tiger's Eye: A Journal of Poetry*, published annually, features both established and undiscovered poets. Acquires one-time rights. Publishes ms 6 months after acceptance. Responds in 6 months after reading period. Journal submissions accepted from September 1-January 31. Guidelines available in magazine or on website.

Tiger's Eye nominates for *The Pushcart Prize*.

MAGAZINES NEEDS "Besides publishing the work of several exceptional poets in each issue, we feature 2 poets in interviews, giving the reader insight into their lives and writing habits." Wants "both free verse and traditional forms; no restrictions on subject or length. We welcome sonnets, haibun, haiku, ghazals, villenelles, etc. We pay special attention to unusual forms and longer poems that may have difficulty being placed elsewhere. Poems with distinct imagery and viewpoint are read and reread by the editors and considered for publication." Length: no more than 5 pages. Pays 1 contributor's copy to each poet, 2 to featured poets.

ALSO OFFERS Tiger's Eye Chapbook Contest (see separate listing in Contests & Awards). "Our annual poetry chapbook contest awards $100 and 25 copies of your chapbook. Chapbook submissions accepted April 1-August 31. Send no more than 20 poems, cover letter with poet's name and contact information (no identifying information on mss pages), SASE, and $15 entry fee.

TIMBER JOURNAL

E-mail: timberjournal@gmail.com. **Website:** www.timberjournal.com. *Timber* is a literary journal, run by students in the MFA program at the University of Colorado Boulder, dedicated to the promotion of innovative literature. Publishes work that explores the boundaries of poetry, fiction, creative nonfiction, and digital literatures. Produces both an online journal that explores the potentials of the digital medium and an annual print anthology. Responds in 2-3 months to mss. Guidelines online.

Reading period: August-March (submit just once during this time). Staff changes regularly; see website for current staff members.

MAGAZINES NEEDS Submit 3-5 poems in single document via online submissions manager. Include 30-50 word bio. Pays 1 contributor's copy.

TIPS "We are looking for innovative poetry, fiction, creative nonfiction, and digital lit (screenwriting, digital poetry, multimedia lit, etc.)."

TIME OF SINGING: A JOURNAL OF CHRISTIAN POETRY

P.O. Box 5276, Conneaut Lake PA 16316. **E-mail:** timesing@zoominternet.net. **Website:** www.timeofsinging.com. **Contact:** Lora Zill, editor. "*Time of Singing* publishes Christian poetry in the widest sense but prefers literary type. Welcomes forms, fresh rhyme, well-crafted free verse. Likes "writers who take chances, who don't feel the need to tie everything up neatly." Acquires first North American serial rights, acquires first rights, acquires one-time rights, acquires second serial (reprint) rights. Publishes ms within 1 year of acceptance. Responds in 3 months to mss. Editorial lead time 6 months. Sample copy: $4/each or 2 for $7 (postage paid). Subscription: $17 USD, $21 USD Canada, $30 USD overseas. Guidelines for SASE or on website.

○ *TOS* is 44 pages, digest-sized, digitally printed. Receives more than 800 submissions/year, accepts about 175. Press run is 250 (150 subscribers).

MAGAZINES NEEDS Wants free verse and well-crafted rhyme; would like to see more forms. Accepts e-mail submissions (pasted into body of message or as attachment). Poems should be single-spaced. Comments "with suggestions for improvement if close to publication." *TOS* has published poets from the U.S., Canada, England, South Africa, Mexico, New Zealand, Scotland, Russia, Australia, Germany, Slovakia, Albania, and Ireland. Has published poetry by John Grey, Luci Shaw, Bob Hostetler, Tony Cosier, Barbara Crooker, and Charles Waugaman. Does not want "collections of uneven lines, sermons that rhyme, greeting card type poetry, unstructured 'prayers,' and trite sing-song rhymes." Length: 3-60 lines. All contributors receive 1 copy of the issue in which their work appears and the opportunity to purchase more at the contributor's rate.

ALSO OFFERS Sponsors theme contests for specific issues. Guidelines available for SASE, by e-mail, or on website.

TIPS "Read widely and study the craft. You need more than feelings and religious jargon to make it into *TOS*. It's helpful to get honest critiques of your work. A cover letter is not necessary. Your poems speak for themselves."

TIN HOUSE

McCormack Communications, P.O. Box 10500, Portland OR 97296. (503)219-0622. **E-mail:** info@tinhouse.com. **Website:** www.tinhouse.com. **Contact:** Cheston Knapp, managing editor; Holly MacArthur, founding editor. "We are a general-interest literary quarterly. Our watchword is quality. Our audience includes people interested in literature in all its aspects, from the mundane to the exalted." Buys first North American serial rights, anthology rights. Pays on publication. Publishes ms an average of 6 months after acceptance. Responds in 6 weeks to queries; in 4 months to mss. Editorial lead time 6 months. Sample copy: $15. Guidelines online.

○ Reading period: September 1-May 31.

MAGAZINES NEEDS Submit via online submissions manager or postal mail. Include cover letter. Pays $50-150.

TOAD SUCK REVIEW

E-mail: toadsuckreview@gmail.com. **Website:** http://toadsuckreview.org. **Contact:** Mark Spitzer, editor in chief. "The innovative *Toad Suck Review* is a cutting-edge mixture of poetry, fiction, creative nonfiction, translations, reviews, and artwork with a provocative sense of humor and an interest in diverse cultures and politics. No previously published work. 'Previously published' work includes: poetry posted on a public website/blog/forum and poetry posted on a private, password-protected forum. Reads mss in the summer." Prefers submissions from skilled, experienced poets; will consider work from beginning poets. Acquires one-time rights. Pays contributor's copy upon publication. Publishes ms 4-8 months after acceptance. Responds to mss in 1 week-9 months. Sample copy: $15. Lifetime subscription: $75. Guidelines available free for SASE or on website.

○ The journal received a *Library Journal* award for being one of the 10 best lit mags published in 2012. Has published work by Charles Bukowski, Lawrence Ferlinghetti, Edward Abbey, Gary Snyder, Anne Waldman, Ed Sanders, Tyrone Jaeger, Jean Genet, Louis-Ferdinand Céline, Antler, David Gessner, C.D. Wright, and Amiri Baraka.

MAGAZINES NEEDS "All forms and styles are welcome, especially those that take risks and shoot for something new." Submit in e-mail as attachment. Receives about 777 poems/year; accepts 17. Sometimes comments on rejected poems. Does not want rhyming, repetitive, pastoral, or religious poetry. Length: 1-111 lines. Pays contributor's copy.

TIPS "Our guidelines are very open and ambiguous. Don't send us too much, and don't make it too long. If you submit in an e-mail, use Word or RTF. We're easy. If it works, we'll be in touch. It's a brutal world—wear your helmet."

TOASTED CHEESE

E-mail: editors@toasted-cheese.com. **E-mail:** submit@toasted-cheese.com. **Website:** www.toasted-cheese.com. "*Toasted Cheese* accepts submissions of previously unpublished fiction, flash fiction, creative nonfiction, poetry, and book reviews. See site for book review requirements and guidelines. Our focus is on quality of work, not quantity. Some issues will therefore contain fewer or more pieces than previous issues. We don't restrict publication based on subject matter. We encourage submissions from innovative writers in all genres." Acquires electronic rights. Responds in 4 months to mss. Sample copy online. Follow online submission guidelines.

MAGAZINES NEEDS Receives 150 unsolicited mss/month. Accepts 1-10 mss/issue; 5-30 mss/year. Publishes 15 new writers/year. Send complete ms in body of e-mail; no attachments. Accepts submissions by e-mail. Sponsors awards/contests "No first drafts."

TIPS "We are looking for clean, professional writing from writers of any level. Accepted stories will be concise and compelling. We are looking for writers who are serious about the craft: tomorrow's literary stars before they're famous. Take your submission seriously, yet remember that levity is appreciated. You are submitting not to traditional 'editors' but to fellow writers who appreciate the efforts of those in the trenches. Follow online submission guidelines."

TRANSFERENCE

Department of World Languages and Literatures at Western Michigan University, 1903 West Michigan Ave., Kalamazoo MI 49008-5338. **E-mail:** lang-transference@wmich.edu; molly.lynde-recchia@wmich.edu. **E-mail:** david.kutzko@wmich.edu. **Website:** scholarworks.wmich.edu/transference. **Contact:** Molly Lynde-Recchia and David Kutzko, editors. Annual literary magazine. Publishes poetry from Arabic, Chinese, French and Old French, German, Classical Greek and Latin, Japanese, and Russian into English, along with short reflections on the art of translation and the choices and challenges involved with the process. Retains first North American serial rights and electronic rights. Does not offer payment. Publishes ms 4 months after acceptance. Responds in 3 months to mss; in 1 month to queries. Editorial lead time is 6 months. Sample copy available online, or send SASE and $10. Guidelines available online at scholarworks.wmich.edu/transference/policies.html.

MAGAZINES NEEDS Poetry must be a translation from another language into English. No minimum or maximum line length. Does not pay.

TIPS "Submitting poets should have a working knowledge of the source language of their poetry and should include a short discussion of their translation approach. Authors should also be sure to have the rights of the original poem they are translating to be submitted along with the original text and the translated poem."

TRAVEL NATURALLY

Internaturally, Inc., P.O. Box 317, Newfoundland NJ 07435-0317. (973)697-3552. **Fax:** (973)697-8313. **E-mail:** naturally@internaturally.com. **Website:** www.internaturally.com. "*Travel Naturally* looks at why millions of people believe that removing clothes in public is a good idea, and at places specifically created for that purpose—with good humor, but also in earnest. *Travel Naturally* takes you to places where your personal freedom is the only agenda and to places where textile-free living is a serious commitment." Buys first rights, buys one-time rights. Pays on publication. Editorial lead time 4 months. Sample copy: $9.95 (back issue).

○ *Travel Naturally* is 72 pages, magazine-sized, printed on glossy paper, saddle-stapled.

MAGAZINES NEEDS Wants poetry about the naturalness of the human body and nature; any length. Considers previously published poems and simultaneous submissions. Accepts e-mail and fax submissions. "Name and address must be submitted with e-mail."

TIPS "*Travel Naturally* invokes the philosophies of naturism and nudism, but also activities and beliefs in the mainstream that express themselves, barely: spiritual awareness, New Age customs, pagan and religious rites, alternative and fringe-lifestyle beliefs, artistic expressions, and many individual nude interests. Our higher purpose is simply to help restore our sense of self. Although the term 'nude recreation' may, for some, conjure up visions of sexual frivolities inappropriate for youngsters—because that can also be technically true—these topics are outside the scope of *Travel Naturally*. Here the emphasis is on the many varieties of human beings, of all ages and backgrounds, recreating in their most natural state, at extraordinary places, their reasons for doing so, and the benefits they derive. We incorporate a travel department to advise and book vacations in locations reviewed in travel articles."

TRIBECA POETRY REVIEW

E-mail: editor@tribecareview.org. **Website:** www.tribecareview.org. **Contact:** Kenlynne Rini Mulroy, editor. *Tribeca Poetry Review*, published biennially in even-numbered years, is "a publication that emerged out of the thick poetic history that is downtown New York. It seeks to expose its readers to the best smattering of poetry we can get our inky hands on. *TPR* showcases new pieces by seasoned poets as well as illuminates the work of fresh voices." Acquires first North American serial rights. Time between acceptance and publication is up to 2 years. Sometimes comments on rejected poems. Responds as soon as possible; can be up to 6 months. Guidelines on website. Now only accepting electronic submissions to editor@tribecareview.org.

○ *Tribeca Poetry Review* is approximately 100 pages, digest-sized, professionally printed, flat-spine bound, with artwork cover. Press run is 1,000. Reads submissions September-May.

MAGAZINES NEEDS Submit up to 5 poems at a time in body of e-mail, *not as attachments*, to editor@tribecareview.org. Cover letter is encouraged. "Please do not use your cover letter as a place to explain your poems. The letter is a place to introduce yourself and your work but not sell or explain either." Wants "the kind of poetry that squirms in your head for days, hopefully longer, after reading it. Send us your best work. Will publish all forms (including traditional poesy, spoken word, or your experimental pieces) providing they translate well on the page, are intelligent, and are well crafted. New York City poets are always encouraged to submit their work, but this is *not* strictly a regional publication. Does not want "overly self-absorbed poems; pieces so abstract that all meaning and pleasure is lost on anyone but the poet; first drafts, goofy word play, trite nostalgia." Considers poetry by teens. "It's the poem itself that needs to resonate with readers, so the age of the poet means little. Occasionally, poetry by a 14-year-old is more profound than the drivel generated by those adults who hang out unnecessarily in coffee shops and believe themselves 'poets.'" Pays 2 contributor's copies.

TRIQUARTERLY

School of Continuing Studies, Northwestern University, 339 E. Chicago Ave., Chicago IL 60611. **E-mail:** triquarterly@northwestern.edu. **Website:** www.triquarterly.org. **Contact:** Adrienne Gunn, managing editor. *TriQuarterly*, the literary magazine of Northwestern University, welcomes submissions of fiction, creative nonfiction, poetry, short drama, and hybrid work. "We also welcome short-short prose pieces." Reading period: February 16-July 15.

MAGAZINES NEEDS Submit up to 6 poems via online submissions manager. Pays honoraria.

TIPS "We are especially interested in work that embraces the world and continues, however subtly, the ongoing global conversation about culture and society that *TriQuarterly* pursued from its beginning in 1964."

TULANE REVIEW

Tulane University, 122 Norman Mayer, New Orleans LA 70118. **E-mail:** tulane.review@gmail.com; litsoc@tulane.edu. **Website:** www.tulane.edu/~litsoc/index.html. *Tulane Review*, published biannually, is a national literary journal seeking quality submissions of prose, poetry, and art. Acquires first North American serial rights, second serial rights. Single copy: $8; subscription: $15. Make checks payable to *Tulane Review*.

○ *Tulane Review* is the recipient of an AWP Literary Magazine Design Award. *Tulane Review* is 70 pages, 7x9, perfect-bound, with 100# cover with full-color artwork.

MAGAZINES NEEDS Considers all types of poetry. Wants imaginative poems with bold, inventive images. Receives about 1,200 poems/year, accepts about 50 per issue. Has published poetry by Tom Chandler, Ace Boggess, Carol Hamilton, and Brady Rhoades. Submit up to 5 poems via online submissions manager. No longer accepts paper and e-mail submissions. Pays 2 contributor's copies.

TULE REVIEW

P.O. Box 160406, Sacramento CA 95816. (916)451-5569. **E-mail:** info@sacpoetrycenter@gmail.com. **Website:** www.sacramentopoetrycenter.org. **Contact:** Frank Dixon Graham, editor-in-chief; Linda Collins, associate editor; Connie Gutowsky, associate editor. *Tule Review*, published 1-2 times/year, uses "poetry, book reviews, and essays concerning contemporary poetry" Acquires first North American serial rights. Publishes ms 1-6 months after acceptance. Responds in 3-4 monts. Guidelines and upcoming themes available by e-mail, or on website.

○ *Tule Review* accepts poetry and cover art submissions on a rolling basis, from May 1 to April 30. All material should be submitted through Submittable.com.

MAGAZINES NEEDS Submit up to 6 poems at a time using online submission form. Provide short, 5 line bio. Reads submissions year round. Wants "all styles and forms of poetry." Primarily publishes poets living in the greater Sacramento area, but accepts work from anywhere. Length: 96 lines maximum. Pays 1 contributor's copy.

☺ URTHONA MAGAZINE

71 The Broadway, Granchester, Cambridge CB3 9NQ, UK. **E-mail:** urthonamag@gmail.com. **Website:** www.urthona.com. *Urthona*, published biannually, explores the arts and Western culture from a Buddhist perspective. Wants "poetry rousing the imagination." Does not want "undigested autobiography, political, or New Age-y poems." Acquires one-time rights. Publishes ms 8 months after acceptance. Responds in 6 months. Sample copy (including guidelines): $7.99 USD, $8.99 CAD."See website for current subscription rates."

Ⓞ *Urthona* is 60 pages, A4, offset-printed, saddle-stapled, with 4-color glossy cover; includes ads. Receives about 300 poems/year, accepts about 40. Press run is 1,200 (200 subscribers, plus shelf sales in Australia and America).

MAGAZINES NEEDS Submit up to 6 poems at a time. Accepts e-mail submissions (as attachment). Cover letter is preferred. Poems are circulated to an editorial board and are read and selected by poetry editor. Other editors have right of veto. Has published poetry by Peter Abbs, Robert Bly, and Peter Redgrove. Pays 1 contributor's copy.

ALSO OFFERS Reviews books/chapbooks of poetry and other magazines in 600 words. Send materials for review consideration.

U.S. 1 WORKSHEETS

U.S. 1 Poets' Cooperative, U.S. 1 Worksheets, P.O. Box 127, Kingston NJ 08528. **E-mail:** us1poets@gmail.com. **Website:** www.us1poets.com. "*U.S. 1 Worksheets*, published annually, uses high-quality poetry and prose poems. We prefer complex, well-written work." Responds in 3-6 months to mss. Guidelines available online.

MAGAZINES NEEDS Submit up to 5 poems at a time, no more than 7 pages total. Considers simultaneous submissions if indicated; no previously published poems. "We are looking for well-crafted poetry with a focused point of view."

ADDITIONAL INFORMATION The U.S. 1 Poets' Cooperative co-sponsors (with the Delaware Valley Poets) a series of monthly poetry readings at the Princeton Public Library. "The group is open to poets who want to share their original work and receive feedback."

TIPS "Mss are accepted from April 15-June 30 and are read by rotating editors from the cooperative. Send us something unusual, something we haven't read before, but make sure it's poetry. Proofread carefully."

⑤ U.S. CATHOLIC

Claretian Publications, 205 W. Monroe St., Chicago IL 60606. (312)236-7782. **Fax:** (312)236-8207. **E-mail:** editors@uscatholic.org. **E-mail:** submissions@uscatholic.org. **Website:** www.uscatholic.org. "*U.S. Catholic* puts faith in the context of everyday life. With a strong focus on social justice, we offer a fresh and balanced take on the issues that matter most in our world, adding a faith perspective to such challenges as poverty, education, family life, the environment, and even pop culture." Buys all rights. Pays on acceptance. Publishes ms an average of 6 months after acceptance. Responds in 1 month to queries; in 2 months to mss. Editorial lead time 8 months. Guidelines on website.

Ⓞ Please include SASE with written ms.

MAGAZINES NEEDS Submit 3-5 poems at a time. Accepts e-mail submissions (pasted into body of message or as attachments). Cover letter is preferred. No light verse. Length: up to 50 lines/poem. Pays $75.

○⑤ VALLUM: CONTEMPORARY POETRY

5038 Sherbrooke West, P.O. Box 23077, CP Vendome, Montreal Quebec H4A 1T0, Canada. (514)937-8946. **Fax:** (514)937-8946. **E-mail:** info@vallummag.com. **E-mail:** editors@vallummag.com. **Website:** www.vallummag.com. **Contact:** Joshua Auerbach and Eleni Zisimatos, editors. Poetry/fine arts magazine published twice/year. Publishes exciting interplay of poets and artists. Content for magazine is selected according to themes listed on website. Material is not filed but is returned upon request by SASE. E-mail response is preferred. Seeking exciting, unpublished, traditional or avant-garde poetry that reflects contemporary experience. Buys first North American serial rights. Copyright remains with the author. Pays on publication. Sample copies available for $10. Guidelines available on website.

Vallum is 100 pages, digest sized (7x8½), digitally printed, perfect-bound, with color images on coated stock cover. Includes ads. Single copy: $12 CDN; subscription: $20/year CDN; $24 U.S. (shipping included). Make checks payable to *Vallum*.

MAGAZINES NEEDS Pays honorarium for accepted poems.

ADDITIONAL INFORMATION "The Vallum Chapbook Series publishes 2-3 chapbooks by both well-known and emerging poets. Past editions include *Gospel of X* by George Elliott Clarke, *The Art of Fugue* by Jan Zwicky and *Address* by Franz Wright. *Vallum* does not currently accept unsolicited mss for this project."

CONTEST/AWARD OFFERINGS "Sponsors annual contest. First Prize: $750, Second Prize: $250 and publication in an issue of *Vallum*. Honourable mentions may be selected but are not eligible for cash prizes. Submit 3 poems. Entry fee: $205USD / CAD (includes subscription to *Vallum*). Deadline: July 15. Guidelines available in magazine, by e-mail, and on website. Poems may be submitted in any style or on any subject; max. 3 poems, up to 60 lines per poem. Entries should be labelled 'Vallum Contest' and submitted online or by regular mail. Submissions are not returned. Winners will be notified via e-mail."

VALPARAISO POETRY REVIEW

Department of English, Valparaiso University, Valparaiso IN 46383-6493. (219)464-5278. **Fax:** (219)464-5511. **E-mail:** vpr@valpo.edu. **Website:** www.valpo.edu/vpr. **Contact:** Edward Byrne, editor. *Valparaiso Poetry Review: Contemporary Poetry and Poetics*, published semiannually online, accepts "submissions of unpublished poetry, book reviews, author interviews, and essays on poetry or poetics that have not yet appeared online and for which the rights belong to the author. Query for anything else." Acquires one-time rights. "All rights remain with author." Publishes ms 6-12 months after acceptance. Responds in 6 weeks. Guidelines online.

MAGAZINES NEEDS Wants poetry of any length or style, free verse, or traditional forms. Submit 3-5 poems at a time. Accepts e-mail submissions only. Reads submissions year round. Seldom comments on rejected poems. Receives about 9,000 poems/year, accepts about 1%. Has published poetry by Charles Wright, Cornelius Eady, Dorianne Laux, Dave Smith, Claudia Emerson, Billy Collins, Brian Turner, Daisy Fried, Stanley Plumly, and Annie Finch.

ALSO OFFERS Reviews books of poetry in single- and multibook formats. Send materials for review consideration.

VAN GOGH'S EAR: BEST WORLD POETRY & PROSE

French Connection Press, 12 Rue Lamartine, Paris 75009, France. (33)(1)4016-1147. **E-mail:** tinafayeayres@gmail.com. **Website:** www.frenchcx.com; theoriginalvangoghsearanthology.com. *Van Gogh's Ear*, published annually in April, is an anthology series "devoted to publishing powerful poetry and prose in English and English translations by major voices and innovative new talents from around the globe." Acquires one-time rights. Time between acceptance and publication is 1 year. Responds in 9 months. Seldom comments on rejections. Always sends prepublication galleys. Single copy: $19; subscription: $36 for 2 years. Guidelines available in anthology or on website. "Every submission is closely read by all members of the editorial board and voted upon. Our continued existence, and continued ability to read your work, depends mainly on subscriptions/donations. Therefore, we must ask that you at least purchase a sample copy before submitting work."

Van Gogh's Ear is 280 pages, digest-sized, offset-printed, perfect-bound, with 4-color matte cover with commissioned artwork. Poetry published in *Van Gogh's Ear* has appeared in *The Best American Poetry*.

MAGAZINES NEEDS Receives about 1,000 poems/year, accepts about 30%. Press run is 2,000 (105 subscribers, 25 libraries, 1,750 shelf/online sales); 120 distributed free to contributors and reviewers. Has published poetry by Tony Curtis, Yoko Ono, James Dean, Xaviera Hollander, and Charles Manson. Submit up to 6 poems by e-mail. Cover letter is preferred, along with a brief bio of up to 120 words. Length: up to 165 lines/poem. Pays 1 contributor's copy.

TIPS "As a 501(c)(3) nonprofit enterprise, *Van Gogh's Ear* needs the support of individual poets, writers, and readers to survive. Any donation, large or small, will help *Van Gogh's Ear* continue to publish the best cross-section of contemporary poetry and prose. Because of being an anglophone publication based in France, *Van Gogh's Ear* is unable to get any grants or funding. Your contribution will be tax-deductible.

Make donation checks payable to Committee on Poetry-*VGE*, and mail them (donations **only**) to the Allen Ginsberg Trust, P.O. Box 582, Stuyvesant Station, New York NY 10009."

VANILLEROTICA LITERARY EZINE

Cleveland OH 44102. (216)799-9775. **E-mail:** talent-dripseroticpublishing@yahoo.com. **Website:** eroti-catalentdrips.wordpress.com. **Contact:** Kimberly Steele, founder. *Vanillerotica*, published monthly online, focuses solely on showcasing new erotic fiction. Acquires electronic rights only. Rights revert to authors and poets upon publication. Work archived on the site for 2 months. Time between acceptance and publication is 2 months. Responds to general and submission queries within a week. Guidelines on website.

MAGAZINES NEEDS Submit by e-mail to talent-dripseroticpublishing@yahoo.com. Accepts e-mail pasted into body of message. Reads submissions during publication months only. Length: up to 30 lines/poem. Pays $10 for each accepted poem.

CONTEST/AWARD OFFERINGS *Vanillerotica Literary EZine* Poet of the Year Contest is held annually. **Prizes:** $75, $50, and certificate. **Deadline:** November 25. Guidelines on website.

TIPS "Please read our take on the difference between *erotica* and *pornography*; it's on the website. *Vanillerotica* does not accept pornography. And please keep poetry 30 lines or less."

VEGETARIAN JOURNAL

P.O. Box 1463, Baltimore MD 21203-1463. (410)366-8343. **E-mail:** vrg@vrg.org. **Website:** www.vrg.org. **Contact:** Debra Wasserman, editor. Quarterly non-profit vegetarian magazine that examines the health, ecological and ethical aspects of vegetarianism. "Highly-educated audience including health professionals." Sample: $4.

○ *Vegetarian Journal* is 36 pages, magazine-sized, professionally printed, saddle-stapled, with glossy card cover. Press run is 20,000.

MAGAZINES NEEDS "Please, no submissions of poetry from adults; 18 and under only."

CONTEST/AWARD OFFERINGS The Vegetarian Resource Group offers an annual contest for ages 18 and under: $50 prize in 3 age categories for the best contribution on any aspect of vegetarianism. "Most entries are essay, but we would accept poetry with enthusiasm." **Deadline:** May 1 (postmark). Details available at website: http://www.vrg.org/essay/

TIPS Areas most open to freelancers are recipe section and feature articles. "Review magazine first to learn our style. Send query letter with photocopy sample of line drawings of food."

VERANDAH LITERARY & ART JOURNAL

Faculty of Arts, Deakin University, 221 Burwood Hwy., Burwood, Victoria 3125, Australia. (61)(3)9251-7134. **E-mail:** verandah@deakin.edu.au. **Website:** www.deakin.edu.au/verandah. *Verandah*, published annually in August, is a high-quality literary journal edited by professional writing students. It aims to give voice to new and innovative writers and artists. Acquires first Australian publishing rights. Sample: $20 AUD. Guidelines available on website.

○ Submission period: February 1-June 5. Has published work by Christos Tsiolka, Dorothy Porter, Seamus Heaney, Les Murray, Ed Burger, and John Muk Muk Burke. *Verandah* is 120 pages, professionally printed on glossy stock, flat-spined, with full-color glossy card cover.

MAGAZINES NEEDS Submit by mail or e-mail. However, electronic version of work must be available if accepted by *Verandah*. Do not submit work without the required submission form (available for download on website). Reads submissions by June 5 deadline (postmark). Length: 100 lines maximum. Pays 1 contributor's copy, "with prizes awarded accordingly."

VERSE

English Department, University of Richmond, Richmond VA 23173. **Website:** http://versemag.blogspot.com. **Contact:** Brian Henry, co-editor; Andrew Zawacki, co-editor. *Verse*, published 3 times/year, is an international poetry journal which also publishes interviews with poets, essays on poetry, and book reviews. Wants no specific kind; looks for high-quality, innovative poetry. Focus is not only on American poetry, but on all poetry written in English, as well as translations. Has published poetry by James Tate, John Ashbery, Barbara Guest, Gustaf Sobin, and Rae Armantrout.

○ *Verse* is 128-416 pages, digest-sized, professionally printed, perfect-bound, with card cover. Receives about 5,000 poems/year, accepts 10%. Press run is 1,000. Single copy: $10; subscription: $18 for individuals, $39 for institutions. Sample: $6. *Verse* has a $10 reading fee for the print edition. Note that *Verse* will sometimes publish individual pieces on the website if they decide not to publish the entire body of work.

MAGAZINES NEEDS Submissions should be chapbook-length (20-40 pages). Pays $10/page, $250 minimum.

TIPS "Read widely and deeply. Avoid inundating a magazine with submissions; constant exposure will not increase your chances of getting accepted."

VINE LEAVES LITERARY JOURNAL

Canada. **E-mail:** vineleaves.editors@gmail.com. **Website:** www.vineleavesliteraryjournal.com. **Contact:** Jessica Bell, publishing editor. Quarterly online/annual print literary magazine. "The world of literature nowadays is so diverse, open-minded, and thriving in experimental works that there doesn't seem to be any single form of written art missing from it ... you would think. But there is. The vignette. It's rare for a literary magazine to accept the 'vignette' as a publishable piece of literature. Why? Because it is not a 'proper story.' We beg to differ. So, what is a vignette? *Vignette* is a word that originally meant 'something that may be written on a vine-leaf.' It's a snapshot in words. It differs from flash fiction or a short story in that its aim doesn't lie within the traditional realms of structure or plot. Instead, the vignette focuses on 1 element, mood, character, setting, or object. It's descriptive, excellent for character or theme exploration and wordplay. Through a vignette, you create an atmosphere. *Vine Leaves* will entwine you in atmosphere, wrap you in a world where literature ferments and then matures." Rights remain with author. Publishes ms 1 month after acceptance. Editorial lead time is 3 months. Sample copy and guidelines available online. See website for payment rates.

MAGAZINES NEEDS Length: up to 40 lines.

TIPS "Please see guidelines on website. Also the vignette-writing tips page."

THE VIRGINIA QUARTERLY REVIEW

P.O. Box 400223, Charlottesville VA 22904. **E-mail:** vqr@vqronline.org. **Website:** www.vqronline.org. **Contact:** W. Ralph Eubanks, editor. "*VQR*'s primary mission has been to sustain and strengthen Jefferson's bulwark, long describing itself as 'A National Journal of Literature and Discussion.' And for good reason. From its inception in prohibition, through depression and war, in prosperity and peace, *The Virginia Quarterly Review* has been a haven—and home—for the best essayists, fiction writers, and poets, seeking contributors from every section of the United States and abroad. It has not limited itself to any special field. No topic has been alien: literary, public affairs, the arts, history, the economy. If it could be approached through essay or discussion, poetry or prose, *VQR* has covered it." Press run is 4,000. Buys first North American print and digital magazine rights; nonexclusive online rights; and other limited rights. Responds in 3 months to mss. Guidelines on website.

MAGAZINES NEEDS Sponsors the Emily Clark Balch Prize for Poetry, an annual award of $1,000 given to the best poem or group of poems published in the *Review* during the year. *The Virginia Quarterly Review* prints approximately 12 pages of poetry in each issue. No length or subject restrictions. Issues have largely included lyric and narrative free verse, most of which features a strong message or powerful voice. Accepts online submissions only at virginiaquarterlyreview.submittable.com/submit. Pays $200/poem (up to 50 lines); $300/poem (50-plus lines).

VOICES ISRAEL

P.O. Box 21, Metulla 10292, Israel. **E-mail:** voicesisraelpoetryanthology@gmail.com. **Website:** www.voicesisrael.com. **Contact:** Dina Yehuda, editor. *Voices Israel*, published annually by The Voices Israel Group of Poets, is "an anthology of poetry in English, with worldwide contributions. We consider all kinds of poetry." Poems must be in English; translations must be accompanied by the original poem. Single copy: $25 for nonmembers. Sample: $15 (back issue). "Members receive the anthology with annual dues ($35)."

Voices Israel is about 300 pages, digest-sized, offset from laser output on ordinary paper, flatspined, with varying cover. Press run is 350.

MAGAZINES NEEDS Submit up to 3 poems/year via online submissions manager. "We do not guarantee publication of any poem. In poems we publish, we reserve the right to correct obviously unintentional errors in spelling, punctuation, etc."

ALSO OFFERS The annual International Reuben Rose Memorial Poetry Competition offers 1st Prize: $500; 2nd Prize $200; 3rd Prize: $100; and Honorable Mentions. Winning poems are published and distributed together with the *Voices Israel* anthology.

THE WALLACE STEVENS JOURNAL

University of Antwerp, Prinsstraat 13, 2000 Antwerp, Belgium. **E-mail:** bart.eeckhout@uantwerp.be; jforjames@aol.com. **Website:** www.press.jhu.edu/journals/wallace_stevens_journal. **Contact:** Bart Eeckhout, editor; James Finnegan, poetry editor. *The Wallace Stevens Journal*, published semiannually by the Wallace Stevens Society, welcomes submissions on all aspects of Wallace Stevens's poetry and life. Subscription: $30 (includes membership in the Wallace Stevens Society).

○ *The Wallace Stevens Journal* is 100-160 pages, digest-sized, typeset, flat-spined, with glossy cover with art. Receives 200 poems/year, accepts 15-20. Press run is 400 + institutional subscriptions through Project Muse (Johns Hopkins University Press).

MAGAZINES NEEDS Has published poetry by David Athey, Jacqueline Marcus, Charles Wright, X.J. Kennedy, A.M. Juster, and Robert Creeley. Submit poems to James Finnegan at jforjames@aol.com.

THE WAR CRY

The Salvation Army, 615 Slaters Lane, Alexandria VA 22314. (703)684-4128. **Fax:** (703)684-5539. **E-mail:** war_cry@usn.salvationarmy.org. **Website:** publications.salvationarmyusa.org. "Inspirational magazine with evangelical emphasis and portrayals that express the mission of the Salvation Army. Fourteen issues published per year, including special Easter and Christmas issues." Buys first rights, buys one-time rights. Pays on publication. Publishes ms an average of 2 months to 1 year after acceptance. Responds in 3-4 weeks to mss. Editorial lead time 2 months before issue date; Christmas and Easter issues: 6 months before issue date. Sample copy, theme list, and writer's guidelines free with #10 SASE or online.

MAGAZINES NEEDS Purchases limited poetry.

WATERWAYS: POETRY IN THE MAINSTREAM

Ten Penny Players, 393 Saint Pauls Ave., Staten Island NY 10304-2127. (718)442-7429. **E-mail:** tenpennyplayers@si.rr.com. **Website:** www.tenpennyplayers.org. **Contact:** Barbara Fisher and Richard Spiegel, poetry editors. *Waterways: Poetry in the Mainstream*, published 11 times/year, prints work by adult poets. "We publish theme issues and are trying to increase an audience for poetry and the printed and performed word. While we do 'themes,' sometimes an idea for a future magazine is inspired by a submission, so we try to remain open to poets' inspirations. Poets should be guided, however, by the fact that we are disabil-

ity, children's, and animal rights advocates and are a NYC press. We are open to reading material from people we have never published, writing in traditional and experimental poetry forms." Acquires one-time rights. Responds in less than 1 month. Sometimes comments on rejected poems. Sample: $5. Subscription: $45. Guidelines available for SASE or on website.

○ *Waterways* is 40 pages, 4.25x7, saddle-stapled. Back issues of *Waterways* are published online at www.tenpennyplayers.org and at scribd.com, in addition to being available in the limited printing paper edition. Accepts 40% of poems submitted. Press run is 150. Has published poetry by Kit Knight, James Penha, William Corner Clarke, Wayne Hogan, Sylvia Manning, and Monique Laforce.

MAGAZINES NEEDS Submit less than 10 poems at a time (for first submission). Accepts e-mail (pasted into body of message) and postal mail submissions (include SASE). Pays 1 contributor's copy.

ALSO OFFERS Ten Penny Players publishes chapbooks "by children and young adults only—not by submission. They come through our workshops in the library and schools. Adult poets are published through our Bard Press imprint, **by invitation only**. Books evolve from the relationship we develop with writers we publish in *Waterways* and to whom we would like to give more exposure."

TIPS "Send for our theme sheet and a sample issue, or view online. Mss that arrive without a return envelope are not sent back."

⑤ WEBER: THE CONTEMPORARY WEST

Weber State University, 1395 Edvalson St., Dept. 1405, Ogden UT 84408-1405. **Website:** www.weber.edu/weberjournal. *Weber: The Contemporary West*, published 2 times/year, "spotlights personal narrative, commentary, fiction, nonfiction, and poetry that speaks to the environment and culture of the American West and beyond." Acquires all rights. Copyright reverts to author after first printing. Publishes ms 15 months after acceptance. Responds in 6 months. Sample: $10 (back issue). Subscription: $20 ($30 for institutions); $40 for outside the U.S. Themes and guidelines available in magazine, for SASE, by e-mail, or on website.

○ Poetry published in *Weber* has appeared in *The Best American Poetry*. *Weber* is 150 pages, offset-printed on acid-free paper, perfect-bound, with color cover. Receives about 250-300 poems/year, accepts 30-40. Press run is 1,000; 80% libraries.

MAGAZINES NEEDS Submit 3-4 poems at a time, 2 copies of each (one without name). "We publish multiple poems from a poet." Cover letter is preferred. Poems are selected by anonymous (blind) evaluation. Always sends prepublication galleys. Has published poetry by Naomi Shihab Nye, Carolyn Forche, Stephen Dunn, Billy Collins, William Kloefkorn, David Lee, Gary Gildner, and Robert Dana. Does not want "poems that are flippant, prurient, sing-song, or preachy." Pays 2 contributor's copies, one-year subscription, and a small honorarium ($100-300) depending on fluctuating grant monies.

ALSO OFFERS The Dr. Sherwin W. Howard Poetry Award, a $500 cash prize, is awarded annually to the author of the best set of poems published in *Weber* during the previous year. The competition is announced each year in the Spring/Summer issue.

WEST BRANCH

Stadler Center for Poetry, Bucknell University, Lewisburg PA 17837-2029. (570)577-1853. **Fax:** (570)577-1885. **E-mail:** westbranch@bucknell.edu. **Website:** www.bucknell.edu/westbranch. **Contact:** G.C. Waldrep, editor. *West Branch* publishes poetry, fiction, and nonfiction in both traditional and innovative styles. Buys first North American serial rights. Pays on publication. Sample copy for $3. Guidelines available online.

Reading period: August 15-April 1. No more than 3 submissions from a single contributor in a given reading period.

MAGAZINES NEEDS Pays $50/submission.

TIPS "All submissions must be sent via our online submission manager. Please see website for guidelines. We recommend that you acquaint yourself with the magazine before submitting."

WESTERLY

University of Wester Australia, The Westerly Centre (M202), Crawley WA 6009, Australia. (61)(8)6488-3403. **Fax:** (61)(8)6488-1030. **E-mail:** westerly@uwa.edu.au. **Website:** westerlymag.com.au. **Contact:** Delys Bird and Tony Hughes-D'Aeth, editors. *Westerly*, published in July and November, prints quality short fiction, poetry, literary criticism, socio-historical articles, and book reviews with special attention given to Australia, Asia, and the Indian Ocean region. "We assume a reasonably well-read, intelligent audience. Past issues of *Westerly* provide the best guides. Not consciously an academic magazine." Acquires first publication rights; requests acknowledgment on reprints. Time between acceptance and publication may be up to 1 year, depending on when work is submitted. "Please wait for a response before forwarding any additional submissions for consideration."

Westerly is about 200 pages, digest-sized, "electronically printed." Press run is 1,200. Subscription information available on website. Deadline for July edition: March 31; deadline for November edition: August 31.

MAGAZINES NEEDS "We don't dictate to writers on rhyme, style, experimentation, or anything else. We are willing to publish short or long poems." Submit up to 3 poems by mail, e-mail, or online submissions form. Pays $75 for 1 page or 1 poem, or $100 for 2 or more pages/poems, and contributor's copies.

ALSO OFFERS The Patricia Hackett Prize (value approximately $750 AUD) is awarded annually for the best contribution published in the previous year's issue of *Westerly*.

WESTERN HUMANITIES REVIEW

University of Utah, English Department, 255 S. Central Campus Dr., Salt Lake City UT 84112-0494. (801)581-6070. **Fax:** (801)585-5167. **E-mail:** whr@mail.hum.utah.edu. **Website:** http://ourworld.info/whrweb/. **Contact:** Barry Weller, editor; Nate Liederbach, managing editor. *Western Humanities Review* is a journal of contemporary literature and culture housed in the University of Utah English Department. Publishes poetry, fiction, nonfiction essays, artwork, and work that resists categorization. Buys one-time rights. Pays in contributor copies. Publishes ms an average of 1 year after acceptance. Responds in 3-5 months. Sample copy for $10. Guidelines available online.

Reading period: September 1-April 15. All submissions must be sent through online submissions manager.

MAGAZINES NEEDS Considers simultaneous submissions but no more than 5 poems or 25 pages per reading period. No fax or e-mail submissions. Reads submissions October 1-April 1 only. Wants quality poetry of any form, including translations. Has published poetry by Charles Simic, Olena Kalytiak Davis, Ravi Shankar, Karen Volkman, Dan Beachy-Quick, Lucie Brock-Broido, Christine Hume, and Dan Chiasson. Innovative prose poems may be submitted as fiction or non-fiction to the appropriate editor. Pays 2 contributor's copies.

CONTEST/AWARD OFFERINGS Sponsors an annual contest for Utah writers.

TIPS "Because of changes in our editorial staff, we urge familiarity with recent issues of the magazine. We do not publish writer's guidelines because we think that the magazine itself conveys an accurate picture of our requirements. Please, no e-mail submissions."

WESTVIEW: A JOURNAL OF WESTERN OKLAHOMA

Southwestern Oklahoma State University, 100 Campus Dr., Weatherford OK 73096. **E-mail:** westview@swosu.edu. **Website:** www.swosu.edu/academics/langarts/westview/. **Contact:** Amanda Smith, editor; Kevin Collins, managing editor. *Westview: A Journal of Western Oklahoma* is published semiannually by the Language Arts Department of Southwestern Oklahoma State University. Publications include previously unpublished fiction, poetry, prose poems, drama, nonfiction, book reviews, literary criticism, and artwork. *Westview* holds only first rights for all works published. Sample: $6.

Has published poetry by Carolynne Wright, Miller Williams, Walter McDonald, Robert Cooperman, Alicia Ostriker, and James Whitehead. *Westview* is 64 pages, magazine-sized, perfect-bound, with full-color glossy card cover. Receives about 500 poems/year; accepts 7%. Press run is 600 (250 subscribers; about 25 libraries). Subscription: $15/2 years; $25/ 2 years international.

WESTWARD QUARTERLY: THE MAGAZINE OF FAMILY READING

Laudemont Press, P.O. Box 369, Hamilton IL 62341. (800)440-4043. **E-mail:** editor@wwquarterly.com. **Website:** www.wwquarterly.com. **Contact:** Shirley Anne Leonard, editor. *WestWard Quarterly: The Magazine of Family Reading* prints poetry. Acquires one-time rights. Responds in "weeks." Often comments on rejected poems. Single copy: $4 ($6 foreign); subscription: $15/year ($18 foreign). Contributors to an issue may order extra copies at a discounted price. Make checks payable to Laudemont Press. Guidelines available for SASE, by e-mail, or on website.

Every issue includes a "Featured Writer" and a piece on improving writing skills or writing different forms of poetry. *WestWard Quarterly* is 32 pages, digest-sized, laser-printed, saddle-stapled, with inkjet color cover with scenic photos, includes ads. Receives about 1,500 poems/year, accepts about 12%. Press run is 150 (60 subscribers).

MAGAZINES NEEDS Wants "all forms, including rhyme—we welcome inspirational, positive, reflective, humorous material promoting nobility, compassion, and courage." Does not want "experimental or avant-garde forms, offensive language, depressing or negative poetry." Submit up to 5 poems at a time. Prefers e-mail submissions (pasted into body of message); no disk submissions. Reads submissions year round. Considers poetry by children and teens. Has published poetry by Wynne Alexander, Leland Jamieson, Joyce I. Johnson, Michael Keshigian, Richard Luftig, Arlene Mandell, Dennis Ross, J. Alvin Speers, Jane Stuart, and Charles Waugaman. Length: up to 40 lines/poem. Pays 1 contributor's copy.

WHISKEY ISLAND MAGAZINE

English Dept., Cleveland State University, Cleveland OH 44115. (216)687-3951. **E-mail:** whiskeyisland@csuohio.edu. **Website:** whiskeyislandmagazine.com. "*Whiskey Island* is a nonprofit literary magazine that has been published in one form or another by students of Cleveland State University for over 30 years." Responds in 3 months to mss. Sample copy: $6.

Reading periods: August 15-November 15 and January 15-April 15. Paper and e-mail submissions are not accepted. No multiple submissions.

MAGAZINES NEEDS "Submit 3-5 poems via online submissions manager. Please combine all the poems you wish to submit into one document." Pays 2 contributor's copies.

WICKED ALICE

E-mail: wickedalicepoetry@yahoo.com. **Website:** www.sundresspublications.com/wickedalice. **Contact:** Kristy Bowen, editor. "*Wicked Alice* is a women-centered poetry journal dedicated to publishing quality work by both sexes, depicting and exploring the female experience." Wants "work that has a strong sense of image and music. Work that is interesting and surprising, with innovative, sometimes unusual, use of language. We love humor when done well, strangeness, wackiness. Hybridity, collage, intertexuality." Acquires one-time rights. Responds in 1-6 months. Guidelines online.

MAGAZINES NEEDS Submit 3-5 poems via e-mail. Has published poetry by Daniela Olszewska, Rebecca Loudon, Robyn Art, Simone Muench, Brandi Homan, and Karyna McGlynn. Receives about 500 poems/year, accepts about 8%. Does not want greeting card verse. Length: open.

WILD GOOSE POETRY REVIEW

Hickory NC 28235-5009. **E-mail:** asowens1@yahoo.com. **Website:** www.wildgoosepoetryreview.com. *Wild Goose Poetry Review* is "looking for good contemporary poetry. No particular biases. We enjoy humor, strong imagery, strong lines, narrative, lyric, etc. Not a fan of abstraction, cliché, form for the sake of form, shock for the sake of shock. As in any good poem, everything should be purposeful." Author retains all rights. Time between acceptance and publication is up to 3 months. Usually responds to mss within 1 month.

Receives more than 1,000 poems/year, accepts less than 10%. Reviews books/chapbooks of poetry. Send materials for review consideration to Scott Owens. Has published poetry by Anthony Abbott, Karen Douglass, and Lisa Zaran.

MAGAZINES NEEDS Accepts e-mail submissions only, pasted into body of e-mail; no attachments; no disk submissions. Cover letter is preferred; include bio. Reads submissions year round.

WILD VIOLET

P.O. Box 39706, Philadelphia PA 19106. **E-mail:** wildvioletmagazine@yahoo.com. **Website:** www.wildviolet.net. **Contact:** Alyce Wilson, editor. *Wild Violet*, published weekly online, aims "to make the arts more accessible, to make a place for the arts in modern life, and to serve as a creative forum for writers and artists. Our audience includes English-speaking readers from all over the world who are interested in both 'high art' and pop culture." Requests limited electronic rights for online publication and archival only. Time between acceptance and publication is 6 months. "Decisions on acceptance or rejection are made by the editor." Responds in 1 week to queries; 3-6 months to mss. Guidelines online by e-mail or on website.

MAGAZINES NEEDS Wants "poetry that is well crafted, that engages thought, that challenges or up-

lifts the reader. We have published free verse, haiku, blank verse, and other forms. If the form suits the poem, we will consider any form." Does not want "abstract, self-involved poetry; poorly managed form; excessive rhyming; self-referential poems that do not show why the speaker is sad, happy, or in love." Has published poetry by Lyn Lifshin, Kimberly Gladman, Andrew H. Oerke, Simon Perchik, John Grey, Joanna Weston, and Amy Barone. Accepts about 15% of work submitted. Submit 3-5 poems at a time. Accepts e-mail submissions (pasted into body of message, or as text or Word attachment) and postal mail submissions; no disk submissions. Cover letter is preferred. Reads submissions year round. Seldom comments on rejected poems, unless requested. Occasionally publishes theme issues.

ALSO OFFERS Reviews books/chapbooks of poetry in 250 words, single-book format. Query for review consideration. Sponsors an annual poetry contest, offering 1st Prize: $100 and publication in *Wild Violet*; 2 Honorable Mentions will also be published. Guidelines available by e-mail or on website. **Entry fee:** $5/poem. Judged by independent judges.

TIPS "We look for stories that are well-paced and show character and plot development. Even short shorts should do more than simply paint a picture. Manuscripts stand out when the author's voice is fresh and engaging. Avoid muddying your story with too many characters, and don't attempt to shock the reader with an ending you have not earned. Experiment with styles and structures, but don't resort to experimentation for its own sake."

WILLARD & MAPLE

163 S. Willard St., Freeman 302, Box 34, Burlington VT 05401. (802)860-2700 ext.2462. **E-mail:** willardandmaple@champlain.edu. **Website:** www.champlain.edu/student-life/campus-life/activities-and-clubs/student-publications/willard-and-maple. *Willard & Maple*, published annually in spring, is a student-run literary magazine from Champlain College's Professional Writing Program that considers short fiction, essays, reviews, fine art, and poetry by adults, children, and teens. Wants creative work of the highest quality. Acquires one-time rights. Time between acceptance and publication is less than 1 year. Responds in 6 months to queries; in 6 months to mss. Single copy: $12. Contact Lulu Press for contributor's copy. Writer's guidelines for SASE or send e-mail.

○ *Willard & Maple* is 200 pages, digest-sized, digitally printed, perfect-bound. Receives about 500 poems/year, accepts about 20%. Press run is 600 (80 subscribers, 4 libraries); 200 are distributed free to the Champlain College writing community.

MAGAZINES NEEDS Send up to 5 poems via e-mail or postal mail. Send SASE for return of ms or send disposable copy of mss and #10 SASE for reply only. Length: up to 100 lines/poem. Pays 2 contributor's copies.

TIPS "The power of imagination makes us infinite."

WILLOW REVIEW

College of Lake County Publications, College of Lake County, 19351 W. Washington St., Grayslake IL 60030-1198. (847)543-2956. **E-mail:** com426@clcillinois.edu. **Website:** www.clcillinois.edu/community/willowreview.asp. **Contact:** Michael Latza, editor. *Willow Review*, published annually, is interested in poetry, creative nonfiction, and fiction of high quality. "We have no preferences as to form, style, or subject, as long as each piece stands on its own as art and communicates ideas." All rights revert to author upon publication. Responds in 3-4 months to mss. Sample: $5 (back issue). Subscription: $18/3 issues, $30/6 issues. International: add $5 per issue. Guidelines available on website.

○ The editors award prizes for best poetry and prose in the issue. Prize awards vary contingent on the current year's budget but normally range from $100-400. There is no reading fee or separate application for these prizes. All accepted mss are eligible. "*Willow Review* can be found on EBSCOhost databases, assuring a broader targeted audience for our authors' work. *Willow Review* is a nonprofit journal partially supported by a grant from the Illinois Arts Council (a state agency), College of Lake County Publications, private contributions, and sales."

MAGAZINES NEEDS Considers simultaneous submissions "if indicated in the cover letter." No e-mail submissions; postal submissions only. Include SASE; mss will not be returned unless requested. Reads submissions September-May. Has published poetry by Lisel Mueller, Lucien Stryk, David Ray, Louis Rodriguez, John Dickson, and Patricia Smith. Pays 2 contributor's copies.

ALSO OFFERS Prizes totaling $400 are awarded to the best poetry and short fiction/creative nonfiction in each issue. The College of Lake County Reading Series (4-7 readings/academic year) has included Thomas Lux, Isabel Allende, Donald Justice, Galway Kinnell, Lisel Mueller, Amiri Baraka, and others. One reading is for contributors to *Willow Review*. Readings, usually held on Thursday evenings and widely publicized in Chicago and suburban newspapers, are presented to audiences of about 150 students and faculty of the College of Lake County and other area colleges, as well as residents of local communities.

WINDFALL: A JOURNAL OF POETRY OF PLACE

Windfall Press, P.O. Box 19007, Portland OR 97280-0007. **E-mail:** bsiverly@comcast.net. **Website:** www.windfalljournal.com. **Contact:** Bill Siverly and Michael McDowell, co-editors. *Windfall: A Journal of Poetry of Place*, published semiannually in March and September, is "looking for poems of place, specifically places in the Pacific Northwest (the broad bioregion extending from the North Slope of Alaska to the San Francisco Bay Area, and from the Rocky Mountains to the Pacific Coast). 'Place' can be named or unnamed, but if unnamed, then location should be clearly implied or suggested by observed detail. The poet does not have to be living in the Pacific Northwest, but the poem does. We favor poetry based on imagery derived from sensory observation. *Windfall* also favors poetry that occurs in lines and stanzas." Does not want "language poetry, metapoetry, surrealism, 'Internet poetry' (constructed from search engine information rather than experience), abstract, or self-centered poetry of any kind." Acquires first North American serial rights. "Poem may appear in sample pages on *Windfall* website." Rights revert to poet upon publication. Publishes ms 2 months after acceptance. Responds within 6 months ("depends on when poems are submitted in the biannual cycle"). Single copy: $7; subscription: $14/year. Make checks payable to Windfall Press. Guidelines available in magazine or on website.

○ Has published poetry by Judith Barrington, Gloria Bird, Barbara Drake, Clem Starck, Tom Wayman, and Robert Wrigley. *Windfall* is 52 pages, digest-sized, stapled, with art on covers ("all are drawings or prints by Portland artist Sharon Bronzan"). Receives about 160 poems/year, accepts about 60. Press run is 250.

MAGAZINES NEEDS Submit 5 poems at a time. Accepts e-mail submissions (as attachment) or postal mail. Cover letter is preferred. "SASE required for submissions by U.S. mail." Reads submissions after the deadlines for each issue: February 1 for spring and August 1 for fall. Length: up to 50 lines/poem.

WINDHOVER

A Journal of Christian Literature, P.O. Box 8008, 900 College St., Belton TX 76513. (254)295-4561. **E-mail:** windhover@umhb.edu. **Website:** undergrad.umhb. edu/english/windhover-journal. **Contact:** Dr. Nathaniel Hansen, editor. "*Windhover* is devoted to promoting writers and literature with Christian perspectives and with a broad definition of those perspectives. We accept poetry, short fiction, nonfiction, and creative nonfiction." Publishes ms 1 year after acceptance. Sample copy: $5. Writer's guidelines available at undergrad.umhb.edu/english/windhover-journal. Accepts electronic submissions only through online submission manager; no e-mailed submissions. Include estimated word count, brief bio, and list of publications.

⊙ Reading period is February 1-August 1.

MAGAZINES NEEDS Pays 1 contributor's copy.

TIPS "We are looking for writing that avoids the didactic, the melodramatic, the trite, the obvious. Eschew tricks and gimmicks. We want writing that invites rereading."

WISCONSIN REVIEW

University of Wisconsin Oshkosh, 800 Algoma Blvd., Oshkosh WI 54901. (920)424-2267. **E-mail:** wisconsinreview@uwosh.edu. **Website:** www.uwosh.edu/wisconsinreview. *Wisconsin Review*, published semiannually, is a "contemporary poetry, prose, and art magazine run by students at the University of Wisconsin Oshkosh." Acquires first North American serial rights. Time between acceptance and publication is 4-6 months. Responds in 6-9 months. Sometimes comments on rejected poems. Single copy: $7.50; subscription: $10 plus $3 extra per issue for shipments outside the U.S. Guidelines available in magazine, for SASE, by e-mail, and on website.

⊙ *Wisconsin Review* is around 100 pages, digest-sized, perfect-bound, with 4-color glossy coverstock. Receives about 400 poetry submissions/year, accepts about 50; Press run is 1,000. Reading period: May through October

for Spring issue; November through April for Fall issue.

MAGAZINES NEEDS Wants all forms and styles of poetry. Considers poetry by children and teens. "Minors may submit material by including a written letter of permission from a parent or guardian." Submit via postal mail or online submission manager. Type 1 poem/page, single-spaced, with name and address of writer on each page. Cover letter is required. Include 3-5 sentence bio and SASE if submitting by mail. Does not want "poetry that is racist, sexist, or unnecessarily vulgar." Pays 2 contributor's copies.

TIPS "We are open to any poetic form and style, and look for outstanding imagery, new themes, and fresh voices—poetry that induces emotions."

⌕ THE WOLF

E-mail: thewolfpoetry@hotmail.com. **Website:** www.wolfmagazine.co.uk. **Contact:** James Byrne, editor. *The Wolf*, published 3 times/year, publishes international translations, critical prose, and interviews with leading contemporary poets, which are frequently mentioned as distinguishing characteristics of the magazine. The poetry, however, comes purely through work submitted. There is no special treatment with regard to the consideration of any poet or poem. Since January 2008, *The Wolf* has benefited from Arts Council funding. Since receiving its grant the magazine has increased its content by a third and is perfect bound. Responds in 6 months. Sample copy on website. Single issue: $12, including postage and packing. Subscription: $35. Accepts PayPal. Guidelines available online.

MAGAZINES NEEDS Submit up to 5 poems at a time. Accepts any poetry of various styles or theme. Advisible to read a few issues of the magazine to see what is accepted. The editor prefers poems to hold a modernist aesthetic over the postmodern, experimental over mainstream, serious over light verse. It's worth seeing how this fits in with recent publications of *The Wolf*. Pays 1 contributor's copy.

ALSO OFFERS Also accepts critical essays on any poetry subject between 2,000-3,000 words. Welcomes artwork or photographs.

THE WORCESTER REVIEW

1 Ekman St., Worcester MA 01607. (508)797-4770. **E-mail:** twr.diane@gmail.com. **Website:** www.theworcesterreview.org. **Contact:** Diane Mulligan, managing editor. *The Worcester Review*, published annually by the Worcester County Poetry Associa-

tion, encourages "critical work with a New England connection; no geographic limitation on poetry and fiction." Wants "work that is crafted, intuitively honest and empathetic. We like high-quality, creative poetry, artwork, and fiction. Critical articles should be connected to New England." Acquires one-time rights. Publishes ms within 1 year of acceptance. Responds in 4-8 months to mss. Sometimes comments on rejected mss. Sample copy: $8. Subscription: $30 (includes membership in WCPA). Guidelines available for SASE or on website.

◯ *The Worcester Review* is 160 pages, digest-sized, professionally printed in dark type on quality stock, perfect-bound, with matte card cover. Press run is 600.

MAGAZINES NEEDS Submit up to 5 poems at a time. Cover letter is optional. Print submissions should be typed on 8.5x11 paper, with poet's name and e-mail address in upper left corner of each page. Include SASE or e-mail for reply. Has published poetry by Kurt Brown, Cleopatra Mathis, and Theodore Deppe. Pays 2 contributor's copies plus small honorarium.

TIPS "We generally look for creative work with a blend of craftsmanship, insight, and empathy. This does not exclude humor. We won't print work that is shoddy in any of these areas."

WORD RIOT

P.O. Box 414, Middletown NJ 07748-3143. (732)706-1272. **Fax:** (732)706-5856. **E-mail:** wr.submissions@gmail.com. **Website:** www.wordriot.org. **Contact:** Jackie Corley, publisher; Kevin O'Cuinn, fiction editor; Doug Paul Case, poetry editor. "*Word Riot* publishes the forceful voices of up-and-coming writers and poets. We like edgy. We like challenging. We like unique voices. Each month we provide readers with book reviews, author interviews, and, most importantly, writing from some of the best and brightest making waves on the literary scene." Acquires electronic rights. Not copyrighted. Publishes ms 1-2 months after acceptance. Responds in 4-6 weeks to ms.

◯ Online magazine. Member CLMP.

MAGAZINES NEEDS Submit via online submissions manager at wordriot.submittable.com/submit. Do not send submissions by mail.

TIPS "We're always looking for something edgy or quirky. We like writers who take risks."

✪ WORKERS WRITE!

Blue Cubicle Press, LLC, P.O. Box 250382, Plano TX 75025. **E-mail:** info@workerswritejournal.com. **Website:** www.workerswritejournal.com. **Contact:** David LaBounty, managing editor. "*Workers Write!* is an annual print journal published by Blue Cubicle Press, an independent publisher dedicated to giving voice to writers trapped in the daily grind. Each issue focuses on a particular workplace; check website for details. Submit your stories via e-mail or send a hard copy." Buys first North American serial rights, electronic rights, one-time rights, second serial (reprint) rights. Pays on acceptance. Publishes mss 6 months after acceptance. Responds in 1 week on queries, 3 months on mss. Sample copy available on website. Writer's guidelines free for #10 SASE and on website.

MAGAZINES NEEDS Pays $5-10.

WRITE ON!! POETRY MAGAZETTE

P.O. Box 901, Richfield UT 84701-0901. **E-mail:** jimnipoetry@yahoo.com. **Contact:** Jim Garman, editor. *Write On!! Poetry Magazette*, published irregularly, features "poetry from poets around the world." Wants poetry of "any style; all submissions must be suitable for all ages to read." Does not want "adult themes or vulgar material." Considers poetry by children and teens. Acquires one-time rights "which return to author upon publication." Time between acceptance and publication is approximately 1 month. Responds in approximately 4 weeks or less. Never comments on rejected poems. Sample copy: $3. Single copy: $4. Make checks payable to Jim Garman. Guidelines available by e-mail.

◯ *Write On!!* is 24 pages, digest-sized, photostat-copied, saddle-stapled. Receives about 200 poems/year, accepts about 50%. Press run is 20.

MAGAZINES NEEDS Submit 1-6 poems at a time. Accepts e-mail submissions (pasted into body of message, no attachments). Reads submissions year round. Occasionally publishes theme issues. Has published poetry by Caryl Calsyn, Roger Singer, Brenda K. Ledford, Robert Martin, and Owen Davis. Length: 6-28 lines/poem. No payment or free copies provided. "*Write On!!* contains no ads, no sponsors; all costs are covered out of pocket or by those desiring a copy."

TIPS "*Write On!!* issues will be published as submissions allow, hopefully once per quarter or more often."

THE WRITE PLACE AT THE WRITE TIME

E-mail: submissions@thewriteplaceatthewritetime.org. **Website:** www.thewriteplaceatthewritetime.org. **Contact:** Nicole M. Bouchard, editor in chief. Online literary magazine, published 3 times/year. Publishes fiction, personal nonfiction, craft essays by professionals, and poetry that "speaks to the heart and mind." Acquires electronic rights, archive rights, and one-time reprint rights. Responds to queries in 2-9 weeks. Frequently comments on rejected mss. Guidelines available on website or by e-mail: questions@ thewriteplaceatthewritetime.org.

○   "Our writers range from previously unpublished to having written for *The New York Times*, *Time* magazine, *The New Yorker*, *The Wall Street Journal*, *Glimmer Train*, *Newsweek*, and *Business Week*, and they come from all over the world. Interview subjects include *NYT* best-selling authors such as Dennis Lehane, Janet Fitch, Alice Hoffman, Joanne Harris, Arthur Golden, Jodi Picoult, and Frances Mayes."

MAGAZINES NEEDS Submit via e-mail—no attachments. Include cover letter with brief bio. Length: up to 30 lines/poem. "If we feel the strength of the submission merits added length, we are happy to consider exceptions."

TIPS "Through our highly personalized approach to content, feedback, and community, we aim to give a very human visage to the publishing process. We wish to speak deeply of the human condition through pieces that validate the entire spectrum of emotions and the real circumstances of life. Every piece has a unique power and presence that stands on its own; we've had writers write about surviving an illness, losing a child, embracing a foreign land, learning of their parent's suicide, discovering love, finding humor in dark hours, and healing from abuse. Our collective voice, from our aesthetic to our artwork to the words, looks at and highlights aspects of life through a storytelling lens that allows for or promotes a universal understanding."

WRITER'S BLOC

MSC 162, Fore Hall Rm. 110, 700 University Blvd., Texas A&M University-Kingsville, Kingsville TX 78363. (361)593-2514. **E-mail:** octavio.quintanilla@ tamuk.edu. **Website:** www.tamuk.edu/artsci/langlit/index4.html. **Contact:** Dr. Octavio Quintanilla. *Writer's Bloc*, published annually, prints poetry, short fiction, flash fiction, one-act plays, interviews, and essays. "About half of our pages are devoted to the works of Texas A&M University-Kingsville students and half to the works of writers and artists from all over the world." Wants quality poetry; no restrictions on content or form. Sample copy: $7. Guidelines online or in magazine.

○   *Writer's Bloc* is 96 pages, digest-sized. Press run is 300. Reading period: February-May.

MAGAZINES NEEDS Submit via postal mail. Include cover letter with contact info, short bio. "Prose poems okay. Submissions should be typed, double-spaced; SASE required for reply. Mss are published upon recommendation by a staff of students and faculty." Seldom comments on rejected poems. Length: no more than 50 lines. Pays 1 contributor's copy.

WRITER'S DIGEST

F+W Media, Inc., 10151 Carver Rd., Suite #200, Blue Ash OH 45242. (513)531-2690. **E-mail:** wdsubmissions@fwmedia.com. **Website:** www.writersdigest.com. *Writer's Digest*, the No. 1 magazine for writers, celebrates the writing life and what it means to be a writer in today's publishing environment. Buys first North American print and perpetual world digital rights. Pays 25% print reprint fee. Pays on acceptance. Publishes ms an average of 4 months after acceptance. Responds in 1-4 months to queries and mss. Guidelines and editorial calendar available online (writersdigest.com/submission-guidelines).

○   The magazine does not accept or read e-queries with attachments.

TIPS "*InkWell* is the best place for new writers to break in. We recommend you consult our editorial calendar before pitching feature-length articles. Check our writer's guidelines for more details."

THE WRITER'S MONTHLY REVIEW MAGAZINE

Rivercity Today / X-Press, 2413 Bethel Rd., Logansport LA 71049. (318)697-5649. **E-mail:** writersmonthlyreviewmag@gmail.com. **Website:** https:// writersmonthlyreview.com. **Contact:** Marcella Simmons, managing editor. Purchases simultaneous rights; rights revert back to author at time of publication. Pays in contributor copies. Publishes 1 month after accepting ms. Responds in 1 week on queries, 1 month on mss. Editorial lead time: 1 month. Submit seasonal material 3 months in advance. Sample copy available for $6.50 and SASE. Guidelines available for SASE or via e-mail.

○ All mss should be submitted with a cover letter, brief bio, and name and address.

THE WRITING DISORDER

P.O. Box 93613, Los Angeles CA 90093. (323)336-5822. **E-mail:** submit@thewritingdisorder.com. **Website:** www.writingdisorder.com. **Contact:** C.E. Lukather, editor; Paul Garson, managing editor; Julianna Woodhead, poetry editor; Pamela Ramos Langley, fiction editor; C.E. Lukather, nonfiction editor. "*The Writing Disorder* is an online literary magazine devoted to literature, art, and culture. The mission of the magazine is to showcase new and emerging writers—particularly those in writing programs—as well as established ones. The magazine also features original artwork, photography, and comic art. Although we strive to publish original and experimental work, *The Writing Disorder* remains rooted in the classic art of storytelling." Acquires first North American serial rights. Pays on publication. Publishes ms an average of 3-6 months after acceptance. Responds in 6-12 weeks to queries; 3-6 months to ms. Editorial lead time 3 months. Sample copy online. Guidelines available online.

MAGAZINES NEEDS Query. Annual print anthology of best work published online. Pays a contributor's copy of anthology to writers whose work has been selected for inclusion.

TIPS "We are looking for work from new writers, writers in writing programs, and students and faculty of all ages."

XAVIER REVIEW

Website: www.xula.edu/review. **Contact:** Ralph Adamo, editor. "*Xavier Review* accepts poetry, fiction, translations, creative nonfiction, and critical essays. Content focuses on African American, Caribbean, and Southern literature, as well as works that touch on issues of religion and spirituality. We do, however, accept quality work on all themes. (Please note: This is not a religious publication.)" Guidelines available online. "Submissions by e-mail are encouraged in all genres."

MAGAZINES NEEDS Submit 3-5 poems at a time via postal mail. Include 2-3 sentence bio and SASE. "Overseas authors only may submit by e-mail attachment." Pays 2 contributor's copies; offers 40% discount on additional copies.

THE YALE REVIEW

Yale University, P.O. Box 208243, New Haven CT 06520-8243. (203)432-0499. **Fax:** (203)432-0510. **Website:** www.yale.edu/yalereview. **Contact:** J.D. McClatchy, editor. "Like Yale's schools of music, drama, and architecture, like its libraries and art galleries, *The Yale Review* has helped give the University its leading place in American education. In a land of quick fixes and short view and in a time of increasingly commercial publishing, the journal has an authority that derives from its commitment to bold established writers and promising newcomers, to both challenging literary work and a range of essays and reviews that can explore the connections between academic disciplines and the broader movements in American society, thought, and culture. With independence and boldness, with a concern for issues and ideas, with a respect for the mind's capacity to be surprised by speculation and delighted by elegance, *The Yale Review* proudly continues into its third century." Buys one-time rights. Pays prior to publication. Publishes ms an average of 6 months after acceptance. Responds in 1-3 months to mss. Sample copy online. Guidelines online.

MAGAZINES NEEDS Submit with SASE. All submissions should be sent to the editorial office. Pays $100-250.

THE YALOBUSHA REVIEW

University of Mississippi, P.O. Box 1848, Dept. of English, University MS 38677. (662)915-3175. **E-mail:** yreditors@gmail.com. **Website:** yr.olemiss.edu. **Contact:** Liam Baranauskas and Marty Cain, senior editors. Acquires first North American serial rights. Responds in 2-4 months to mss. Sample copy for $5. Guidelines for #10 SASE.

MAGAZINES NEEDS Submit 3-5 poems via online submissions manager. Pays honorarium when funding is available.

YEMASSEE

University of South Carolina, Department of English, Columbia SC 29208. (803)777-2085. **Fax:** (803)777-9064. **E-mail:** editor@yemasseejournalonline.org. **Website:** yemasseejournalonline.org. **Contact:** Jennifer Blevins, Brandon Rushton, or Matthew Fogarty, co-editors. "*Yemassee* is the University of South Carolina's literary journal. Our readers are interested in high-quality fiction, poetry, drama, and creative nonfiction. We have no editorial slant; quality of work is our only concern. We publish in the fall and spring, printing 5-7 stories, 2-3 essays, and 12-15 poems per issue. We tend to solicit reviews, essays, and interviews but welcome unsolicited queries. We do not favor any particular aesthetic or school of writing." Buys first North American serial rights; buys electronic rights. Publishes ms an average of 4-6 months after acceptance. Responds in 1-4 months to queries and mss. Editorial lead time 3 months. Sample copy: $5. Guidelines available online.

○ Stories from *Yemassee* have been published in *New Stories From the South*. As of 2012, only accepts submissions through online submissions manager.

MAGAZINES NEEDS Submit 3-5 poems combined into a single document. "Submissions for all genres should include a cover letter that lists the titles of the pieces included, along with your contact information (including author's name, address, e-mail address, and phone number)." Does not want workshop poems, unpolished drafts, generic/unoriginal themes, or bad Hemingway. Does not want "poems of such a highly personal nature that their primary relevance is to the author; bad Ginsberg." Length: 1-120 lines. Pays 2 contributor's copies.

CONTEST/AWARD OFFERINGS Pocataligo Poetry Contest: $500 award. Check website for deadline.

ZEEK: A JEWISH JOURNAL OF THOUGHT AND CULTURE

125 Maiden Ln., 8th Floor, New York NY 10038. (212)453-9435. **E-mail:** zeek@zeek.net. **Website:** www.zeek.net. **Contact:** Erica Brody, editor in chief. *ZEEK* "relaunched in late February 2013 as a hub for the domestic Jewish social justice movement, one that showcases the people, ideas, and conversations driving an inclusive and diverse progressive Jewish community. At the same time, we've reaffirmed our commitment to building on *ZEEK*'s reputation for original, ahead-of-the-curve Jewish writing and arts, culture and spirituality content, incubating emerging voices and artists, as well as established ones." *ZEEK* seeks "great writing in a variety of styles and voices, original thinking, and accessible content. That means we're interested in hearing your ideas for first-person essays, reflections and commentary, reporting, profiles, Q&As, analysis, infographics, and more. For

the near future, *ZEEK* will focus on domestic issues. Our discourse will be civil." Responds in 6 weeks to queries.

MAGAZINES NEEDS "Pitches should be sent to zeek@zeek.net, with 'submission' or 'pitch' in the subject line. And please include a little bit about yourself and why you think your pitch is a good fit for *ZEEK*."

ZYLOPHONE POETRY JOURNAL

E-mail: rogerbarrow52@yahoo.com. **Website:** www. poetezines.4mg.com. **Contact:** J. Rogers Barrow. *Zylophone* is published semiannually in print and online. Wants all common formats. Has published poetry by Edward W. Cousins, Daisy Whitmore, and David Barger. Publishes ms 6 weeks after acceptance. Sample copy: $6. Guidelines by e-mail.

○ *Zylophone* is 16 pages, tabloid-sized, staple-bound with line-drawing artwork. Receives about 60 poems/year; accepts about 12. Press run is 20.

MAGAZINES NEEDS Submit up to 3 poems at a time by e-mail. Cover letter is preferred. Reads submissions year round. Length: 4-16 lines/poem. Pays 1 contributor's copy.

⊛ ZYZZYVA

57 Post St., Suite 604, San Francisco CA 94104. (415)757-0465. **E-mail:** editor@zyzzyva.org. **Website:** www.zyzzyva.org. **Contact:** Laura Cogan, editor; Oscar Villalon, managing editor. "Every issue is a vibrant mix of established talents and new voices, providing an elegantly curated overview of contemporary arts and letters with a distinctly San Francisco perspective." Buys first North American serial and one-time anthology rights. Pays on acceptance. Publishes ms an average of 3 months after acceptance. Responds in 1 week to queries; in 1 month to mss. Sample copy: $12. Guidelines online.

○ Accepts submissions January 1-May 31 and August 1-November 30. Does not accept online submissions.

MAGAZINES NEEDS Submit by mail. Include SASE and contact information. Length: no limit. Pays $50

TIPS "We are not currently seeking work about any particular theme or topic; that said, reading recent issues is perhaps the best way to develop a sense for the length and quality we are looking for in submissions."

BOOK/CHAPBOOK PUBLISHERS

Every poet dreams of publishing a collection of his or her work. However, it's surprising how many poets still envision putting out a thick, hardbound volume containing hundreds of poems. In reality, poetry books are usually slim, often paperback, with varying levels of production quality, depending on the publisher.

More common than full-length poetry books (i.e., 50-150 pages by modern standards) are poetry *chapbooks*, small editions of approximately 24-32 pages. They may be printed on quality paper with beautiful cover art on heavy stock; or they may be photocopied sheets of plain printer paper, folded and stapled or hand-sewn along the spine.

In this section you'll find a variety of presses and publishers of poetry books and chapbooks. However, it's a reflection of how poetry publishing works in the early 21st century that many book/chapbook publishing opportunities appear in the Contest & Awards section instead.

GETTING STARTED, FINDING A PUBLISHER

If you don't have a publisher in mind, read randomly through the listings, making notes as you go. (Don't hesitate to write in the margins, underline, use highlighters; it also helps to flag markets that interest you with Post-It Notes). Browsing the listings is an effective way to familiarize yourself with the kind of information presented and the publishing opportunities that are available at various skill levels. If you're thinking of a specific publisher by name, however, begin with the General Index. Here all *Poet's Market* listings are alphabetized.

AHSAHTA PRESS

MFA Program in Creative Writing, Boise State University, 1910 University Dr., MS 1525, Boise ID 83725. (208)426-3414. **E-mail:** ahsahta@boisestate.edu. **E-mail:** jholmes@boisestate.edu. **Website:** ahsahtapress.org. **Contact:** Janet Holmes, director. Publishes trade paperback originals. Pays 8% royalty on retail price for first 1,000 sold; 10% thereafter. Publishes ms 2 years after acceptance. Responds in 3 months to mss. Book catalog online. Guidelines online; submit through submissions manager.

NEEDS "We hold an open submissions period in May as well as the Sawtooth Poetry Prize competition, from which we publish 2-3 mss per year."

HOW TO CONTACT Submit complete ms. The press publishes runners-up as well as winners of the Sawtooth Poetry Prize. Forthcoming, new, and backlist titles available on website. Most backlist titles: $9.95; most current titles: $18.

TIPS "Ahsahta's motto is that poetry is art, so our readers tend to come to us for the unexpected—poetry that makes them think, reflect, and even do something they haven't done before."

ANHINGA PRESS

P.O. Box 3665, Tallahassee FL 32315. Phone/**Fax:** (850)577-0745. **E-mail:** info@anhinga.org. **Website:** www.anhinga.org. **Contact:** Kristine Snodgrass, editor. Publishes only full-length collections of poetry (60-80 pages). No individual poems or chapbooks. Publishes hardcover and trade paperback originals. Pays 10% royalty on retail price. Responds in 3 months. Guidelines online.

NEEDS Not accepting any unsolicited submissions at this time. Enter Robert Dana-Anhinga Prize for Poetry.

ANVIL PRESS

P.O. Box 3008 MPO, Vancouver BC V6B 3X5, Canada. (604)876-8710. **Fax:** (604)879-2667. **E-mail:** info@anvilpress.com. **Website:** www.anvilpress.com. "Anvil Press publishes contemporary adult fiction, poetry, and drama, giving voice to up-and-coming Canadian writers, exploring all literary genres, discovering, nurturing, and promoting new Canadian literary talent. Currently emphasizing urban/suburban themed fiction and poetry; de-emphasizing historical novels." Canadian authors only. No e-mail submissions. Publishes trade paperback originals. Pays advance. Average advance is $500-2,000, depending on the genre.

Publishes book 8 months after acceptance of ms. Responds in 2 months to queries; 6 months to mss. Book catalog for 9×12 SAE with 2 first-class stamps. Guidelines online.

NEEDS "Get our catalog, look at our poetry. We do very little poetry-maybe 1-2 titles per year."

HOW TO CONTACT Query with 8-12 poems and SASE.

TIPS "Audience is informed, educated, aware, with an opinion, culturally active (films, books, the performing arts). No U.S. authors. Research the appropriate publisher for your work."

ARC PUBLICATIONS

Nanholme Mill, Shaw Wood Rd., Todmorden, Lancashire OL14 6DA, England. **E-mail:** editorarcuk@btinternet.com. **E-mail:** international-editor@arc-publications.co.uk. **Website:** www.arcpublications.co.uk. **Contact:** John W. Clarke, domestic editor; James Byrne, international editor (outside Ireland/England). Responds in 6 weeks.

NEEDS Publishes "contemporary poetry from new and established writers from the UK and abroad, specializing in the work of world poets writing in English, and the work of overseas poets in translation."

HOW TO CONTACT Send 16-24 pages of poetry and short cover letter.

ARTE PUBLICO PRESS

University of Houston, 4902 Gulf Fwy, Bldg 19, Rm 100, Houston TX 77204-2004. **Fax:** (713)743-2847. **E-mail:** submapp@uh.edu. **Website:** artepublicopress.com. **Contact:** Nicolas Kanellos, editor. Arte Publico Press is the oldest and largest publisher of Hispanic literature for children and adults in the United States. "We are a showcase for Hispanic literary creativity, arts and culture. Our endeavor is to provide a national forum for U.S.-Hispanic literature." Publishes hardcover originals, trade paperback originals and reprints. Pays 10% royalty on wholesale price. Provides 20 author's copies; 40% discount on subsequent copies. Pays $1,000-3,000 advance. Publishes book 2 years after acceptance of ms. Responds in 1 month to queries and proposals; 4 months to mss. Book catalog available free. Guidelines online.

HOW TO CONTACT Submissions made through online submission form.

TIPS "Include cover letter in which you 'sell' your book—why should we publish the book, who will want to read it, why does it matter, etc. Use our ms submission online form. Format files accepted are: Word, plain/text, rich/text files. Other formats will not be accepted. Manuscript files cannot be larger than 5MB. Once editors review your ms, you will receive an e-mail with the decision. Revision process could take up to 4 months."

ASHLAND POETRY PRESS

401 College Ave., Ashland OH 44805. (419)289-5098. **Fax:** (419)289-5255. **E-mail:** app@ashland.edu. **Website:** www.ashlandpoetrypress.com. **Contact:** Wendy Hall, managing editor. Publishes trade paperback originals. Makes outright purchase of $500-1,000. Publishes book 10 months after acceptance. Responds in 1 month to queries; 6 months to mss. Book catalog online. Guidelines online.

NEEDS "We accept unsolicited manuscripts through the Snyder Prize competition each spring-the deadline is April 30. Judges are mindful of dedication to craftsmanship and thematic integrity."

TIPS "We rarely publish a title submitted off the transom outside of our Snyder Prize competition."

AUTUMN HOUSE PRESS

87½ Westwood St., Pittsburgh PA 15211. (412)381-4261. **E-mail:** info@autumnhouse.org. **Website:** www.autumnhouse.org. Fiction Editor: Sharon Dilworth. **Contact:** Michael Simms, editor-in-chief (fiction). "We are a non-profit literary press specializing in high-quality poetry, fiction, and nonfiction. Our editions are beautifully designed and printed, and they are distributed nationally. Approximately one-third of our sales are to college literature and creative writing classes." Member CLMP and Academy of American Poets. "We distribute our own titles. We do extensive national promotion through ads, web-marketing, reading tours, bookfairs and conferences. We are open to all genres. The quality of writing concerns us, not the genre." You can also learn about our annual Fiction Prize, Poetry Prize, Nonfiction Prize, and Chapbook Award competitions, as well as our online journal, *Coal Hill Review*. (Please note that Autumn House accepts unsolicited mss *only* through these competitions.) Publishes hardcover, trade paperback, and electronic originals. Format: acid-free paper; offset printing; perfect and casebound (cloth) bound; sometimes contains illustrations. Average print order: 1,000. Debut novel print order: 1,000. Pays 7% royalty on wholesale price. Pays $0-2,500 advance. Publishes 9 months after acceptance. Responds in 1-3 days on queries and proposals; 3 months on mss Catalog free on request. Guidelines online.

NEEDS "*We ask that all submissions from authors new to Autumn House come through one of our annual contests.*" All finalists will be considered for publication.

HOW TO CONTACT Submit only through our annual contest. See guidelines online.

TIPS "The competition to publish with Autumn House is very tough. Submit only your best work."

THE BACKWATERS PRESS

3502 N. 52nd St., Omaha NE 68104. **Website:** www.thebackwaterspress.org. **Contact:** James Cihlar, editor.

NEEDS Only considers submissions to Backwaters Prize. More details on website.

BEAR STAR PRESS

185 Hollow Oak Dr., Cohasset CA 95973. (530)891-0360. **Website:** www.bearstarpress.com. **Contact:** Beth Spencer, publisher/editor. "Bear Star is committed to publishing the best poetry it can attract. Each year it sponsors the Dorothy Brunsman contest, open to poets from Western and Pacific states. From time to time we add to our list other poets from our target area whose work we admire." Publishes trade paperback originals. Pays $1,000, and 25 copies to winner of annual Dorothy Brunsman contest. Publishes book 9 months after acceptance. Responds in 2 weeks to queries. Guidelines online.

NEEDS Wants well-crafted poems. No restrictions as to form, subject matter, style, or purpose. "Poets should enter our annual book competition. Other books are occasionally solicited by publisher, sometimes from among contestants who didn't win."

HOW TO CONTACT Online submissions strongly preferred.

TIPS "Send your best work, consider its arrangement. A 'wow' poem early keeps me reading."

BIRCH BOOK PRESS

P.O. Box 81, Delhi NY 13753. **Fax:** (607)746-7453. **E-mail:** birchbrook@copper.net. **Website:** www.birchbrookpress.info. **Contact:** Tom Tolnay, editor/publisher; Leigh Eckmair, art & research editor. Birch Brook Press "is a letterpress book printer/typesetter/designer that uses monies from these activities to publish several titles of its own each year with cultural and literary interest." Specializes in literary work, fly-fishing, baseball, outdoors, theme anthologies, and books about books. Occasionally publishes trade paperback originals. Pays modest royalty on acceptance. Publishes ms 10-18 months after acceptance. Responds in 3 to 6 months. Book catalog online.

HOW TO CONTACT Query first with a few sample poems or chapters, or send entire ms. No e-mail submissions; submissions by postal mail only. Must include SASE with submissions. Occasionally comments on rejected poems. Royalty on co-op contracts.

TIPS "Write well on subjects of interest to BBP, such as outdoors, flyfishing, baseball, music, literary stories, fine poetry, and occasional novellas, books about books."

BKMK PRESS

University of Missouri - Kansas City, 5101 Rockhill Rd., Kansas City MO 64110-2499. (816)235-2558. **Fax:** (816)235-2611. **E-mail:** bkmk@umkc.edu. **Website:** newletters.org. "BkMk Press publishes fine literature. Reading period January-June." Publishes trade paperback originals. Responds in 4-6 months to queries. Guidelines online.

HOW TO CONTACT Submit 10 sample poems and SASE.

TIPS "We skew toward readers of literature, particularly contemporary writing. Because of our limited number of titles published per year, we discourage apprentice writers or 'scattershot' submissions."

BLACK LAWRENCE PRESS

326 Bigham St., Pittsburgh PA 15211. **E-mail:** editors@blacklawrencepress.com. **Website:** www.blacklawrencepress.com. **Contact:** Diane Goettel, executive editor. Black Lawrence press seeks to publish intriguing books of literature—novels, short story collections, poetry collections, chapbooks, anthologies, and creative nonfiction. Will also publish the occasional translation from German. Publishes 15-20 books/year, mostly poetry and fiction. Mss are selected through open submission and competition. Books are 20-400 pages, offset-printed or high-quality POD, perfect-bound, with 4-color cover. Pays royalties. Responds in 6 months to mss.

HOW TO CONTACT Submit complete ms.

BLACK OCEAN

P.O. Box 52030, Boston MA 02205. **Fax:** (617)849-5678. **E-mail:** carrie@blackocean.org. **Website:** www.blackocean.org. **Contact:** Carrie Olivia Adams, poetry editor. Responds in 6 months to mss.

NEEDS Wants poetry that is well-considered, risks itself, and by its beauty and/or bravery disturbs a tiny corner of the universe. Mss are selected through open submission. Books are 60+ pages.

HOW TO CONTACT Book/chapbook mss may include previously published poems. "We have an open submission period in June of each year; specific guidelines are updated and posted on our website in the months preceding."

BLAZEVOX [BOOKS]

131 Euclid Ave., Kenmore NY 14217. **E-mail:** editor@blazevox.org. **Website:** www.blazevox.org. **Contact:** Geoffrey Gatza, editor/publisher. "We are a major publishing presence specializing in innovative fictions and wide-ranging fields of innovative forms of poetry and prose. Our goal is to publish works that are challenging, creative, attractive, and yet affordable to individual readers. Articles of submission depend on many criteria, but overall items submitted must conform to one ethereal trait, your work must not suck. This put plainly, bad art should be punished; we will not promote it. However, all submissions will be reviewed and the author will receive feedback. We are human too." Pays 10% royalties on fiction and poetry books, based on net receipts. This amount may be split across multiple contributors. "We do not pay advances." Guidelines online.

HOW TO CONTACT Submit complete ms via e-mail.

TIPS "We actively contract and support authors who tour, read and perform their work, play an active part of the contemporary literary scene, and seek a readership."

BLUE LIGHT PRESS

1563 45th Ave., San Francisco CA 94122. **E-mail:** bluelightpress@aol.com. **Website:** www.bluelightpress.com. **Contact:** Diane Frank, chief editor. "We like poems that are imagistic, emotionally honest, and push the edge—where the writer pushes through the imagery to a deeper level of insight and understanding. No rhymed poetry." Has published poetry by Rustin Larson, Mary Kay Rummel, Philip Kobylarz, Daniel J. Langton, and K.B. Ballentine. "Books are elegantly designed and artistic. Our books are professionally printed, with original cover art, and we publish full-length books of poetry and chapbooks."

NEEDS "We have an online poetry workshop with a wonderful group of American and international poets—open to new members 3 times/year. Send an e-mail for info."

HOW TO CONTACT Does not accept e-mail submissions. Deadlines: January 30 full-sized ms. and June 15 for chapbooks. "Read our guidelines before sending your ms."

BLUE MOUNTAIN PRESS

Blue Mountain Arts, Inc., P.O. Box 4549, Boulder CO 80306. (800)525-0642. **E-mail:** editorial@sps.com. **Website:** www.sps.com. **Contact:** Patti Wayant, editorial director. *"Please note: We are not accepting works of fiction, rhyming poetry, children's books, chapbooks, or memoirs."* Publishes hardcover originals, trade paperback originals, electronic originals. Pays royalty on wholesale price. Publishes ms 6-8 months after acceptance. Responds in 2-4 months. Guidelines by e-mail.

NEEDS "We publish poetry appropriate for gift books, self-help books, and personal growth books. We do not publish chapbooks or literary poetry."

HOW TO CONTACT Query. Submit 10+ sample poems.

BOA EDITIONS, LTD.

P.O. Box 30971, Rochester NY 14603. (585)546-3410. **Fax:** (585)546-3913. **E-mail:** contact@boaeditions.org. **Website:** www.boaeditions.org. **Contact:** Peter Conners, publisher; Melissa Hall, development director/office manager. "BOA Editions publishes distinguished collections of poetry, fiction and poetry in translation. Our goal is to publish the finest American contemporary poetry, fiction and poetry in translation." Publishes hardcover and trade paperback originals. Negotiates royalties. Pays variable advance. Publishes ms 18 months after acceptance. Responds in 1 week to queries; 5 months to mss. Book catalog online. Guidelines online.

NEEDS "Readers who, like Whitman, expect of the poet to 'indicate more than the beauty and dignity which always attach to dumb real objects... They expect him to indicate the path between reality and their souls,' are the audience of BOA's books." BOA Editions, a Pulitzer Prize-winning, not-for-profit publishing house acclaimed for its work, reads poetry mss for the American Poets Continuum Series (new poetry by distinguished poets in mid- and late career), the Lannan Translations Selection Series (publication of 2 new collections of contemporary international poetry annually, supported by The Lannan Founda-

tion of Santa Fe, NM), The A. Poulin, Jr. Poetry Prize (to honor a poet's first book; mss considered through competition), and The America Reader Series (short fiction and prose on poetics).

HOW TO CONTACT Check website for reading periods for the American Poets Continuum Series and The Lannan Translation Selection Series. "Please adhere to the general submission guidelines for each series." Guidelines online.

BOTTOM DOG PRESS, INC.

P.O. Box 425, Huron OH 44839. **E-mail:** lsmithdog@smithdocs.net. **Website:** smithdocs.net. **Contact:** Larry Smith, director; Allen Frost, Laura Smith, Susanna Sharp-Schwacke, associate editors. Bottom Dog Press, Inc., "is a nonprofit literary and educational organization dedicated to publishing the best writing and art from the Midwest and Appalachia."

◑   "Query via e-mail first."

BOYDS MILLS PRESS

Highlights for Children, Inc., 815 Church St., Honesdale PA 18431. (570)253-1164. **Website:** www.boydsmillspress.com. Boyds Mills Press publishes picture books, nonfiction, activity books, and paperback reprints. Their titles have been named notable books by the International Reading Association, the American Library Association, and the National Council of Teachers of English. They've earned numerous awards, including the National Jewish Book Award, the Christopher Medal, the NCTE Orbis Pictus Honor, and the Golden Kite Honor. Boyds Mills Press welcomes unsolicited submissions from published and unpublished writers and artists. Submit a ms with a cover letter of relevant information, including experience with writing and publishing. Label the package "Manuscript Submission" and include an SASE. For art samples, label the package "Art Sample Submission." Responds to mss within 3 months. Catalog online. Guidelines online.

HOW TO CONTACT Send a book-length collection of poems. Do not send an initial query. Keep in mind that the strongest collections demonstrate a facility with multiple poetic forms.

◔ BRICK BOOKS

Box 20081, 431 Boler Rd., London ON N6K 4G6, Canada. (519)657-8579. **E-mail:** brick.books@sympatico.ca. **Website:** www.brickbooks.ca. **Contact:** Don McKay, Stan Dragland, Barry Dempster, editors. Brick Books has a reading period of January

1-April 30. Mss received outside that period will be returned. No multiple submissions. Pays 10% royalty in book copies only. Publishes trade paperback originals. Publishes ms 2 years after acceptance. Responds in 3-4 months to queries. Book catalog free or online. Guidelines online.

◯ "We publish only poetry."

HOW TO CONTACT Submit only poetry.

TIPS "Writers without previous publications in literary journals or magazines are rarely considered by Brick Books for publication."

BRICK ROAD POETRY PRESS, INC.

P.O. Box 751, Columbus GA 31902. (706)649-3080. **Fax:** (706)649-3094. **E-mail:** editor@brickroadpoetrypress.com. **Website:** www.brickroadpoetrypress.com. **Contact:** Ron Self and Keith Badowski, co-editors/founders.

NEEDS Publishes poetry only: books (single author collections), e-zine, and annual anthology. "We prefer poetry that offers a coherent human voice, a sense of humor, attentiveness to words and language, narratives with surprise twists, persona poems, and/or philosophical or spiritual themes explored through the concrete scenes and images." Does not want overemphasis on rhyme, intentional obscurity or riddling, highfalutin vocabulary, greeting card verse, overt religious statements of faith and/or praise, and/or abstractions. Publishes 10-12 poetry books/year and 1 anthology/year. Accepted poems meeting our theme requirements are published on our website. Mss accepted through open submission and competition.

HOW TO CONTACT "We accept .doc, .rtf, or .pdf file formats. We prefer electronic submissions but will reluctantly consider hard copy submissions by mail if USPS Flat Rate Mailing Envelope is used and with the stipulation that, should the author's work be chosen for publication, an electronic version (.doc or .rtf) must be prepared in a timely manner and at the poet's expense." Please include cover letter with poetry publication/recognition highlights and something intriguing about your life story or ongoing pursuits. "We would like to develop a connection with the poet as well as the poetry." Please include the collection title in the cover letter. "We want to publish poets who are engaged in the literary community, including regular submission of work to various publications and participation in poetry readings, workshops, and writers' groups. That said, we would never rule

out an emerging poet who demonstrates ability and motivation to move in that direction." Pays royalties and 15 author copies. Initial print run of 150, print-on-demand thereafter.

TIPS "The best way to discover all that poetry can be and to expand the limits of your own poetry is to read expansively. We recommend the following poets: Kim Addonizio, Ken Babstock, Coleman Barks, Billy Collins, Morri Creech, Alice Friman, Beth A. Gylys, Jane Hirshfield, Jane Kenyon, Ted Kooser, Stanley Kunitz, Thomas Lux, Barry Marks, Michael Meyerhofer, Linda Pastan, Mark Strand, and Natasha D. Trethewey."

BRONZE MAN BOOKS

Millikin University, 1184 W. Main, Decatur IL 62522. (217)424-6264. **E-mail:** rbrooks@millikin.edu. **Website:** www.bronzemanbooks.com. **Contact:** Dr. Randy Brooks, editorial board; Edwin Walker, editorial board. Publishes hardcover, trade paperback, and mass market paperback originals. Outright purchase based on wholesale value of 10% of a press run. Publishes book 6 months after acceptance. Responds in 1-3 months.

HOW TO CONTACT Submit completed ms.

TIPS "The art books are intended for serious collectors and scholars of contemporary art, especially of artists from the Midwestern US. These books are published in conjunction with art exhibitions at Millikin University or the Decatur Area Arts Council. The children's books have our broadest audience, and the literary chapbooks are intended for readers of contemporary fiction, drama, and poetry."

⊘ CALAMARI PRESS

Via Titta Scarpetta #28, Rome 00153, Italy. **E-mail:** derek@calamaripress.net. **Website:** www.calamaripress.com. Calamari Press publishes books of literary text and art. Mss are selected by invitation. Occasionally has open submission period—check website. Helps to be published in *SleepingFish* first. Publishes paperback originals. Pays in author's copies. Ms published 2-6 months after acceptance. Responds to mss in 2 weeks. Guidelines online.

CARCANET PRESS

Alliance House, 4th Floor, 30 Cross St., Manchester England M2 7AQ, United Kingdom. **E-mail:** info@carcanet.co.uk. **E-mail:** schmidt@carcanet.co.uk. **Website:** www.carcanet.co.uk. **Contact:** Michael Schmidt, editorial and managing director. "Carcanet Press is one of Britain's leading poetry publishers. It provides a comprehensive and diverse list of modern and classic poetry in English and in translation." Publishes hardcover and trade paperback originals.

NEEDS Familiarize yourself with our books, and then submit between 6 and 10 pages or work (poetry or translations) and SASE. Replies are usually sent within 6 weeks. Writers wishing to propose other projects should send a full synopsis and cover letter, with sample pages, having first ascertained that the kind of book proposed is suitable for our programme. Do not call in person.

CARNEGIE MELLON UNIVERSITY PRESS

5032 Forbes Ave., Pittsburgh PA 15289-1021. (412)268-2861. **Fax:** (412)268-8706. **E-mail:** carnegiemellonuniversitypress@gmail.com. **Website:** www.cmu.edu/universitypress/. **Contact:** Cynthia Lamb, senior editor. Publishes hardcover and trade paperback originals. Book catalog and guidelines online.

NEEDS Holds annual reading period. "This reading period is only for poets who have not previously been published by CMP."

HOW TO CONTACT Submit complete ms. **Requires reading fee of $15.**

CAROLINA WREN PRESS

120 Morris St., Durham NC 27701. (919)560-2738. E-mail: carolinawrenpress@earthlink.net. **Website:** www.carolinawrenpress.org. **Contact:** Andrea Selch, president. "We publish poetry, fiction, and memoirs by, and/or about people of color, women, gay/lesbian issues, and work by writers from, living in, or writing about the U.S. South." Publishes ms 2 year after acceptance. Responds in 3 months to queries; 6 months to mss. Guidelines online.

○ Accepts simultaneous submissions, but "let us know if work has been accepted elsewhere."

NEEDS Publishes 2 poetry books/year, "usually through the Carolina Wren Press Poetry Series Contest. Otherwise we primarily publish women, minorities, and authors from, living in, or writing about the U.S. South." Not accepting unsolicited submissions except through Poetry Series Contest.

HOW TO CONTACT Accepts e-mail queries, but send only letter and description of work, no large files. Carolina Wren Press Poetry Contest for a First or Second Book takes submissions, electronically, from January to March of odd-numbered years.

TIPS "Best way to get read is to submit to a contest."

CLEVELAND STATE UNIVERSITY POETRY CENTER

2121 Euclid Ave., RT 1841, Cleveland OH 44115. (216)687-3986. **Fax:** (216)687-6943. **E-mail:** poetry-center@csuohio.edu. **Website:** www.csupoetrycenter.com. **Contact:** Amber Allen, managing editor.

NEEDS The Cleveland State University Poetry Center publishes "full-length collections by established and emerging poets, through competition and solicitation, as well as occasional poetry anthologies, texts on poetics, and novellas. Eclectic in its taste and inclusive in its aesthetic, with particular interest in lyric poetry and innovative approaches to craft. Not interested in light verse, devotional verse, doggerel, or poems by poets who have not read much contemporary poetry."

HOW TO CONTACT Most mss are accepted through the competitions. All mss sent for competitions are considered for publication. Outside of competitions, mss are accepted by solicitation only.

☺ COACH HOUSE BOOKS

80 bpNichol Lane, Toronto ON M5S 3J4, Canada. (416)979-2217. **Fax:** (416)977-1158. **E-mail:** editor@chbooks.com. **Website:** www.chbooks.com. **Contact:** Alana Wilcox, editorial director. Publishes trade paperback originals by Canadian authors. Pays 10% royalty on retail price. Publishes ms 1 year after acceptance. Responds in 6 months to queries. Guidelines online.

TIPS "We are not a general publisher, and publish only Canadian poetry, fiction, artist books and drama. We are interested primarily in innovative or experimental writing."

COFFEE HOUSE PRESS

79 13th NE, Suite 110, Minneapolis MN 55413. (612)338-0125. **Fax:** (612)338-4004. **E-mail:** info@coffeehousepress.org. **Website:** www.coffeehousepress.org. **Contact:** Molly Fuller, production editor. This successful nonprofit small press has received numerous grants from various organizations including the NEA, the McKnight Foundation and Target. Books published by Coffee House Press have won numerous honors and awards. Example: The Book of Medicines by Linda Hogan won the Colorado Book Award for Poetry and the Lannan Foundation Literary Fellowship. Publishes hardcover and trade paperback originals. Responds in 4-6 weeks to queries; up to 6 months to mss. Book catalog and ms guidelines online.

HOW TO CONTACT Coffee House Press will not accept unsolicited poetry submissions. Please check our web page periodically for future updates to this policy.

TIPS "Look for our books at stores and libraries to get a feel for what we like to publish. No phone calls, e-mails, or faxes."

COTEAU BOOKS

Thunder Creek Publishing Co-operative Ltd., 2517 Victoria Ave., Regina SK S4P 0T2, Canada. (306)777-0170. **Fax:** (306)522-5152. **E-mail:** coteau@coteaubooks.com. **Website:** www.coteaubooks.com. **Contact:** Geoffrey Ursell, publisher. "Our mission is to publish the finest in Canadian fiction, nonfiction, poetry, drama, and children's literature, with an emphasis on Saskatchewan and prairie writers. De-emphasizing science fiction, picture books." Publishes trade paperback originals and reprints. Pays 10% royalty on retail price. Publishes book 1 year after acceptance. Responds in 3 months. Book catalog available free. Guidelines online.

HOW TO CONTACT Submit 20-25 sample poems.

TIPS "Look at past publications to get an idea of our editorial program. We do not publish romance, horror, or picture books but are interested in juvenile and teen fiction from Canadian authors. Submissions, even queries, must be made in hard copy only. We do not accept simultaneous/multiple submissions. Check our website for new submission timing guidelines."

CRESCENT MOON PUBLISHING

P.O. Box 393, Maidstone Kent ME14 5XU, United Kingdom. (44)(162)272-9593. **E-mail:** cresmopub@yahoo.co.uk. **Website:** www.crmoon.com. **Contact:** Jeremy Robinson, director (arts, media, cinema, literature); Cassidy Hushes (visual arts). "Our mission is to publish the best in contemporary work, in poetry, fiction, and critical studies, and selections from the great writers. Currently emphasizing nonfiction (media, film, music, painting). De-emphasizing children's books." Publishes hardcover and trade paperback originals. Pays royalty. Pays negotiable advance. Publishes ms 18 months after acceptance. Responds in 2 months to queries; 4 months to proposals and mss. Book catalog and ms guidelines free.

NEEDS "We prefer a small selection of the poet's very best work at first. We prefer free verse or non-rhyming poetry. Do not send too much material."

HOW TO CONTACT Query and submit 6 sample poems.

TIPS "Our audience is interested in new contemporary writing."

CROSS-CULTURAL COMMUNICATIONS

239 Wynsum Ave., Merrick NY 11566. (516)869-5635. **Fax:** (516)379-1901. **E-mail:** info@cross-culturalcommunications.com. **Website:** www.cross-culturalcommunications.com. Publishes hardcover and trade paperback originals. Publishes book 1 year after acceptance. Responds in 1 month to proposals; 2 months to mss. Book catalog (sample flyers) for #10 SASE.

HOW TO CONTACT For bilingual poetry submit 3-6 short poems in original language with English translation, a brief (3-5 lines) bio of the author and translator(s).

TIPS "Best chance: poetry from a translation."

DIAL BOOKS FOR YOUNG READERS

Imprint of Penguin Group (USA), 345 Hudson St., New York NY 10014. (212)366-2000. **Website:** www.penguin.com/youngreaders. **Contact:** Lauri Hornik, president/publisher. "Dial Books for Young Readers publishes quality picture books for ages 18 months-6 years; lively, believable novels for middle readers and young adults; and occasional nonfiction for middle readers and young adults." Publishes hardcover originals. Pays royalty. Pays varies advance. Responds in 4-6 months to queries. Book catalog and guidelines online.

TIPS "Our readers are anywhere from preschool age to teenage. Picture books must have strong plots, lots of action, unusual premises, or universal themes treated with freshness and originality. Humor works well in these books. A very well-thought-out and intelligently presented book has the best chance of being taken on. Genre isn't as much of a factor as presentation."

DUFOUR EDITIONS

P.O. Box 7, 124 Byers Rd., Chester Springs PA 19425. (610)458-5005 or (800)869-5677. **Fax:** (610)458-7103. **Website:** www.dufoureditions.com. "We publish literary fiction by good writers which is well received and achieves modest sales. De-emphsazing poetry and nonfiction." Publishes hardcover originals, trade paperback originals and reprints. Pays $100-500 advance. Publishes ms 18 months after acceptance. Responds in 3-6 months. Book catalog available free.

HOW TO CONTACT Query.

ÉCRITS DES FORGES

992-A, rue Royale, Trois-Rivières QC G9A 4H9, Canada. (819)840-8492. **Website:** www.ecritsdesforges.

com. **Contact:** Bernard Pozier, director. Pays royalties of 10-20%. Responds to queries in 6 months.

NEEDS Écrits des Forges publishes poetry only that is "authentic and original as a signature. We have published poetry from more than 1,000 poets coming from most of the francophone countries." Publishes 45-50 paperback books of poetry/year. Books are usually 80-88 pages, digest-sized, perfect-bound, with 2-color covers with art.

HOW TO CONTACT Query first with a few sample poems and a cover letter with brief bio and publication credits. Order sample books by writing or faxing.

ÉDITIONS DU NOROÎT

4609 D'Iberville, Bureau 202, Montreal QC H2H 2L9, Canada. (514)727-0005. **Fax:** (514)723-6660. **E-mail:** lenoroit@lenoroit.com. **Website:** www.lenoroit. com. **Contact:** Paul Belanger, director. "Editions du Noiroît publishes poetry and essays on poetry." Publishes trade paperback originals and reprints. Pays 10% royalty on retail price. Publishes ms 1 year after acceptance. Responds in 4 months to mss.

HOW TO CONTACT Submit 40 sample poems.

FARRAR, STRAUS & GIROUX

18 W. 18th St., New York NY 10011. (646)307-5151. **Website:** us.macmillan.com. **Contact:** Editorial Department. "We publish original and well-written material for all ages." Publishes hardcover originals and trade paperback reprints. Pays 2-6% royalty on retail price for paperbacks, 3-10% for hardcovers. Pays $3,000-25,000 advance. Publishes ms 18 months after acceptance. Responds in 2-3 months. Catalog available by request. Guidelines online.

HOW TO CONTACT Send cover letter describing submission with 3-4 poems. By mail only.

FARRAR, STRAUS & GIROUX FOR YOUNG READERS

Macmillan Children's Publishing Group, 175 Fifth Ave., New York NY 10010. (212)741-6900. **Fax:** (212)633-2427. **E-mail:** childrens.editorial@fsgbooks. com. **Website:** www.fsgkidsbooks.com. Book catalog available by request. Ms guidelines online.

HOW TO CONTACT Submit cover letter, 3-4 poems by mail only.

TIPS "Study our catalog before submitting. We will see illustrators' portfolios by appointment. Don't ask for criticism and/or advice—due to the volume of submissions we receive, it's just not possible. Never send originals. Always enclose SASE."

FENCE BOOKS

Science Library 320, Univ. of Albany, 1400 Washington Ave., Albany NY 12222. (518)591-8162. **E-mail:** fencesubmissions@gmail.com. **E-mail:** peter.n.fence@gmail.com. **Website:** www.fenceportal. org. **Contact:** Submissions Manager. Closed to submissions until June 15. Check website for details. Publishes hardcover originals. Guidelines online.

HOW TO CONTACT Submit via contests and occasional open reading periods.

FLARESTACK POETS

69 Beaks Hill Rd., Birmingham B38 8BL, United Kingdom. **E-mail:** flarestackpoets@gmail.com. **Website:** www.flarestackpoets.co.uk. **Contact:** Meredith Andrea and Jacqui Rowe. Pays 25% royalty and 6 contributor's copies. Responds in 6 weeks.

NEEDS Flarestack Poets wants "poems that dare outside current trends, even against the grain." Publishes 6 chapbooks/year. Chapbooks are 20-30 pages, professional photocopy, saddle-stitched, card cover.

HOW TO CONTACT See website for current submission arrangements.

FLOATING BRIDGE PRESS

909 NE 43rd St., #205, Seattle WA 98105. **E-mail:** floatingbridgepress@yahoo.com. **Website:** www. floatingbridgepress.org.

NEEDS Floating Bridge Press publishes chapbooks and anthologies by Washington State poets, selected through an annual competition.

FOLDED WORD

79 Tracy Way, Meredith NH 03253. **E-mail:** editors@ foldedword.com. **Website:** www.foldedword.com. Editor-in-Chief: J.S. Graustein. Poetry Editor: Rose Auslander. Fiction Editor: Casey Murphy. "Folded Word is an independent literary press. Our focus? Connecting new voices to readers. Our goal? To make poetry and fiction accessible for the widest audience possible both on and off the page."

TIPS "We are seeking non-formulaic narratives that have a strong sense of place and/or time, especially the exploration of unfamiliar place/time."

FOUR WAY BOOKS

Box 535, Village Station, New York NY 10014. **E-mail:** editors@fourwaybooks.com. **Website:** www.fourwaybooks.com. **Contact:** Martha Rhodes, director. "Four Way Books is a not-for-profit literary press dedicated to publishing poetry and short fiction by emerging and established writers. Each year, Four Way Books publishes the winners of its national poetry competitions, as well as collections accepted through general submission, panel selection, and solicitation by the editors."

NEEDS Four Way Books publishes poetry and short fiction. Considers full-length poetry mss only. Books are about 70 pages, offset-printed digitally, perfect-bound, with paperback binding, art/graphics on covers. Does not want individual poems or poetry intended for children/young readers.

HOW TO CONTACT See website for complete submission guidelines and open reading period in June. Book mss may include previously published poems. Responds to submissions in 4 months. Payment varies. Order sample books from Four Way Books online or through bookstores.

FUTURECYCLE PRESS

Website: www.futurecycle.org. **Contact:** Diane Kistner, director/editor-in-chief. Publishes English-language poetry books, chapbooks, and anthologies in print-on-demand and digital editions. Awards the FutureCycle Poetry Book Prize and honorarium for the best full-length book the press publishes each year. Pays in deeply discounted author copies (no purchase required). Responds in 3 months. Guidelines, sample contract, and detailed *Guide for Authors* online.

NEEDS Wants "poetry from imaginative, highly skilled poets, whether well known or emerging. We abhor the myopic, self-absorbed, and sloppy, but otherwise are eclectic in our tastes." Does not want concrete or visual poetry. Publishes 15+ poetry books/year and 5+ chapbooks/year. Ms. selected through open submission. Books average 62-110 pages; chapbooks 30-42 pages; anthologies 100+ pages.

HOW TO CONTACT Submit complete ms. No need to query.

GERTRUDE PRESS

P.O. Box 83948, Portland OR 97283. (503)515-8252. **E-mail:** edelehoy@fc.edu. **Website:** www.gertrudepress.org. **Contact:** Justus Ballard (all fiction). "Gertrude Press is a nonprofit organization developing and showcasing the creative talents of lesbian, gay, bisexual, trans, queer-identified and allied individuals. We publish limited-edition fiction and poetry chapbooks plus the biannual literary journal, *Gertrude*." Reads chapbook mss only through contests.

TIPS Sponsors poetry and fiction chapbook contest. Prize is $50 and 50 contributor's copies. Submission guidelines and fee information on website. "Read the journal and sample published work. We are not impressed by pages of publications; your work should speak for itself."

GINNINDERRA PRESS

P.O. Box 3461, Port Adelaide 5015, Australia. **E-mail:** stephen@ginninderrapress.com.au. **Website:** www.ginninderrapress.com.au. **Contact:** Stephen Matthews, publisher. Ginninderra Press works "to give publishing opportunities to new writers." Has published poetry by Alan Gould and Geoff Page. Books are usually up to 72 pages, A5, laser-printed, saddle-stapled or thermal-bound, with board covers. *Publishes books by Australian authors only.* Responds to queries within 1 week; mss in 2 months.

HOW TO CONTACT Query first, with a few sample poems and a cover letter with brief bio and publication credits. Considers previously published poems.

GIVAL PRESS

Gival Press, LLC, P.O. Box 3812, Arlington VA 22203. (703)351-0079. **E-mail:** givalpress@yahoo.com. **Website:** www.givalpress.com. **Contact:** Robert L. Giron, editor-in-chief (area of interest: literary). Publishes trade paperback, electronic originals, and reprints. Pays royalty. Publishes ms 12 months after acceptance. Responds in 3-5 months. Book online. Guidelines online.

HOW TO CONTACT Query via e-mail; provide description, bio, etc.; submit 5-6 sample poems via e-mail.

TIPS "Our audience is those who read literary works with depth to the work. Visit our website—there is much to be read/learned from the numerous pages."

DAVID R. GODINE, PUBLISHER

15 Court Square, Suite 320, Boston MA 02108. (617)451-9600. **Fax:** (617)350-0250. **E-mail:** info@godine.com. **Website:** www.godine.com. "We publish books that matter for people who care." This publisher is no longer considering unsolicited mss of any type. Only interested in agented material.

GOODMAN BECK PUBLISHING

E-mail: info@goodmanbeck.com. **Website:** www.goodmanbeck.com. "Our primary interest at this time is mental health, personal growth, aging well, positive psychology, accessible spirituality, and self-help. Our audience is adults trying to cope with this 'upside down world.' With our self-help books, we are trying to improve the world one book at a time." Publishes trade paperback originals. Pays 10% royalty on retail price. Publishes book 6-9 months after acceptance. "Due to high query volume, response not guaranteed."

NEEDS "We are interested in zen-inspired haiku and non-embellished, non-rhyming, egoless poems. Read Mary Oliver."

HOW TO CONTACT Query, submit 3 sample poems. E-mail submissions only.

TIPS "Your book should be enlightening and marketable. Be prepared to have a comprehensive marketing plan. You will be very involved."

GOOSE LANE EDITIONS

500 Beaverbrook Ct., Suite 330, Fredericton NB E3B 5X4, Canada. (506)450-4251. **Fax:** (506)459-4991. **E-mail:** submissions@gooselane.com. **Website:** www.gooselane.com. **Contact:** Angela Williams, publishing assistant. "Goose Lane publishes literary fiction and nonfiction from well-read and highly skilled Canadian authors." Publishes hardcover and paperback originals and occasional reprints. Pays 8-10% royalty on retail price. Pays $500-3,000, negotiable advance. Responds in 6 months to queries.

NEEDS Considers mss by Canadian poets only.

HOW TO CONTACT Submit cover letter, list of publications, synopsis, entire ms, SASE.

TIPS "Writers should send us outlines and samples of books that show a very well-read author with highly developed literary skills. Our books are almost all by Canadians living in Canada; we seldom consider submissions from outside Canada. We consider submissions from outside Canada only when the author is Canadian and the book is of extraordinary interest to Canadian readers. We do not publish books for children or for the young adult market."

GRAYWOLF PRESS

250 Third Ave. N., Suite 600, Minneapolis MN 55401. **E-mail:** wolves@graywolfpress.org. **Website:** www.graywolfpress.org. **Contact:** Lucia Cowles, editorial and administrative assistant. "Graywolf Press is an independent, nonprofit publisher dedicated to the creation and promotion of thoughtful and imaginative contemporary literature essential to a vital and diverse culture." Publishes trade cloth and paperback originals. Pays royalty on retail price. Pays $1,000-25,000 advance. Publishes 18 months after acceptance. Responds in 3 months to queries. Book catalog free. Guidelines online.

NEEDS "We are interested in linguistically challenging work."

HOW TO CONTACT Agented submissions only.

GROVE/ATLANTIC, INC.

841 Broadway, 4th Floor, New York NY 10003. (212)614-7850. **Fax:** (212)614-7886. **E-mail:** info@groveatlantic.com. **Website:** www.groveatlantic.com. "Due to limited resources of time and staffing, Grove/Atlantic cannot accept manuscripts that do not come through a literary agent. In today's publishing world, agents are more important than ever, helping writers shape their work and navigate the main publishing houses to find the most appropriate outlet for a project." Publishes hardcover and trade paperback originals, and reprints. Pays 7 ½-12 ½% royalty. Makes outright purchase of $5-500,000. Book published 9 months after acceptance of ms. Responds in 1 month to queries; 2 months to proposals; 4 months to mss. Book catalog available online.

HOW TO CONTACT Agented submissions only.

GUERNICA EDITIONS

1569 Heritage Way, Oakville Ontario L6M 2Z7, Canada. (905)599-5304. **Fax:** (416)981-7606. **E-mail:** michaelmirolla@guernicaeditions.com. **Website:** www.guernicaeditions.com. **Contact:** Michael Mirolla, editor/publisher (poetry, nonfiction, short stories, novels). Guernica Editions is a literary press that produces works of poetry, fiction and nonfiction often by writers who are ignored by the mainstream. Publishes trade paperback originals and reprints. Pays 8-10% royalty on retail price, or makes outright purchase of $200-5,000. Pays $450-750 advance. Publishes 24-36 months after acceptance. Responds in 1 month to queries. Responds in 6 months to proposals. Responds in 1 year to manuscripts Book catalog available online.

NEEDS Feminist, gay/lesbian, literary, multicultural, poetry in translation. We wish to have writers in translation. Any writer who has translated Italian poetry is welcomed. Full books only. No single poems by different authors, unless modern, and used as an anthology. First books will have no place in the next couple of years.

HOW TO CONTACT Query.

⊘ HARPERCOLLINS

195 Broadway, New York NY 10007. (212)207-7000. **Website:** www.harpercollins.com. HarperCollins, one of the largest English language publishers in the world, is a broad-based publisher with strengths in academic, business and professional, children's, educational, general interest, and religious and spiritual books, as well as multimedia titles. Publishes hardcover and paperback originals and paperback reprints. Pays royalty. Pays negotiable advance.

TIPS "We do not accept any unsolicited material."

HIGH PLAINS PRESS

P.O. Box 123, 403 Cassa Rd., Glendo WY 82213. (307)735-4370. **Fax:** (307)735-4590. **E-mail:** editor@highplainspress.com. **Website:** www.highplainspress.com. **Contact:** Nancy Curtis, publisher. High Plains Press is a regional book publishing company specializing in books about the American West, with special interest in things relating to Wyoming. Publishes hardcover and trade paperback originals. Pays 10% royalty on wholesale price. Pays $200-1,200 advance. Publishes book 2 years after acceptance of ms. Responds in 1 month to queries and proposals; 12 months on mss. Book catalog and guidelines online.

NEEDS "We publish 1 poetry volume a year. Require connection to West. Consider poetry in August."

HOW TO CONTACT Submit 5 sample poems.

TIPS "Our audience comprises general readers interested in history and culture of the Rockies."

🌑 HIPPOPOTAMUS PRESS

22 Whitewell Rd., Frome Somerset BA11 4EL, United Kingdom. (44)(173)466-6653. **E-mail:** rjhippopress@aol.com. **Contact:** R. John, editor; M. Pargitter (poetry); Anna Martin (translation). "Hippopotamus Press publishes first, full collections of verse by those well represented in the mainstream poetry magazines of the English-speaking world." Publishes hardcover and trade paperback originals. Pays 7½-10% royalty on retail price. Pays advance. Publishes book 10 months after acceptance. Responds in 1 month to queries. Book catalog available free.

NEEDS "Read one of our authors—poets often make the mistake of submitting poetry without knowing the type of verse we publish."

HOW TO CONTACT Query and submit complete ms.

TIPS "We publish books for a literate audience. We have a strong link to the Modernist tradition. Read what we publish."

⊙⊘ HOUSE OF ANANSI PRESS

110 Spadina Ave., Suite 801, Toronto ON M5V 2K4, Canada. (416)363-4343. **Fax:** (416)363-1017. **Website:** www.anansi.ca. House of Anansi publishes literary fiction and poetry by Canadian and international writers. Pays 8-10% royalties. Pays $750 advance and 10 author's copies. Responds to queries within 1 year; to mss (if invited) within 4 months.

NEEDS "We seek to balance the list between well-known and emerging writers, with an interest in writing by Canadians of all backgrounds. We publish Canadian poetry only, and poets must have a substantial publication record—if not in books, then definitely in journals and magazines of repute." Does not want "children's poetry or poetry by previously unpublished poets."

HOW TO CONTACT Canadian poets should query first with 10 sample poems (typed double-spaced) and a cover letter with brief bio and publication credits. Considers simultaneous submissions. Poems are circulated to an editorial board. Often comments on rejected poems.

IBEX PUBLISHERS

P.O. Box 30087, Bethesda MD 20824. (301)718-8188. **Fax:** (301)907-8707. **E-mail:** info@ibexpub.com. **Website:** www.ibexpublishers.com. "IBEX publishes books about Iran and the Middle East and about Persian culture and literature." Publishes hardcover and trade paperback originals and reprints. Payment varies. Book catalog available free.

NEEDS "Translations of Persian poets will be considered."

ILIUM PRESS

2407 S. Sonora Dr., Spokane WA 99037. (509)701-8866. **E-mail:** contact@iliumpress.com; submissions@iliumpress.com. **Website:** www.iliumpress.com. **Contact:** John Lemon, owner/editor (literature, epic poetry). Publishes trade paperback originals and reprints, electronic originals and reprints. Pays 20-50% royalties on receipts. Publishes ms up to 1 year after acceptance. Responds in 6 months. Guidelines online.

NEEDS "Submit only narrative epic poems in metered or sprung blank non-rhyming verse. All others will be rejected. See submission guidelines on website."

HOW TO CONTACT Query with first 20 pages and SASE.

INNOVATIVE PUBLISHERS INC.

133 Clarendon St., Box 170021, Boston MA 02117. (617)963-0886. **Fax:** (617)861-8533. **E-mail:** admin@innovative-publishers.com. **Website:** www.innovative-publishers.com. Publishes hardcover, trade paperback, mass market, and electronic originals; trade paperback and mass market reprints. Pays 5-17% royalty on retail price. Offers $1,500-125,000 advance. Publishes ms 2 years after acceptance. Responds in 3 months to queries; 4-6 months to mss and proposals. Book catalog for 9x12 SASE with 7 first-class stamps. Guidelines for #10 SASE.

NEEDS "Some works may be slated for anthologies. Readers are from diverse demographic. Seeking innovative styles. Especially seeking emerging ethnic poets from Asia, Europe, and Spanish-speaking countries."

☺ INSOMNIAC PRESS

520 Princess Ave., London ON N6B 2B8, Canada. (416)504-6270. **E-mail:** mike@insomniacpress.com. **Website:** www.insomniacpress.com. **Contact:** Mike O'Connor, publisher. Publishes trade paperback originals and reprints, mass market paperback originals, and electronic originals and reprints. Pays 10-15% royalty on retail price. Pays $500-1,000 advance. Publishes ms 6 months after acceptance. Guidelines online.

NEEDS "Our poetry publishing is limited to 2-4 books per year and we are often booked up a year or two in advance."

HOW TO CONTACT Submit complete ms.

TIPS "We envision a mixed readership that appreciates up-and-coming literary fiction and poetry as well as solidly researched and provocative nonfiction. Peruse our website and familiarize yourself with what we've published in the past."

ITALICA PRESS

595 Main St., Suite 605, New York NY 10044-0047. (917)371-0563. **E-mail:** inquiries@italicapress.com. **Website:** www.italicapress.com. **Contact:** Ronald G. Musto and Eileen Gardiner, publishers. "Italica Press publishes English translations of modern Italian fiction and medieval and Renaissance nonfiction." Publishes hardcover and trade paperback originals. Pays 7-15% royalty on wholesale price; author's copies. Publishes ms 1 year after acceptance. Responds in 1 month to queries; 4 months to mss. Book catalog and guidelines online.

NEEDS Poetry titles are always translations and generally dual language.

HOW TO CONTACT Query with 10 sample translations of medieval and Renaissance Italian poets. Include cover letter, bio, and list of publications.

TIPS "We are interested in considering a wide variety of medieval and Renaissance topics (not historical fiction), and for modern works we are only interested in translations from Italian fiction by well-known Italian authors. *Only* fiction that has been previously published in Italian. A *brief* e-mail saves a lot of time. 90% of proposals we receive are completely off base—but we are very interested in things that are right on target."

ALICE JAMES BOOKS

114 Prescott St., Farmington ME 04938. (207)778-7071. **Fax:** (207)778-7766. **E-mail:** alicejamesea@alicejamesbooks.org. **Website:** www.alicejamesbooks.org. **Contact:** Alyssa Neptune, managing editor; Carey Salerno, executive director; Nicole Wakefield, senior editorial assistant. "Alice James Books is a nonprofit cooperative poetry press. The founders' objectives were to give women access to publishing and to involve authors in the publishing process. The cooperative selects mss for publication through both regional and national competitions." Publishes trade paperback originals. Pays through competition awards. Publishes ms 1 year after acceptance. Responds promptly to queries; 4 months to mss. Book catalog online. Guidelines online.

NEEDS "Alice James Books is a nonprofit cooperative poetry press. The founders' objectives were to give women access to publishing and to involve authors in the publishing process. The cooperative selects mss for publication through both regional and national competitions." Does not want children's poetry or light verse.

TIPS "Send SASE for contest guidelines or check website. Do not send work without consulting current guidelines."

THE JOHNS HOPKINS UNIVERSITY PRESS

2715 N. Charles St., Baltimore MD 21218. (410)516-6900. **Fax:** (410)516-6968. **E-mail:** gb@press.jhu.edu. **Website:** www.press.jhu.edu. **Contact:** Jacqueline C. Wehmueller, executive editor (consumer health, psychology and psychiatry, and history of medicine; jcw@press.jhu.edu); Matthew McAdam, editor (mxm@jhu.press.edu); Robert J. Brugger, senior acquisitions editor (American history; rjb@press.jhu. edu); Vincent J. Burke, exec. editor (biology; vjb@ press.jhu.edu). Publishes hardcover originals and reprints, and trade paperback reprints. Pays royalty. Publishes ms 1 year after acceptance.

NEEDS "One of the largest American university presses, Johns Hopkins publishes primarily scholarly books and journals. We do, however, publish short fiction and poetry in the series Johns Hopkins: Poetry and Fiction, edited by John Irwin."

KAYA PRESS

USC ASE, 3620 S. Vermont Ave. KAP 462, Los Angeles CA 90089. (213)740-2285. **E-mail:** info@kaya. com. **Website:** www.kaya.com. **Contact:** Sunyoung Lee, editor. Kaya is an independent literary press dedicated to the publication of innovative literature from the Asian diaspora. "We are looking for innovative writers with a commitment to quality literature." Publishes hardcover originals and trade paperback originals and reprints. Responds in 6 months to mss. Book catalog available free. Guidelines online.

HOW TO CONTACT Submit complete ms.

TIPS "Audience is people interested in a high standard of literature and who are interested in breaking down easy approaches to multicultural literature."

KELSEY STREET PRESS

Poetry by Women, 2824 Kelsey St., Berkeley CA 94705. **E-mail:** amber@kelseyst.com. **Website:** www.kelseyst. com. "A Berkeley, California press publishing collaborations between women poets and artists. Many of the press's collaborations focus on a central theme or conceit, like the sprawl and spectacle of New York in *Arcade* by Erica Hunt and Alison Saar." Hardcover and trade paperback originals and electronic originals.

HOW TO CONTACT Query.

KNOPF

Imprint of Random House, 1745 Broadway, New York NY 10019. **Fax:** (212)940-7390. **Website:** knopfdoubleday.com/imprint/knopf. **Contact:** The editors. Publishes hardcover and paperback originals. Royalties vary. Offers advance. Publishes ms 1 year after acceptance. Responds in 2-6 months to queries.

❾❷ LAPWING PUBLICATIONS

1 Ballysillan Dr., Belfast BT14 8HQ, Northern Ireland. (44)2890-500-796. **Fax:** (44)2890-295-800. **E-mail:** lapwing.poetry@ntlworld.com. **Website:** www.lapwingpoetry.com. **Contact:** Dennis Greig, editor. Pays

20 author's copies, no royalties. Responds to queries in 1 month; mss in 2 months.

❷ Lapwing will produce work only if and when resources to do so are available.

NEEDS Lapwing publishes "emerging Irish poets and poets domiciled in Ireland, plus the new work of a suitable size by established Irish writers. Non-Irish poets are also published. Poets based in continental Europe have become a major feature. Emphasis on first collections preferrably not larger than 80 pages.

HOW TO CONTACT "Submit 6 poems in the first instance; depending on these, an invitation to submit more may follow." Considers simultaneous submissions. Accepts e-mail submissions in body of message or in DOC format. Cover letter is required. "All submissions receive a first reading. If these poems have minor errors or faults, the writer is advised. Those which appeal at first reading are retained, and a conditional offer is sent." Often comments on rejected poems. "After initial publication, irrespective of the quantity, the work will be permanently available using 'print-on-demand' production; such publications may not always be printed exactly as the original, although the content will remain the same."

TIPS "We are unable to accept new work from beyond mainland Europe and the British Isles due to delivery costs."

LEE & LOW BOOKS

95 Madison Ave., #1205, New York NY 10016. (212)779-4400. **E-mail:** general@leeandlow.com. **Website:** www.leeandlow.com. Jessica Echeverria, associate editor; Samantha Wolf, editorial assistant. **Contact:** Louise May, vice president/editorial director (multicultural children's fiction/nonfiction). "Our goals are to meet a growing need for books that address children of color, and to present literature that all children can identify with. We only consider multicultural children's books. Sponsors a yearly New Voices Award for first-time picture book authors of color. Contest rules online at website or for SASE." Publishes hardcover originals and trade paperback reprints. Pays net royalty. Pays authors advances against royalty. Pays illustrators advance against royalty. Photographers paid advance against royalty. Publishes book 2 years after acceptance. Responds in 6 months to mss if interested. Book catalog available online. Guidelines available online or by written request with SASE.

HOW TO CONTACT Submit complete ms.

TIPS "Check our website to see the kinds of books we publish. Do not send mss that don't fit our mission."

LES FIGUES PRESS

P.O. Box 7736, Los Angeles CA 90007. **E-mail:** info@lesfigues.com. **Website:** www.lesfigues.com. **Contact:** Teresa Carmody and Vanessa Place, co-directors. Les Figues Press is an independent, nonprofit publisher of poetry, prose, visual art, conceptual writing, and translation. With amission is to create aesthetic conversations between readers, writers, and artists, Les Figues Press favors projects which push the boundaries of genre, form, and general acceptability. Submissions are only reviewed through its annual NOS Book Contest.

LETHE PRESS

118 Heritage Ave., Maple Shade NJ 08052. (609)410-7391. **E-mail:** editor@lethepressbooks.com. **Website:** www.lethepressbooks.com. **Contact:** Steve Berman, publisher. "Welcomes submissions from authors of any sexual or gender identity." Guidelines online.

NEEDS "Lethe Press is a small press seeking gay and lesbian themed poetry collections." Lethe Books are distributed by Ingram Publications and Bookazine, and are available at all major bookstores, as well as the major online retailers.

HOW TO CONTACT Query with 7-10 poems, list of publications.

LOST HORSE PRESS

105 Lost Horse Lane, Sandpoint ID 83864. (208)255-4410. **E-mail:** losthorsepress@mindspring.com. **Website:** www.losthorsepress.org. **Contact:** Christine Holbert, publisher. Distributed by University of Washington Press. Publishes hardcover and paperback originals. Publishes ms 3-9 months after acceptance. "Does not accept unsolicited mss. However, we welcome submissions for the *Idaho Prize for Poetry*, a national competition offering $1,000 prize money plus publication for a book-length ms. Please check the submission guidelines for the *Idaho Prize for Poetry* online."

LUNA BISONTE PRODS

137 Leland Ave., Columbus OH 43214-7505. **E-mail:** bennettjohnm@gmail.com. **Website:** www.johnmbennett.net. **Contact:** John M. Bennett, editor/publisher.

NEEDS "Interested in avant-garde and highly experimental work only." Has published poetry by Jim Leftwich, Sheila E. Murphy, Al Ackerman, Richard Kostelanetz, Carla Bertola, Olchar Lindsann, and many others.

HOW TO CONTACT Query first, with a few sample poems and cover letter with brief bio and publication credits. "Keep it brief. Chapbook publishing usually depends on grants or other subsidies, and is usually by solicitation. **Will also consider subsidy arrangements on negotiable terms.**" A sampling of various Luna Bisonte Prods products is available for $20.

MAGE PUBLISHERS, INC.

(202)342-1642. **Fax:** (202)342-9269. **E-mail:** as@mage.com. **Website:** www.mage.com. Mage publishes books relating to Persian/Iranian culture. Publishes hardcover originals and reprints, trade paperback originals. Pays royalty. Responds in 1 month to queries. Book catalog available free. Guidelines online.

NEEDS Must relate to Persian/Iranian culture.

HOW TO CONTACT Query.

TIPS "Audience is the Iranian-American community in America and Americans interested in Persian culture."

MANOR HOUSE PUBLISHING, INC.

452 Cottingham Crescent, Ancaster ON L9G 3V6, Canada. **E-mail:** mbdavie@manor-house.biz. **Website:** www.manor-house.biz. **Contact:** Mike Davie, president (novels, poetry, and nonfiction). Publishes hardcover, trade paperback, and mass market paperback originals reprints. Pays 10% royalty on retail price. Publishes book 1 year after acceptance. Queries and mss to be sent by e-mail only. "We will respond in 30 days if interested-if not, there is no response. Do not follow up unless asked to do so." Book catalog online. Guidelines available via e-mail.

NEEDS Poetry should engage, provoke, involve the reader.

TIPS "Our audience includes everyone-the general public/mass audience. Self-edit your work first, make sure it is well written with strong Canadian content."

MAVERICK DUCK PRESS

E-mail: maverickduckpress@yahoo.com. **Website:** www.maverickduckpress.com. Assistant Editors: Kayla Marie Middlebrook and Brielle Kelton. **Contact:** Kendall A. Bell, editor. Maverick Duck Press is a "publisher of chapbooks from undiscovered talent. We are looking for fresh and powerful work that shows a sense of innovation or a new take on passion or emotion. Previous publication in print or online journals could increase your chances of us accepting your manuscript." Does not want "unedited work." Pays 20 author's copies (out of a press run of 50).

HOW TO CONTACT Send ms in Microsoft Word format with a cover letter with brief bio and publication credits. Chapbook mss may include previously published poems. "Previous publication is always a plus, as we may be more familiar with your work. Chapbook mss should have 16-24 poems, but no more than 24 poems."

○ MCCLELLAND & STEWART, LTD.

The Canadian Publishers, One Toronto St., Unit 300, Toronto ON M5A 2P9, Canada. (416)364-4449. **Fax:** (416)598-7764. **Website:** www.mcclelland.com. Publishes hardcover, trade paperback, and mass market paperback originals and reprints. Pays 10-15% royalty on retail price (hardcover rates). Pays advance. Publishes ms 1 year after acceptance. Responds in 3 months to proposals.

NEEDS Only Canadian poets should apply. We publish only 4 titles each year. Query. *No unsolicited mss.*

MERRIAM PRESS

133 Elm St., Suite 3R, Bennington VT 05201. (802)447-0313. **E-mail:** ray@merriam-press.com. **Website:** www.merriam-press.com. "Merriam Press specializes in military history, particularly World War II history. We are also branching out into other genres." Publishes hardcover and softcover trade paperback originals and reprints. Pays 10% royalty on actual selling price. Publishes ms 6 months or less after acceptance. Responds quickly (e-mail preferred) to queries. Book catalog and guidelines online.

NEEDS Especially but not limited to military topics.

HOW TO CONTACT Query with SASE or by e-mail first.

TIPS "Our military history books are geared for military historians, collectors, model kit builders, wargamers, veterans, general enthusiasts. We now publish some historical fiction and poetry and will consider well-written books on a variety of non-military topics."

⊘ MIAMI UNIVERSITY PRESS

356 Bachelor Hall, Miami University, Oxford OH 45056. **E-mail:** tumakw@miamioh.edu. **Website:** www.miamioh.edu/mupress. **Contact:** Keith Tuma, editor; Amy Toland, managing editor. Publishes 1-2 books of poetry/year and 1 novella, in paperback editions.

HOW TO CONTACT Miami University Press is unable to respond to unsolicited mss and queries.

MICHIGAN STATE UNIVERSITY PRESS

1405 S. Harrison Rd., Suite 25, East Lansing MI 48823-5202. (517)355-9543. **Fax:** (517)432-2611. **E-mail:** msupress@msu.edu. **Website:** msupress.org. **Contact:** Alex Schwartz and Julie Loehr, acquisitions. Michigan State University Press has notably represented both scholarly publishing and the mission of Michigan State University with the publication of numerous award-winning books and scholarly journals. In addition, they publish nonfiction that addresses, in a more contemporary way, social concerns, such as diversity and civil rights. They also publish literary fiction and poetry. Publishes hardcover and softcover originals. Pays variable royalty. Book catalog and ms guidelines online.

NEEDS Publishes poetry collections.

HOW TO CONTACT Submit proposal with sample poems.

MILKWEED EDITIONS

1011 Washington Ave. S., Suite 300, Minneapolis MN 55415. (612)332-3192. **Fax:** (612)215-2550. **Website:** www.milkweed.org. **Contact:** Patrick Thomas, editor and program director. "Milkweed Editions publishes with the intention of making a humane impact on society, in the belief that literature is a transformative art uniquely able to convey the essential experiences of the human heart and spirit. To that end, Milkweed Editions publishes distinctive voices of literary merit in handsomely designed, visually dynamic books, exploring the ethical, cultural, and esthetic issues that free societies need continually to address." Publishes hardcover, trade paperback, and electronic originals; trade paperback and electronic reprints. Pays authors variable royalty based on retail price. Offers advance against royalties. Pays varied advance from $500-10,000. Publishes book in 18 months. Responds in 6 months. Book catalog online. Guidelines online.

NEEDS Milkweed Editions is "looking for poetry manuscripts of high quality that embody humane values and contribute to cultural understanding." Not limited in subject matter. Open to writers with previously published books of poetry or a minimum of 6 poems published in nationally distributed commercial or literary journals. Considers translations and bilingual mss.

HOW TO CONTACT Query with SASE; submit completed ms.

TIPS "We are looking for excellent writing with the intent of making a humane impact on society. Please read submission guidelines before submitting and acquaint yourself with our books in terms of style and quality before submitting. Many factors influence our selection process, so don't get discouraged. Nonfiction is focused on literary writing about the natural world, including living well in urban environments."

⊘ MOVING PARTS PRESS

10699 Empire Grade, Santa Cruz CA 95060. (831)427-2271. **E-mail:** frice@movingpartspress.com. **Website:** www.movingpartspress.com. **Contact:** Felicia Rice, poetry editor. Moving Part Press publishes handsome, innovative books, broadsides, and prints that "explore the relationship of word and image, typography and the visual arts, the fine arts and popular culture."

HOW TO CONTACT *Does not accept unsolicited mss.*

NEW DIRECTIONS

80 Eighth Ave., New York NY 10011. **Fax:** (212)255-0231. **E-mail:** editorial@ndbooks.com. **Website:** www.ndpublishing.com. **Contact:** Editorial Assistant. "Currently, New Directions focuses primarily on fiction in translation, avant garde American fiction, and experimental poetry by American and foreign authors. If your work does not fall into one of those categories, you would probably do best to submit your work elsewhere." Hardcover and trade paperback originals. Responds in 3-4 months to queries. Book catalog and guidelines online.

HOW TO CONTACT Query.

TIPS "Our books serve the academic community."

⊙ NEWEST PUBLISHERS LTD.

201, 8540-109 St., Edmonton AB T6G 1E6, Canada. (780)432-9427. **Fax:** (780)433-3179. **E-mail:** submissions@newestpress.com. **Website:** www.newestpress.com. NeWest publishes Western Canadian fiction, nonfiction, poetry, and drama. Publishes trade paperback originals. Pays 10% royalty. Publishes ms 2-3 years after acceptance. Responds in 6-8 months to queries. Book catalog for 9×12 SASE. Guidelines online.

NEW ISSUES POETRY & PROSE

Western Michigan University, 1903 W. Michigan Ave., Kalamazoo MI 49008-5463. (269)387-8185. **Fax:** (269)387-2562. **E-mail:** new-issues@wmich.edu.

Website: wmich.edu/newissues. **Contact:** Managing Editor. Publishes 18 months after acceptance. Guidelines online.

NEEDS New Issues Poetry & Prose offers two contests annually. The Green Rose Prize is awarded to an author who has previously published at least one full-length book of poems. The New Issues Poetry Prize, an award for a first book of poems, is chosen by a guest judge. Past judges have included Philip Levine, C.K. Williams, C.D. Wright, and Campbell McGrath. New Issues does not read mss outside our contests. Graduate students in the Ph.D. and M.F.A. programs of Western Michigan Univ. often volunteer their time reading mss. Finalists are chosen by the editors. New Issues often publishes up to 2 additional mss selected from the finalists.

NEW RIVERS PRESS

MSU Moorhead, 1104 Seventh Ave. S., Moorhead MN 56563. **E-mail:** kelleysu@mnstate.edu. **Website:** www.newriverspress.com. **Contact:** Suzanne Kelley, managing editor. New Rivers Press publishes collections of poetry, novels, nonfiction, translations of contemporary literature, and collections of short fiction and nonfiction. "We continue to publish books regularly by new and emerging writers, but we also welcome the opportunity to read work of every character and to publish the best literature available nationwide. Each fall through the Many Voices Project competition, we choose 2 books: 1 poetry and 1 prose."

NEEDS The Many Voices Project awards $1,000, a standard book contract, publication of a book-length ms by New Rivers Press, and national distribution. All previously published poems must be acknowledged. "We will consider simultaneous submissions if noted as such. If your manuscript is accepted elsewhere during the judging, you must notify New Rivers Press immediately. If you do not give such notification and your manuscript is selected, your entry gives New Rivers Press permission to go ahead with publication."

HOW TO CONTACT Guidelines online.

⊘ NINETY-SIX PRESS

Furman University, 3300 Poinsett Hwy., Greenville SC 29613. (864)294-3152. **Fax:** (864)294-2224. **E-mail:** gil.allen@furman.edu. **Website:** library.furman.edu/specialcollections/96Press/index.htm. **Contact:** Gilbert Allen, editor. For a sample, send $10.

TIPS "South Carolina poets only. Check our website for guidelines."

NODIN PRESS

5114 Cedar Lake Rd., Minneapolis MN 55416. (952)546-6300. **Fax:** (952)546-6303. **E-mail:** nstill4402@aol.com. **Contact:** Norton Stillman, publisher. "Nodin Press publishes Minnesota regional titles: nonfiction, memoir, sports, poetry." Publishes hardcover and trade paperback originals Pays 5% royalty. Publishes book 6 months after acceptance. Responds in 6 months to queries. Book catalog and ms guidelines free.

NEEDS Regional (Minnesota poets).

HOW TO CONTACT Submit 10 sample poems.

NORTH ATLANTIC BOOKS

2526 MLK Jr. Way, Berkeley CA 94704. **Website:** www.northatlanticbooks.com. **Contact:** Acquisitions Board. Publishes hardcover, trade paperback, and electronic originals; trade paperback and electronic reprints. Pays royalty percentage on wholesale price. Publishes ms 14 months after acceptance. Responds in 3-6 months. Book catalog free on request (if available). Guidelines online.

HOW TO CONTACT Submit 15-20 sample poems.

⊘ W.W. NORTON & COMPANY, INC.

500 Fifth Ave., New York NY 10110. (212)354-5500. **Fax:** (212)869-0856. **Website:** www.wwnorton.com. "W. W. Norton & Company, the oldest and largest publishing house owned wholly by its employees, strives to carry out the imperative of its founder to 'publish books not for a single season, but for the years' in fiction, nonfiction, poetry, college textbooks, cookbooks, art books and professional books. Due to the workload of our editorial staff and the large volume of materials we receive, *Norton is no longer able to accept unsolicited submissions.* If you are seeking publication, we suggest working with a literary agent who will represent you to the house."

OBERLIN COLLEGE PRESS

50 N. Professor St., Oberlin College, Oberlin OH 44074. (440)775-8408. **Fax:** (440)775-8124. **E-mail:** oc.press@oberlin.edu. **Website:** www.oberlin.edu/ocpress. **Contact:** Marco Wilkinson, managing editor. Publishes hardcover and trade paperback originals. Pays 7½-10% royalty. Responds promptly to queries; 2 months to mss.

NEEDS *FIELD Magazine*—submit 2-6 poems through website "submissions" tab; FIELD Translation Series—query with SASE and sample poems; FIELD Poetry Series—*no unsolicited mss.* Enter mss in FIELD Poetry Prize ($1,000 and a standard royalty contract) held annually in May.

HOW TO CONTACT Submit complete ms.

TIPS "Queries for the FIELD Translation Series: send sample poems and letter describing project. Winner of the annual FIELD poetry prize determines publication. Do not send unsolicited manuscripts."

OHIO STATE UNIVERSITY PRESS

1070 Carmack Rd., 180 Pressey Hall, Columbus OH 43210-1002. (614)292-6930. **Fax:** (614)292-2065. **E-mail:** eugene@osupress.org. **E-mail:** lindsay@osupress.org. **Website:** www.ohiostatepress.org. **Contact:** Eugene O'Connor, acquisitions editor (medieval studies and classics); Lindsay Martin, acquisitions editor (literary studies). The Ohio State University Press publishes scholarly nonfiction, and offers short fiction and short poetry prizes. Currently emphasizing history, literary studies, political science, women's health, classics, Victoria studies. Pays royalty. Pays advance. Responds in 3 months to queries. Guidelines online.

NEEDS Offers poetry competition through *The Journal.*

☺ OOLICHAN BOOKS

P.O. Box 2278, Lantzville BC V0R 1M0, Canada. (250)390-4839. **Fax:** (866)299-0026. **E-mail:** oolichanbooks@telus.net. **Website:** www.oolichan.com. Publishes hardcover and trade paperback originals and reprints. Pays royalty on retail price. Publishes ms 6-12 months after acceptance. Responds in 1-3 months. Book catalog online. Guidelines online.

☺ Only publishes Canadian authors.

NEEDS "We are one of the few small literary presses in Canada that still publishes poetry. We try to include 2-3 poetry titles each year. We attempt to balance our list between emerging and established poets. Our poetry titles have won or been shortlisted for major national awards, including the Governor General's Award, the BC Book Prizes, and the Alberta Awards."

HOW TO CONTACT Submit 10 sample poems.

TIPS "Our audience is adult readers who love good books and good literature. Our audience is regional and national, as well as international. Follow our submission guidelines. Check out some of our titles at your local library or bookstore to get an idea of what we publish. Don't send us the only copy of your manuscript. Let us know if your submission is simultaneous, and inform us if it is accepted elsewhere. Above all, keep writing!"

OOLIGAN PRESS

369 Neuberger Hall, 724 SW Harrison St., Portland OR 97201. (503)725-9410. **E-mail:** acquisitions@ooliganpress.pdx.edu. **Website:** ooligan.pdx.edu. Publishes trade paperback, and electronic originals and reprints. Pays negotiable royalty on retail price. Book catalog online. Guidelines online.

NEEDS Ooligan is a not-for-profit general trade press that publishes books honoring the cultural and natural diversity of the Pacific Northwest. "We are limited in the number of poetry titles that we publish as poetry represents only a small percentage of our overall acquisitions. We are open to all forms of style and verse; however, we give special preference to prose poetry and traditional verse. Although spoken word, slam, and rap poetry are of interest to the press, we will consider such work if it does not translate well to the written page." Ooligan does not publish chapbooks.

HOW TO CONTACT Query, submit 20 sample poems, submit complete ms.

TIPS "For children's books, our audience will be middle grades and young adult, with marketing to general trade, libraries, and schools. Good marketing ideas increase the chances of a manuscript succeeding."

⊘ ORCHARD BOOKS

557 Broadway, New York NY 10012. **E-mail:** mcroland@scholastic.com. **Website:** www.scholastic.com. **Contact:** Ken Geist, vice president/editorial director; David Saylor, vice president/creative director. *Orchard is not accepting unsolicited mss.* Most commonly offers an advance against list royalties.

⊘ ORCHISES PRESS

P.O. Box 320533, Alexandria VA 22320. (703)683-1243. **E-mail:** lathbury@gmu.edu. **Website:** mason.gmu.edu/~lathbury. **Contact:** Roger Lathbury, editor-in-chief. Orchises Press is a general literary publisher specializing in poetry with selected reprints and textbooks. No new fiction or children's books. Publishes hardcover and trade paperback originals and reprints. Pays 36% of receipts after Orchises has recouped its costs. Publishes book 1 year after acceptance. Responds in 3 months to queries. Guidelines online.

NEEDS Poetry must have been published in respected literary journals. *Orchises Press no longer reads unsolicited mss.* Publishes free verse, but has strong formalist preferences.

HOW TO CONTACT Query and submit 5 sample poems.

PALETTES & QUILLS

1935 Penfield Road, Penfield NY 14526. (585)456-0217. **E-mail:** palettesnquills@gmail.com. **Website:** www.palettesnquills.com. **Contact:** Donna M. Marbach, publisher/owner.

NEEDS Palettes & Quills "is at this point, a poetry press only, and produces only a handful of publications each year, specializing in anthologies, individual chapbooks, and broadsides." Wants "work that should appeal to a wide audience." Does not want "poems that are sold blocks of text, long-lined and without stanza breaks. Wildly elaborate free-verse would be difficult and in all likelihood fight with art background, amateurish rhyming poem, overly sentimental poems, poems that use excessive profanity, or which denigrate other people, or political and religious diatribes."

HOW TO CONTACT Query first with 3-5 poems and a cover letter with brief bio and publication credits for individual unsolicited chapbooks. May include previously published poems. Chapbook poets would get 20 copies of a run; broadside poets and artists get 5-10 copies and occasionally paid $10 for reproduction rights. Anthology poets get 1 copy of the anthology. All poets and artists get a discount on purchases that include their work.

PAYCOCK PRESS

3819 N. 13th St., Arlington VA 22201. (703)525-9296. **E-mail:** rchrdpeabody9@gmail.com. **Website:** www.gargoylemagazine.com. **Contact:** Richard Peabody. "Too academic for the underground, too outlaw for the academic world. We tend to be edgy and look for ultra-literary work." Publishes paperback originals. Books: POD printing. Average print order: 500. Averages 1 total title/year. Member CLMP. Distributes through Amazon and website. Publishes ms 1 year after acceptance. Responds to queries in 1 month; mss in 4 months.

NEEDS Considers experimental, edgy poetry collections.

HOW TO CONTACT Accepts unsolicited mss. Accepts queries by e-mail. Include brief bio. Send SASE for return of ms or send a disposable ms and SASE for reply only.

TIPS "Check out our website. Two of our favorite writers are Paul Bowles and Jeanette Winterson."

PELICAN PUBLISHING COMPANY

1000 Burmaster St., Gretna LA 70053. (504)368-1175. **Fax:** (504)368-1195. **E-mail:** editorial@pelicanpub.

com. **Website:** www.pelicanpub.com. "We believe ideas have consequences. One of the consequences is that they lead to a best-selling book. We publish books to improve and uplift the reader. Currently emphasizing business and history titles." Publishes 20 young readers/year; 1 middle reader/year. "Our children's books (illustrated and otherwise) include history, biography, holiday, and regional. Pelican's mission is to publish books of quality and permanence that enrich the lives of those who read them." Publishes hardcover, trade paperback and mass market paperback originals and reprints. Pays authors in royalties; buys ms outright "rarely." Illustrators paid by "various arrangements." Advance considered. Publishes a book 9-18 months after acceptance. Responds in 1 month to queries; 3 months to mss. Book catalog and ms guidelines online.

NEEDS Considers poetry for "hardcover children's books only (1,100 words maximum), preferably with a regional focus. However, our needs for this are very limited; we publish 20 juvenile titles per year, and most of these are prose, not poetry." Books are 32 pages, magazine-sized, include illustrations.

TIPS "We do extremely well with cookbooks, popular histories, and business. We will continue to build in these areas. The writer must have a clear sense of the market and knowledge of the competition. A query letter should describe the project briefly, give the author's writing and professional credentials, and promotional ideas."

PERSEA BOOKS

277 Broadway, Suite 708, New York NY 10007. (212)260-9256. **Fax:** (212)267-3165. **E-mail:** info@ perseabooks.com. **Website:** www.perseabooks.com. The aim of Persea is to publish works that endure by meeting high standards of literary merit and relevance. "We have often taken on important books other publishers have overlooked, or have made significant discoveries and rediscoveries, whether of a single work or writer's entire oeuvre. Our books cover a wide range of themes, styles, and genres. We have published poetry, fiction, essays, memoir, biography, titles of Jewish and Middle Eastern interest, women's studies, American Indian folklore, and revived classics, as well as a notable selection of works in translation." Responds in 8 weeks to proposals; 10 weeks to mss. Guidelines online.

NEEDS "We have a longstanding commitment to publishing extraordinary contemporary poetry and

maintain an active poetry program. At this time, due to our commitment to the poets we already publish, we are limited in our ability to add new collections."

HOW TO CONTACT Send an e-mail to poetry@ perseabooks.com describing current project and publication history, attaching a pdf or Word document with up to 12 sample pages of poetry. "If the timing is right and we are interested in seeing more work, we will contact you."

PERUGIA PRESS

P.O. Box 60364, Florence MA 01062. **Website:** www. perugiapress.com. **Contact:** Susan Kan, director. Celebrating poetry by women since 1997. "Contact us through our website."

PIÑATA BOOKS

Imprint of Arte Publico Press, University of Houston, 4902 Gulf Fwy., Bldg. 19, Room 100, Houston TX 77204-2004. (713)743-2845. **Fax:** (713)743-3080. **E-mail:** submapp@uh.edu. **Website:** www.artepublicopress.com. "Piñata Books is dedicated to the publication of children's and young adult literature focusing on U.S. Hispanic culture by U.S. Hispanic authors. Arte Publico's mission is the publication, promotion and dissemination of Latino literature for a variety of national and regional audiences, from early childhood to adult, through the complete gamut of delivery systems, including personal performance as well as print and electronic media." Publishes hardcover and trade paperback originals. Pays 10% royalty on wholesale price. Pays $1,000-3,000 advance. Publishes book 2 years after acceptance. Responds in 2-3 months to queries; 4-6 months to mss. Book catalog and guidelines online.

NEEDS Appropriate to Hispanic theme.

HOW TO CONTACT Submissions made through online submission form.

TIPS "Include cover letter with submission explaining why your manuscript is unique and important, why we should publish it, who will buy it, etc."

PLAN B PRESS

2714 Jefferson Dr., Alexandria VA 22303. (215)732-2663. **E-mail:** planbpress@gmail.com. **Website:** www.planbpress.com. **Contact:** Steven Allen May, president. Plan B Press is a "small publishing company with an international feel. Our intention is to have Plan B Press be part of the conversation about the direction and depth of literary movements and genres. Plan B Press's new direction is to seek out authors rarely-to-never published, sharing new voices that might not otherwise be heard. Plan B Press is determined to merge text with image, writing with art." Publishes poetry and short fiction. Wants "experimental poetry, concrete/visual work." Pays author's copies. Responds to queries in 1 month; mss in 3 months.

NEEDS Wants to see: experimental, concrete, visual poetry. Does not want "sonnets, political or religious poems, work in the style of Ogden Nash."

PRESA PRESS

P.O. Box 792, 8590 Belding Rd. NE, Rockford MI 49341. **E-mail:** presapress@aol.com. **Website:** www. presapress.com. **Contact:** Roseanne Ritzema, editor. Presa Press publishes perfect-bound paperbacks and saddle-stitched chapbooks of poetry. Wants "imagistic poetry where form is an extension of content, surreal, experimental, and personal poetry." Does not want "overtly political or didactic material." Pays 10-25 author/quotes copies. Time between acceptance and publication is 8-12 weeks. Responds to queries in 2-4 weeks; to mss in 8-12 weeks

NEEDS Acquires first North American serial rights and the right to reprint in anthologies. Rights include e-book publishing rights. Rights revert to poets upon publication. Accepts postal submissions only. Cover letter is preferred. Reads submissions year round. Poems are circulated to an editorial board. Send materials for review consideration to Roseanne Ritzema.

HOW TO CONTACT Query first, with a few sample poems and a cover letter with brief bio and publication credits. Book/chapbook mss may include previously published poems.

PRESS 53

560 N. Trade St., Suite 103, Winston-Salem NC 27101. **E-mail:** kevin@press53.com. **Website:** www.press53. com. **Contact:** Kevin Morgan Watson, publisher. "Press 53 was founded in October 2005 and quickly began earning a reputation as a quality publishing house of short story and poetry collections." Responds in 6 months to mss. Guidelines online.

NEEDS "We love working with poets who have been widely published and are active in the poetry community. We publish roughly 4-6 full-length poetry collections of around 70 pages or more each year, plus the winner of our Press 53 Award for Poetry." Prefers that at least 30-40% of the poems in the collection be previously published.

HOW TO CONTACT Finds mss through contest and referrals.

TIPS "We are looking for writers who are actively involved in the writing community, writers who are submitting their work to journals, magazines and contests, and who are getting published, building readership, and earning a reputation for their work."

PRESS HERE

22230 NE 28th Place, Sammamish WA 98074-6408. **Website:** www.gracecuts.com/press-here. Press Here publishes award-winning books of haiku, tanka, and related poetry by the leading poets of these genres, as well as essays, criticism, and interviews about these genres. "We publish work only by those poets who are already frequently published in the leading haiku and tanka journals." Publishes 1-2 poetry books/year, plus occasional books of essays or interviews. Mss are selected through open submission. Pays a negotiated percentage of author's copies (out of a press run of 200-1,000). Responds to queries in up to 1 month; to mss in up to 2 months. Catalog available for #10 SASE.

○ Press Here publications have won the 1st-place Merit Book Award and other awards from the Haiku Society of America.

NEEDS Does not want any poetry other than haiku, tanka, and related genres. Has published poetry by Lee Gurga, paul m., Paul O. Williams, Pat Shelley, Cor van den Heuvel, and William J. Higginson.

HOW TO CONTACT Query first, with a few sample poems and a cover letter with brief bio and publication credits. Book mss may include previously published poems ("previous publication strongly preferred"). "All proposals must be by well-established haiku or tanka poets, and must be for haiku or tanka poetry, or criticism/discussion of these genres. If the editor does not already know your work well from leading haiku and tanka publications, then he is not likely to be interested in your manuscript."

PRINCETON UNIVERSITY PRESS

41 William St., Princeton NJ 08540. (609)258-4900. **Fax:** (609)258-6305. **Website:** www.pupress.princeton.edu. **Contact:** Brigitta van Rheinberg, editor-in-chief. "The Lockert Library of Poetry in Translation embraces a wide geographic and temporal range, from Scandinavia to Latin America to the subcontinent of India, from the Tang Dynasty to Europe of the modern day. It especially emphasizes poets who are established in their native lands and who are being

introduced to an English-speaking audience. Manuscripts are judged with several criteria in mind: the ability of the translation to stand on its own as poetry in English; fidelity to the tone and spirit of the original, rather than literal accuracy; and the importance of the translated poet to the literature of his or her time and country." Responds in 3-4 months. Guidelines online.

NEEDS Submit hard copy of proposal with sample poems or full ms. Cover letter is required. Reads submissions year round. Mss will not be returned. Comments on finalists only.

RAGGED SKY PRESS

P.O. Box 312, Annandale NJ 08801. **E-mail:** raggedskyanthology@gmail.com. **Website:** www.raggedsky.com. **Contact:** Ellen Foos, publisher; Vasiliki Katsarou, managing editor; Arlene Weiner, editor. Produces poetry anthologies and single-author poetry collections along with occasional inspired prose. Ragged Sky is a small, highly selective cooperative press. "We work with our authors closely." Individual poetry collections currently by invitation only. Learn more online.

RED HEN PRESS

P.O. Box 40820, Pasadena CA 91114. (818)831-0649. **Fax:** (818)831-6659. **Website:** www.redhen.org. **Contact:** Mark E. Cull, publisher/editor (fiction). "At this time, the best opportunity to be published by Red Hen is by entering one of our contests. Please find more information in our award submission guidelines." Publishes trade paperback originals. Publishes ms 1 year after acceptance. Responds in 1-2 months. Book catalog available free. Guidelines online.

HOW TO CONTACT Submit to Benjamin Saltman Poetry Award.

TIPS "Audience reads poetry, literary fiction, intelligent nonfiction. If you have an agent, we may be too small since we don't pay advances. Write well. Send queries first. Be willing to help promote your own book."

⊘ RED MOON PRESS

P.O. Box 2461, Winchester VA 22604. (540)722-2156. **E-mail:** jim.kacian@redmoonpress.com. **Website:** www.redmoonpress.com. **Contact:** Jim Kacian, editor/publisher. Red Moon Press "is the largest and most prestigious publisher of English-language haiku and related work in the world." Publishes 6-8 volumes/year, usually 3-5 anthologies and individual collec-

tions of English-language haiku, as well as 1-3 books of essays, translations, or criticism of haiku. Under other imprints, the press also publishes chapbooks of various sizes and formats.

HOW TO CONTACT Query with book theme and information, and 30-40 poems or draft of first chapter. Responds to queries in 2 weeks, to mss (if invited) in 3 months. "Each contract separately negotiated."

☺ RONSDALE PRESS

3350 W. 21st Ave., Vancouver BC V6S 1G7, Canada. (604)738-4688. **Fax:** (604)731-4548. **E-mail:** ronsdale@shaw.ca. **Website:** ronsdalepress.com. **Contact:** Ronald B. Hatch (fiction, poetry, nonfiction, social commentary); Veronica Hatch (YA novels and short stories). "Ronsdale Press is a Canadian literary publishing house that publishes 12 books each year, four of which are young adult titles. Of particular interest are books involving children exploring and discovering new aspects of Canadian history." Publishes trade paperback originals. Pays 10% royalty on retail price. Publishes book 1 year after acceptance. Responds to queries in 2 weeks; mss in 2 months. Book catalog for #10 SASE. Guidelines online.

NEEDS Poets should have published some poems in magazines/journals and should be well-read in contemporary masters.

HOW TO CONTACT Submit complete ms.

TIPS "Ronsdale Press is a literary publishing house, based in Vancouver, and dedicated to publishing books from across Canada, books that give Canadians new insights into themselves and their country. We aim to publish the best Canadian writers."

ROSE ALLEY PRESS

4203 Brooklyn Ave. NE, #103A, Seattle WA 98105. (206)633-2725. **E-mail:** rosealleypress@juno.com. **Website:** www.rosealleypress.com. **Contact:** David D. Horowitz. "Rose Alley Press primarily publishes books featuring rhymed metrical poetry and an annually updated booklet about writing and publication. We do not read or consider unsolicited manuscripts."

SAKURA PUBLISHING & TECHNOLOGIES

P.O. Box 1681, Hermitage PA 16148. (330)360-5131. **E-mail:** skpublishing124@gmail.com. **Website:** www.sakura-publishing.com. **Contact:** Derek Vasconi, talent finder and CEO. Mss that don't follow guidelines will not be considered. Publishes hardcover, trade paperback, mass market paperback and electronic originals and reprints. Pays royalty of 20-60% on wholesale price or retail price. Publishes ms 6 months after acceptance. Responds in 1 week. Book catalog available for #10 SASE. Guidelines online.

HOW TO CONTACT Follow guidelines online.

TIPS "Please make sure you visit our submissions page at our website and follow all instructions exactly as written. Also, Sakura Publishing has a preference for fiction/nonfiction books specializing in Asian culture."

SALINA BOOKSHELF

3120 N. Caden Ct., Suite 4, Flagstaff AZ 86004. (928)527-0070. **Fax:** (928)526-0386. **Website:** www.salinabookshelf.com. Publishes trade paperback originals and reprints. Pays varying royalty. Pays advance. Publishes ms 1 year after acceptance. Responds in 3 months to queries.

NEEDS "We accept poetry in English/Southwest language for children."

HOW TO CONTACT Submit 3 sample poems.

SALMON POETRY

Knockeven, Cliffs of Moher, County Clare , Ireland. 353(0)65-7081941. **E-mail:** info@salmonpoetry.com. **E-mail:** jessie@salmonpoetry.com. **Website:** www.salmonpoetry.com. **Contact:** Jessie Lendennie, editor. Publishes mass market paperback originals and e-books.

NEEDS "Salmon Press has become one of the most important publications in the Irish literary world, specialising in the promotion of new poets, particularly women poets. Established as an alternative voice. Walks tightrope between innovation and convention. Was a flagship for writers in the west of Ireland. Salmon has developed a cross-cultural, internatonal literary dialog, broadening Irish Literature and urging new perspectives on established traditions."

HOW TO CONTACT E-mail query with short biographical note and 5-10 sample poems.

TIPS "If we are broad minded and willing to nurture the individual voice inherent in the work, the artist will emerge."

SARABANDE BOOKS, INC.

2234 Dundee Rd., Suite 200, Louisville KY 40205. (502)458-4028. **Fax:** (502)458-4065. **E-mail:** info@sarabandebooks.org. **Website:** www.sarabandebooks.org. **Contact:** Sarah Gorham, editor-in-chief. "Sarabande Books was founded to publish poetry, short fiction, and creative nonfiction. We look for works of lasting literary value. Please see our titles to get an idea of our taste. Accepts submissions through contests and open submissions." Publishes trade paperback originals. Pays royalty. 10% on actual income received. Also pays in author's copies. Pays $500-1,000 advance. Publishes ms 18 months after acceptance. Book catalog available free. Contest guidelines for #10 SASE or on website.

◯ Charges $15 handling fee with alternative option of purchase of book from website (e-mail confirmation of sale must be included with submission).

NEEDS Poetry of superior artistic quality; otherwise no restraints or specifications. Sarabande Books publishes books of poetry of 48 pages minimum. Wants "poetry that offers originality of voice and subject matter, uniqueness of vision, and a language that startles because of the careful attention paid to it—language that goes beyond the merely competent or functional."

HOW TO CONTACT Mss selected through literary contests, invitation, and recommendation by a well-established writer.

TIPS "Sarabande publishes for a general literary audience. Know your market. Read-and buy-books of literature. Sponsors contests for poetry and fiction. Make sure you're not writing in a vacuum, that you've read and are conscious of contemporary literature. Have someone read your manuscript, checking it for ordering, coherence. Better a lean, consistently strong manuscript than one that is long and uneven. We like a story to have good narrative, and we like to be engaged by language."

SATURNALIA BOOKS

105 Woodside Rd., Ardmore PA 19003. (267) 278-9541. **E-mail:** info@saturnaliabooks.com. **Website:** www.saturnaliabooks.org. **Contact:** Henry Israeli, publisher. "We do not accept unsolicited submissions. We hold a contest, the Saturnalia Books Poetry Prize, annually in which 1 anonymously submitted title is chosen by a poet with a national reputation for publication. Submissions are accepted during the month of March. The submission fee is $30, and the prize is $2,000 and 20 copies of the book. See website for details." Publishes trade paperback originals and digital versions for e-readers. Pays authors 4-6% royalty on retail price. Pays $400-2,000 advance. Responds in 4 months on mss. Catalog online. Guidelines online.

HOW TO CONTACT "Saturnalia Books has no bias against any school of poetry, but we do tend to publish writers who take chances and push against convention in some way, whether it's in form, language, content, or musicality." Submit complete ms to contest only.

TIPS "Our audience tend to be young avid readers of contemporary poetry. Read a few sample books first."

SHEARSMAN BOOKS, LTD

50 Westons Hills Dr., Emersons Green Bristol BS16 7DF, United Kingdom. **E-mail:** editor@shearsman. com. **Website:** www.shearsman.com. **Contact:** Tony Frazer, editor. Publishes trade paperback originals. Pays 10% royalty on retail price after 150 copies have sold; authors also receive 10 free copies of their books. Responds in 2-3 months to mss. Book catalog online. Guidelines online.

NEEDS "Shearsman only publishes poetry, poetry collections, and poetry in translation (from any language but with an emphasis on work in Spanish & in German). Some critical work on poetry and also memoirs and essays by poets. Mainly poetry by British, Irish, North American, and Australian poets." No children's books.

TIPS "Book ms submission: most of the ms must have already appeared in the UK or USA magazines of some repute, and it has to fill 70-72 pages of half letter or A5 pages. You must have sufficient return postage. Submissions can also be made by email. It is unlikely that a poet with no track record will be accepted for publication as there is no obvious audience for the work. Try to develop some exposure to UK and US magazines and try to assemble a ms only later."

SHIPWRECKT BOOKS PUBLISHING COMPANY LLC

P.O. Box 20, Lanesboro MN 55949. (507)458-8190. **E-mail:** editor@shipwrecktbooks.com. **E-mail:** contact@shipwrecktbooks.com. **Website:** www.shipwrecktbooks.com. **Contact:** Tom Driscoll, managing editor. Publishes trade paperback originals, mass market paperback originals, and electronic originals. Authors receive a maximum of 35% royalties. Average length of time between acceptance of a book-length ms and publication is 6 months. Responds to queries within 2 months. Catalog and guidelines online.

HOW TO CONTACT Submit 3 sample poems by e-mail.

TIPS "Quality writing. Query first. Development and full editorial services available."

SILVERFISH REVIEW PRESS

P.O. Box 3541, Eugene OR 97403. (541)344-5060. **E-mail:** sfrpress@earthlink.net. **Website:** www.silverfishreviewpress.com. "Sponsors the Gerald Cable Book Award. This prize is awarded annually to a book length manuscript of original poetry by an author who has not yet published a full-length collection. There are no restrictions on the kind of poetry or subject matter; translations are not acceptable. Winners will receive $1,000, publication, and 25 copies of the book. Entries must be postmarked by October 15. Entries may be submitted by e-mail. See website for instructions." Publishes trade paperback originals. Guidelines online.

TIPS "Read recent Silverfish titles."

SOUTHERN ILLINOIS UNIVERSITY PRESS

1915 University Press Dr., SIUC Mail Code 6806, Carbondale IL 62901. (618)453-6626. **Fax:** (618)453-1221. **E-mail:** kageff@siu.edu. **Website:** www.siupress.com. **Contact:** Karl Kageff, editor-in-chief. Scholarly press specializes in film and theater studies, rhetoric and composition studies, American history, Civil War, regional and nonfiction trade, poetry. No fiction. Currently emphasizing film, theater and American history, especially Civil War. Publishes hardcover and trade paperback originals and reprints. Pays 5-10% royalty on wholesale price. Rarely offers advance. Publishes ms 1 year after acceptance. Responds in 2 months to queries. Book catalog and ms guidelines free.

NEEDS Crab Orchard Series in Poetry.

HOW TO CONTACT Guidelines online.

STEEL TOE BOOKS

Department of English, Western Kentucky University, 1906 College Heights Blvd. #11086, Bowling Green KY 42101. (270)745-5769. **E-mail:** tom.hunley@wku. edu. **Website:** www.steeltoebooks.com. **Contact:** Dr. Tom C. Hunley, director. Steel Toe Books publishes "full-length, single-author poetry collections. Our books are professionally designed and printed. We look for workmanship (economical use of language, high-energy verbs, precise literal descriptions, original figurative language, poems carefully arranged as a book); a unique style and/or a distinctive voice; clarity; emotional impact; humor (word plays, hyperbole, comic timing); performability (a Steel Toe poet is at home on the stage as well as on the page)." Does not want "dry verse, purposely obscure language, poetry by people who are so wary of being called 'sentimental' they steer away from any recognizable human emotions, poetry that takes itself so seriously that it's unintentionally funny." Has published poetry by Allison Joseph, Susan Browne, James Doyle, Martha Silano, Mary Biddinger, John Guzlowski, Jeannine Hall Gailey, and others. Publishes 1-3 poetry books/year. Mss are normally selected through open submission. **HOW TO CONTACT** "Check the website for news about our next open reading period." Book mss may include previously published poems. Responds to mss in 3 months. Pays $500 advance on 10% royalties and 10 author's copies. Order sample books by sending $12 to Steel Toe Books. *Must purchase a manuscript in order to submit.* See website for submission guidelines.

SUBITO PRESS

University of Colorado at Boulder, Dept. of English, 226 UCB, Boulder CO 80309-0226. **E-mail:** subitopressucb@gmail.com. **Website:** www.subitopress.org. Subito Press is a non-profit publisher of literary works. Each year Subito publishes one work of fiction and one work of poetry through its contest. Publishes trade paperback originals. Guidelines online.
HOW TO CONTACT Submit complete ms to contest.
TIPS "We publish 2 books of innovative writing a year through our poetry and fiction contests. All entries are also considered for publication with the press."

SUNBURY PRESS, INC.

P.O. Box 548, Boiling Springs PA 17007. **E-mail:** info@sunburypress.com. **E-mail:** proposals@sunburypress.com. **Website:** www.sunburypress.com. "Please use our online submission form." Publishes trade paperback originals and reprints; electronic originals and reprints. Pays 10% royalty on wholesale price. Publishes ms 3 months after acceptance. Responds in 2 months. Catalog and guidelines online.
HOW TO CONTACT Submit complete ms.
TIPS "Our books appeal to very diverse audiences. We are building our list in many categories, focusing on many demographics. We are not like traditional publishers—we are digitally adept and very creative. Don't be surprised if we move quicker than you are accustomed to!"

SWAN ISLE PRESS

P.O. Box 408790, Chicago IL 60640. (773)728-3780. **E-mail:** info@swanislepress.com. **Website:** www.swanislepress.com. *"We do not accept unsolicited mss."* Publishes hardcover and trade paperback originals. Pays

7-10% royalty on wholesale price. Publishes book 18 months after acceptance. Responds in 6-12 months. Book catalog online. Guidelines online.
HOW TO CONTACT Query with SASE.

SWAN SCYTHE PRESS

1468 Mallard Way, Sunnyvale CA 94087. **E-mail:** robert.pesich@gmail.com. **Website:** www.swanscythe.com. **Contact:** Robert Pesich, editor.
NEEDS "After publishing 25 chapbooks, a few full-sized poetry collections, and 1 anthology, then taking a short break from publishing, Swan Scythe Press is now re-launching its efforts with some new books, under a new editorship. We have also begun a new series of books, called Poetas/Puentes, from emerging poets writing in Spanish, translated into English. We will also consider mss in indigenous languages from North, Central and South America, translated into English."
HOW TO CONTACT Query first before submitting a ms via e-mail or through website.

TARPAULIN SKY PRESS

P.O. Box 189, Grafton VT 05146. **E-mail:** editors@tarpaulinsky.com. **Website:** www.tarpaulinsky.com. **Contact:** Resh Daily, managing editor. Tarpaulin Sky Press publishes cross- and trans-genre works as well as innovative poetry and prose. Produces full-length books and chapbooks, hand-bound books and trade paperbacks, and offers both hand-bound and perfect-bound paperback editions of full-length books. "We're a small, author-centered press endeavoring to create books that, as objects, please our authors as much their texts please us."
HOW TO CONTACT Writers whose work has appeared in or been accepted for publication in *Tarpaulin Sky* may submit chapbook or full-length mss at any time, with no reading fee. Tarpaulin Sky Press also considers chapbook and full-length mss from writers whose work has not appeared in the journal, but **asks for a $20 reading fee.** Make checks/money orders to Tarpaulin Sky Press. Cover letter is preferred. Reading periods may be found on the website.

TEBOT BACH

P.O. Box 7887, Huntington Beach CA 92615. (714)968-0905. **E-mail:** info@tebotbach.org. **Website:** www.tebotbach.org. **Contact:** Mifanwy Kaiser, editor/publisher. Publishes mss 2 years after acceptance. Responds in 3 months.

NEEDS Offers 2 contests per year. The Patricia Bibby First Book Contest and The Clockwise Chapbook contest. Go online for more information.

HOW TO CONTACT Query first via e-mail, with a few sample poems and cover letter with brief bio.

TEXAS TECH UNIVERSITY PRESS

3003 15th St., Suite 901, Lubbock TX 79409. (806)834-5821. **Fax:** (806)742-2979. **E-mail:** ttup.editorial@ttu.edu. **Website:** www.ttupress.org. **Contact:** Joanna Conrad, editor-in-chief. Texas Tech University Press, the book publishing office of the university since 1971 and an AAUP member since 1986, publishes nonfiction titles in the areas of natural history and the natural sciences; 18th century and Joseph Conrad studies; studies of modern Southeast Asia, particularly the Vietnam War; costume and textile history; Latin American literature and culture; and all aspects of the Great Plains and the American West, especially history, biography, memoir, sports history, and travel. In addition, the Press publishes several scholarly journals, acclaimed series for young readers, an annual invited poetry collection, and literary fiction of Texas and the West. Guidelines online.

NEEDS "TTUP publishes an annual invited first-book poetry manuscript (please note that we cannot entertain unsolicited poetry submissions)."

☺ THISTLEDOWN PRESS LTD.

410 2nd Ave., Saskatoon SK S7K 2C3, Canada. (306)244-1722. **Fax:** (306)244-1762. **E-mail:** editorial@thistledownpress.com. **Website:** www.thistledownpress.com. **Contact:** Allan Forrie, publisher. "Thistledown originates books by Canadian authors only, although we have co-published titles by authors outside Canada. We do not publish children's picture books." Pays authors royalty of 10-12% based on net dollar sales. Pays illustrators and photographers by the project (range: $250-750). Publishes book 1 year after acceptance. Responds to queries in 4 months. Book catalog free on request.

NEEDS "We do not publish cowboy poetry, inspirational poetry, or poetry for children."

TIPS "Send cover letter including publishing history and SASE."

TIA CHUCHA PRESS

P.O. Box 328, San Fernando CA 91341. **E-mail:** info@tiachucha.com. **Website:** www.tiachucha.com. **Contact:** Luis Rodriguez, director. Tia Chucha's Centro Cultural is a nonprofit learning and cultural arts center. "We support and promote the continued growth, development and holistic learning of our community through the many powerful means of the arts. Tia Centra provides a positive space for people to activate what we all share as humans: the capacity to create, to imagine and to express ourselves in an effort to improve the quality of life for our community." Publishes hardcover and trade paperback originals. Pays 10% royalty on wholesale price. Publishes ms 1 year after acceptance. Responds in 9 months to mss. Guidelines online.

NEEDS No restrictions as to style or content. "We only publish poetry at this time. We do cross-cultural and performance-oriented poetry. It has to work on the page, however."

HOW TO CONTACT Query and submit complete ms.

TIPS "We will cultivate the practice. Audience is those interested."

☺❂ TIGHTROPE BOOKS

#207-2 College St., Toronto ON M5G 1K3, Canada. (416)928-6666. **E-mail:** tightropeasst@gmail.com. **Website:** www.tightropebooks.com. **Contact:** Jim Nason, publisher. Publishes hardcover and trade paperback originals. Pays 5-15% royalty on retail price. Pays advance of $200-300. Publishes book 1 year after acceptance. Responds if interested. Catalog and guidelines online.

○ Accepting submissions for new mystery imprint, Mysterio.

TIPS "Audience is young, urban, literary, educated, unconventional."

TORREY HOUSE PRESS, LLC

2806 Melony Dr., Salt Lake City UT 84124. (801)810-9THP. **E-mail:** mark@torreyhouse.com. **Website:** torreyhouse.com. **Contact:** Mark Bailey, publisher. "Torrey House Press (THP) publishes literary fiction and creative nonfiction about the world environment with a tilt toward the American West. Want submissions from experienced and agented authors only." Publishes hardcover, trade paperback, and electronic originals. Pays 5-15% royalty on retail price. Publishes ms 12-18 months after acceptance. Responds in 3 months. Catalog online. Guidelines online.

HOW TO CONTACT Query; submit complete ms.

TIPS "Include writing experience (none okay)."

☺ TRADEWIND BOOKS

202-1807 Maritime Mews, Granville Island, Vancouver BC V6H 3W7, Canada. (604)662-4405. **Website:**

www.tradewindbooks.com. **Contact:** R. David Stephens, senior editor. "Tradewind Books publishes juvenile picture books and young adult novels. Requires that submissions include evidence that author has read at least 3 titles published by Tradewind Books." Publishes hardcover and trade paperback originals. Pays 7% royalty on retail price. Pays variable advance. Publishes book 3 years after acceptance. Responds to mss in 2 months. Book catalog and ms guidelines online.

HOW TO CONTACT Please send a book-length collection only.

TRUMAN STATE UNIVERSITY PRESS

100 E. Normal Ave., Kirksville MO 63501. (660)785-7336. **Fax:** (660)785-4480. **E-mail:** tsup@truman.edu. **E-mail:** bsm@truman.edu. **Website:** tsup.truman.edu. **Contact:** Barbara Smith-Mandell, editor-in-chief. Truman State University Press (TSUP) publishes peer-reviewed research in the humanities for the scholarly community and the broader public, and publishes creative literary works. Guidelines online.

NEEDS Not accepting unsolicited mss. Submit to annual T.S. Eliot Prize for Poetry.

TUPELO PRESS

P.O. Box 1767, North Adams MA 01247. (413)664-9611. **E-mail:** publisher@tupelopress.org. **E-mail:** www.tupelopress.org/submissions. **Website:** www.tupelopress.org. **Contact:** Jeffrey Levine, publish/editor-in-chief; Jim Schley, managing editor. "We're an independent nonprofit literary press. We accept book-length poetry, poetry collections (48+ pages), short story collections, novellas, literary nonfiction/memoirs and up to 80 pages of a novel." Guidelines online.

NEEDS "Our mission is to publish thrilling, visually and emotionally and intellectually stimulating books of the highest quality, inside and out. We want contemporary poetry, etc. by the most diverse list of emerging and established writers in the U.S."

HOW TO CONTACT Submit complete ms. **Charges $28 reading fee.**

TURNING POINT

WordTech Communications LLC, P.O. Box 541106, Cincinnati OH 45254. **E-mail:** connect@wordtechcommunications.com. **Website:** www.turningpointbooks.com. Pays in royalties. Catalog and guidelines online.

NEEDS "Dedicated to the art of story in poetry. We seek to publish collections of narrative poetry that tell the essential human stories of our times."

HOW TO CONTACT No e-mail submissions. No calls for book-length poetry right now.

☺ TURNSTONE PRESS

Artspace Building, 206-100 Arthur St., Winnipeg MB R3B 1H3, Canada. (204)947-1555. **Fax:** (204)942-1555. **Website:** www.turnstonepress.com. **Contact:** Submissions Assistant. "Turnstone Press is a literary publisher, not a general publisher, and therefore we are only interested in literary fiction, literary nonfiction—including literary criticism—and poetry. We do publish literary mysteries, thrillers, and noir under our Ravenstone imprint. We publish only Canadian authors or landed immigrants, we strive to publish a significant number of new writers, to publish in a variety of genres, and to have 50% of each year's list be Manitoba writers and/or books with Manitoba content." Publishes ms 2 years after acceptance. Responds in 4-7 months. Guidelines online.

HOW TO CONTACT Poetry mss should be a minimum 70 pages. Submit complete ms. Include cover letter.

TIPS "As a Canadian literary press, we have a mandate to publish Canadian writers only. Do some homework before submitting works to make sure your subject matter/genre/writing style falls within the publishers area of interest."

THE UNIVERSITY OF AKRON PRESS

120 E. Mill St., Suite 415, Akron OH 44325. (330)972-6953. **Fax:** (330)972-8364. **E-mail:** uapress@uakron.edu. **Website:** www.uakron.edu/uapress. **Contact:** Thomas Bacher, director and acquisitions. "The University of Akron Press is the publishing arm of The University of Akron and is dedicated to the dissemination of scholarly, professional, and regional books and other content." Publishes hardcover and paperback originals and reissues. Pays 7-15% royalty. Publishes book 9-12 months after acceptance. Responds in 2 weeks to queries/proposals; 3-4 months to solicited mss. Query prior to submitting. Guidelines online.

NEEDS Follow the guidelines and submit mss only for the contest: www.uakron.edu/uapress/poetry.html. "We publish two books of poetry annually, one of which is the winner of The Akron Poetry prize. We also are interested in literary collections based around one theme, especially collections of translated works."

HOW TO CONTACT If you are interested in publishing with The University of Akron Press, please fill out form online.

THE UNIVERSITY OF ARKANSAS PRESS

McIlroy House, 105 N. McIlroy Ave., Fayetteville AR 72701. (479)575-3246. **Fax:** (479)575-6044. **E-mail:** mbieker@uark.edu. **Website:** uapress.com. **Contact:** Mike Bieker, director. "The University of Arkansas Press publishes series on Ozark studies, the Civil War in the West, poetry and poetics, and sport and society." Publishes hardcover and trade paperback originals and reprints. Publishes book 1 year after acceptance. Responds in 3 months to proposals. Book catalog and ms guidelines online.

HOW TO CONTACT University of Arkansas Press publishes 4 poetry books per year through the Miller Williams Poetry Prize.

⊘ THE UNIVERSITY OF CHICAGO PRESS

1427 E. 60th St., Chicago IL 60637. Voicemail: (773)702-7700. **Fax:** (773)702-9756. **Website:** www. press.uchicago.edu. **Contact:** Randolph Petilos, poetry and medieval studies editor. "The University of Chicago Press has been publishing scholarly books and journals since 1891. Annually, we publish an average of four books in our Phoenix Poets series and two books of poetry in translation. Occasionally, we may publish a book of poetry outside Phoenix Poets, or as a paperback reprint from another publisher." Has recently published work by Peter Balakian, Charles Bernstein, Peg Boyers, Killarney Clary, Milo De Angelis, Nate Klug, Robert Pack, Pier Paolo Pasolini, Vanesha Pravin, and Connie Voisine.

UNIVERSITY OF IOWA PRESS

100 Kuhl House, 119 W. Park Rd., Iowa City IA 52242. (319)335-2000. **Fax:** (319)335-2055. **E-mail:** james-mccoy@uiowa.edu; elisabeth-chretien@uiowa.edu; cathcampbell@uiowa.edu. **Website:** www.uiowapress.org. **Contact:** James McCoy, director (short fiction, poetry, general trade); Elisabeth Chretien, acquisitions editor (literary criticism, literary and general nonfiction, military and veterans' studies); Catherine Cocks, acquisitions editor (book arts, fan studies, food studies, midwestern history and culture, theatre history and culture). "We publish authoritative, original nonfiction that we market mostly by direct mail to groups with special interests in our titles, and by advertising in trade and scholarly publications." Publishes hardcover and paperback originals. Pays 7-10% royalty on net receipts. Publishes book 1 year after acceptance. Book catalog available free. Guidelines online.

NEEDS Currently publishes winners of the Iowa Poetry Prize Competition, Kuhl House Poets, poetry anthologies. Competition guidelines available on website.

UNIVERSITY OF NORTH TEXAS PRESS

1155 Union Circle, #311336, Denton TX 76203. (940)565-2142. **Fax:** (940)565-4590. **E-mail:** ronald. chrisman@unt.edu; karen.devinney@unt.edu. **Website:** untpress.unt.edu. **Contact:** Ronald Chrisman, director; Karen De Vinney, assistant director; Lori Belew, administrative assistant. "We are dedicated to producing the highest quality scholarly, academic, and general interest books. We are committed to serving all peoples by publishing stories of their cultures and experiences that have been overlooked. Currently emphasizing military history, Texas history, music, Mexican-American studies." Publishes hardcover and trade paperback originals and reprints. Publishes ms 1-2 years after acceptance. Responds in 1 month to queries. Book catalog for 8 ½×11 SASE. Guidelines online.

NEEDS "The only poetry we publish is the winner of the Vassar Miller Prize in Poetry, an annual, national competition with a $1,000 prize and publication of the winning ms each Spring."

HOW TO CONTACT Query.

TIPS "We publish series called War and the Southwest; Texas Folklore Society Publications; the Western Life Series; Practical Guide Series; Al-Filo: Mexican-American studies; North Texas Crime and Criminal Justice; Katherine Anne Porter Prize in Short Fiction; and the North Texas Lives of Musicians Series."

UNIVERSITY OF SOUTH CAROLINA PRESS

1600 Hampton St., 5th Floor, Columbia SC 29208. (803)777-5243. **Fax:** (803)777-0160. **Website:** www. sc.edu/uscpress. **Contact:** Linda Fogle, assistant director for operations (trade books); Jim Denton, acquisitions editor (literature, religious studies, rhetoric, communication, social work); Alexander Moore, acquisitions editor (history, regional studies). "We focus on scholarly monographs and regional trade books of lasting merit." Publishes hardcover originals, trade paperback originals and reprints. Publishes ms 1 year after acceptance. Responds in 3 months to mss. Book catalog available free. Guidelines online.

NEEDS Palmetto Poetry Series, a South Carolina-based original poetry series edited by Nikky Finney.

Director: Jonathan Haupt, director (jhaupt@mailbox. sc.edu).

UNIVERSITY OF TAMPA PRESS

University of Tampa, 401 W. Kennedy Blvd., Tampa FL 33606. (813)253-6266. **Fax:** (813)258-7593. **E-mail:** utpress@ut.edu. **Website:** www.utpress.ut.edu. **Contact:** Richard Mathews, editor. Publishes hardcover originals and reprints; trade paperback originals and reprints. Responds in 3-4 months to queries. Book catalog online.

HOW TO CONTACT Submit to the Tampa Review Prize for Poetry.

UNIVERSITY OF WISCONSIN PRESS

1930 Monroe St., 3rd Floor, Madison WI 53711. (608)263-1110. **Fax:** (608)263-1132. **E-mail:** gcwalker@wisc.edu. **E-mail:** kadushin@wisc.edu. **Website:** uwpress.wisc.edu. **Contact:** Raphael Kadushin, senior acquisitions editor; Gwen Walker, acquisitions editor. Publishes hardcoveroriginals, paperback originals, and paperback reprints. Pays royalty. Publishes ms 9-18 months after acceptance. Responds in 2 weeks to queries; 8 weeks to mss. Rarely comments on rejected mss. Guidelines online.

NEEDS The University of Wisconsin Press Awards the Brittingham Prize in Poetry and Felix Pollack Prize in Poetry. More details online.

TIPS "Make sure the query letter and sample text are well-written, and read guidelines carefully to make sure we accept the genre you are submitting."

○ VÉHICULE PRESS

P.O.B. 42094 BP Roy, Montreal QC H2W 2T3, Canada. (514)844-6073. **Fax:** (514)844-7543. **E-mail:** vp@vehiculepress.com. **E-mail:** esplanade@vehiculepress.com. **Website:** www.vehiculepress.com. **Contact:** Simon Dardick, president/publisher. "Montreal's Véhicule Press has published the best of Canadian and Quebec literature-fiction, poetry, essays, translations, and social history." Publishes trade paperback originals by Canadian authors mostly. Pays 10-15% royalty on retail price. Pays $200-500 advance. Publishes ms 1 year after acceptance. Responds in 4 months to queries. Book catalog for 9 x 12 SAE with IRCs.

NEEDS Vehicule Press is a "literary press with a poetry series, Signal Editions, publishing the work of Canadian poets only." Publishes flat-spined paperbacks. Publishes Canadian poetry that is "first-rate, original, content-conscious."

TIPS "Quality in almost any style is acceptable. We believe in the editing process."

⊘ WAKE FOREST UNIVERSITY PRESS

P.O. Box 7333, Winston-Salem NC 27109. (336)758-5448. **Fax:** (336)758-5636. **E-mail:** wfupress@wfu.edu. **Website:** wfupress.wfu.edu. **Contact:** Jefferson Holdridge, director/poetry editor; Dillon Johnston, advisory editor. "We publish only poetry from Ireland. I am able to consider only poetry written by native Irish poets. I must return, unread, poetry from American poets." Query with 4-5 samples and cover letter. Sometimes sends prepublication galleys. Buys North American or U.S. rights. Pays on 8% list royalty contract, plus 6-8 author's copies. Negotiable advance. Responds to queries in 1-2 weeks; to submissions (*if invited*) in 2-3 months.

WASHINGTON WRITERS' PUBLISHING HOUSE

P.O. Box 15271, Washington DC 20003. **E-mail:** wwphpress@gmail.com. **Website:** www.washingtonwriters.org. **Contact:** Kathleen Wheaton, president. Offers $1,000 and 50 copies of published book plus additional copies for publicity use. Guidelines online.

NEEDS Washington Writers' Publishing House considers book-length mss for publication by poets living within 75 driving miles of the U.S. Capitol (Baltimore area included) through competition only. Publishes 1-2 poetry books/year.

HOW TO CONTACT "No specific criteria, except literary excellence."

WAVE BOOKS

1938 Fairview Ave. E., Suite 201, Seattle WA 98102. (206)676-5337. **E-mail:** info@wavepoetry.com. **Website:** www.wavepoetry.com. **Contact:** Charlie Wright, publisher; Joshua Beckman and Matthew Zapruder, editors; Heidi Broadhead, managing editor. "Wave Books is an independent poetry press based in Seattle, Washington, dedicated to publishing the best in contemporary American poetry, poetry in translation, and writing by poets. The Press was founded in 2005, merging with established publisher Verse Press. By publishing strong innovative work in finely crafted trade editions and handmade ephemera, we hope to continue to challenge the values and practices of readers and add to the collective sense of what's possible in contemporary poetry." Publishes hardcover and trade paperback originals. Catalog online.

HOW TO CONTACT "Please no unsolicited mss or queries. We will post calls for submissions on our website."

⊘ WESLEYAN UNIVERSITY PRESS

215 Long Ln., Middletown CT 06459. (860)685-7711. **Fax:** (860)685-7712. **E-mail:** stamminen@wesleyan.edu. **E-mail:** psmathers@wesleyan.edu. **Website:** www.wesleyan.edu/wespress. **Contact:** Suzanna Tamminen, director and editor-in-chief; Parker Smathers, editor. "Wesleyan University Press is a scholarly press with a focus on poetry, music, dance and cultural studies." Wesleyan University Press is one of the major publishers of poetry in the nation. Poetry publications from Wesleyan tend to get widely (and respectfully) reviewed. **"We are accepting manuscripts by invitation only until further notice."** Publishes hardcover originals and paperbacks. Pays royalties, plus 10 author's copies. Responds to queries in 2 months; to mss in 4 months. Book catalog available free. Guidelines online.

NEEDS *Does not accept unsolicited mss.*

⊘ WHITE PINE PRESS

P.O. Box 236, Buffalo NY 14201. (716)627-4665. **Fax:** (716)627-4665. **E-mail:** wpine@whitepine.org. **Website:** www.whitepine.org. **Contact:** Dennis Maloney, editor. Publishes trade paperback originals. Pays contributor's copies. Publishes ms 18 months after acceptance. Responds in 1 month to queries and proposals; 4 months to mss. Catalog online. Guidelines online.

NEEDS "Only considering submissions for our annual poetry contest."

WORDSONG

815 Church St., Honesdale PA 18431. **Fax:** (570)253-0179. **Website:** www.wordsongpoetry.com. "We publish fresh voices in contemporary poetry." Pays authors royalty or work purchased outright. Responds to mss in 3 months.

HOW TO CONTACT *Agented submissions only.*

TIPS "Collections of original poetry, not anthologies, are our biggest need at this time. Keep in mind that the strongest collections demonstrate a facility with multiple poetic forms and offer fresh images and insights. Check to see what's already on the market and on our website before submitting."

YALE UNIVERSITY PRESS

P.O. Box 209040, New Haven CT 06520. (203)432-0960. **Fax:** (203)432-0948. **E-mail:** christopher.rogers@yale.edu. **Website:** yalepress.yale.edu/yupbooks. **Contact:** Christopher Rogers, editorial director. "Yale University Press publishes scholarly and general interest books." Publishes hardcover and trade paperback originals. Book catalog and ms guidelines online.

NEEDS Submit to Yale Series of Younger Poets Competition.

HOW TO CONTACT Guidelines online.

TIPS "Audience is scholars, students and general readers."

CONTESTS & AWARDS

This section contains a wide array of poetry competitions and literary awards. These range from state poetry society contests (with a number of modest monetary prizes) to prestigious honors bestowed by private foundations, elite publishers and renowned university programs. Because these listings reflect such a variety of skill levels and degrees of competitiveness, it's important to read each carefully and note its unique requirements. *Never* enter a contest without consulting the guidelines and following directions to the letter (including manuscript formatting, number of lines or pages of poetry accepted, amount of entry fee, entry forms needed and other details).

IMPORTANT NOTE: As we gathered information for this edition of *Poet's Market*, we found that some competitions hadn't yet established their 2016 fees and deadlines. In such cases, we list the most recent information available as a general guide. Always consult current guidelines for updates before entering any competition.

WHAT ABOUT ENTRY FEES?

Most contests charge entry fees, and these are usually quite legitimate. The funds are used to cover expenses such as paying the judges, putting up prize monies, printing prize editions of magazines and journals, and promoting the contest through mailings and ads. If you're concerned about a poetry contest or other publishing opportunity, see "Is It a 'Con'?" for advice on some of the more questionable practices in the poetry world.

10 MINUTE PLAY CONTEST & FESTIVAL

Weathervane Playhouse, 1301 Weathervane Lane, Akron OH 44313. (330)836-2626. **E-mail:** 10minuteplay@weathervaneplayhouse.com. **Website:** www.weathervaneplayhouse.com. **Contact:** Eileen Moushey. Annual 8x10 TheatreFest. Must be US citizen 18 years or older. All rights remain with writers. The mission of the Weathervane Playhouse 8x10 TheatreFest is to promote the art of play writing, present new works, and introduce area audiences to the short play form. The competition will provide Weathervane with recognition for quality and innovative theatre. Deadline: May 15. Submission period begins December 1. Prizes: Each of 8 finalists receive full productions of their plays during the Festival, held in mid-July. 1st Place: $350; 2nd Place: $250; 3rd Place: $150; 5 runners-up: $50 each. First round judges include individuals with experience in every area of stagecraft, including tech designers, actors, directors, stage managers, and playwrights.

49TH PARALLEL AWARD FOR POETRY

Western Washington University, Mail Stop 9053, Bellingham WA 98225. (360)650-4863. **E-mail:** bellingham.review@wwu.edu. **Website:** www.bhreview.org. **Contact:** Brenda Miller, editor-in-chief; Kaitlyn Teer, managing editor. Annual poetry contest, supported by the *Bellingham Review,* given for a poem or group of poems of any style or length. Deadline: March 15. Submissions period begins December 1. Prize: $1,000.

☻ J.M. ABRAHAM POETRY PRIZE

(902)423-8116. **Fax:** (902)422-0881. **E-mail:** director@writers.ns.ca. **Website:** www.writers.ns.ca. The J.M. Abraham Poetry Prize is an annual award designed to honor the best book of poetry by a resident of Atlantic Canada. Formerly known as the Atlantic Poetry Prize. Deadline: First Friday in December. Prize: Valued at $2,000 for the winning title.

☻ ACORN-PLANTOS AWARD FOR PEOPLES POETRY

Acorn-Plantos Award Committee, 36 Sunset Ave., Hamilton ON L8R 1V6, Canada. **E-mail:** jeffhamiltonjeff@gmail.com. **Contact:** Jeff Seffinga. Annual contest for work that appeared in print in the previous calender year. This award is given to the Canadian poet who best (through the publication of a book of poems) exemplifies populist or peoples poetry in the tradition of Milton Acorn, Ted Plantos, et al. Work may be entered by the poet or the publisher; the award goes to the poet. Entrants must submit 5 copies of each title. Poet must be a citizen of Canada or a landed immigrant. Publisher need not be Canadian. Deadline: June 30. Prize: $500 (CDN) and a medal. Judged by a panel of poets in the tradition who are not entered in the current year.

AKRON POETRY PRIZE

The University of Akron Press, 120 E. Mill St., Suite 415, Akron OH 44308. **E-mail:** uapress@uakron.edu. **Website:** www.uakron.edu/uapress/akron-poetry-prize/. **Contact:** Mary Biddinger, editor/award director. Submissions must be unpublished. Considers simultaneous submissions (with notification of acceptance elsewhere). Submit 48 or more pages, typed, single-spaced; optional self-addressed postcard for confirmation. Mss will not be returned. Do not send mss bound or enclosed in covers. See website for complete guidelines. Competition receives 500+ entries. 2014 winner was John Repp for *Pictures at an Exhibition.* Winner posted on website by September 30. Deadline: April 15-June 15. Prize: $1,500, plus publication of a book-length ms.

MARIE ALEXANDER POETRY SERIES

English Department, 2801 S. University Ave., Little Rock AR 72204. **E-mail:** editor@mariealexanderseries.com. **Website:** mariealexanderseries.com. **Contact:** Nickole Brown. Annual contest for a collection of previously unpublished prose poems or flash fiction by a U.S. writer. Deadline: July 1-31. Prize: $1,000, plus publication.

AMERICAN LITERARY REVIEW CONTESTS

American Literary Review, P.O. Box 311307, University of North Texas, Denton TX 76203-1307. (940)565-2755. **E-mail:** americanliteraryreview@gmail.com. **Website:** www.americanliteraryreview.com. Contest to award excellence in short fiction, creative nonfiction, and poetry. Multiple entries are acceptable, but each entry must be accompanied with a reading fee. Do not put any identifying information in the file itself; include the author's name, title(s), address, e-mail address, and phone number in the boxes provided in the online submissions manager. Short fiction: Limit 8,000 words per work. Creative nonfiction: Limit 6,500 words per work. Deadline: October 1. Submission period begins June 1. Prize: $1,000 prize for each category, along with publication in the Spring online issue of the *American Literary Review.*

THE AMERICAN POETRY JOURNAL BOOK PRIZE

P.O. Box 2080, Aptos CA 95001-2080. **E-mail:** dreamhorsepress@yahoo.com. **Website:** www.dreamhorsepress.com. Deadline: February 28 for snail mail postmarks, five days later for electronic submissions. Prize: $1,000, publication and 20 copies. All entries will be considered for publication.

AMERICAN-SCANDINAVIAN FOUNDATION TRANSLATION PRIZE

(212)779-3587. **E-mail:** grants@amscan.org; info@amscan.org. **Website:** www.amscan.org. **Contact:** Matthew Walters, director of fellowships & grants. The annual ASF translation competition is awarded for the most outstanding translations of poetry, fiction, drama, or literary prose written by a Scandinavian author born after 1800. Deadline: June 1. Prize: The Nadia Christensen Prize includes a $2,500 award, publication of an excerpt in *Scandinavian Review*, and a commemorative bronze medallion; The Leif and Inger Sjöberg Award, given to an individual whose literature translations have not previously been published, includes a $2,000 award, publication of an excerpt in *Scandinavian Review*, and a commemorative bronze medallion.

ANABIOSIS PRESS CHAPBOOK CONTEST

2 South New St., Bradford MA 01835. (978)469-7085. **E-mail:** rsmyth@anabiosispress.org. **Website:** www.anabiosispress.org. **Contact:** Richard Smyth, editor. Deadline: June 30 (postmarked). Prize: $100, plus publication of the winning chapbook, and 100 copies of the first run.

THE ANHINGA PRESS-ROBERT DANA PRIZE FOR POETRY

Anhinga Press, P.O. Box 3665, Tallahassee FL 32315. **E-mail:** info@anhinga.org. **Website:** www.anhinga.org. **Contact:** Kristine Snodgrass, poetry editor. Offered annually for a book-length collection of poetry by an author writing in English. Guidelines on website. Past winners include Frank X. Gaspar, Earl S. Braggs, Julia Levine, Keith Ratzlaff, Lynn Aarti Chandhok, and Rhett Iseman Trull. Deadline: Submissions will be accepted from February 15-May 15. Prize: $2,000, a reading tour of selected Florida colleges and universities, and the winning ms will be published. Past judges include Jan Beatty, Richard Blaco, Denise Duhamel, Donald Hall, Joy Harjo, Robert Dana, Mark Jarman, and Tony Hoagland.

ANNUAL GIVAL PRESS OSCAR WILDE AWARD

Gival Press, LLC, P.O. Box 3812, Arlington VA 22203. (703)351-0079. **E-mail:** givalpress@yahoo.com. **Website:** www.givalpress.com. **Contact:** Robert L. Giron. Award given to the best previously unpublished original poem—written in English of any length, in any style, typed, double-spaced on 1 side only—which best relates gay/lesbian/bisexual/transgendered life, by a poet who is 18 years or older. Deadline: June 27 (postmarked). Prize: $100 and the poem, along with information about the poet, will be published on the Gival Press website.

ANNUAL VENTURA COUNTY WRITERS CLUB POETRY CONTEST IN HONOR OF JOYCE LA MERS

Ventura County Writers Club Poetry Contest, P.O. Box 3373, Thousand Oaks CA 91362. **E-mail:** poetrycontest@venturacountywriters.com. **Website:** www.venturacountywriters.com. **Contact:** Poetry Contest Chair. Annual poetry contest for youth and adult poets. Youth division for poets under 18: Division A is open to entrants ages 13-18; and, Division B is open to poets ages 12 and under. Adult division for poets 18 and older. Club mebership not required to enter and entries accepted worldwide as long as fees are paid and the poem is in English. Enter through website. Deadline: February 15. Entries accepted beginning January 1. Prize: The adult winners will be awarded $100 for first place, $75 for second and $50 for third place. The two youth categories will receive $50 for first place, $35 for second and $25 for third place.

ANNUAL WORLD HAIKU COMPETITION & ANNUAL WORLD TANKA CONTEST

P.O. Box 17331, Arlington VA 22216. **E-mail:** LPEzineSubmissions@gmail.com. **Website:** http://lyricalpassionpoetry.yolasite.com. **Contact:** Raquel D. Bailey. Contest is open to all writers. Promotes Japanese short form poetry. Deadline: See website for details. Prize: Monetary compensation and publication. Judged by experienced editors and award-winning writers from the contemporary writing community.

ARIZONA LITERARY CONTEST & BOOK AWARDS

6145 W. Echo Lane, Glendale AZ 85302. (623)847-9343. **E-mail:** info@azauthors.com. **Website:** www.azauthors.com. Arizona Authors Association sponsors annual literary contest in poetry, short story, essay, unpublished novels, and published books (fiction, nonfiction, and children's literature). Awards publication in *Arizona Literary Magazine*, and prizes by Five Star Publications, Inc. Deadline: July 1. Begins reading submissions on January 1. Prizes: Grand Prize, Arizona Book of the Year Award: $500. All categories: 1st Prize: $150 and publication; 2nd Prize: $75 and publication; 3rd Prize: $30 and publication. Features in *Arizona Literary Magazine* can be taken instead of money and publication. 1st Prize Published Fiction and Nonfiction: Listing on AuthorsandExperts.com. 1st Prize Chilren's Literature: Listing on SchoolBookings.com. 1st and 2nd Prize winners in Poetry, Essay, Short Story: Nomination for the Pushcart Prize. Judged by Arizona authors, editors, and reviewers. Winners announced at an award banquet by November 8.

Competition receives 1,000 entries/year.

ART AFFAIR POETRY CONTEST

P.O. Box 54302, Oklahoma City OK 73154. **E-mail:** okpoets@aol.com. **Website:** www.shadetreecreations.com. **Contact:** Barbara Shepherd, contest chair. The annual Art Affair Poetry Contest is open to any poet. Multiple entries accepted with entry fee for each and may be mailed in the same packet. Guidelines available on website. Winners' list will be published on the Art Affair website in December. Deadline: October 1. Prizes: 1st Prize: $40 and certificate; 2nd Prize: $25 and certificate; and 3rd Prize: $15 and certificate. Honorable Mention certificates will be awarded at the discretion of the judges.

ATLANTIC WRITING COMPETITION FOR UNPUBLISHED MANUSCRIPTS

Writers' Federation of Nova Scotia, 1113 Marginal Rd., Halifax NS B3H 4P7. (902)423-8116. **Fax:** (902)422-0881. **E-mail:** programs@writers.ns.ca. **Website:** www.writers.ns.ca. **Contact:** Robin Spittal, communications and development officer. Annual program designed to honor work by unpublished writers in all 4 Atlantic Provinces. Entry is open to writers unpublished in the category of writing they wish to enter. Prizes are presented in the fall of each year. Categories include: novel, writing for children, poetry, short story, juvenile/young adult novel, creative non-fiction, and play. Judges return written comments when competition is concluded. Deadline: February 2. Prizes vary based on categories. See website for details.

ATLANTIS AWARD

The Poet's Billow, 245 N. Collingwood, Syracuse NY 13206. **E-mail:** thepoetsbillow@gmail.com. **Website:** http://thepoetsbillow.org. **Contact:** Robert Evory. Annual award open to any writer to recognize one outstanding poem from its entries. Finalists with strong work will also be published. Submissions must be previously unpublished. Deadline: October 1. Submissions open July 1. Prize: $100 and winning poet will be featured in an interview on The Poet's Billow website. Poem will be published and displayed in The Poet's Billow Literary Art Gallery and nominated for a Pushcart Prize. If the poet qualifies, the poem will also be submitted to The Best New Poets anthology. Judged by the editors, and, occasionally, a guest judge.

AUTUMN HOUSE POETRY, FICTION, AND NONFICTION PRIZES

P.O. Box 60100, Pittsburgh PA 15211. (412)381-4261. **E-mail:** gcerto@autumhouse.org; info@autumnhouse.org. **E-mail:** autumnh420@gmail.com. **Website:** http://autumnhouse.org. **Contact:** Giuliana Certo, managing editor. Offers annual prize and publication of book-length ms with national promotion. Submission must be unpublished as a collection, but individual poems, stories, and essays may have been previously published elsewhere. Considers simultaneous submissions. "Autumn House is a nonprofit corporation with the mission of publishing and promoting poetry and other fine literature. We have published books by Gerald Stern, Ruth L. Schwartz, Ed Ochester, Andrea Hollander Budy, George Bilgere, Jo McDougall, and others." Deadline: June 30. Prize: The winner (in each of three categories) will receive book publication, $1,000 advance against royalties, and a $1,500 travel/publicity grant to promote his or her book. Judged by Dorianne Laux (poetry), Sharon Dilworth (fiction), and Dinty W. Moore (nonfiction). **TIPS** "Include only your best work."

AWP AWARD SERIES

Association of Writers & Writing Programs, George Mason University, 4400 University Drive, MSN 1E3, Fairfax VA 22030. **E-mail:** supriya@awpwriter.org. **Website:** www.awpwriter.org. **Contact:** Supriya Bhatnagar, director of publications. AWP sponsors the Award Series, an annual competition for the publication of excellent new book-length works. The competition is open to all authors writing in English regardless of nationality or residence, and is available to published and unpublished authors alike. Offered annually to foster new literary talent. Deadline: Postmarked between January 1 and February 28. Prize: AWP Prize for the Novel: $2,500 and publication by New Issues Press; Donald Hall Prize for Poetry: $5,500 and publication by the University of Pittsburgh Press; Grace Paley Prize in Short Fiction: $5,500 and publication by the University of Massachusetts Press; and AWP Prize for Creative Nonfiction: $2,500 and publication by the University of Georgia Press.

THE BALTIMORE REVIEW CONTESTS

The Baltimore Review, 6514 Maplewood Rd., Baltimore MD 21212. **Website:** www.baltimorereview. org. **Contact:** Barbara Westwood Diehl, senior editor. Each summer and winter issue includes a contest theme (see submissions guidelines for theme). Prizes are awarded for first, second, and third place among all categories—poetry, short stories, and creative nonfiction. All entries are considered for publication. Deadline: May 31 and November 30. Prize: 1st Place: $500; 2nd Place: $200; 3rd Place: $100. All entries are considered for publication. Judged by the editors of *The Baltimore Review* and a guest, final judge.

BARROW STREET PRESS BOOK CONTEST

P.O. Box 1558, Kingston RI 02881. **E-mail:** submissions@barrowstreet.org. **Website:** www.barrowstreet. org. The Barrow Street Press Book Contest award will be given for the best previously unpublished ms of poetry in English. Deadline: June 30. Prize: $1,000. Judged by Denise Duhamel.

THE BASKERVILLE PUBLISHERS POETRY AWARD & THE BETSY COLQUITT POETRY AWARD

(817)257-5907. **Fax:** (817)257-6239. **E-mail:** descant@ tcu.edu. **Website:** www.descant.tcu.edu. **Contact:** Alex Lemon, poetry editor. Annual award for an outstanding poem published in an issue of *descant*. Deadline: September-April. Prize: $250 for Baskerville Award; $500 for Betsy Colquitt Award. Publication retains copyright, but will transfer it to the author upon request.

ELINOR BENEDICT POETRY PRIZE

Passages North, Northern Michigan University, 1401 Presque Isle Ave., Marquette MI 49855. **E-mail:** passages@nmu.edu. **Website:** passagesnorth.com/contests/. **Contact:** Jennifer A. Howard, Editor-in-Chief. Prize given biennially for a poem or a group of poems. Deadline: March 22. Submission period begins January 15. Prize: $1,000 and publication for winner; 2 honorable mentions are also published; all entrants receive a copy of *Passages North*.

GEORGE BENNETT FELLOWSHIP

Phillips Exeter Academy, 20 Main St., Exeter NH 03833. **E-mail:** teaching_opportunities@exeter.edu. **Website:** www.exeter.edu/bennettfellowship. Annual award for fellow and family to provide time and freedom from material considerations to a person seriously contemplating or pursuing a career as a writer. Applicants should have a manuscript in progress which they intend to complete during the fellowship period. Manuscript should be fiction, nonfiction, novel, short stories, or poetry. Duties: To be in residency at the Academy for the academic year; to make oneself available informally to students interested in writing. Committee favors writers who have not yet published a book with a major publisher. Deadline for application: November 30. A choice will be made, and all entrants notified in mid-April. Cash stipend (currently $14,933), room and board. Judged by committee of the English department.

BERMUDA TRIANGLE PRIZE

The Poet's Billow, 245 N. Collingwood, Syracuse NY 13206. **E-mail:** thepoetsbillow@gmail.com. **Website:** http://thepoetsbillow.org. **Contact:** Robert Evory. Annual award open to any writer to recognize three poems that address a theme set by the editors. Finalists with strong work will also be published. Submissions must be previously unpublished. Please submit online. Deadline: March 15. Submission period begins November 15. Prize: $50 each to three poems. The winning poems will be published and displayed in The Poet's Billow Literary Art Gallery and nominated for a Pushcart Prize. If the poet qualifies, the poem will also be submitted to The Best New Poets anthology. Judged by the editors, and, occasionally, a guest judge.

THE PATRICIA BIBBY FIRST BOOK AWARD

Patricia Bibby Award, Tebot Bach, P.O. Box 7887, Huntington Beach CA 92615-7887. **E-mail:** mifanwy@tebotbach.org; info@tebotbach.org. **Website:** www.tebotbach.org. **Contact:** Mifanwy Kaiser. Annual competition open to all poets writing in English who have not committed to publishing collections of poetry of 36 poems or more in editions of over 400 copies. Offers award and publication of a book-length poetry ms by Tebot Bach. Deadline: October 31. Prize:

$500 and book publication. Judges for each year's competition announced online.

BINGHAMTON UNIVERSITY MILT KESSLER POETRY BOOK AWARD

Binghamton University Creative Writing Program, Department of English, General Literature, and Rhetoric, Library North Room 1149, Vestal Parkway East, P.O. Box 6000, Binghamton NY 13902-6000. (607)777-2713. **Fax:** (607)777-2408. **E-mail:** cwpro@binghamton.edu. **Website:** www2.binghamton.edu/english/creative-writing/binghamton-center-for-writers. **Contact:** Maria Mazziotti Gillan, creative writing program director. Annual award for a book of poems written in English, 48 pages or more in length, selected by judges as the strongest collection of poems published in that year. Deadline: March 1. Prize: $1,000.

THE BITTER OLEANDER PRESS LIBRARY OF POETRY AWARD

The Bitter Oleander Press, 4983 Tall Oaks Dr., Fayetteville NY 13066-9776. (315)637-3047. **Fax:** (315)637-5056. **E-mail:** info@bitteroleander.com. **Website:** www.bitteroleander.com. **Contact:** Paul B. Roth. The Bitter Oleander Press Library of Poetry Book Award replaces the 15-year long run of the Frances Locke Memorial Poetry Award. Guidelines available on website. Deadline: June 15 (postmarked). Open to submissions on May 1. Early or late entries will be disqualified. Prize: $1,000, plus book publication of the winning ms.

THE BLACK RIVER CHAPBOOK COMPETITION

Black Lawrence Press, 326 Bingham St., Pittsburgh PA 15211. **E-mail:** editors@blacklawrencepress.com. **Website:** www.blacklawrencepress.com. Twice each year, Black Lawrence Press runs the Black River Chapbook Competition for an unpublished chapbook of poems or short fiction between 18-36 pages in length. Spring deadline: May 31. Fall deadline: October 31. Prize: $500, publication, and 10 copies. Judged by a revolving panel of judges, in addition to the Chapbook Editor and other members of the BLP editorial staff.

BLUE MOUNTAIN ARTS/SPS STUDIOS POETRY CARD CONTEST

P.O. Box 1007, Boulder CO 80306. (303)449-0536. **Fax:** (303)447-0939. **E-mail:** poetrycontest@sps.com; editorial@sps.com. **Website:** www.sps.com. Biannual poetry card contest. All entries must be the original creation of the submitting author. Looking for original poetry that is rhyming or non-rhyming, although non-rhyming poetry reads better. Poems may also be considered for possible publication on greeting cards or in book anthologies. Guidelines available online. Deadline: December 31 and June 30. Prize: 1st Place: $300; 2nd Place: $150; 3rd Place: $50. Judged by the Blue Mountain Arts editorial staff.

TIPS "We suggest that you write about real emotions and feelings and that you have some special person or occasion in mind as you write."

THE BOARDMAN TASKER PRIZE FOR MOUNTAIN LITERATURE

The Boardman Tasker Charitable Trust, 8 Bank View Rd., Darley Abbey Derby DE22 1EJ, UK. 01332 342246. **E-mail:** steve@people-matter.co.uk. **Website:** www.boardmantasker.com. **Contact:** Steve Dean. Offered annually to reward a work with a mountain theme, whether fiction, nonfiction, drama, or poetry, written in the English language (initially or in translation). Subject must be concerned with a mountain environment. Previous winners have been books on expeditions, climbing experiences, a biography of a mountaineer, novels. Guidelines available in January by e-mail or on website. Entries must be previously published. Open to any writer. The award is to honor Peter Boardman and Joe Tasker, who disappeared on Everest in 1982. Deadline: August 1. Prize: £3,000. Judged by a panel of 3 judges elected by trustees.

THE FREDERICK BOCK PRIZE

(312)787-7070. **Fax:** (312)787-6650. **E-mail:** editors@poetrymagazine.org. **Website:** www.poetryfoundation.org. Several prizes are awarded annually for the best work printed in *Poetry* during the preceding year. Only poems already published in the magazine are eligible for consideration, and no formal application is necessary. The winners are announced in the November issue. Upon acceptance, *Poetry* licenses exclusive worldwide first serial rights, including electronic rights, for publication, as well as non-exclusive rights to reprint, reuse, and archive the work, in any format, in perpetuity. Copyright reverts to author upon first publication. Any writer may submit poems to *Poetry*. Prize: $500.

BOSTON GLOBE-HORN BOOK AWARDS

The Boston Globe, Horn Book, Inc., 300 The Fenway, Palace Road Building, Suite P-311, Boston MA 02115. (617)628-0225. **Fax:** (617)628-0882. **E-mail:** info@hbook.com; khedeen@hbook.com. **Website:** hbook.com/bghb/. **Contact:** Katrina Hedeen. Offered annually for excellence in literature for children and young adults (published June 1-May 31). Categories: picture book, fiction and poetry, nonfiction. Judges may also name up to 2 honor books in each category. Books must be published in the US, but may be written or illustrated by citizens of any country. The Horn Book Magazine publishes speeches given at awards ceremonies. Guidelines for SASE or online. Deadline: May 15. Prize: $500 and an engraved silver bowl; honor book recipients receive an engraved silver plate. Judged by a panel of 3 judges selected each year.

THE BOSTON REVIEW ANNUAL POETRY CONTEST

Poetry Contest, Boston Review, P.O. Box 425786, Cambridge MA 02142. (617)324-1360. **Fax:** (617)452-3356. **E-mail:** review@bostonreview.net. **Website:** www.bostonreview.net. Offers $1,500 and publication in *Boston Review* (see separate listing in Magazines/Journals). Deadline: June 1. Winner announced in early November on website. Prize: $1,500 and publication.

BOULEVARD POETRY CONTEST FOR EMERGING POETS

PMB 325, 6614 Clayton Rd., Richmond Heights MO 63117. **E-mail:** richardburgin@att.net; jessicarogen@boulevardmagazine.org. **Website:** www.boulevardmagazine.org. **Contact:** Jessica Rogen, managing editor. Annual Emerging Poets Contest offers $1,000 and publication in *Boulevard* (see separate listing in Magazines/Journals) for the best group of 3 poems by a poet who has not yet published a book of poetry with a nationally distributed press. All entries will be considered for publication and payment at regular rates. Deadline: June 1. Prize: $1,000 and publication.

BARBARA BRADLEY PRIZE

New England Poetry Club, 376 School St., Watertown MA 02472 . **E-mail:** contests@nepoetryclub.org. **Website:** www.nepoetryclub.org. **Contact:** Audrey Kalajin. For a lyric poem under 20 lines, written by a woman. Deadline: May 31. Prize: $200. Judged by well-known poets and sometimes winners of previous NEPC contests.

THE BRIAR CLIFF REVIEW FICTION, POETRY, AND CREATIVE NONFICTION COMPETITION

The Briar Cliff Review, Briar Cliff University, 3303 Rebecca St., Sioux City IA 51104-0100. **E-mail:** tricia.currans-sheehan@briarcliff.edu (editor); jeanne.emmons@briarcliff.edu (poetry). **Website:** www.bcreview.org. **Contact:** Tricia Currans-Sheehan, editor.

The Briar Cliff Review sponsors an annual contest offering $1,000 and publication to each 1st Prize winner in fiction, poetry, and creative nonfiction. Previous year's winner and former students of editors ineligible. Winning pieces accepted for publication on the basis of first-time rights. Considers simultaneous submissions, "but notify us immediately upon acceptance elsewhere. We guarantee a considerate reading." No mss returned. Award to reward good writers and showcase quality writing. Deadline: November 1. Prize: $1,000 and publication to each 1st Prize winner in fiction, poetry, and creative nonfiction.

BRICK ROAD POETRY BOOK CONTEST

Brick Road Poetry Press, Inc., P.O. Box 751, Columbus GA 31902. (706)649-3080. **Fax:** (706)649-3094. **E-mail:** editor@brickroadpoetrypress.com. **Website:** www.brickroadpoetrypress.com. **Contact:** Ron Self and Keith Badowski, co-editors/founders. Annual competition for an original collection of 50-100 pages of poetry. Deadline: November 1. Submission period begins August 1. Prize: $1,000, publication in both print and e-book formats, and 25 copies of the book. May also offer publication contracts to the top finalists.

TIPS "The best way to discover all that poetry can be and to expand the limits of your own poetry is to read expansively."

● THE BRIDPORT PRIZE

P.O. Box 6910, Dorset DT6 9QB, United Kingdom. **E-mail:** info@bridportprize.org.uk; kate@bridportprize.org.uk. **Website:** www.bridportprize.org.uk. **Contact:** Kate Wilson, Bridport Prize administrator. Award to promote literary excellence, discover new talent. Categories: Short stories, poetry, flash fiction. Deadline: May 31. Open for submissions starting November 15. Prize: £5,000 ; £1,000 ; £500 ; various runners-up prizes and publication of approximately 13 best stories and 13 best poems in anthology; plus 6 best flash fiction stories. £1,000 1st Prize for the best short, short story of under 250 words. Judged by 1 judge for short stories (in 2014, Andrew Miller), 1 judge for poetry (in 2014, Liz Lochhead) and 1 judge for flash fiction (in 2014, Tania Hershman).

BRIGHT HILL PRESS POETRY CHAPBOOK COMPETITION

Bright Press Hill & Literary Center, 94 Church St., Treadwell NY 13846. (607)829-5055. **E-mail:** brighthillpress@stny.rr.com; wordthur@stny.rr.com. **Website:** www.brighthillpress.org. The annual Bright Hill Press Chapbook Award recognizes an outstanding collection of poetry. Guidelines available for SASE, by e-mail, or on website. Deadline: December 15. Submission period begins October 25. Prize: A publication contract with Bright Hill Press and $1,000, publication in print format, and 30 copies of the printed book. Judged by a nationally-known poet.

TIPS "Publish your poems in literary magazines before trying to get a whole ms published. Publishing individual poems is the best way to hone your complete ms."

BRITTINGHAM PRIZE IN POETRY

University of Wisconsin Press, 1930 Monroe Street, 3rd Floor, Madison WI 5311-2059. (608)263-1110. **Fax:** (608)263-1132. **E-mail:** rwallace@wisc.edu. **E-mail:** uwiscpress@uwpress.wisc.edu. **Website:** www.wisc. edu/wisconsinpress/poetryguide.html. **Contact:** Ronald Wallace, contest director. The annual Brittingham Prize in Poetry is 1 of 2 prizes awarded by The University of Wisconsin Press (see separate listing for the Felix Pollak Prize in Poetry in this section). The Brittingham Prize in Poetry is awarded annually to the best book-length manuscript of original poetry submitted in an open competition. The award is administered by the University of Wisconsin–Madison English Department, and the winner is chosen by a nationally recognized poet. The resulting book is published by the University of Wisconsin Press. Deadline: Submit August 15-September 15. Prize: Offers $1,000, plus publication. Judged by a distinguished poet who will remain anonymous until the winners are announced in mid-February.

BOB BUSH MEMORIAL AWARD FOR FIRST BOOK OF POETRY

Website: www.texasinstituteofletters.org. Offered annually for best first book of poetry published in previous year. Writer must have been born in Texas, have lived in the state at least 2 consecutive years at some time, or the subject matter should be associated with the state. Deadline: See website for exact date. Prize: $1,000.

GERALD CABLE BOOK AWARD

Silverfish Review Press, P.O. Box 3541, Eugene OR 97403. (541)344-5060. **E-mail:** sfrpress@earthlink. net. **Website:** www.silverfishreviewpress.com. **Contact:** Rodger Moody, editor. Awarded annually to a book-length ms of original poetry by an author who has not yet published a full-length collection. There are no restrictions on the kind of poetry or subject

matter; translations are not acceptable. Deadline: October 15. Prize: $1,000, publication, and 25 copies of the book. The winner will be announced in March.

CAKETRAIN COMPETITION

P.O. Box 82588, Pittsburgh PA 15218. **E-mail:** editors@caketrain.org. **Website:** www.caketrain.org. **Contact:** Amanda Raczkowski, editor; Joseph Reed, editor. Annual contest for full length works of fiction and poetry chapbooks sponsored by *Caketrain* literary journal. Can submit by mail with SASE or by e-mail. See website for guidelines. Deadline: October 1. Prize: $250 cash and 25 copies of their book.

CALIFORNIA BOOK AWARDS

Commonwealth Club of California, 595 Market St., San Francisco CA 94105. (415)597-6700. **Fax:** (415)597-6729. **E-mail:** bookawards@commonwealthclub.org. **Website:** www.commonwealthclub. org/. Offered annually to recognize California's best writers and illuminate the wealth and diversity of California-based literature. Award is for published submissions appearing in print during the previous calendar year. Can be nominated by publisher or author. Open to California residents (or residents at time of publication). Deadline: December 31. Prize: Medals and cash prizes to be awarded at publicized event. Judged by 12-15 California professionals with a diverse range of views, backgrounds, and literary experience.

☉ CANADIAN AUTHORS ASSOCIATION AWARD FOR POETRY

(705)325-3926. **E-mail:** admin@canadianauthors. org. **Website:** www.canadianauthors.org. **Contact:** Anita Purcell, executive director. Offered annually for a full-length English-language book of poems for adults, by a Canadian writer. Deadline: January 15. Prize: $2,000 and a silver medal. Judging: Each year a trustee for each award appointed by the Canadian Authors Association selects up to 3 judges. Identities of the trustee and judges are confidential.

CAROLINA WREN PRESS POETRY SERIES CONTEST

120 Morris St., Durham NC 27701. (919)560-2738. **Fax:** (919)560-2759. **E-mail:** carolinawrenpress@ earthlink.net. **Website:** www.carolinawrenpress.org. **Contact:** Ravi Shankar, founding editor. Carolina Wren Press is a nonprofit organization whose mission is to publish quality writing, especially by writers his-

torically neglected by mainstream publishing, and to develop diverse and vital audiences through publishing, outreach, and educational programs. Deadline: March 31. Prize: $1,000 and publication.

JAMIE CAT CALLAN HUMOR PRIZE

Category in the Soul-Making Keats Literary Competition, The Webhallow House, 1544 Sweetwood Dr., Broadmoor Village CA 94015-2029. **E-mail:** SoulKeats@mail.com. **Website:** www.soulmaking-contest.us. **Contact:** Eileen Malone. Deadline: November 30. Prize: First Place: $100; Second Place: $50; Third Place: $25. Judged by Jamie Cat Callan. **TIPS** "Make me laugh out loud."

THE CENTER FOR BOOK ARTS POETRY CHAPBOOK COMPETITION

The Center for Book Arts, 28 W. 27th St., 3rd Floor, New York NY 10001. (212)481-0295. **Fax:** (866)708-8994. **E-mail:** info@centerforbookarts.org. **Website:** www.centerforbookarts.org. Annual competition for unpublished collections of poetry. Individual poems may have been previously published. Collection must not exceed 500 lines or 24 pages (does not include cover page, title pages, table of contents, or acknowledgements pages). Copies of winning chapbooks available through website. Deadline: December 15. Prize: $500 award, $500 honorarium for a reading, publication, and 10 copies of chapbook.

JOHN CIARDI PRIZE FOR POETRY

BkMk Press, University of Missouri-Kansas City, 5100 Rockhill Rd., Kansas City MO 02903-1803. (816)235-2558. **E-mail:** bkmk@umkc.edu. **Website:** www.newletters.org. Offered annually for the best book-length collection (unpublished) of poetry in English by a living author. Translations are not eligible. Guidelines for SASE, by e-mail, or on website. Deadline: January 15. Prize: $1,000, plus book publication by BkMk Press. Judged by a network of published writers. Final judging is done by a writer of national reputation.

CIDER PRESS REVIEW BOOK AWARD

P.O. Box 33384, San Diego CA 92163. **E-mail:** editor@ciderpressreview.com. **Website:** http://ciderpressreview.com/. Annual award from *Cider Press Review*. Deadline: November 30. Open to submissions on September 1. Prize: $1,500, publication, and 25 author's copies of a book length collection of poetry. Author receives a standard publishing contract. Initial print run is not less than 1,000 copies. CPR acquires first publication rights. Judged by Jeffrey Harrison in 2014. Previous judge was Charles Harper Webb.

☁ THE CITY OF VANCOUVER BOOK AWARD

Cultural Services Dept., Woodward's Heritage Building, 111 W. Hastings St., Suite 501, Vancouver BC V6B 1H4, Canada. (604) 829-2007. **Fax:** (604)871-6005. **E-mail:** marnie.rice@vancouver.ca; culture@vancouver.ca. **Website:** https://vancouver.ca/people-programs/city-of-vancouver-book-award.aspx. The annual City of Vancouver Book Award recognizes authors of excellence of any genre who contribute to the appreciation and understanding of Vancouver's history, unique character, or the achievements of its residents. The book must exhibit excellence in one or more of the following areas: content, illustration, design, format. Deadline: May 14. Prize: $3,000. Judged by an independent jury.

CLOCKWISE CHAPBOOK COMPETITION

Tebot Bach, Tebot Bach, Clockwise, P.O. Box 7887, Huntington Beach CA 92615. (714)968-0905. **Fax:** (714)968-4677. **E-mail:** mifanwy@tebotbach.org. **Website:** www.tebotbach.org/clockwise.html. Annual competition for a collection of poetry. Submit 24-32 pages of original poetry in English. Deadline: April 15. Prize: $500 and a book publication in Perfect Bound Editions. Winner announced in September with publication the following April. Judged by Gail Wronsky.

CLOUDBANK CONTEST

P.O. Box 610, Corvallis OR 97339. **E-mail:** michael@cloudbankbooks.com. **Website:** www.cloudbankbooks.com. **Contact:** Michael Malan. Prize: $200 and publication, plus an extra copy of the issue in which the winning poem appears. Two contributors' copies will be sent to writers whose work appears in the magazine. Judged by Michael Malan and Peter Sears.

☁ TOM COLLINS POETRY PRIZE

Fellowship of Australian Writers (WA), P.O. Box 6180, Swanbourne WA 6910, Australia. (61)(8)9384-4771. **Fax:** (61)(8)9384-4854. **E-mail:** fellowshipaustralian-writerswa@gmail.com. **Website:** www.fawwa.org. Annual contest for unpublished poems, maximum 60 lines. Reserves the right to publish entries in a FAW-WA publication or on its website. Guidelines online or for SASE. Deadline: December 15. Submission period begins September 1. Prize: 1st Place: $1,000; 2nd Place; $400; 4 Highly Commended: $150 each.

COLORADO BOOK AWARDS

(303)894-7951, ext. 19. **Fax:** (303)864-9361. **E-mail:** stephanie@coloradohumanities.org. **Website:** www. coloradohumanities.org. **Contact:** Stephanie March. An annual program that celebrates the accomplishments of Colorado's outstanding authors, editors, illustrators, and photographers. Awards are presented in at least ten categories including anthology/collection, biography, children's, creative nonfiction, fiction, history, nonfiction, pictorial, poetry, and young adult. Deadline: January 2.

THE COLORADO PRIZE FOR POETRY

Colorado Review/Center for Literary Publishing, Department of English, Colorado State University, 9105 Campus Delivery, Ft. Collins CO 80523. (970)491-5449. **E-mail:** creview@colostate.edu. **Website:** http://coloradoprize.colostate.edu. **Contact:** Stephanie G'Schwind, editor; Donald Revell, poetry editor. Submission must be unpublished as a collection, but individual poems may have been published elsewhere. Submit mss of 48-100 pages of poetry on any subject, in any form, double- or single-spaced. Include 2 titles pages: 1 with ms title only, the other with ms title and poet's name, address, and phone number. Enclose SASP for notification of receipt and SASE for results; mss will not be returned. Guidelines available for SASE or by e-mail. Guidelines available for SASE or online at website. Poets can also submit online via our online submission manager through our website. Deadline: Early January. Check website for exact deadline Prize: $2,000 and publication of a book-length ms.

CONCRETE WOLF POETRY CHAPBOOK CONTEST

P.O. Box 1808, Kingston WA 98346. **E-mail:** concrete-wolf@yahoo.com. **Website:** http://concretewolf.com. Prefers chapbooks that have a theme, either obvious (i.e., chapbook about a divorce) or understated (i.e., all the poems mention the color blue). Likes a collection that feels more like a whole than a sampling of work. No preference as to formal or free verse. Slightly favors lyric and narrative poetry to language and concrete, but excellent examples of any style will grab their attention. Considers simultaneous submissions if notified of acceptance elsewhere. Deadline: Novem-

ber 30. Prize: Publication and 100 author copies of a perfectly-bound chapbook.

THE CONNECTICUT RIVER REVIEW POETRY CONTEST

P.O. Box 270554, W. Hartford CT 06127. **Website:** ct-poetry.net. Deadline: September 30. 1st Place: $400; 2nd Place: $100; 3rd Place: $50.

CPR EDITOR'S PRIZE FIRST OR SECOND BOOK AWARD

P.O. Box 33384, San Diego CA 92163. **E-mail:** editor@ ciderpressreview.com. **Website:** http://ciderpressreview.com/bookaward. Annual award from *Cider Press Review*. Deadline: submit between April 1-June 30. Prize: $1,000, publication, and 25 author's copies of a book length collection of poetry. Author receives a standard publishing contract. Initial print run is not less than 1,000 copies. CPR acquires first publication rights. Judged by *Cider Press Review* editors.

CRAB ORCHARD SERIES IN POETRY FIRST BOOK AWARD

First Book Award, Dept. of English, Mail Code 4503, Southern Illinois University Carbondale, 1000 Faner Drive, Carbondale IL 62901. (618)453-6833. **E-mail:** jtribble@siu.edu. **Website:** www.craborchardreview. siu.edu. **Contact:** Jon Tribble, series editor. Annual award that selects a first book of poems for publication from an open competition of manuscripts, in English, by a U.S. citizen or permanent resident who has neither published, nor committed to publish, a volume of poetry 48 pages or more in length in an edition of over 500 copies (individual poems may have been previously published; for the purposes of the Crab Orchard Series in Poetry, a ms which was in whole or in part submitted as a thesis or dissertation as a requirement for the completion of a degree is considered unpublished and is eligible). Deadline: July 8. Submission period begins May 15. Prize: Offers $4,000 and a publication contract.

CRAB ORCHARD SERIES IN POETRY OPEN COMPETITION AWARDS

Department of English, Mail Code 4503, Faner Hall 2380, Southern Illinois University at Carbondale, Carbondale IL 62901. **E-mail:** jtribble@siu.edu. **Website:** www.craborchardreview.siu.edu. **Contact:** Jon Tribble, series editor. Annual competition to award unpublished, original collections of poems written in English by United States citizens and permanent residents (individual poems may have been previously published). Two volumes of poems will be selected from the open competition of mss. Deadline: December 5. Submission period begins October 1. Prize: Both winners will be awarded a $2500 prize and $1500 as an honorarium for a reading at Southern Illinois University Carbondale. Both readings will follow the publication of the poets' collections by Southern Illinois University Press.

THE CRAZYHORSE PRIZE IN POETRY

Crazyhorse, Department of English, College of Charleston, 66 George St., Charleston SC 29424. (843)953-4470. **E-mail:** crazyhorse@cofc.edu. **Website:** http://crazyhorse.cofc.edu. **Contact:** Prize Director. The *Crazyhorse* Prize in Poetry is for a single poem. All entries will be considered for publication. Submissions must be unpublished. Deadline: January 31. Submissions period begins January 1. Prize: $2,000 and publication in *Crazyhorse*. Judged by genre judges for first round, guest judge for second round. Judges change on a yearly basis.

THE CUTBANK CHAPBOOK CONTEST

CutBank Literary Magazine, *CutBank*, University of Montana, English Dept., LA 133, Missoula MT 59812. **E-mail:** editor.cutbank@gmail.com. **Website:** www. cutbankonline.org. **Contact:** Allison Linville, editor-in-chief. This competition is open to original English language mss in the genres of poetry, fiction, and creative nonfiction. While previously published standalone pieces or excerpts may be included in a ms, the ms as a whole must be an unpublished work. Looking for startling, compelling, and beautiful original work. "We're looking for a fresh, powerful manuscript. Maybe it will overtake us quietly; gracefully defy genres; satisfyingly subvert our expectations; punch us in the mouth page in and page out. We're interested in both prose and poetry—and particularly work that straddles the lines between genres." Deadline: January 15. Submissions period begins November 1. Prize: $1,000 and 25 contributor copies. Judged by a guest judge each year.

CWW ANNUAL WISCONSIN WRITERS AWARDS

Council for Wisconsin Writers, 6973 Heron Way, De Forest WI 53532. **E-mail:** karlahuston@gmail.com. **Website:** www.wiswriters.org. **Contact:** Geoff Gilpin, president and annual awards co-chair; Karla Huston, secretary and annual awards co-chair; Marilyn L. Taylor, annual awards chair; Alice D'Allesio, annual awards co-chair. Offered annually for work published by Wisconsin writers during the previous calendar year. Nine awards: Major Achievement (presented in alternate years); short fiction; short nonfiction; nonfiction book; poetry book; fiction book; children's literature; Lorine Niedecker Poetry Award; Christopher Latham Sholes Award for Outstanding Service to Wisconsin Writers p(resented in alternate years); Essay Award for Young Writers. Open to Wisconsin residents. Deadline: January 31. Submissions open on November 1. Prizes: First place prizes: $500. Honorable mentions: $50.

DANA AWARDS IN THE NOVEL, SHORT FICTION, AND POETRY

200 Fosseway Dr., Greensboro NC 27445. (336)644-8028. **E-mail:** danaawards@gmail.com. **Website:** www.danaawards.com. **Contact:** Mary Elizabeth Parker, chair. Three awards offered annually for unpublished work written in English. Works previously published online are not eligible. Purpose is monetary award for work that has not been previously published or received monetary award, but will accept work published simply for friends and family. Deadline: October 31 (postmarked). Prizes: $1,000 for each of the 3 awards.

DANCING POETRY CONTEST

AEI Contest Chair, Judy Cheung, 704 Brigham Ave., Santa Rosa CA 95404-5245. (707)528-0912. **E-mail:** jhcheung@comcast.net. **Website:** www.dancingpoetry.com. **Contact:** Judy Cheung, contest chair. Deadline: May 15. Prizes: Three Grand Prizes will receive $100 each plus the poems will be danced and videotaped at this year's Dancing Poetry Festival; six First Prizes will receive $50 each; twelve Second Prizes will receive $25 each; and thirty Third Prizes will receive $10 each.

TIPS "We always look for something new and different including new twists to old themes, different looks at common situations, inovative concepts for dynamic, thought provoking entertainment."

DER-HOVANESSIAN PRIZE

New England Poetry Club, 376 School St., Watertown MA 02472. **E-mail:** contests@nepoetryclub. org. **Website:** www.nepoetryclub.org. **Contact:** Audrey Kalajin. For a translation from any language into English. Send a copy of the original. Funded by John Mahtesian. Deadline: May 31 Prize: $200. Judges are well-known poets and sometimes winners of previous NEPC contests.

DIAGRAM/NEW MICHIGAN PRESS CHAPBOOK CONTEST

New Michigan Press, P.O. Box 210067, English, ML 424, University of Arizona, Tucson AZ 85721. **E-mail:** nmp@thediagram.com. **Website:** www.thediagram. com. **Contact:** Ander Monson, editor. The annual *DIAGRAM*/New Michigan Press Chapbook Contest offers $1,000, plus publication and author's copies, with discount on additional copies. Deadline: April 27. Prize: $1,000, plus publication. Finalist chapbooks also considered for publication.

DOBIE PAISANO WRITER'S FELLOWSHIP

The Graduate School, The University of Texas at Austin, Attn: Dobie Paisano Program, 110 Inner Campus Drive Stop G0400, Austin TX 78712-0531. (512)232-3609. **Fax:** (512)471-7620. **E-mail:** gbarton@austin. utexas.edu. **Website:** www.utexas.edu/ogs/Paisano. **Contact:** Gwen Barton. Sponsored by the Graduate School at The University of Texas at Austin and the Texas Institute of Letters, the Dobie Paisano Fellowship Program provides solitude, time, and a comfortable place for Texas writers or writers who have written significantly about Texas through fiction, nonfiction, poetry, plays, or other mediums. The Dobie Paisano Ranch is a very rural and rustic setting, and applicants should read the guidelines closely to insure their ability to reside in this secluded environment. Deadline: January 15. Applications are accepted beginning December 1 and must be post-marked no later than January 15. The Ralph A. Johnston memorial Fellowship is for a period of 4 months with a stipend of $6,250 per month. It is aimed at writers who have already demonstrated some publishing and critical success. The Jesse H. Jones Writing Fellowship is for a period of approximately 6 months with a stipend of $3,000 per month. It is aimed at, but not limited to, writers who are early in their careers.
TIPS "Three sets of each complete application must be submitted. Electronic submissions are not allowed. Guidelines and application forms are on the website (http://www.utexas.edu/ogs/Paisano/info.html) or may be requested by sending a SASE (3-ounce postage) to the above address, attention of 'Dobie Paisano Fellowship Project.'"

DREAM HORSE PRESS NATIONAL POETRY CHAPBOOK PRIZE

P.O. Box 2080, Aptos CA 95001-2080. **E-mail:** dreamhorsepress@yahoo.com. **Website:** www.dreamhorse-press.com. **Contact:** J.P. Dancing Bear, Editor/Publisher. Deadline: June 30. Prize: $500, publication, and 25 copies of a handsomely printed chapbook. Judged by C.J. Sage.

EDITORS LOYALTY READING PERIOD

E-mail: editor@wordworksbooks.org. **Website:** www.wordworksbooks.org. **Contact:** Nancy White, editor. The Word Works now reads mss during May by its past authors and anyone who has ever placed as a semi-finalist or finalist in the past. Prize: 1-4 books per year published from reading period.

T.S. ELIOT PRIZE FOR POETRY

Truman State University Press, 100 E. Normal Ave., Kirksville MO 63501. (660)785-7336. **Fax:** (660)785-4480. **E-mail:** tsup@truman.edu. **Website:** tsup.truman.edu. The ms may include individual poems previously published in journals or anthologies, but may not include a significant number of poems from a published chapbook or self-published book. Deadline: October 31. Prize: $2,000 and publication. Judge announced after close of competition.
Competition receives about 500 entries/year.

FAR HORIZONS AWARD FOR POETRY

The Malahat Review, University of Victoria, P.O. Box 1700, Stn CSC, Victoria BC V8W 2Y2, Canada. (250)721-8524. **Fax:** (250)472-5051. **E-mail:** malahat@uvic.ca. **Website:** www.malahatreview.ca. **Contact:** John Barton, editor. The biennial Far Horizons Award for Poetry offers $1,000 CAD and publication in *The Malahat Review* (see separate listing in Magazines/Journals). 2010 winner: Darren Bifford; 2012 winner: Kayla Czaga. 2014 winner: Laura Ritland. Winner and finalists contacted by e-mail. Winner published in fall in *The Malahat Review* and announced on website, Facebook page, and in quarterly e-newsletter, *Malahat lite*. Open to "emerging poets from Canada, the United States, and elsewhere" who have not yet published a full-length book (48 pages or more). Deadline: May 1 of even-numbered years. Prize: $1,000.

JANICE FARRELL POETRY PRIZE CATEGORY

Soul-Making Keats Literary Competition, The Webhallow House, 1544 Sweetwood Dr., Broadmoor Village CA 94015. **E-mail:** SoulKeats@mail.com. **Website:** www.soulmakingcontest.us. **Contact:** Eileen Malone. Deadline: November 30. Prize: Cash prizes.

Judged by a local San Francisco successfully published poet.

THE JEAN FELDMAN POETRY PRIZE

E-mail: wwphpress@gmail.com. **Website:** www.washingtonwriters.org. Poets living within 75 miles of the Capitol are invited to submit a ms of either a novel or a collection of short stories. Ms should be 50-70 pages, single spaced. Deadline: November 1. Submission period begins July 1. Prize: $1,000 and 50 copies of the book.

FIELD POETRY PRIZE

Oberlin College Press/FIELD, 50 N. Professor St., Oberlin OH 44074-1095. (440)775-8408. **Fax:** (440)775-8124. **E-mail:** oc.press@oberlin.edu. **Website:** www.oberlin.edu/ocpress/prize.htm. **Contact:** Marco Wilkinson, managing editor. Offered annually for an unpublished book-length collection of poetry (mss of 50-80 pages). Contest seeks to encourage the finest in contemporary poetry writing. Open to any writer. Deadline: Submit in May only. Prize: $1,000 and a standard royalty contract.

FINELINE COMPETITION FOR PROSE POEMS, SHORT SHORTS, AND ANYTHING IN BETWEEN

(419)372-2725. **E-mail:** mar@bgsu.edu. **Website:** www.bgsu.edu/midamericanreview. **Contact:** Abigail Cloud, editor-in-chief. Offered annually for previously unpublished submissions. Contest open to all writers not associated with current judge or *Mid-American Review*. Deadline: June 1. Prize: $1,000, plus publication in fall issue of *Mid-American Review*; 10 finalists receive notation plus possible publication. 2015 judge: Michael Czyzniejewski.

FIRST BOOK AWARD FOR POETRY

Zone 3, Austin Peay State University, Austin Peay State University, PO Box 4565, Clarksville TN 37044. (931)221-7031. **Fax:** (931)221-7149. **E-mail:** spofforda@aspu.edu; wallacess@apsu.edu. **Website:** www.apsu.edu/zone3/. **Contact:** Andrea Spofford, poetry editor; Susan Wallace, managing editor. Annual poetry award for anyone who has not published a full-length collection of poems (48 pages or more). Deadline: April 1. Prize: $1,000 and publication.

FISH POETRY PRIZE

Durrus, Bantry Co. Cork , Ireland. **E-mail:** info@fishpublishing.com. **Website:** www.fishpublishing.com. For poems up to 300 words. Age Range: Adult.

The best 10 will be published in the Fish Anthology, launched in July at the West Cork Literary Festival. Entries must not have been published before. Enter online or by post. See website for full details of competitions, and information on the Fish Editorial and Critique Services, and the Fish Online Writing Courses. The aim of the competition is to discover and publish new writers. Deadline: March 30. Prize: $1,200. Results announced April 30.

FIVE POINTS JAMES DICKEY PRIZE FOR POETRY

(404)413-5812. **Website:** www.fivepoints.gsu.edu. Offered annually for unpublished poetry. Deadline: December 1. Prize: $1,000, plus publication.

THE LEVIS POETRY PRIZE

Four Way Books, Box 535, Village Station, New York NY 10014. (212)334-5430. **Fax:** (212)334-5435. **E-mail:** editors@fourwaybooks.com. **Website:** www.fourwaybooks.com. **Contact:** Martha Rhodes, director. The Levis Poetry Prize, offered biennially in odd-numbered years, offers publication by Four Way Books (see separate listing in Book Publishers), honorarium, and a reading at one or more participating series. Open to any poet writing in English. Entry form and guidelines available on website. Deadline: March 31 (postmark or online submission). Winner announced by e-mail and on website. Prize: Publication and $1,000. Copies of winning books available through Four Way Books online and at bookstores (to the trade through University Press of New England).

FREEFALL SHORT PROSE AND POETRY CONTEST

Freefall Literary Society of Calgary, 922 9th Ave. SE, Calgary AB T2G 0S4, Canada. **E-mail:** editors@freefallmagazine.ca. **Website:** www.freefallmagazine.ca. **Contact:** Ryan Stromquist, managing editor. Offered annually for unpublished work in the categories of poetry (5 poems/entry) and prose (3,000 words or less). Recognizes writers and offers publication credits in a literary magazine format. Contest rules and entry form online. Acquires first Canadian serial rights; ownership reverts to author after one-time publication. Deadline: December 31. Prize: 1st Place: $500 (CAD); 2nd Place: $250 (CAD); 3rd Place: $75; Honorable Mention: $25. All prizes include publication in the spring edition of *FreeFall Magazine*. Winners will also be invited to read at the launch of that issue, if such a launch takes place. Honorable mentions in each category will be published and may be asked to read. Travel expenses not included. Judged by current guest editor for issue (who are also published authors in Canada).

GERTRUDE PRESS POETRY CHAPBOOK CONTEST

P.O. Box 28281, Portland OR 97228. **E-mail:** editor@gertrudepress.org; poetry@gertrudepress.org. **Website:** www.gertrudepress.org. Annual chapbook contest for 25-30 pages of poetry. Deadline: May 15. Submission period begins September 15. Prize: $250, publication, 50 complimentary copies of the chapbook, and 2 e-book files.

ALLEN GINSBERG POETRY AWARDS

The Poetry Center at Passaic County Community College, One College Blvd., Paterson NJ 07505. (973)684-6555. **Fax:** (973)523-6085. **E-mail:** mgillan@pccc.edu. **Website:** www.pccc.edu/poetry. **Contact:** Maria Mazziotti Gillan, executive director. All winning poems, honorable mentions, and editor's choice poems will be published in *The Paterson Literary Review*. Winners will be asked to participate in a reading that will be held in the Paterson Historic District. Submissions must be unpublished. Deadline: April 1 (postmark). 1st Prize: $1,000; 2nd Prize: $200; 3rd Prize: $100.

GIVAL PRESS POETRY AWARD

Gival Press, LLC, P.O. Box 3812, Arlington VA 22203. (703)351-0079. **E-mail:** givalpress@yahoo.com. **Website:** www.givalpress.com. **Contact:** Robert L. Giron, editor. Offered annually for a previously unpublished poetry collection as a complete ms, which may include previously published poems; previously published poems must be acknowledged, and poet must hold rights. Guidelines for SASE, by e-mail, or online. Open to any writer, as long as the work is original, not a translation, and is written in English. The copyright remains in the author's name; certain rights fall to the publisher per the contract. The competition seeks to award well-written, origional poetry in English on any topic, in any style. Deadline: December 15 (postmarked). Prize: $1,000, publication, and 20 copies of the publication. The editor narrows entries to the top 10; previous winner selects top 5 and chooses the winner—all done anonymously.

PATRICIA GOEDICKE PRIZE IN POETRY

CutBank Literary Magazine, *CutBank*, University of Montana, English Dept., LA 133, Missoula MT 59812.

E-mail: editor.cutbank@gmail.com. **Website:** www.cutbankonline.org. **Contact:** Allison Linville, editor-in-chief. The Patricia Goedicke Prize in Poetry seeks to highlight work that showcases an authentic voice, a boldness of form, and a rejection of functional fixedness. Deadline: January 15. Submissions period begins November 1. Prize: $500 and featured in the magazine. Judged by a guest judge each year.

GOLDEN ROSE AWARD

New England Poetry Club, 654 Green St., No. 2, Cambridge MA 02139. **Website:** www.nepoetryclub.org. **Contact:** NEPC contest coordinator. Given annually to the poet, who by their poetry and inspiration to and encouragement of other writers, has made a significant mark on American poetry. Traditionally given to a poet with some ties to New England so that a public reading may take place. Deadline: May 31. Judged by well-known poets and sometimes winners of previous NEPC contests.

⬦ GOVERNOR GENERAL'S LITERARY AWARDS

Canada Council for the Arts, 150 Elgin St., P.O. Box 1047, Ottawa ON K1P 5V8, Canada. (613)566-4414, ext. 5573. **Website:** www.canadacouncil.ca. Established by Parliament, the Canada Council for the Arts provides a wide range of grants and services to professional Canadian artists and art organizations in dance, media arts, music, theater, writing, publishing, and the visual arts. The Governor General's Literary Awards are given annually for the best English-language and French-language work in each of 7 categories, including fiction, nonfiction, poetry, drama, children's literature (text), children's literature (illustration), and translation. Deadline: Depends on the book's publication date. See website for details. Prize: Each GG winner receives $25,000. Non-winning finalists receive $1,000. Judged by fellow authors, translators, and illustrators. For each category, a jury makes the final selection.

GRANDMOTHER EARTH NATIONAL AWARD

Grandmother Earth Creations, P.O. Box 2018, Cordova TN 38088. (901)309-3692. **E-mail:** gmoearth@gmail.com. **Website:** www.grandmotherearth.org. **Contact:** Frances Cowden, Award Director. Annual national award open to anyone. Submissions may be published or unpublished. Considers simultaneous submissions. Submit at least 3 poems, any subject, in any form. See website for changes in the rules. Include SASE for winners list. Guidelines available for SASE or on website. Winners will be announced in October at the Life Press Writers Conference in August in Cordova, TN. Copies of winning poems or books available from Grandmother Earth Creations. Deadline: July 7. Prize: Offers annual award of $1,250 with varying distributions each year; separate contest for students ages 2-12; $1,250 minimum in awards for poetry and prose; $100 first, etc., plus publication in anthology; non-winning finalists considered for anthology if permission is given.

GREAT LAKES COLLEGES ASSOCIATION NEW WRITERS AWARD

535 W. William, Suite 301, Ann Arbor MI 48103. (734)661-2350. **Fax:** (734)661-2349. **E-mail:** wegner@glca.org. **Website:** www.glca.org. **Contact:** Gregory R. Wegner. Annual award for a first published volume of poetry, fiction, and creative nonfiction. Deadline: July 25. Prize: Honorarium of at least $500. Each award winner has the opportunity to tour the 13 colleges giving readings, meetings students and faculty, and leading discussions or classes. Judged by professors of literature and writers in residence at GLCA colleges.

THE GREEN ROSE PRIZE IN POETRY

New Issues Poetry & Prose, Deptartment of English, Western Michigan University, 1903 W. Michigan Ave., Kalamazoo MI 49008-5331. (269)387-8185. **Fax:** (269)387-2562. **Website:** www.wmich.edu/newissues. Offered annually for unpublished poetry. The university will publish a book of poems by a poet writing in English who has published 1 or more full-length collections of poetry. *New Issues* may publish as many as 3 additional mss from this competition. Guidelines for SASE or online. *New Issues Poetry & Prose* obtains rights for first publication. Book is copyrighted in the author's name. Deadline: Submit May 1-September 30. Winner is announced in January or February on website. Prize: $2,000 and publication of a book of poems.

THE GRUB STREET NATIONAL BOOK PRIZE

Grub Street, 162 Boylston Street, 5th Floor, Boston MA 02116. (617) 695-0075. **Fax:** (617) 695-0075. **E-mail:** info@grubstreet.org; chris@grubstreet.org. **Website:** http://grubstreet.org. **Contact:** Christopher Castellani, artistic director. The Grub Street National Book Prize is awarded once annually to an American writer outside New England publishing his or her second, third, fourth (or beyond...) book. First books are not

eligible. Writers whose primary residence is Massachusetts, Vermont, Maine, New Hampshire, Connecticut or Rhode Island are also not eligible. Genre of the prize rotates from year to year, between fiction, nonfiction, and poetry. Deadline: October 1. Prize: $5,000.

GREG GRUMMER POETRY AWARD

E-mail: phoebeliterature@gmail.com. **Website:** www.phoebejournal.com. **Contact:** Elizabeth Deanna Morris Lakes, poetry editor. Offered annually for unpublished work. Submit up to 4 poems, no more than 10 pages total. Guidelines online. Requests first serial rights, if work is to be published. The purpose of the award is to recognize new and exciting poetry. Deadline: February 15. Prize: $800 and publication in the *Phoebe*. Judged by a recognized poet.

HACKNEY LITERARY AWARDS

1305 2nd Ave. N, #103, Birmingham AL 35203. (205)226-4921. **E-mail:** info@hackneyliteraryawards.org. **Website:** www.hackneyliteraryawards.org. **Contact:** Myra Crawford, PhD, executive director. Offered annually for unpublished novels, short stories (maximum 5,000 words), and poetry (50 line limit). Guidelines on website. Deadline: September 30 (novels), November 30 (short stories and poetry). Prize: $5,000 in annual prizes for poetry and short fiction ($2,500 national and $2,500 state level). 1st Place: $600; 2nd Place: $400; 3rd Place: $250); plus $5,000 for an unpublished novel. Competition winners will be announced on the website each March.

⬤ THE HODDER FELLOWSHIP

Lewis Center for the Arts, 185 Nassau St., Princeton NJ 08544. (609)258-6926. **E-mail:** ysabelg@princeton.edu. **Website:** arts.princeton.edu. **Contact:** Ysabel Gonzalez, fellowships assistant. The Hodder Fellowship will be given to writers of exceptional promise to pursue independent projects at Princeton University during the current academic year. Typically the fellows are poets, playwrights, novelists, creative nonfiction writers and translators who have published one highly acclaimed work and are undertaking a significant new project that might not be possible without the "studious leisure" afforded by the fellowship. Deadline: October 1. Open to applications in July. Prize: $75,000 stipend.

ERIC HOFFER AWARD

Hopewell Publications, LLC, P.O. Box 11, Titusville NJ 08560-0011. **Fax:** (609)964-1718. **E-mail:** info@hopepubs.com. **Website:** www.hofferaward.com. **Contact:** Christopher Klim, chair. Annual contest for previously published books. Recognizes excellence in independent publishing in many unique categories: Art (titles capture the experience, execution, or demonstration of the arts); Poetry (all styles); General Fiction (nongenre-specific fiction); Commercial Fiction (genre-specific fiction); Children (titles for young children); Young Adult (titles aimed at the juvenile and teen markets); Culture (titles demonstrating the human or world experience); Memoir (titles relating to personal experience); Business (titles with application to today's business environment and emerging trends); Reference (titles from traditional and emerging reference areas); Home (titles with practical applications to home or home-related issues, including family); Health (titles promoting physical, mental, and emotional well-being); Self-help (titles involving new and emerging topics in self-help); Spiritual (titles involving the mind and spirit, including relgion); Legacy (titles over 2 years of age that hold particular relevance to any subject matter or form). Open to any writer of published work within the last 2 years, including categores for older books. This contest recognizes excellence in independent publishing in many unique categories. Also awards the Montaigne Medal for most though-provoking book, the Da Vinci Eye for best cover, and the First Horizon Award for best new authors. Results published in the US Review of Books.

THE BESS HOKIN PRIZE

Poetry, 61 W. Superior St., Chicago IL 60654. (312)787-7070. **Fax:** (312)787-6650. **E-mail:** editors@poetry-magazine.org. **Website:** www.poetrymagazine.org. Offered annually for poems published in *Poetry* during the preceding year (October-September). Upon acceptance, *Poetry* licenses exclusive worldwide first serial rights, including electronic rights, for publication, as well as non-exclusive rights to reprint, reuse, and archive the work, in any format, in perpetuity. Copyright reverts to author upon first publication. "Established in 1947 through the generosity of our late friend and guarantor, Mrs. David Hokin, and is given annually in her memory." Prize: $1,000.

FIRMAN HOUGHTON PRIZE

New England Poetry Club, 376 School St., Watertown MA 02472. **E-mail:** contests@nepoetryclug.org. **Website:** www.nepoetryclub.org. **Contact:** Audrey Kalajin. For a lyric poem in honor of the former president of NEPC. Deadline: May 31 Prize: $250. Judged by well-known poets and sometimes winners of previous NEPC contests.

TOM HOWARD/MARGARET REID POETRY CONTEST

Sponsored by Winning Writers, Winning Writers, 351 Pleasant St., PMB 222, Northampton MA 01060-3961. **E-mail:** adam@winningwriters.com. **Website:** www.winningwriters.com. **Contact:** Adam Cohen. Offers annual awards of Tom Howard Prize, for a poem in any style or genre, and Margaret Reid Prize, for a poem that rhymes or has a traditional style. See website for guidelines and to submit your poem. Nonexclusive right to publish submissions online, in e-mail newsletters, in e-books, and in press releases. Deadline: September 30. Submission period begins April 15. Prizes: Each prize is $1,500, with 10 Honorable Mentions of $100 each (any style).

THE HUNGER MOUNTAIN CREATIVE NONFICTION PRIZE

Vermont College, 36 College St., Montpelier VT 05602. (802)828-8517. **E-mail:** hungermtn@vcfa.edu. **Website:** www.hungermtn.org. **Contact:** Miciah Bay Gault, editor. Annual contest for the best writing in creative nonfiction. Submit essays under 10,000 words. Guidelines available on website. Deadline: September 10. Prize: $1,000 and publication. Two honorable mentions receive $100 each.

ILLINOIS STATE POETRY SOCIETY ANNUAL CONTEST

Illinois State Poetry Society, 543 E. Squirrel Trail Dr., Tucson AZ 85704. **Website:** www.illinoispoets.org. **Contact:** Alan Harris. Annual contest to encourage the crafting of excellent poetry. Guidelines and entry forms available for SASE. Deadline: September 30. Prize: Cash prizes of $50, $30, and $10. Three Honorable Mentions. Poet retains all rights. Judged by out-of-state professionals.

INDIANA REVIEW ½ K PRIZE

Indiana Review, Ballantine Hall 465, 1020 E. Kirkwood Ave., Indiana University, Bloomington IN 47405-7103. (812)855-3439. **Fax:** (812)855-9535. **E-mail:** inreview@indiana.edu. **Website:** http://indianareview.org. **Contact:** Katie Moulton, consulting editor. Offered annually for unpublished work. Maximum story/poem length is 500 words. Guidelines available in March for SASE, by phone, e-mail, on website, or in publication. Deadline: May 31. Submission period begins August 1. Prize: $1,000, plus publication, contributor's copies, and a year's subscription to *Indiana Review*.

INDIANA REVIEW POETRY PRIZE

Indiana Review, Poetry Prize, Indiana Review, Ballantine Hall 465, 1020 E. Kirkwood Ave., Bloomington IN 47405-7103. (812)855-3439. **Fax:** (812)855-9535. **E-mail:** inreview@indiana.edu. **Website:** www.indianareview.org. **Contact:** Michael Mlekoday, Poetry Editor. Offered annually for unpublished work. Open to any writer. Guidelines available on website. All entries are considered for publication. Deadline: March 15. Submission period begins February 1. Prize: $1,000 and publication. Judged by Edward C. Corral in 2015. Different judge every year.

IOWA POETRY PRIZE

University of Iowa Press, 119 West Park Rd., 100 Kuhl House, Iowa City IA 52242. (319)335-2000. **Fax:** (319)335-2055. **E-mail:** uipress@uiowa.edu. **Website:** www.uiowapress.org. Offered annually to encourage poets and their work. Submissions must be postmarked during the month of April; put name on title page only. This page will be removed before ms is judged. Open to writers of English (US citizens or not). Mss will not be returned. Previous winners are not eligible. Deadline: April 30. Prize: Publication under standard royalty agreement.

THE IOWA REVIEW AWARD IN POETRY, FICTION, AND NONFICTION

308 EPB, University of Iowa, Iowa City IA 52242. **E-mail:** iowa-review@uiowa.edu. **Website:** www.iowareview.org. *The Iowa Review* Award in Poetry, Fiction, and Nonfiction presents $1,500 to each winner in each genre, $750 to runners-up. Winners and runners-up published in *The Iowa Review*. Deadline: Submit January 1-31. Judged by Srikanth Reddy, Kevin Brockmeier, and Wayne Koestenbaum in 2015.

ALICE JAMES AWARD

Alice James Books, University of Maine at Farmington, 114 Prescott St., Farmington ME 04938. (207)778-7071. **Fax:** (207)778-7766. **E-mail:** ajb@alicejamesbooks.org; info@alice jamesbooks.org. **Website:** www.alicejamesbooks.org. **Contact:** Alyssa Neptune, managing editor. Offered annually for unpublished, full-length poetry collections. Emerging and established poets are welcome. Deadline: November 1. Prize: $2,000, publication, and distribution through Consortium.

JUNIPER PRIZE FOR POETRY

University of Massachusetts Press, East Experiment Station, 671 North Pleasant St., Amherst MA 01003. (413)545-2217. **Fax:** (413)545-1226. **E-mail:** info@umpress.umass.edu; kfisk@umpress.umass.edu. **E-mail:** poetry@umpress.umass.edu. **Website:** www.umass.edu/umpress. **Contact:** Karen Fisk, competition coordinator. The University of Massachusetts Press offers the annual Juniper Prize for Poetry, awarded in alternate years for the first and subsequent books. Deadline: September 30. Submissions period begins August 1. Winners announced online in April on the press website. Prize: Publication and $1,500 in addition to royalties.

○ In even-numbered years, only subsequent books will be considered—mss whose authors have had at least 1 full-length book or chapbook (of at least 30 pages) of poetry published or accepted for publication. Self-published work is not considered to lie within this books and chapbooks category. In odd-numbered years, only first books will be considered—mss by writers whose poems may have appeared in literary journals and/or anthologies but have not been published or accepted for publication in book form.

BARBARA MANDIGO KELLY PEACE POETRY AWARDS

(805)965-3443. **Fax:** (805)568-0466. **E-mail:** wagingpeace@napf.org; cwarner@napf.org. **Website:** www.wagingpeace.org; www.peacecontests.org. **Contact:** Carol Warner, poetry award coordinator. The Barbara Mandigo Kelly Peace Poetry Contest was created to encourage poets to explore and illuminate positive visions of peace and the human spirit. The annual contest honors the late Barbara Kelly, a Santa Barbara poet and longtime supporter of peace issues. Awards are given in 3 categories: adult (over 18 years), youth between 12 and 18 years, and youth under 12. All submitted poems should be unpublished. Deadline: July 1 (postmarked). Prize: Adult: $1,000; Youth (13-18): $200; Youth (12 and under): $200. Honorable Mentions may also be awarded. Judged by a committee of poets selected by the Nuclear Age Peace Foundation. The foundation reserves the right to publish and distribute the award-winning poems, including honorable mentions.

TIPS "Poets should keep copies of all entries as we will be unable to return them. Copies of the winning poems from the 2003 Awards will be posted on the Nuclear Age Peace Foundation website after October 1, 2009."

THE LEAGUE OF MINNESOTA POETS CONTEST

2029 103rd Ave. NW, Coon Rapids MN 55433. **E-mail:** pwilliamstein@yahoo.com; schambersmediator@yahoo.com. **Website:** www.mnpoets.com. **Contact:** Peter Stein; Sue Chambers. Annual contest offers 22 different categories, with 3 prizes in each category. See guidelines for poem lengths, forms, and subjects. Guidelines available for #10 SASE, by e-mail, or on website. Additional information regarding LOMP membership available on website. Deadline: July 31. Submissions period begins May 1. Prize: See specific categories. Prize amounts vary from $10 up to $125, depending on category and place. Judged by nationally known, non-Minnesota judges. Winners will be announced at the October LOMP Conference and by mail.

LEAGUE OF UTAH WRITERS CONTEST

The League of Utah Writers, The League of Utah Writers, P.O. Box 64, Lewiston UT 84320. (435)755-7609. **E-mail:** luwcontest@gmail.com. **Website:** www.luwriters.org. Open to any writer, the LUW Contest provides authors an opportunity to get their work read and critiqued. Multiple categories are offered; see website for details. Entries must be the original and unpublished work of the author. Winners are announced at the Annual Writers Round-Up in September. Those not present will be notified by e-mail. Deadline: June 15. Submissions period begins March 15. Prize: Cash prizes are awarded. Judged by professional authors and editors from outside the League.

LES FIGUES PRESS NOS BOOK CONTEST

P.O. Box 7736, Los Angeles CA 90007. (323)734-4732. **E-mail:** info@lesfigues.com. **Website:** www.lesfigues. com. **Contact:** Teresa Carmody and Vanessa Place, co-directors. Les Figues Press creates aesthetic conversations between writers/artists and readers, especially those interested in innovative/experimental/ avant-garde work. The Press intends in the most premeditated fashion to champion the trinity of Beauty, Belief, and Bawdry. Deadline: September 15. Prize: $1,000, plus publication by Les Figues Press. Each entry receives LFP book.

LET'S WRITE LITERARY CONTEST

The Gulf Coast Writers Association, P.O. Box 952, Long Beach MS 39560. **E-mail:** writerpllevin@gmail.

com. **Website:** www.gcwriters.org. **Contact:** Philip Levin. The Gulf Coast Writers Association sponsors this nationally recognized contest, which accepts unpublished poems and short stories from authors all around the US. This is an annual event which has been held for over 20 years. Deadline: April 10. Prize: 1st Prize: $100; 2nd Prize: $60; 3rd Prize: $25.

LEVIS READING PRIZE

(804)828-1329. **Fax:** (804)828-8684. **E-mail:** detischc@ mymail.vcu.edu. **Website:** www.english.vcu.edu/mfa/ levis. **Contact:** Christian Detisch, Levis Fellow. Offered annually for books of poetry published in the previous year to encourage poets early in their careers. The entry must be the writer's first or second published book of poetry. Previously published books in other genres, or previously published chapbooks or self-published material, do not count as books for this purpose. Deadline: February 1. Prize: $2,000 and an expense-paid trip to Richmond to present a public reading.

THE RUTH LILLY POETRY PRIZE

(312)787-7070. **Fax:** (312)787-6650. **E-mail:** editors@ poetrymagazine.org. **Website:** www.poetrymagazine. org. Awarded annually, the $100,000 Ruth Lilly Poetry Prize honors a living U.S. poet whose lifetime accomplishments warrant extraordinary recognition. Established in 1986 by Ruth Lilly, the Prize is one of the most prestigious awards given to American poets and is one of the largest literary honors for work in the English language. Deadline: No submissions or nominations considered. Prize: $100,000.

LITERAL LATTÉ POETRY AWARD

Literal Latté, 200 E. 10th St., Suite 240, New York NY 10003. (212)260-5532. **E-mail:** LitLatte@aol.com. **Website:** www.literal-latte.com. **Contact:** Jenine Gordon Bockman, editor. Offered annually to any writer for unpublished poetry (maximum 2,000 words per poem). All styles welcome. Winners published in *Literal Latté*. Deadline: Postmark by July 15. 1st Place: $1,000; 2nd Place: $300; 3rd Place: $200. Judged by the editors.

THE HUGH J. LUKE AWARD

Prairie Schooner, 123 Andrews Hall, University of Nebraska-Lincoln, Lincoln NE 68588-0334. (402)472-0911. **Fax:** (402)472-1817. **E-mail:** prairieschooner@ unl.edu. **Website:** www.prairieschooner.unl.edu. **Contact:** Kwame Dawes. Offered annually for work published in *Prairie Schooner* in the previous year. Results announced in the Spring issue. Winners notified by mail in February or March. Prize: $250. Judged by editorial staff of *Prairie Schooner*.

LUMINA POETRY CONTEST

Website: www.luminajournal.com. Annual poetry competition held by the Sarah Lawrence College's graduate literary journal. Deadline: October 15. Prize: 1st Place: $500 and publication; 2nd Place: $250 and publication; 3rd Place: $100 and online publication.

LUMINA POETRY CONTEST

E-mail: lumina@gm.slc.edu. **Website:** www.lumina-journal.com/contests. *Lumina* is the literary magazine of the graduate writing program of Sarah Lawrence College. This contest provides a place for the publication of some of the best original poetry written in English. Deadline: October 15. 1st Place: $500 and publication; 2nd Place: $250 and publication; 3rd Place: $100 and publication online. Judged by Patricia Lockwood in 2014.

THE MACGUFFIN NATIONAL POET HUNT CONTEST

The MacGuffin, The MacGuffin, Schoolcraft College, 18600 Haggerty Rd., Livonia MI 48152. (734)462-4400, ext. 5327. **Fax:** (734)462-4679. **E-mail:** macguffin@schoolcraft.edu. **Website:** www.schoolcraft.edu/a-z-index/the-macguffin. **Contact:** Gordon Krupsky, managing editor. *The MacGuffin* is a national literary magazine from Schoolcraft College in Livonia, Michigan. The mission of *The MacGuffin* is to encourage, support, and enhance the literary arts in the Schoolcraft College community, the region, the state, and the nation. Deadline: June 3. Submissions period begins April 1. Prize: $500. Judged by Carl Dennis.

NAOMI LONG MADGETT POETRY AWARD

Lotus Press, Inc., 8300 East Jefferson Ave., #504, Detroit MI 48214. (313)736-5338. **E-mail:** broadsidelotus@gmail.com. **Website:** www.lotuspress.org. **Contact:** Gloria House. Offered annually to recognize an unpublished book-length poetry ms by an African American. Guidelines available online. Deadline: March 1. Submission period begins January 2. Prize: $500 and publication by Lotus Press.

MAIN STREET RAG'S ANNUAL POETRY BOOK AWARD

P.O. Box 690100, Charlotte NC 28227. (704)573-2516. **E-mail:** editor@mainstreetrag.com. **Website:** www.MainStreetRag.com. **Contact:** M. Scott Douglass, edi-

tor/publisher. Deadline: January 31. Prize: 1st Place: $1,200 and 50 copies of book; runners-up are also be offered publication.

☉ THE MALAHAT REVIEW LONG POEM PRIZE

The Malahat Review, Box 1700 STN CSC, Victoria BC V8W 2Y2, Canada. **E-mail:** malahat@uvic.ca. **Website:** www.malahatreview.ca. **Contact:** John Barton, editor. Long Poem Prize offered in alternate years with the Novella Contest. Open to any writer. Offers 2 awards of $1,000 CAD each for a long poem or cycle (10-20 printed pages). Includes publication in *The Malahat Review* and a 1-year subscription. Open to entries from Canadian, American, and overseas authors. Obtains first world rights. Publication rights after revert to the author. Deadline: February 1 (odd-numbered years). Prize: Two $1,000 prizes. Winners published in the summer issue of *The Malahat Review*, announced in summer on website, Facebook page, and in quarterly e-newsletter *Malahat lite*. Judged by 3 recognized poets. Preliminary readings by editorial board.

THE MORTON MARR POETRY PRIZE

Southwest Review, Southern Methodist University, P.O. Box 750374, Dallas TX 75275. (214)768-1037. **Fax:** (214)768-1408. **E-mail:** swr@mail.smu.edu. **Website:** www.smu.edu/southwestreview. **Contact:** Prize coordinator. Annual award for poem(s) by a writer who has not yet published a book of poetry. Submit no more than 6 poems in a "traditional" form (e.g., sonnet, sestine, villanelle, rhymed stanzas, blank verse, et al.). Submissions will not be returned. All entrants will receive a copy of the issue in which the winning poems appear. Deadline: September 30. Prizes: $1,000 for 1st place; $500 for 2nd place; plus publication in the Southwest Review.

MARSH HAWK PRESS POETRY PRIZE

P.O. Box 206, East Rockaway NY 11518-0206. **E-mail:** marshhawkpress1@aol.com. **Website:** www.Marsh-HawkPress.org. **Contact:** prize director. The Marsh Hawk Press Poetry Prize offers $1,000, plus publication of a book-length ms. Additionally, The Robert Creeley Poetry Prize and The Rochelle Ratner Poetry Award go to the runners-up. Deadline: April 30.

KATHLEEN MCCLUNG SONNET PRIZE CATEGORY

Soul-Making Keats Literary Competition, The Webhallow House, 1544 Sweetwood Dr., Broadmoor Village CA 94015-2029. **E-mail:** soulkeats@mail.com. **Website:** www.soulmakingcontest.us. **Contact:** Eileen Malone. Call for Shakespearean and Petrarchan sonnets on the theme of the "beloved." Deadline: November 30. Prize:1st Place: $100; 2nd Place: $50; 3rd Place: $25.

VASSAR MILLER PRIZE IN POETRY

University of North Texas Press, 1155 Union Circle, #311336, Denton TX 76203. (940)565-2142. **Fax:** (940)565-4590. **Website:** http://untpress.unt.edu. **Contact:** John Poch. Annual prize awarded to a collection of poetry. Deadline: Mss may be submitted between 9 A.M. on September 1 and 5 P.M. on October 31, through online submissions manager only. Prize: $1,000 and publication by University of North Texas Press. Judged by a different eminent writer selected each year. Some prefer to remain anonymous until the end of the contest.

MISSISSIPPI REVIEW PRIZE

Mississippi Review, 118 College Dr., #5144, Hattiesburg MS 39406-0001. (601)266-4321. **Fax:** (601)266-5757. **E-mail:** msreview@usm.edu. **Website:** www. mississippireview.com. Annual contest starting August 1 and running until January 1. Winners and finalists will make up next winter's print issue of the national literary magazine *Mississippi Review*. Each entrant will receive a copy of the prize issue. Deadline: January1. Prize: $1,000 in fiction and poetry.

THE KATHRYN A. MORTON PRIZE IN POETRY

Sarabande Books, Inc., 2234 Dundee Rd., Suite 200, Louisville KY 40205. (502)458-4028. **E-mail:** info@ sarabandebooks.org. **Website:** www.sarabandebooks.org. **Contact:** Sarah Gorham, editor-in-chief. The Kathryn A. Morton Prize in Poetry is awarded annually to a book-length ms (at least 48 pages). All finalists are considered for publication. Competition receives approximately 1,400 entries. Deadline: February 15. Submissions period begins January 1. Prize: $2,000, publication, and a standard royalty contract.

THE HOWARD FRANK MOSHER SHORT FICTION PRIZE

Vermont College, 36 College St., Montpelier VT 05602. (802)828-8517. **E-mail:** hungermtn@vcfa.edu. **Website:** www.hungermtn.org. **Contact:** Miciah Bay Gault, editor. The Howard Frank Mosher Short Fiction Prize is an annual contest for short fiction. Deadline: June 30. Prize: One first place winner receives $1,000 and publication. Two honorable mentions receive $100 each, and are considered for publication.

SHEILA MARGARET MOTTON PRIZE

New England Poetry Club, 2 Farrar St., Cambridge MA 02138. (617)744-6034. **E-mail:** info@nepoetryclub.org. **Website:** www.nepoetryclub.org. **Contact:** Audrey Kalajin. Awarded for a book of poems published in the last 2 years. Deadline: May 31. Prize: $500. Judged by well-known poets and sometimes winners of previous NEPC contests.

ERIKA MUMFORD PRIZE

New England Poetry Club, 376 School St., Watertown MA 02472. **E-mail:** contests@nepoetryclub.org. **Website:** www.nepoetryclub.org/contests.htm. **Contact:** Audrey Kalajin. Offered annually for a poem in any form about foreign culture or travel. Funded by Erika Mumford's family and friends. Deadline: May 31. Prize: $250. Judged by well-known poets and sometimes winners of previous NEPC contests.

NATIONAL BOOK AWARDS

The National Book Foundation, 90 Broad St., Suite 604, New York NY 10004. (212)685-0261. **E-mail:** nationalbook@nationalbook.org; agall@nationalbook.org. **Website:** www.nationalbook.org. **Contact:** Amy Gall. The National Book Foundation and the National Book Awards celebrate the best of American literature, expand its audience, and enhance the cultural value of great writing in America. The contest offers prizes in 4 categories: fiction, nonfiction, poetry, and young people's literature. Books should be published between December 1 and November 30 of the past year. Deadline: Entry form and payment by May 15; a copy of the book by July 1. Prize: $10,000 in each category. Finalists will each receive a prize of $1,000. Judged by a category specific panel of 5 judges for each category.

NATIONAL WRITERS ASSOCIATION POETRY CONTEST

The National Writers Association, 10940 S. Parker Rd. #508, Parker CO 80134. (303)841-0246. **E-mail:** natlwritersassn@hotmail.com. **Website:** www.nationalwriters.com. **Contact:** Sandy Whelchel, director. Annual contest to encourage the writing of poetry, an important form of individual expression but with a limited commercial market. Deadline: October 1. Prize: 1st Place: $100; 2nd Place: $50; 3rd Place: $25.

THE PABLO NERUDA PRIZE FOR POETRY

Nimrod International Journal, 800 S. Tucker Dr., Tulsa OK 74104. (918)631-3080. **Fax:** (918)631-3033. **E-mail:** nimrod@utulsa.edu. **Website:** www.utulsa.edu/nimrod. **Contact:** Eilis O'Neal. Annual award to discover new writers of vigor and talent. Open to US residents only. Deadline: April 30. Prizes: 1st Place: $2,000 and publication; 2nd Place: $1,000 and publication. Judged by the *Nimrod* editors (finalists). A recognized author selects the winners.

THE NEUTRINO SHORT-SHORT CONTEST

(906)227-1203. **Fax:** (906)227-1096. **E-mail:** passages@nmu.edu. **Website:** www.passagesnorth.com. **Contact:** Jennifer Howard. Offered every 2 years to publish new voices in literary fiction, nonfiction, hybrid-essays and prose poems (maximum 1,000 words). Guidelines available for SASE or online. Deadline: March 15. Submission period begins January 15. Prize: $1,000, and publication for the winner; 2 honorable mentions also published; all entrants receive a copy of *Passages North*. Judged by Connie Voisine in 2014.

THE NEW ISSUES POETRY PRIZE

New Issues Poetry & Prose, New Issues Poetry & Prose, Department of English, Western Michigan University, 1903 W. Michigan Ave., Kalamazoo MI 49008-5331. (269)387-8185. **Fax:** (269)387-2562. **E-mail:** new-issues@wmich.edu. **Website:** www.wmich.edu/newissues. Offered annually for publication of a first book of poems by a poet writing in English who has not previously published a full-length collection of poems in an edition of 500 or more copies. *New Issues Poetry & Prose* obtains rights for first publication. Book is copyrighted in author's name. Guidelines for SASE or online. Additional mss will be considered from those submitted to the competition for publication. Considers simultaneous submissions, but *New Issues* must be notified of acceptance elsewhere. Deadline: November 30. Prize: $2,000, plus publication of a book-length ms. A national judge selects the prize winner and recommends other manuscripts. The editors decide on the other books considering the judge's recommendation, but are not bound by it. 2015 judge: Major Jackson.

NEW LETTERS LITERARY AWARDS

New Letters, UMKC, University House, Room 105, 5101 Rockhill Rd., Kansas City MO 64110-2499. (816)235-1168. **Fax:** (816)235-2611. **Website:** www.newletters.org. Award has 3 categories (fiction, poetry, and creative nonfiction) with 1 winner in each. Offered annually for previously unpublished work. For guidelines, send an SASE to *New Letters*, or visit www.newletters.org. Deadline: May 18. 1st place: $1,500, plus publication; first runners-up: a copy of a recent book of poetry or fiction courtesy of our affiliate BkMk Press. Judged by regional writers of prominence and experience. Final judging by someone of national repute. Previous judges include Maxine Kumin, Albert Goldbarth, Charles Simic, and Janet Burroway.

NEW LETTERS PRIZE FOR POETRY

New Letters Awards for Writers, UMKC, University House, 5101 Rockhill Rd., Kansas City MO 64110-2499. **E-mail:** newletters@umkc.edu. **Website:** www.newletters.org. The annual New Letters Poetry Prize awards $1,500 and publication in *New Letters* (see separate listing in Magazines/Journals) to the best group of 3-6 poems. All entries will be considered for publication in *New Letters*. Deadline: May 18 (postmarked). Prize: $1,500 and publication.

NEW MILLENNIUM AWARDS FOR FICTION, POETRY, AND NONFICTION

New Millennium Writings, 4021 Garden Dr., Knoxville TN 37918. (865)254-4880. **Website:** www.newmillenniumwritings.com/awards. No restrictions as to style, content or number of submissions. Previously published pieces acceptable if online or under 5,000 print circulation. Simultaneous and multiple submissions welcome. Deadline: postmarked on or before July 31 for the Summer Awards and January 31 for the Winter Awards. Prize: $1,000 for Best Poem; $1,000 for Best Fiction; $1,000 for Best Nonfiction; $1,000 for Best Short-Short Fiction.

NORTHERN CALIFORNIA BOOK AWARDS

Northern California Book Reviewers Association, c/o Poetry Flash, 1450 Fourth St. #4, Berkeley CA 94710. (510)525-5476. **E-mail:** ncbr@poetryflash.org; editor@poetryflash.org. **Website:** www.poetryflash.org. **Contact:** Joyce Jenkins, executive director. Annual Northern California Book Award for outstanding book in literature, open to books published in the current calendar year by Northern California authors. NCBR presents annual awards to Bay Area (northern California) authors annually in fiction, nonfiction, poetry and children's literature. Encourages writers and stimulates interest in books and reading. Deadline: December 28. Prize: $100 honorarium and award certificate. Judging by voting members of the Northern California Book Reviewers.

☺ OPEN SEASON AWARDS

The Malahat Review, University of Victoria, P.O. Box 1700, Stn CSC, Victoria BC V8V 2Y2, Canada. (250)721-8524. **Fax:** (250)472-5051. **E-mail:** malahat@ uvic.ca. **Website:** www.malahatreview.ca. **Contact:** John Barton, editor. The Open Season Awards accepts entries of poetry, fiction, and creative nonfiction. Winners published in spring issue of *Malahat Review* announced in winter on website, facebook page, and in quarterly e-newsletter, *Malahat lite*. Deadline: November 1. Prize: $1,000 CAD and publication in *The Malahat Review* in each category.

OREGON BOOK AWARDS

925 SW Washington St., Portland OR 97205. (503)227-2583. **Fax:** (503)241-4256. **E-mail:** la@literary-arts. org. **Website:** www.literary-arts.org. **Contact:** Susan Denning, director of programs and events. The annual Oregon Book Awards celebrate Oregon authors in the areas of poetry, fiction, nonfiction, drama and young readers' literature published between August 1 and July 31 of the previous calendar year. Awards are available for every category. See website for details. Deadline: August 29. Prize: Grant of $2,500. (Grant money could vary.) Judged by writers who are selected from outside Oregon for their expertise in a genre. Past judges include Mark Doty, Colson Whitehead and Kim Barnes.

OREGON LITERARY FELLOWSHIPS

925 S.W. Washington, Portland OR 97205. (503)227-2583. **E-mail:** susan@literary-arts.org. **Website:** www. literary-arts.org. **Contact:** Susan Denning, director of programs and events. Oregon Literary Fellowships are intended to help Oregon writers initiate, develop or complete literary projects in poetry, fiction, literary nonfiction, drama and young readers literature. Writers in the early stages of their career are encouraged to apply. The awards are merit-based. Deadline: Last Friday in June. Prize: $2,500 minimum award, for approximately 10 writers and 2 publishers. Judged by out-of-state writers

PANGAEA PRIZE

The Poet's Billow, 245 N. Collingwood, Syracuse NY 13206. **E-mail:** thepoetsbillow@gmail.com. **Website:** http://thepoetsbillow.org. **Contact:** Robert Evory. An-

nual award open to any writer to recognize the best series of poems, ranging between two and up to seven poems in a group. Finalists with strong work will also be published. Submissions must be previously unpublished. Please submit online. Deadline: May 1. Prize: $100. The winning poem will be published and displayed in The Poet's Billow Literary Art Gallery and nominated for a Pushcart Prize. If the poet qualifies, the poem will also be submitted to The Best New Poets anthology. Judged by the editors, and, occasionally, a guest judge.

THE PATERSON POETRY PRIZE

(973)684-6555. **Fax:** (973)523-6085. **E-mail:** mgillan@ pccc.edu. **Website:** www.pccc.edu/poetry. **Contact:** Maria Mazziotti Gillan, executive director. The Paterson Poetry Prize offers an annual award for the strongest book of poems (48 or more pages) published in the previous year. The winner will be asked to participate in an awards ceremony and to give a reading at The Poetry Center. Minimum press run: 500 copies. Publishers may submit more than 1 title for prize consideration; 3 copies of each book must be submitted. Include SASE for results; books will not be returned (all entries will be donated to The Poetry Center Library). Guidelines and application form (required) available for SASE or on website. Deadline: February 1. Prize: $1,000.

THE KATHERINE PATERSON PRIZE FOR YOUNG ADULT AND CHILDREN'S WRITING

Hunger Mountain, Vermont College of Fine Arts, 36 College St., Montpelier VT 05602. (802)828-8517. **E-mail:** hungermtn@vcfa.edu. **Website:** www.hungermtn.org. **Contact:** Miciah Bay Gault, editor. The annual Katherine Paterson Prize for Young Adult and Children's Writing honors the best in young adult and children's literature. Submit young adult or middle grade mss, and writing for younger children, short stories, picture books, or novel excerpts, under 10,000 words. Guidelines available on website. Deadline: June 30. Prize: $1,000 and publication for the first place winner; $100 each and publication for the three category winners. Judged by a guest judge every year. The 2014 judge is Katherine Applegate, the Newbery Award-winning author of *The One and Only Ivan*.

PAVEMENT SAW PRESS CHAPBOOK AWARD

321 Empire St., Montpelier OH 43543-1301. **E-mail:** info@pavementsaw.org. **E-mail:** editor@pavementsaw.

org. **Website:** www.pavementsaw.org. **Contact:** David Baratier, editor. Pavement Saw Press has been publishing steadily since the fall of 1993. Each year since 1999, they have published at least 4 full-length paperback poetry collections, with some printed in library edition hard covers, 1 chapbook, and a yearly literary journal anthology. Theyspecialize in finding authors who have been widely published in literary journals but have not published a chapbook or full-length book. **Deadline:** December 31 (postmark). **Prize:** Chapbook Award offers $500, publication, and 50 author copies.

JEAN PEDRICK PRIZE

New England Poetry Club, 2 Farrar St., Cambridge MA 02138. **E-mail:** contests@nepoetryclub.org. **Website:** www.nepoetryclub.org. **Contact:** Audrey Kalajin. Prize for a chapbook of poems published in the last two years. **Deadline:** May 31. **Prize:** $100. Judged by well-known poets and sometimes winners of previous NEPC contests.

PEN AWARD FOR POETRY IN TRANSLATION

(212)334-1660, ext. 108. **E-mail:** awards@pen.org. **Website:** www.pen.org. **Contact:** Arielle Anema. This award recognizes book-length translations of poetry from any language into English, published during the current calendar year. All books must have been published in the US. Translators may be of any nationality. US residency/citizenship not required. **Deadline:** November 15. **Prize:** $3,000. Judged by a single translator of poetry appointed by the PEN Translation Committee.

PEN CENTER USA LITERARY AWARDS

PEN Center USA, P.O. Box 6037, Beverly Hills CA 90212. (323)424-4939. **E-mail:** awards@penusa.org. **E-mail:** pen@penusa.org. **Website:** www.penusa.org. Offered for work published or produced in the previous calendar year. Open to writers living west of the Mississippi River. Award categories: fiction, poetry, research nonfiction, creative nonfiction, translation, children's/young adult, graphic literature, drama, screenplay, teleplay, journalism. Deadline for book categories: 4 copies must be received by December 31. Deadline for non-book categories: 4 copies must be received by February 28. **Prize:** $1,000.

PEN/JOYCE OSTERWEIL AWARD FOR POETRY

PEN American Center, 588 Broadway, Suite 303, New York NY 10012. (212)334-1660, ext. 126. **E-mail:** awards@pen.org. **Website:** www.pen.org. **Contact:** Arielle Anema. *Candidates may only be nominated by members of PEN.* This award recognizes the high literary character of the published work to date of a new and emerging American poet of any age, and the promise of further literary achievement. Nominated writer may not have published more than 1 book of poetry. Offered in odd-numbered years and alternates with the PEN/Voelcker Award for Poetry. **Deadline:** November 15 **Prize:** $5,000. Judged by a panel of 3 judges selected by the PEN Awards Committee.

PNWA LITERARY CONTEST

(452)673-2665. **Fax:** (452)961-0768. **E-mail:** pnwa@pnwa.org. **Website:** www.pnwa.org. Annual literary contest with 12 different categories. See website for details and specific guidelines. Each entry receives 2 critiques. Winners announced at the PNWA Summer Conference, held annually in mid-July. **Deadline:** February 20. **Prize:** 1st Place: $700; 2nd Place: $300. Judged by an agent or editor attending the conference.

POETS & PATRONS ANNUAL CHICAGOLAND POETRY CONTEST

Sponsored by Poets & Patrons of Chicago, 416 Gierz St., Downers Grove IL 60515. **E-mail:** eatonb1016@aol.com. **Website:** www.poetsandpatrons.net. **Contact:** Barbara Eaton, director. Annual contest for unpublished poetry. Guidelines available for self-addressed, stamped envelope. The purpose of the contest is to encourage the crafting of poetry. **Deadline:** September 1. **Prize:** 1st Place: $45; 2nd Place: $20; 3rd Place: $10 cash. Poet retains rights. Judged by out-of-state professionals.

FELIX POLLAK PRIZE IN POETRY

University of Wisconsin Press, 1930 Monroe St., 3rd Floor, Madison WI 53711. (608)263-1110. **Fax:** (608)263-1120. **E-mail:** uwiscpress@wisc.edu. **Website:** uwpress.wisc.edu. The Felix Pollak Prize in Poetry is awarded annually to the best book-length ms of original poetry submitted in an open competition. The award is administered by the University of Wisconsin–Madison English department, and the winner is chosen by a nationally recognized poet. The resulting book is published by the University of Wisconsin Press. **Deadline:** September 15. **Prize:** $1,000 cash prize, plus publication.

A. POULIN, JR. POETRY PRIZE

BOA Editions, Ltd., BOA Editions, Ltd., P.O. Box 30971, Rochester NY 14603. **E-mail:** fisher@boaeditions.org. **Website:** www.boaeditions.org. The A. Poulin, Jr. Poetry Prize is awarded to honor a poet's first book, while also honoring the late founder of BOA Editions, Ltd., a not-for-profit publishing house of poetry, poetry in translation, and short fiction. Published books in other genres do not disqualify contestants from entering this contest. Deadline: Submit between August 1-Nov. 30. Prize: Awards $1,500 honorarium and book publication in the A. Poulin, Jr. New Poets of America Series.

PRESS 53 AWARD FOR POETRY

Press 53, 560 N. Trade St., Suite 103, Winston-Salem NC 27101. **E-mail:** kevin@press53.com. **Website:** www.press53.com. **Contact:** Kevin Morgan Watson, publisher. Awarded to an outstanding, unpublished collection of poetry. Deadline: July 31. Submission period begins April 1. Finalists announced October 1. Winner announced on December 1. Publication in April. Prize: Publication of winning poetry collection as a Tom Lombardo Poetry Selection, $1,000 cash advance, travel expenses and lodging for a special reading and book signing in Winston-Salem, NC, attendance as special guest to the Press 53/Jacar Press Gathering of Writers, and 10 copies of the book. Judged by Press 53 poetry series editor Tom Lombardo.

PRIME NUMBER MAGAZINE AWARDS

Press 53, 560 N. Trade St., Suite 103, Winston-Salem NC 27101. **E-mail:** kevin@press53.com. **Website:** www.press53.com. **Contact:** Kevin Morgan Watson, publisher. Awards $1,000 in each of 3 categories: poetry, short fiction, and creative nonficiton. Deadline: March 30. Submission period begins January 1. Finalists announced June 1. Winner announced on August 1. Prize: $1,000 cash. All winners receive publication in Prime Number Magazine online. Judged by industry professionals to be named when the contest begins.

PUSHCART PRIZE

Pushcart Press, P.O. Box 380, Wainscott NY 11975. (631)324-9300. **Website:** www.pushcartprize.com. **Contact:** Bill Henderson. Published every year since 1976, The Pushcart Prize - Best of the Small Presses series "is the most honored literary project in America. Hundreds of presses and thousands of writers of short stories, poetry and essays have been represented in the pages of our annual collections." Little magazine and small book press editors (print or online) may make up to six nominations from their year's publi-

catoins by the deadline. The nominations may be any combination of poetry, short fiction, essays or literary whatnot. Editors may nominate self-contained portions of books — for instance, a chapter from a novel. Deadline: December 1.

RATTLE POETRY PRIZE

RATTLE, 12411 Ventura Blvd., Studio City CA 91604. (818) 505-6777. **E-mail:** tim@rattle.com. **E-mail:** prize@rattle.com. **Website:** www.rattle.com. **Contact:** Timothy Green, editor. *Rattle*'s mission is to promote the practice of poetry. "More than anything, our goal is to promote a community of active poets." Deadline: July 15. Prize: One $10,000 winner and ten $200 finalists will be selected in a blind review by the editors of *Rattle* and printed in the Winter issue; one $1,000 Readers' Choice Award will then be chosen from among the Finalists by subscriber and entrant vote. Judged by the editors of *Rattle*.

✪ THE RBC BRONWEN WALLACE AWARD FOR EMERGING WRITERS

The Writers' Trust of Canada, 460 Richmond St. W., Suite 600, Toronto ON M5C 1P1, Canada. (416)504-8222. **Fax:** (416)504-9090. **E-mail:** info@writerstrust.com. **Website:** www.writerstrust.com. **Contact:** Amanda Hopkins. Presented annually to a Canadian writer under the age of 35 who is not yet published in book form. The award, which alternates each year between poetry and short fiction, was established in memory of poet Bronwen Wallace. Deadline: Check website, to be announced. Prize: $5,000 and $1,000 to 2 finalists.

✪ REGINA BOOK AWARD

Saskatchewan Book Awards, Inc., 315-1102 8th Ave., Regina SK S4R 1C9, Canada. (306)569-1585. **E-mail:** director@bookawards.sk.ca. **Website:** www.bookawards.sk.ca. **Contact:** Courtney Bates-Hardy, administrative director. Offered annually. In recognition of the vitality of the literary community in Regina, this award is presented to a Regina author for the best book, judged on the quality of writing. Books from the following categories will be considered: Children's; drama; fiction (short fiction by a single author, novellas, novels); nonfiction (all categories of nonfiction writing except cookbooks, directories, how-to books, or bibliographies of minimal critical content); poetry. Part of a larger group of awards, the Saskatchewan Book Awards. Deadline: November 3. Prize: $2,000 (CAD).

RHINO FOUNDERS' PRIZE

RHINO, The Poetry Forum, P.O. Box 591, Evanston IL 60204. **E-mail:** editors@rhinopoetry.org. **Website:** rhinopoetry.org. **Contact:** Editors. Send best, unpublished poetry, translations, and flash fiction (750 words max). Visit website for previous winners and more information. Deadline: September 1-October 31. Prize: $300, publication, featured on website, and nominated for a Pushcart Prize. Two runners-ups will receive $50, publication, and will be featured on website. Occasionally nominates runner-up for a Pushcart Prize.

TIPS "RHINO values original voice, musicality, fresh language, and respect for the reader."

ROANOKE-CHOWAN POETRY AWARD

The North Carolina Literary & Historical Assoc., 4610 Mail Service Center, Raleigh NC 27699-4610. (919)807-7290. **Fax:** (919)733-8807. **E-mail:** michael.hill@ncdcr.gov. **Website:** www.history.ncdcr.gov/affiliates/lit-hist/awards/awards.htm. **Contact:** Michael Hill, awards coordinator. Offers annual award for an original volume of poetry published during the 12 months ending June 30 of the year for which the award is given. Deadline: July 15.

Competition receives about 15 entries.

BENJAMIN SALTMAN POETRY AWARD

Red Hen Press, P.O. Box 40820, Pasadena CA 91114. (818)831-0649. **Fax:** (818)831-6659. **E-mail:** productioncoordinator@redhen.org. **Website:** www.redhen.org. **Contact:** Alisa Trager, production coordinator. Offered annually for unpublished work to publish a winning book of poetry. Open to any writer. Deadline: August 31. $3,000 and publication.

SASKATCHEWAN FIRST BOOK AWARD

Saskatchewan Book Awards, Inc., 315-1102 8th Ave., Regina SK S4R 1C9, Canada. (306)569-1585. **E-mail:** director@bookawards.sk.ca. **Website:** www.bookawards.sk.ca. **Contact:** Courtney Bates-Hardy, administrative director. Offered annually. This award is presented to a Saskatchewan author for the best first book, judged on the quality of writing. Books from the following categories will be considered: Children's; drama; fiction (short fiction by a single author, novellas, novels); nonfiction (all categories of nonfiction writing except cookbooks, directories, how-to books, or bibliographies of minimal critical content); and poetry. Deadline: November 3. Prize: $2,000 (CAD).

THE SCARS EDITOR'S CHOICE AWARDS

829 Brian Court, Gurnee IL 60031-3155. **E-mail:** editor@scars.tv. **Website:** http://scars.tv. **Contact:** Janet Kuypers, editor/publisher (whom all reading fee checks need to be made out to). Award to showcase good writing in an annual book. Deadline: Revolves for appearing in different upcoming books as winners. Prize: Publication of story/essay and 1 copy of the book.

THE MONA SCHREIBER PRIZE FOR HUMOROUS FICTION & NONFICTION

E-mail: brad.schreiber@att.net. **Website:** www.bradschreiber.com. **Contact:** Brad Schreiber. The purpose of the contest is to award the most creative humor writing, in any form less than 750 words, in either fiction or nonfiction, including but not limited to stories, articles, essays, speeches, shopping lists, diary entries, and anything else writers dream up. Complete rules and previous winning entries on website. Deadline: December 1. Prize: 1st Place: $500; 2nd Place: $250; 3rd Place: $100. Judged by Brad Schreiber, author, journalist, consultant, and instructor.

SCREAMINMAMAS MOTHER'S DAY POETRY CONTEST

1911 Cleveland St., Hollywood FL 33020. **E-mail:** screaminmamas@gmail.com. **Website:** www.screaminmamas.com/contests. **Contact:** Darlene Pistocchi, editor/managing director. "What does it mean to be a mom? There is so much to being a mom—get deep, get creative! We challenge you to explore different types of poetry: descriptive, reflective, narrative, lyric, sonnet, ballad, limerick... you can even go epic!" Open only to moms. Deadline: December 31. Prize: complementary subscription to magazine, publication.

SHORT GRAIN CONTEST

Box 67, Saskatoon SK S7K 3K1, Canada. (306)244-2828. **E-mail:** grainmag@skwriter.com. **Website:** www.grainmagazine.ca/short-grain-contest. **Contact:** Jordan Morris, business administrator (inquiries only). The annual Short Grain Contest includes a category for poetry of any style up to 100 lines and fiction of any style up to 2,500 words, offering 3 prizes. Deadline: April 1. Prize: $1,000, plus publication in *Grain Magazine*.

SKIPPING STONES HONOR (BOOK) AWARDS

P.O. Box 3939, Eugene OR 97403. (541)342-4956. **Fax:** (541)342-4956. **E-mail:** editor@skippingstones.org. **Website:** www.skippingstones.org. **Contact:** Arun N. Toké. *Skipping Stones* is a well respected, multicultural literary magazine now in its 27th year. Annual award to promote multicultural and/or nature awareness through creative writings for children and teens and their educators. Seeks authentic, exceptional, child/youth friendly books that promote intercultural, international, intergenerational harmony, or understanding through creative ways. Deadline: February 1. Prize: Honor certificates; gold seals; reviews; press release/publicity. Judged by a multicultural committee of teachers, librarians, parents, students and editors.
TIPS "Writings that come out of their own experiences and cultural understanding seem to have an edge."

SKIPPING STONES YOUTH AWARDS

P.O. Box 3939, Eugene OR 97403-0939. (541)342-4956. **Fax:** (541)342-4956. **E-mail:** editor@skippingstones.org. **Website:** www.skippingstones.org. **Contact:** Arun N. Toké. Annual awards to promote creativity as well as multicultural and nature awareness in youth. Deadline: June 25. Prize: Publication in the autumn issue of *Skipping Stones*, honor certificate, subscription to magazine, plus 5 multicultural and/or nature books.
TIPS "Be creative. Do not use stereotypes or excessive violent language or plots. Be sensitive to cultural diversity."

SLIPSTREAM ANNUAL POETRY CHAPBOOK CONTEST

E-mail: editors@slipstreampress.org. **Website:** www.slipstreampress.org. **Contact:** Dan Sicoli, co-editor. Slipstream Magazine is a yearly anthology of some of the best poetry you'll find today in the American small press. Offered annually to help promote a poet whose work is often overlooked or ignored. Open to any writer. Deadline: December 1. Prize: $1,000 plus 50 professionally-printed copies of your book.

HELEN C. SMITH MEMORIAL AWARD FOR BEST BOOK OF POETRY

E-mail: tilsecretary@yahoo.com. **Website:** http://texasinstituteofletters.org/. Offered annually for the best book of poems published January 1-December 31 of previous year. Poet must have been born in Texas, have lived in the state at some time for at least 2 con-secutive years, or the subject matter must be associated with the state. Deadline: January 10. Prize: $1,200.

KAY SNOW WRITING CONTEST

Willamette Writers, Willamette Writers, 2108 Buck St., West Linn OR 97068. (503)305-6729. **Fax:** (503)344-6174. **E-mail:** reg@willamettewriters.com. **Website:** www.willamettewriters.com. Willamette Writers is the largest writers' organization in Oregon and one of the largest writers' organizations in the United States. It is a non-profit, tax-exempt Oregon corporation led by volunteers. Elected officials and directors administer an active program of monthly meetings, special seminars, workshops and annual writing conference. Continuing with established programs and starting new ones is only made possible by strong volunteer support. The purpose of this annual writing contest, named in honor of Willamette Writer's founder, Kay Snow, is to help writers reach professional goals in writing in a broad array of categories and to encourage student writers. Deadline: April 23. Submission deadline begins January 15. Prize: One first prize of $300, one second place prize of $150, and a third place prize of $50 per winning entry in each of the six categories.

THE RICHARD SNYDER MEMORIAL PUBLICATION PRIZE

Ashland Poetry Press, 401 College Ave., Ashland University, Ashland OH 44805. **E-mail:** app@ashland.edu. **Website:** www.ashlandpoetrypress.com. **Contact:** Wendy Hall, managing editor. Offers annual award of $1,000 plus book publication. Submissions must be unpublished in book form. Considers simultaneous submissions. Submit 50-96 pages of poetry. Competition receives 400+ entries/year. Winners will be announced in *Writer's Chronicle* and *Poets & Writers*. Copies of winning books available from Small Press Distribution and directly from the Ashland University Bookstore online. The Ashland Poetry Press publishes 2-4 books of poetry/year. Deadline: April 30. Judged by David St. John in 2015.

SOCIETY OF MIDLAND AUTHORS AWARD

Society of Midland Authors, Society of Midland Authors, P.O. Box 10419, Chicago IL 60610-0419. **E-mail:** marlenetbrill@comcast.net. **Website:** www.midlandauthors.com. **Contact:** Marlene Targ Brill, awards chair. Since 1957, the Society has presented annual awards for the best books written by Midwestern authors. The Society of Midland Authors (SMA) Award is presented to one title in each of six categories: adult nonfiction, adult fiction, adult biography and memoir, children's nonfiction, children's fiction, and poetry. Books and entry forms must be mailed to the 3 judges in each category; for a list of judges and the entry form, visit the website. Do not mail books to the society's P.O. box. Deadline: January 3. Prize: cash prize of $500 and a plaque that is awarded at the SMA banquet in May in Chicago.

SOUL-MAKING KEATS LITERARY COMPETITION

The Webhallow House, 1544 Sweetwood Dr., Broadmoor Vlg CA 94015-2029. **E-mail:** SoulKeats@mail.com. **Website:** www.soulmakingcontest.us. **Contact:** Eileen Malone, award director. Annual open contest offers cash prizes in each of 13 literary categories. Competition receives 600 entries/year. Names of winners and judges are posted on website. Winners announced in January by SASE and on website. Winners are invited to read at the Koret Auditorium, San Francisco. Event is televised. Deadline: November 30. Prizes: 1st Prize: $100; 2nd Prize: $50; 3rd Prize: $25.

THE SOW'S EAR POETRY COMPETITION

The Sow's Ear Poetry Review, P.O. Box 127, Millwood VA 22646. **E-mail:** rglesman@gmail.com. **Website:** www.sows-ear.kitenet.net. **Contact:** Robert G. Lesman, managing editor. Deadline: November 1. Prize: $1,000, publication, and the option of publication for approximately 20 finalists.

STAGE OF LIFE ESSAY WRITING CONTESTS

StageofLife.com, P.O. Box 580950, Minneapolis MN 55458-0950. **Fax:** (717)650-3855. **E-mail:** contact@stageoflife.com. **Website:** www.stageoflife.com. Monthly writing contests for teens, college students, brides, grooms, married couples, homeowners, parents, and grandparents using a nonfiction, memoir, blogging, essay-style format. Submitted essays must be 500 words or less. Style, grammar, point of view, and authentic voice are all important aspects in the submissions. Press for the StageofLife.com writing contest has appeared on Time.com, ABC TV'S "Mary Talks Money", *The Wall Street Journal*'s MarketWatch, Socialtimes.com, and other media outlets. Deadline: 12am PST the last day of the month. Offers $25-50 cash prize or equivalent gift card from current contest sponsor, "Featured Writer" status on StageofLife.com, and mention in the site's monthly press release.

Editorial staff headed by Eric Thiegs, CEO; Rebecca Thiegs, senior editor; Michelle Pease, essay editor; and a panel of 12 freelance editors judge monthly contests. **TIPS** "Writer must be in the life stage for the contest they are entering."

THE RUTH STONE POETRY PRIZE

Vermont College, 36 College St., Montpelier VT 05602. (802)828-8517. **E-mail:** hungermtn@vcfa.edu. **Website:** www.hungermtn.org. **Contact:** Miciah Bay Gault, editor. The Ruth Stone Poetry Prize is an annual poetry contest. Deadline: December 10. Prize: One first place winner receives $1,000 and publication on Hunger Mountain online. Two honorble mentions receive $100 and publication on Hunger Mountain online.

THE ELIZABETH MATCHETT STOVER MEMORIAL AWARD

Southwest Review, Southern Methodist University, P.O. Box 750374, Dallas TX 75275-0374. (214)768-1037. **Fax:** (214)768-1408. **E-mail:** swr@mail.smu.edu. **Website:** www.smu.edu/southwestreview. **Contact:** Jennifer Cranfill, senior editor, and Willard Spiegelman, editor-in-chief. Offered annually to the best works of poetry that have appeared in the magazine in the previous year. Please note that mss are submitted for publication, not for the prizes themselves. Guidelines for SASE and online. Prize: $300. Judged by Jennifer Cranfill and Willard Spiegelman.
TIPS "Not an open contest. Annual prize in which winners are chosen from published pieces during the preceding year."

THE TAMPA REVIEW PRIZE FOR POETRY

University of Tampa, 401 W. Kennedy Blvd., Tampa FL 33606. **E-mail:** utpress@ut.edu. **Website:** www.utpress.ut.edu. Annual award for the best previously unpublished collection of poetry (at least 48 pages, though preferably 60-100). Deadline: December 31. Prize: $2,000, plus publication.

THE TENTH GATE PRIZE

c/o Leslie McGrath, Series Editor, The Tenth Gate Prize, English Department, Central CT State University, 1615 Stanley St., New Britain CT 06050. **E-mail:** editor@wordworksbooks.org. **Website:** www.wordworksbooks.org. Publication and cash prize awarded annually by The Word Works to a full-length ms by a poet who has already published at least 2 full-length collections. Deadline: July 15. Open to submissions on June 1. Prize: $1,000 and publication.

THE TEXAS INSTITUTE OF LETTERS LITERARY AWARDS

E-mail: Betwx@aol.com. **Website:** www.texasinstituteofletters.org. The Texas Institute of Letters gives annual awards for books by Texas authors and writers who have produced books about Texas, including Best Books of Poetry, Fiction, and Nonfiction. Awards are also given for best Short Story, Magazine or Newspaper Article, Essay, and best Books for Children and Young Adults. Work submitted must have been published in the year stipulated, and entries may be made by authors or by their publishers. Complete guidelines and award information is available on the Texas Institute of Letters website.

THE HILARY THAM CAPITAL COLLECTION

The Word Works, Nancy White, c/o SUNY Adiorndack, 640 Bay Rd., Queensbury NY 12804. **E-mail:** editor@wordworksbooks.org. **Website:** www.wordworksbooks.org. **Contact:** Nancy White, editor. The Hilary Tham Capital Collection publishes only poets who volunteer for literary nonprofits. Every nominated poet is invited to submit; authors have until May 1 to send their ms via online submissions at website, or to Nancy White. Deadline: April 15 to send nomination.

TOR HOUSE PRIZE FOR POETRY

Robinson Jeffers Tor House Foundation, Poetry Prize Coordinator, Tor House Foundation, Box 223240, Carmel CA 93922. (831)624-1813. **Fax:** (831)624-3696. **E-mail:** thf@torhouse.org. **Website:** www.torhouse.org. **Contact:** Eliot Ruchowitz-Roberts, Poetry Prize Coordinator. The annual Prize for Poetry is a living memorial to American poet Robinson Jeffers (1887-1962). Open to well-crafted poetry in all styles, ranging from experimental work to traditional forms, including short narrative poems. Poems must be original and unpublished. Deadline: March 14. Prize: $1,000 honorarium for award-winning poem; $200 Honorable Mention.

TRANSCONTINENTAL POETRY AWARD

Pavement Saw Press, 321 Empire St., Montpelier OH 43543. (419)485-0524. **E-mail:** info@pavementsaw.org. **Website:** pavementsaw.org. **Contact:** David Baratier, editor. Offered annually for a first or second book of poetry. Each year, Pavement Saw Press will seek to publish at least 1 book of poetry and/or prose poems from manuscripts received during this competition, which is open to anyone who has not previously published a volume of poetry or prose. Poets who have not published a book, who have published 1 collection, or who have published a second collection of fewer than 40 pages, or who have published a second full-length collection with a print run of no more than 500 copies are eligible. More than 1 prize may be awarded. Deadline: Reads submissions in June, July, and until August 15 (must have August 15 or earlier postmark). Prize: $1,000, publication, and a percentage of the print run for a first or second book. Judged by the editor and a guest judge.

TUFTS POETRY AWARDS

Kingsley & Kate Tufts Poetry Awards, Claremont Graduate University, 160 E. Tenth St., Harper East B7, Claremont CA 91711-6165. (909)621-8974. **E-mail:** tufts@cgu.edu. **Website:** www.cgu.edu/tufts. Unlike many literary awards, which are coronations for a successful career or body of work, the Kingsley Tufts Poetry Award was created to both honor the poet and provide the resources that allow artists to continue working towards the pinnacle of their craft. "Any poet will tell you that the only thing more rare than meaningful recognition is a meaningful payday. For two outstanding poets each year, the Kingsley and Kate Tufts awards represent both." Deadline: September 1. Submissions period begins June 30. Prize: $100,000 for the Kingsley Tufts Poetry Award and $10,000 for the Kate Tufts Discovery Award.

UTMOST CHRISTIAN POETRY CONTEST

Utmost Christian Writers Foundation, 121 Morin Maze, Edmonton Alberta T6K 1V1, Canada. (780)265-4650. **E-mail:** nnharms@telusplanet.net. **Website:** www.utmostchristianwriters.com. **Contact:** Nathan Harms, executive director. Utmost is founded on—and supported by—the dreams, interests and aspirates of individual people. Deadline: February 28. Prizes: 1st Place: $1,000; 2nd Place: $500; 10 prizes of $100 are offered for honorable mention; $300 for best rhyming poem and $200 for an honorable mention rhyming poem. Judged by a committee of the Directors of Utmost Christian Writers Foundation (who work under the direction of Barbara Mitchell, chief judge).

TIPS "Besides providing numerous resources for Christian writers and poets, Utmost also provides a marketplace where Christian writers and poets can sell their work. Please follow our guidelines. We receive numerous unsuitable submissions from writers. We encourage writers to submit suitable material. The best way to do this is to read the guidelines specific to your project—poetry, book reviews, articles—and then take time to look at the material we have already published in that area. The final step is to evaluate your proposed submission in comparison to the material we have used previously. If you complete these steps and strongly feel that your material is appropriate for us, we encourage you to submit it."

DANIEL VAROUJAN AWARD

New England Poetry Club, 376 School St., Watertown MA 02472. **E-mail:** contests@nepoetryclub.org. **Website:** www.nepoetryclub.org. **Contact:** Audrey Kalajin. For an unpublished poem (not a translation) worthy of Daniel Varoujan, a poet killed by the Turks in the genocide which destroyed three-fourths of the Armenian population. Deadline: May 31. Prize: $1,000. Judged by well-known poets and sometimes winners of previous NEPC contests.

MARICA AND JAN VILCEK PRIZE FOR POETRY

Bellevue Literary Review, New York University School of Medicine, OBV-A612, 550 First Ave., New York NY 10016. (212)263-3973. **E-mail:** info@BLReview.org. **Website:** www.BLReview.org. **Contact:** Stacy Bodziak. The annual Marica and Jan Vilcek Prize for Poetry recognizes outstanding writing related to themes of health, healing, illness, the mind, and the body. All entries will be considered for publication. No previously published poems (including Internet publication). Submit up to 3 poems (5 pages maximum). Electronic (online) submissions only; combine all poems into 1 document and use first poem as document title. See guidelines for additional submission details. Guidelines available for SASE or on website. Deadline: July 1. Prize: $1,000 for best poem and publication in *Bellevue Literary Review*. Previous judges include Mark Doty, Cornelius Eady, Naomi Shihab Nye, and Tony Hoagland.

WABASH PRIZE FOR POETRY

Sycamore Review, Department of English, 500 Oval Dr., Purdue University, West Lafayette IN 47907. **E-mail:** sycamore@purdue.edu; sycamorepoetry@pur-

due.edu. **Website:** www.sycamorereview.com/contest/. **Contact:** Kara Krewer, editor-in-chief. Annual contest for unpublished poetry. Deadline: December 1. Prize: $1,000 and publication.

THE WASHINGTON PRIZE

Dearlove Hall, SUNY Adirondack, 640 Bay Rd., Queensbury NY 12804. **E-mail:** editor@wordworksbooks.org. **Website:** www.wordworksdc.com. **Contact:** Rebecca Kutzer-Rice, Washington Prize administrator. Sponsors an ongoing poetry reading series, educational programs, and and three additional imprints: The Tenth Gate, International Editions, and the Hilary Tham Capital Collection. Sponsors The Washington Prize, one of the older manuscript publishing prizes, and The Jacklyn Potter Young Poets Competition. Additional information available on website. Winners announced in August. Book publication planned for January of the following year. Deadline: Submit January 15-March 15 (postmark). Prize: $1,500 and publication of a book-length ms of original poetry in English by a living American poet (US or Canadian citizen).

THE ROBERT WATSON LITERARY PRIZE IN FICTION AND POETRY

The Robert Watson Literary Prizes, *The Greensboro Review*, MFA Writing Program, 3302 MHRA Building, Greensboro NC 27402-6170. (336)334-5459. **E-mail:** jlclark@uncg.edu. **Website:** www.greensbororeview.org. **Contact:** Jim Clark, editor. Offered annually for fiction (up to 25 double-spaced pages) and poetry (up to 10 pages). Entries must be unpublished. No submissions by e-mail. Open to any writer. Deadline: September 15. Prize: $1,000 each for best short story and poem. Judged by editors of *The Greensboro Review*.

WERGLE FLOMP HUMOR POETRY CONTEST

Winning Writers, 351 Pleasant St., PMB 222, Northampton MA 01060. (866)946-9748. **Fax:** (413)280-0539. **E-mail:** adam@winningwriters.com. **Website:** www.winningwriters.com. **Contact:** Adam Cohen. This annual contest seeks today's best humor poems. One poem of any length should be submitted. Poem may be published or unpublished. The poem should be in English. Inspired gibberish is also accepted. See website for guidelines, examples, and to submit your poem. Nonexclusive right to publish submissions on WinningWriters.com, in e-mail newsletters, in e-books, and in press releases. Deadline:

April 1 Prize: 1st prize of $1,000, plus 10 honorable mentions of $100 each. Judged by Jendi Reiter (final). Submissions may be previously published and may be entered in other contests. Competition receives about 4,000 entries/year. Winners are announced on August 15 at WinningWriters.com. Entrants who provide a valid e-mail address will also receive notification.

WESTERN AUSTRALIAN PREMIER'S BOOK AWARDS

State Library of Western Australia, Perth Cultural Centre, 25 Francis St., Perth WA 6000, Australia. (61)(8)9427-3151. **E-mail:** premiersbookawards@slwa.wa.gov.au. **Website:** pba.slwa.wa.gov.au. **Contact:** Karen de San Miguel. Annual competition for Australian citizens or permanent residents of Australia, or writers whose work has Australia as its primary focus. Categories: children's books, digital narrative, fiction, nonfiction, poetry, scripts, writing for young adults, West Australian history, and Western Australian emerging writers. Deadline: January 31. Prize: Awards $25,000 for Premier's Prize; awards $15,000 each for the Children's Books, Digital Narrative, Fiction, and Nonfiction categories; awards $10,000 each for the Poetry, Scripts, Western Australian History, Western Australian Emerging Writers, and Writing for Young Adults; awards $5,000 for People's Choice Award.

WESTERN HERITAGE AWARDS

National Cowboy & Western Heritage Museum, 1700 NE 63rd St., Oklahoma City OK 73111-7997. (405)478-2250. **Fax:** (405)478-4714. **Website:** www.nationalcowboymuseum.org. **Contact:** Jessica Limestall. The National Cowboy & Western Heritage Museum Western Heritage Awards were established to honor and encourage the legacy of those whose works in literature, music, film, and television reflect the significant stories of the American West. Accepted categories for literary entries: western novel, nonfiction book, art book, photography book, juvenile book, magazine article, or poetry book. The WHA are presented annually to encourage the accurate and artistic telling of great stories of the West through 16 categories of western literature, television, film and music; including fiction, nonfiction, children's books and poetry. See website for details and category definitions. Deadline: November 30. Prize: Awards a Wrangler bronze sculpture designed by famed western artist,

John Free. Judged by a panel of judges selected each year with distinction in various fields of western art and heritage.

WESTMORELAND POETRY & SHORT STORY CONTEST

Westmoreland Arts & Heritage Festival, 252 Twin Lakes Rd., Latrobe PA 15650-9415. (724)834-7474. **Fax:** (724)850-7474. **E-mail:** info@artsandheritage.com. **Website:** www.artsandheritage.com. **Contact:** Adam Shaffer. Offered annually for unpublished work. Two categories: Poem & Short Story. Short story entries no longer than 4,000 words. Family-oriented festival and contest. Deadline: February 16. Prizes: Award: $200; 1st Place: $125; 2nd Place: $100; 3rd Place: $75.

STAN AND TOM WICK POETRY PRIZE

301 Satterfield Hall, Kent State University, P.O. Box 5190, Kent OH 44242-0001. (330)672-2067. **E-mail:** dhassle1@kent.edu. **Website:** www2.kent.edu/wick/competitions. **Contact:** David Hassler, director. Offered annually to a poet who has not previously published a full-length collection of poetry (a volume of 50 or more pages published in an edition of 500 or more copies). Deadline: May 1. Submissions period begins February 1. Prize: $2,500 and publication of full-length book of poetry by Kent State University Press.

WILLA LITERARY AWARD

E-mail: cynipid@comcast.net. **Website:** www.womenwritingthewest.org. **Contact:** Cynthia Becker. The WILLA Literary Award honors the year's best in published literature featuring women's or girls' stories set in the West. Women Writing the West (WWW), a nonprofit association of writers and other professionals writing and promoting the Women's West, underwrites and presents the nationally recognized award annually (for work published between January 1 and December 31). The award is named in honor of Pulitzer Prize winner Willa Cather, one of the country's foremost novelists. The award is given in 7 categories: historical fiction, contemporary fiction, original softcover fiction, creative nonfiction, scholarly nonfiction, poetry, and children's/young adult fiction/nonfiction. Entry forms available on the website. Deadline: November 1-February 1. Prize: $100 and a trophy. Finalist receives a plaque. Both receive digital and sticker award emblems for book covers. Notice of Winning and Finalist titles mailed to more than 4,000 booksellers, libraries, and others. Award announcement is in early August, and awards are presented to the winners and finalists at the annual WWW Fall Conference. Judged by professional librarians not affiliated with WWW.

MILLER WILLIAMS POETRY PRIZE

University of Arkansas Press, McIlroy House, 105 N. McIlroy Avenue, Fayetteville AR 72701. (479)575-7258. **Fax:** (479)575-6044. **E-mail:** info@uapress.com; mbieker@uark.edu. **Website:** www.uapress.com. **Contact:** Billy Collins, judge and series editor; Mike Bieker, director. Each year, the University of Arkansas Press accepts submissions for the Miller Williams Poetry Series and from the books selected awards the Miller Williams Poetry Prize in the following summer. Deadline: September 30. Accepts submissions all year long. Prize: $5,000, publication, and featured reading at the University of Arkansas. Judged by Billy Collins, series editor.

THE J. HOWARD AND BARBARA M.J. WOOD PRIZE

Poetry, 61 W. Superior St., Chicago IL 60654. (312)787-7070. **Fax:** (312)787-6650. **E-mail:** editors@poetrymagazine.org. **Website:** www.poetrymagazine.org. Offered annually for poems published in *Poetry* during the preceding year (October-September). Upon acceptance, *Poetry* licenses exclusive worldwide first serial rights, including electronic rights, for publication, as well as non-exclusive rights to reprint, reuse, and archive the work, in any format, in perpetuity. Copyright reverts to author upon first publication. Prize: $5,000.

WORKING PEOPLE'S POETRY COMPETITION

Blue Collar Review, P.O. Box 11417, Norfolk VA 23517. **E-mail:** red-ink@earthlink.net. **Website:** www.partisanpress.org. Deadline: May 15. Prize: $100, 1-year subscription to *Blue Collar Review* (see separate listing in Magazines/Journals) and 1-year posting of winning poem to website.

WORLD'S BEST SHORT-SHORT STORY CONTEST, NARRATIVE NONFICTION CONTEST & SOUTHEAST REVIEW POETRY CONTEST

E-mail: southeastreview@gmail.com. **Website:** www.southeastreview.org. **Contact:** Erin Hoover, editor. Annual award for unpublished short-short stories (500 words or less), poetry, and narrative nonfiction (6,000 words or less). Visit website for details. Deadline: March 15. Prize: $500 per category. Winners and finalists will be published in *The Southeast Review*.

JAMES WRIGHT POETRY AWARD

Mid-American Review, Dept. of English, Bowling Green State University, Bowling Green OH 43403. (419)372-2725. **Fax:** (419)372-4642. **E-mail:** clouda@bgsu.edu. **Website:** www.bgsu.edu/midamericanreview. **Contact:** Abigail Cloud, editor. Offered annually for unpublished poetry. Open to all writers not associated with *Mid-American Review* or judge. Deadline: November 1. Prize: $1,000 and publication in spring issue of *Mid-American Review*. Judged by editors and a well known writer, i.e., Kathy Fagan, Bob Hicok, Michelle Boisseau.

WRITER'S DIGEST ANNUAL WRITING COMPETITION

Writer's Digest, a publication of F+W Media, Inc., 10151 Carver Rd., Suite 200, Cincinnati OH 45242. (715)445-4612, ext. 13430. **E-mail:** writing-competition@fwmedia.com. **Website:** www.writersdigest.com. **Contact:** Nicki Howard. Writing contest with 10 categories: Inspirational Writing (spiritual/religious, maximum 2,500 words); Memoir/Personal Essay (maximum 2,000 words); Magazine Feature Article (maximum 2,000 words); Short Story (genre, maximum 4,000 words); Short Story (mainstream/literary, maximum 4,000 words); Rhyming Poetry (maximum 32 lines); Nonrhyming Poetry (maximum 32 lines); Stage Play (first 15 pages and 1-page synopsis); TV/Movie Script (first 15 pages and 1-page synopsis). Entries must be original, in English, unpublished/unproduced (except for Magazine Feature Articles), and not accepted by another publisher/producer at the time of submission. *Writer's Digest* retains one-time publication rights to the winning entries in each category. Deadline: May (early bird); June. Grand Prize: $3,000 and a trip to the Writer's Digest Conference to meet with editors and agents; 1st Place: $1,000 and $100 of Writer's Digest Books; 2nd Place: $500 and $100 of Writer's Digest Books; 3rd Place: $250 and $100 of Writer's Digest Books; 4th Place: $100 and $50 of *Writer's Digest* Books.

WRITER'S DIGEST SELF-PUBLISHED BOOK AWARDS

Writer's Digest, 10151 Carver Road, Suite #200, Blue Ash OH 45242. (715)445-4612, ext. 13430. **E-mail:** WritersDigestSelfPublishingCompetition@fwmedia.com. **Website:** www.writersdigest.com. **Contact:** Nicole Howard. Contest open to all English-language, self-published books for which the authors have paid the full cost of publication, or the cost of printing has been paid for by a grant or as part of a prize. Categories include: Mainstream/Literary Fiction, Genre Fiction, Nonfiction, Inspirational (spiritual/new age), Life Stories (biographies/autobiographies/family histories/memoirs), Children's Books, Reference Books (directories/encyclopedias/guide books), Poetry, and Middle-Grade/Young Adult Books. Judges reserve the right to re-categorize entries. Judges reserve the right to withhold prizes in any category. All winners will be notifed by October 12. Early bird deadline: April 1; Deadline: May 1. Prizes: Grand Prize: $8,000, a trip to the Writer's Digest Conference, promotion in *Writer's Digest*, 10 copies of the book will be sent to major review houses, and a guaranteed review in *Midwest Book Review*; 1st Place (9 winners): $1,000 and promotion in *Writer's Digest*; Honorable Mentions: $50 worth of Writer's Digest Books and promotion on writersdigest.com. All entrants will receive a brief commentary from one of the judges.

WRITER'S DIGEST SELF-PUBLISHED E-BOOK AWARDS

Writer's Digest, 10151 Carver Road, Suite #200, Blue Ash OH 45242. (715)445-4612, ext. 13430. **E-mail:** WritersDigestSelfPublishingCompetition@fwmedia.com. **Website:** www.writersdigest.com. **Contact:** Nicole Howard. Contest open to all English-language, self-published e-books for which the authors have paid the full cost of publication, or the cost of publication has been paid for by a grant or as part of a prize. Categories include: Mainstream/Literary Fiction, Genre Fiction, Nonfiction (includes reference books), Inspirational (spiritual/new age), Life Stories (biographies/autobiographies/family histories/memoirs), Children's Books, Poetry, and Middle-Grade/Young Adult Books. Judges reserve the right to re-categorize entries. Judges reserve the right to withhold prizes in any category. All winners will be notifed by December 31. Early bird deadline: August 1; Deadline: September 19. Prizes: Grand Prize: $3,000, promotion in *Writer's Digest*, a full 250-word (minimum) editorial review, $200 worth of Writer's Digest Books, and more; 1st Place (9 winners): $1,000 and promotion in *Writer's Digest*; Honorable Mentions: $50 worth of Writer's Digest

Books and promotion on writersdigest.com. All entrants will receive a brief commentary from one of the judges.

WRITERS-EDITORS NETWORK INTERNATIONAL WRITING COMPETITION

E-mail: contestentry@writers-editors.com. **E-mail:** info@writers-editors.com. **Website:** www.writers-editors.com. **Contact:** Dana K. Cassell, executive director. Annual award to recognize publishable talent. Categories: Nonfiction (previously published article/essay/column/nonfiction book chapter; unpublished or self-published article/essay/column/nonfiction book chapter); fiction (unpublished or self-published short story or novel chapter); children's literature (unpublished or self-published short story/nonfiction article/book chapter/poem); poetry (unpublished or self-published free verse/traditional). Guidelines available online. Deadline: March 15. Prize: 1st Place: $100; 2nd Place: $75; 3rd Place: $50. All winners and Honorable Mentions will receive certificates as warranted. Judged by editors, librarians, and writers.

☯ WRITERS GUILD OF ALBERTA AWARDS

Writers Guild of Alberta, Percy Page Centre, 11759 Groat Rd., Edmonton AB T5M 3K6, Canada. (780)422-8174. **Fax:** (780)422-2663. **E-mail:** mail@writersguild.ab.ca. **Website:** www.writersguild.ab.ca. **Contact:** Executive Director. Offers the following awards: Wilfrid Eggleston Award for Nonfiction; Georges Bugnet Award for Fiction; Howard O'Hagan Award for Short Story; Stephan G. Stephansson Award for Poetry; R. Ross Annett Award for Children's Literature; Gwen Pharis Ringwood Award for Drama; Jon Whyte Memorial Essay Prize; James H. Gray Award for Short Nonfiction. Deadline: December 31. Prize: Winning authors receive $1,500; essay prize winners receive $700.

THE YALE SERIES OF YOUNGER POETS

Yale University Press, P.O. Box 209040, New Haven CT 06520-9040. **Website:** www.youngerpoets.org; yalepress.yale.edu/yupbooks/youngerpoets.asp. The Yale Series of Younger Poets champions the most promising new American poets. The Yale Younger Poets prize is the oldest annual literary award in the United States. Deadline: November 15. Submissions period begins October 1.

ZONE 3 POETRY AWARD

Zone 3, Austin Peay State University, Austin Peay State University, PO Box 4565, Clarksville TN 37044. (931)221-7031. **Fax:** (931)221-7149. **E-mail:** spofforda@aspu.edu; wallacess@apsu.edu. **Website:** www.apsu.edu/zone3/. **Contact:** Andrea Spofford, poetry editor; Susan Wallace, managing editor. Offered annually for unpublished poetry. Submit up to 3 poems via online submissions manager. Deadline: April 1. Prize: $250 and publication.

GRANTS

State & Provincial

//

Arts councils in the United States and Canada provide assistance to artists (including poets) in the form of fellowships or grants. These grants can be substantial and confer prestige upon recipients; however, only state or province residents are eligible. Because deadlines and available support vary annually, query first (with a SASE) or check websites for guidelines.

UNITED STATES ARTS AGENCIES

ALABAMA STATE COUNCIL ON THE ARTS, 201 Monroe St., Montgomery AL 36130-1800. (334)242-4076. E-mail: staff@arts.alabama.gov. Website: www.arts.state.al.us.

ALASKA STATE COUNCIL ON THE ARTS, 411 W. Fourth Ave., Suite 1-E, Anchorage AK 99501-2343. (907)269-6610 or (888)278-7424. E-mail: aksca_info@eed.state.ak.us. Website: www.eed.state.ak.us/aksca.

ARIZONA COMMISSION ON THE ARTS, 417 W. Roosevelt St., Phoenix AZ 85003-1326. (602)771-6501. E-mail: info@azarts.gov. Website: www.azarts.gov.

ARKANSAS ARTS COUNCIL, 1500 Tower Bldg., 323 Center St., Little Rock AR 72201.

(501)324-9766. E-mail: info@arkansasarts.com. Website: www.arkansasarts.com.

CALIFORNIA ARTS COUNCIL, 1300 I St., Suite 930, Sacramento CA 95814. (916)322-6555. E-mail: info@caartscouncil.com. Website: www.cac.ca.gov.

COLORADO COUNCIL ON THE ARTS, 1625 Broadway, Suite 2700, Denver CO 80202. (303)892-3802. E-mail: online form. Website: www.coloarts.state.co.us.

COMMONWEALTH COUNCIL FOR ARTS AND CULTURE (Northern Mariana Islands), P.O. Box 5553, CHRB, Saipan MP 96950. (670)322-9982 or (670)322-9983. E-mail: galaidi@vzpacifica.net. Website: www.geocities.com/ccacarts/ccacwebsite.html.

CONNECTICUT COMMISSION ON CULTURE & TOURISM, Arts Division, One Financial Plaza, 755 Main St., Hartford CT 06103. (860)256-2800. Website: www.cultureand-tourism.org.

DELAWARE DIVISION OF THE ARTS, Carvel State Office Bldg., 4th Floor, 820 N. French St., Wilmington DE 19801. (302)577-8278 (New Castle Co.) or (302)739-5304 (Kent or Sussex Counties). E-mail: delarts@state.de.us. Website: www.artsdel.org.

DISTRICT OF COLUMBIA COMMISSION ON THE ARTS & HUMANITIES, 410 Eighth St. NW, 5th Floor, Washington DC 20004. (202)724-5613. E-mail: cah@dc.gov. Website: http://dcarts.dc.gov.

FLORIDA ARTS COUNCIL, Division of Cultural Affairs, R.A. Gray Building, Third Floor, 500 S. Bronough St., Tallahassee FL 32399-0250. (850)245-6470. E-mail: info@florida-arts.org. Website: http://dcarts.dc.gov.

GEORGIA COUNCIL FOR THE ARTS, 260 14th St., Suite 401, Atlanta GA 30318. (404)685-2787. E-mail: gaarts@gaarts.org. Website: www.gaarts.org.

GUAM COUNCIL ON THE ARTS & HUMANITIES AGENCY, P.O. Box 2950, Hagatna GU 96932. (671)646-2781. Website: www.guam.net.

HAWAII STATE FOUNDATION ON CULTURE & THE ARTS, 2500 S. Hotel St., 2nd Floor, Honolulu HI 96813. (808)586-0300. E-mail: ken.hamilton@hawaii.gov. Website: http.state.hi.us/sfca.

IDAHO COMMISSION ON THE ARTS, 2410 N. Old Penitentiary Rd., Boise ID 83712. (208)334-2119 or (800)278-3863. E-mail: info@arts.idaho.gov. Website: www.arts.idaho.gov.

ILLINOIS ARTS COUNCIL, James R. Thompson Center, 100 W. Randolph, Suite 10-500, Chicago IL 60601. (312)814-6750. E-mail: iac.info@illinois.gov. Website: www.state.il.us/agency/iac.

INDIANA ARTS COMMISSION, 150 W. Market St., Suite 618, Indianapolis IN 46204. (317)232-1268. E-mail: IndianaArtsCommission@iac.in.gov. Website: www.in.gov/arts.

INSTITUTE OF PUERTO RICAN CULTURE, P.O. Box 9024184, San Juan PR 00902-4184. (787)724-0700. E-mail: www@icp.gobierno.pr. Website: www.icp.gobierno.pr.

IOWA ARTS COUNCIL, 600 E. Locust, Des Moines IA 50319-0290. (515)281-6412. Website: www.iowaartscouncil.org.

KANSAS ARTS COMMISSION, 700 SW Jackson, Suite 1004, Topeka KS 66603-3761. (785)296-3335. E-mail: KAC@arts.state.ks.us. Website: http://arts.state.ks.us.

KENTUCKY ARTS COUNCIL, 21st Floor, Capital Plaza Tower, 500 Mero St., Frankfort KY 40601-1987. (502)564-3757 or (888)833-2787.

E-mail: kyarts@ky.gov. Website: http:// artscouncil.ky.gov.

LOUISIANA DIVISION OF THE ARTS, Capitol Annex Bldg., 1051 N. 3rd St., 4th Floor, Room #420, Baton Rouge LA 70804. (225)342-8180. Website: www.crt.state. la.us/arts.

MAINE ARTS COMMISSION, 193 State St., 25 State House Station, Augusta ME 04333-0025. (207)287-2724. E-mail: MaineArts. info@maine.gov. Website: www.mainearts. com.

MARYLAND STATE ARTS COUNCIL, 175 W. Ostend St., Suite E, Baltimore MD 21230. (410)767-6555. E-mail: msac@msac.org. Website: www.msac.org.

MASSACHUSETTS CULTURAL COUNCIL, 10 St. James Ave., 3rd Floor, Boston MA 02116-3803. (617)727-3668. E-mail: mcc@art.state. ma.us. Website: www.massculturalcouncil. org.

MICHIGAN COUNCIL OF HISTORY, ARTS, AND LIBRARIES, 702 W. Kalamazoo St., P.O. Box 30705, Lansing MI 48909-8205. (517)241-4011. E-mail: artsinfo@michigan.gov. Website: www.michigan.gov/ hal/0,1607,7-160-17445_19272---,00.html.

MINNESOTA STATE ARTS BOARD, Park Square Court, 400 Sibley St., Suite 200, St. Paul MN 55101-1928. (651)215-1600 or (800)866-2787. E-mail: msab@arts.state. mn.us. Website: www.arts.state.mn.us.

MISSISSIPPI ARTS COMMISSION, 501 N. West St., Suite 701B, Woolfolk Bldg., Jackson MS 39201. (601)359-6030. Website: www.arts.state.ms.us.

MISSOURI ARTS COUNCIL, 815 Olive St., Suite 16, St. Louis MO 63101-1503. (314)340-6845 or (866)407-4752. E-mail: moarts@ ded.mo.gov. Website: www.missouri-artscouncil.org.

MONTANA ARTS COUNCIL, 316 N. Park Ave., Suite 252, Helena MT 59620-2201. (406)444-6430. E-mail: mac@mt.gov. Website: www.art.state.mt.us.

NATIONAL ASSEMBLY OF STATE ARTS AGENCIES, 1029 Vermont Ave. NW, 2nd Floor, Washington DC 20005. (202)347-6352. E-mail: nasaa@nasaa-arts.org. Website: www.nasaa-arts.org.

NEBRASKA ARTS COUNCIL, 1004 Farnam St., Plaza Level, Omaha NE 68102. (402)595-2122 or (800)341-4067. Website: www.ne-braskaartscouncil.org.

NEVADA ARTS COUNCIL, 716 N. Carson St., Suite A, Carson City NV 89701. (775)687-6680. E-mail: online form. Website: http:// dmla.clan.lib.nv.us/docs/arts.

NEW HAMPSHIRE STATE COUNCIL ON THE ARTS, 21/2 Beacon St., 2nd Floor, Concord NH 03301-4974. (603)271-2789. Website: www.nh.gov/nharts.

NEW JERSEY STATE COUNCIL ON THE ARTS, 225 W. State St., P.O. Box 306, Trenton NJ 08625. (609)292-6130. Website: www.njartscouncil.org.

NEW MEXICO ARTS, DEPT. OF CULTURAL AFFAIRS, P.O. Box 1450, Santa Fe NM 87504-1450. (505)827-6490 or (800)879-4278. Website: www.nmarts.org.

NEW YORK STATE COUNCIL ON THE ARTS, 175 Varick St., New York NY 10014. (212)627-4455. Website: www.nysca.org.

NORTH CAROLINA ARTS COUNCIL, 109 East Jones St., Cultural Resources Building, Raleigh NC 27601. (919)807-6500. E-mail: ncarts@ncmail.net. Website: www.ncarts.org.

NORTH DAKOTA COUNCIL ON THE ARTS, 1600 E. Century Ave., Suite 6, Bismarck ND 58503. (701)328-7590. E-mail: comserv@state.nd.us. Website: www.state.nd.us/arts.

OHIO ARTS COUNCIL, 727 E. Main St., Columbus OH 43205-1796. (614)466-2613. Website: www.oac.state.oh.us.

OKLAHOMA ARTS COUNCIL, Jim Thorpe Building, 2101 N. Lincoln Blvd., Suite 640, Oklahoma City OK 73105. (405)521-2931. E-mail: okarts@arts.ok.gov. Website: www.arts.state.ok.us.

OREGON ARTS COMMISSION, 775 Summer St. NE, Suite 200, Salem OR 97301-1280. (503)986-0082. E-mail: oregon.artscomm@state.or.us. Website: www.oregonartscommission.org.

PENNSYLVANIA COUNCIL ON THE ARTS, 216 Finance Bldg., Harrisburg PA 17120. (717)787-6883. Website: www.pacouncil-onthearts.org.

RHODE ISLAND STATE COUNCIL ON THE ARTS, One Capitol Hill, Third Floor, Providence RI 02908. (401)222-3880. E-mail: info@arts.ri.gov. Website: www.arts.ri.gov.

SOUTH CAROLINA ARTS COMMISSION, 1800 Gervais St., Columbia SC 29201. (803)734-8696. E-mail: info@arts.state.sc.us. Website: www.southcarolinaarts.com.

SOUTH DAKOTA ARTS COUNCIL, 711 E. Wells Ave., Pierre SD 57501-3369. (605)773-3301. E-mail: sdac@state.sd.us. Website: www.artscouncil.sd.gov.

TENNESSEE ARTS COMMISSION, 401 Charlotte Ave., Nashville TN 37243-0780. (615)741-1701. Website: www.arts.state.tn.us.

TEXAS COMMISSION ON THE ARTS, E.O. Thompson Office Building, 920 Colorado, Suite 501, Austin TX 78701. (512)463-5535. E-mail: front.desk@arts.state.tx.us. Website: www.arts.state.tx.us.

UTAH ARTS COUNCIL, 617 E. South Temple, Salt Lake City UT 84102-1177. (801)236-7555. Website: http://arts.utah.gov.

VERMONT ARTS COUNCIL, 136 State St., Drawer 33, Montpelier VT 05633-6001. (802)828-3291. E-mail: online form. Website: www.vermontartscouncil.org.

VIRGIN ISLANDS COUNCIL ON THE ARTS, 5070 Norre Gade, St. Thomas VI 00802-6872. (340)774-5984. Website: http://vi-councilonarts.org.

VIRGINIA COMMISSION FOR THE ARTS, Lewis House, 223 Governor St., 2nd Floor, Richmond VA 23219. (804)225-3132. E-mail: arts@arts.virginia.gov. Website: www.arts.state.va.us.

WASHINGTON STATE ARTS COMMISSION, 711 Capitol Way S., Suite 600, P.O. Box 42675, Olympia WA 98504-2675. (360)753-3860. E-mail: info@arts.wa.gov. Website: www.arts.wa.gov.

WEST VIRGINIA COMMISSION ON THE ARTS, The Cultural Center, Capitol Complex, 1900 Kanawha Blvd. E., Charleston WV 25305-0300. (304)558-0220. Website: www.wvculture.org/arts.

WISCONSIN ARTS BOARD, 101 E. Wilson St., 1st Floor, Madison WI 53702. (608)266-0190. E-mail: artsboard@arts.state.wi.us. Website: www.arts.state.wi.us.

WYOMING ARTS COUNCIL, 2320 Capitol Ave., Cheyenne WY 82002. (307)777-7742. E-mail: ebratt@state.wy.us. Website: http://wyoarts.state.wy.us.

CANADIAN PROVINCES ARTS AGENCIES

ALBERTA FOUNDATION FOR THE ARTS, 10708-105 Ave., Edmonton AB T5H 0A1. (780)427-9968. Website: www.affta.ab.ca/index.shtml.

BRITISH COLUMBIA ARTS COUNCIL, P.O. Box 9819, Stn. Prov. Govt., Victoria BC V8W 9W3. (250)356-1718. E-mail: BCArtsCouncil@gov.bc.ca. Website: www.bcartscouncil.ca.

THE CANADA COUNCIL FOR THE ARTS, 350 Albert St., P.O. Box 1047, Ottawa ON K1P 5V8. (613)566-4414 or (800)263-5588 (within Canada). Website: www.canadacouncil.ca.

MANITOBA ARTS COUNCIL, 525-93 Lombard Ave., Winnipeg MB R3B 3B1. (204)945-2237 or (866)994-2787 (in Manitoba). E-mail: info@artscouncil.mb.ca. Website: www.artscouncil.mb.ca.

NEW BRUNSWICK ARTS BOARD (NBAB), 634 Queen St., Suite 300, Fredericton NB E3B 1C2. (506)444-4444 or (866)460-2787. Website: www.artsnb.ca.

NEWFOUNDLAND & LABRADOR ARTS COUNCIL, P.O. Box 98, St. John's NL A1C 5H5. (709)726-2212 or (866)726-2212. E-mail: nlacmail@nfld.net. Website: www.nlac.nf.ca.

NOVA SCOTIA DEPARTMENT OF TOURISM, CULTURE, AND HERITAGE, Culture Division, 1800 Argyle St., Suite 601, P.O. Box 456, Halifax NS B3J 2R5. (902)424-4510. E-mail: cultaffs@gov.ns.ca. Website: www.gov.ns.ca/dtc/culture.

ONTARIO ARTS COUNCIL, 151 Bloor St. W., 5th Floor, Toronto ON M5S 1T6. (416)961-1660 or (800)387-0058 (in Ontario). E-mail: info@arts.on.ca. Website: www.arts.on.ca.

PRINCE EDWARD ISLAND COUNCIL OF THE ARTS, 115 Richmond St., Charlottetown PE C1A 1H7. (902)368-4410 or (888)734-2784. E-mail: info@peiartscouncil.com. Website: www.peiartscouncil.com.

QUÉBEC COUNCIL FOR ARTS & LITERA-TURE, 79 boul. René-Lévesque Est, 3e étage, Quebec QC G1R 5N5. (418)643-1707 or (800)897-1707. E-mail: info@calq.gouv.qc.ca. Website: www.calq.gouv.qc.ca.

THE SASKATCHEWAN ARTS BOARD, 2135 Broad St., Regina SK S4P 1Y6. (306)787-4056 or (800)667-7526 (Saskatchewan only). E-mail: sab@artsboard.sk.ca. Website: www.artsboard.sk.ca.

YUKON ARTS FUNDING PROGRAM, Cultural Services Branch, Dept. of Tourism & Culture, Government of Yukon, Box 2703 (L-3), Whitehorse YT Y1A 2C6. (867)667-8589 or (800)661-0408 (in Yukon). E-mail: arts@gov.yk.ca. Website: www.tc.gov.yk.ca/216.html.

CONFERENCES, WORKSHOPS & FESTIVALS

///

There are times when we want to immerse ourselves in learning. Or perhaps we crave a change of scenery, the creative stimulation of being around other artists, or the uninterrupted productivity of time alone to work.

That's what this section of *Poet's Market* is all about, providing a selection of writing conferences and workshops, artist colonies and retreats, poetry festivals, and even a few opportunities to go traveling with your muse. These listings give the basics: contact information, a brief description of the event, lists of past presenters, and offerings of special interest to poets. Contact an event that interests you for additional information, including up-to-date costs and housing details. (Please note that most directors had not finalized their 2016 plans when we contacted them for this edition of *Poet's Market*. However, where possible, they provided us with their 2015 dates, costs, faculty names or themes to give you a better idea of what each event has to offer.)

Before you seriously consider a conference, workshop or other event, determine what you hope to get out of the experience. Would a general conference with one or two poetry workshops among many other types of sessions be acceptable? Or are you looking for something exclusively focused on poetry? Do you want to hear poets speak about poetry writing, or are you looking for a more participatory experience, such as a one-on-one critiquing session or a group workshop? Do you mind being one of hundreds of attendees, or do you prefer a more intimate setting? Are you willing to invest in the expense of traveling to a conference, or would something local better suit your budget? Keep these questions and others in mind as you read these listings, view websites and study conference brochures.

ABROAD WRITERS CONFERENCES

17363 Sutter Creek Rd., Sutter Creek CA 95685. (209)296-4050. **E-mail:** abroadwriters@yahoo.com; nancy@abroadwritersconference.com. **Website:** http://abroadwritersconference.com/. "Abroad Writers Conferences are devoted to introducing our participants to world views here in the United States and Abroad. Throughout the world we invite several authors to come join us to give readings and to participate on a panel. Our discussion groups touch upon a wide range of topics from important issues of our times to publishing abroad and in the United States. Our objective is to broaden our cultural and scientific perspectives of the world through discourse and writing." Conferences are held throughout the year in various places worldwide. See website for scheduling details. Conference duration: 7-10 days. "Instead of being lost in a crowd at a large conference, Abroad Writers' Conference prides itself on holding small group meetings where participants have personal contact with everyone. Stimulating talks, interviews, readings, Q&A's, writing workshops, film screenings, private consultations and social gatherings all take place within a week to ten days. Abroad Writers' Conference promises you true networking opportunities and full detailed feedback on your writing."

See the complete schedule online. Recent events include Italy, Spain and England in 2014-2015.

COSTS/ACCOMMODATIONS See website for pricing details.

ADDITIONAL INFORMATION Agents participate in conference. Application is online at website.

AMERICAN CHRISTIAN WRITERS CONFERENCES

P.O. Box 110390, Nashville TN 37222-0390. (800)219-7483. **Fax:** (615)834-7736. **E-mail:** acwriters@aol.com. **Website:** www.acwriters.com. **Contact:** Reg Forder, director. ACW hosts dozens of annual two-day writers conferences and mentoring retreats across America taught by editors and professional freelance writers. These events provide excellent instruction, networking opportunities, and valuable one-on-one time with editors. Annual conferences promoting all forms of Christian writing (fiction, nonfiction, scriptwriting). Conferences are held between March and November during each year.

COSTS/ACCOMMODATIONS Special rates are available at the host hotel (usually a major chain like Holiday Inn). Costs vary based on conference. Prices also depend on whether it is a conference or a mentoring retreat.

ADDITIONAL INFORMATION Send a SASE for conference brochures/guidelines.

ANAM CARA WRITER'S AND ARTIST'S RETREAT

Eyeries, Beara, Co. Cork , Ireland. (353)(027)74441. **Fax:** (353)(027)74448. **E-mail:** anamcararetreat@gmail.com. **Website:** www.anamcararetreat.com. **Contact:** Sue Booth-Forbes, director. Offers up to one-month individual retreats as well as workshops on a variety of creative subjects for writers and artists. Length of workshops varies with subject and leader/facilitator. Location: "Beara is a rural and hauntingly beautiful part of Ireland that is kept temperate by the Gulf Stream. The retreat sits on a hill overlooking Coulagh Bay, the mountains of the Ring of Kerry, and the Slieve Mishkish Mountains of Beara. The village of Eyeries is a short walk away." Average attendance: 5 residents at the retreat when working individually; 12-18 workshop participants.

COSTS/ACCOMMODATIONS 2015 cost: residency fee ranges from 600-700 Euro/week for individual retreats (full room and board). The event also features editorial consulting, laundry, sauna, hot tub overlooking Coulagh Bay, 5 acres of gardens, meadows, riverbank and cascades, river island, swimming hole, and several unique working spots, such as the ruin of a stone mill and a sod-roofed beehive hut. Overflow from workshops stay in nearby B&Bs, a 10-minute walk or 2-minute drive away. Transportation provided if needed. Details regarding workshops scheduled for 2015 and their fees as well as transportation to Anam Cara are available on the website.

ADDITIONAL INFORMATION Requests for specific information about rates and availability can be made through the website.

ANNUAL SPRING POETRY FESTIVAL

City College, 160 Convent Ave., New York NY 10031. (212)650-6356. **Website:** www1.ccny.cuny.edu/prospective/humanities/poetry. Writer workshops geared to all levels. **Open to students.** Annual poetry festival. 2015 dates: May 8, 2015. Registration limited to 325. Cost of workshops and festival: free. Write for more information. Site: Theater B of Aaron Davis Hall.

ART WORKSHOPS IN GUATEMALA

4758 Lyndale Ave. S., Minneapolis MN 55419-5304. (612)825-0747. **E-mail:** info@artguat.org. **Website:** www.artguat.org. **Contact:** Liza Fourre, director. Art & cultural workshops held year-round. Maximim class size: 10 students per class.

COSTS/ACCOMMODATIONS All transportation and accommodations included in price of conference. See website. ncludes tuition, lodging, breakfast, ground transportation.

ADDITIONAL INFORMATION Conference information available now. For brochure/guidelines visit website, e-mail or call. Accepts inquiries by e-mail, phone.

ASPEN SUMMER WORDS LITERARY FESTIVAL & WRITING RETREAT

Aspen Words, 110 E. Hallam St., #116, Aspen CO 81611. (970)925-3122. **Fax:** (970)925-5700. **E-mail:** aspenwords@aspeninstitute.org. **Website:** www.aspenwords.org. **Contact:** Caroline Tory, programs coordinator. 2015 dates: June 21-26. The 39th annual Aspen Summer Words Writing Retreat and Literary Festival offers workshops in fiction, memoir, novel editing, and playwriting. The faculty includes fiction writers Ann Hood, Richard Russo, Akhil Sharma, and Hannah Tinti; memoir writers Andre Dubus III and Dani Shapiro; and playwright Sharr White. Aspen Summer Words features lectures, readings, panel discussions, and the opportunity to meet with agents and editors. Tuition for the writing workshops ranges from $1,100 to $1,375, which includes some meals. Financial aid is available on a limited basis. To apply for a juried workshop, submit up to 10 pages of prose with a $30 application fee by February 27. Registration to non-juried workshops (Beginning Fiction and Playwriting) is first-come, first-served. A pass to all the public panels is $150, tickets to individual events are $20. Call, e-mail, or visit the website for an application and complete guidelines.

ASSOCIATION OF WRITERS & WRITING PROGRAMS ANNUAL CONFERENCE

Association of Writers & Writing Programs, George Mason University, 4400 University Drive, MSN 1E3, Fairfax VA 22030-4444. (703)993-4317. **Fax:** (703)993-4302. **E-mail:** conference@awpwriter.org; events@awpwriter.org. **Website:** www.awpwriter.org/awp_conference. Each year, AWP holds its Annual Conference & Bookfair in a different city to celebrate the authors, teachers, writing programs, literary centers, and independent publishers of that region. The conference typically features hundreds of readings, lectures, panel discussions, and forums, as well as hundreds of book signings, receptions, dances, and informal gatherings. AWP's is now the largest literary conference in North America.

ADDITIONAL INFORMATION Upcoming conference locations include Minneapolis (2015), Los Angeles (March 30 - April 2, 2016), and Washington, D.C. (February 8-11, 2017).

AUSTIN INTERNATIONAL POETRY FESTIVAL

(512)777-1888. **E-mail:** joe@aipf.org; james@aipf.org. **Website:** www.aipf.org. **Contact:** Joe Brundidge or James Jacobs. The 23rd Austin International Poetry Festival (AIPF) will be held April 9-12, 2015. Registration is required for all poets. Nikki Giovanni will be featured April 11, 2015 - additional ticket required for this special reading, AIPF registered poets get in free. All additional events are free to the general public. This four-day citywide, all-inclusive celebration of poetry and poets has grown to become "the largest non-juried poetry festival in the U.S." The festival will include a minimum of the following: 20 readings, one youth anthology read, 10 workshops, 5 open mics, 2 music and poetry presentations, 2 anthology competitions and complete readings, 2 poetry slams, an all-night open mic and a poetry panel symposium. Additional information available online at www.aipf.org. Discount registration fees available for retired, college students, and military poets.

COSTS/ACCOMMODATIONS Includes anthology submission fee, program bio, scheduled reading at one of AIPF's 15 venues, participation in all events, 1 catered meal, workshop participation, and more.

ADDITIONAL INFORMATION Offers multiple poetry contests as part of festival. Guidelines available on website. Registration form available on website. "Largest non-juried poetry festival in the U.S."

BREAD LOAF WRITERS' CONFERENCE

(802)443-5286. **Fax:** (802)443-2087. **E-mail:** blwc@middlebury.edu. **Website:** www.middlebury.edu/bread-loaf-conferences/bl_writers. Annual conference held in late August. Conference duration: 10 days. Offers workshops for fiction, nonfiction, and poetry. Agents and editors will be in attendance.

COSTS/ACCOMMODATIONS Bread Loaf Campus in Ripton, Vermont.

ADDITIONAL INFORMATION 2015 Conference Dates: August 12-22. Location: mountain campus of Middlebury College in Vermont. Average attendance: 230. The application deadline for the 2015 event is March 1, 2015; there is $15 application fee.

CAPE COD WRITERS CENTER ANNUAL CONFERENCE

P.O. Box 408, Osterville MA 02655. **E-mail:** writers@capecodwriterscenter.org. **Website:** www.capecodwriterscenter.org. **Contact:** Nancy Rubin Stuart, executive director. Duration: 3 days; held during first week in August. Offers workshops in fiction, commercial fiction, nonfiction, poetry, writing for children, memoir, pitching your book, screenwriting, digital communications, and getting published. There are ms evaluation and mentoring sessions with faculty.

COSTS/ACCOMMODATIONS Held at Resort and Conference Center of Hyannis, Hyannis, MA. Vary, depending on the number of courses selected.

CELEBRATION OF SOUTHERN LITERATURE

Southern Lit Alliance, 3069 S. Broad St., Suite 2, Chattanooga TN 37408-3056. (423)267-1218. **Fax:** (866)483-6831. **E-mail:** srobinson@southernlitalliance.org. **Website:** www.southernlitalliance.org. **Contact:** Susan Robinson. "The Celebration of Southern Literature stands out because of its unique collaboration with the Fellowship of Southern Writers, an organization founded by towering literary figures like Eudora Welty, Cleanth Brooks, Walker Percy, and Robert Penn Warren to recognize and encourage literature in the South. The 2015 celebration marked 26 years since the Fellowship selected Chattanooga for its headquarters and chose to collaborate with the Celebration of Southern Literature. The Fellowship awards 11 literary prizes and induct new members, making this event the place to discover up-and-coming voices in Southern literature. The Southern Lit Alliance's Celebration of Southern Literature attracts more than 1,000 readers and writers from all over the U.S. It strives to maintain an informal atmosphere where conversations will thrive, inspired by a common passion for the written word. The Southern Lit Alliance (formerly The Arts & Education Council) started as 1 of 12 pilot agencies founded by a Ford Foundation grant in 1952. The Alliance is the only

organization of the 12 still in existence. The Southern Lit Alliance celebrates southern writers and readers through community education and innovative literary arts experiences."

◔   This event happens every other year in odd-numbered years.

THE COLRAIN POETRY MANUSCRIPT CONFERENCE

Website: www.colrainpoetry.com. "Colrain is the original, one-of-a-kind manuscript conference. Faculty includes nationally-renowned poet-editors and publishers. Work with the best for the best results. Our unique, realistic method of manuscript evaluation sets poets with a manuscript-in-progress on a path toward publication. Poets also get a look into the publication world and make important contacts with leading editors, teachers, and publishers."

COSTS/ACCOMMODATIONS The Colrain Practicum is April 25-26, 2015 in Massachusetts. The Colarin Classic is May 15-18, 2015 in Vermont. The second Colrain Classic is June 5-8, 2015 in New Mexico.

ADDITIONAL INFORMATION Details, application, and registration form available on website.

FINE ARTS WORK CENTER

24 Pearl St., Provincetown MA 02657. (508)487-9960, ext. 103. **Fax:** (508)487-8873. **E-mail:** workshops@fawc.org. **Website:** www.fawc.org. Weeklong workshops in creative writing and the visual arts. Location: The Fine Arts Work Center in Provincetown.

COSTS/ACCOMMODATIONS Summer Workshop Program fees range $600-725. Limited accommodations available at the Work Center for $700 for 6 nights. Additional accommodations available locally. Cost: $600-725/week, $675/week (housing).

ADDITIONAL INFORMATION See website for details and an application form.

HAIKU NORTH AMERICA CONFERENCE

1275 Fourth St., PMB 365, Santa Rosa CA 95404. **E-mail:** welchm@aol.com. **Website:** www.haikunorthamerica.com. **Contact:** Michael Dylan Welch. Biennial conference. 2015 dates: Oct 15-18, 2015. Haiku North America (HNA) is the largest and oldest gathering of haiku poets in the United States and Canada. There are no membership fees and HNA provides breaking news and interaction at the HNA blog. All haiku poets and interested parties are welcome. HNA is a long weekend of papers, panels, workshops, readings, performances, book sales, and much socialization with fellow poets, translators, scholars, editors, and publishers. Both established and aspiring haiku poets are welcome.

COSTS/ACCOMMODATIONS Accommodations at discounted hotels nearby are an additional cost. Information available on website as details are finalized closer to the conference date. Typically around $200, including a banquet and a conference anthology

HIGHLAND SUMMER CONFERENCE

Box 7014, Radford University, Radford VA 24142-7014. **E-mail:** tburriss@radford.edu; rbderrick@radford.edu. **Website:** tinyurl.com/q8z8ej9. **Contact:** Dr. Theresa Burriss, Ruth Derrick. 2015 dates: June 15-19. The Highland Summer Writers' Conference is a 4-day lecture-seminar workshop combination conducted by well-known guest writers. It offers the opportunity to study and practice creative and expository writing within the context of regional culture. The course is graded on Pass/Fail basis for undergraduates and letter grades for graduate students. It may be taken twice for credit. The evening readings are free and open to the public. Services at a reduced rate for continuing education credits or to simply participate.

INDIANA UNIVERSITY WRITERS' CONFERENCE

464 Ballantine Hall, 1020 E. Kirkwood Ave., Bloomington IN 47405-7103. (812)855-1877. **Fax:** (812)855-9535. **E-mail:** writecon@indiana.edu. **Website:** www.indiana.edu/~writecon. Annual. Conference/workshops held in May. 2015 dates: May 30 - June 3. Average attendance: 115. "The Indiana University Writers' Conference believes in a craft-based teaching of fiction writing. We emphasize an exploration of creativity through a variety of approaches, offering workshop-based craft discussions, classes focusing on technique, and talks about the careers and concerns of a writing life."

COSTS/ACCOMMODATIONS Information on accommodations available on website.

ADDITIONAL INFORMATION Connect on Twitter at @iuwritecon.

IOWA SUMMER WRITING FESTIVAL

The University of Iowa, C215 Seashore Hall, University of Iowa, Iowa City IA 52242. (319)335-4160. **Fax:** (319)335-4743. **E-mail:** iswfestival@uiowa.edu. **Website:** uiowa.edu/~iswfest. Annual festival held in June and July. 2015 event will have 138 workshops with 72 instructors. Conference duration: Workshops are 1 week or a weekend. Average attendance: Limited to 12 people/class, with over 1,500 participants throughout the summer. "We offer courses across the genres: novel, short story, poetry, essay, memoir, humor, travel, playwriting, screenwriting, writing for children, and women's writing. Held at the University of Iowa campus." Speakers have included Marvin Bell, Lan Samantha Chang, John Dalton, Hope Edelman, Katie Ford, Patricia Foster, Bret Anthony Johnston, Barbara Robinette Moss, among others.

COSTS/ACCOMMODATIONS Accommodations available at area hotels. Information on overnight accommodations available by phone or on website.

ADDITIONAL INFORMATION Brochures are available in February. Inquire via e-mail or on website.

IWWG ANNUAL CONFERENCE

(212)737-7536. **Fax:** (212)737-9469. **E-mail:** iwwgquestions@gmail.com. **Website:** www.iwwg.org. Writer and illustrator workshops geared toward all levels. Offers over 50 different workshops—some are for children's book writers and illustrators. Also sponsors other events throughout the U.S. Annual workshops. Workshops held every summer for a week. Length of each session: 90 minutes; sessions take place for an entire week. Registration limited to 500. Write for more information. The 2015 spring conference was March 15 in Los Angeles.

JACKSON HOLE WRITERS CONFERENCE

PO Box 1974, Jackson WY 83001. (307)413-3332. **E-mail:** nicole@jacksonholewritersconference.com. **Website:** jacksonholewritersconference.com. Annual conference held June 27-29. Conference duration: 4 days. Average attendance: 110. Covers fiction, creative nonfiction, and young adult and offers ms critiques from authors, agents, and editors. Agents in attendance will take pitches from writers. Paid manuscript critique programs are available.

COSTS/ACCOMMODATIONS $365 if registered by May 12. Accompanying teen writer: $175. Pre-Conference Writing Workshop: $150.

ADDITIONAL INFORMATION Held at the Center for the Arts in Jackson, Wyoming and online.

KENTUCKY WOMEN WRITERS CONFERENCE

University of Kentucky College of Arts & Sciences, 232 E. Maxwell St., Lexington KY 40506. (859)257-2874. **E-mail:** kentuckywomenwriters@gmail.com. **Website:** kentuckywomenwriters.org. **Contact:** Julie

Wrinn, director. Conference held in second or third weekend of September. The 2014 dates were Sept. 12-13. The location is the Carnegie Center for Literacy in Lexington, Kentucky. Conference duration: 2 days. Average attendance: 150-200. Conference covers poetry, fiction, creative nonfiction, playwriting. Writing workshops, panels, and readings featuring contemporary women writers. The 2014 conference featured prize-winning poet Tracy K. Smith as its keynote speaker.

COSTS/ACCOMMODATIONS $175 early bird discount, $200 thereafter; $125 without workshop; $30 for students; includes boxed lunch on Friday; $20 for writers' reception. Other meals and accommodations are not included.

ADDITIONAL INFORMATION Sponsors prizes in poetry ($200), fiction ($200), nonfiction ($200), playwriting ($500), and spoken word ($500). Winners also invited to read during the conference. Pre-registration opens May 1.

KENYON REVIEW WRITERS WORKSHOP

Kenyon College, Gambier OH 43022. (740)427-5207. **Fax:** (740)427-5417. **E-mail:** kenyonreview@kenyon.edu; writers@kenyonreview.org. **Website:** www.kenyonreview.org. **Contact:** Anna Duke Reach, director. Annual 8-day workshop held in June. Participants apply in poetry, fiction, creative nonfiction, literary hybrid/book arts or writing online, and then participate in intensive daily workshops which focus on the generation and revision of significant new work. Held on the campus of Kenyon College in the rural village of Gambier, Ohio. Workshop leaders have included David Baker, Carl Phillips, Mary Szybist, Rebecca McClanahan, Dinty Moore, Caitlin Horrocks, Lee K. Abbott, and Nancy Zafris.

COSTS/ACCOMMODATIONS The workshop operates a shuttle to and from Gambier and the airport in Columbus, Ohio. Offers overnight accommodations. Participants are housed in Kenyon College student housing. The cost is covered in the tuition. $1,995; includes tuition, room and board.

ADDITIONAL INFORMATION Application includes a writing sample. Admission decisions are made on a rolling basis. Workshop information is available online at www.kenyonreview.org/workshops in November. For brochure send e-mail, visit website, call, or fax. Accepts inquiries by SASE, e-mail, phone, fax.

⊙ KUNDIMAN POETRY RETREAT

P.O. Box 4248, Sunnyside NY 11104. **E-mail:** info@kundiman.org. **Website:** kundiman.org/retreat. **Contact:** June W. Choi, executive director. Held annually. 2015 dates: June 24-28. Held at Fordham University's Rose Hill campus. "This is a special event for Asian American poets. Renowned faculty will conduct workshops and provide one-on-one mentorship sessions with fellows. Readings and informal social gatherings will also be scheduled. Fellows selected based on sample of 6-8 poems and short essay answer.

COSTS/ACCOMMODATIONS Room and board is free to accepted Fellows.

ADDITIONAL INFORMATION Additional information, guidelines, and online application available on website.

MENDOCINO COAST WRITERS CONFERENCE

1211 Del Mar Dr., second address is P.O. Box 2087, Fort Bragg CA 95437. (707)485-4032. **E-mail:** info@mcwc.org. **Website:** www.mcwc.org. Annual summer conference. 2015 dates: August 6-8, 2015. Average attendance: 90. Offers intensive workshops in fiction, creative nonfiction, poetry, YA, and seminars/panels about writing and publishing. Located at a community college on the Northern California Coast. Workshop leaders at the 2015 event: Ellen Bass, David Corbett, Catherine Ryan Hyde, Albert DeSilver, Lisa Locascio. Opportunities to meet informally or in private manuscript consultations with agents and editors.

COSTS/ACCOMMODATIONS $525 (minimum) includes morning intensives, afternoon panels and seminars, social events, and most meals. Scholarships available. Early application advised.

ADDITIONAL INFORMATION Emphasis is on encouragement, expertise and inspiration in a literary community where authors are also fantastic teachers. Registration opens March 15.

MONTEVALLO LITERARY FESTIVAL

Sta. 6420, University of Montevallo, Montevallo AL 35115. (205)665-6420. **Fax:** (205)665-6422. **E-mail:** murphyj@montevallo.edu. **Website:** http://www.montevallo.edu/arts-sciences/college-of-arts-sciences/departments/english-foreign-languages/student-organizations/montevallo-literary-festival/. **Contact:** Dr. Jim Murphy, director. 2015 dates: March 20. "Each April, the University of Montevallo's Department of English and Foreign Languages hosts the annual Montevallo Literary Festival, a celebration of creative writing dedicated to bringing literary writers and readers together on a personal scale. Our friendly, relaxed festival runs all day into the evening featuring readings by all invited writers, book signings, a Q&A panel, social gatherings and dinner with live music."

JENNY MCKEAN MOORE COMMUNITY WORKSHOPS

English Department, George Washington University, 801 22nd St. NW, Rome Hall, Suite 760, Washington DC 20052. (202)994-6180. **Fax:** (202)994-7915. **E-mail:** lpageinc@gwu.edu. **Website:** www.gwu. edu/~english/creative_jennymckeanmoore.html. **Contact:** Lisa Page, acting director of creative writing. Workshop held each semester at the university. Average attendance: 15. Concentration varies depending on professor—usually fiction or poetry. The Creative Writing department brings an established poet or novelist to campus each year to teach a writing workshop for GW students and a free community workshop for adults in the larger Washington community. Details posted on website in June, with an application deadline at the end of August or in early September. **ADDITIONAL INFORMATION** Admission is competitive and by decided by the quality of a submitted ms.

⊙ MOUNT HERMON CHRISTIAN WRITERS CONFERENCE

PO Box 413, Mount Hermon CA 95041. **E-mail:** info@mounthermon.org. **Website:** writers.mounthermon.org. Annual professional conference. 2015 dates: March 27-31. Average attendance: 450. Sponsored by and held at the 440-acre Mount Hermon Christian Conference Center near San Jose, California in the heart of the coastal redwoods, we are a broad-ranging conference for all areas of Christian writing, including fiction, nonfiction, fantasy, children's, teen, young adult, poetry, magazines, inspirational and devotional writing. This is a working, how-to conference, with Major Morning tracks in all genres (including a track especially for teen writers), and as many as 20 optional workshops each afternoon. Faculty-to-student ratio is about 1 to 6. The bulk of our more than 70 faculty members are editors and publisher representatives from major Christian publishing houses nationwide. Speakers have included T. Davis Bunn, Debbie Macomber, Jerry Jenkins, Bill Butterworth, Dick Foth and others.

NAPA VALLEY WRITERS' CONFERENCE

Napa Valley College, 1088 College Ave., St. Helena CA 94574. (707)967-2900. **E-mail:** writecon@napa-valley.edu. **Website:** www.napawritersconference.org. **Contact:** Andrea Bewick, managing director. Established 1981. Annual weeklong event. 2015 dates: July 26 - July 31. Location: Upper Valley Campus in the historic town of St. Helena, 25 miles north of Napa in the heart of the valley's wine growing community. Average attendance: 48 in poetry and 48 in fiction. "Serious writers of all backgrounds and experience are welcome to apply." Offers poets and fiction writers workshops, lectures, faculty readings at Napa Valley wineries, and one-on-one faculty counseling. "Poetry session provides the opportunity to work both on generating new poems and on revising previously written ones."

◯ On Twitter as @napawriters and on Facebook as facebook.com/napawriters.

COSTS/ACCOMMODATIONS $975; $25 application fee.

PIMA WRITERS' WORKSHOP

Pima College, 2202 W. Anklam Rd., Tucson AZ 85709. (520)206-6084. **Fax:** (520)206-6020. **E-mail:** mfiles@pima.edu. **Contact:** Meg Files, director. Annual conference geared toward beginner, intermediate and advanced levels. **Open to students.** The conference features presentations and writing exercises on writing and publishing stories for children and young adults, among other genres. Participants may attend for college credit. Meals and accommodations not included. Features a dozen authors, editors, and agents talking about writing and publishing fiction, nonfiction, poetry, and stories for children. E-mail us for more info, or check the website.

SAN DIEGO STATE UNIVERSITY WRITERS' CONFERENCE

SDSU College of Extended Studies, 5250 Campanile Dr., San Diego State University, San Diego CA 92182-1920. (619)594-3946. **Fax:** (619)594-8566. **E-mail:** sdsuwritersconference@mail.sdsu.edu. **Website:** ces.sdsu.edu/writers. Annual conference held in January. Conference duration: 2.5 days. Average attendance: 350. Covers fiction, nonfiction, scriptwriting and e-books. Held at the San Diego Marriott Mission Valley Hotel. Each year the conference offers a variety of workshops for the beginner and advanced writers. This conference allows the individual writer to choose which workshop best suits his/her needs. In addition to the workshops, editor reading appointments and agent/editor consultation appointments are provided so attendees may meet with editors and agents one-on-one to discuss specific questions. A reception is offered Saturday immediately following the workshops, offering attendees the opportunity to socialize with the faculty in a relaxed atmosphere. Last year, approximately 60 faculty members attended.

COSTS/ACCOMMODATIONS Attendees must make their own travel arrangements. A conference rate for attendees is available at the event hotel (Marriott Mission Valley Hotel). Approximately $399-435. Parking is available for $8/day.

SANTA BARBARA WRITERS CONFERENCE

27 W. Anapamu St., Suite 305, Santa Barbara CA 93101. (805)568-1516. **E-mail:** info@sbwriters.com. **Website:** www.sbwriters.com. Annual conference held in June. 2015 dates: June 7-12. Average attendance: 200. Covers fiction, nonfiction, journalism, memoir, poetry, playwriting, screenwriting, travel writing, young adult, children's literature, humor, and marketing. Speakers have included Ray Bradbury, William Styron, Eudora Welty, James Michener, Sue Grafton, Charles M. Schulz, Clive Cussler, Fannie Flagg, Elmore Leonard, and T.C. Boyle. Agents will appear on a panel; in addition, there will be an agents and editors day that allows writers to pitch their projects in one-on-one meetings.

COSTS/ACCOMMODATIONS Hyatt Santa Barbara. Early conference registration is $575, and regular registration is $650.

ADDITIONAL INFORMATION Register online or contact for brochure and registration forms.

☺ SASKATCHEWAN FESTIVAL OF WORDS

217 Main St. N., Moose Jaw SK S6J 0W1, Canada. **Website:** www.festivalofwords.com. Annual 4-day event, third week of July (2015 dates: July 16-19). Location: Moose Jaw Library/Art Museum complex in Crescent Park. Average attendance: about 4,000 admissions. "Canadian authors up close and personal for readers and writers of all ages in mystery, poetry, memoir, fantasy, graphic novels, history, and novel. Each summer festival includes more than 60 events within 2 blocks of historic Main Street. Audience favorite activities include workshops for writers, audi-

ence readings, drama,performance poetry, concerts, panels, and music."

COSTS/ACCOMMODATIONS Information available at www.templegardens.sk.ca, campgrounds, and bed and breakfast establishments. Complete information about festival presenters, events, costs, and schedule also available on website.

☺ THE SCHOOL FOR WRITERS FALL WORKSHOP

The Humber School for Writers, Humber Institute of Technology & Advanced Learning, 3199 Lake Shore Blvd. W., Toronto ON M8V 1K8, Canada. (416)675-6622. **E-mail:** antanas.sileika@humber.ca; hilary.higgins@humber.ca. **Website:** www.humber.ca/scapa/programs/school-writers. The School for Writers Workshop has moved to the fall with the International Festival of Authors. The workshop runs during the last week in October. Conference duration: 1 week. Average attendance: 60. New writers from around the world gather to study with faculty members to work on their novels, short stories, poetry, or creative nonfiction. Agents and editors participate in the conference. Include a work-in-progress with your registration. Faculty has included Martin Amis, David Mitchell, Kevin Barry, Rachel Kuschner, Peter Carey, Roddy Doyle, Tim O'Brien, Andrea Levy, Barry Unsworth, Edward Albee, Ha Jin, Julia Glass, Mavis Gallant, Bruce Jay Friedman, Isabel Huggan, Alistair MacLeod, Lisa Moore, Kim Moritsugu, Francine Prose, Paul Quarrington, Olive Senior, D.M. Thomas, Annabel Lyon, Mary Gaitskill, and M.G. Vassanji.

COSTS/ACCOMMODATIONS around $850 (in 2014). Some limited scholarships are available.

ADDITIONAL INFORMATION Accepts inquiries by e-mail, phone, and fax.

SEWANEE WRITERS' CONFERENCE

735 University Ave., 119 Gailor Hall, Stamler Center, Sewanee TN 37383-1000. (931)598-1654. **E-mail:** allatham@sewanee.edu. **Website:** www.sewaneewriters.org. **Contact:** Adam Latham. Annual conference. 2015 dates: July 21 - Aug. 2. Average attendance: 150. "The University of the South will host the 26th session of the Sewanee Writers' Conference. Thanks to the generosity of the Walter E. Dakin Memorial Fund, supported by the estate of the late Tennessee Williams, the Conference will gather a distinguished faculty to provide instruction and criticism through workshops and craft lectures in poetry, fiction, and playwriting.

During an intense 12-day period, participants will read and critique each other's manuscripts under the leadership of some of our country's finest fiction writers, poets, and playwrights. All faculty members and fellows give scheduled readings; senior faculty members offer craft lectures; open-mic readings accommodate many others. Additional writers, along with a host of writing professionals, visit to give readings, participate in panel discussions, and entertain questions from the audience. Receptions and mealtimes offer opportunities for informal exchange. This year's faculty includes fiction writers Richard Bausch, Tony Earley, Adrianne Harun, Randall Kenan, Jill McCorkle, Alice McDermott, Tim O'Brien, Christine Schutt, Allen Wier, and Steve Yarbrough; and poets Daniel Anderson, Claudia Emerson, B.H. Fairchild, Andrew Hudgins, Maurice Manning, Charles Martin, Mary Jo Salter, and A.E. Stallings. Dan O'Brien and Paula Vogel will lead the playwriting workshop. Erin McGraw and Wyatt Prunty will read from their work. The conference fee reflects but two-thirds of the actual cost to attend. Additional funding is awarded to fellows and scholars."

COSTS/ACCOMMODATIONS Participants are housed in single rooms in university dormitories. Bathrooms are shared by small groups. $1,000 for tuition and $800 for room, board, and activity costs

THE SOUTHAMPTON WRITERS CONFERENCE

(631)632-5030. **E-mail:** southamptonarts@stonybrook.edu. **Website:** www.stonybrook.edu/southampton/mfa/summer/cwl_home.html. 2015 dates: July 8-19. "Since 1976, the Southampton Writers Conference has brought together writers at all stages of their careers with world-class novelists, essayists, editors, poets and children's book authors for lectures, readings, panels and workshops. All writers are welcome to attend the Conference, including those who seek a 12-day writers residency in the Hamptons. This year's offerings include a 5-part craft lecture series with Roger Rosenblatt. Admission to a 5-day writing workshop is competitive and requires additional application materials."

SOUTH CAROLINA WRITERS WORKSHOP

4840 Forest Drive, Suite 6B: PMB 189, Columbia SC 29206. **E-mail:** scwwliaison@gmail.com; scww2013@gmail.com. **Website:** www.myscww.org. Conference in October held at the Hilton Myrtle Beach Resort in Myrtle Beach, SC. Held almost every year. Conference duration: 3 days. The conference features critique sessions, open mic readings, presentations from agents and editors and more. The conference features more than 50 different workshops for writers to choose from, dealing with all subjects of writing craft, writing business, getting an agent and more. Agents will be in attendance.

SOUTH COAST WRITERS CONFERENCE

Southwestern Oregon Community College, P.O. Box 590, 29392 Ellensburg Ave., Gold Beach OR 97444. (541)247-2741. **Fax:** (541)247-6247. **E-mail:** scwc@socc.edu. **Website:** www.socc.edu/scwriters. Annual conference held Presidents Day weekend in February. Conference duration: 2 days. Covers fiction, poetry, children's, nature, songwriting, and marketing. Melissa Hart is the next scheduled keynote speaker, and presenters include Stevan Allred, Mark Bennion, Dan Berne, Mark Graham, Nina Kiriki Hoffman, Elena Passarello, Liz Prato, Jeffrey Shultz, Tess Thompson.

ADDITIONAL INFORMATION See website for cost and additional details.

STEAMBOAT SPRINGS WRITERS CONFERENCE

Steamboat Springs Arts Council, Eleanor Bliss Center for the Arts at the Depot, 1001 13th St., Steamboat Springs CO 80487. (970)879-9008. **Fax:** (970)879-8138. **E-mail:** info@steamboatwriters.com. **Website:** www.steamboatwriters.com. **Contact:** Susan de Wardt. Writers' workshops geared toward intermediate levels. Open to professionals and amateurs alike.

COSTS/ACCOMMODATIONS Tuition: $60 early registration, $75 after May 16

ADDITIONAL INFORMATION For additional information, please consult the website.

SUMMER WRITING PROGRAM

Naropa University, 2130 Arapahoe Ave., Boulder CO 80302. (303)245-4862. **Fax:** (303)546-5287. **E-mail:** swpr@naropa.edu. **Website:** www.naropa.edu/swp. **Contact:** Kyle Pivarnik, special projects manager. Annual event in summer. Workshop duration: 4 weeks. Average attendance: 250. Offers college credit. Accepts inquiries by e-mail, phone. With 13 workshops to choose from each of the 4 weeks of the program, students may study poetry, prose, hybrid/cross-genre writing, small press printing, or book arts. Site: All workshops, panels, lectures and readings are hosted on the Naropa University main campus. Located in downtown Boulder, the campus is within easy walking distance of restaurants, shopping, and the scenic Pearl Street Mall.

ADDITIONAL INFORMATION Writers can elect to take the Summer Writing Program for noncredit, graduate, or undergraduate credit. The registration procedure varies, so consider whether or not you'll be taking the SWP for academic credit. All participants can elect to take any combination of the first, second, third, and/or fourth weeks. To request a catalog of upcoming program or to find additional information, visit naropa.edu/swp. Naropa University also welcomes participants with disabilities.

TAOS SUMMER WRITERS' CONFERENCE

Department of English Language and Literature, MSC 03 2170, 1 University of New Mexico, Albuquerque NM 87131-0001. **E-mail:** swarner@unm.edu. **Website:** taosconf.unm.edu. **Contact:** Sharon Oard Warner. Annual conference held in July. 2015 dates: July 12-19. Offers workshops and master classes in the novel, short story, poetry, creative nonfiction, memoir, prose style, screenwriting, humor writing, yoga and writing, literary translation, book proposal, the query letter and revision.Participants may also schedule a consultation with a visiting agent/editor.

COSTS/ACCOMMODATIONS Week-long workshop registration $700, weekend workshop registration $400, master classes between $1,350 and $1,625, publishing consultations are $175.

UNIVERSITY OF NORTH DAKOTA WRITERS CONFERENCE

(701)777-2393. **Fax:** (701)777-2373. **E-mail:** crystal.alberts@email.und.edu. **Website:** http://und.edu/orgs/writers-conference. **Contact:** Crystal Alberts, director. Location: the University of North Dakota Memorial Union, which has a variety of small rooms and a 600-seat main hall. Average attendance: 3,000-5,000. "Some individual events have as few as 20, some over 1,000." Annual event of 3-5 days. 2015 dates: March 25-27. Offers panels, readings, and films focused around a specific theme. Almost all events take place in the UND Memorial Union, which has a variety of small rooms and a 1,000-seat main hall. Past speakers include Art Spiegelman, Truman Capote, Sir Salman Rushdie, Allen Ginsberg, Alice Walker, and Louise Erdrich.

COSTS/ACCOMMODATIONS Accommodations available at area hotels. Information on overnight accommodations available on website. All events are free and open to the public. Donations accepted.

ADDITIONAL INFORMATION Schedule and other information available on website.

WESLEYAN WRITERS CONFERENCE

Wesleyan University, 294 High St., Room 207, Middletown CT 06459. (860)685-3604. **Fax:** (860)685-2441. **E-mail:** agreene@wesleyan.edu. **Website:** www.wesleyan.edu/writing/conference. Annual conference. 2015 dates: June 10-14. Average attendance: 100. Focuses on the novel, fiction techniques, short stories, poetry, screenwriting, nonfiction, literary journalism, memoir, mixed media work and publishing. The conference is held on the campus of Wesleyan University, in the hills overlooking the Connecticut River. Features a faculty of award-winning writers, seminars and readings of new fiction, poetry, nonfiction and mixed media forms - as well as guest lectures on a range of topics including publishing. Both new and experienced writers are welcome. Participants may attend seminars in all genres. Speakers have included Esmond Harmsworth (Zachary Schuster Agency), Daniel Mandel (Sanford J. Greenburger Associates), Amy Williams (ICM and Collins McCormick), and many others. Agents will be speaking and available for meetings with attendees. Participants are often successful in finding agents and publishers for their mss. Wesleyan participants are also frequently featured in the anthology *Best New American Voices*.

COSTS/ACCOMMODATIONS Meals are provided on campus. Lodging is available on campus or in town.

ADDITIONAL INFORMATION Ms critiques are available, but not required.

WESTERN RESERVE WRITERS & FREELANCE CONFERENCE

7700 Clocktower Dr., Kirtland OH 44094. (440)525-7812. **E-mail:** deencr@aol.com. **Website:** www.deannaadams.com. **Contact:** Deanna Adams, director/conference coordinator. Biannual. Last conference held September 27, 2014. Conference duration: 1 day or half-day. Average attendance: 120. "The Western Reserve Writers Conferences are designed for all writers, aspiring and professional, and offer presentations in all genres—nonfiction, fiction, poetry, essays, creative nonfiction, and the business of writing, including Web writing and successful freelance writing." Site: "Located in the main building of Lakeland Community College, the conference is easy to find and just off the I-90 freeway. The Fall 2013 conference featured top-notch presenters from newspapers and magazines, along with published authors, freelance writers, and professional editors. Presentations included 'Writing Believable Dialogue,' 'Creating a Sense of Place,' 'Writing Your Life Story,' 'First Fiction,' 'Writing and Researching Crime Stories,' as well as tips on submissions, getting books into stores, and storytelling for both fiction and nonfiction writers. Included throughout the day are one-on-one editing consults, Q&A panel, and book sale/author signings."

COSTS/ACCOMMODATIONS Fall all-day conference includes lunch: $105. Spring half-day conference, no lunch: $69.

ADDITIONAL INFORMATION Brochures for the conferences are available by January (for spring conference) and July (for fall). Also accepts inquiries by e-mail and phone.

WILDACRES WRITERS WORKSHOP

(336)255-8210. **E-mail:** judihill@aol.com. **Website:** www.wildacreswriters.com. **Contact:** Judi Hill, Director. 2015 summer workshop dates: July 4-11. Conference duration: 1 week. Average attendance: 100. Workshop focuses on novel, short story, flash fiction, poetry, and nonfiction. 10 on faculty include Ron Rash, Carrie Brown, Dr. Janice Fuller, Phillip Gerard, Luke Whisnant, Dr. Joe Clark, John Gregory Brown, Dr. Phebe Davidson, Lee Zacharias, and Vicki Lane. This group also has a week-long writing retreat that is different from the workshop.

COSTS/ACCOMMODATIONS The current price is $790. Check the website for more info.

ADDITIONAL INFORMATION Include a 1-page writing sample with your registration. See the website for information.

WINTER POETRY & PROSE GETAWAY

(888)887-2105. **E-mail:** info@wintergetaway.com; amanda@murphywriting.com. **Website:** www.wintergetaway.com. **Contact:** Peter Murphy. Annual January conference at the Jersey Shore. 2016 dates: January 15-18. "This is not your typical writers' conference. Advance your craft and energize your writing at the Winter Getaway. Enjoy challenging and supportive workshops, insightful feedback, and encouraging community. Choose from small, intensive workshops in memoir, novel, YA, nonfiction, and poetry."

COSTS/ACCOMMODATIONS See website or call for current fee information.

ADDITIONAL INFORMATION Previous faculty has included Julianna Baggott, Christian Bauman, Laure-Anne Bosselaar, Kurt Brown, Mark Doty (National Book Award winner), Stephen Dunn (Pulitzer Prize winner), Dorianne Laux, Carol Plum-Ucci, James Richardson, Mimi Schwartz, Terese Svoboda, and more.

WRITER'S DIGEST CONFERENCES

F+W Media, Inc., 10151 Carver Rd., Suite 200, Blue Ash OH 45242. **E-mail:** jill.ruesch@fwmedia.com. **E-mail:** phil.sexton@fwmedia.com. **Website:** www.writersdigestconference.com. The Writer's Digest conferences feature an amazing line up of speakers to help writers with the craft and business of writing. Each calendar year typically features multiple conferences around the country. In 2015, the New York conference will be July 31 - Aug 2. The most popular feature of the east coast conference is the agent pitch slam, in which potential authors are given the ability to pitch their books directly to agents. For the 2015 conference, there will be more than 50 agents in attendance. For more details, see the website.

COSTS/ACCOMMODATIONS A block of rooms at the event hotel are reserved for guests. Cost varies by location and year. There are typically different pricing options for those who wish to stay for the entire event vs. daylong passes.

WRITING WORKSHOPS AT CASTLE HILL

10 Meetinghouse Rd., P.O. Box 756, Truro MA 02666. (508)349-7511. **Fax:** (508)349-7513. **E-mail:** info@castlehill.org. **Website:** www.castlehill.org/workshop-writing.html. Workshops about poetry, fiction, narrative nonfiction, memoir, and more; these writing workshops are geared toward intermediate and advanced levels. **Open to students.** The dates, courses, and instructors change each year, so check the website for individual details of upcoming events. Held at the Truro Center for the Arts at Castle Hill in Massachusetts.

THE HELENE WURLITZER FOUNDATION

P.O. Box 1891, Taos NM 87571. (575)758-2413. **Fax:** (575)758-2559. **E-mail:** hwf@taosnet.com. **Website:** www.wurlitzerfoundation.org. **Contact:** Michael A. Knight, executive director.

COSTS/ACCOMMODATIONS "Provides individual housing in fully furnished studio/houses (casitas), rent and utility free. Artists are responsible for transportation to and from Taos, their meals, and materials for their work. Bicycles are provided upon request."

ORGANIZATIONS

//

There are many organizations of value to poets. These groups may sponsor workshops and contests, stage readings, publish anthologies and chapbooks or spread the word about publishing opportunities. A few provide economic assistance or legal advice. The best thing organizations offer, though, is a support system to which poets can turn for a pep talk, a hard-nosed (but sympathetic) critique of a manuscript or simply the comfort of talking and sharing with others who understand the challenges, and joys, of writing poetry.

Whether national, regional or as local as your library or community center, each organization has something special to offer. The listings in this section reflect the membership opportunities available to poets with a variety of organizations. Some groups provide certain services to both members and nonmembers.

To find out more about groups in your area (including those that may not be listed in *Poet's Market*), contact your YMCA, community center, local colleges and universities, public library and bookstores (and don't forget newspapers and the Internet). If you can't find a group that suits your needs, consider starting one yourself. You might be surprised to discover there are others in your locality who would welcome the encouragement, feedback and moral support of a writer's group.

92ND STREET Y UNTERBERG POETRY CENTER

1395 Lexington Ave., New York NY 10128. (212)415-5500. **E-mail:** unterberg@92y.org. **Website:** www.92y.org/poetry. The Unterberg Poetry Center offers "students of all ages the opportunity to hone their skills as writers and deepen their appreciation as readers."Offers annual series of readings by major literary figures (weekly readings late September through May), writing workshops, master classes in fiction and poetry, and lectures and literary seminars. Also co-sponsors the "Discovery"/Boston Review Poetry Contest.

THE ACADEMY OF AMERICAN POETS

75 Maiden Ln., Suite 901, New York NY 10038. (212)274-0343. **Fax:** (212)274-9427. **E-mail:** academy@poets.org. **Website:** www.poets.org. The Academy of American Poets was founded to support the nation's poets at all stages of their careers and to foster the appreciation of contemporary poetry. Administers The Walt Whitman Award; The James Laughlin Award; The Harold Morton Landon Translation Award; The Lenore Marshall Poetry Prize; The Raiziss/de Palchi Translation Award; and The Wallace Stevens Award. Also awards The Fellowship of the Academy of American Poets and The University & College Poetry Prizes. Publishes *American Poet*, an informative semiannual journal sent to all Academy members. The Academy's other programs include National Poetry Month (April), the largest literary celebration in the world; the Poetry Audio Archive, a 700-volume audio library capturing the voices of contemporary American poets for generations to come; an annual series of poetry readings and special events; and Poets.org, which includes thousands of poems, hundreds of essays and interviews, lesson plans for teachers, a National Poetry Almanac, a national Calendar of Events, and the National Poetry Map.

AMERICAN BOOKSELLERS FOUNDATION FOR FREE EXPRESSION

19 Fulton St., Suite 407, New York NY 10038. (212)587-4025 ext. 15. **Fax:** (212)587-2436. **E-mail:** chris@abffe.com. **Website:** www.abffe.com. "The American Booksellers Foundation for Free Expression is the bookseller's voice in the fight against censorship. Founded by the American Booksellers Association, ABFFE's mission is to promote and protect the free exchange of ideas, particularly those contained in books, by opposing restrictions on the freedom of speech; issuing statements on significant free expression controversies; participating in legal cases involving First Amendment rights; collaborating with other groups with an interest in free speech; providing education about the importance of free expression to booksellers, other members of the book industry, politicians, the press and the public." Additional information online.

AMERICAN HAIKU ARCHIVES

California State Library, Library & Courts II Bldg, 900 N St., Sacramento CA 95814. **E-mail:** welchm@aol.com. **Website:** www.americanhaikuarchives.org. **Contact:** Michael Dylan Welch. The American Haiku Archives is "the world's largest public collection of haiku and related poetry books and papers outside Japan." This repository is housed at the California State Library in Sacramento, California, and is dedicated to preserving the history of North American haiku. Materials are publicly available for research purposes through the library's California History Room. The American Haiku Archives actively seeks donations of books, journals, recordings, letters, ephemera, and personal papers relating to haiku poetry in all languages, but especially North American languages. The American Haiku Archives also appoints an honorary curator every July for a one-year term. The intent of this appointment is to honor leading haiku poets, translators, or scholars for their accomplishments or service in support of haiku poetry as a literary art. Past honorary curators have been Gary Snyder, Stephen Addiss, George Swede, H. F. Noyes, Hiroaki Sato, Francine Porad, Makoto Ueda, William J. Higginson, Leroy Kanterman, Lorraine Ellis Harr, Robert Spiess, Cor van den Heuvel, Jerry Kilbride, and Elizabeth Searle Lamb. Additional information online.

THE AMERICAN POETS' CORNER

The Cathedral Church of St. John the Divine, 1047 Amsterdam Ave., New York NY 10025. (212)316-7540. **Website:** www.stjohndivine.org. Initiated in 1984 with memorials for Emily Dickinson, Walt Whitman, and Washington Irving. Similar in concept to the British Poets' Corner in Westminster Abbey, was established and dedicated to memorialize this country's greatest writers. A board of electors chooses one deceased author each year for inclusion in The American Poets' Corner. The Cathedral is also home to the Muriel Rukeyser Poetry Wall, a public space for posting poems, which was dedicated in 1976 by Ms. Rukeyser and the Cathedral's Dean. Send poems for the Poetry Wall to the above address. Designated a National Poetry Landmark by the Academy of American Poets.

ARIZONA AUTHORS ASSOCIATION

6145 West Echo Ln., Glendale AZ 85302. (623)847-9343. **E-mail:** info@azauthors.com. **Website:** www.azauthors.com. **Contact:** Toby Heathcotte, president. Purpose of organization: to offer professional, educational and social opportunities to writers and authors, and serve as a network. Members must be authors, writers working toward publication, agents, publishers, publicists, printers, illustrators, etc. Publishes bimonthly newsletter and *Arizona Literary Magazine*. Sponsors Annual Literary Contest in poetry, essays, short stories, novels, and published books with cash prizes and awards bestowed at a public banquet. Winning entries are also published or advertised in the *Arizona Literary Magazine*. First and second place winners in poetry, essay and short story categories are entered in the Pushcart Prize. Learn more online.

THE AUTHORS GUILD, INC.

31 E. 32nd St., 7th Floor, New York NY 10016. (212)564-5904. **Fax:** (212)564-5363. **E-mail:** staff@authorsguild.org. **Website:** www.authorsguild.org. **Contact:** Mary Rasenberger, executive director. Purpose of organization: to offer services and materials intended to help authors with the business and legal aspects of their work, including contract problems, copyright matters, freedom of expression and taxation. Guild has 8,000 members. Qualifications for membership: Must be book author published by an established American publisher within 7 years or any author who has had 3 works (fiction or nonfiction) published by a magazine or magazines of general circulation in the last 18 months. Associate membership also available. Different levels of membership include: associate membership with all rights except voting available to an author who has a firm contract offer or is currently negotiating a royalty contract from an established American publisher. "The Guild offers free contract reviews to its members. The Guild conducts several symposia each year at which experts provide information, offer advice and answer questions on subjects of interest and concern to authors. Typical subjects have been the rights of privacy and publicity, libel, wills and estates, taxation, copyright, editors and editing, the art of interviewing, standards of criticism and book reviewing. Transcripts of these symposia are published and circulated to members. The *Authors Guild Bulletin*, a quarterly journal, contains articles on matters of interest to writers, reports of Guild activities, contract surveys, advice on problem clauses in contracts, transcripts of Guild and League symposia and information on a variety of professional topics. Subscription included in the cost of the annual dues."

BOWERY POETRY CLUB

308 Bowery St., New York NY 10012. (212)614-0505. **Fax:** (212)614-8539. **E-mail:** mail@bowerypoetry.com. The Bowery Poetry Club and Cafe hosts regional open mic and poetry events. "Hosting between 20 and 30 shows a week, the Bowery Poetry Club (BPC) is proud of our place in the lineage of populist art: The Yiddish theater, burlesque, vaudeville, beat poetry, jazz, and punk that gave the Bowery its name." Offers workshops for adults and young poets. "Each Tuesday night at 6:30 pm touring Slam poets give a craft talk as part of our WordShop series." Nationally known writers give readings that are open to the public. Sponsors open mic readings for the public each Tuesday night at 7 pm as part of the Urbana Poetry Slam; format: open mic, featured poet, poetry slam. See website for more information and schedule.

BRIGHT HILL LITERARY CENTER

94 Church St., Treadwell NY 13846. (607)829-5055. **E-mail:** wordthur@stny.rr.com. **Website:** www.brighthillpress.org. Bright Hill Literary Center serves residents in the Catskill Mountain region, greater New York, and throughout the U.S. Includes the Bright Hill Library and Internet Center, with "thousands of volumes of literary journals, literary prose and poetry, literary criticism and biography, theater, reference, art, and children's books available for reading and research (noncirculating, for the time being). Wireless Internet access is available." Sponsors workshops for children and adults. Learn more online.

☺ BURNABY WRITERS' SOCIETY

6584 Deer Lake Ave., Burnaby BC V5G 3T7, Canada. **E-mail:** info@bws.bc.ca. **Website:** burnabywritersnews.blogspot.com. Corresponding membership in the society, including a newsletter subscription, is open to anyone, anywhere. Currently has 100 members. Members of the society stage regular public readings of their own work. Sponsors open mic readings for the public. Sponsors a poetry contest open

ORGANIZATIONS

to British Columbia residents. Competition receives about 100-200 entries/year. Past contest winners include Mildred Tremblay, Irene Livingston, and Kate Braid. Additional information online.

COLUMBINE POETS OF COLORADO

P.O. Box 6245, Broomfield CO 80021. (303)431-6774. **E-mail:** anitajg5@aol.com. **Website:** columbinepoetsofcolorado.com. **Contact:** Anita Jepson-Gilbert, secretary/treasurer. Statewide organization open to anyone interested in poetry. Currently has around 100 members in 3 Chapters, now in Denver, Salida, and Loveland, CO. An affiliate of the National Federation of State Poetry Societies (NFSPS). Offerings for the Denver Foothills Chapter include weekly workshops and monthly critiques. Sponsors contests, awards for students and adults, an Annual Poetry Fest and some publications. Additional information available with SASE, by phone or e-mail.

CONNECTICUT POETRY SOCIETY

P.O. Box 702, Manchester CT 06040. **E-mail:** connpoetry@comcast.net. **Website:** ctpoetry.net. **Contact:** Tony Fusco, president. The Connecticut Poetry Society is a nonprofit organization dedicated to the promotion and enjoyment of poetry through chapter meetings, contests, and poetry-related events. Statewide organization open to non-Connecticut residents. Currently has about 175 members. Membership benefits include automatic membership in The National Federation of State Poetry Societies (NFSPS); a free copy of *The Connecticut River Review*, a national poetry journal published by CPS; opportunity to publish in *Long River Run II*, a members-only poetry journal; quarterly CPS and NFSPS newsletters; annual April poetry celebration; and membership in any of 10 state chapters. Sponsors conferences and workshops. Sponsors The Connecticut River Review Annual Poetry Contest, The Brodinsky-Brodine Contest, The Winchell Contest, and The Lynn Decaro High School Competition. Members and nationally known writers give readings that are open to the public. Members meet monthly. Additional information online.

COUNCIL OF LITERARY MAGAZINES AND PRESSES (CLMP)

154 Christopher St., Suite 3C, New York NY 10014. (212)741-9110. **E-mail:** info@clmp.org. **Website:** www.clmp.org. "Dedicated to supporting and actively promoting the field of independent literary publishing." Open to publishers who are primarily literary in na-ture, have published at least 1 issue/title prior to applying for membership, publish at least 1 issue/title annually on an ongoing basis, have a minimum print run of 500 per issue or title, do not charge authors a fee, are not primarily self-publishing, and do not primarily publish children's/students' work. Currently has over 500 members. Levels of membership/dues: based on publishing organization's annual budget. See website for complete member application process. Benefits include free and discounted monographs, subscription to e-mail listserves and online databases, annual copy of *The Literary Press and Magazine Directory*, plus many valuable services. Additional information online.

FURIOUS FLOWER POETRY CENTER

500 Cardinal Dr., MSC3802, James Madison University, Harrisonburg VA 22807. (540)568-8883. **Fax:** (540)568-8888. **E-mail:** gabbinjv@jmu.edu. **Website:** www.jmu.edu/furiousflower. **Contact:** Joanne Gabbin, executive director. The mission of the Furious Flower Poetry Center is to advance the genre of African American Poetry by providing opportunities for education, research, and publication. Furious Flower Poetry Center serves as a resource for the campus and local Harrisonburg community. The Center hosts visiting poets, sponsors poetry workshops for emerging poets, holds an annual poetry camp for children in the community, and produces scholarly texts, videos and DVDs on African American poetry. Furious Flower has sponsored two decade-defining conferences celebrating the African American poetic tradition.

GEORGIA POETRY SOCIETY

P.O. Box 2184, Columbia GA 31902. **E-mail:** gps@georgiapoetrysociety.org. **Website:** www.georgiapoetrysociety.org. Statewide organization open to any person who is in accord with the objectives to secure fuller public recognition of the art of poetry, stimulate an appreciation of poetry, and enhance the writing and reading of poetry. Currently has 200 members. Membership includes affiliation with NFSPS. Holds at least 1 workshop annually. Contests are sponsored throughout the year, some for members only. "Our contests have specific general rules, which should be followed to avoid the disappointment of disqualification. See the website for details." Publishes Georgia Poetry Society Newsletter, a quarterly, and *The Reach of Song*, an annual anthology devoted to contest-winning poems and member works. Each quarterly meeting (open to the public) features at least 1 poet of regional prominence. Also sponsors a monthly open mic at the Columbus Library (Macon Rd) in Columbus, GA (open to the public). Sponsors Poetry in the Schools project. Additional information online.

GREATER CINCINNATI WRITERS' LEAGUE

E-mail: ignatius@gmail.com. **Website:** www.cincinnatiwritersleague.org. **Contact:** Bucky Ignatius, president. Purpose is to "support those who write poetry in the Cincinnati area and to promote excellence in poetry writing. We believe in creative freedom, with open, constructive critique as a learning tool." Offerings include monthly meetings with critique or a workshop on a subject of interest to poets. Poems submitted by members are critiqued by guest critics (published poets who are also teachers or professors of poetry and/or creative writing). Group discussion of critiqued poems follows. Sponsors fall poetry contest with cash prizes; also sponsors a category of the annual Ohio Poetry Day contest with cash prizes. Occasionally publishes an anthology. Members occasionally give readings that are open to the public (see website for meeting time and place). Additional information online.

HAIKU SOCIETY OF AMERICA

1921 Joseph St., New Orleans LA 70115. **E-mail:** david1gerard@hotmail.com. **Website:** www.hsa-haiku.org. The Haiku Society of America is composed of haiku poets, editors, critics, publishers, and enthusiasts dedicated to "promoting the creation and appreciation of haiku and related forms (haibun, haiga, renku, senryu, sequences, and tanka) among its members and the public." Currently has over 800 members. Membership benefits include a year's subscription to the Society's journal, *Frogpond*, and to the quarterly HSA newsletter *Ripples*; the annual information sheet; an annual address/e-mail list of HSA members; and eligibility to submit work to the members' anthology. Administers the following annual awards: The Harold G. Henderson Awards for haiku, The Gerald Brady Awards for senryu, The Bernard Lionel Einbond Awards for renku, The Merit Book Awards, and The Nicholas Virgilio Haiku Awards for youth. Additional information online.

THE HUDSON VALLEY WRITERS' CENTER

300 Riverside Dr., Sleepy Hollow NY 10591. (914)332-5953. **Fax:** (914)332-4825. **E-mail:** info@writerscenter.org. **Website:** www.reading.org. **Contact:** Jo Ann Clark, executive director. "The Hudson Valley Writers' Center is a nonprofit organization devoted to furthering the literary arts in our region. Its mission is to promote the appreciation of literary excellence, to stimulate and nurture the creation of literary works in all sectors of the population, and to bring the diverse works of gifted poets and prose artists to the attention of the public." Open to all. Currently has 350 members. Offerings include public readings by established and emerging poets/writers, workshops and classes, monthly open mic nights, paid and volunteer outreach opportunities, and an annual chapbook competition with Slapering Hol Press. Additional information online.

INTERNATIONAL READING ASSOCIATION

P.O. Box 8139, Newark DE 19714. (302)731-1600 ext. 293. **Fax:** (302)731-1057. **E-mail:** councils@reading.org. **Website:** www.reading.org. "The International Reading Association seeks to promote high levels of literacy for all by improving the quality of reading instruction through studying the reading process and teaching techniques; serving as a clearinghouse for the dissemination of reading research through conferences, journals, and other publications; and actively encouraging the lifetime reading habit. Its goals include professional development, advocacy, partnerships, research, and global literacy development." Sponsors annual convention. Publishes a newsletter called "Reading Today." Sponsors a number of awards and fellowships. More information online.

INTERNATIONAL WOMEN'S WRITING GUILD

International Women's Writing Guild, 274 Madison Ave., Suite 1202, New York NY 10016. (917)720-6959. **E-mail:** iwwgquestions@gmail.com. **Website:** www.iwwg.org. **Contact:** Kristin Rath, director of operations. IWWG is "a network for the personal and professional empowerment of women through writing." Open to any woman connected to the written word regardless of professional portfolio. "IWWG sponsors several annual conferences a year in all areas of the U.S. The major conference is held in June of each year at Yale University in New Haven, Connecticut. It is a week-long conference attracting 350 women internationally." Also publishes a 32-page newsletter, *Network*, 4 times/year; offers dental and vision insurance at group rates, referrals to literary agents.

IOWA POETRY ASSOCIATION

2325 61st St., Des Moines IA 50322. (515)279-1106. **Website:** www.iowapoetry.com. **Contact:** Lucille Morgan Wilson, editor. Statewide organization open to "anyone interested in poetry, with a residence or valid address in the state of Iowa." Offerings include "semiannual workshops to which a poem may be sent in advance for critique; annual contest--also open to nonmembers--with no entry fee; IPA Newsletter, published 5 or 6 times/year, including a quarterly national publication listing of contest opportunities; and an annual poetry anthology, *Lyrical Iowa*, containing prize-winning and high-ranking poems from contest entries. No requirement for purchase to ensure publication." Semiannual workshops "are the only 'meetings' of the association." Additional information online.

THE KENTUCKY STATE POETRY SOCIETY

E-mail: libby_jones@berea.edu. **Website:** www.kys-tatepoetrysociety.org. **Contact:** Libby Jones, president. Regional organization open to all. Member of The National Federation of State Poetry Societies (NFSPS). Currently has about 230 members. Offerings include association with other poets; information on contests and poetry happenings across the state and nation; annual state and national contests; national and state annual conventions with workshops, selected speakers, and open poetry readings. Sponsors workshops, contests, awards. Membership includes the quarterly KSPS Newsletter. Also includes a quarterly newsletter, *Strophes*, of the NFSPS; and the KSPS journal, *Pegasus*, published 3 times/year: a Spring/ Summer and Fall/ Winter issue which solicits good poetry for publication (need not be a member to submit), and a Prize Poems issue of 1st Place contest winners in over 30 categories. Members or nationally known writers give readings that are open to the public. Members meet annually. More information online.

☺ THE LEAGUE OF CANADIAN POETS

312-192 Spadina Ave., Toronto ON M5T 2C2, Canada. (416)504-1657. **E-mail:** readings@poets.ca. **Website:** www.poets.ca. **Contact:** Ingrel Madrus, readings/membership coordinator. A nonprofit national association of professional publishing and performing poets in Canada. Its purpose is "to enhance the status of poets and nurture a professional poetic community to facilitate the teaching of Canadian poetry at all levels of education and to develop the audience for poetry by encouraging publication, performance, and recognition of Canadian poetry nationally and internationally. As well as providing members and the public with many benefits and services, the League speaks for poets on many issues such as freedom of expression, Public Lending Right, CanCopy, contract advice, and grievance." Open to all Canadian citizens and landed immigrants; applications are assessed by a membership committee. Currently has 600 members. Membership benefits include a 1-year subscription to monthly e-newsletter, discount on Gift Shop purchases, listing in online members' catalog, and more (benefits increase with membership level). Sponsors The Pat Lowther Memorial Award (for a book of poetry by a Canadian woman published in the preceding year; $1,000 CAD prize) and The Gerald Lampert Memorial Award (recognizes the best first book of poetry published by a Canadian in the preceding year; $1,000 CAD). Additional information online.

THE LOFT LITERARY CENTER

Suite 200, Open Book, 1011 Washington Ave. S., Minneapolis MN 55415. (612)215-2575. **E-mail:** loft@loft.org. **Website:** www.loft.org. "The Loft is the largest and most comprehensive literary center in the country, serving both writers and readers with a variety of readings, Spoken Word performances, educational programs, contests and grants, and writing facilities." Supporting members receive benefits including discounted tuition, admission charges, and contest fees; check-out privileges at The Loft's Rachel Anne Gaschott Resource Library; rental access to the Book Club Meeting Room and writers' studios and more. Additional information online.

MASSACHUSETTS STATE POETRY SOCIETY

64 Harrison Ave., Lynn MA 01905. **E-mail:** msps.jc-maes@comcast.net. **Website:** mastatepoetrysociety.tripod.com. Dedicated to the writing and appreciation of poetry and promoting the art form. Statewide organization open to anyone with an interest in poetry. Currently has 200 members. Member benefits include subscription to *Bay State Echo*, published 5 times/year with members' news and announcements; members-only contests; round-robin critique groups; members-only annual anthology; workshops at society meetings; and automatic membership in National Federation of State Poetry Societies (NFSPS). Sponsors contests open to all poets. Guidelines online.

Members or nationally known writers give readings that are open to the public. Sponsors open mic readings for members and the public for National Poetry Day. Members meet 5 times/year. Additional information online.

MISSISSIPPI POETRY SOCIETY, INC.

608 N. Pearl St., Luka MS 38852. **E-mail:** judydavies@cableone.net. **Website:** misspoetry.net. **Contact:** Judy Davies, president. Purpose is "to foster interest in the writing of poetry through a study of poetry and poetic form; to provide an opportunity for, and give recognition to, individual creative efforts relating to poetry; and to create an audience for poetry; and suggest or otherwise make known markets and contests for poetry to its members." Statewide organization, affiliated with the National Federation of State Poetry Societies (NFSPS), consisting of 3 branches open to "anyone who writes poetry or is interested in fostering the interests of poetry." Currently has 100 members. Offerings include monthly meetings, annual contests, an annual awards banquet, and opportunities to have poems critiqued in sessions at state and branch meetings. State also holds a 1-day Mini-Festival in the fall and an annual 2-day Spring Festival; includes noted speakers and contests. Publishes bimonthly newsletter *Magnolia Muse* (members who win places in contests are published in *The Mississippi Poetry Journal*; student winners are published in *Fledglings*). Additional information online.

MOUNTAIN WRITERS SERIES

Mountain Writers Center, 2804 S.E. 27th Ave., #2, Portland OR 97202. **E-mail:** pdxmws@mountainwriters.org. **Website:** www.mountainwriters.org. "Mountain Writers Series is an independent nonprofit organization dedicated to supporting writers, audiences, and other sponsors by promoting literature and literacy through artistic and educational literary arts events in the Pacific Northwest." Currently has about 150 members. Mountain Writers Series offers intensive one-day and 2-day workshops, weekend master classes, 5-week, 8-week, and 10-week courses about writing. Sponsors readings that are open to the public. Nationally and internationally known writers are sponsored by the Mountain Writers Series Northwest Regional Residencies Program (reading tours) and the campus readings program (Pulitzer Prize winners, Nobel Prize winners, MacArthur Fellows, etc.). Additional information online.

NATIONAL FEDERATION OF STATE POETRY SOCIETIES (NFSPS)

E-mail: paperlesspoetsonline@hotmail.com. **Website:** www.nfsps.com. "NFSPS is a nonprofit organization exclusively educational and literary. Its purpose is to recognize the importance of poetry with respect to national cultural heritage. It is dedicated solely to the furtherance of poetry on the national level and serves to unite poets in the bonds of fellowship and understanding." Currently has 7,000 members. Any poetry group located in a state not already affiliated, but interested in affiliating with NFSPS, may contact the membership chairman (see website). In a state where no valid group exists, help may also be obtained by individuals interested in organizing a poetry group for affiliation. Most reputable state poetry societies are members of the National Federation and advertise their various poetry contests through the NFSPS quarterly newsletter *Strophes*. NFSPS holds an annual 3-day convention in a different state each year with workshops, an awards banquet, and addresses by nationally known poets. Sponsors an annual 50-category national contest. Additional information online.

NATIONAL WRITERS ASSOCIATION

10940 S. Parker Rd., #508, Parker CO 80138. (303)841-0246. **Fax:** (303)841-2607. **E-mail:** natlwritersassn@hotmail.com. **Website:** www.nationalwriters.com. Association for freelance writers. Qualifications for membership: associate membership--must be serious about writing; professional membership--must be published and paid writer (cite credentials). Sponsors workshops/conferences: TV/screenwriting workshops, NWAF Annual Conferences, Literary Clearinghouse, editing and critiquing services, local chapters, National Writer's School. Open to non-members. Publishes industry news of interest to freelance writers; how-to articles; market information; member news and networking opportunities. Sponsors poetry contest; short story contest; article contest; novel contest. Awards cash for top 3 winners; books and/or certificates for other winners; honorable mention certificate places 5-10. Contests open to nonmembers.

NATIONAL WRITERS UNION

256 W. 38th St., Suite 703, New York NY 10018. (212)254-0279. **Fax:** (212)254-0673. **E-mail:** nwu@nwu.org. **Website:** www.nwu.org. Advocacy for freelance writers. Qualifications for membership: "Membership in the NWU is open to all qualified

writers, and no one shall be barred or in any manner prejudiced within the Union on account of race, age, sex, sexual orientation, disability, national origin, religion or ideology. You are eligible for membership if you have published a book, a play, three articles, five poems, one short story or an equivalent amount of newsletter, publicity, technical, commercial, government or institutional copy. You are also eligible for membership if you have written an equal amount of unpublished material and you are actively writing and attempting to publish your work." Holds workshops throughout the country. Members only section on website offers rich resources for freelance writers. Skilled contract advice and grievance help for members.

NEW HAMPSHIRE WRITERS' PROJECT

2500 North River Rd., Manchester NH 03106. (603)314-7980. **Fax:** (603)314-7981. **E-mail:** info@nhwritersproject.org. **Website:** www.nhwritersproject.org. Statewide organization open to writers at all levels in all genres. Currently has 600+ members. Offerings include workshops, seminars, an annual conference, and a literary calendar. Sponsors daylong workshops and 4- to 6-week intensive courses. Also sponsors the biennial New Hampshire Literary Awards for outstanding literary achievement (including The Jane Kenyon Award for Outstanding Book of Poetry). Publishes *NH Writer*, a quarterly newsletter for and about New Hampshire writers. Members and nationally known writers give readings that are open to the public. Additional information online.

THE NORTH CAROLINA POETRY SOCIETY

NCPS, 3814 Hulon Dr., Durham NC 27705. **Website:** www.ncpoetrysociety.org. The North Carolina Poetry Society holds poetry-related contests and gives away several awards each year, for both Adults and Students (which includes 3rd Graders all the way to University Undergraduates). Statewide organization open to non-NC residents. Purpose: to encourage the reading, writing, study, and publication of poetry. NCPS brings poets together in meetings that feature workshops, presentations by noted poets and publishers, book and contest awards, and an annual anthology of award-winning poems. Currently has 350 members from NC and beyond. Sponsors annual Poetry Contest with categories for adults and students. Contests are open to anyone, with small fee for nonmembers. Winning poems are published in *Pinesong*, NCPS's annual anthology. A free copy is given to all winners, who are also invited to read at Awards Day. NCPS also sponsors the annual Brockman-Campbell Book Award for a book of poetry over 20 pages by a North Carolina poet (native-born or current resident for 3 years. NCPS also cosponsors the Gilbert-Chappell Distinguished Poet Series with The North Carolina Center for the Book, for the purpose of mentoring young poets across the state. Additional information online.

NORTH CAROLINA WRITERS' NETWORK

P.O. Box 21591, Winston-Salem NC 27120. (336)293-8844. **E-mail:** mail@ncwriters.org. **Website:** www.ncwriters.org. Supports the work of writers, writers' organizations, independent bookstores, little magazines and small presses, and literary programming statewide. Currently has 1,000 members. Membership benefits include *The Writers' Network News*, a 24-page quarterly newsletter containing organizational news, trend in writing and publishing, and other literary material of interest to writers; and access to the NCWN online resources, other writers, workshops, writer's residencies, conferences, readings and competitions, and NCWN's critiquing and editing service. Annual fall conference features nationally known writers, publishers, and editors, held in a different North Carolina location each November. Sponsors competitions in short fiction, nonfiction, and poetry for North Carolina residents and NCWN members. Guidelines online.

OHIO POETRY ASSOCIATION

E-mail: chuck@ohiopoetryassn.org. **Website:** www.ohiopoetryassn.org. Promotes the art of poetry, and furthers the support of poets and others who support poetry. Statewide membership with additional members in several other states, Japan, and England. Affiliated with the National Federation of State Poetry Societies (NFSPS). Open to poets and writers of all ages and ability, as well as to non-writing lovers of poetry. Currently has about 215 members. Member benefits include regular contests; meeting/workshop participation; assistance with writing projects; networking; twice-yearly magazine, *Common Threads*, publishing only poems by members; quarterly Ohio Poetry Association Newsletter ; quarterly NFSPS newsletters (*Strophes*); automatic NFSPS membership; and contest information and lower entry fees for NFSPS contests. Members are automatically on the mailing list for Ohio Poetry Day contest guidelines (OPA financially supports Ohio Poetry Day). Individual chapters regularly host workshops and seminars. Members and nationally known writers give readings that are open to the public (at quarterly meetings; public is invited). Sponsors open mic readings for members and the public. Members meet quarterly (September, December, March, May). Additional information available online. "In short, OPA provides poets with opportunities to share info, critique, publish, sponsor contests, and just socialize."

PEN AMERICAN CENTER

588 Broadway, Suite 303, New York NY 10012. (212)334-1660. **Fax:** (212)334-2181. **E-mail:** info@pen.org. **Website:** www.pen.org. "An association of writers working to advance literature, to defend free expression, and to foster international literary fellowship. The standard qualification for a writer to become a member of PEN is publication of two or more books of a literary character, or one book generally acclaimed to be of exceptional distinction. Also eligible for membership: editors who have demonstrated commitment to excellence in their profession (usually construed as five years' service in book editing); translators who have published at least two book-length literary translations; playwrights whose works have been produced professionally; and literary essayists whose publications are extensive even if they have not yet been issued as a book. Candidates for membership may be nominated by a PEN member or they may nominate themselves with the support of two references from the literary community or from a current PEN member. PEN members receive a subscription to the PEN journal, the PEN Annual Report, and have access to medical insurance at group rates. Members living in the New York metropolitan and tri-state area, or near the Branches, are invited to PEN events throughout the year. Membership in PEN American Center includes reciprocal privileges in PEN American Center branches and in foreign PEN Centers for those traveling abroad. Application forms are available online. PEN American Center is the largest of the 141 centers of PEN International, the world's oldest human rights organization and the oldest international literary organization. PEN International was founded in 1921 to dispel national, ethnic, and racial hatreds and to promote understanding among all countries. PEN American Center, founded a year later, works to advance literature, to defend free expression, and to foster international literary fellowship. The Center has a membership of 3,400 distinguished writers, editors, and translators. In addition to defending writers in prison or in danger of imprisonment for their work, PEN American Center sponsors public literary programs and forums on current issues, sends prominent authors to inner-city schools to encourage reading and writing, administers literary prizes, promotes international literature that might otherwise go unread in the United States, and offers grants and loans to writers facing financial or medical emergencies."

PITTSBURGH POETRY EXCHANGE

P.O. Box 4279, Pittsburgh PA 15203. (412)481-POEM. **E-mail:** ppepoets@yahoo.com. **Website:** pghpoetryexchange.pghfree.net. **Contact:** Michael Wurster, coordinator. A community-based volunteer organization for local poets, it functions as a service organization and information exchange, conducting ongoing workshops, readings, forums, and other special events to promote poets and poetry. No dues or fees. "Any monetary contributions are voluntary, often from outside sources. We've managed not to let our reach exceed our grasp." Currently has about 30 members (with a mailing list of 400). Reading programs are primarily committed to local and area poets, with honorariums of $25-85. Sponsors a minimum of 3 major events each year in addition to a monthly workshop (first Monday, 8 p.m, City Books); these include reading programs in conjunction with community arts festivals, such as South Side Poetry in October--a series of readings throughout the evening at various shops, galleries, and bookstores. Poets from out of town may contact the Exchange for assistance in setting up readings at bookstores to help sell their books. "We have been partnering with Autumn House Press in co-sponsoring events and bringing some of its authors to town." Members meet on an ongoing basis, at least twice monthly. Additional information online. "Pittsburgh is a very exciting literary town."

⊙ POETRY BOOK SOCIETY

The Dutch House, 307-308 High Holborn, London WC1V 7LL, United Kingdom. **E-mail:** info@poetrybooks.co.uk. **Website:** www.poetrybooks.co.uk. **Contact:** Ms. Chris Holifield. A book club that promotes "the best newly published contemporary poetry to as wide an audience as possible." Membership: 2,200. All members receive a subscription to the quarterly *PBS Bulletin*, 25% discount on almost all poetry books published in the UK, and advance notice of poetry events; Full Members also receive 4 PBS Choice selections free. New members receive a welcome gift. The PBS selectors also recommend other books of special merit each quarter. Sponsors the T.S. Eliot Prize for the best new single author collection published in the UK and Ireland in the calendar year. The Poetry Book Society is subsidized by the Arts Council of England. Additional information online.

THE POETRY FOUNDATION

61 W. Superior St., Chicago IL 60654. (312)787-7070. **Fax:** (312)787-6650. **E-mail:** mail@poetryfoundation.org. **Website:** poetryfoundation.org. "The Poetry Foundation is an independent literary organization committed to a vigorous presence for poetry in our culture. It exists to discover and celebrate the best poetry and to place it before the largest possible audience. Initiatives include publishing *Poetry* magazine; distributing Ted Kooser's *American Life in Poetry* newspaper project; funding and promotion of Poetry Out Loud: National Recitation Contest (in partnership with the National Endowment for the Arts and state arts associations); *Poetry Everywhere*, a series of short poetry films airing on public television and on transportation systems across the country; *The Essential American Poets* podcast series featuring seminal recordings of major American Poets reading from their work, as selected by former Poet Laureate Donald Hall; and www.poetryfoundation.org, an award-winning comprehensive online resource for poetry featuring an archive of more than 6,500 poems by more than 600 classic and contemporary poets. The site also includes the poetry blog "Harriet," poetry-related articles, a bestseller list, video programming, a series of poetry podcasts, and reading guides about poets and poetry. The Poetry Foundation annually awards the Ruth Lilly Poetry Prize, of $100,000, and the Ruth Lilly Poetry Fellowships, 5 annual awards of $15,000 to young poets to support their further studies in poetry." More information online.

POETRY LIBRARY

The Saison Poetry Library, Level 5, Royal Festival Hall, London SE1 8XX, United Kingdom. (44)(207)921-0943/0664. **Fax:** (44)(207)921-0607. **E-mail:** info@poetrylibrary.org.uk. **Website:** www.poetrylibrary.org.uk. **Contact:** Chris McCabe, librarian. A "free public library of modern poetry. It contains a comprehensive collection of all British poetry published since 1912 and an international collection of poetry from all over the world, either written in or translated into English. As the United Kingdom's national library for poetry, it offers loan and information services and a large collection of poetry magazines, cassettes, compact discs, videos, records, poem posters, and cards; also press cuttings and photographs of poets."

THE POETRY SOCIETY

22 Betterton St., London WC2H 9BX, United Kingdom. (44)(207)420-9880. **E-mail:** info@poetrysociety.org.uk. **Website:** www.poetrysociety.org.uk. One of Britain's most dynamic arts organizations, with membership open to all. "The Poetry Society exists to help poets and poetry thrive in Britain today. Our members come from all over the world, and their support enables us to promote poetry on a global scale." Publishes *Poetry Review*, Britain's most prominent poetry magazine, and *Poetry News*, the Society's newsletter, as well as books and posters to support poetry in the classroom. Runs the National Poetry Competition and The Foyle Young Poets of the Year Award (for poets aged 11-17), as well as many other competitions, services, and education projects for readers and writers of poetry. More information online.

POETRY SOCIETY OF AMERICA

15 Gramercy Park, New York NY 10003. (212)254-9628. **Fax:** (212)673-2352. **Website:** www.poetrysociety.org. The Poetry Society of America is a national nonprofit organization for poets and lovers of poetry. All paid members receive *Crossroads: The Journal of the Poetry Society of America*; additional benefits available as membership levels increase. Sponsors readings and lectures as well as the Poetry in Motion program. Provides free-to-join PSA electronic mailing list for news of upcoming events. PSA also sponsors a number of competitions for members and nonmembers.

POETRY SOCIETY OF NEW HAMPSHIRE

170 Browns Ridge Rd., Ossipee NH 03864. **E-mail:** info@poetrysocietyofnewhampshire.org. **Website:** www.poetrysocietyofnewhampshire.org. A statewide organization for anyone interested in poetry. Currently has 200 members. Offerings include annual subscription to quarterly magazine, *The Poet's Touchstone*; critiques, contests, and workshops; public readings; and quarterly meetings with featured poets.

Members and nationally known writers give readings that are open to the public. Sponsors open mic readings for members and the public. Additional information available for SASE or by e-mail. "We do sponsor a national contest four times a year. People from all over the country enter and win."

THE POETRY SOCIETY OF SOUTH CAROLINA

P.O. Box 1090, Charleston SC 29402. **E-mail:** president@poetrysocietysc.org. **Website:** www.poetrysocietysc.org. The Poetry Society of South Carolina supports "the reading, writing, study, and enjoyment of poetry." Statewide organization open to anyone interested in poetry. Offers programs in Charleston that are free and open to the public September-May (except for members-only holiday party in December). Currently has 150 members. Membership benefits include discounts to PSSC-sponsored seminars and workshops held in various SC locations; a copy of the annual Yearbook of contest-winning poems; eligibility to read at the open mic and to enter contests without a fee; and an invitation to the annual holiday party. Sponsors a monthly Writers' Group, a January open mic reading featuring PSSC members, a Charleston Poetry Walk during Piccolo Spoleto in June, and a May Forum leading to an audience-selected poetry prize. Sponsors two yearly contests, totaling 20-25 contest categories, some with themes; some are open to all poets, others open only to SC residents or PSSC members. Guidelines available online. Also offers the Skylark Prize, a competition for SC high school students. Sometimes offers a chapbook competition. Members and nationally known writers give readings that are open to the public. Additional information online.

POETRY SOCIETY OF TENNESSEE

18 S. Rembert, Memphis TN 38104. **Website:** poetrysocietytn.org. **Contact:** Russell H. Strauss. Purpose is "to promote writing, reading, and appreciation of poetry among members of the society and the community; to improve poetry writing skills of members and local students." State poetry society, with some out-of-state members. Affiliate of National Federation of State Poetry Societies (NFSPS). Current membership about 70. Yearbook contains names, addresses, e-mail addresses of officers and members; winning poems by members and student members; and more. Society activities include programs with speakers; po-etry contests, readings, and workshops; one meeting a year dedicated to students; plus Mid-South Poetry Festival first Saturday in October with workshop and prizes. Poetry readings about four times a year in local restaurants and bookstores.

THE POETRY SOCIETY OF TEXAS

518 Grinnell Dr., Garland TX 75043. (972)270-4994. **E-mail:** catherinepoet@juno.com. **Website:** www.poetrysocietyoftexas.org. "The purpose of the society shall be to secure fuller public recognition of the art of poetry, to encourage the writing of poetry by Texans, and to kindle a finer and more intelligent appreciation of poetry, especially the work of living poets who interpret the spirit and heritage of Texas." Poetry Society of Texas is a member of the National Federation of State Poetry Societies (NFSPS). Has 25 chapters in cities throughout the state. Currently has 300 members. Offerings include annual contests with prizes in excess of $5,000 as well as monthly contests (general and humorous); 8 monthly meetings; annual awards banquet; annual summer conference in a different location each year; round-robin critiquing opportunities sponsored at the state level; and Poetry in Schools with contests at state and local chapter levels. "Our monthly state meetings are held at the Preston Royal Branch of the Dallas Public Library. Our annual awards banquet is held at the Crown Plaza Suites in Dallas. Our summer conference is held at a site chosen by the hosting chapter. Chapters determine their meeting sites." PST publishes *A Book of the Year*, which presents annual and monthly award-winning poems, coming contest descriptions, minutes of meetings, by-laws of the society, history, and information. Also publishes the *Poetry Society of Texas Bulletin*, a monthly newsletter that features statewide news documenting contest winners, state meeting information, chapter and individual information, news from the NFSPS, and announcements of coming activities and offerings for poets. Members and nationally known writers give readings. "All of our meetings are open to the public." Additional information online.

POETS & WRITERS, INC.

90 Broad St, Suite 2100, New York NY 10004. (212)226-3586. **Website:** www.pw.org. Poets & Writers' mission is "to foster the professional development of poets and writers, to promote communication throughout the U.S. literary community, and to help create an environment in which literature can be

appreciated by the widest possible public." The largest nonprofit literary organization in the nation, P&W offers information, support, resources, and exposure to poets, fiction writers, and nonfiction writers at all stages in their careers. Sponsors the Readings/Workshops Program, through which P&W sponsors more than 1,700 literary events in New York, California, and other cities in the U.S. Sponsors the Writers Exchange Contest; the Jacobson Poetry Prize; and the Amy Award. Additional information online.

POETS HOUSE

10 River Terrace, New York NY 10282. (212)431-7920. **Fax:** (212)431-8131. **E-mail:** info@poetshouse.org. **Website:** www.poetshouse.org. Poets House, a national poetry library and literary center, is a "home for all who read and write poetry." Resources include the 50,000-volume poetry collection, conference room, exhibition space, a programming hall, and a Children's Room. Over 200 annual public programs include panel discussions and lectures, readings, seminars and workshops, and children's events. In addition, Poets House continues its collaboration with public library systems, Poetry in The Branches, a multi-faceted program model to help libraries nationwide create a complete environment for poetry locally (see website for information). Finally, each year Poets House hosts the Poets House Showcase, a comprehensive exhibit of the year's new poetry releases from commercial, university, and independent presses across the country. "Poets House depends, in part, on tax-deductible contributions of its nationwide members." Additional information online.

SCIENCE FICTION POETRY ASSOCIATION

P.O. Box 907, Winchester CA 92596. **E-mail:** sfpatreasurer@gmail.com. **Website:** www.sfpoetry.com. The Science Fiction Poetry Association was founded "to bring together poets and readers interested in science fiction poetry (poetry with some element of speculation, usually science fiction, fantasy, or horror)." Membership benefits include 6 issues/year of *Star*Line*, a journal filled with poetry, reviews, articles, and more; one issue of the annual Rhysling Anthology of the best science fiction poetry of the previous year; opportunity to nominate one short poem and one long poem to be printed in the anthology, and to vote for which poems should receive that year's Rhysling award; half-priced advertising on the SFPA

website, with greater subject matter leeway than non-members; eligibility to vote for SFPA officers (or run for officer); mailings with the latest news. Additional information online.

SCOTTISH POETRY LIBRARY

5 Crichton's Close, Edinburgh EH8 8DT, Scotland. (44)(131)557-2876. **Fax:** (44)(131)557-8393. **E-mail:** reception@spl.org.uk. **Website:** www.spl.org.uk. A reference information source and free lending library; also lends by post. Arranges poetry-writing workshops throughout Scotland, mainly for young people. The library has a web-based catalog available that allows searches of all the library's resources, including books, magazines, and audio material--over 30,000 items of Scottish and international poetry. Need not be a member to borrow material; memberships available strictly to support the library's work. Benefits include semiannual newsletter, annual report, new publications listings, and book offers. The School of Poets is open to anyone; "at meetings, members divide into small groups in which each participatn reads a poem, which is then analyzed and discussed." Also offers a Critical Service in which groups of up to 6 poems, not exceeding 200 lines in all, are given critical comment by members of the School: 15 for each critique (with SAE). Additional information online.

SMALL PUBLISHERS ASSOCIATION OF NORTH AMERICA

Box 715, Avon CT 06001. (860)675-1344. **E-mail:** brianjud@bookapss.org. **Website:** www.spannet.org. **Contact:** Brian Jud, executive director. Founded to "advance the image and profits of independent publishers and authors through education and marketing opportunities." Open to "authors, small- to medium-sized publishers, and the vendors who serve them." Currently has 1,300 members. Offers marketing ideas, sponsors annual conference. Additional information online.

TANKA SOCIETY OF AMERICA

439 S. Catalina Ave., #306, Pasadena CA 91106. **Website:** www.tankasocietyofamerica.org. **Contact:** Kathabela Wilson, secretary. The Tanka Society of America, a nonprofit volunteer organization, aims to further the writing, reading, study, and appreciation of tanka poetry in English. Open to anyone interested in tanka. Membership dues for USA, Canada, and International are available online. Membership of-

ferings include the quarterly *Ribbons: Tanka Society of America Journal* and eligibility to submit poems to annual members' anthology. The Tanka Society of American also conducts an annual international tanka competition with cash awards and publication of winning poems. Additional information online.

UNIVERSITY OF ARIZONA POETRY CENTER

1508 E. Helen St., P.O. Box 210129, Tucson AZ 85721. (520)626-3765. **E-mail:** poetry@email.arizona.edu. **Website:** www.poetrycenter.arizona.edu. **Contact:** Gail Browne, executive director. "Open to the public, the University of Arizona Poetry Center is a contemporary poetry archive and a nationally acclaimed poetry collection that includes over 70,000 items. Programs and services include a library with a noncirculating poetry collection and space for small classes; online lesson plan library; High School Bilingual Corrido Contest; K-16 field trip program; summer camps; poetry-related meetings and activities; facilities, research support, and referral information about poetry and poets for local and national communities; reading series; community creative writing classes and workshops; a summer residency offered each year to two writers (one prose, one poetry) selected by jury; and poetry awards, readings, and special events for high school, undergraduate, and graduate students. Additional information available by phone, e-mail, or website. Become a 'Friend of the Poetry Center' by making an annual contribution."

UTAH STATE POETRY SOCIETY

Utah Arts Council & NEA, 864 N. Bonita Way, Centerville UT 84014. (801)292-0283. **E-mail:** poetkmm@msn.com. **Website:** www.utahpoets.com. Purpose is to secure a wider appreciation of the poetry arts and to promote excellence in writing poetry. Statewide organization. Membership is open to all citizens of the State of Utah and to interested people from any other state in the union, without consideration of age, race, regional, religious, educational, or other backgrounds. Currently has about 200 members. Membership benefits include membership in National Federation of State Poetry Societies (NFSPS) and subscription to their newsletter *Strophes*, copy of the *Book of the Year* and other publications, and full contest privileges. Sponsors conferences, workshops, contests, awards. USPS publishes, semiannually, work of members in a chapbook anthology. Publishes *Poet Tree*, a semi-

annual newsletter (also available online). Publishes one winning manuscript annually. Members or nationally known writers give readings/workshops that are open to the public. Chapters meet at least once a month, with open readings, critiques, lessons. Annual Awards Festival includes open reading. Additional information online. "We welcome all potential members."

WISCONSIN FELLOWSHIP OF POETS

301 E. Kent St., Apt. C, Wausau WI 54403. **E-mail:** krieselmichaela@gmail.com. **Website:** www.wfop.org. Statewide organization open to residents and former residents of Wisconsin who are interested in the aims and endeavors of the organization. Currently has 485 members. Sponsors biannual conferences, workshops, contests and awards. Publishes *Wisconsin Poets' Calendar*, poems of Wisconsin (resident) poets. Also publishes *Museletter*, a quarterly newsletter. Members or nationally known writers give readings that are open to the public. Sponsors open mic readings. Additional information online.

WORCESTER COUNTY POETRY ASSOCIATION

1 Ekman St., Worcester MA 01607. (508)797-4770. **E-mail:** wcpaboard@yahoo.com. **Website:** wcpa.homestead.com. **Contact:** Membership Chair. The Worcester County Poetry Association is "open to all who appreciate poetry and wish to support the vibrant Worcester poetry community." Membership benefits include annual subscription to *The Worcester Review*; all WCPA mailings, including broadsides, calendars, and *The Issue*; and fee-free submission to the WCPA Annual Poetry Contest. Additional information online.

WORDS WITHOUT BORDERS

P.O. Box 1658, New York NY 10276. **E-mail:** info@wordswithoutborders.org. **Website:** www.wordswithoutborders.org. "Words Without Borders opens doors to international exchange through translation, publications, and promotion of the world's best writing. Our ultimate aim is to introduce exciting international writing to the general public--travelers, teachers, students, publishers, and a new generation of eclectic readers-- by presenting international literature not as a static, elite phenomenon, but a portal through which to explore the world. The heart of WWB's work is its online magazine. Monthly issues feature new selections of contemporary world literature, most of which would never have been accessible to English-speaking readers without WWB. Members and international writers give readings that are open to the public. Finally, Words without Borders is building an education program in order to expose students at both the high school and college levels to a broader spectrum of contemporary international literature. Our goal is to provide content and resources fostering the use of contemporary literature in the classroom. We hope that in reaching out to students we can create a passion for international literature, a curiosity about other cultures, and help cultivate true world citizens. See website for additional information."

THE WORD WORKS

P.O. Box 42164, Washington DC 20015. **E-mail:** editor@wordworksdc.com. **Website:** www.wordworksdc. com. Word Works is "a nonprofit literary organization publishing contemporary poetry in single-author editions." Membership benefits at the basic level include choice of 2 books from The Word Works book list, newsletter, and 20% discount on additional book orders; in addition to these benefits, sustaining members are eligible for online critique of several poems via e-mail. Sponsors an ongoing poetry reading series, educational programs, and the Hilary Tham Capital Collection. Sponsors The Washington Prize, one of the older ms publishing prizes, and The Jacklyn Potter Young Poets Competition. Additional information online.

THE WRITER'S CENTER

4508 Walsh St., Bethesda MD 20815. (301)654-8664. **E-mail:** post.master@writer.org. **Website:** www. writer.org. **Contact:** Stewart Moss, executive director. Voluntary, membership organization open to all skill levels. "The Writer's Center is a nonprofit community of writers supporting each other in the creation and marketing of literary texts." Annually conducts hundreds of workshops; hosts literary events, readings, and conferences; publishes *Writer's Carousel*, a quarterly magazine of articles and writing news for members. Also publishes *Poet Lore*, America's oldest poetry journal. Additional information online.

WRITERS' FEDERATION OF NOVA SCOTIA

1113 Marginal Rd., Halifax NS B3H 4P7, Canada. (902)423-8116. **Fax:** (902)422-0881. **E-mail:** director@writers.ns.ca. **Website:** www.writers.ns.ca. Purpose of organization: "to foster creative writing and the profession of writing in Nova Scotia; to provide advice and assistance to writers at all stages of their careers; and to encourage greater public recognition of Nova Scotian writers and their achievements." Regional organization open to anybody who writes. Currently has 800+ members. Offerings include resource library with over 2,500 titles, promotional services, workshop series, annual festivals, mentorship program. Publishes *Eastword*, a bimonthly newsletter containing "a plethora of information on who's doing what; markets and contests; and current writing events and issues." Members and nationally known writers give readings that are open to the public. Additional information online.

WRITERS GUILD OF ALBERTA

11759 Groat Rd., Edmonton AB T5M 3K6, Canada. (780)422-8174. **E-mail:** mail@writersguild.ab.ca. **Website:** www.writersguild.ab.ca. Purpose of organization: to support, encourage and promote writers and writing, to safeguard the freedom to write and to read, and to advocate for the well-being of writers in Alberta. Currently has over 1,000 members. Offerings include retreats/conferences; monthly events; bimonthly magazine that includes articles on writing and a market section; weekly electronic bulletin with markets and event listings; and the Stephan G. Stephansson Award for Poetry (Alberta residents only). Holds workshops/conferences. Publishes a newsletter focusing on markets, competitions, contemporary issues related to the literary arts (writing, publishing, censorship, royalties etc.). Sponsors annual literary awards in 5 categories (novel, nonfiction, children's literature, poetry, drama). Awards include $1,500, leather-bound book, promotion and publicity. Open to nonmembers.

THE WRITERS ROOM

740 Broadway, 12th Floor, New York NY 10003. (212)254-6995. **E-mail:** writersroom@writersroom. org. **Website:** www.writersroom.org. Provides a "home away from home" for any writer who needs space to work. Currently has about 350 members. Emerging and established writers may apply. Large loft provides desk space, Internet access, storage, and more. Call for application or download from website.

W.B. YEATS SOCIETY OF NEW YORK

National Arts Club, 15 Gramercy Park S., New York NY 10003. **Website:** www.yeatssociety.org. **Contact:** Andrew McGowan, president. Founded "to promote the legacy of Irish poet and Nobel Laureate William Butler Yeats through an annual program of lectures, readings, poetry competition, and special events." National organization open to anyone. Currently has 450 members. Sponsors The W.B. Yeats Society Annual Poetry Competition. Also sponsors conferences/workshops. Each April, presents an all-day Saturday program, "A Taste of Yeats Summer School in Ireland." Nationally known writers give readings that are open to the public. Members meet approximately monthly, September to June. Additional information online.

POETS IN EDUCATION

Whether known as PITS (Poets in the Schools), WITS (Writers in the Schools), or similar names, programs exist nationwide that coordinate residencies, classroom visits and other opportunities for experienced poets to share their craft with students. Many state arts agencies include such "arts in education" programs in their activities. Another good source is the National Assembly of State Arts Agencies, which offers an online directory of contact names and addresses for arts education programs state-by-state. The following list is a mere sampling of programs and organizations that link poets with schools.

THE ACADEMY OF AMERICAN POETS, 584 Broadway, Suite 604, New York NY 10012-5243. (212)274-0343. E-mail: academy@poets.org. Website: www.poets.org.

ARKANSAS WRITERS IN THE SCHOOLS, WITS Director, 333 Kimpel Hall, University of Arkansas, Fayetteville AR 72701. (479)575-5991. E-mail: wits@cavern.uark.edu. Website: www.uark.edu/~wits.

CALIFORNIA POETS IN THE SCHOOLS, 1333 Balboa St. #3, San Francisco CA 94118. (415)221-4201. E-mail: info@cpits.org. Website: www.cpits.org.

E-POETS.NETWORK, a collective online cultural center that promotes education through videoconferencing (i.e., "distance learning"); also includes the *Voces y Lugares* project. Website: http://learning.e-poets.net (includes online contact form).

IDAHO WRITERS IN THE SCHOOLS, Log Cabin Literary Center, 801 S. Capitol Blvd., Boise ID 83702. (208)331-8000. E-mail: info@thecabinidaho.org. Website: www.thecabin idaho.org.

INDIANA WRITERS IN THE SCHOOLS, University of Evansville, Dept. of English, 1800 Lincoln Ave., Evansville IN 47722. (812)488-2962. E-mail: rg37@evansville.edu. Website: http://english.evansville.edu/WritersintheSchools.htm.

MICHIGAN CREATIVE WRITERS IN THE SCHOOLS, ArtServe Michigan, 17515

W. Nine Mile Rd., Suite 1025, Southfield MI 48075. (248)557-8288. Website: www. artservemichigan.org.

NATIONAL ASSEMBLY OF STATE ARTS AGENCIES, 1029 Vermont Ave. NW, 2nd Floor, Washington DC 20005. (202)347-6352. E-mail: nasaa@nasaa-arts.org. Website: www.nasaa-arts.org.

NATIONAL ASSOCIATION OF WRITERS IN EDUCATION (NAWE), P.O. Box 1, Sheriff Hutton, York YO60 7YU England. (44)(1653)618429. Website: www.nawe.co.uk.

OREGON WRITERS IN THE SCHOOLS, Literary Arts, 224 NW 13th Ave., Suite 306, Portland OR 97209. (503)227-2583. E-mail: john@literary-arts.org. Website: www.literary-arts.org/wits.

PEN IN THE CLASSROOM (PITC), Pen Center USA, Ðco Antioch University, 400 Corporate Pointe, Culver City CA 90230. (310)862-1555. E-mail: pitc@penusa.org. Website: www.penusa.org/go/classroom.

"PICK-A-POET," The Humanities Project, Arlington Public Schools, 1439 N. Quincy St., Arlington VA 22207. (703)228-6299. E-mail: online form. Website: www.humanitiesproject.org.

POTATO HILL POETRY, 6 Pleasant St., Suite 2, South Natick MA 01760. (888)5-POET-RY. E-mail: info@potatohill.com. Website: www.potatohill.com (includes online contact form).

SEATTLE WRITERS IN THE SCHOOLS (WITS), Seattle Arts & Lectures, 105 S. Main St., Suite 201, Seattle WA 98104. (206)621-2230. Website: www.lectures.org/wits.html.

TEACHERS & WRITERS COLLABORATIVE, 520 Eighth Ave., Suite 2020, New York NY 10018. (212)691-6590 or (888)BOOKS-TW (book orders). E-mail: info@twc.org. Website: www.twc.org. "A catalog of T&W books is available online, or call toll-free to request a print copy.

TEXAS WRITERS IN THE SCHOOLS, 1523 W. Main, Houston TX 77006. (713)523-3877. E-mail: mail@witshouston.org. Website: www.writersintheschools.org.

WRITERS & ARTISTS IN THE SCHOOLS (WAITS), COMPAS, Landmark Center, Suite 304, 75 Fifth St. West, St. Paul MN 55102-1496. (651)292-3254. E-mail: daniel@compas.org. Website: www.compas.org.

YOUTH VOICES IN INK, Badgerdog Literary Publishing, Inc., P.O. Box 301209, Austin TX 78703-0021. (512)538-1305. E-mail: info@badgerdog.org. Website: www.badgerdog.org

GLOSSARY

This glossary is provided as a quick-reference only, briefly covering poetic styles and terms that may turn up in articles and listings in *Poet's Market*.

A3, A4, A5. Metric equivalents of 11¾×16½, 8¼×11¾, and 5⅞×8¼ respectively.

ABSTRACT POEM: conveys emotion through sound, textures, and rhythm and rhyme rather than through the meanings of words.

ACKNOWLEDGMENTS PAGE. A page in a poetry book or chapbook that lists the publications where the poems in the collection were originally published; may be presented as part of the copyright page or as a separate page on its own.

ACROSTIC: initial letters of each line, read downward, form a word, phrase, or sentence.

ALLITERATION: close repetition of consonant sounds, especially initial consonant sounds. (Also known as *consonance*.)

ALPHABET POEM: arranges lines alphabetically according to initial letter.

AMERICAN CINQUAIN: derived from Japanese haiku and tanka by Adelaide Crapsey; counted syllabic poem of 5 lines of 2-4-6-8-2 syllables, frequently in iambic feet.

ANAPEST: foot consisting of 2 unstressed syllables followed by a stress.

ANTHOLOGY. A collection of selected writings by various authors.

ASSONANCE: close repetition of vowel sounds. Avant-garde: work at the forefront—cutting edge, unconventional, risk-taking.

ATTACHMENT. A computer file electronically "attached" to an e-mail message.

AUD. Abbreviation for Australian Dollar.

B&W. Black & white (photo or illustration).

BALLAD: narrative poem often in ballad stanza (4-line stanza with 4 stresses in lines 1 and 3, 3 stresses in lines 2 and 4, which also rhyme).

BALLADE: 3 stanzas rhymed *ababbcbC* (*C* indicates a refrain) with envoi rhymed *bcbC*.

BEAT POETRY: anti-academic school of poetry born in '50s San Francisco; fast-paced free verse resembling jazz.

BIO. A short biographical statement often requested with a submission.

BLANK VERSE: unrhymed iambic pentameter.

CAD. Abbreviation for Canadian Dollar.

CAESURA: a deliberate rhetorical, grammatical, or rhythmic pause, break, cut, turn, division, or pivot in poetry.

CAMERA-READY. Poems ready for copy camera platemaking; camera-ready poems usually appear in print exactly as submitted.

CHANT: poem in which one or more lines are repeated over and over.

CHAPBOOK. A small book of about 24-50 pages.Circulation. The number of subscribers to a magazine/journal.

CINQUAIN: any 5-line poem or stanza; also called "quintain" or "quintet." (See also *American cinquain*.)

CLMP. Council of Literary Magazines and Presses; service organization for independent publishers of fiction, poetry, and prose.

CONCRETE POETRY: see *emblematic poem*.

CONFESSIONAL POETRY: work that uses personal and private details from the poet's own life.

CONSONANCE: see *alliteration*.

CONTRIBUTOR'S COPY. Copy of book or magazine containing a poet's work, sometimes given as payment.

COUPLET: stanza of 2 lines; pair of rhymed lines.

COVER LETTER. Brief introductory letter accompanying a poetry submission.

COVERSTOCK. Heavier paper used as the cover for a publication.

DACTYL: foot consisting of a stress followed by 2 unstressed syllables.

DIDACTIC POETRY: poetry written with the intention to instruct.

DIGEST-SIZED. About 5½×8½, the size of a folded sheet of conventional printer paper.

DOWNLOAD. To "copy" a file, such as a registration form, from a website.

ECLECTIC: open to a variety of poetic styles (as in "eclectic taste").

EKPHRASTIC POEM: verbally presents something originally represented in visual art, though more than mere description.

ELECTRONIC MAGAZINE. See *online magazine*.

ELEGY: lament in verse for someone who has died, or a reflection on the tragic nature of life.

EMBLEMATIC POEM: words or letters arranged to imitate a shape, often the subject of the poem.

ENJAMBMENT: continuation of sense and rhythmic movement from one line to the next; also called a "run-on" line.

ENVOI: a brief ending (usually to a ballade or sestina) no more than 4 lines long; summary.

EPIC POETRY: long narrative poem telling a story central to a society, culture, or nation.

EPIGRAM: short, satirical poem or saying written to be remembered easily, like a punchline.

EPIGRAPH: a short verse, note, or quotation that appears at the beginning of a poem or section; usually presents an idea or theme on which the poem elaborates, or contributes background information not reflected in the poem itself.

EPITAPH: brief verse commemorating a person/group of people who died.

EURO. Currency unit for the 27 member countries of the European Union; designated by EUR or the INSERT EURO symbol.

EXPERIMENTAL POETRY: work that challenges conventional ideas of poetry by exploring new techniques, form, language, and visual presentation.

FAQ. Frequently Asked Questions.

FIBS: short form based on the mathematical progression known as the Fibonacci sequence; syllable counts for each line are 1/1/2/3/5/8/13 (count for each line is derived by adding the counts for the previous two lines).

FLARF: a malleable term that may refer to 1) poetic and creative text pieces by the Flarflist Collective; any poetry created from search engine (such as Google) results; any intentionally bad, zany, or trivial poetry.

FONT. The style/design of type used in a publication; typeface.

FOOT: unit of measure in a metrical line of poetry. Found poem: text lifted from a nonpoetic source such as an ad and presented as a poem.

FREE VERSE: unmetrical verse (lines not counted for accents, syllables, etc.).

GALLEYS. First typeset version of a poem, magazine, or book/chapbook.

GHAZAL: Persian poetic form of 5-15 unconnected, independent couplets; associative jumps may be made from couplet to couplet.

GLBT. Gay/lesbian/bisexual/transgender (as in "GLBT themes").

GREETING CARD POETRY: resembles verses in greeting cards; sing-song meter and rhyme.

HAIBUN: originally, a Japanese form in which elliptical, often autobiographical prose is interspersed with haiku.

HAIKAI NO RENGA: see *renku*.

HAY(NA)KY: a 3-line form, with 1 word in line 1, 2 words in line 2, and 3 words in line 3.

HAIKU: originally, a Japanese form of a single vertical line with 17 sound symbols in a 5-7-5 pattern. In English, typically a 3-line poem with fewer than 17 syllables in no set pattern, but exhibiting a 2-part juxtapositional structure, seasonal reference, imagistic immediacy, and a moment of keen perception of nature or human nature. The term is both singular and plural.

HOKKU: the starting verse of a renga or renku, in 5, 7, and then 5 sound symbols in Japanese; or in three lines, usually totaling fewer than 17 syllables, in English; the precursor for what is now called haiku. (See also *haiku*.)

HONORARIUM. A token payment for published work.

IAMB: foot consisting of an unstressed syllable followed by a stress.

IAMBIC PENTAMETER: consists of 5 iambic feet per line.

IMAGIST POETRY: short, free verse lines that present images without comment or explanation; strongly influenced by haiku and other Oriental forms.

IRC. International Reply Coupon; a publisher can exchange IRCs for postage to return a manuscript to another country.

JPEG. Short for *Joint Photographic Experts Group*; an image compression format that allows digital images to be stored in relatively small files for electronic mailing and viewing on the Internet.

KYRIELLE: French form; 4-line stanza with 8-syllable lines, the final line a refrain.

LANGUAGE POETRY: attempts to detach words from traditional meanings to produce something new and unprecedented.

LIMERICK: 5-line stanza rhyming *aabba*; pattern of stresses/line is traditionally 3-3-2-2-3; often bawdy or scatalogical.

LINE: basic compositional unit of a poem; measured in feet if metrical.

LINKED POETRY: written through the collaboration of 2 or more poets creating a single poetic work.

LONG POEM: exceeds length and scope of short lyric or narrative poem; defined arbitrarily, often as more than 2 pages or 100 lines.

LYRIC POETRY: expresses personal emotion; music predominates over narrative or drama.

MAGAZINE-SIZED. About 8½×11, the size of an unfolded sheet of conventional printer paper.

METAPHOR: 2 different things are likened by identifying one as the other (A=B).

METER: the rhythmic measure of a line.

MINUTE: a 12-line poem consisting of 60 syllables, with a syllabic line count of 8,4,4,4,8,4,4,4, 8,4,4,4; often consists of rhyming couplets.

MODERNIST POETRY: work of the early 20th century literary movement that sought to break with the past, rejecting outmoded literary traditions, diction, and form while encouraging innovation and reinvention.

MS. Manuscript.

MSS. Manuscripts.

MULTI-BOOK REVIEW. Several books by the same author or by several authors reviewed in one piece.

NARRATIVE POETRY: poem that tells a story.

NEW FORMALISM: contemporary literary movement to revive formal verse.

NONSENSE VERSE: playful, with language and/or logic that defies ordinary understanding.

OCTAVE: stanza of 8 lines.

ODE: a songlike, or lyric, poem; can be passionate, rhapsodic, and mystical, or a formal address to a person on a public or state occasion.

OFFSET-PRINTED. Printing method in which ink is transferred from an image-bearing plate to a "blanket" and then from blanket to paper.

ONLINE MAGAZINE. Publication circulated through the Internet or e-mail.

P&H. Postage & handling.

P&P. Postage & packing.

PANTOUM: Malayan poetic form of any length; consists of 4-line stanzas, with lines 2 and 4 of one quatrain repeated as lines 1 and 3 of the next; final stanza reverses lines 1 and 3 of the previous quatrain and uses them as lines 2 and 4; traditionally each stanza rhymes *abab*.

"PAYS IN COPIES." See *contributor's copy*.

PDF. Short for *Portable Document Format*, developed by Adobe Systems, that captures all elements of a printed document as an electronic image, allowing it to be sent by e-mail, viewed online, and printed in its original format.

PERFECT-BOUND. Publication with glued, flat spine; also called "flat-spined."

PETRARCHAN SONNET: octave rhymes *abbaabba*; sestet may rhyme *cdcdcd, cdedce, ccdccd, cddcdd, edecde,* or *cddcee.*

POD. See *print-on-demand.*

PRESS RUN. The total number of copies of a publication printed at one time.

PREVIOUSLY PUBLISHED. Work that has appeared before in print, in any form, for public consumption.

PRINT-ON-DEMAND. Publishing method that allows copies of books to be published as they're requested, rather than all at once in a single press run.

PROSE POEM: brief prose work with intensity, condensed language, poetic devices, and other poetic elements.

PUBLISHING CREDITS. A poet's magazine publications and book/chapbook titles.

QUATRAIN: stanza of 4 lines.

QUERY LETTER. Letter written to an editor to raise interest in a proposed project.

READING FEE. A monetary amount charged by an editor or publisher to consider a poetry submission without any obligation to accept the work.

REFRAIN: a repeated line within a poem, similar to the chorus of a song.

REGIONAL POETRY: work set in a particular locale, imbued with the look, feel, and culture of that place.

RENGA: originally, a Japanese collaborative form in which 2 or more poets alternate writing 3 lines, then 2 lines for a set number of verses (such as 12, 18, 36, 100, and 1,000). There are specific rules for seasonal progression, placement of moon and flower verses, and other requirements. (See also *linked poetry.*)

RENGAY: an American collaborative 6-verse, thematic linked poetry form, with 3-line and 2-line verses in the following set pattern for 2 or 3 writers (letters represent poets, numbers indicate the lines in each verse): A3-B2-A3-B3-A2-B3 or A3-B2-C3-A2-B3-C2. All verses, unlike renga or renku, must develop at least one common theme.

RENKU: the modern term for renga, and a more popular version of the traditionally more aristocratic renga. (See also *linked poetry.*)

RHYME: words that sound alike, especially words that end in the same sound.

RHYTHM: the beat and movement of language (rise and fall, repetition and variation, change of pitch, mix of syllables, melody of words).

RICH TEXT FORMAT. Carries the .rtf filename extension. A file format that allows an exchange of text files between different word processor operating systems with most of the formatting preserved.

RIGHTS. A poet's legal property interest in his/her literary work; an editor or publisher may acquire certain rights from the poet to reproduce that work.

RONDEAU: French form of usually 15 lines in 3 parts, rhyming *aabba aabR aabbaR* (*R* indicates a refrain repeating the first word or phrase of the opening line).

ROW. "Rest of world."

ROYALTIES. A percentage of the retail price paid to the author for each copy of a book sold.

SADDLE-STAPLED. A publication folded, then stapled along that fold; also called "saddle-stitched."

SAE. Self-addressed envelope.

SASE. Self-addressed, stamped envelope.

SASP. Self-addressed, stamped postcard.

SENRYU: originally, a Japanese form, like haiku in form, but chiefly humorous, satirical, or ironic, and typically aimed at human foibles. (See also *haiku* and *zappai*.)

SEQUENCE: a group or progression of poems, often numbered as a series.

SESTET: stanza of 6 lines.

SESTINA: fixed form of 39 lines (6 unrhymed stanzas of 6 lines each, then an ending 3-line stanza), each stanza repeating the same 6 non-rhyming end-words in a different order; all 6 end-words appear in the final 3-line stanza.

SHAKESPEAREAN SONNET: rhymes *abab cdcd efef gg.*Sijo: originally a Korean narrative or thematic lyric form. The first line introduces a situation or problem that is countered or developed in line 2, and concluded with a twist in line 3. Lines average 14-16 syllables in length.

SIMILE: comparison that uses a linking word (*like, as, such as, how*) to clarify the similarities.

SIMULTANEOUS SUBMISSION. Submission of the same manuscript to more than one publisher at the same time.

SONNET: 14-line poem (traditionally an octave and sestet) rhymed in iambic pentameter; often presents an argument but may also present a description, story, or meditation.

SPONDEE: foot consisting of 2 stressed syllables.

STANZA: group of lines making up a single unit; like a paragraph in prose.

STROPHE: often used to mean "stanza"; also a stanza of irregular line lengths.

SUBSIDY PRESS. Publisher who requires the poet to pay all costs, including typesetting, production, and printing; sometimes called a "vanity publisher."

SURREALISTIC POETRY: of the artistic movement stressing the importance of dreams and the subconscious, nonrational thought, free associations, and startling imagery/juxtapositions.

TABLOID-SIZED. 11×15 or larger, the size of an ordinary newspaper folded and turned sideways.

TANKA: originally, a Japanese form in one or 2 vertical lines with 31 sound symbols in a 5-7-5-7-7 pattern. In English, typically a 5-line lyrical poem with fewer than 31 syllables in no set syllable pattern, but exhibiting a caesura, turn, or pivot, and often more emotional and conversational than haiku.

TERCET: stanza or poem of 3 lines.

TERZA RIMA: series of 3-line stanzas with interwoven rhyme scheme (*aba, bcb, cdc* . . .).

TEXT FILE. A file containing only textual characters (i.e., no graphics or special formats).

TROCHEE: foot consisting of a stress followed by an unstressed syllable.

UNSOLICITED MANUSCRIPT. A manuscript an editor did not ask specifically to receive.

URL. Stands for "Uniform Resource Locator," the address of an Internet resource (i.e., file).

USD. Abbreviation for United States Dollar.

VILLANELLE: French form of 19 lines (5 tercets and a quatrain); line 1 serves as one refrain (repeated in lines 6, 12, 18), line 3 as a second refrain (repeated in lines 9, 15, 19); traditionally, refrains rhyme with each other and with the opening line of each stanza.

VISUAL POEM: see *emblematic poem.*

WAKA: literally, "Japanese poem," the precursor for what is now called tanka. (See also *tanka.*)

WAR POETRY: poems written about warfare and military life; often written by past and current soldiers; may glorify war, recount exploits, or demonstrate the horrors of war.

ZAPPAI: originally Japanese; an unliterary, often superficial witticism masquerading as haiku or senryu; formal term for joke haiku or other pseudo-haiko.

ZEUGMA: a figure of speech in which a single word (or, occasionally, a phrase) is related in one way to words that precede it, and in another way to words that follow it.

GEOGRAPHICAL INDEX

SUBJECT INDEX

GENERAL INDEX